THE BEST PLAYS OF 1939-40

THE BEST PLAYS
OF 1939-40

AND THE
YEAR BOOK OF THE DRAMA
IN AMERICA

EDITED BY
BURNS MANTLE

DODD, MEAD AND COMPANY
NEW YORK

INTRODUCTION

THE second year of the World's Fair and the first year of the second World's War did not appear greatly to affect the theatre season of 1939-40 in New York. It was, if anything, a little gayer than most seasons have been recently. Gayer in both the auditoriums and the box offices. It was, in fact, a comedy year. Seven of the plays selected for inclusion in this year book are on the comedy side and only three of serious import.

It was a comedy year, too, in its more exciting interludes. Such, for example, as the re-emergence of our erstwhile leading American actor, John Barrymore. Mr. Barrymore, having spent seventeen years in making motion pictures, returned to the stage in a slightly fantastic comedy called "My Dear Children," which had to do with the home life of an actor who had been frequently married and frequently a father. Being a co-operative worker, on and off the stage, Mr. Barrymore proceeded to do a bit of clowning which won him a new public of the curious, and considerably amused what was left of the legitimate public he had deserted seventeen years before.

There was a touch of comedy too, some of us thought, in the awarding of the major prizes of the season to the author of the best American play. The New York Drama Critics' Circle, after struggling through a number of ballots, hoping to find three-fourths of its membership convinced of the superlative qualities of a single play, was obliged to resort to a plain and simple majority vote to get a decision. The majority vote went to William Saroyan's "The Time of Your Life," which received eleven votes to four for Robert E. Sherwood's excessively timely story of the Russians' invasion of Finland, "There Shall Be No Night," two that were given to Maxwell Anderson's "Key Largo" and one to "The Man Who Came to Dinner."

By the record, Russel Crouse's and Howard Lindsay's "Life with Father" was the most successful of the year's comedies. "Father" was looked upon as a sure contender for the Critics' Circle Award and practically a certainty for the Pulitzer committee award. But when the votes were counted Mr. Saroyan's "The Time of Your Life" was the victor in both instances. Proving something, probably, but nothing of more importance than the defiant independence of the critical American mind, both lay and professional. Digests of both prize-winning plays are included in this volume.

Mr. Sherwood's drama seems to this editor to be one of the finer plays of the American theatre record, and to base its superiority on human values rather than upon those ephemeral emotional reactions born of its subject, which stems from the invasion of Finland. It will still be a fine drama, though probably a dated argument, fifty years from now. By then it is hoped the struggle of men for freedom from the appalling thraldom of ignorance and bestiality expressed through war and the emotions bred by war will have been in some measure resolved and consummated.

Mr. Saroyan's "The Time of Your Life," Mr. Brooks Atkinson of the New York *Times* advised his clients, "is something worth cherishing—a prose poem in ragtime with a humorous and lovable point of view." "It is ambling and almost plotless; fantasy and gags and nitwit stories, bound together very lightly with melodrama; it is two-thirds sheer delight, a third mere fumbling," Mr. Richard Lockridge told his readers in the New York *Sun*. Whatever individual reactions to the Saroyan drama may be, it has brought a freshness of viewpoint and attack, and a sympathetic and understanding study of character to the theatre that has been good for the cause.

Mr. Anderson's "Key Largo" is definitely on the serious side, being an intimate and revealing analysis of a coward's conscience —not a coward in the physical sense but a coward who tried unsuccessfully to meet reality with reasoning dictated by self-interest. "No dramatist writing for the contemporary theatre can claim a nobler vision of the timeless function of high tragedy than Maxwell Anderson," wrote John Mason Brown in the New York *Evening Post*. To which conviction "Key Largo" bears eloquent witness.

Mr. Kingsley's "The World We Make" presents a combination of realistic drama and a fairly sound sentimentalism in which current domestic problems are exposed; both psychological and sociological problems. The play's setting and treatment are theatrical, but the Kingsley intent and purpose are sincere and fine.

A fourth play of serious intent, but with a definite comedy overlay, is Clare Boothe's "Margin for Error," the one play of frankly anti-Nazi inspiration that has proved successful in this prejudiced section.

The three comedy leaders were the Lindsay-Crouse "Life with Father," the Kaufman-Hart "The Man Who Came to Dinner" and the Thurber-Nugent "The Male Animal." A financial statement from each would probably place them in this same relative order as playgoers' favorites, though naturally there were the usual divisions of opinion as to which furnished the most satisfying entertainment.

Samson Raphaelson's "Skylark" was happily given to the popular Gertrude Lawrence to have and to hold, to make or to mar. She brought it through triumphantly as one of the season's better jobs.

Paul Osborn's "Morning's at Seven" was too gentle a comedy, too sensitively written, too delicately played to stand against the sturdier comedy competition. It deserves a place, however, among the more adult and satisfying plays of the season, and is therefore included herein.

"The Best Plays" series was begun in 1919 with a volume that covered the season of 1919-20. The first twenty years are therefore completed with this volume, devoted to the season of 1939-40. An additional ten-year coverage of preceding theatre seasons is contained in "The Best Plays of 1909-19," in the assembling of which Garrison P. Sherwood was a collaborator. It is our hope and expectation shortly to complete a volume covering the period between 1900 and 1909, and when that addition is ready there will be available a complete record of the American theatre from its earliest organization in 1750 to the productions of today.

B. M.

Forest Hills, L. I., 1940.

CONTENTS

x CONTENTS

THE BEST PLAYS OF 1939-40

THE BEST PLAYS OF 1939-40

THE SEASON IN NEW YORK

WHILE little novelty attaches nowadays to the play that runs a year on Broadway, there is still a bit of wonder, sometimes a touch of mystery, surrounding the entertainment that threatens to run continuously through a generation. When we were summing up last year's New York theatre record "Tobacco Road," having started away back in the depression year of 1933, was breezing through its sixth year and still playing to profitable, though not greatly profitable, returns at a scale of prices that gave the motion pictures fair competition. As we begin this compilation of the season's events for 1939-40 "Tobacco Road" is breezing through its seventh year. There are now rumors, however, that the end of the run is in sight.

Similarly the production made by the needle trades in November of 1937, a Labor Stage revue called "Pins and Needles," had passed its 1,100th performance and was headed for a three-year record. The Labor folk, however, decided to give its players a Summer's rest preparatory to sending them touring in the Fall, and "Pins and Needles," having run through a number of new editions, was withdrawn in late June.

Now we face the prospect of having the revue called "Hellzapoppin" practically always with us. The Messrs. Olsen and Johnson, comedians, have added fresh material to their entertainment in new editions and are blithely, even confidently, approaching the 1,000th performance mark. Whether they will go on through 1940-41 on Broadway or seek greater profits on tour has not at this writing been determined, but there seems to be no reason why they should not go on indefinitely if they wish to. Their audiences contain more repeaters probably than do those of any of their competitors.

"The Philadelphia Story," with Katharine Hepburn, "The Little Foxes," with Tallulah Bankhead, "Abe Lincoln in Illinois," with Raymond Massey, and the High School farce, "What a Life"— all these spanned a year's playing without resorting to forced runs for the benefit of the advertising, though the "Abe Lincoln"

3

play did wind up with nine weeks of performances in the huge Adelphi Theatre at popular prices, with Richard Gaines replacing Mr. Massey in the name part.

As the attractions of the World's Fair became increasingly potent last Summer producers of popular plays thought to suspend their runs and pick them up again later. "The American Way" was closed for a month, reopened in late July and continued for an additional ten weeks. "Leave It to Me," closing in July, reopened in September, but for only two weeks before taking to the road.

The Summer was barren of new offerings, with the exception of a musical comedy called "Yokel Boy," in which Lew Brown undertook to make something of Buddy Ebsen and Judy Canova as featured entertainers, succeeding quite well, and a new George White "Scandals," following Mr. White's desertion of Broadway for six or seven years. "Yokel Boy," missing Christmas week, ran through until January for 207 performances. "Scandals," without a very enthusiastic start, Mr. White having depended too generously on his burlesque inspirations of long ago, changed theatres once and hung around until December for 120 performances.

The season proper did not get under way until late September, and not too hilariously then. A George Abbott farce, "See My Lawyer," which was rather an Abbott staff production, with Milton Berle featured, did fairly well, and made a run of it after having been moved to the Adelphi and offered at more reasonable tariffs. Ezra Stone did the directing. An assembled "Straw Hat Revue" that had been uncovered in Pennsylvania by Harry Kaufman brought in a touch of novelty and lasted until the competition shut it out with seventy-five performances.

It remained for Gertrude Lawrence to start things really with Samson Raphaelson's "Skylark" the second week in October. Miss Lawrence had been practicing with the comedy in Chicago and in the Summer theatres, and by the time she brought it to Broadway it was good entertainment. It ran the season out to the generous profit of Miss Lawrence, both in friends and money, and her producer, the fortunate John Golden.

A week later "The Man Who Came to Dinner" struck Broadway squarely between the eyes, as you might say, and immediately became the comedy sensation of the new season. George Kaufman and Moss Hart, the authors; Sam H. Harris, the producer; Monty Woolley, the featured player, who assumed a rôle inspired by the humors and habits of Alexander Woollcott, according to a Kaufman-Hart confession—all these were surprised and, naturally, delighted, and so were we, their screeching patrons.

Helen Hayes, bringing "Ladies and Gentlemen" to town, immediately following the Kaufman-Hart success, had to depend pretty much upon her personal appeal to her own particular public to meet the competition. Fortunately Miss Hayes, with two seasons of "Victoria Regina" back of her, is still a playgoers' idol. "Ladies and Gentlemen" proved a light but pleasant jury-room comedy, written by Miss Hayes' husband, Charles MacArthur, and Ben Hecht. It gave the actress a pleasant run of 105 performances. After which she stayed at home with her family, doing a bit of radio work now and then and becoming increasingly interested in War Relief work as the European trouble developed.

Now we had the first musical comedy hit of the year—the George Abbott production of "Too Many Girls," which Robert Rodgers and Lorenz Hart had prepared for him as a successor to the "Boys from Syracuse" of the year before. Here was a cast studded with talent, a better than average book by George Marion, Jr., and an agreeably clean entertainment that missed being stuffy. The combination richly deserved the season's run it got.

There were two other October hits, neither sensational but both fairly substantial. One, in fact, that of William Saroyan's "The Time of Your Life," lived to win both major awards as the best play of American authorship the season produced. Mr. Saroyan, whose first full length play this happened to be, was given the Critics' Circle plaque by a vote of 11 to 4, and also the Pulitzer Prize. The other was Clare Boothe's "Margin for Error," the first anti-Nazi play to score in these prejudiced parts, thanks to its author's gifts of humor, satire and a nice sense of proportion. The Saroyan comedy continued until April. The Boothe drama, with the help of a supplemental season at popular prices, went through till June. Both are included in this collection of digests.

Now the season began to take on character as one definitely favoring comedy. The first week in November saw the production of Howard Lindsay's and Russel Crouse's "Life with Father," which was literally a roaring success at the Empire (and still is, for that matter). A great deal of happiness was engendered by this adventure. The authors, naturally, were lightly hysterical; Oscar Serlin, who had been working two years to get the play written and staged; Mrs. Clarence Day, the widow of the Clarence Day whose short stories had inspired it; Howard Lindsay and Dorothy Stickney, his wife, both of whom had scored successes in the chief rôles, and literally thousands of auditors who were willing to vote "Life with Father" the best comedy of their time—these were all made very happy, for reasons which should later more fully appear in this book.

The veteran and popular composer of music, Jerome Kern, came back hopefully with his old book partner, Oscar Hammerstein, Jr., but their "Very Warm for May" was a little too cluttered for the crowd. Sidney Kingsley made a re-entry as author-producer with a serious drama, "The World We Make," which he took from a novel by Millen Brand called "The Outward Room." Here, too, the effort was worthy and deserving, but the box office enthusiasm was not sufficient to keep Mr. Kingsley interested after he had sold the motion picture rights for a profit and scored eighty performances on Broadway.

Again the serious note, and the second play inspired by a war theme, came in with Maxwell Anderson's beautifully written "Key Largo." Paul Muni, coming on from Hollywood to play the hero, did a great deal for the play's popularity, Mr. Anderson's poetic text not appealing to a wide public. Ethel Barrymore, having been happy playing a 100-year-old lady in "Whiteoak," decided to risk a second ancient with "Farm of Three Echoes," in which she was only ninety-seven. Again the Barrymore public was pleased, but fairly quickly satisfied. Six weeks' playing was all "The Farm" got.

The Center Theatre, seating 3,000 and being something of a headache for the Rockefeller interests who brought it into being with Radio City, was given over to the production of "Swinging the Dream," a huge colored musical show founded on Shakespeare's "Midsummer Night's Dream." Nice for the boys and girls having parts, but not to the liking of the public. Two weeks and it was withdrawn.

Another happy comedy, Paul Osborn's "Morning's at Seven," in which all the characters were past middle age except the young lovers, and they 38 and 40 respectively, made many friends but was not sturdy enough to meet the musical comedy competition. The play is herein included to prove how sensitively written it is, and how pleasant is its gentle character humor.

The holiday period was pretty dull. Only one outstanding success brightened the December evenings. This was "Du Barry Was a Lady," with Ethel Merman playing the name part and Bert Lahr her comic opposite. Cole Porter wrote the score, which greatly helped a book by B. G. De Sylva, the producer, and Herbert Fields. "Du Barry" ran riotously through the season.

It was not until the second week in January that the season took a turn for the better. Then a new comedy, "The Male Animal," written by James Thurber, cartoonist of the *New Yorker* magazine, and Elliott Nugent, one-time comedian favorite in the East, and lately picture favorite in the West, set the town laughing almost as heartily as "Life with Father" had done. Also for reasons which are later revealed in these pages.

Paul Robeson had an unhappy experience with an ambitious undertaking, a musicalized version of Roark Bradford's Negro legend, "John Henry." The colored baritone sang gorgeously in the title rôle, that of the boastfulest colored hero in all the deep South, and generous sums were spent on the production and the cast. But as entertainment "John Henry" lagged and playgoers refused to pay for voice quality alone.

Earl Carroll also had an unhappy experience with the importation of his restaurant show from the Coast, decked out with the old Carroll trademark, "Earl Carroll's Vanities." The girls were beauties, the production fairly elaborate and the comedy interludes of standard quality. But again the reviewers decided that there was not enough novelty to warrant the tariff, and there evidently was not a large enough Carroll bankroll to overcome this discouraging blast.

Sara Allgood and Barry Fitzgerald of the original Abbey Theatre company, being in town and out of jobs, it was decided to revive the Sean O'Casey "Juno and the Paycock." The response for these star performances was immediate and practically unanimous. With the aid of a cut-rate campaign the O'Casey comedy ran for 105 performances, which was a record of sorts.

A story of John Wilkes Booth called "The Man Who Killed Lincoln" proved unpopular, and was quickly withdrawn. Elmer Rice, having overcome his disappointment in the failure of "American Landscape," came forward with a novel treatment of a trite story, that of innocence abroad in Broadway. "Two on an Island" was the familiar tale of boy meets girl when both are trying to conquer the Big City. Happily it had the advantage of being intelligently told and splendidly cast. Betty Field and John Craven played the young people appealingly, there was a novel setting by Jo Mielziner and ninety-six performances were the result. George Bernard Shaw's international satire, "Geneva," was liked by only those of us who still insist that a weak Shaw is still more interesting than 90 per cent of the stalwart and strong moderns.

And then John Barrymore obliged. John had been obliging in

Chicago for many months, playing a comedy about an actor who was amusing, on and off the stage, and often very, very funny in his cups. In the West "My Dear Children" had earned a new reputation for the youngest of the Barrymores, who for seventeen years had been in pictures. Coming back to the stage the once great Hamlet and Richard became a great clown, given to ad libbing whenever the situation or his condition so moved him. In New York Mr. Barrymore was welcomed with an honest display of affection and respect for the past. He responded by giving as "straight" a performance as the part and the play permitted. The text had gradually absorbed most of his pat impromptu speeches, and it was quite impossible for anyone not acquainted with the original script to know when Mr. Barrymore was "gagging" and when he wasn't. "My Dear Children" continued for nearly four months. During the engagement Elaine Barrie Barrymore succeeded in rejoining the cast. She took back the rôle of the heroine which had been played by Doris Dudley from the day that Mrs. Barrymore had walked out in a huff and a rash, caused, she was willing to swear, by the spanking Mr. Barrymore had taken some delight in administering as a part of the business of the play. "My Dear Children" was withdrawn in May. There were no closing demonstrations.

In early February Alfred Lunt and Lynn Fontanne, having been stirred by the courageous defense the Finns were presenting against the Russians, wound up a 20,000-mile tour of the country with eight performances of "The Taming of the Shrew," which was the main item of their repertory. These were given for the benefit of the Finnish Relief Fund. The week added $25,000 to the Fund. The Lunts thereupon started for their home in Genesee Depot, Wisconsin, hoping to enjoy a long rest. But they were patriotically diverted a second time when they read the finished script of a new play by Robert E. Sherwood called "There Shall Be No Night." An account of what followed will be found elsewhere in these pages.

Stanley Gilkey and Gertrude Macy, having done well with an informal musical show called "One for the Money" last season, came forward again with one called "Two for the Show." We may expect "Three to Make Ready" and "Four to Go" in good time. The second of the series emphasized the virtue of good taste and something known usually as class in the selection of both the players and the material with which they worked. Again Nancy Hamilton was responsible for the book and lyrics and Norman Lewis for the score. A wild young jitterbug named

Betty Hutton scored a considerable personal success, and Richard Haydn, an English monologist, was a favored member of the company.

There was another assembling of sketches and songs to occupy the talents of refugee artists under the title of "Reunion in New York." It kept eighteen or twenty refugees working more or less happily and co-operatively for eighty-nine performances. Clifford Odets, who up to this time had been more concerned with his domestic affairs than with the theatre, now came forward with a drama of New York called "Night Music." It was well plotted, well, though not too wisely, cast, and earnestly played. Elia Kazan, Morris Carnovsky and Jane Wyatt had the chief rôles. The Odets public, however, did not respond and the play was taken off after twenty performances.

The month of March was pretty much a month of failures. One, two and three-week trials and a dozen plays were discarded. Only "Ladies in Retirement," a remarkably good mystery drama from England, with Flora Robson, a London favorite, at the head of the cast; Franchot Tone as the hero of a Hemingway-Glazer version of "The Fifth Column," and "Lady in Waiting," a farcical comedy with Gladys George its star, broke through for respectable runs. A light piece staged and played by three Hollywood personalities, Alan Dinehart, Glenda Farrell and Lyle Talbot dismissed by the critics, held on for the balance of the season with the help of a cut-rate campaign and co-operative playing. A revival of Molnar's "Liliom," with Burgess Meredith and Ingrid Bergman, got fifty-six performances.

April came in with three good promises. Maurice Evans revived his "Richard II" for four weeks, Ethel Barrymore tried a new comedy, "An International Incident," written by Vincent Sheehan, war correspondent, and a musical troupe headed by Jack Haley, Marta Eggert, prima donna, and Shirley Ross, film favorite, appeared in one called "Higher and Higher." The Evans and Haley engagements were fairly successful, though not big, but Miss Barrymore's comedy was out in two weeks.

Molly Picon, an East Side darling of the Yiddish theatre these many seasons, came to Broadway to play in English in a comedy drama called "Morning Star," by Sylvia Regan, with Joseph Bulov, a popular East Side comedian, to help her. Pleasant reception but only six or eight weeks' business. Private capital took a hint from the success the Federal theatre had enjoyed with the Living Newspaper type of topical criticism and produced a nicely staged number, "Medicine Show" written by Oscar Saul and H. R. Hays. The authors took the larger Medical Associations apart and revealed much in their conduct that should be corrected, but there was no active response on the part of the people, especially from those "Medicine Show" hoped to benefit.

John (was Jules) Garfield became enthused over "Heavenly Express," a drama script by Albert Bein, author of "Little Ol' Boy" and "Let Freedom Ring." A production was arranged, the play proved a rather earnest satirical fantasy about a hobo's heaven and the reviews were friendly. No response from the paying public, however. At least not response enough.

William Saroyan, not yet resting nervously on his laurels as a prize winner, the season's awards not having been made, offered a second play called "Love's Old Sweet Song" to go with his "The Time of Your Life." Not so good, according to several of his critics, but still more original than the output of his contemporaries, declared the others.

The production of Sherwood's "There Shall Be No Night" gave a great lift to the closing weeks of the season, which the regretted disappointment of the Laurence Olivier-Vivien Leigh revival of "Romeo and Juliet" could not entirely dispel. The Sherwood drama, with the Lunts, continued on until late Summer. The "Romeo and Juliet" revival got five weeks, when the stars withdrew under the stress of Hollywood commitments and a threat of war duty calls from England.

George Cohan tried to recapture something of the wild, careless rapture of "The Tavern," a minor sensation of the season of 1920. He could not quite make it. "The Return of the Vagabond" used the same scenic setting and the same characters "The Tavern" used, but too many "kidding melodramas" had come in between and the impact of freshness and novelty was gone.

There was one more hit before the season closed. As a matter of record there were a hit and a half. "Louisiana Purchase," with a score by Irving Berlin and a lightly satirical book by the Morrie Ryskind who helped George Kaufman with "Of Thee I Sing," and with the popular Victor Moore and William Gaxton to head a cast that included Vera Zorina and Irene Bordoni—this happy combination duplicated the early season success of "DuBarry Was a Lady," and became the most desired of the Summer musical shows. The fact that they were both B. G. De Sylva productions probably means something. Means at least that the De Sylva finger rests at the moment securely upon the playgoing pulse.

Resuming after four years its custom of reviving a classic in the Spring, the Players' Club stepped in with William Congreve's "Love for Love" and a star-studded cast. Peggy Wood was in it, and so were Cornelia Otis Skinner, Violet Hemming and Dorothy Gish. Bobby Clark was in it, to the surprise and delight of all, and so were Thomas Chalmers, Leo G. Carroll, Romney Brent, Dudley Digges, Barry Jones, A. G. Andrews and a lot of others. No one raved much about the Congreve art, or even the Congreve wit, but there was a lot of satisfaction expressed that the Players had restored a widely favored custom to its yearly activities.

There was one more comedy with music, "Keep Off the Grass," with Kitty Carlisle, Mitzi Green, Jack Whiting, Stepin Fetchit of the films and Frances Williams, but not much of a book. After which the season went into the record. A better than average season, as seasons go. Fewer productions, more hits. Fewer performances, heavier receipts.

THE SEASON IN CHICAGO

By Cecil Smith

Dramatic Critic of the *Chicago Tribune*

FOR the first time in a decade it is possible to submit a reasonably bright and cheery account of the theatrical year in Chicago. Both statistics of theatre tenancy and reports of box office grosses reveal greatly and consistently increased prosperity—at least until repercussions of European events sent the late spring season into an abrupt and ignominious tailspin.

Without daring to vouch for the authority of my own peculiarly subjective arithmetic processes, I have computed that Chicago supported precisely 39.5 per cent more playing weeks between June 1, 1939, and June 1, 1940, than it supported in the preceding twelve-month span. Translated into more tangible terms, this means that the Chicago legitimate theatres offered public entertainment to a total of 180 playing weeks, not including three tag-end WPA productions given before the demise of the Federal Theatre Project on June 30, 1939.

Such an expansion of business naturally increased the demand for playing time in the established theatres. The Selwyn, thanks partly to John Barrymore's magnetic power over summer visitors, kept busy for fifty weeks, though a fortnight must be subtracted for a lapse caused by Mr. Barrymore's illness, during which the Messrs. Aldrich and Myers paid rent but presented no performances. The two other Shubert-controlled houses, the Harris and the Grand Opera house, also did well, with 39 and 29 playing weeks respectively. Along about the first of March business seemed so booming that the Shuberts signed a lease on the Studebaker, but ultimately did not provide it with any bookings.

The rehabilitation of the Blackstone Theatre by Oscar Serlin, for "Life with Father," restored an important name to the list of Chicago's class A theatres. Opened in 1911, and for 22 years thereafter the home of more major carriage trade attractions than any other Chicago playhouse, the Blackstone had since 1933 lapsed first into total darkness and later into the careless charge of the Federal Theatre Project. Mr. Serlin rented its four walls, and proceeded to freshen the sumptuous French interior attractively. His virtue was rewarded, for the success of "Life with

12

Father" demonstrated that Chicago playgoers do not seriously object to patronizing a theatre a mile away from the main Rialto.

The independent Erlanger showed a tally of 27 weeks, including three of the six Theatre Guild-American Theatre Society subscription offerings. The Auditorium, still cherishing the illusion that spectacles of normal dimensions can be satisfactorily projected within its vast space, chalked up ten and a half weeks exclusive of opera, concert and ballet. The handsomely equipped Civic Theatre, a small unit in the colossal Civic Opera building, survived through seven weeks of its own summer repertory, and then was heard from no more. The Great Northern ($4\frac{1}{2}$ weeks) and the Studebaker ($1\frac{1}{2}$ weeks) were tenanted only by productions whose professionalism was subject to some question.

John Barrymore's unique spectacle of exhibitionism, "My Dear Children," attained the year's long-run record, with 29 weeks of actual playing in the period now under survey, and two previous weeks in 1938-1939—a total of 31 weeks. I described this unstable carnival in relentless detail a year ago in these pages, and shall not repeat myself. Suffice it to say that Mr. Barrymore's performances from day to day were utterly unpredictable, and that the final curtain time ranged from 11:10 to 12:15. Two changes in cast took place during the run, Patricia Waters and Kenneth Treseder replacing Dorothy McGuire and Lloyd Gough. Doris Dudley stayed with the show throughout the Chicago engagement, and was not forced out by Elaine Barrie until after the New York opening, though this eventuality had been threatened before the play finished in Chicago.

The season's runner-up was "The Man Who Came to Dinner," with 23 weeks, though "Life with Father" will have outstripped it before this volume comes off the press. For the second company of the Kaufman-Hart lampoon, Sam H. Harris and George Kaufman brought together the best cast they could find. Clifton Webb's interpretation of the Sheridan Whiteside wheelchair part far surpassed Monty Woolley's in technical resourcefulness, and not a line or a gesture was wasted. But his humor was harsher and more biting, so that the comedy in total effect became edgy and bellicose. I am inclined to believe that Monty Woolley's mellower performance would have achieved a longer run with the unsophisticated Chicago audience.

If "The Man Who Came to Dinner" strayed from the orbit of Chicago's usual taste in humor, "Life with Father" proved to be a complete natural. In the face of world tumult and calamity, it is the only play strong enough to remain open during the early summer doldrums in which these paragraphs are written. New Yorkers may not like to believe it, but the Chicago company of "Life with Father" is actually every bit as good as the Empire Theatre cast, and possibly even better. (I employ the present tense with confidence, for if indications may be trusted the Chicago company will still be working when this résumé comes off the press.) Lillian Gish, as Vinnie, is captivating, for she never quite flutters down to earth. In Dorothy Stickney's performance in New York a note of shrewd calculation may sometimes be detected. Miss Gish, on the other hand, seems the embodiment of every clause in Father's frustrated definition of female psychology. This conception of the rôle also draws strength from Percy Waram's Father, who is effective by being blunt and bellowing, without the constant play of nuance Howard Lindsay discovers in the same part in New York.

In the course of the year Chicago saw nine professional productions which, for better or for worse, were denied to New York. The repertory at the Civic Theatre, instituted on May 28, 1939, under the direction of J. Charles Gilbert, offered three attractions in 1939-1940, shutting up shop permanently on July 22. The final bill, for three weeks, was a revival of "Seventh Heaven." It drew fairly impressive audiences because of the co-stars, Francis Lederer and Margo. Mr. Lederer handled the heavy hokum of his part remarkably well, in view of the fact that he was also rehearsing with Guthrie McClintic in nearly all his spare hours for the rôle he took over in "No Time for Comedy" on July 24.

The two preceding Civic Theatre undertakings were even less significant, if that is possible. They were a revival of "The Thirteenth Chair," with Margaret Wycherly, and what was, oddly, the first professional Chicago presentation of Samson Raphaelson's "Accent on Youth," with a feeble cast. Two more of the nine productions referred to above, though not given at the Civic, were not more important. The Chicago Mummers, a semi-professional group of good reputation, overreached itself in a version of "Night Must Fall" that did not make the grade. And a group of social-minded sponsors underwrote a colored musical, "Tropical Pinafore," drawn from Gilbert and Sullivan with none of the acumen witnessed by the original WPA swing "Mikado."

Ruth Chatterton, convinced that she was haunted by a jinx, did not bring "Tonight We Dance" into New York. It might have fared better than the play she did choose, for it really was not half bad. Written by Marcella Burke and the late Gladys Unger, the *prétexte*, as the French so knowingly call a plot, concerned the breezy disagreement, separation, and reunion (with offstage bed) of a volatile couple of bright intelligence, living, for obscure reasons, on a ranch in the middle of the central California fruit area. Three delightful children—I use the adjective at full face value—roamed about the stage, and a lot of their repartee, together with that of Miss Chatterton and Barry Thomson, was highly diverting. The comedy was almost wholly disorganized structurally, and occasionally it drew the world's oldest chestnuts (called Joe Millers, aren't they?) out of the grab-bag. But it was funny, and Miss Chatterton is a beautifully competent, economical actress.

From somewhere or other Constance Bennett conceived the notion of plunging onto the stage for the first time with a revival of Noel Coward's "Easy Virtue." I bow to nobody in my regard for Mr. Coward at his best, but this attitude has nothing to do with "Easy Virtue," a thin dish of treacle if ever there was one. The burden of its message, that the British ought to try to get along with an American girl because Americans are really all right if you dig deep enough, took on an ironic cast at a time when the British, everyone knew, were making a frantic attempt to induce the Americans to get along with *them*. Of Miss Bennett's performance, the most that can be said is that it seemed genuine, and that her talent seemed sufficient to warrant a serious study of the technique of acting.

When it comes to Edward Everett Horton's revival of Benn W. Levy's "Springtime for Henry," we can neatly save space. The star's double takes and extreme mugging were rather hysterical for an act or two, but the cumulative monotony of his method reduced his effectiveness by the time he arrived at the final curtain. The performance had a good deal of popular appeal, however, and no doubt deserved its successful eight weeks. "A Night at the Moulin Rouge," on the other hand, did not deserve the single week it got. Glorying in the services of Helen Morgan (she does those numbers from "Show Boat," you know) and the incontrovertibly shapely Ada Leonard, this uneventful hangover from a dead era merely succeeded momentarily in transplanting burlesque from Van Buren street six blocks north to Randolph.

Two other items, both bad, played Chicago before New York—"Thanks for My Wife," which became "Separate Rooms," and the musical "Three after Three," which, after replacing Simone Simon and Mary Brian with Kitty Carlisle and Betty Lawford, became "Walk with Music." In the latter piece the best song was withdrawn before the New York opening because it dealt with the already defunct "Confucius say" fad.

Laurence Olivier's "Romeo and Juliet," with himself and Vivien Leigh, also tried out in the Auditorium before moving to New York. I should prefer to call this misguided and overambitious rather than bad, though its reception in Chicago was as lukewarm as the treatment it later received in New York.

The rest of the season's product consisted of works well known to Broadway. Raymond Massey in "Abe Lincoln in Illinois" drew good houses for twelve weeks, a record not equaled by any other serious drama in more than a decade. Katharine Cornell's first visit in "No Time for Comedy," for three weeks in the fall, was a complete sellout. A fortnight's return engagement in April turned out to be an unhappy error in managerial judgment. Box office triumphs were achieved by Ethel Waters in "Mamba's Daughters" (5 weeks); Maurice Evans' full length "Hamlet" (2 weeks); Katharine Hepburn in "The Philadelphia Story" (5 weeks). The following plays were not more, at best, than moderate successes: "Easy Virtue" (3 weeks); "Thanks for My Wife" (6 weeks); "Key Largo" (3 weeks); Tallulah Bankhead in "The Little Foxes" (6 weeks); "Tonight We Dance" (4 weeks); Laurette Taylor and Florence Reed in "Outward Bound" (3 weeks); "The White Steed" (with Whitford Kane bogged down by an inferior cast) (3 weeks); Helen Hayes in "Ladies and Gentlemen" (3 weeks); Laurence Olivier and Vivien Leigh in "Romeo and Juliet" (2½ weeks); "Margin for Error" (an unfortunate road company) (3 weeks).

Nine musical productions were provided during the year. "One for the Money," Nancy Hamilton's charming "intimate" revue, picked the slim period of June and early July for a six weeks engagement, but even so it was said to have prospered better in Chicago than in New York. "Leave It to Me," with Victor Moore, William Gaxton and Sophie Tucker, did not draw well at the Auditorium, a place much too large for the subtlety of Mr. Moore's style. Michael Todd's rowdy "Hot Mikado" did better there, with five weeks to three for "Leave It to Me." (It should be noted that the box office potentiality of even a single week at the 3,500-seat Auditorium is tremendous.) Most successful of the musicals was George White's "Scandals," which had the foresight to play during the winter's most concentrated convention period, for five big weeks. The other musical entrants were "A Night at the Moulin Rouge (one week); "Three after Three" (4 weeks); "Tropical Pinafore" (3 weeks); Earl Carroll "Hollywood Vanities" (one week), and "The Streets of Paris" (2 weeks).

The last named of these was headed toward success, but it was removed and turned into a tabloid at the New York World's Fair.

Six plays were presented on the combined subscription list of the Theatre Guild and the American Theatre Society: "The White Steed," "Outward Bound," "Ladies and Gentlemen," "Romeo and Juliet," "The Philadelphia Story," and "Margin for Error."

Amateur and semi-professional activity continues in a crescendo in Chicago. None of the productions in this category reached a big-time level. If a palm is to be awarded, it should go to the left-wing Chicago Repertory Group for an original musical comedy, full of social satire, entitled "The Lady Is Right." Its musical score brought to light the considerable gifts of a young composer named Sonny Vale.

The number of summer theatres in the Chicago area of the Midwest has grown. Twenty-one groups, to my knowledge, are operating as I write in mid-July. While only three of these make use of Equity players, the general standard of production and performance is improving, and the future augury is hopeful.

By way of final summary: 33 professional plays (24 nonmusical, 9 musical) were seen in Chicago for a total of 180 weeks. To this tally may be added three WPA productions ("As You Like It," 4 weeks; "Street Scene," 2 weeks; "The Emperor's New Clothes," 2 performances), and two Yiddish plays (Maurice Schwartz in "Salvation," 4 performances; "The Whole World Trembles," a musical revue, 9 performances).

THE SEASON IN SAN FRANCISCO

By Fred Johnson

Drama Editor of *The Call-Bulletin*

SAN FRANCISCO'S reputation as a "good show" town is still something to be mentioned with a studied placing of quotation marks.

The season, locally figured as ending one month later than Broadway's due to the customary lag in road show visits, brought new proof that a good show will receive as generous support here as anywhere.

A few producers, perhaps led to believe the town's theatre taste might be even a little more discriminating than that in some other centers, again elected to premiere their plays in this city.

That the estimate may not have been so complimentary is suspected in one or two cases, where customers were convinced they were guinea pigs less highly regarded, who might be lured into approval of entertainments obviously conceived in doubt.

So any show-going San Franciscan who may have been giving himself airs over the rumor of his superior judgment in rendering a first verdict has subsided with the thought that any crossroads juror might have been of equally astute mind.

Such a reflection might have followed four of the five new productions given premieres in San Francisco during the season.

The exception was "Ladies and Gentlemen," the MacArthur-Hecht vehicle written for Helen Hayes and based on a play by L. Bush-Fekete. After it had received the critics' agreement that it was an undistinguished play, redeemed by the acting of Miss Hayes and Herbert Marshall, it continued to the tune of a $60,000 gross in receipts for the two weeks' engagement in mid-July, a season record.

First metropolitan audiences to view the comedy anywhere also were in agreement that they preferred seeing one of their favorite stars in a play that more nearly matched her talents. But this view interfered in no wise with their filling the Curran Theatre to capacity at all performances. For this some minor credit went to Mr. Marshall as a name of Hollywood potency.

With nursery duties more in mind than the adding of luster to the premiere, Producer Gilbert Miller had hurried from London

18

for a "personal appearance" scene and Authors Charles Mac-
Arthur and Ben Hecht were in anxious attendance, armed with
revising typewriters.

Should readers of the Broadway play reviews be in the least
interested, they should also be amused by learning that the four
San Francisco press critics were evenly divided on the merits of
"Romeo and Juliet" as acted by Laurence Olivier and Vivien
Leigh; produced and directed by the former.

This and one other scribe, in passing the salve through their
columns after a specific panning of Olivier's acrobatic Romeo,
reminded him of his luck in drawing a fifty-fifty critical score.
But not without a warning of the worse to come in Chicago and
New York should he elect to stand on his "original" interpretation.

Miss Leigh's Juliet, more fortunately for her, followed locally
close upon her screen Scarlett O'Hara, to win the actress praise
for her facile switch to a contrasting rôle.

Between Helen Hayes' well-accepted offering and the Olivier-
Leigh debacle came two new productions of less pretension but
seemingly no less belief in the credulity rather than the reputed
discrimination of San Francisco audiences.

The worst stinging was from Leo Carrillo's "Red Bumble-Bee,"
the comedy of an imagined romance between Joaquin Murietta,
the California outlaw, and the exotic Lola Montez. Opposite
Carrillo appeared Tamara Geva, who failed in a dramatic rôle
to follow up either her dancing success in Broadway musicals or
her acceptance in a London production of "Idiot's Delight."
Carrillo, with a financial share in the play, gave of his acting best,
but it was not enough to ward off a personal two weeks' stinging
from both ends—of the house.

Broadway was spared this one, but was less fortunate in the
case of Earl Carroll's "Vanities," which had its one week San
Francisco tryout in December. His Hollywood restaurant-café
girls were greatly admired and he had something in Coast Comedian Jerry Lester. But the Carroll stamp, vastly in need of re-
inking, wasn't enough. And an optimistic week's stop on the
Hollywood return trip three months later was too much.

As this is written, A. H. Woods is again casting a menacing
eye at Broadway with his threat to revive the bedroom farce in
that sector. But before this is printed he may have thought
better of re-venturing there with a new comedy called "Goodbye
to Love," which ended the local season—and practically itself—
with Joan Blondell's temporary good-by to the movies.

Sheldon Davis' play, staged by John Hayden and financed by

Dick Powell, was a showcase of dubious worth to the actress, who had promised Woods, on his releasing her from Broadway a decade ago, to do another play for him should she ever return to the stage.

Who was doing who a favor now, or the reverse, had its answer in the unknown Davis' play, filthier than any trick either could have played on the other. Miss Blondell's only confessed consolation is that she has given her talented sister, Gloria, a theatre hearing after indifferent rôles on the screen.

However luckless San Francisco may have been in the attractions starting here, it was a record season on the receiving end for top-flight touring entertainments. By spring they were crowding each other so closely that managers of the jointly-operated Curran and Geary Theatres faced a jam that cut short the expected run of more than one attraction.

Maurice Evans' "Hamlet" was so heartily received for two weeks and added performances in January that he returned four months later in "King Richard II" for the three weeks that ended his tour. His second engagement, however, failed of the same popular appeal and rated only as "satisfactory."

Preceding him was Paul Muni in "Key Largo," who met with two weeks' disappointing patronage, as measured by his motion picture vogue. Raymond Massey in "Abe Lincoln in Illinois," competing with Muni in his one limited week, played to virtual capacity. Katharine Cornell in "No Time for Comedy," and accompanied by Producer Guthrie McClintic, met with less response than in her dramatic vehicles, which was not construed as a decline in her popularity here.

In her S. N. Behrman comedy, Robert E. Sherwood's "Abe Lincoln" and Maxwell Anderson's "Key Largo" San Francisco theatre-goers had their first mass introduction to the Playwrights' Company attractions.

Alfred Lunt and Lynn Fontanne, who had previously won an excited following with their premiere of "Amphitryon 38," with "Idiot's Delight" added, met with expectant and still excited audiences for their successful two weeks in "The Taming of the Shrew."

"I Married an Angel," ending its tour here in January, was oddly lacking in expected drawing power, as it had on the road—to the extent of making the jaunt profitable. But Producer Dwight Deere Wiman had pledged its continuation to the coast, although with Zorina among the absent.

Ruth Draper, whose character sketches had crowded the Curran on a former week's visit two years ago, stretched her February engagement to two, with disastrous results. But it was different with Alexander Woollcott in "The Man Who Came to Dinner," playing himself, as he refused to do in the New York production. He was about to break "Tobacco Road's" early season record of seven weeks when illness cut him off at six, with the expectation of another fortnight at least. Those two weeks he passed in his bed at a local hotel, exchanged for his invalid's chair in the comedy, before being removed to his physician in the East.

The mid-summer season opened with this same "Tobacco Road," again starring John Barton. Besides the other attractions named, the year brought a revival of 'Outward Bound," a coast production by the new Stage League, with a Hollywood cast that included Dorothy Jordan, Richard Cromwell, Reginald Denny and Cecilia Loftus. It lacked the spirit and atmosphere of either the original stage play or the screen version and won little attention.

A similar fate was that of "The Great American Family," adapted from a Lee Shippey novel and done originally at the Pasadena Playhouse. A revival of "The Desert Song," however, had a successful month's run. Perry Askam and Elvira Tanzi of the original cast headed the company.

Eva Le Gallienne and Earl Larrimore devoted a profitless week to the playing of "Hedda Gabler" and "The Master Builder" and Max Reinhardt's Workshop Players were stranded after one week in Goldoni's "At Your Service," Maeterlinck's "Sister Beatrice" (a streamlined "Miracle") and Pirandello's "Six Characters in Search of an Author." The plays, staged and directed by Reinhardt, were tastefully done and revealed excellent talent. Front office trouble added to the week's disaster.

George White's "Scandals," with Willie and Eugene Howard, Ann Miller and others of the Broadway company, ended its season with a two weeks' run and White then took a tabloid edition on tour.

The failure of "Oscar Wilde" to follow up its six weeks' Hollywood vogue with a like success in San Francisco was laid to war excitement and exposition show competition. In its lean two weeks the Robert Morley hit vehicle drew a distinctly class patronage, mainly of the literati. But there was the same enthusiastic acclaim for Laird Cregar, young actor discovery in the title rôle, who accounted for much of the film colony's interest in the play and immediately signed a movie contract with Twentieth Century-Fox. Producer Arthur Hutchinson, granting a loan out of his newly-made star, then made plans to tour him in "Wilde," later in the year. He would be a strong contender for the part of "Henry the Eighth" in the play on Ann Boleyn now being written by Francis Hackett.

San Francisco's first annual light opera festival of four weeks, by arrangement with Edwin Lester's Los Angeles civic organization, was so successful as to assure its becoming a yearly fixture. John Charles Thomas, the main attraction in previous two week seasons, was starred in "H.M.S. Pinafore" and an afterpiece called "Serenade Serenade." The ensuing operettas were "Show Boat," with John Boles, Norma Terris, Paul Robeson and Guy Kibbee; "The Merry Widow," starring Jarmila Novotna of the Metropolitan, with Walter Woolf King, and "The Red Mill," with Natalie Hall, Dorothy Stone and Sterling Holloway.

The Golden Gate International Exposition's second year brought the return to Treasure Island of a new "Folies Bergère" and the coast inaugural of Billy Rose's Aquacade, so novel to Californians that it has steadily packed a 7,000 seat indoor theatre. Swimmers Johnny Weissmuller, Esther Williams and Gertrude Ederle, with Morton Downey as vocalist and announcer, head the principals.

The near-by universities have had a season of significance in campus theatricals. The University of California Little Theatre, under Edwin Duerr's direction for seven years, made O'Neill's "All God's Chillun Got Wings" its outstanding production, along with "The Merchant of Yonkers," "Shadow and Substance" and Saroyan's "My Heart's in the Highlands." The organization, still without an adequate playhouse, has recently contributed numerous players to the Broadway and other stages.

Stanford, with its new theatre and F. Cowles Strickland, from the Washington, D. C., Civic Theatre, as new director, preceded Maurice Evans here with a production of "King Richard II" and a first coast staging of "The Headless Horseman," among others.

Not far from the Stanford campus, the Palo Alto Community Players, also well housed, has grown in strength and versatility in proven vehicles. In San Francisco the Wayfarers, whose fame has spread since their outgrowth of a waterfront loft, have continued to delve in heavier pieces with skill and effectiveness. Their more successful productions for the season were Capek's "R.U.R." and four Grand Guignol plays. But they have also conquered such classics as "The Taming of the Shrew" and "Measure for Measure," in modern dress, and The Passion Play of Oberammergau.

THE SEASON IN SOUTHERN CALIFORNIA

By Edwin Schallert

Drama Editor of the *Los Angeles Times*

AN erratic season, the most erratic in the past decade, undoubtedly, ended June 30, 1940, in Southern California theatrical territory. It was good, bad, and fair-to-middlin' all at once; but it was not dull and uneventful.

Signs of advancement can even be discerned. There has been more of the spirit of the stage in the air than in a dozen years. Creative impulses are making themselves felt, even though there are no wild realizations. Dreams are dreamt by the dozen, but their actual fulfillment is calculated to keep observers guessing as to how and when.

Even Orson Welles talked of a branch of the Mercury Theatre, but this seemed almost as visionary as his plans for making a motion picture during the better part of a year. Ideas for subscription performances continued to germinate off and on during the twelve-month, but mostly died a-borning.

A. H. Woods did accomplish a Coast production of "Goodbye to Love" with Joan Blondell, Patric Knowles and others in the cast, but this came to Los Angeles July 1, and therefore too late for full appraisal. Advance presentation at Santa Barbara indicated a light comedy. There were no signs at this writing that it would arrive on Broadway with the present company, and in its present substance and design.

Early in the season (Summer of 1939) the Ben Hecht-Charles MacArthur show, "Ladies and Gentlemen," with Helen Hayes, was tried out in Los Angeles, but encountered very little genuine approval, though it had audiences. This, too, started on its way in Santa Barbara as recorded by this writer in the chapter covering the 1938-39 season. It's all too far in the dim past now to merit more than this passing mention.

Most noteworthy of dramatic productions—the play having first been seen in New York—was "The Man Who Came to Dinner," with Alexander Woollcott. This had the best of popular favor. The presence of Woollcott, despite his limitations as an actor, seemed to connote the valuable attribute of glamour. The company playing with him included Claudia Morgan, Doris Nolan, Rex O'Malley, who scored a hit in the so-called Noel Coward impersonation, Mabel Taliaferro, Robert Allen and Renie

Riano as its more important members. Presence of Woollcott
from the showmanship standpoint endowed the play with unique
attractions.

While Woollcott was indisposed, George S. Kaufman, co-author,
undertook the leading rôle for a few performances, thus providing
another novelty of the engagement. The entire venture deserved
praise for maintaining the best standards of theatre as rendered
apparent in this general locality. The effort was made to invest
the enterprise with befitting class, and this unquestionably pleased
the showgoers.

Barring the musicals, which we will come to later, one of the
most effective productions of a stage piece previously seen in New
York obtained with "Oscar Wilde" at El Capitan Theatre, former
habitat of the Henry Duffy shows. This was presented by the
Stage League, headed by Charles O'Neal and Arthur Hutchinson,
with Arthur Ripley as director. Laird Cregar, playing the title
rôle enacted by Robert Morley in New York, gained an outstanding success, becoming for the time being the talk of the town.
Cregar is still new in the theatre, and was formerly with the
Pasadena Community Playhouse. He had always wanted to
assume the Wilde rôle in the play, and justified that ambition.
His closest rival was Howard Johnson who appeared as the star
witness against the Victorian poet. This play had an engagement
of six weeks at the theatre, whereas "The Man Who Came to
Dinner" was present for three.

Probably the most important engagement, aside from these, was
Maurice Evans in "Hamlet," which was met with enthusiasm not
only by devotees of Shakespeare, of whom there seem a constantly
diminishing number, but also others. Evans fared less well,
though, with his "Richard II," probably because the play lacks
the familiarity of the Melancholy Dane's tragedy. Evans gave
this later in the season.

Alfred Lunt and Lynn Fontanne, with their "Taming of the
Shrew," proffered rather belatedly on the Coast, enjoyed a fair
engagement, but not one to compare with either "Idiot's Delight"
or "Amphitryon" in drawing super-capacity houses. It is not a
Shakespearean epoch in the West, despite "Hamlet" nearly always
seems an exception.

Of the plays favored by Burns Mantle as the ten best of the
1939-40 season, four were given in Los Angeles, "The Man Who
Came to Dinner" being one of them. The other three included
"Key Largo," in which Paul Muni paid a visit toward the close of
the season; "The Male Animal," which was first seen on the

Coast, though benefiting by only a mild reaction, and Clare Boothe's "Margin for Error," which had Fay Wray as a motion picture "name," and in which Lionel Stander was highly successful.

The record for the production of Mantle-approved plays is better than last season when only one reached Southern California audiences during the same theatrical period. Since that last chronicle "Rocket to the Moon," per Pasadena Community rendition and "Family Portrait" have been made visible out of the 1938-39 list, as well as "Abe Lincoln in Illinois," starring Raymond Massey, and "No Time for Comedy" with Katharine Cornell. "The Little Foxes" will also be here ere 1940 is over. But the western area is running well over a year behind on some of these attractions.

Why "The Male Animal" did not make an impression in Los Angeles requires, perhaps, no extensive explanations. It had not been whipped into shape at the time, and the casting was considerably revised for the New York premiere, with only Leon Ames, who had been commended exceedingly, Robert Scott and Richard Beckhard retained. At the time it was viewed out here the critical were inclined to carp at the final act, and did not respond as markedly to the comedy as did New York a few months later. But in a sense this was just a Coast tryout.

Life really begins theatrically in Los Angeles during 1939-40 with the musical show—one musical show, above all others, to be accurate. This is "Meet the People," presented first at the Assistance League Playhouse Christmas night, missed there by the first-string critics because "I Married an Angel" happened to move into town the same evening, and later transferred to the Hollywood Playhouse, former locale of "Two-a-Day" the Federal Theatre attraction.

"Meet the People" qualifies for top-rating as the most original event of the theatre seen hereabouts in any recent year. It has set a pace which others have attempted to follow less fortunately. There has been money in this production for those concerned. It will have reeled off a thirty-week run before it goes into its second edition, which is beyond the purview of this chronicle.

An intimate revue, "Meet the People," has most often been compared with "Pins and Needles," yet it is not a workers' effort in the same sense at all. Its biting satire and irony stretch far and wide, and it is rich in universal human elements. It dares besides to become "browish" even in its musical effervescence, as for example a number based on the idea of why not steal a tune from Offenbach—words to that effect. Its ace number, "The

Same Old South," is a strangely sharp sort of jab and jibe in a territorial way, yet still amuses even southerners.

The show discovered Virginia O'Brien, who subsequently went into "Keep Off the Grass," the New York musical with Jimmy Durante, Ray Bolger, Jane Froman and Ilka Chase. It has an ensemble of leading performers that from time to time is "raided" by the studios, but still seems merrily to go along even with altering membership. The co-operative character of the whole business is such that it is hard, even, to determine a roster of credits for this smart sophisticated achievement.

The popularity of the show is attested to by the fact that the same people go to see it again and again, and incidentally they're pretty nearly certain to find some new entertainment, no matter how often their pilgrimage. It promises to become as much of an institution as the Earl Carroll "World of Pleasure," which is now in its fourth edition, and there are no added restaurateur's inducements either.

William Orr is probably the most consistent hit with his take-offs on celebrated people, but the audiences always acclaimed Miss O'Brien as long as she was in the company. It's hard to single out anybody who "makes" this show; it represents the best in a united endeavor.

Light opera attained a much better standard than during any prior year. John Charles Thomas was a star for the third season, this time in "Pinafore." However, the production that quite surprised was "The Red Mill," which closed the series of four offerings, with Dorothy Stone, Sterling Holloway, Ernie Stanton, Odette Myrtil, John Garrick and others in the cast. Here again it was ensemble that made the show effective.

"Show Boat" opened the season with John Boles, Norma Terris, Paul Robeson, Guy Kibbee and Helen Morgan, and leading lights in "The Merry Widow" were Walter Woolf King, Jarmila Novotna, Hope Manning and Melville Cooper. There were other light opera revivals during the year including "Blossom Time," "The Desert Song" and "The Vagabond King," but they were overshadowed by the "Mikado in Swing," a "hot" attraction of the summer of 1939. And it *was* exceptionally good.

"Folies Bergère," another edition, came back for a successful stay. George White's "Scandals" with Willie and Eugene Howard for comedy, the new "Merry Wives in Swing," musical based on "Merry Wives of Windsor," sponsored by George Houston, "Tattle Tales of 1940," "Hit and Run" were among the other tuneful events of varying appeal. The general trend seemed to be toward more activity in this department.

Comedy on the mad side without music was supplied by Noel Langley's "Walrus and the Carpenter," scherzo of family life, which had a fairly successful session at a small theatre called the Pelican. Here, too, Langley presented "Cage Me a Peacock," burlesque in ancient Greek style on Lucrece.

Among the perennials both the Pilgrimage Play and the Mission Play were revived. The Mission Play was not given in its usual theatre in San Gabriel, but in the Civic Auditorium at Pasadena. And of course, "The Drunkard" is still firmly entrenched in its eighth year. That surpasses Producer Galt Bell's expectations for a seven-year run, and upsets most other predictions.

"Shadow and Substance" had a presentation; Max Reinhardt staged "Too Many Husbands" in colorful style; Pauline Lord acted in "Suspect," once destined to display the talents of the late Pauline Frederick, who appeared in the play for a brief while just before her death; "Love Life of Dorian Gray," "White Cargo," which had a long engagement; "Dead We Live" were in the procession of shows designated as professional, or at least semi-professional. "The Penguin," written by Jan Boris about Hollywood, and "Milan in May," musical with Jane Winton, were also in this realm, as was "The Wary Quarry" ("Dance of Spring") by Philip Barry, and (of all things) "She Lost It in Campeche." Nice title!

The Federal Theatre Project meanwhile did its fadeout, which had aspects of glory, because it closed in Los Angeles with "Run, Little Chillun" and "Two-a-Day." Efforts were made to keep one or the other alive for a while beyond the term of government subsidy.

As always the Pasadena Community Playhouse remained a dominating influence for progress in theatrical affairs, and a highly cultivated center of entertainment. The Maxwell Anderson festival season of 1939 was followed by the James M. Barrie festival in the Summer of 1940. During the Anderson season, "Elizabeth the Queen" was notable, and followed by especially excellent productions of "Wingless Victory," "Masque of Kings," "Winterset" and other plays. There were eight scheduled for the Barrie sequence, which started in June with "Quality Street."

"Rocket to the Moon," "Dear Octopus," "Our Town" and "Comedy of Errors" were very brilliantly put on during the winter season. Brightest of the premieres was "Young April" by Aurania Rouverol. Other plays comprised "Morning Glory," "Kiss the Boys Goodbye," "David Harum," "Cricket on the

Hearth," "Father Malachy's Miracle" (first time on Coast), "She Loves Me Not," "Susan and God," "Pancho" by Lowell Barrington (premiere), "Room Service," "The Texas Nightingale" and "What a Life" (first time on Coast), "Heritage of the Desert," adaptation from Zane Grey by Robert Chapin and Charley King, and "The Dictator's Boots" by B. Harrison Orkow (premieres), "Glorious Morning" (first time on Coast), and "The Queen Was in the Parlour." Even more comprehensive than usual, it appeared, was the repertoire of this remarkably progressive playhouse.

THERE SHALL BE NO NIGHT
A Drama in Three Acts

By Robert E. Sherwood

THE most stirring event of the theatre season of 1939-40 was the production of Robert E. Sherwood's drama of the Russian invasion of Finland, "There Shall Be No Night," on April 30, 1940. It was an event unequaled in many ways in all the recent history of the American theatre.

Mr. Sherwood, who had been working on a new version of a drama called "Acropolis," which he had written for Alfred Lunt and Lynn Fontanne, and which they had tried a year ago in London, was inspired by a broadcast from Helsinki to put his convictions concerning the betrayal of Finland into dramatic form.

Quietly, almost secretly, he started work upon the new play, discovered that his inspiration increased with his progress and devoted himself to the task with something like a feverish intensity. He finished the play a few days before Mr. Lunt and Miss Fontanne brought to a close a 20,000-mile-tour of the country by devoting a week to a series of Finnish relief fund benefits in New York, playing their revival of "The Taming of the Shrew."

The Lunts were leaving for a long-delayed vacation on their Wisconsin farm when Mr. Sherwood handed them the script of "There Shall Be No Night" (then bearing the tentative title of "Revelation"). They were to read it when they got home as a possible drama for their use the following season. Before their train reached Chicago Mr. Sherwood had wires from them announcing that they would be ready for rehearsals as soon as they could get back.

It then became known that, not only had Mr. Sherwood's eloquent script made a profound impression upon America's favorite acting couple, but that Mr. Lunt, having been reared by a Finnish stepfather, was devoted heart and soul to the patriotic little republic of the North, and excited in his eagerness to spread the message of the character and quality of its courageous citizens.

Within a fortnight "There Shall Be No Night" was in rehearsal and a trial week set for Washington, D. C. The Washington reception was enthused and positive. An exciting but less unanimous welcome followed in New York, the critics being strong in their endorsement of the staging and acting, the eloquence of the text and the sincerity of purpose backing the author and the actors in their effort, but intimating with professional caution that perhaps the timeliness of subject had much to do with the play's popularity.

Audience reaction, however, was immediately favorable and enthusiastic receptions continued through a Summer run. "There Shall Be No Night," produced jointly by The Playwrights' Company, of which Mr. Sherwood is a member, and The Theatre Guild, with which Mr. Lunt and Miss Fontanne have long been associated, will be the chief offering of these producing groups for the theatre season of 1940-41.

In the play we enter the living room of the Dr. Kaarlo Valkonens in the suburbs of Helsinki on an afternoon in early October, 1938. The Doctor and Miranda Valkonen his wife, are being posed for their pictures by an American radio commentator, Dave Corween, who represents the Columbia Broadcasting System.

"This is a nice, neat, old-fashioned house, with large windows, through which one sees a lovely view of the harbor and the islands," writes Mr. Sherwood.

The living room is comfortably furnished. "On the walls, surprisingly, are pictures from an American house, several family portraits, a number of pallid little water colors of Louisiana scenes. . . . On the piano and tables are portraits of many famous doctors—Pavlov, Freud, the Mayos, Carrel, etc."

In the center of the room is a sofa and in front of it a table with a microphone and a telephone. Wires run into the adjoining dining room. Below the table the Valkonens are being instructed in their pose by the camera men. Dr. Valkonen "is between forty-five and fifty years old—gentle, amused, vague, and now pretty self-conscious." Mrs. Valkonen "is beautiful, chic and enjoying the whole situation intensely. Kaarlo is a native Finn; Miranda comes from New Bedford, Massachusetts."

Corween, the radio commentator, is about thirty-five, a pleasant, active, dark young man who was formerly foreign newspaper correspondent but has been doing the radio job for some time.

The pose is agreed upon, the bulbs flash and the self-conscious Valkonens are released. The Doctor, however, must go now to the microphone that his voice may be tested as it is sent into a "mixer" in the dining room. He obliges by trying to speak as naturally as possible: "How do you do, my dear friends in America? How are you? I am well. I hope you are likewise. And do you know that the human digestive tract or alimentary

canal extends for a distance of twenty-five to thirty feet, and
consists of the following main parts: the mouth, pharynx,
esophagus—"

By the time he has finished with the organs of the alimentary
canal the test is pronounced entirely satisfactory. Everyone is
pleased except Dr. Valkonen who is still doubtful. Mrs. Valkonen
would put in a word of advice—

"Now, Kaarlo—when you do speak to the American people,
please don't forget yourself and go through all those disgusting
organs again. People don't like to be reminded of such things."

While Mrs. Valkonen has gone to put the finishing touches to
her translation of the Doctor's speech, Dr. Valkonen would learn
a little something more about the marvels of radio. "Wonderful
business, this," he ventures to Corween.

"Wonderful and awful."

KAARLO—More complicated than the alimentary canal, eh?

DAVE—Perhaps. But less essential.

KAARLO—How does my voice get from here all the way to
America? Can you explain that to me?

DAVE—No, Doctor—I can't. But I can give you the outline.
The voice travels from the microphone along that wire into the
next room. It goes into that box in there. That's called the
mixer. From there, it goes over your own telephone line to the
broadcasting station, where various things happen that I don't
understand. It's then transmitted on another line under the Gulf
of Finland to Geneva, where it's broadcast by short wave from
the League of Nations station.

KAARLO—Really. So that's what the League of Nations is
doing!

DAVE—Well, they've got to do something. They send your
voice to some place on Long Island, where it's transmitted to
C.B.S. in New York, and then rebroadcast from coast to coast.

KAARLO—My word! Do you think anyone will listen?

DAVE (laughing)—Certainly. They'll listen to all sorts of
strange things on Sunday.

KAARLO—I knew I should never have agreed to this nonsense.
I'll make a fool of myself.

DAVE—Oh, please, Doctor—I didn't mean to suggest that.

KAARLO—I know you didn't. But I'm still sorry. My wife's
relatives will be listening, and then they will write to her and say,
"Kaarlo sounds older." They live in New Bedford, Massachusetts. Have you ever been there?

DAVE—I couldn't be sure.

KAARLO—A depressing place. But good people. Terrifying—
but good. All of these paintings on the wall came from the house
in New Bedford. (*He points to the 1812 officer.*) There's a fine-
looking fellow. They must have been gayer in those days. But
look at that one over there. Miranda's grandfather. Did you
ever see such a brigand? That's a drawing of her father on the
piano. A very sensitive face. He didn't come from New Bedford—Louisiana, I think. He painted all those water colors—
swamps, and things. Miranda loved him. He must have been
very charming. But he was surely a very bad painter.

Kaarlo's Uncle Waldemar has arrived. A fine musician, he is
only casually interested in the broadcasting preparations. "Uncle
Waldemar is a moody, disenchanted old man," but he knows
what he thinks. When the conversation turns to Dave Corween's experiences in the recent crises in Prague and Munich, it
is Uncle Waldemar who understands.

"Uncle Waldemar always looks on the dark side of things,"
Kaarlo explains. "There's been too much Sibelius in his life."

"I can understand what happened at Munich because I know
Germany," announces Uncle Waldemar. "I've lived there—I've
studied music there—I've read Goethe. He knew his own people.
He stood on the heights, and he said that from his point of view
all life looks like some malignant disease."

"Well, he should see it now. I can tell you I was glad when
they ordered me to come up here. You don't know what it means
to be in a really free country again. To read newspapers that
print *news*—to sit around cafés and hear people openly criticizing
their government. Why—when I saw a girl in the street who
wasn't afraid to use lipstick, I wanted to go right up and kiss her."

"Why didn't you? She'd have been very flattered. Our girls
here like Americans, especially those gay young college boys who
come here on tours—"

The speech is ready, and there are a few minutes in which
Dr. Valkonen can go to his room and read it over carefully.
Miranda manages that. Then she is pleased to add a little to
what Kaarlo has told Mr. Corween of her New England background.

"Did he tell you his idea—that they represent the whole cycle
of modern history?" she queries, pointing to the family portraits.
"Rugged heroism—that's him—developing into ruthless material-
ism—that's him—and then degenerating into intellectual im-

potence and decay—that's him."

She has picked up a sketch of her father from the piano and is holding it fondly. "Rugged heroism—that's old Great-grand-father Eustis—he fought in the navy in the War of 1812."

"Did he?"

"Yes—and he lived to sail a clipper ship to California in the Gold Rush. He didn't get any gold, but he died happy. His son, my sainted grandfather—that's the one with the beard—bought his way out of the Civil War for three hundred dollars. Then he made a nice fortune selling shoddy uniforms to the army. He did even better after the war when he packed his carpet bag and went south. He married a beautiful daughter of the ruined aristocracy, and my father was the result. (She holds out the drawing.) You can see he was more New Orleans than New Bedford. Sargent drew that. Beautiful, isn't it?"

"Wonderful."

"I'm supposed to take after him. They always said in New Bedford, 'Miranda and her father are as like as two peas in a pod.' And they didn't mean that as a compliment, either."

Dave would know how she happened to meet Dr. Valkonen. He may want to write something about this visit later—"when the public gets tired of being fed through the ears."

"Well, Kaarlo and I met in Russia in 1914," Mrs. Valkonen recalls. "That was when my father was coming to the end of his brilliant career as a spendthrift. Kaarlo was a medical officer in St. Petersburg—that's what they called it then. Oh, he was so handsome! Thin—dark—tragic looking. I was seventeen— I'd never seen anyone like him. Of course he didn't know I was alive. Then came the war and we had to leave for America. It was the end of the world for me. I pestered him with letters regularly, and he replied—once. Then he had to come to America to study, and we met again, and after considerable effort on my part, we were married. And that's all there is to that."

The time set for the broadcast is approaching. Dr. Valkonen is back with his speech, which he has found pretty dull. Now they have taken their places. There is a brief pause and then the loud speaker—

"This is Station WABC in New York—"

"Great God!" mutters Kaarlo.

"We now take you to the Finnish Capital. Go ahead, Hel-sinki—"

Dave Corween has shuffled his notes on the table and is now talking into the microphone—

"Hello, America—this is David Corween, in Helsinki. We're bringing you the first of a series of broadcasts from Finland, Sweden and Norway, those little countries in the far north of Europe which are at peace, and intend to remain at peace. . . . I am now speaking from the home of one of Finland's most distinguished citizens, Dr. Kaarlo Valkonen, the eminent neurologist, who has received high honors in the United States, England, the Soviet Union and other nations, and has just been awarded the Nobel prize in medicine. . . . Many of you have read his book, 'The Defense of Man,' and to some of you now listening he is known personally, as he has lived much in America, and his wife comes from that fine old Massachusetts town, New Bedford. It gives me great pleasure to bring you—Dr. Kaarlo Valkonen."

He moves the microphone over to Dr. Valkonen and gestures for him to go ahead. With a muttered "I never heard so much introduction," Kaarlo turns to the microphone and begins—

"To tell the truth, I think the Nobel prize is premature. The work I am doing will be finished by someone else many years from now. . . . Dr. Carrel has said, 'For the first time in history, a crumbling civilization is capable of discerning the causes of its decay. For the first time it has at its disposal the gigantic strength of science.' And he asks, 'Will we utilize this knowledge and this power?' That's a question far more important than speculating about the possible results of the Munich crisis. In fact, behind this question are the real causes of all the problems we now must face.

"It is no doubt well known to you that insanity is increasing at an alarming rate. Indeed, the day is within sight when the few remaining sane people are put into confinement and the lunatics are at large.

"Does this seem a ridiculous exaggeration? Then look about you, at the present world. You see the spectacle of a great, brilliant nation, which has contributed perhaps more than all others to scientific progress. Today, the spiritual resistance of its people has been lowered to such an extent that they are willing to discard all their moral sense, all the essential principles of justice and civilization. They glorify a theory of government which is no more than co-ordinated barbarism, under the leadership of a megalomaniac who belongs in a psychopathic ward rather than a chancellery. He seeks to create a race of moral cretins whom science has rendered strong and germless in their bodies, but feeble and servile in their minds. We now know how quickly such men can be converted into brutes.

"Science has considered disease as mechanical phenomena, to be cured by mechanical means. And we have been remarkably successful. Examine the achievements in the fight against tuberculosis—typhoid—all the ancient plagues. You will see that the number of fatalities is steadily being reduced. Then look at the degenerative diseases—insanity, which is the degeneration of the brain—and cancer, which is degeneration of the tissues. These diseases are going up, almost in the same proportion as the others are going down. . . .

"We count too heavily upon pills and serums to protect us from our enemies, just as we count too heavily upon vast systems of concrete fortifications and big navies to guard our frontiers. Of what avail are these artificial protections if each man lacks the power of resistance within himself?

"You have heard it said that the days of exploration are over—that there are no more lost continents—no more Eldorados. But I promise you that the greatest of all adventures in exploration is still before us—the exploration of man himself—his mind—his spirit—the thing we call his character—the quality which has raised him above the beasts. 'Know thyself,' said the oracle. And after thousands of years, we still don't know. Can we learn before it is too late—before the process of man's degeneration has been completed and he is again a witless ape, groping his way back into the jungle?"

Kaarlo has thrust his manuscript aside as his voice takes on a greater intimacy in tone. "But why should I go on spoiling your Sunday? I want to send my greetings to New Bedford, Massachusetts. I want to send especial greetings to Minnesota, home of my dear good friends, the Mayos. Perhaps I have an especial feeling of love for Minnesota because it is so much like Finland, with many beautiful lakes, and forests of birch and pine and spruce. And I know so many fine people there, with good blood that came from Finland, and our neighboring countries of Sweden, Norway and Denmark. To them, and to all my friends in the United States of America I say, 'Thank you and God bless you and good-by.' "

He has turned to Miranda with a shrug, as though to say, "I'm sorry, but that's the best I could do." Corween takes over the microphone: "Thank you, Dr. Kaarlo Valkonen. This is David Corween in Helsinki, returning you now to New York."

"Never will I speak to one of those damned things again," swears Dr. Valkonen, but the others are greatly pleased. Miranda is sure he was quite wonderful and Corween is convinced the

Doctor has a definite radio personality. Even Gus, who was in charge of the "mixer," insists the Doctor's voice came through fine.

The Valkonens' son, Erik, who has been away on a holiday, is home. With him is his girl friend, Kaatri Alquist. Erik "is seventeen years old, but mature and calm. He is handsome and healthy." Kaatri "is very pretty, very young and quite serious."

The young people are affectionately welcomed. They have brought gifts from Viipuri—chocolates for Mrs. Valkonen and some Viipurin Rinkelia, a favorite bread, for the Doctor. Gifts following a trip are a custom of the country. And so is politeness.

"I've noticed that here—and in Sweden, too—everybody is insufferably polite," notes Dave Corween. "Why, yesterday, in Stockholm, my cab side-swiped another cab, so the two drivers got out and apologized to each other. It's unnatural."

"I know," admits Miranda. "I've lived here for twenty years. I've never got used to it."

"I used to think, Mr. Corween, in my ignorance, that you Americans have no national character," the Doctor is saying. "My wife has taught me my error. Her character is strong enough to resist all civilizing influences. And sometimes I think our son has inherited too much from her."

MIRANDA—That's what Kaatri thinks. Kaatri is the girl friend I was telling you about. I'm afraid she disapproves of me. Too shallow—too frivolous.

KAARLO—Oh, Kaatri comes from a typically Finnish military family. Her father is a colonel and her brothers are all brought up to be fighters. Very formidable! Maybe she does disapprove of you, my dear, but in her heart she wishes she could be more like you. She wishes she could have as much fun as we do.

MIRANDA—I'll have a good talk with her some time.

DAVE—I'm interested in that work your son is doing.

KAARLO—I tell him it's silly—but he won't listen.

DAVE—It seems a sensible thing for anyone to be preparing for trouble these days.

KAARLO—Yes—eminently sensible. But they don't know how to prepare. That's the trouble. They build those concrete pillboxes, and tank traps—as if such things could save anybody when Armageddon comes.

MIRANDA—What does it matter, darling? They enjoy doing the work.

KAARLO—Yes—and I suppose it's good exercise. (ERIK *and*

KAATRI *come in.*) Erik and hundreds of other students spend
all their free time on the Mannerheim Line. Kaatri is there, too,
with the women's organization, to do the cooking and cleaning.
Oh, they have a lot of fun—and maybe a little romance in the
long evenings, eh, Kaatri?

KAATRI (*she giggles, then answers soberly*)—In the evening we
have discussions, Dr. Valkonen.

DAVE—And may I ask—what sort of things do you discuss?

KAATRI—Last night we tried to arrive at some conclusions
about the consequences of the Munich treaty.

DAVE—I'd like to know what your conclusions were?

ERIK—Just what you would probably hear in a similar discussion in America, Mr. Corween. We thanked heaven for the ge-
ography which puts us so far from the scene of action. We were
grateful that we do not live in Czechoslovakia or the Balkans, or
even England or France.

Miranda has been serving coffee, and now a pitcher of Parker
House Punch arrives. It is a special preparation of Miranda's in
honor of her American visitors. They drink it in a toast to Dr.
Valkonen's benefactor, the late Alfred Nobel. . . .

Corween has drawn young Erik into conversation respecting his
studies—economics and sociology. "And ski-ing," puts in Dr.
Valkonen. "He can't make up his mind whether he wants to be
another Karl Marx, or another Olympic champion."

"Have you been much in the Soviet Union?"

"Oh, yes. We lived there when Father was working with
Pavlov."

"And you really believe they might invade this country?"

"If there were counter revolution in Russia, anything might
happen. Or the Nazis might come that way. We have to be
prepared."

"I know the Russians," Dr. Valkonen is saying. "I was a medical officer in their army and I was with them in prison camp in
Germany all through 1916. And during the revolution I was right
there in Leningrad on the staff of the Strelka Hospital. I treated
Lenin for a sore throat! And I can tell you about these Russians:
they love to plot—but they don't love to fight. And the reason
they don't love to fight is that they're a little like the Italians—
they're too charming—they really don't know how to hate."

Dr. Ziemssen has called. He is a neighbor, and also the German Consul General. "He is a mild, scholarly, correct German
of thirty-five," and he has come to report that he has just talked

with Berlin about Dr. Valkonen's broadcast, which had been picked up at his government's short wave station.

"Good God! I seem to remember that I said some things that were not for your government to hear."

"Have no worries on that score, Herr Doktor," says Dr. Ziemssen. "We are well accustomed to hearing the worst about ourselves. We have heard you frequently, Mr. Corween."

"Don't be frightened by Dr. Ziemssen," advises Dr. Valkonen. "He was an anthropologist before he became a diplomat. He's very broadminded."

The talk has turned to the Finnish defenses, which Dr. Ziemssen is convinced are magnificent. But the Czechs had fine defenses, too, Erik reminds them.

"Ah, but you are more intelligent than the Czechs," ventures Dr. Ziemssen. "You have no allies to betray you." He is laughing as he turns to Corween. "How do you feel about that, Mr. Corween? You were at Munich?"

"If you had asked me that question a few years ago," Corween answers; "if you had asked me any questions of cosmic significance, I could have answered without a moment's hesitation. I was the youngest genius ever to be given a by-line in the *Chicago Daily News*. I was on intimate terms with both God and Mammon. The wisdom of the ages was set before me on a half-shell. All I had to do was add horse-radish and eat."

"You have become a little less confident in recent years?"

"Well, since then I have been de-educated, if there is such a word. I've covered Manchukuo, Ethiopia, Spain, China, Austria, Czechoslovakia. And all I can say is—I'm bewildered. But I suspect, Dr. Valkonen, that when you say the human race is in danger of going insane, you're not so much a prophet of future doom as a reporter of current fact." He is suddenly conscious of holding the floor. "I seem to be sounding off," he adds. "That punch is powerful."

"Good! Then have some more and tell us what it was like in Ethiopia," cheerily suggests Miranda.

But Dave is through. He must be about his business of finding out what it is like in Finland. He is hoping to get a glimpse of the Mannerheim Line. And he is also hoping to see them all again. At the Olympic games in 1940 if not before. Now he has gone.

"Do you like him, Erik? He's nice, isn't he?" asks Miranda.

ERIK—Yes. I wish I could do work like that. To be able to wander all over the earth—and see things—without being a part of them.

KAATRI (*darting a worried look at* ERIK)—I'd hate such a life.

MIRANDA—Why, Kaatri?

KAATRI—When you see too much of the world it makes you cynical. I'd never want to be that.

MIRANDA—I agree with you, but I've traveled all over and it hasn't made me cynical. Perhaps that's because I'm just plain stupid.

ZIEMSSEN—Ah, no, Frau Valkonen. It is only because you are an American.

ERIK—A journalist like Mr. Corween has the opportunity to see the *truth*. Maybe the ultimate truth is the ultimate futility—

MIRANDA (*laughing at this*)—Oh, dear. That boy really should have a beard.

ERIK—Even so—I'd like to know it. (UNCLE WALDEMAR *starts to play a gay tune.*)

MIRANDA—Kaatri, the next time we go to America, I'll ask your father and mother if you can go with us. Would you like that?

KAATRI—Oh, I think I should love that!

KAARLO—I hope some of your relatives will send us a cable so we'll know how I really sounded.

MIRANDA—If I know New Bedford, they'll send a postcard . . . What's that you're playing now, Uncle Waldemar? (UNCLE WALDEMAR *doesn't hear. She turns to* DR. ZIEMSSEN.) What is that?

ZIEMSSEN (*listening, appreciatively*)—I believe that is Meri-kantor's "Tolari Ja Huotari," isn't it? (*He listens a moment.*) Yes—a delightful little Finnish folk song. (UNCLE WALDEMAR *continues to play variations on the theme—and plays it like a music-box.*)

MIRANDA—Oh—I love that.

"She pats Kaarlo's hand. They listen silently, happily to the music." The curtain falls.

ACT II

It is a year later—an evening late in November, 1939. In the Valkonen living room, Kaatri is sitting on the couch crocheting. Erik is at the window looking at millions of stars, he says, but Kaatri is convinced he is looking for bombers. Erik is sure there will be no bombings, but that, Kaatri reminds him, with some spirit, is what Poland thought. True, it was the Nazis who bombed Poland, but the Russians went in, too—

"But they know perfectly well if they attack us it would mean betrayal of the revolution!" insists Erik. "The suffering they might inflict on us would be insignificant compared to the murder of their own honor."

"Honor!"

"That's what my father says," persists Erik, "and he knows them."

"I don't believe they ever had any honor—Tsarists or Bolshevists either. My father knows them, too. That's why he has spent his life preparing to fight them when they invade our country."

But Erik would talk of other things; of their engagement; of his going to work to earn money for their support; of their being always together and being happy. They are in each other's arms now and wondering what their wedding will be like.

"It will be in the Agricola church, and there'll be lots of flowers," says Kaatri.

"Your father will be looking stern and magnificent in his colonel's uniform," visions Erik. "And my father, in his black coat, looking bored. And Mother behaving like a grand duchess, and Uncle Waldemar playing da-da-de-dum—" (*He hums a bar of Mendelssohn's "Wedding March."*)

"And then we'll escape from all of them, and go home, and have several children."

"Erik!" They are laughing happily as they kiss each other.

"Oh, Kaatri! We'll be happy people, you and I. That's all that matters, isn't it, dearest?"

"Yes." Suddenly the happiness fades from her face. "No! It isn't all that matters," she says.

"What else is there?"

"There's *now!*" She is looking away from him, but still holding him close. "There may be war. Next summer may never come to us. There's this—"

"I tell you we don't have to think about those things. We're young and we're free. We have only our own love, for each other—"

They break apart guiltily as Uncle Waldemar comes through the door. They would explain their embarrassment, but he stops them. Uncle Waldemar is carrying a newspaper and is measurably excited. The newspaper reports that the United States has offered its good services to settle the Soviet-Finnish dispute. He doesn't think that will come to anything and he is sure Russia will attack Finland.

"My father doesn't agree with you," objects Erik.

"And what does *he* know about it?"

"As much as anyone could. He understands the Russians. He was the good friend of Pavlov and Gorki, and even Lenin himself."

"All those gentlemen you mention are dead. And the revolution—that's dead, too. It's embalmed and exposed in a glass coffin in front of the Kremlin. It is respected—but dead. Now comes the true disintegration—the end of the world. Your father said—men might become again like apes, groping their way back into the jungle. Well—it has come to pass. Men are groping their way through the night. The lights are out in Berlin, Paris, London. And in Warsaw, they crawl through the ruins like rats. It will be the same here. This is war in the jungle, and the winner will be crowned 'King of Beasts.' "

Miranda Valkonen, "looking very smart in her furs and her Paris hat," is home from an errand. She had stopped in at the laboratory and found Dr. Valkonen surrounded by dozens of barking, howling dogs. She could do nothing about it. She had stopped in at the American Legation where they had told her the United States State Department had ordered all Americans to leave Finland. "He was very guarded in his choice of words," she says, "but he seems to think that things are rather serious."

"So does Uncle Waldemar," answers Erik. "But that doesn't mean anything. The American government—all governments—are being pulverized with fear by this Soviet propaganda. (*He picks up the paper from the piano.*) They want to pulverize us, too, so that we'll give them what they want without a struggle. It's all bluff—it's all imitation of the Nazis."

"But when the bluff doesn't work, suppose they go on imitating the Nazis—suppose they do attack?"

"Then—we'll have to fight—that's all."

Would Erik fight? Of course he would. So would everybody. For as long as they could. Which would be long enough to prove that Finland has a right to live.

"And who will derive any benefit from that proof?" demands Miranda. "Are you anxious to die just to get applause from the civilized world—applause and probably nothing else? The Czechs are fine, brave people—but they didn't offer any resistance to the Germans."

ERIK—They couldn't. Their resistance was stolen from them at Munich.

MIRANDA—Even so—they're better off now than the Poles, who did resist.

ERIK—That doesn't affect my feeling. I only know that if anyone is going to take my freedom from me, he's going to have to pay for it.

MIRANDA—Now you're talking like a boy scout.

ERIK—I'm your son, Mother. I have the same blood in me that you have—the blood of that gentleman up there. (*He points to the portrait of Great-grandfather Eustis.*) He fought pirates in the Mediterranean. He fought with Jackson at New Orleans.

MIRANDA—Yes—and when he died, in honored old age, they had to pass the hat around among the neighbors to get enough to bury him. (*Pointing to the portrait of her grandfather.*) Whereas that unselfish hero who paid another man to take his place in the conscript army—when he died—the whole town turned out—the Chamber of Commerce, the Republican Club, the Knights of Pythias—all paying tribute to the memory of a good, substantial citizen. If you have to look to your ancestry for guidance, look to him. He was no hero. He was a despicable, slimy cheat. But he did very well. . . . You say someone will have to pay for your freedom. But who will receive the payment? Not you, when you're dead.

KAATRI (*fiercely*)—Don't listen to her, Erik! Don't listen to her!

MIRANDA—Why shouldn't he listen to me, Kaatri?

KAATRI (*with too much vehemence*)—Because you're an American! You don't understand.

MIRANDA (*patiently*)—I understand one thing, Kaatri. Erik is my son. I want to save his life.

KAATRI—What good is his life if it has to be spent in slavery? (*To* ERIK.) And that's what it would be if he gave in to them. Slavery for you—for all of us. Oh, I know that you Americans don't like to think of such terrible things.

ERIK—Kaatri! You mustn't say that—

MIRANDA (*gently*)—You may say what you please about me, Kaatri. But you can't say it about Erik. He's as loyal as you are. He was born in this house, as his father was before him.

KAATRI—Dr. Valkonen is like you. He doesn't really belong

to this country. He is a great scientist. He has an international mind.

MIRANDA—And is that a bad thing?

KAATRI—Oh, no—it's a good thing—a noble thing. But for Erik—it would be weakness. I'm afraid for Erik—afraid that he belongs more to America than he does to us. Oh—I don't want to be rude, Mrs. Valkonen—to you or your country. But we're desperate people now. All the men in my family—my father, my brothers—they're all in the army now, on the frontier. It's the same with all families, rich and poor, men and women. All our lives we've had to be ready to fight, for everything we are, everything we believe in. Oh, I know—it's hard for you to understand that—or to see the *need* for it that is in our souls.

ERIK—Kaatri! Of course Mother can understand! Americans fought for that same thing—for the same reason—the same need, that was in their souls. It was the Americans who taught the whole world that it was worth *fighting* for!

KAATRI—Yes. But—it's just as Dr. Valkonen says. When life becomes too easy for people, something changes in their character, something is lost. Americans now are too lucky. (*She looks straight at* MIRANDA.) In your blood is the water of those oceans that have made your country safe. But—don't try to persuade Erik that life here is as easy as it is in America. (*She is speaking passionately, desperately.*) He's a Finn, and the time has come when he must behave like one.

Erik has gone to Kaatri and taken her in his arms. "Kaatri, my dearest—don't—don't cry," he is saying, as she buries her head against him. The word "dearest" impresses Miranda. She had not before been fully conscious of Erik's and Kaatri's love for each other, nor of their being engaged to be married. They were still children to her. But now she is glad, glad to know of what has happened. When, a moment later, Dr. Valkonen comes in, all excitement about his dogs and a recent experiment, she would stop him to give him the good news. "Erik and Kaatri are going to be married!"

The news is also a little unbelievable to Kaarlo. Erik! Married! He has to laugh at that. At first. But soon he has hold of himself and has gone to Erik and kissed him and congratulated him, and Kaatri, too, because he will be delighted to have her as a daughter-in-law.

"Ever since Erik was born I've been training him to be a gentleman of taste and discrimination, and, by God, I've succeeded," exclaims Kaarlo. And now he is all for having some schnapps as a toast to the happy couple, and then supper.

Supper, however, is going to be late, Miranda explains. Everybody is going to church to pray that Finland will be able to defend itself. Kaarlo will have to go, too, and wear his tail coat. Kaarlo may submit to church, but he doesn't want to hear any war talk—

"Neither do I, Kaarlo. But I've had to hear it. Erik is ready to fight," says Miranda.

KAARLO—Erik? You're a child. It seems to me that you are deciding too suddenly that you are grown up. If you want to consider yourself engaged to be married, I have no objection— I'm delighted. But I don't want to hear that you are talking to your mother, or to anyone else about going to war.

ERIK—I'm sorry, Father—but I have to do what I think best.

KAARLO—And are you *able* to think?

MIRANDA—Oh, Kaarlo!—Of course Erik knows—

KAARLO—No, Miranda. Don't interrupt. (*To* ERIK.) I repeat—in forming this heroic resolve to fight—have you used one grain of the intelligence that I know you possess?

ERIK—I hope I have.

KAARLO—Hoping is not good enough. You have seen those celebrations in Red Square—all those aeroplanes, those huge tanks, those troops marching—hundreds of thousands of them?

ERIK—Yes, Father—I've seen them.

KAARLO—And yet you dare to pretend that you're competent to stand up against such a force as that?

ERIK—That's why I've trained with the volunteer ski troops and why I've worked to help make the Mannerheim Line so strong they can never break through.

KAARLO—All that nonsensical child's play on skis—

ERIK—Kaatri's brother Vaino is younger than I am—but he's with his father's regiment at the frontier . . .

KAARLO (*bitterly*)—Oh! If we are at war with the Soviet Union, *I* shall be at the frontier, too. Surely we'll need everybody, including the aged and decrepit.

MIRANDA—Now, really, Kaarlo, that is just simply ridiculous—

KAARLO (*sitting*)—I can press the trigger of a machine gun just as well as Erik— So that's what we're going to pray for? Ability to imitate our enemies in the display of force. It is all nothing but a substitute for intelligent thinking.

ERIK—This is not a time for intelligent thinking! That doesn't do any good.

KAARLO—No?

ERIK—When your enemies are relying on force, you can't meet them with theories. You can't throw books at them—even good books. What else can anybody do but fight?

KAARLO—This is no time for intelligent thinking! So this is the climax of a century of scientific miracles. This is what the great men worked for—what *they* fought for in their laboratories. Pasteur, Koch, Ehrlich, Lister. They saved lives that we might build Mannerheim Lines in which to die.

Faintly in the distance the church bells are ringing. Kaarlo decides to put on his tail coat and go to church to "join in asking God to grant the impossible." But he will provide his own prayer. Miranda has gone to get her things. Kaatri is again in Erik's arms, assuring him of her love and asking forgiveness for the things she said that might have made him unhappy.

Erik understands. He understands his father and mother, too. And how natural it is for them to live, not in this country, nor in this time, but in a future of their own imagining. "They are wonderful people—wonderful and unreal," he says to Kaatri. "You *are* real. You know what we have to face—and we will face it without fear."

Kaarlo is back and in his tail coat. It smells terribly of moth balls, he insists, and will be a church scandal. But Miranda reassures him. There will be so much of that smell in the church no one will notice.

They have started now. "Come, Miranda, we go to pray," Kaarlo is saying. "O God, have pity, for that which we have greatly feared has come upon us."

He switches off the light and they go through the door as the curtain falls.

It is the next afternoon. The appearance of the Valkonens' living room is unchanged, save for the long black curtains that have been hung at the windows. At the moment these are drawn apart to let the sun in.

Uncle Waldemar is at the piano playing softly. Miranda, coming from the dining room, carrying a dust cloth and wearing an apron, is eager to know if he has seen either Kaarlo or Erik.

Uncle Waldemar can tell her of having seen Kaarlo at the hospital. He was all right. As for Erik, he has neither seen nor heard of him. The air raid? Yes, several bombs had fallen.

Perhaps thirty people were killed, the police said.

Uncle Waldemar is in a confessional mood. He would like to apologize for having been so poor a companion to Kaarlo and Miranda in the past. Especially does he want to apologize to Miranda—"You have worked so hard and so well to make this a happy home," he is saying.

"I've never done any work in my life, and I've never wanted to," insists Miranda, dusting a chair.

"You have filled this house with laughter—your own peculiar American kind of laughter. And here I have been, in the midst of all this happiness, an apostle of despair."

He should not be asking forgiveness for having told the truth, Miranda reminds him. But Uncle Waldemar cannot be turned from his convictions. He should have had more philosophy. He who had lived for forty years under the tyranny of the Tsars, and then seen his country rise from its ashes, should have been reconciled to what is happening.

". . . I have always believed in God's mercy," Uncle Waldemar is saying. "I have served Him in His church. Whenever I was in doubt and fear, I would go back to the teachings of Martin Luther—to the doctrine of 'The Freedom of the Christian Man.' And then I would believe again that the virtues of simple faith would always triumph over intolerance. Whenever I had enough money saved, I would go to Germany, to Eisenach, to the room in the Wartburg where Luther worked. 'A mighty fortress is our God.' But last year when I was there I saw the Nazis. I saw old friends of mine, living in terror—some of them because they have Jewish blood—some just because they retain a sense of common decency. Even ministers of the gospel—afraid that if they preached the true devotion to God's word they would go into concentration camps. I saw men marching—marching—marching. Day and night singing, 'Today we own Germany—tomorrow the whole world.' They didn't know where they were marching to. They didn't care. They had been drilled and lectured down to the level where marching itself was enough."

"They can't win, Uncle Waldemar."

"Can we prevent them from winning? All we can do is defend ourselves to the end. And then they sweep over us to the next goal—and the next—"

"You're a good Christian, Uncle Waldemar. You have to believe that they can't win."

"I can believe in the coming of the Antichrist. I can believe in the Apocalypse," says Uncle Waldemar, passionately. " 'And

Satan shall be loosed out of his prison, and shall go out to deceive the nations which are in the four quarters of the Earth.' "

Erik has come. He is wearing the uniform of the ski-troops. He has only a few minutes. He must pack his things and be back for assembly at the station. His troop is leaving for the North. He tries to avoid his mother's gaze. He kisses her cheek as he goes to get his things.

Miranda is in the kitchen getting what food she can find for Erik when Kaarlo comes, bringing Dave Corween with him. The broadcaster is back in Helsinki temporarily, but he doesn't know for how long. He has sought out the Valkonens partly at the request of Jim Walsh of the American Legation. Mr. Walsh is eager that they should take advantage of a ship that is sailing from the Swedish port of Goteborg the following Tuesday carrying refugees to New York. Dr. Valkonen is grateful for both Mr. Walsh's and Mr. Corween's interest, but—

"I am needed here for the time being," he says. "There is a great shortage of doctors. All of the young men in all the hospitals are going to the front, for service with the army medical corps. There will be many more casualties here from air-raids."

DAVE—It is not my business to say so, Doctor—but that isn't suitable work for a winner of the Nobel prize.

KAARLO (*with great sadness*)—It is not suitable work for any member of the human race, Mr. Corween. But someone must do it.

DAVE—I realize that you're a patriotic citizen of this country—

KAARLO—I am not a patriotic citizen of this country, Mr. Corween. I hope I am aware of the fact that "patriotism" as now practiced is one of the most virulent manifestations of evil.

DAVE—Yes, Doctor. That's just what I mean. You're a citizen of the world. You're of importance to the whole world, not just to these few gallant men who are going to fight and die for Finland. . . . Oh—I know it's presumptuous of me to be talking to you. But—I beg you, please, for God's sake, while you still have the chance, go to a country where you can carry on your work— your own fight—to bring men to consciousness—

KAARLO—But I shall carry on that work as long as I live, Mr. Corween—wherever I am.

DAVE—As long as you live! I'm sorry if I seem unduly emotional about it, Doctor—but—I have seen too many men of intellectual distinction forced into uniform, forced to pick up guns and shoot because they had discovered that their intelligence was

impotent to cope with brutal reality. You may be forced into
that situation, Dr. Valkonen. You who have devoted yourself
to discovering the inward defenses of man. You may find yourself, crouching behind a sand-bag, shooting at an illiterate Russian
peasant.

KAARLO—Yes, Mr. Corween. You know whereof you speak.
And I should be the last to dispute you. Now—we feel like
heroes, strong in the armor of the justice of our own cause.
Tomorrow—we may be corpses. It is all very foolish—very
temporary. But, you see, I am accustomed to this sort of thing.
In my youth, this country was ruled by the Romanovs. I survived that oppression. I am prepared to endure it again. Let the
forces of evil engulf us. If the truth is in here, my friend—
(*He taps his chest.*)

Miranda and Erik have come back. Dave has left with the
expressed hope that he will see them soon again. Erik is notice-
ably anxious as he faces his father—

"I take it you know what you're doing—what chances you have
of accomplishing anything," Kaarlo is saying.

"Yes, Father. I think I know about that."

"Very well, then. There's nothing I can say to you but
good-by."

"Father, before I go, I want you to know that I'm sorry for
you. I think I understand what this is for you. It's worse for
you than it is for any of us. But—if it's any consolation to you—
I hope you'll remember—you have a son who at least obeys the
Fourth Commandant. I honor my father and my mother."

The emotion is a bit too much for Erik. He hides his face in
his hands as his father leans over and kisses his cheek tenderly.
"Go on, go on, Erik," Kaarlo mutters. Erik turns to his mother.
"I'll go to the door with you, darling," says Miranda.

Dr. Ziemssen has called. He, too, is eager that Dr. Valkonen
should leave Finland at once. He is not surprised to hear that
Mr. Corween also has urged the move—

"Mr. Corween is a remarkably well-informed man. He is aware
of the inevitable outcome of this war, as you yourself must be,
Herr Doktor. Oh—I have all admiration for the Little Finnish
army. But two hundred thousand against ten million—"

"Yes, we will be conquered, as we have been conquered before.
And then we will be ruled from Moscow—as we were formerly
ruled from Petersburg. But as I was just saying to Mr. Corween,
I shall continue with my experiments."

"Dr. Valkonen—I must warn you—you are making a serious mistake. . . . You think your enemies are these—these Communists who now invade your country? . . . The Russians think so, too, but they are wrong. *We* are your enemies, Herr Doktor. This Finnish incident is one little item in our vast scheme. We make good use of our esteemed allies of the Soviet Union. All the little communist cells, in labor movements, youth movements, in all nations—they are now working for *us*, although they may not know it. Communism is a good laxative to loosen the constricted bowels of democracy. When it has served that purpose, it will disappear down the sewer with the excrement that must be purged."

KAARLO—It seems to me, Dr. Ziemssen, you are talking with extremely undiplomatic frankness.

ZIEMSSEN—I know I can do so to you, Herr Doktor. You are a scientist. You are accustomed to face facts—even those facts which to the ordinary, dull mind are too terrible to contemplate.

KAARLO—What is it you are threatening, Doctor? What is going to happen to Finland?

ZIEMSSEN—You do not know the whole story of what happened to Poland. (KAARLO *looks at him, rises and walks away.*) You will hear the Pope in Rome weeping publicly and proclaiming that the Polish nation will rise again. I assure you it will not rise again, because, as a nation, it is dead. The remnants of its people are scattered all the way from the Rhine to the Pacific Coast of Siberia. This is the process of annihilation. It is a studied technique, and it was not invented in Moscow. You will find the blue-prints of it, not in "Das Kapital," but in "Mein Kampf." It is all there for you to read. It involves, first, liquidation of all leaders of thought—political, religious, economic, intellectual. (KAARLO *sits down. He seems to slump.*) Among the masses—the difficult ones are killed—the weaklings are allowed to die of starvation—the strong ones are enslaved.

KAARLO—You are an anthropologist—a man of learning, Dr. Ziemssen. Do you approve of this technique?

ZIEMSSEN—Naturally, I regret the necessity for it. But I *admit* the necessity. And so must you, Dr. Valkonen. Remember that every great state of the past in its stages of construction has required slavery. Today, the greatest world state is in process of formation. There is a great need for slave labor. And these Finns and Scandinavians would be useful. They are strong;

they have great capacity for endurance. Is that brutal—ruthless? Yes. But I am now talking to a scientist, not a sniveling sentimentalist. Vivisection has been called brutal, ruthless—but it is necessary for the survival of man. So it is necessary that inferior races be considered merely as animals. . . . Do you believe me, Herr Doktor?

KAARLO—I believe you. Although—still talking as one scientist to another—I cannot help wondering just how you establish proof that these other races are inferior, especially when you know it is a lie.

ZIEMSSEN—Of course it is a lie, biologically. But we can prove it by the very simple expedient of asserting our own superiority—just as the Romans did before they decayed—and the Anglo-Saxons, before *they* decayed. View this objectively, Herr Doktor, and then you will be able to proceed with your experiments. You have made important progress in an important field—conditioning men to their environment. That can be of extraordinary value to us in the future. You can help to postpone, perhaps indefinitely, the time when we will be conquered by decay. But, first—you must accept the theory of the new world state, for that *is* the environment of the future. If you refuse to accept, and stay here and attempt to resist destiny, you will die.

KAARLO—Where can one go to escape this world state?

ZIEMSSEN (*smiles*)—An intelligent question, Herr Doktor. I assure you that the United States is secure for the present. It may continue so for a long time, if the Americans refrain from interfering with us in Mexico and South America and Canada. And I believe they will refrain. They are now showing far greater intelligence in that respect than ever before. They are learning to mind their own shrinking business.

KAARLO—I appreciate your motives in warning me, Dr. Ziemssen. And I understand that all you have told me is confidential.

ZIEMSSEN (*laughing*)—You *are* an innocent, my friend. Nothing that I have said is confidential. You may repeat it all. And you will not be believed. There is the proof of our superiority—that our objectives are so vast that our pigmy-minded enemies simply have not the capacity to believe them. They are eager to accept the big lies we give them, because they cannot comprehend the big truth. (*Rises.*) And the big truth is this: For the first time since the whole surface of the earth became known, one dynamic race is on the march to occupy that surface and rule it. When you have absorbed that huge conception, you will

find that your own theories can be adjusted to it. And now I
must go.

Uncle Waldemar has come to switch on the lights and close
the black curtains. Kaarlo would have him go at once to the
American Legation, see Mr. Walsh, and make arrangements for
Miranda to leave for America on the ship that is to sail from
Goteborg. Yes, Kaarlo is sending Miranda away alone. If she
should refuse to go Kaarlo will find some way of persuading her.
It may hurt her to think he wants her to go, but it will be a hurt
from which she will recover.

And now Kaarlo is employing his most persuasive arguments
to convince Miranda that she should go home, to her own country. He wishes it. He is needed in Finland, but Miranda is not.
What has she been trained to do, except wear lovely clothes and
be a charming hostess—

"You are an intelligent woman, Miranda," Kaarlo is saying.
"Reason this out for yourself. You will see that this is a time
when everyone who eats bread must have worked to earn it.
And, God help us, there is only one form of work that matters
now—resistance—blind, dogged, desperate resistance."

"You've said yourself—that kind of resistance is useless."

"You don't know what I've said. Or—if you know the words,
you have less idea of their meaning than the youngest of the
students who hear my lectures at the Institute. I'm not insulting
your courage, Miranda. Nor your good will. I'm sure you would
like to be useful. But you can't. You know you can't."

Still Miranda will not give up. Finland is the country of her
husband and her son. She doesn't think that Erik would be
particularly proud of his mother if she were "to scurry to safety
at the first sound of a shot fired." It is obvious what Kaarlo is
trying to say—that he doesn't want her, doesn't need her—

"Miranda! You don't understand why I want you to go," cries
Kaarlo out of his misery.

"It makes no difference to me whether I understand it or not,"
she says. "There's one thing I do know, and you'd better know
it, too: I am not going. Probably, you *don't* need me. You have
important work to do—and I'm sure that's enough, for you. But
the time may come when Erik might need me, and when that
time comes, I intend to be here. . . ."

KAARLO—No, please—for God's sake—don't keep on bringing
Erik into it! Wasn't it bad enough to see him going away like

that, in his uniform? That poor, hopeful, defenseless child! (*He sees that he has hurt her terribly with that.*) Oh—I'm sorry, darling. You must see that I've been making a desperate attempt to drive you to safety with lies. It's no use. You always can make me tell the truth. The *real* trouble is—you've had too much confidence in me. How could you know that I was living in a dream—a beautiful, wishful dream in which you played your own unsubstantial but exciting part? And now—there is war—and our own son goes to fight—and I wake up to discover that reality itself is a hideous nightmare. (*He is looking into her eyes, desperately.*)

MIRANDA—What has happened, Kaarlo? What have you heard?

KAARLO—I have suddenly realized what and where I am. I am a man working in the apparent security of a laboratory. I am working on a theory so tentative that it may take hundreds of years of research, and generations of workers to prove it. I am trying to defeat insanity—degeneration of the human race. And then—a band of pyromaniacs enters the building in which I work. And that building is the world—the whole planet—not just Finland. They set fire to it. What can I do? Until that fire is put out, there can be no peace—no freedom from fear—no hope of progress for mankind. . . . (*Despairing.*) Every day that we hold them off—will only serve to increase the terror of the vengeance which must surely descend upon us. All the pathetic survivors of this war will have to pay in torture for the heroism of the dead. And it isn't just us—not just this one little breed that wants to be free. This is a war for everybody—yes—even for the scientists who thought themselves immune behind their test tubes. (*He looks into her eyes again.*) Darling! I can stand this ordeal if I know it is only for myself. I can stand it if I know you are safe—that you are beyond their reach. . . . I love you. That is the only reality left to me. I love you. (*They are in each other's arms. For a moment, they are silent.*)

MIRANDA—Then I can stand it, too, darling, whatever it is. I can stand it as long as I know that you love me—that you do need me—that I am essential, after all. Even if I am a woman who is nothing but a woman. Even at a time when the whole life of the world is marching with men. . . . (*She kisses him fiercely.*)

KAARLO—I'm sorry, Miranda, I hadn't intended to talk like this. I'm frightened.

MIRANDA—You should talk to me, Kaarlo. You always have.

Why should you change now? Now come and have some coffee. (*They cross to the piano.*) It's not very warm.
KAARLO—Oh. That's all right.

It is New Year's Day of 1940. There is a Christmas tree in the Valkonens' living room. Uncle Waldemar is at the piano, playing something surprisingly gay and spirited. Now Dr. Valkonen is there, wearing the uniform coat of a colonel in the Medical Corps, and feeling a little self-conscious. Shortly he will be leaving for the front—

"When Erik went—I—I thought our world had come to an end," Kaarlo is saying to Uncle Waldemar. "Since then—I have been struggling to adjust myself—to find in all this tragedy some intimation of hope for the future."

"I know, Kaarlo."

"This—represents the final stage in that attempt at adjustment. It is like the moment when a scientist knows he can no longer experiment with guinea pigs—he must now test his theories on human life itself. It is kill or cure."

In the kitchen Miranda has been making a pitcher of egg-nog, which she brings in. Kaarlo's uniform is something of a shock to her. She had not known that he was leaving that afternoon for Viipuri. Nor is she entirely satisfied with his explanation that he is only going up for a few days to inspect some new hospital space. Dave Corween is going with him, he explains, and several others. They are riding up in a new American ambulance recently arrived from France.

There has been no word from Erik, but they must believe that he is all right. There isn't much chance for sending letters from the Arctic.

Now Dave Corween has arrived, and brought with him four others—Major Rutkowski, "a tired, tragic young Polish officer;" Joe Burnett, "tall, lean, about 40, wearing a uniform assembled from various wars;" Ben Geichner and Frank Olmstead, of the American Ambulance Corps, with Red Cross insignia on their sleeves.

There is a babel of greetings which merges finally into a toast offered by Dave. "I'm not at my best without a mike and a coast-to-coast hook-up," admits Dave, lifting his glass to Miranda. "However, we want to tell you we're glad to be here, enjoying your gracious hospitality, and we hope that this New Year will bring you and yours health and happiness."

Again a babel of small talk that includes the visitors' admiration for the nice Victorian quality of the Valkonen home, and personal confessions from them as to why they are, or are not, militarily minded. And how they happen to be doing what they are doing: of Maj. Rutkowski, who had been with the Polish cavalry and escaped by way of Riga, hoping to join the Polish Legion in France; of Ben, who had been working for the American Express in Paris and thought he would like to see the countries to which he had sold many tours; of Joe Burnett, who had spent the last two years in one of Gen. Franco's dungeons, after having been kicked out of Princeton for having thrown a few forward passes in chapel, and of Frank, who really wanted to be a poet and who is admittedly a pacifist at heart. Why is Frank there? "Because I'm a crazy fool, that's why," answers Frank.

"That's interesting," says Miranda. "How many crazy fools do you suppose there are in America?"

"I can name four hundred and seventy-three of my own acquaintance."

"The pioneers were fools. And as for that goof, Columbus— why didn't he stay home and mind his own business?"

"Have you ever met any Americans before, Major?" Miranda asks of Rutkowski.

"No, I'm sorry, I have not."

"Then this will give you a faint idea."

"I am glad of the opportunity," responds the Major. "I have often wondered what it would be like to be an American—to believe, even for a moment, that such things as peace and security are possible. You see, we have never been permitted such belief. For us, the sun rose each morning among our enemies—and it set among our enemies. And now, it is high noon, and our enemies have joined together over our country—and we are gone."

"It isn't always so completely delightful to be an American, Major," confesses Dave Corween. "Sometimes even we have an uncomfortable feeling of insecurity. I imagine that Pontius Pilate didn't feel entirely at peace with himself. He knew that this was a good, just man, who didn't deserve death. He was against the crown of thorns on principle. But when they cried, 'Crucify Him!' all Pilate could say was, 'Bring me a basin of water, so that I can wash my hands of the whole matter.'"

All the guests have risen as Dr. Valkonen, in full uniform, and Uncle Waldemar come in. Now they are gathered around the pitcher of egg-nog, have filled their glasses and are drinking a toast to the friends from the United States and Poland, and long life to the Republic of Finland. And now they have formed a group around the piano and, as Frank plays, they sing "Auld Lang Syne" fairly lustily.

Suddenly Kaatri has appeared at the door. She is wearing her Lotta uniform, is very pale and is looking wildly around at all the strangers as Miranda goes to her. Kaatri is plainly in need of help. Sensing the situation, Dave and the others are quick to say their good-bys and leave.

"I've written every day to Erik," Kaatri is saying, half sobbingly. "I haven't heard from him since that first letter two weeks ago. I've got to see him, Mrs. Valkonen. Don't you think they could give him a little leave?"

MIRANDA—He'll surely have leave soon, dear. The Russians have to stop attacking some time. Isn't that so, Kaarlo?

KAARLO—Of course it is. Erik's all right. In fact, he's probably enjoying himself. He likes that energetic life. Now—I must go—

KAATRI—No—please, Dr. Valkonen. There's something I have to ask you. I'm going to have a baby.

MIRANDA (*rising*)—Darling! (*She takes her in her arms.*)

KAARLO—Well! I'm very happy to hear it.

KAATRI—I'm not happy. I don't want it! Dr. Valkonen! What can I do to stop it? Please tell me what I can do.

MIRANDA—You're not ashamed, Kaatri? There's nothing for you to be ashamed of.

KAATRI—No—I'm not! But I don't want it. You've got to help me, Dr. Valkonen.

KAARLO—Have you told your family of this?

KAATRI—No. It wouldn't be easy for them to understand, as you do, about Erik and me.

MIRANDA—Why don't you want to have a baby, Kaatri?

KAATRI—I'm working. It would make me useless—just another person to be cared for—

MIRANDA—That's not being useless.

KAATRI—It is now! What good would it be to bring a child into a world like this? He would have no country—no hope. *Please,* Dr. Valkonen. I'm sorry to be troubling you. But—just tell me some doctor that I can see.

KAARLO—You will see Dr. Palm. Miranda—you know him.

MIRANDA—Yes, Kaarlo.

KAARLO—You take Kaatri to see him. Tell him that this is our daughter-in-law, and her baby will be our grandchild. (KAATRI *looks at him with terror.*) Yes, my dear, you are going to have that child.

KAATRI (*hysterical*)—No—no! I won't have it! (*She tries desperately to break away from them.*) I won't have a child born under a curse!

MIRANDA—Quiet, dear. Please. (*She seats* KAATRI *beside her.*)

KAATRI (*another attempt to get away*)—No! You won't help me. I'll find a doctor—

KAARLO—Do as my wife tells you, Kaatri! You love Erik, and he loves you. You are willing to be married to him. You have taken responsibility. The highest responsibility! You are not going to evade it.

MIRANDA—Kaatri—Kaatri! (KAATRI *submits.* KAARLO *leans over her.*)

KAARLO—Whatever happens to our country, your child will not be born under a curse. It will be born to the greatest opportunity that any child has ever known, since the beginning of time. Remember that, and be brave. . . . Now—I can't keep them waiting. Good-by, Uncle Waldemar. I'll be back soon.

UNCLE WALDEMAR—Yes, Kaarlo. Good-by. (*They kiss.* KAARLO *leans over and kisses* KAATRI'S *head. Then he takes* MIRANDA'S *hand. She rises, looks back, motions to* UNCLE WALDEMAR *to come to* KAATRI.)

KAARLO—Come on, darling. (*They exit.* KAATRI *is crumpled up on the couch. Uncle Waldemar goes over to her, sits down beside her, and takes her in his arms.*)

UNCLE WALDEMAR—Now—don't cry, Kaatri. Pay attention to what Dr. Valkonen told you. He knows what he is saying. If he tells you there is good hope, you can believe him.

The curtain falls.

ACT III

In his room at the Hotel Kamp, in Helsinki, Dave Corween is sitting before a microphone with a type-script in front of him, awaiting a "Go ahead" signal. Beside him, Gus, his assistant, is fooling with the mixer. It is an evening in February.

The room is pretty much of a mess. Dave's typewriter is on a chair in the center of the room, deep in copy paper and carbon sheets. The signal comes and Dave goes on with his broadcast—

"In an attempt to surround the main force of the Finnish army on the Karelian Isthmus, the Russians are now making determined attacks across Viipuri Bay," is his report. "The Mannerheim Line, supposedly impregnable bulwark of Finland's defense, has been shattered. The bombardment of these defenses, and of Viipuri itself, has now reached the terrible total of three hundred thousand shells a day. Looking at the ruination in Viipuri, I could not help thinking of the despairing prophecies made by H. G. Wells in 'The Shape of Things to Come.' Here was the awful picture of the collapse of our Western civilization, the beginning of the Age of Frustration . . ."

Dave has finished. He has, Joe Burnett thinks, held his own with the serialized "Renfrew of the Mounted," but more than that, he is probably wasting his breath, because nobody in America is listening.

Joe is just back from the North and reports that Dr. Valkonen, with his Red Cross aids, have established several hospitals and are now working day and night to evacuate them. No, he has not seen anything of Erik Valkonen. But he had come through one rather startling adventure. He was flying low, looking for the greatest point of Russian concentration, when he came suddenly upon a row of staff cars filled with Nazis. The revelation that the Nazis, as suspected, were fighting with the Russians, had given Joe such a turn that he let them have it—

"It was a beautiful sight to see 'em diving into the ditches, mussing their slick gray uniforms in the mud," says Joe.

"Did you get any of them?"

"I'm afraid I'll never know. . . . Is there any news from home?"

"Yes. . . . This has been the biggest season in the history of Miami Beach. The University of Southern California won the national basketball championship. The Beaux Arts Ball was an outstanding success."

There is a knock at the door. It is Miranda Valkonen. She is very pale. She has come to ask a favor. She is eager to get her daughter-in-law, Kaatri, out of the country. Kaatri and Erik had been married at the hospital just before Erik died—

"Kaatri is going to have a baby. She's very ill. I've made all the arrangements to get her to Norway, and then to New York. But she has to leave right away. I need some American money, Dave. Could you lend me fifty dollars? It will be paid back."

"Will that be enough?"

"Oh, yes—that will be plenty." She opens her handbag and takes out a sheet of paper. "Here is the name and address of my aunt in Boston. When you get back to America, just write to her and tell her where to send the money. You see—the

Finnish money is worth very little in foreign exchange now. By the time Kaatri arrives in New York, it might be completely worthless. That's why I had to have dollars."

"I wish you were going with her."

"I wish I could. I should like to be present at the birth of my grandchild. Poor Kaatri. She'll have a bad time of it, all alone there. I'm afraid my relatives won't be of much comfort. Perhaps she'll have a son, and he'll grow up a nice, respectable New Englander and go to Harvard and wonder why he has an odd name like Valkonen. . . . Erik wasn't very badly wounded. He might have pulled through if he hadn't been in such a state of terrible exhaustion. It was a lucky thing that we learned where he was and got to him. I sent word to Kaarlo. I don't know where he is—somewhere around Viipuri. They're getting closer, aren't they, Dave?"

"Yes."

"I'm very grateful for that loan," says Miranda, rising. "I hope you will come to see Uncle Waldemar and me. We're always there."

"Thank you, Mrs. Valkonen. I—I wish to God you'd let me really *do* something."

"But you've done a lot, Dave. That fifty dollars—"

"It's not much satisfaction to know that fifty dollars is the best I can do."

"It's all I want, Dave. All I can use. I was desperately anxious to get Kaatri out of the country. You can understand why. It means one little link with the future. It gives us the illusion of survival—and perhaps it isn't just an illusion . . . Good-by, Dave."

"Good-by." The curtain has fallen.

A few days later we are in the classroom of a little country school in eastern Finland. It is the afternoon of a gloomy day. At the back of the room is a dais, with a row of desks facing it. "The size of the pupils' desks indicates that this is a classroom for little children of nine or ten. . . . There is a blackboard with arithmetical problems. On the walls are tacked rows of sketches done by the pupils. Around the room on the walls are painted, in decorative, colored Finnish script, the first ten lines of the Kalevala."

At one of the desks a soldier is sitting, solemnly playing solitaire. "He is a mild, tired Englishman, about thirty-five years old. He wears the uniform of an infantry soldier." His name is Gosden.

A scuffle at the door brings Gosden to his feet, with his rifle in position. The two Red Cross ambulance men, Ben Gichner and Frank Olmstead are the intruders. They come in with their hands up, but as soon as they explain that they are not Russians and unarmed, their welcome is hearty. Gosden has been pretty lonesome.

In an exchange of explanatory confidences the ambulance men learn that Gosden as a volunteer is easily accounted for—

"I came because I was bored, fed up," Gosden is saying. "My wife and two little children were sent to Cornwall in the evacuation. Then I lost my job. I was working in the furniture department at Harrod's—and who wants to buy furniture in war time? I couldn't join up with our own army—too old. All I could do was walk the streets looking at nothing. There was no news to read in the papers—except about heroic little Finland. On Christmas, I felt I couldn't stick it out any longer. So—I thought— why not have a go at heroic little Finland? And here I am. Where I shall be tomorrow, I really couldn't say."

Major Rutkowski and Dr. Valkonen have arrived. The Doctor is wearing a Red Cross arm-band on his uniform. He is, once he has shaken off the numbness of the cold, greatly interested in the little schoolroom.

"You know—they must have left this school very quickly— right in the midst of an arithmetic lesson," Dr. Valkonen is saying. "Look—there's a multiplication problem that was never finished. The pupils were probably delighted but—(*Pointing to the sketches.*)—they had to leave without knowing which picture won first prize."

Fascinated, his eyes wander about the room. He notes the desks where the children sat and the sketches they have left pinned to the wall. His listeners catch something of his fascination as he reads from the epic poem of Finland, the Kalevala, to them.

"It had its beginnings in the songs of our minstrels a thousand years ago," he is explaining. "Your poet Longfellow knew the Kalevala and used its rhythm in 'Hiawatha,'—

> " 'Let us clasp our hands together,
>   Let us interlock our fingers;
>   Let us sing a cheerful measure,
>   Let us use our best endeavors—'

"Every Finnish child learns about the Kalevala—just as Americans learn those words about Life, Liberty and the Pursuit of Happiness."

They are quiet for a moment. Then Frank would ask a question. Frank has been carrying Dr. Valkonen's book about with him ever since he arrived in Finland, and he has found himself puzzled by it—especially at the very end—which he reads aloud—

" 'How long, O Lord, before we shall hear the sound of the Seventh Angel of the Apocalypse? Have you forgotten the promise of St. John? "And they shall see his face, and his name shall be in their foreheads. And there shall be no night there and they need no candle, neither light of the sun; for the Lord giveth them light; and they shall reign forever and ever." How long, O Lord, before we shall be given to see the true revelation?' (FRANK *closes the book and looks at* KAARLO.) Why did you conclude a scientific work with Biblical words—and what do you mean by the true revelation?"

KAARLO—It's the revealing to us of ourselves—of what we are —and what we may be. (*Smiles.*) Of course—we can all use the Book of Revelation to substantiate our own theories. It's an eternally effective device. I have heard evangelist charlatans quote it to prove that if you do not accept their nonsense and pay for it, you will most surely burn in hell. But there is something profound in those words I quoted. That unknown Jewish mystic who wrote that—somehow, unconsciously, he knew that man will find the true name of God in his own forehead, in the mysteries of his own mind. "And there shall be no night there." That is the basis of all the work I have done.

FRANK—And how do you feel about that work now, Dr. Valkonen?

KAARLO—I think I've learned a great deal in the last few months. Research work in the field! I never dreamed I would have such a vast laboratory, with so many specimens.

BEN—Have you arrived at any new conclusions, Doctor?

KAARLO—Not conclusions, I'm afraid. Just—somewhat stronger suspicions. It is wonderful to see what men are capable of—what courage—what endurance—what utter lack of selfishness. And what a tragedy that these heroic qualities can be tested only by disease. That's what all this is, you know—disease. All of this— reasonless war—aimless revolution—it's a psychological epidemic. (*He rises. It is as though he were lecturing to a class.*) We had seen it coming, for a long time, long before 1914, even. But we had no conception of its extent. And now the very belief of men that they can insulate themselves against it is in itself a sign of lunacy. The germs of that disease travel on the air waves. The only defenses are still here—behind the forehead. I apologize, . . . for carrying on a conversation which must be extremely boring to you.

GOSDEN—I'm an ignorant man, sir. I haven't read this book—didn't even know I was in the presence of anyone who had written a book. But—from what you've said—I have a feeling it's all hopeless. I shouldn't care to die believing *that*.

KAARLO—Then you won't die believing it's hopeless. That's the point, my friend. You have lived in faith—the light is in you—and it is the light which gives the strength that defeats death. It's only the fearful—the unbelieving—those who have sold themselves to the murderers and the liars—they are the only ones who can really die.

FRANK—But how can you deny that the light is going out—it's going fast—everywhere?

KAARLO (*on platform*)—It is just beginning to burn with a healthy flame. I know this, because I have seen it. I have seen it in all kinds of men, of all races, and all varieties of faith. They are coming to consciousness. Look at all the millions of men now under arms, and all those that are fearful that arms may be thrust upon them. Are there any illusions of glory among any of them? None whatever! Isn't that progress?

BEN—Far be it from me to argue, Doctor, but I can't see the difference whether men go to war because of illusions of glory, or just in a spirit of grim resignation.

KAARLO—There is all the difference. Because those illusions, when shattered, leave men hollow. They say, "Oh, what's the use? What have we got to live for?" They are devitalized by the conviction of futility. But grim resignation, as you call it, that makes a man say, "This is an evil job—but I have to do it." And when men say that, they are already beginning to ask, "But why do I have to do it? Why must this evil go on forever?" And when men start asking questions, they are not satisfied until they find the answers. That is consciousness. And for the first time in history, consciousness is not just the privilege of a few secluded philosophers. It is free for all. For the first time, individual men are fighting to know themselves. . . . Forgive me, gentlemen. I forget myself. I think I am lecturing at the Medical Institute. But—(*He pauses to listen to the guns.*)—the Russians are only one kilometer away. This may be my last lecture. So—please permit me to finish. (*He is speaking deliberately but with a sense of excitement.*) Listen! What you hear now—this terrible sound that fills the earth—it is the death rattle. One may say easily and dramatically that it is the death rattle of civilization. But—I choose to believe differently. I believe it is the long deferred death rattle of the primordial beast. We are conquering bestiality, not with our muscles and our swords, but with the power of the light that is in our minds. What a thrilling challenge this is to all Science! To play its part in the ultimate triumph of evolution. To help speed the day when man becomes genuinely human, instead of the synthetic creature—part bogus angel, part actual brute—that he has imagined himself in the dark past—

The sound of an approaching motorcycle is heard. Shortly Joe Burnett is with them. Joe had been shot down from the air and just managed to make a landing. Now he is looking for headquarters and another plane.

Joe comes from Helsinki, too. He has seen Dave Corween. He has heard about Dr. Valkonen's son, and is the bearer of the sad news of Erik's death in hospital. The blow is a hard one for Dr. Valkonen to take. With great dignity he accepts it, and their sympathy—

". . . Thank you for telling me, Mr. Burnett. I imagine my wife has written me all this, but we have moved about so much that there have been no letters in weeks. I'm sorry you had to undergo this embarrassment."

Major Rutkowski is back. He reports the Russians approaching rapidly. They are bringing tanks over the ice. The Finns are forming to drive them back. They need more men. There are no reserves. Rutkowski has brought a revolver and belt salvaged from an officer who was killed. He thinks Dr. Valkonen had better take them. There are rifles for the others. There is no compulsion. They don't have to go if they don't wish to.

Dr. Valkonen has gone to an adjoining schoolroom to write a letter to his wife, hoping Joe will be able to get it through to Helsinki. The thought to Frank Olmstead is depressing—

"Do you know that Dr. Valkonen believes in the teachings of Christ?" demands Frank, a little excitedly. "He believes in them as if they were scientific facts, which can yet be proved. He says

so in his book. He says you can't resist evil by building Maginot
Lines and big navies. So now—there's nothing left for him to do
but take a gun and go up there and shoot."

It is all wrong, this fighting and dying. Frank is convinced of
that. He would be a conscientious objector—if he had the
courage. And if his conscience would let him. Even with the
choice of quitting or dying now he hasn't the guts to say, "No, I
won't fight." Let them kid him if they like.

The others have no idea of kidding anybody. Major Rutkowski is frank in admitting that he believes they are all condemned
to death. They take that opinion calmly.

"I can't help agreeing with you, Frank," says Ben Gichner.
"It seems a silly way to end your life."

"Any way is silly," puts in Joe Burnett. "A cousin of mine
was killed—he and his girl both—driving home from a debutante
party at the Ritz in New York. He was a little tight, and he
didn't notice the Dead End sign—and—phft!—right into the East
River!"

"Every one of us can find plenty of reasons for *not* fighting,"
agrees the Englishman, Gosden; "and they're the best reasons in
the world. But—the time comes when you've bloody well got to
fight—and you might just as well go cheerfully."

They are adjusting their equipment, getting ready to move.
Their good-bys are casual. There is no attempt at a false gaiety.
They wish each other luck and promise, if they do get through, to
get in touch with each other's relatives. "I wish I'd written to
my missus to tell her I'm going up the line in good company,"
says Gosden.

Joe has taken Dr. Valkonen's letter. The others have gone on.
Major Rutkowski is watching the Doctor with silent sympathy.
"Forgive me, Dr. Valkonen," he says. "I hadn't known of the
great loss you have suffered."

"Thank you. I had been expecting that news for a long time.
I was prepared for it. My son had a good character—part Finnish, part American. He was not afraid."

Dr. Valkonen has put on his coat and strapped the revolver belt
around his waist.

"Doctor, I think you had better take off that Red Cross arm
band," suggests Rutkowski, as he goes out.

For a second Dr. Valkonen stands in silhouette as he rips off
the band. Then, with a final, pitying look around the room at
the inscription of the Kalevala, he starts to pick up his Red

Cross pack, but turns away. He will not need that. Not ever again. He is going through the door as the curtain falls.

A few days later, Uncle Waldemar is standing at a window in the Valkonens' living room. Dave Corween and Joe Burnett come from the dining room. They have just finished lunch and Mrs. Valkonen has refused to let them help her clear the dishes. Uncle Waldemar goes to take their place.

The boys have found it difficult to express themselves in the face of Miranda's stoicism. "She's lost everybody that she loves, and now she's in terrible danger of losing her own life," Dave is saying. "But it's a matter of principle that neither she nor anyone else must ever admit that there are certain undertones of tragedy in the situation. After all the centuries, New England is still New England. You might even go so far as to say that it's still England. Keeping a stiff upper lip."

Dave has tried to get Miranda and Uncle Waldemar to leave Helsinki, but they won't leave. "They're going to wait here for whatever comes, the Russians, or the Nazis, or both," he explains to Joe. "They've even planned how they'll burn the house down. That's required by Finnish tradition. It's like the scorched earth in China. Mrs. Valkonen wants to stay here and die, just as her husband did. She doesn't care what happens."

"It's a pity."

"That's what it is, Joe. A wholesale pity. Three months ago, the Soviet troops marched in. They had brass bands and truckloads of propaganda with them. They thought it would be just a grand parade through Finland, like May Day in the Red Square. So now—several hundred thousand men have been killed—millions of other lives ruined. The cause of revolution all over the world has been set back incalculably. The Soviet Union has been reduced from the status of a great power to that of a great fraud. And the Nazis have won another bloodless victory."

Miranda and Uncle Waldemar join them, and Joe takes his leave. Miranda is very grateful to Joe for having brought her the letter from Kaarlo, and for telling her about the little schoolhouse.

"He's the only one left of those young men who went to Viipuri with Kaarlo," she says, when Joe has gone.

And now Dave must be going, too. He doesn't know whether he is to be sent to Stockholm to investigate peace rumors or not. He is still worried about Mrs. Valkonen. But Miranda and Uncle Waldemar have their plans all made. From the hospital they have recovered a couple of army rifles discarded by wounded soldiers, and have learned how to use them. When the Russians had first come their Finnish President had promised that they would fight—all of them, even the women and the old people— and so they will. Miranda has taken a rifle, and stands facing the window, showing Dave how she can slip a cartridge into place, and throw out the empty shell.

"When we see them coming from the shore down there, we'll light the fire," she says. "It's all ready down in the cellar. Then we'll go out into the garden behind the stone wall with the guns and ammunition. . . . What do you think of that, Dave?" She looks up at the 1812 portrait. "Great-grandfather Eustis thinks it's fine."

Miranda has found a package that she wants Dave to take back to America with him. It contains Kaarlo's signed pictures of Freud and Pavlov, of Carrel and the Mayos. "He was very proud of those pictures," she says. "There's also the Nobel gold medal. I want you to take the package and the letter and give them to Kaatri, to keep for her child. You have that address in Boston —my aunt, who is going to pay you back the fifty dollars I borrowed?"

"Yes, I have the address."

MIRANDA (*looking at the letter*)—Kaarlo had just heard from me about Erik's death. He wanted to comfort me in his curious way. Do you mind if I read you the letter?

DAVE—Please do.

MIRANDA (*reading*)—"In this time of our own grief it is not easy to summon up the philosophy which has been formed from long study of the sufferings of others. But I must do it, and you must help me." You see he wanted to make me feel that I'm stronger—wiser. "I have often read the words which Pericles spoke over the bodies of the dead in the dark hour when the light of Athenian democracy was being extinguished by the Spartans. He told the mourning people that he could not give them any of the old words which tell how fair and noble it is to die in battle. Those empty words were old even then, twenty-four centuries ago. But he urged them to find revival in the memory of the commonwealth which they together had achieved, and he promised them that the story of their commonwealth would never die, but would live on, far away, woven into the fabric of other men's lives. I believe that these words can be said now of our own dead and our own commonwealth. I have always believed in the mystic truth of the resurrection. The great leaders of the mind and the spirit—Socrates, Christ, Lincoln—were all done to death that the full measure of their contribution to human experience might never be lost. Now—the death of our son is only a fragment in the death of our country. But Erik and the others who give their lives are also giving to mankind a symbol—a little symbol, to be sure, but a clear one—of man's unconquerable aspiration to dignity and freedom and purity in the sight of God. When I made that radio speech—you remember?—I quoted from St. Paul. I repeat those words to you now, darling: 'We glory in tribulations; knowing that tribulation worketh patience; and patience, experience; and experience, hope.' There are men here from all different countries. Fine men. Those Americans who were at our house on New Year's Day—and that nice Polish officer Major Rutkowski—they are all here. They are waiting for me now, so I must close this, with all my love." (*She folds the letter and hands it to* DAVE.) There it is, Dave. Take good care of it.

DAVE—I shall, Mrs. Valkonen. But it may be a long time before I can deliver it.

MIRANDA—It will be a long time before my grandchild learns to read.

DAVE (*after a moment's silence*)—I—I have to be going now. . . . (*He goes quickly to* UNCLE WALDEMAR.) Good-by, Mr. Sederstrum.

UNCLE WALDEMAR (*shaking hands with* DAVE)—Good-by, Mr. Corween.

MIRANDA—You'll surely let us know if you're going to Stockholm?

DAVE—Oh, yes, Mrs. Valkonen.

MIRANDA—We'll miss you very much, Dave. You've really become part of our life here in Helsinki.

"Miranda and Dave have gone out on that. Uncle Waldemar looks after them, then he sits down at the piano. Still looking toward the door, he starts to play the little Finnish folk song heard at the end of the first scene. After a moment, Miranda returns. She goes to the couch and sits down where she had sat beside Kaarlo at the end of the first act. She listens to Uncle Waldemar's playing. She looks to the left, where Erik had been, and to the right, where Kaarlo had been."

THE CURTAIN FALLS

KEY LARGO

A Tragedy in a Prologue and Two Acts

By Maxwell Anderson

PAUL MUNI had been in Hollywood for seven years when he came back to Broadway this season to play the disillusioned hero of Maxwell Anderson's "Key Largo." The return was at once felicitous and eloquent. Mr. Anderson, too, had been taking a rest from the serious drama that has engaged his attention the last several seasons. He had spent a year toying with a play with music, the "Knickerbocker Holiday" of pleasant memory. Now he was back writing his stirring blank verse in something of the mood which produced "Winterset."

There was some little doubt in the minds of most of his play's reviewers as to whether or not Mr. Anderson had read his title clear in all that he wrote in "Key Largo," but there was no doubt expressed of his high purpose nor of his great gifts as a dramatist. And there was fine praise for Mr. Muni's sympathetic and understanding performance of the young crusader who led a little band of idealists into Loyalist Spain and left them when he counted the cause lost.

"Bright moonlight comes down across a rocky hilltop in northern Spain, revealing four young men on outpost guard duty," writes Mr. Anderson in describing the opening scene of "Key Largo." "They are Americans, dressed haphazardly in nondescript uniforms, zipper overalls and mufti, well worn and uncared for."

There is a pup-tent at the side, and three of the four young men are sprawled about trying to catch a bit of sleep. The fourth sits at the top of the hill, writing on a pad on his knee, humming softly to himself and evidently taking his guard duty quite casually. Occasionally, from afar off, there is a flash of light in the sky, followed by a low, rumbling detonation.

It is the humming that disturbs the sleepers rather than the faraway booming, but their protests leave the guard quite unmoved. He is writing poetry—meaningless poetry, it may be, as one soldier insists, but excellent poetry for all that, having to do with the moon and a mood.

The poet, who is called Victor, is also writing a letter to his sister in Key Largo, which is in Florida. But there is no time to talk about that. Shadows have appeared down the hill, and they probably mean that the two who are missing, King and Shippy, are returning—returning, it is the pious hope of the four, with food.

The shadow proves to be King, and he has two sacks of food. But he is alone. He is also a little angered that Victor should stand up, exposing himself with his silhouette neatly outlined against the sky. They are not as far from danger as they may think. The enemy is closing in. Where there was no one between them and the road this morning, there are now two trucks parked below.

And where is Shippy? Shippy is in the hospital. "That big gun laid one down right outside the village," King reports. "We both dropped and Shippy didn't get up." King would have stayed with Shippy, but he had to get their grub back to them. And here it is—mostly dry-pack-chocolate and biscuits. And one cut of salami. They can cut the salami in five pieces. They're only five now, instead of the eight they started with—

"We've been lucky, comparatively," observes one named Monte. "Whole companies have been wiped out, not a man left to turn in a report. We're used to being lucky and it hits us hard when somebody goes."

"You're sure he (Shippy) won't come to enough to talk?" asks Victor.

"Positive. . . ."

"This is the God-damndest loneliest mountain this side of hell," bursts out a soldier called Jerry.

"Well, take your section," commands another named Nimmo, who is dividing the sausage. "Salami's salami whether it's in six cuts or five."

"Aren't we beginning to talk like a lot of drafted men with a choice between prison and the front line?" demands Monte. "We volunteered, mind you. It isn't our fight, and it never was our fight, but we made it our fight. We said that to each other before we came over here—we said if a lot of good, healthy men don't die for Spain right now there won't be any place on earth where a free man can live in a couple of years. Well, we're in Spain, and three of us are dead in Spain—and will stay dead for the rest of time. Maybe we'll all die and stay dead—but the original proposition remains unchanged. I admit it's getting pretty close, and I don't find it very comfortable, but if I can manage to keep my food down maybe I'll stick it out."

"To say nothing of the fact that you'd damn well better stick it out now you're here. Because if you don't they'll stand you up against an outhouse and shoot you."

"I guess we all know the honeymoon's over."

"It's not that so much. It's mostly you don't like yourself as much as you did—or respect yourself. When you're in a fight it doesn't count how you got in it, or what you're out to get. You have to crawl on your belly and rip up the other fellow's guts just the same. And it does something to you. Because it's a stinking business, and it makes you stink."

"Quit talking, and eat your food. You'll need it before the night's over."

The talk goes on just the same. They are a pretty confused group it soon appears. Jerry would like to know what they're really out to get. Nimmo thinks he knows, as they all did, when they volunteered, but on the other hand, if they're fighting for freedom and the right to keep it, and they believe in the rights of minorities, and there are already fifty-seven minorities in Loyalist Spain—

". . . if they won and it came to a vote, and one party was in power, would it make hash of the other fifty-six varieties!" Nimmo would know. "They're very intense about politics, these Spanish. Once they get in an argument, they don't care how long they live, and they don't think it matters about you, either. Each one of them intends to live as he God damn pleases, and he intends to see to it that everybody else lives the way he wants them to!"

"Hasn't it always looked the same, the fight for freedom?" demands Victor. "It's never respectable. It's led by unscrupulous fanatics, each one eyeing the others' throats. They're followed by a rabble that pulls down all the walls and lets the roofs fall in on them. A lot of people die, good and bad, but there is more freedom later, for the next generation, there is. If you want a clean, Armageddon battle, all the beasts of hell against the angels of light, you won't get that, not in this world!"

"No. Well, I'm not complaining, except about the food," says Nimmo.

Now their attention is drawn to King, who has dragged his kit from the tent and is apparently doing a job of sewing. As it happens, King is not sewing. He's ripping—ripping out all the tags and marks of identification. King is preparing to leave, and

they had better be preparing, too. "We're changing names and
seeping out of here," advises King.

MONTE—Are we ordered out?

KING—No. But I led you here. I'm responsible, and I mean
to get you out.

JERRY (*saluting*)—As you say, commandante. Here's to hell
or Paris. But I prefer Paris.

MONTE—Remember, King, this is a democratic army, and even
anarchistic in spots—we'd want to know what's on your mind,
because we have minds of our own, all of us.

KING—Why, certainly. Take a vote. I was at that wine-shop
back of the convent waiting to hear how Shippy came out, when
in walked a couple of officers, spread out their maps and went to
work. I guess they didn't see me. I was up in the alcove.
Well, there's to be a general retirement along this line; our ridge
is being abandoned; they're falling back three miles to the rear.

VICTOR—When?

KING—Tonight and part of tomorrow. There's a lot of stuff
to move, and it takes time; they want to be out before Mr.
Franco's scouts begin to notice. Have we had marching orders?
Are we going anywhere?

MONTE—Not that I know of.

KING—No, and you won't get any. We're left to hold the
ridge.

MONTE—How do you know?

KING—I heard something vague about Hill 4—how it would
take them anyway twenty-four hours to blast us out of here, and
by that time they'd be dug in three miles back.

MONTE—They're leaving us to cover the retreat?

KING—That's what I gathered. And why not? It's good
strategy. This salient's way out of line, and never could be held
in a general assault. But if they withdrew without a rear-guard
action they'd be caught in the valley and massacred. They have
to choose between losing a lot of men and losing a few, and we're
picked for the few. Personally I don't take it. I'm fed up with
the war, and the whole damn setup from God and Chamberlain
on down. I'm ripping a few identification marks and labels off
my clothes and leaving. And so are you.

There is some talk of passports and of how they can probably
trick the enemy when they reach the enemy lines with a sob story
of some sort. But the boys aren't quite ready to accept King's

plan with enthusiasm. After all they are supposed to hold the ridge. And if they do quit and are caught they'll be shot anyway.

It is better to take the chance than not to take it, argues King. Even though, as Monte muses, sadly, "An ignominious exit from our crusade." King has an answer for that, too. Says he—

> "Was there ever a crusade
> without an ignominious end? Before
> we came to Spain we should have thought of that.
> The knights in rusty armor crippling home
> with an increment of blood and bone diseases
> from Palestine—leaving the infidels
> in charge as usual. Or the A.E.F.
> over-seas for democracy, and winning—
> along with other diseases—
> this Mussolini and Hitler. Yes, and Franco,
> very likely."

VICTOR—Isn't this a graver matter than you pretend, King?

KING— It's running for your life. That's grave enough.

VICTOR—If we go it's more than an end
to our crusade. It's an end to everything
we were, everything we talked of in your room
under the skylight, an end to all the meaning
you found in the world. We haven't talked much
lately.
I thought it was only because there wasn't time,
but maybe you've changed and haven't told us.

KING— I have.
I was trying to hold on. When you've believed
that right wins in the end it's a little hard
to turn round suddenly on a battle-front
and say the hell with it.

VICTOR—But you've turned round now
and said it?

KING— Yes.

VICTOR—But right does win in the end.

KING— Only if you believe whoever wins
is right in the end. Because we're losing here—
and dying here!

VICTOR—You have been our leader, King.
Certainly you've been mine. We haven't been cow‹
ards,

           any of us, but we've let you show the way
           most of the time. Are we suddenly afraid
           to die, when suddenly it's necessary?
           Are you afraid? If you are then it's come about
           between tonight and this morning.
KING— Nobody's afraid
           to die when he sees good reason for it. Hell,
           we're not here for fun! We came believing
           there was some use in it! Maybe some of us think
           there still is use. I've been trying to hold on
           this last half-year—I've been trying to believe
           the whole world would rise up and step on this evil
           that crawls over Spain—and it has risen up,
           and stepped on us. And now I'm beginning to wonder
           if a cause is sacred when it's lost. Did we volunteer
           to die in a lost cause?
VICTOR—What's gone? What's changed
           since yesterday?
KING— Our cause is lost, that's all.
           Maybe because there isn't any God
           and nobody cares who wins. Anyway if you win
           you never get what you fight for, never get
           the least approximation of the thing
           you were sold on when you enlisted. No, you find
           instead that you were fighting to impose
           some monstrous, bloody injustice, some revenge
           that would end in another war.

What does he think the war has lost for them? Monte would know. Because of what he heard and read between the lines, King answers. So let them get their duffle and come on.

"Look," King is saying: "We were children, suckled in one of these nutmeg Alma Maters, and Spain was a bugle call. Up and to Spain and save the world! Byron went out to Greece about a hundred years ago and died in a swamp of the fever. Don Quixote went out against the windmills. It was a Spaniard who knew his Spain well enough to write Quixote—and we should have read it.—I know I'm a turncoat; it was my romantic notion to save Spain, and I was eloquent about it. Yes, maybe I thought I talked like Rupert Brooke—for all I know maybe I thought I looked like that poor Galahad of Gallipoli, saving heaven for the angels.—The best I can do now is to be fairly honest about it,

and get you out and get myself out. They say there's just one
test for whether a man's a fool—it's how long he lives and how
well."

They're getting ready to pack now. Jerry and Nimmo are
ready. Monte still hangs back a little. And Victor. Victor is
decided. He isn't going. If he stays alone, well, he'll be alone.
Nor can King argue him out of his determination. Victor has
been brought up to think of Spain and freedom "first in the
morning, and first at night. It took the place of prayers with us,"
he explains, "but that's because my father's a little crazy, according to the neighbors, and I'm infected—not that I mind."

VICTOR—I have to believe
            there's something in the world that isn't evil—
            I have to believe there's something in the world
            that would rather die than accept injustice—something
            positive for good—that can't be killed—
            or I'll die inside. And now that the sky's found empty
            a man has to be his own god for himself—
            has to prove to himself that a man can die
            for what he believes—if ever the time comes to him
            when he's asked to choose, and it just so happens
            it's up to me tonight.—And I stay here.
            I don't say it's up to you—I couldn't tell
            about another man—or any of you—
            but I know it's up to me.
KING—   Is it up to us still,
            after all the betrayals, after the game's changed
            and we're cheated on both sides? After the Russian
            secret police taking over our own brigade? And
              Munich,
            and Czechoslovakia, and this last betrayal
            of Spain by France and England? We should know
            by this time—we've looked at Europe long enough
            to know there's nothing to fight for here—that nothing
            you win means freedom or equality
            or justice—that all the formulas are false—
            and known to be false—democracy, communism,
            socialism, naziism—dead religions
            nobody believes in—or if he does believe
            he's quietly made use of by the boys
            who long ago learned better, and believe

in nothing but themselves. Let it end—let them end
   it—
these idiot ideologies that snarl
across borders at each other. Stalin walking
his swamps in blood, Hitler's swastikas
in blood above the lintels, the English and French
desperate because everything has failed,
because life itself has failed, and capitalism,
and they may even lose their colonies,
unless God can be revived. And here in Spain,
Franco will win in Spain, they'll see to that—
but if he didn't, Stalin would win in Spain,
and it's one blood-purge or the other, but never justice,
only the rat-men ratting on each other
in a kind of rat despair.—I tell you it was a dream,
all a dream we had, in a dream world,
of brothers who put out a helping hand
to brothers, and might save them.—Long ago
men found out the sky was empty; it follows
that men are a silly accident, meaningless,
here in the empty sky, like a flag on the moon,
as meaningless as an expedition led
to take possession of it—in the name of Marx—
or maybe democracy—or social justice!
Why should we die here for a dead cause, for a symbol,
on these empty ramparts, where there's nothing to win,
even if you could win?
VICTOR—Yes, but if I die
then I know men will never give in;
then I'll know there's something in the race
of men, because even I had it, that hates injustice
more than it wants to live.—Because even I had it—
and I'm no hero.—And that means the Hitlers
and the Mussolinis always lose in the end—
force loses in the long run, and the spirit wins,
whatever spirit is. Anyway it's the thing
that says it's better to sit here with the moon
and hold them off while I can. If I went with you
I'd never know whether the race was turning
down again, to the dinosaurs—this way
I keep my faith. In myself and what men are.
And in what we may be.

KING— Well—
VICTOR—Oh, I know all this
         sounds priggish—it's the manly thing to joke
         in extremis—but just for the record let it stand,
         and now we'll forget it.
KING—   If you won't argue
         there's no arguing. I only wish
         we could all stick together. Are we ready?

They're not ready. First Monte decides to stick with Victor.
Then Jerry. And then Nimmo. "With the four of us we might
hold them. Long enough—while the shock troops got away!"
says Nimmo. It gives them a new thought. King is packed and
ready. As he stands silhouetted on the embankment he turns
to them.
"It's not cowardice, you know," he says, "it's plain, common,
everyday horse-sense; it's not me that's crazy." They are looking at him silently. "Don't you see I can't save you, but you
can save yourselves, and if you don't I'll run from you all like a
pack of ghosts?"

VICTOR—But you shouldn't.
         You shouldn't, King. Why can't you think of us
         as among the fortunate few whose lives have had
         a meaning right up to the end? And not as heroes—
         just ordinary fellows who ate breakfast
         on a certain morning—and then ate lunch and dinner
         and slept exceptionally long that night—
         as why shouldn't they?
KING—   Well, anything I can do?
         You were writing a letter.
VICTOR—It isn't finished,
         and it wasn't important. Give me your hand, though.
KING—   Good-by.
VICTOR—You're doing what you believe, and that's all that
matters. (KING *comes down and takes* VICTOR's *hand, then turns
and goes down the hill.*)
MONTE—Has it occurred to you—here in the moonlight—
there's a resemblance between these Spanish mountains and the
mountains of the moon?

Again the flash, and the detonation, as the curtain falls.

ACT I

Some months later we are facing a wharf and a small thatched summer house on Key Largo, Florida. "The planks (of the wharf) end at the water and the blue sea runs out into a blue sky." A table and some chairs are on the porch of the cottage.

Presently Sheriff Gash, "a tall, middle-aged man in leather boots," comes to knock on the door and demand of an elderly man wearing dark glasses who answers the knock whether or not he is Bruno d'Alcala.

He is d'Alcala, and he is blind. No, he has seen nothing of a couple of Seminole boys for whom the Sheriff is searching. Yes, he had a son called Victor. Victor was killed in Spain early in the year. There was some charge on the Sheriff's books against Victor. Victor had given aid, or shelter, to a fellow escaping from a road gang. But—if Victor is dead—

Is there anyone else who might have seen the Seminole boys? There is Alegre, the d'Alcala daughter. But Alegre, a pretty girl who at this moment comes around the corner of the house wearing a wide sun-hat and carrying a basket, has seen no one.

As for others who are staying there, they are a party of transients and d'Alcala would like to do a little complaining against them himself. They are gamblers and they are not honest. They have rented all the d'Alcala rooms, set up their paraphernalia on the wharf, and refused to leave. They fleece the tourists and will give the place a bad name.

Sheriff Gash is not interested in the complaint. If the visitors pay their rent and there is nothing against them the d'Alcalas will have to submit. The county's wide open about gambling just now.

"If you wish them well—if you have any personal concern," says d'Alcala, "if you know anyone who has, then tell him they've burned out their welcome here, and it's high time they leave the Key. There's misfortune in the wind, particularly for Murillo."

"You don't want him here, and I don't blame you, but that's hardly news," says Gash. "The law can't deal with prophecy, you know, only with facts."

The only fact d'Alcala has to offer is his conviction that the Sheriff is taking money from Murillo. That, the Sheriff is quick to retort, as he turns to go, is in the nature of a threat, and doesn't make for friendliness.

And now Alegre is troubled. She has a confession to make to her father—

ALEGRE—   I lied to him. There are two Indians hiding
under water in the mangrove swamp. I saw them
from the clam-flats yesterday, and again today—
I've just come from there.

D'ALCALA—Well, that's God's lie,
as your mother would have said. And modern
science
is less and less insistent on the truth,
seeing there is none.

ALEGRE—   But we're so constructed,
what with our antique conscience, and whatever
makes us blush, that we can't prevaricate
without a sense of fear. It was worse than I told
you.
I put some of Victor's old clothes in my basket
when I went for clams this morning, and left them
there
out of the reach of the tide. They'll find them,
because I saw
where they'd been digging clams.

D'ALCALA—May they find them, and Godspeed
to all poor fugitives. We've seen no one and nothing,
and you were quite right to say so.

ALEGRE—   Then that's all clear—
For a moment I thought it might be sacrilege
to let his clothes go walking down the beach
on some lost vagrant. They were all he left
and had his shape still in them.—

D'ALCALA—It doesn't help
to hang things in a closet, and take them out
on rainy days when you are lonely. I tried that
and it doesn't help.—The Indians are still there,
still hiding among the mangroves?

ALEGRE—   Yes. They must be.
They won't dare leave till dark. Only two black
heads
bobbing behind the roots. They won't be seen
even if there's a search.

D'Alcala—Would they do something for us?
　　　　　Would they do us a favor?　A favor in return?
Alegre—　I think they would.
　　　　　Yes, I saw their faces.
D'Alcala—If I had my eyes
　　　　　I wouldn't need an Indian or anyone else
　　　　　to teach this sheriff!　God, if I had my eyes!
Alegre—　If I could see for you—
D'Alcala—You could take a message
　　　　　and leave it with the clothes.
Alegre—　The truth is, father,
　　　　　I meant to put some breakfast in a basket
　　　　　and take it down later on.　What shall I tell them?
D'Alcala—Only that I must talk to one of them,
　　　　　tonight, if it's possible.

The gamblers have come in with their crudely made wheel of
fortune.　Gage and Corky are a couple of fly city fellows and
experts at their business.　They set up the table and the wheel
that spins above it, being careful to set the bolts tight so the
controls will work.

Alegre passes through the yard as they work.　Corky is wondering how long it would take a guy to make Alegre, who has deter-
minedly ignored all his advances.　It would take much longer than
they will have time to spend in these parts, Gage is quick to answer.　They, and particularly their boss, are in trouble, and trouble of a sort for which they cannot buy protection.

The night before, relates Gage, there had been a little brawl.
The big fellow who had lost all his expense money and made a
play for the boss's girl, was in it.　Gage didn't see anything of
what happened to the big fellow, and doesn't know anything
about anything, but, says he, "I'm willing to bet he's sunk out
there in forty feet of water with a turn of steel clothesline around
his arms, a bag of coral hung on his feet, and a school of these
tropical fishes taking little bites out of his ears."

Gage has an idea that they will not be hanging around there
much longer.　Corky, however, is not convinced.　The boss isn't
easily frightened.　"He's been followed by dead meat before and
it never catches up with him.　He never even worries about it,"
says Corky.　"He wouldn't think of pulling out on account of dead
meat in the water."

Murillo, the boss, flashy as to clothes and domineering and
sinister as to manner, has come to inspect the preparations.　Hunk,

another of his followers, is with him, and there are two rather flashy young women, Priscilla and Killarney.

Murillo is surly and out of temper. Killarney, his girl, is of a mood to meet him in the same spirit. There is fire in her eye and disgust in her voice when she reminds him of the mess he has got himself in for no reason at all. "How long do you think anybody's going to stick with you? With that around your neck?" demands Killarney.

Murillo ignores her and turns to the wheel. As Corky spins it Murillo calls the orders. "Stop it on red. Stop it on zero. Stop it on seven." They are intent on the wheel when King McCloud enters the yard. He is still wearing his bedraggled khaki uniform. Hunk has warned Murillo, who stops the wheel and turns to King.

"Looking for something, neighbor?" he asks.

"Can you tell me who lives here?"

"We all live here."

"Thanks." And King has gone on around the corner of the house without further comment. With a quick motion of his hand Murillo orders Hunk to follow. A moment later Hunk is back with the report that the stranger is only strolling. Walked down to the water's edge and took off his shoes; fixing to wash his feet in the Gulf of Mexico. Must be tired. "I guess we don't worry about him," says Murillo.

Now they have sighted a big car on the way in. A Packard Twelve, which stands for plenty of money. Quickly, at Murillo's command, the group snaps into action, taking positions around the wheel and pretending a deep personal interest in the game.

"Get around to that side, you girls," orders Murillo, giving the wheel a spin. "Spread out a little. And this time no off-hand remarks, if you don't mind. Nothing except what's been rehearsed, and if you can't remember your lines keep quiet. I run this show alone, and you can count on it anything you think of to say is wrong. It just so happens you never queered anything yet, but you will if you go on trying."

A Mr. and Mrs. Aaronson and a Mr. and Mrs. Wheeler, typical tourists, stroll in. They are quite charmed with the place. It's an inn, where they might get rooms and special dinners, according to the sign. And now they have discovered the group at the wheel—

"Well, there you are, ladies and gentlemen! Red again!" Murillo is preparing to count out the money. "Forty dollars for this gentleman, fifty dollars for this other gentleman; am I right, please—? Correct me if I'm wrong! Seventy-five dollars for this lady, and eighty dollars to the lady in red! Count your winnings, ladies and gentlemen, count your winnings! I want to see everybody satisfied! A satisfied customer is the best advertisement to an established house! Correct, sir, correct, madam?"

CORKY—Absolutely!

KILLARNEY—Mac, I won eighty dollars! Look!

CORKY—Don't throw it around, now!

MURILLO—That's right, lady. Money saved is money earned, as the old saying goes. Looks like the house was the big loser today, but we'll have to take it and smile, ladies and gentlemen. When I bought this machine they told me the house makes a percentage in the long run—and I'm depending on that, ladies and gentlemen. So far the house is a big loser, but you can count on it, win or lose, lose or win, we play the game square and pay up in the end. Count your money, lady.

PRISCILLA—Yes, sir. Look, John!

MRS. AARONSON—This is where I spend the day! Oh, darling, it's a betting machine. Where's my money!

AARONSON—Wait a minute! Wait a minute!

MRS. WHEELER—Look at the funny home-made wheel!

Mrs. Aaronson—Please don't let them start till I've got my money down!

WHEELER—What do you call this game?

MURILLO—Does anybody else wish to join in our backwoods pastime? This, sir, is a wheel-of-fortune, the rural version of what they call roulette in the gilded halls of Monaco!—Only here we play it straight, gentlemen, on a home-made contrivance, absolutely uncontrollable and honest; anybody can spin it, anybody can win! Everybody does win, as these folks will tell you! Round it goes like this, ladies and gentlemen—that's right, the lady may spin it if she wishes—and every time it stops on red you get double your money! Every time it stops on black we double the bet! You can't lose; you honestly and truly can't lose! Only a dollar to get in the game, folks; anybody can afford a dollar! Here's a lady put down a dollar and picked up eighty— here's a gentleman put down a dollar and picked up seventy-five! A little hard on the house, friends, but we can still pay!

Mrs. Aaronson is convinced now. You simply can't lose. So everybody plays. And everybody wins. With a generous sweep of both language and funds Murillo pays off at the rate of five to one. There is considerable excitement now. Again everybody

plays, and again the whirling arrow stops at red and Murillo
pays. Twenty-five dollars apiece for the one they invested. Even
King has drifted in, put down five dollars and taken his winnings.

"What the hell? It's Roosevelt money anyway," remarks the
happy Murillo; "fiat money, unsupported by specie, badly in-
flated and negotiable only because Barnum was right! Take the
money! Who wants to try one more spin at five to one? You
can't lose, friends—you've got one dollar invested and if it comes
up red you win a hundred and twenty-five!"

They have all put their money in now except King. He keeps
his thirty dollars and is content, a little to Murillo's disgust.
As a further stroke of complete honesty Murillo lets Mrs. Aaronson spin the wheel, watching it craftily as it whirls and begins to
slow down—

". . . It's coming red again, it's coming red, watch the indi-
cator, it's creeping, ladies and gentlemen—it's creeping. Luckiest
wheel you ever saw in your lives! It'll make red yet, just a little
more, just a little more! Let me call your attention to the fact
that there's three times as many red as black spaces! Come now,
come—creep, creep a shade more— Sorry, ladies and gentlemen,
it's black, and the game's five to one. I'd much rather it came
out the other way, because I took a liking to you at once, but
there it is, and nothing we can do about it. Pay the house a
hundred and twenty-five."

"What?" demands an outraged Wheeler.

"Pay the house a hundred and twenty-five," smiles a confident
Murillo.

"I don't see that."

"It's a very simple game, sir. If it had come up red, I'd have
paid you a hundred and twenty-five. It came up black, which
means you pay me a hundred and twenty-five."

"Each of us?"

"Naturally, each of you."

"But how did this happen?"

"I simply don't follow you," protests a puzzled Mrs. Aaronson.

"I won't pay it. It's a gyp, by God!" swears Mr. Aaronson.

"I think you will. It's a perfectly fair and honest game, sir.
You came into it of your own free will. You took my money
without question. I think you'll all pay."

There is a show of further defiance from Aaronson, but the
threat in Murillo's eyes and manner deters him. The gambler
puts a detaining hand on Aaronson's arm and warns them all of a
partner who is watching and is likely to make trouble if they don't

pay. Presently they have paid $400 altogether—and moved on, grumbling about the trap of the banditti.

Murillo collects the money his group has been playing with and is curt in his refusal to divide any of it. He also would like to contact King, that guy in uniform who may fancy he is going to keep his winnings. "He's too God-damn smart for his uniform!" insists Murillo. "We're going to get that thirty out of him if we have to melt it out of his teeth!"

The Murillo group has moved on now, laughing at the dumb things tourist suckers always say. Murillo is also about to leave when Alegre d'Alcala comes from the house with a tray of things to set the table. Murillo's eye is appraising, his manner intimate.

"You know, when I look at you I get all starry-eyed and impractical," he is saying. "For a thin dime, one-tenth of a dollar, I'd put on a pair of overalls and go in the fishing business with your father.—Did you hear what I said?"

"Yes."

Murillo—Well, do I get an answer? Did you take it in? You can't be as dumb as you are beautiful! That would be too good to be true.

Alegre—I understand very little of what you say, and what little I do understand I dislike.

Murillo—I'll tell you what I'll do, I'll cut your old man in on the gambling take, an honest five per cent. You'll make more money than you ever saw in your life. We're doing well here and we want to stay. There's plenty in it for all of us.

Alegre—If we could have got rid of you legally you'd be gone now, but it seems the law protects you. It seems that we can do no more than say that you are unwelcome. You are unwelcome, and any percentage you might offer, large or small, would be quite unacceptable.

Murillo—Listen, do you think, for God's sake, there's anything I want I can't have? I'm offering to pay because I'm a gentleman, but look at the situation, baby. Your old man's blind, and you haven't got so much as a gun in the house, and if you had one you couldn't use it. I can have this place, and I can pay what I like for it, and I can have you too any time you look good to me! What's more I probably will, so come down to earth and talk my language and maybe we can make a deal! (King *slips in from the left and stands listening.*)

Alegre—You're mistaken about the fire-arms. I have a revolver, and I have a rifle, and I handle them both very well.

Murillo—Now you're talking. Now I have some respect for you.

Alegre—But I have none for you.

Murillo—You will have, baby. You will have. It's the same with women as with nations, baby; the fellow with the most guns and the most money wins. Always. Because that's what the nations want! And what the women want!

Alegre (*turning on him*)—Don't count on it too much.

Murillo—Why not?

Alegre (*more gently*)—I don't know what you've wanted—or what you want now—but whatever it is you'll never have it.

Murillo—They all come round in time, girl, every one of them comes round in time.

Alegre—But not to you. Nothing will come to you.

Murillo—If you mean you'll make a noise, lady, and people will come—and I'll be in trouble, don't rely on it. That's all different now. You go ahead and scream and if anybody hears you he'll turn over and say, "That's Murillo and his woman; why the hell can't he keep his women quiet?" And before long you won't mind; before long you'll be asking me to come home early nights. That's the way it goes with a man and his women.

Murillo has followed his group around the house. A moment later Alegre has seen King. Frightened, she calls to her father, and when he comes confesses her fright and the fear that she has seen a ghost—the ghost of King McCloud, who had gone out with Victor, and was reported dead with Victor and the others. Perhaps it was because she wanted to see King that the stranger took his form. For long months she had had a framed snapshot of King in her room, and it had become a kind of altar to her—

". . . He was the gayest, the proudest, the one they all loved most, and who figured most in all the letters," she says. "I'm punished for it now wanting him too much—and seeing him between me and the sky."

It was no ghost that Alegre saw. D'Alcala is sure of that. He had heard the step and it was the step of the one who had played a round with the gamblers and won. . . . D'Alcala has gone back into the house when King comes again, and this time makes himself known.

Yes, he is the King McCloud who had joined the Loyalists with Victor back in April, 1937. There were eight of them who went out together and he, being the one survivor, has taken it upon himself to bring back reports personally to the nearest of kin of each. There is something he wants to tell, yet he is hesitant in the telling—

"I've come here last," King explains. "The others were mostly from New England—and this seemed a long way south, almost out of the world—at least the world I've known. But it was Victor whom I'd known best, and loved most, and felt surely had been most loved at home."

ALEGRE—We did love him, and knew
　　　　　that he'd know how to die well if it came
　　　　　to dying. But to know just how and where
　　　　　is something—almost as if you'd saved a trace
　　　　　of life for him too. And that's a thing so precious
　　　　　one can hardly give thanks.—My father will want to
　　　　　　hear.
　　　　　Shall I call him?
KING—　There's something—it would be easier
　　　　　if I spoke to you for a moment—
ALEGRE—Yes, surely.
KING—　I've told
　　　　　this all so often—and yet the oftener told
　　　　　and the longer in between—the harder it is
　　　　　to bring myself to begin. I can't help knowing
　　　　　that it's a shock to see me. Wherever I go
　　　　　(and I can't blame them, mind you)
　　　　　they look at me and say, he's above the earth,
　　　　　he walks about and breathes—and my boy's dead—
　　　　　and might have been alive like him—no older—
　　　　　not so old by a year or two, but dead—
　　　　　underground and beginning the long cycle
　　　　　of being dead forever. You thought of that
　　　　　when you first saw me. You looked about for Victor,
　　　　　and then looked back to me.
ALEGRE—No, for at first
　　　　　I thought you were a ghost.
KING—　I've learned this much—
　　　　　that I'm not easily forgiven.
ALEGRE—Forgiven?
　　　　　But it's not your fault—and couldn't have been your
　　　　　　fault
　　　　　that some came home and others stayed in Spain.
　　　　　No one could hold it was.
　　　　　Have the others been cruel, or silent? Or only silent.
　　　　　For that would be cruel.

KING— The home I came to first
was in New England. I can see it now,
the elm, the honey-locust, and the sea,
the twelve-foot tide lapping up and down the piers
and I watching from the red diner across the common
afraid of the blind door.—Then, after that
I looked them all up, one by one, the homes
of all the boys that died there on Hill 4:
only each time it took longer to steel myself—
and I'd wear my shoes out pacing up and down
across from every house. Then suddenly I'd go in
and tell them. One by one I told them all,
how the boys came to die—and how I was alive—
and I can see now it was natural
they'd give me little thanks.
There in New England a man goes down with his ship
or he's not a man. And so at last, in the end,
it came down to Key Largo. That was the name
on Victor's letter. I had some reluctance
about deciding on so many miles,
on foot—and I hesitated. Then a month ago
I noticed there were buzzards overhead
along the road I took, and the pine was slashed
for turpentine, and I knew I was drifting south
to see you. Then I followed the buzzards down
and left the turpentine and followed the palms—
and watched the moss grow thick and the shacks grow
    thin
and came on down the keys.

ALEGRE—Do you mean you came
without quite knowing what roads you had taken
nor why you took them?

KING— Something like that.

ALEGRE—As if
some compulsion lay over you?

KING— Have I said so?

ALEGRE—No,
but, how have you lived?

KING— It's not so hard to get money
if you don't care how you get it.

ALEGRE—If this is a story
that harrows you to tell—or if you're weary
and would find it easier later—come in now

and be our guest—and let it all go till evening
or as long as you like. Victor wrote me about you
long ago, and nothing you can say
will alter your welcome.

KING— I'd better say it now.
It's fair to tell you there was an argument
that night before the last battle—and I held
that the war was lost, and everything was lost,
and it was better to abandon Spain
and save our lives. And it was true; we lost,
and the war's lost, and the others are all dead—
and they might be alive if they'd followed me—
yet Victor said I was wrong, and even now
he'd say I was wrong, and that's what tortures me—

ALEGRE—But why should you be tortured? When men differ
they must follow what they believe. Victor believed
so
and would have said so.

KING— Yes, he said so then.
And over and over I say it to myself—
that I meant their good and mine—that I tried to
save them—
could have saved them if they'd only followed
when I left the lines. And it's true. I was cool and
sane
and chose to live. But some insanity
came over them there in the moonlight, and they chose
to stay and die. They chose it, and all I could say
meant nothing to them. Why should I feel a guilt
or be looked upon as guilty?

ALEGRE—You shouldn't.

KING— No,
and yet I do. Something within myself
accuses me. They accuse me. Without warrant,
without reason, day and night, incessantly,
till I look at a bed with horror, as a place
where a man can't sleep, and look at a road with
horror
as something I must walk along forever
followed by the dead!—Will you forgive? All this—
this is just raving—

ALEGRE—If there was something said
or done that tortures you—

KING— Something done, perhaps.
ALEGRE—And if what you seek's forgiveness, then pass it over
in silence, and consider it forgiven.
Forget it utterly. It won't help to remember
some fatal awkwardness.
KING— But I have to say it
and say it honestly, and then wait to hear
a verdict from you.
ALEGRE—Shall I call my father?
KING— Not yet.—Yes, do call him. He must hear it now
or I go through it again.—I'll put it off
while there's excuse. But call him.

To d'Alcala the story is repeated, with something added, and
something more explained of the fear that has driven King on, and
tortured him out of sleep. Finally there is the story of the last night
when he had left Victor and the others on the hill; of how he had
made his way down and met Franco's men coming on in a surprise
attack; of how he had started back to be in the fight, but had
been too late; of how finally he found himself prisoner and how,
deepest hurt of all, to save himself he had fought out the war
with the Insurgents—

"Something broke inside me—my nerve, maybe," says King.
"I was willing to eat dirt and be damned if I could live. I ate
dirt, and I'm damned. I had to tell them I was one of them—
and then there was no way out. And now you know me. I
deserted, and left my friends to die alone—and fought on Franco's
side—and I'm alive—and better men are dead—

"That's why I'm here, and why I've gone from door to door.
Not because I deserted, and left the lines
when the fighting was no use, for I was right
there on Hill 4—but once having saved my life
by slipping away, there never came a time
when I could say to myself, make a stand here,
this is too low—even to save your life
this is too low. So I went on and down
keeping myself alive, till the very maggots
cleansing the earth, took more pride in their work
than I in mine—or in myself."

Osceola, one of the Seminoles for whom d'Alcala has sent, comes
silently into the group. He reports to d'Alcala, and is told of the

murdered man whose body has been sunk in the sea. D'Alcala
would have the Indians bring up the body at the turn of the tide
and let it float to the bar below, that the crime may be brought
home to the man who committed it. The Indian, understanding,
leaves as quietly as he came and d'Alcala turns again to King.
"And still, I don't know why you're here," he says. And King
answers him:

> "Because my mind
> says even now I was right, that I should live,
> that one's better living on carrion, beast among beasts,
> than dead in the earth's shell. But I have a demon
> that won't hear any of this, that lives in my soul
> and cries out day and night—that I should have died
> before I gave the lie to what I was
> there with the rebels! This demon tore me inside,
> saying, very well, let them decide it
> whose sons died on Hill 4! Tell your tale to them
> and if one answers, ye, it was well done,
> lift up your head and go on. But they said nothing,
> and the demon drove me here."

There is still something else for which King must beg forgiveness. This would be a love for Alegre, for Victor's sister, that has
grown within his heart from what Victor, through the long nights
in Spain, had told him of that sister—"that there was no one else
in all the world to whom a man could go with a man's crime and
say, I did this, and get understanding for the lowest he could do.

> ". . . Out of a desperate loneliness and fear—
> out of an outcast's life, with no God to pray to—
> and never having seen your face—I've dared to love
>   you—
> have even imagined you from knowing Victor—
> and find you as I knew you'd be. Never saying,
> never admitting it even to myself,
> I've put what little hope was left on you
> and kept on south toward you. Now you owe me
>   nothing
> except a parting curse, and I ask for nothing
> but I have said it at last, and said it to you.
> If I said more I'd go beyond all begging.—"

ALEGRE—Why must you tell me?
　　　　About this betrayal—and then about—this love?
　　　　Why should you tell me, and make me live through it,
　　　　　　too?
　　　　How could a woman love you?
　　　　We're all less for it, the whole world's less because
　　　　of what you are! A woman can hesitate
　　　　forever—but a man must be something sometime
　　　　bright and clear, like a plowshare in the sun
　　　　or a mountain above the cloud!

King would go now, but they would have him stay a little.
Alegre will be safer with him there in their present trouble, suggests d'Alcala, and Alegre would have him rest while they try to
forget all that has happened to lengthen their misery.

"One can get over love—oh, any kind, except for someone
dead," Alegre is saying. "That doesn't end."

"For someone dead in Spain?" asks King.

"For a boy who went to Spain and won't come back. One of
the leaders. With a beauty on his face that comes to a man with
being more a man than other men." But Alegre will not say of
whom she's thinking. . . .

Murillo has come back with his group, ready to go to work
again fleecing tourists. King has tried blindly to leave the yard,
but misses the exit and is called back. Murillo would like to talk
with him. Murillo would like his thirty dollars back. But King
is of no mind to return it. He gambled on Murillo's invitation,
and won, and he'll keep what he won. If there is trouble he, too,
has a gun that is loose in its holster.

Murillo and King stand eyeing each other, each with his hand
on the butt of his gun. Murillo is boasting that he never yet has
lost any sucker money and King is answering that there is a new
experience awaiting him—

　　　　　　　"I know your kind," says King.
　　　　　　　"I've watched a dozen like you, up and down
　　　　　　　the fairs and carnivals—sneaking into town
　　　　　　　and sneaking out—setting up three-card
　　　　　　　　monte
　　　　　　　and disappearing like a bad smell when they
　　　　　　　　try
　　　　　　　to get their fingers on you—always just three
　　　　　　　　jumps

ahead of the police—always an eye on the
    exit—
a species of gangster rabbit! Don't threaten
    me
with that hand on your pocket. You know
    your shifty game
too well to make a noise!

MURILLO—   Well, it just happens
you've got me wrong. I know the kind you
    mean,
but personally I've used a gun before
and I'll maybe use it again, because it gets
to be a kind of thirst, and maybe a soldier
knows what that means. I want my money
    back
and I'm going to get it. (*He reaches slowly
    into his pocket and takes out an auto-
    matic.* KING *extracts his revolver at the
    same time.*)
Look, bo, that was your chance
to shoot, and you didn't do it. In my game
you learn that there are just two kinds of men,
those who are not afraid to die, and those
who are. A man who's not afraid to die,
he's dangerous. The others you can handle.
You have to learn to pick 'em out in a crowd
and pick 'em fast—and you can't make mis-
    takes—
so I don't make any—

KING—   Maybe your world
is over-simplified. I think you'll find
there are more than two kinds of men. Just
    for example
some can think, some have nerve reactions
beyond the solar plexus.

MURILLO—   I'm warning you.
This is trained on your belly, see; if you
kill me, you die. I'm not afraid to die,
and you are. You're all afraid, all your lives,
afraid of gods and churches and the law—
but if a man gets up who's afraid of nothing,
and he'll kill you as soon as look at you, and
    spit in your face

after it's over—because there aren't any ghosts
to follow a man—well, men do what he tells them—
they do what I tell them. And so will you all. I know.
I've watched it plenty often.

KING— Your poor, darkened, ophidian mind,
what kind of triumph is there for you or me
in killing each other here for a poker bluff
with spectators looking on? Is there no other way
you can make yourself believe that you're alive
except by holding a gun on a fellow's entrails
and daring him to shoot? You're a fool, Murillo.
If you rated beyond a ten-year-old I.Q.
you'd have other satisfactions. Look at Hunk.
You'd better watch your jumpy gun-man.

MURILLO (*to* HUNK)—Drop it! (HUNK *lowers his gun.*)
You're playing for time, no doubt. You think, later on,
when he isn't looking, I'll get him. You'll call the police,
you think. Well, times have changed in the manner of police
and what they can do for you. The whole damn world's
quite different from what it was. Here on Key Largo
I say what's what. Call the police and tell them
and hear what they say about it.
Maybe you haven't noticed, but the bars are down
and the water's over the sea-wall nowadays.
You can have what you can pay for
or what you can take. And no questions asked. Anyway
not here, not now. Remember that's
a delicate trigger on those army models,

	so let go easy. Give me the gun. (KING *lets go.*)
	And now
	give me the money. (KING *hands the money over.*)
KING—	What do you think you gain by that? (*He sits.*)
MURILLO—	Thirty dollars. And take back your gun. I don't want it.
	Right at this moment you haven't got a thing
	I can't take from you. (*He lays a hand on* ALEGRE'S *shoulder.*)
	There's a champion!
	There's a hero! I've paid up my protection
	another two weeks. And there's two weeks' more rent.
	We're staying on. (*He turns away, tossing* ALEGRE *two ten-dollar bills.*)
CORKY—	There's a party of monkeys walking in. Two men and
	two women, Packard sedan. Flash tourists.
MURILLO	Get ready. (*The gang gathers round the wheel.*)
	You too, third rail. Get in the game. Yes, I mean you.
	I'm about to lose a couple of stooges and I need an under-
	study. Get in there and look interested. (KING *obeys orders.* MURILLO *spins the wheel. Two couples enter.*)
FIRST WOMAN—	What a darling place! But really darling!
MURILLO—	The house loses, ladies and gentlemen. Loses heavily
	but we're still game. Eighty dollars to this lady. Eighty
	dollars to the two gentlemen. (*He pays off in bills.*)
SECOND WOMAN—	Harry! An outdoor casino! Where's my purse?
	I left my purse in the car!

The curtain falls.

ACT II

Inside the d'Alcala cottage King McCloud is asleep on a couch, his face to the wall. Alegre and her father are talking quietly. The girl's gaze is out the window, and the blind d'Alcala is telling her something of what she sees, by what he hears.

"The tide's three-quarters out, by the clanking of the chain where the boat's tethered. Murillo and the others are holding some kind of conference in his room; one of the women's crying. Out on the gulf there's a government cutter heading in this way—no, it may be a fisherman; but a Chrysler engine, too new for a fisherman. . . . The eyes can look only one way at a time, but the ears reach out in every direction. It makes for a full world. . . ."

Alegre is troubled. That she still loves King she confesses. But it were better that he never knew. Whether it were also better that King should die and keep his faith, or lose his faith and live, as her father demands, she cannot answer.

The shadow of a man's figure has passed the window. A man bent over, completely double. That would be the Seminoles, d'Alcala decides. Indians walk that way. A second later Horn, the Indian, and Osceola, his son, stand in the doorway. They have come to express their thanks for the clothes and the help. They must leave Key Largo. If they could take an old boat of d'Alcala's they have found in the inlet and caulked with Spanish moss they think they can get to the Everglades.

They have floated the body, as d'Alcala asked, Horn reports, and seen to it that it floated where fishermen would find it. There is a boat playing a flashlight on the cottage. The Indians must wait until it passes. Then they leave quietly. . . .

King has awakened. A delegation, Corky, Gage and Hunk, has come to deliver Murillo's new set of rules.

First, Corky reports, nobody's to leave the place without permission. And after sunset nobody's to leave the house without permission from Murillo. Anyone who wants to send out for supplies can make a list and it will be attended to. There are to be other changes. Murillo has taken a fancy to eating and sleeping in the cottage. King can have his place in the cabin.

D'Alcala would send word back to Murillo. His conditions are acceptable, with the exception of the last. King will continue to sleep in the cottage and Murillo can stay where he is. Hunk is willing to take that message, but it won't mean anything. Murillo is sure to get what he wants.

King, too, is doubtful that Murillo will be stopped by d'Alcala's reply. He is puzzled as to what he should do.

"Sleep in your bed, because it's yours," calmly answers d'Alcala.

KING— But you see what you've done?

D'ALCALA—It was done deliberately.

KING— You accept the conditions
only that I'm to eat where he wants to eat
and sleep where he wants to sleep.

D'ALCALA—He won't sleep here.

KING— Don't think I won't stand up and do what I can
against him! He wants Alegre, and my blood can burn
like yours when he looks at her—burns in me now
and I can feel it.—But, God, how can I explain?
If it came to dying I don't trust my brain,
my busy, treacherous, casuistic brain,
presenting me with scientific facts
and cunning reasons. It's separate from myself,
separate from my will—a traitor brain,
an acid eating away at all the faiths
by which we live, questioning all the rules,
and leaving us bare—naked white animals
without poetry or God.

ALEGRE— But say these things.

KING— I lived with the worms so long
and ran away so often, that my mind's trained
to find excuses, like a poacher's ferret
finding himself a warren underground
and running wild among the rabbit-holes,
sleeping among the bodies, and forgetting
the master above ground.

D'ALCALA—If we ask too much
it's possible a man could slip away
to the west of the house, in the shadow.

KING— I couldn't do that,
and wouldn't try. But could we all go together
or are we watched?

D'ALCALA—We're watched quite carefully.

KING— If you stay here
then I must stay.

D'Alcala—Then it won't come to dying.
          If we can only hold him off tonight
          someone will find the evidence on the point
          and Murillo will move on. Perhaps even this eve-
              ning.
          The mullet fishermen are out at night
          this time of year. (*A pause.*)
Alegre—   What does your mind
          think traitorously underneath sometimes to betray
              you
          when you're in danger?
King—   I can't tell you that.
Alegre—   Does it begin by saying that we live—
          all of us—on illusions? That we live
          and lay our lives down for things unsubstantial
          as a sunrise or a rainbow?
King—   That's how it begins.
Alegre—   Then I have it too. It's not peculiar
          to soldiers out of Spain, or even to men
          who've left a line against orders. It's all of us
          in this age of dying fires.
King—   Do you wish to live
          by truth or by illusion?
Alegre—   By the truth.
          Always by the truth.
King—   But that's an illusion.
          Because by the truth no man can live at all,
          even a day. We die when we look at truth.
          And one by one the illusions
          wear themselves out.

Murillo has come in person, first to tell them that Corky and
Killarney are leaving and that their places are to be filled in the
group by King and Alegre. They will start working tomorrow.
Secondly, Murillo has come to deliver his own order as to the
change of sleeping arrangements. He is moving in tonight and
King is moving out. Are there any objections?
   There are objections. There is something King had forgotten
to tell Murillo. He (King) is supposed to be dead and there are
reasons why he is traveling under a name not his own. He is
really Victor d'Alcala, Alegre's brother. For that reason he cannot
permit Murillo to move into the cabin—
   "You didn't know this, of course," King concludes. "Nobody

knew it, and I don't hold it against you, but a man's sister's his sister. He has a right to say hands off."

Murillo is in agreement with that code. But he is not alto-gether satisfied that King is telling the truth. He would do a little cross-questioning. Where was King born and when? When did he come to this country? Where are his passports?

He turns to Alegre. Is King her brother? Yes. To d'Alcala. Is King his son, Victor? Yes. What's the color of his hair? How tall is he? And so on. The answers come quick and sure until Murillo snaps:

"There's a scar on his face. Where?"

"He had no scar when he went away," answers d'Alcala.

"What's the color of his eyes?" At this d'Alcala hesitates. "You should have told him that before you lied to me," Murillo smirks, turning triumphantly on King. "You're no more Victor than I am!"

Before Murillo can follow up this advantage Sheriff Gash ap-pears in the doorway. The sheriff is worried and he wants to see Murillo outside. Murillo refuses to move. "Let me finish this, and then I'll see you," he says.

GASH—   I can talk from here.
            Would you maybe want to know what we found, Murillo,
            washed up below on the bar with a gag in his mouth and tied with wire?
MURILLO—What?
GASH—   That road gang boss.
            Dead about twenty-four hours. It seems he was tangled
            with a cray-fish line.
MURILLO—Who?
GASH—   That boss of the road gang
            that disappeared yesterday. You may know the fellow.
            I heard some talk he'd been seen gambling here—
            yesterday sometime. And there was some kind of quarrel
            over the game and a woman.
MURILLO—Not to my knowledge.
            I can't keep track who gambles.
GASH—   Well, all I say, I wish whoever did it
            had sunk him deep enough so he wouldn't come floating

around to cause a stink.
We've got a body, and it was certainly murder,
and when a fellow's working for the state
and drawing checks you can be God damn sure
he's got connections somewhere. He'll be missed,
and there'll be an investigation. It'll come to me—
I've had to swear in extra deputies
already—and, Jesus, there was enough to explain,
without explaining murder.

MURILLO—Don't look at me,
for Christ's sake! It's not my murder!

GASH—   Who said it was?
I said I wished to God whoever did it
had sunk him deep enough so he wouldn't wash up
     in my territory! (*He goes to the door and calls
     in a* DEPUTY.)
Hey, Sam, take these three out,
and hold them on the porch. They're all of 'em
     suspects.
I'm questioning Murillo.
(*To* D'ALCALA.)
If you don't mind,
we'll use this room.
(*To the* DEPUTY.)
Shut the door.
(*The door is closed and* GASH *and* MURILLO *face
     each other.*)

MURILLO—You're serious.

GASH—   You're God damn right I'm serious.

MURILLO—But what about?
You're not accusing me?

GASH—   It's not my business
to accuse anybody, mind you. But I'm supposed
to make arrests of suspicious characters
found near the scene of a crime!

MURILLO—Good God! I hope
I'm not a suspicious character.

GASH—   Get me right,
Mr. Murillo, what I think about you
or anybody here, won't matter a damn—
but if other people think you should be arrested
and I didn't arrest you, then I begin to worry
about my job! You have to hold the votes

> to get re-elected sheriff, and most of the time
> you can just play along, and it's easy, but when it's
>   murder
> you've got to watch your step, for they're watching
>   you.
> They're watching me now. Watching both of us.

MURILLO—I shouldn't be here.

GASH—   No.

> You should have left. When anything suspicious
> happens, you should trek it. Innocent or guilty.
> For your own protection—and mine. And the trou-
>   ble is
> this stink's bigger than you are, and bigger than I
>   am,
> and you're right here in my hands, and the deputies
> want to know who you are.

MURILLO—I'm getting out.

GASH—   You can't.

> Not now. But why the hell you aren't in Georgia
> or Alabama gripes me. You could have been,
> easy, by now.

MURILLO—I had something particular here.

GASH—   She must have been pretty. They hang in this state,
> you know.
> They don't burn or smother.

MURILLO—Are you holding me up
> for money?

GASH—   Son, if I take my hand away
> and you start running, you'll never get off this Key,
> you won't get fifty yards! I wish to God
> I could get you out of this, and into Cuba,
> because you're around my neck! And you'll cross
>   me up
> if you ever get in the dock.

MURILLO—I wouldn't say that.

GASH—   Well, I would.

MURILLO—Then, for Christ's sake, use your head,
> and pin this on somebody.

The most likely suspects would be the two niggers who were
there this morning. They were members of the dead man's own
gang. They had killed him and run, suggests Murillo.

Gash is willing to accept that story as perfect—if he can find the niggers. But until he can he has to arrest someone nearer the crime. He has called the others in, and is questioning them. D'Alcala denies the visit of any Negroes, but admits the visit of the Indians. However, there is little evidence to connect them with the crime. Nor any evidence that Victor had helped them get away.

"You have no need for suspects, because I know
the murderer and what happened," adds d'Alcala.
"The gambler Murillo,
who sits there, in that corner, even now,
because I hear him breathe,—this man Murillo
(by God, I should have learned to shoot by ear)
surprised the road gang boss and the girl who's
        called
Killarney, and struck him over the head, and tied
        him
with wire from our clothes-line. This was near the
        wharf-end
at two o'clock. He made Killarney help him
and they dragged the body to the rowboat, towed it
some fifty yards or so out into the gulf,
weighted it with pockets full of stones,
or so I judge, and let it sink."

MURILLO— God damn you,
        who told you that?
D'ALCALA—Told me? I knew so well
        where you had sunk that body that today
        at my direction it was fished to the surface,
        and freed of weights and floated to the bar
        where it was found to use against you!
MURILLO— Damn you,
        I say who told you this? For he can't see!
        He's blind as dirt!
GASH—   He's drawing you out, you lunk
        and you fall in the trap! Where did you get this
            story?
        Can you substantiate it?
D'ALCALA—I hear better
        than most men see.

This is not evidence that could be accepted in a court of law, Gash is convinced. Alegre knows who fished the body up but she cannot tell. D'Alcala admits that he is the one who wanted to fasten the crime upon Murillo. "I wanted to send his murder home to him because he's fixed himself here on my house like a cancer on the heart!" says d'Alcala.

Sheriff Gash has decided upon his theory of the crime and is ready to proceed. Two convicts had killed a foreman to get away. They got scared and towed the body to the Murillo doorstep to shift the blame to him, and Victor, who has been mixed up in a similar business before, helped them to get away. He will put Victor under arrest, though he is frank to say that he'd rather have the Indians.

Gash has searched the cottage. He has found Alegre's revolver and her rifle, and the snapshot of King. "Maybe he is your brother," muses Gash. "Either that or you've known him a damned long time, because there's a date here on the picture— May, 1936." Gash is also prepared to bargain with Alegre. Let her tell him where the Indians are and he will let her brother go.

"For your own good, and his, and his—I tell you, give me a line on those Indians and from now on we're friends," the Sheriff says.

"We'd be dishonored by such a friendship," Alegre answers.

But in the end Alegre tells the Sheriff of the Indians' hiding place under the mangroves. To King she has no other justification for telling than that she could not see him die for them, nor let them die for him. Gash will bring the Indians back and then the choice will be up to King—

"Yes, he'll bring them here—and they'll stand before me—and this big-mouth Gash will ask are these the men—" says King.

"Yes."

"Will you say they are? Could you say that?"

"Yes, if you say it. Yes, if you say they're guilty, I'll say it too. It must be your decision."

"I'll choose to live then!"

And why not? King is demanding. Why, if there has to be a scapegoat to pay for Murillo's fun, why should he walk off gallantly to a death on the gallows to save two drones from a reservation?

"No, I haven't said that," protests Alegre, quietly. "But can you stand face to face with two innocent fugitives, and stand there silent and load them with a crime to save yourself? How could one do it and live? Would you wish to live after they were gone?"

"How else can I live?"

"Anyway that squares with what a man, waking, may think of himself in the night and not want to die before morning."

Still King would argue that the ancient code established by the knights of the middle ages is dead; that men no longer "live by faith or honor or justice," but rather as they can, "as the animals they are, because it's impossible to arrange a life by these fantastic, inexcusable rules." . . . "Isn't it a question whether I'm more useful here, and alive, and trying, at least, to ward off Murillo?"

"But we cannot choose, either you or I, to purchase your safety or mine, by offering up those two poor, wandering children to Murillo and the sheriff. We simply can't, whatever happens to us."

KING—   Whatever happens?
         Have you envisioned that?
ALEGRE— I have a revolver,
         and I can use it.
KING—   And would you?
ALEGRE— Do you doubt it?
KING—   Then we both die—as a sacrifice to the rules.
         It would be something to know who it is arranges
             these little ironies.
         I came here running from a civil war
         where madmen and morons tore a continent
         apart to share it, where death and rape were com-
             mon
         as flies on a dead soldier, and alien men
         were weary of native women. I ran from that storm
         of rape and murder, because I couldn't help
         and nobody could help, and I wanted at least
         to save my life, in any crawling way,
         and the great master of the laboratory
         (wearing spectacles, probably), drives me down
         to this bloody wharf, where I must choose again
         between death and the rape of a woman, between
             death
         and the murder of innocent men. I made my choice
         long ago, and ran, and left them bleeding
         there in the field.   And I say it's better to live—
         if one could live alone in the Everglades
         and fill his stomach with fish, and sleep at night,
         and knock his oysters from the mangrove roots,

and let the dead bury their dead, for there's no faith sure,
no magnanimity that won't give way
if you test it often enough, no love of woman
or love of man, that won't dry up in the end
if the drouth lasts long enough, no modesty
that isn't relative. There's no better than you
among all women—and yet when you envisioned
the choice between Murillo and your death
there was a flash when your mind asked itself,
must it be death? Is even the man Murillo
worse than death? And if you can ask the question
then there's more than one answer.

ALEGRE—   How did you know that!

KING—   Because the mind, the bright, quicksilver mind,
has but one purpose, to defend the body
and ward off death. Because it's the law of earth
where life was built up from the very first
on rape and murder—where the female takes what she gets
and learns to love it, and must learn to love it,
or the race would die! Show me one thing secure
among these names of virtues—justice and honor
and love and friendship—and I'll die for it gladly,
but where's justice, and where's honor, and where's friendship,
and what's love, under the rose?

ALEGRE—   Then you've never loved.

KING—   Not as you've loved, perhaps, for you assume
that it's forever, and I've known, and know,
that it's till the fire burns down, till the stimulant
of something new or something stolen's gone,
till you know all the intimate details
and the girl's with child, and cries. And if that's true
of love, it's true of all the other doors—
the doors of all the illusions, and one by one
we all jump at them. We jump first at the door
with Christ upon it, hanging on the cross,
then the door with Lenin, legislating heaven,
then the emblem of social security, representing
eighteen dollars a week, good luck or bad,

jobs or no jobs—then the door with the girl ex-
    pectant,
the black triangle door, and they all give meaning
to life, and mental sustenance, but then
there comes a day when there's no sustenance,
and you jump, and there's nothing you want to buy
    with money,
and Christ hangs dead on the cross, as all men die,
and Lenin legislates a fake paradise,
and the girl holds out her arms, and she's made of
    sawdust,
and there's sawdust in your mouth!

ALEGRE—   But if this were true,
             then why would one live—woman or man or beast,
             or grub in the dark?

KING—   To eat and sleep and breed
             and creep in the forest.

ALEGRE—   Answer him, father, answer,
             because it sounds like truth—but if it were true
             one couldn't live! There is something in women
             that is as he says, and there is something in men
             that merely wants to live, but answer him!
             We're not like this!

D'ALCALA—   Why, girl, we're all alone,
             here on the surface of a turning sphere
             of earth and water, cutting a great circle
             round the sun, just as the sun itself
             cuts a great circle round the central hub
             of some great constellation, which in turn
             wheels round another. Where this voyage started
             we don't know, nor where it will end, nor whether
             it has a meaning, nor whether there is good
             or evil, whether man has a destiny
             or happened here by chemical accident—
             all this we never know. And that's our challenge—
             to find ourselves in this desert of dead light-years,
             blind, all of us, in a kingdom of the blind,
             living by appetite in a fragile shell
             of dust and water; yet to take this dust
             and water and our range of appetites
             and build them toward some vision of a god
             of beauty and unselfishness and truth—
             could we ask better of the mud we are

> than to accept the challenge, and look up
> and search for god-head? If it's true we came
> from the sea-water—and children in the womb
> wear gills a certain time in memory
> of that first origin—we've come a long way;
> so far there's no predicting what we'll be
> before we end. It may be women help
> this progress choosing out the men who seem
> a fractional step beyond sheer appetite—
> and it may be that's sacred, though my values
> are hardly Biblical—and perhaps men help
> by setting themselves forever, even to the death,
> against cruelty and arbitrary power,
> for that's the beast—the ancient, belly-foot beast
> from which we came, which is strong within us yet
> and tries to drag us back down. Somehow or other,
> in some obscure way, it's the love of woman
> for man, and a certain freedom in her love
> to choose tomorrow's men, and the leverage
> in the interplay of choice between men and women,
> that's brought us here—to this forking of the
> roads—
> and may take us farther on.

KING—   And where are we going?

D'ALCALA—To a conquest of all there is, whatever there is
        among the suns and stars.

In the end there is no answer, d'Alcala admits. None that he
knows:

> "You should have asked the fish what would come of him
>   before the earth shrank and the land thrust up
>   between the oceans. You should have asked the fish
>   or asked me, or asked yourself, for at that time
>   we were the fish, you and I, or they were we—
>   and we, or they, would have known as much about it
>   as I know now—yet it somehow seems worth while
>   that the fish were not discouraged, and did keep on—
>   at least as far as we are.—"

The boats are at the point now and the searching party is returning. For a moment King and Alegre are alone. He has
found the snapshot of himself, and on it noted a sonnet to love
that Alegre had written that spring when Victor had first gone
away and she felt most alone. Victor had talked much about

King that spring. "You were the singing hero of their venture
into the world, leading the great crusade to make over the face
of things," she says. "It was on your face—this light of the
future. It's on your face there yet, on the picture in your hand."

"Have I changed so much?"

"You've changed."

"And all this happened in the spring three years ago?"

"It happened in the spring and lasted till this morning."

"You said you loved someone who died in Spain."

"You died in Spain. . . ."

For a moment King is silent. When he speaks again, there is a
new conviction in his voice.

> "Yes. I did die in Spain.
> And maybe this is what I came looking for,
> this picture of the athlete who died young,
> the portrait of one dead. I came a long way to get it,
> and tried to stay away, but now I have it
> and I'll know what to do. (*A pause.*)
> And yet it's unfair somehow."

> "Is it unfair?"

> "It doesn't come to us all. It comes to many
> in certain generations, comes to only a few
> in others; and it says, if you want to live
> you must die now—this instant—or the food
> you eat will rot at your lips, and the lips you kiss
> will turn to stone, and the very ground you tread
> will curl up under your footsteps like a snake
> and hiss behind you.—Yet if you're chosen out,
> or choose yourself, and go out to die, you die
> forever after, and that's farther away
> than one can say in light-years;—and the thing
> you die for is as far away as that.
> You die to bring about a race of men
> who'll walk the heavens on a rope of sines
> and cosines, looking like Wells' Martian polyp,
> and operating on the womb of night
> with a long sharp equation. It's no fun
> to perish in your own person, when you're young
> for this remote eventuality—
> even if it were attractive, which it's not;

and so in the last analysis one dies
because it's part of the bargain he takes on
when he agrees to live.—A man must die
for what he believes—if he's unfortunate
enough to have to face it in his time—
and if he won't then he'll end up believing
in nothing at all—and that's death, too."

Gash and Murillo are back. They have the Indians with them.
The Sheriff had found them where Alegre had told him they would
be. She having kept her bargain, he is prepared to keep his.
And there is another thing he would like to have settled. He has
heard there had been trouble with Murillo in that house. He
would like to have that all cleared up. ". . . I'll be watching you
from now on," he says, "and listening to reports—and I want to
hear it's all peaceful here on Key Largo, and doing business as
usual." So far as Gash is concerned he has the Indians and King
is discharged.

King will not have it that way. He had thought, he says, that
he could let the Indians die, but now, seeing their faces, he knows
he can't. He is the man who murdered the foreman. There's a
sort of satisfaction in that confession, King insists, and he's glad
it's over. He would like to point out, too, that he will offer certain
advantages as a defendant. He will convict himself, whereas the
Indians would probably protest their innocence. Mr. Murillo
might even be involved, and that would be unnecessary. So the
Sheriff takes their handcuffs off and lets the Indians go.

King has picked up Alegre's revolver, a heavy forty-five, which
once was Victor's, and is pointing it at Murillo—

"Look, atom-smasher, we played a game this morning, you and
I, revolver-on-the-belly or atom-smash-atom, and it seems to me
you won—"

GASH (*to his* DEPUTY)—Take that gun from him!
MURILLO— Wait! Don't move, for God's sake! The fool
            means it!
            Don't move or he'll kill me!
KING—   Yes, I certainly would!
            If anybody jumps at me you're done
            because the triggers on these forty-fives
            are tender as young love. I think you said
            you weren't afraid to die, but what you meant
            was that you knew I didn't have the guts

to shoot you. And I didn't. Only tonight
I have, and strangely enough, it's the other way round,
and I'm not afraid to die!

GASH— What are you trying to do?

KING— Once in a thousand years a mortal man
gets the same chance twice. Where we stood this morning
we stand now again. Give us elbow-room.
(*The others draw slowly back from them.*)
And now, my friend,
let me explain that we won't either of us
emerge from this predicament. This is curtains
for me and you. Black curtains and the end
as sure as you're a gambler. To save my soul
I have to get rid of you, and if you're to go
you'll certainly want me along.

MURILLO— Listen, boy, I'm licked.
I know when I'm licked. Put up your gun, for God's sake
and I'll put mine up.

KING— Not at all. What I want now, atom-smasher,
is that you back out gently through that door,
putting out your hand behind you so you won't stumble
and die before your time. We'll go together—
always the gun-point on your belly-button—
and then we'll climb together into your car—
you first, climbing in backwards—and then we'll drive,
or rather you'll drive, Mr. Murillo, turning
to right or left as indicated, the gun
still on your unathletic periphery.
You may begin,
one foot behind the other, very softly;
and as we go, I'd like to say that for sheer
unadulterated pleasure to the heart,
for a happiness that beats against the side
and almost makes you weep, this game of yours
is tops with me. There was another door,
and one I never leaped at, and there's food
for the soul and mental sustenance, and mirth
to last out all the long night after dying

                in the winning of this last hand.   And thanks where
                    they're due:
                I thank you, Mr. Murillo, from my teeth,
                for appearing out of the darkness of that hell
                which is probably your home, to teach me the
                    game,
                and take me with you to earth!

MURILLO— Hold it, for God's sake!
                Don't shoot at him!
                (HUNK *shoots* KING *and* KING's *gun fells* MU-
                    RILLO, *who falls half outside the door.* KING
                    staggers to a chair and sits.)

GASH— God damn you, have you no brains?

HUNK— I had to do it!

KING— Oh, you lunk, you lunk-head,
                I knew you couldn't stand it!   You must be shoot-
                    ing.
                I counted on you—and you did it!—Nevertheless
                it looks as if you might have to do it again!
                That first wasn't enough!

GASH— Sam, get those Indians
                before they get away.   No, wait a minute,
                I can't use them now.

KING— Right, right, Mr. Sheriff;
                now that Murillo's gone, there's not much point
                in proving he was or wasn't.   Let the Indians go.
                Give them a chance at their happy hunting grounds.
                They waited long enough for it!

ALEGRE— King, I was wrong!
                You didn't have to die!

KING— Is this dying, Alegre?
                Then it's more enviable than the Everglades,
                to fight where you can win, in a narrow room,
                and to win, dying.

GASH— Where's he hurt?   Get him down here
                flat, so he won't lose blood.

KING— No, let me alone.
                Let me sit up and look him in the face
                whoever he is.   They say when they bury an Indian
                they bury him seated upright in his grave
                with his weapons around him.   That's very sensible.
                Very sensible.
                (*He slumps down.*)

GASH—   You can't be sorry
             for a man that planned it, and it all worked out,
             and he got what he wanted.—
             Just for the record, sir, this was your son?
D'ALCALA—He was my son.

THE CURTAIN FALLS

THE WORLD WE MAKE
A Drama in a Prologue and Three Acts

BY SIDNEY KINGSLEY

(Based on a Novel by Millen Brand)

SIDNEY KINGSLEY, who is a deliberate worker in the theatre, is not one to rush a play into production. He waited long for his first success, which came in 1935 with "Men in White," and another two years for his second, which was the "Dead End" that later spilled over into the motion picture field and created a group of "Dead End Kid" stars.

He was a bit precipitous with the next try, because of his eagerness to have a hand in settling, or at least in pointing out, the evils of a world in turmoil, and indicating a possible way of adjustment. He produced an anti-war drama called "Ten Million Ghosts" in 1936, and when that failed he again withdrew from the scene temporarily.

Last Fall Mr. Kingsley came back with a dramatization of Millen Brand's novel, "The Outward Room," done in a prologue and three acts which he called "The World We Make." The play was generally well received, but with something less than the enthusiasm the author had naturally hoped for. The play ran for ten weeks, and the motion picture rights were sold for a reported $150,000.

Mr. Kingsley has used the second world war as a contributing motivation in the hazards faced by the mentally unstable, which, I believe, was not a factor in the story of Virginia McKay and her reclamation through service and a normal life in Mr. Brand's novel. This, it seems to me, has added a suggestion of timeliness to the story and pointed up certain of the dramatic scenes with good effect. The story swings without too great effort between the realism and romance of the physical theatre and the deeper significance of the causes leading to mental and nervous breakdowns that have of late years crowded public and private sanitariums.

It is in such an institution that the first scene of the play is laid. The view is of a corner in Dr. Schiller's office in Greendale Sanitarium, and of several of the nearby corridors. The walls are of translucent glass. Against them the shadow of hospital attendants

110

and patients are plainly silhouetted. We see a nurse select a key from a ring, let herself through a second door at the end of the corridor, close the door and lock it again.

Dr. Schiller is a "middle-aged, kindly-faced" man whose professional manner is gentle but serious. He is at the moment examining a middle-aged man patient, whose wife stands anxiously by. A second physician, Dr. Blane, is assisting. As they conclude the examination the report to the patient's wife is that conditions are, in general, favorable. There is a test or two they still wish to make, and to these the wife is entirely agreeable.

As the couple disappears the Head Nurse, a commanding, professional person, comes with a report. Back of her a second nurse, with a young girl, has appeared and stopped in the outer corridor. The Head Nurse's report covers several rooms—Mr. Swanson, 12, who shows no change; Mrs. Cunningham, 28, who has been disturbed and treated by Dr. Somnes, etc. The Nurse in the corridor knocks to announce her arrival with Virginia McKay. Dr. Schiller's interest is quickened. He would know more about Miss McKay. The Head Nurse reports that Virginia had had an uneasy night, in spite of a sedative; that she had cried out several times in her sleep; that in the morning she was "resistive;" that she would say nothing and had refused to go for a walk.

When they have Virginia in she is revealed as a girl about twenty, "with a sad, lost little face," quite timid and, at first, almost inaudible. After the Nurse has been dismissed Virginia admits to Dr. Schiller that she is worried. "Yesterday everything was so clear, and today, I don't know. I'm afraid again," she says.

Virginia has been expecting her parents. In fact she has asked that they be sent for. Now she begins to dread their coming. That may have had something to do with her restless night and her bad dreams. But she is loathe to talk about that. The Doctor's effort to re-establish her confidence in him is only partially successful. Virginia is eager to be well again. She might be happy if she were well and at home and everything was as it used to be, but— Can they bring her brother back? There is a suggestion of mounting hysteria with that demand which Dr. Schiller is at pains to quiet.

"Would you be less unhappy if you were outside, whether you were well or not?" Dr. Schiller asks.

"Yes."

"But why?"

"Isn't there reason enough? Here everybody knows. They see my brother's death. They see my death."

"Why do you start that again? . . . If you fight me again, Virginia, I can't help you. And I'm trying to help you. Do you trust me?"

"Yes, I do, Dr. Schiller. You're the only friend I have."

Slowly, gently, Dr. Schiller retraces the progress that Virginia has made. She has begun to take interest in the other patients, to be concerned about them. She admits that even were she outside it would not be possible for her to forget her brother's death, even though, as she says, she "would have it alone, to herself—"

"You see, Virginia, everybody at one time or another has to face unpleasant things?" Dr. Schiller is saying. "We can't always avoid them. The only thing we can do is to make ourselves tougher—stronger—in order to face them whenever they arise. If an individual tries to wrap himself in cotton as a protection against the outside world, then he becomes a fragile, artificial thing. In trying to escape from life he makes himself unfit for life. He can only be protected in a hospital, as you are. No normal human being lives alone in the world. He lives with other people and other things, and must accommodate himself to them— to their impact—to the differences of viewpoint and feeling. Possibly in your case, living with your parents is such an impact. You will have at least to be strong enough to withstand it if you want to go out into life."

VIRGINIA—Yes.

DR. SCHILLER—See them or not—just as you please. Now, what about your dream? Is it still upsetting you?

VIRGINIA—I can't think.

DR. SCHILLER—You can. Now come on! What was it?

VIRGINIA (after a pause, slowly)—I was alone in a long dark hallway. I was frightened and I wanted to find a lighted room. I heard voices behind a door. I opened it. There was no one there. It was dark and empty. I started to run. Suddenly I was carrying a doll. I ran, hugging the doll. My heart was beating so hard it hurt. I wanted to scream, but I couldn't. All at once the doll slipped out of my hands and broke. (She pauses.)

DR. SCHILLER—Go on.

VIRGINIA—That's all. Then I woke up.

DR. SCHILLER—Why are you upset now about this dream? Does it remind you of something in the past?

VIRGINIA—That's it. I can't . . . I don't know.

DR. SCHILLER—Think of your brother. Does it have anything to do with him?

VIRGINIA (*after a long pause*)—I don't know.

DR. SCHILLER—How about those voices in the dream? Did you recognize them?

VIRGINIA—I'm not sure.

DR. SCHILLER—What were they saying?

VIRGINIA—It was jumbled. They were whispering. (*Phone buzzes*—DR. SCHILLER *answers it.*)

DR. SCHILLER—In a little while. Have them wait outside.

VIRGINIA—Are they here?

DR. SCHILLER—Yes, Virginia.

VIRGINIA—Dr. Schiller . . .

DR. SCHILLER—Let's continue. If you don't want to see them later—I'll send them away. All right?

VIRGINIA—All right.

DR. SCHILLER—What about the doll? Do you remember that clearly?

VIRGINIA—No.

DR. SCHILLER—Did it resemble a doll that your brother had something to do with? (*A man and a woman appear outside with a nurse. Even as a shadow, the woman is obviously over-fashionable. An extreme hat, extravagant feathers, dripping furs, flaring coat.*)

VIRGINIA—I tell you, they don't want to see me.

DR. SCHILLER—They're here. Your father's a busy man. He's put aside his business—you wrote the letter, you asked them, and they came at once.

VIRGINIA—Before I was here they never had any time for us. When my brother and I were little, we never saw them.

DR. SCHILLER—All that's past, Virginia. I'm not saying they were right or wrong. It's past. You've got to grow up. You see, Virginia, you're living in the past. You never developed emotionally beyond your brother's death . . . You want to get well, don't you?

VIRGINIA (*torn between the desire to get well and the desire not to get well, reflects the anguish of this emotional struggle in her face. Finally, in a low voice, she answers*)—Yes, I want to.

DR. SCHILLER—Then you've got to live in the present. Today! Now! Why don't you go through with the original plan? Talk to them, and try to understand their viewpoint. Once you do that you can go home with them and there you'll have a chance to grow up, to adjust yourself to the world, to be free.

VIRGINIA—All right, I'll see them.

DR. SCHILLER—Fine.   One thing.   You mustn't hurt them.

VIRGINIA—I'll try, Dr. Schiller.

DR. SCHILLER—It's up to you.   And remember!   Even if this doesn't work out, there's still hope.

VIRGINIA—Hope?

DR. SCHILLER—Yes.   You ready now?

VIRGINIA—I'm ready.

DR. SCHILLER—I'll bring them in.

Mr. and Mrs. McKay are ushered down the corridor and through the door. "Mrs. McKay is a tall, too fashionably slim woman of forty-five, elegantly groomed. . . . She possesses a frigid, viscous beauty. . . . Mr. McKay, shorter than his wife, considerably older, wizened, homely, soured, clipped, precise authority that hints of violent energy."

Dr. Schiller meets them and brings them to Virginia.   Mrs. McKay's greeting is effusive.   Mr. McKay's "Hello" is curtly paternal, but friendly.   Virginia is a little reserved, but eager to make a good impression.   She is, she insists, quite all right.   Yes, as Dr. Schiller admits, she has gained fifteen pounds.   But whether or not she is pretty—like her Aunt Grace—as her father insists— Well, Mrs. McKay doesn't think so, anyway.

Her father has brought Virginia a box of candy.   The blue ribbon with which it is tied attracts her attention.   "Do you remember—you once had a dress this color, Mother," she says.   "It had silver stars embroidered on it.   I was in love with that dress. Once when you and Daddy were away . . . I put it on.   I put on your high-heeled slippers, too, and I pinned my hair up, and I sat in front of your dressing table and played that I was you. It was a beautiful dress."

"Yes, I remember it.   Darling!   Dr. Schiller tells us you'll soon be coming home.   And the very first thing we'll do is to go shopping for a blue evening gown with silver stars."

"Would you really, Mother?"

"We'll have such a good time, darling.   The country club's been completely done over.   It's perfectly charming now.   Very gay.   I can see it.   You'll steal all my beaux away."

"I don't like boys."

"You know, darling.   I've been planning a trip to Europe this summer.   Now we can go together.   Would you like that, dear?"

"If war doesn't break out," puts in Mr. McKay.

"Nonsense! There'll be no war."

"I'm glad you settled that, too," snaps Mr. McKay.

A shadow has passed over Virginia's face at this first suggestion of a familiar home atmosphere. She wonders if her father would come to Europe with them, but Mr. McKay sees no hope of that. Nor Mrs. McKay. Virginia's father, says she, is too preoccupied to pay any attention to anything. "One-trace Roger" is what she calls him.

"That's right," snaps Mr. McKay, bitingly. "I haven't your choice variety of interests."

"And exactly what do you mean by that?"

"Nothing . . . nothing."

"No! Go on! Say it! You're always building a mountain of—"

Now Virginia has drawn away from them and turned her head. They have noticed the action and for the moment stop their quarrel. Suddenly Virginia has turned back to them to ask about her brother. Where is he buried? Where is his grave? Is it covered with flowers? Mrs. McKay hesitates a little at that. And Virginia would know why.

"Is he resting in peace?" she demands.

"We trust so."

"I'm not," cries Virginia. "I'm dead, too, but I can't rest in peace!"

They have gone to her, trying to comfort, trying to reassure her that she is well now and should not think of such things. But Virginia tears her arms away from her mother's grasp and moves away from them.

"Stop! Get out of here!" she screams. "Leave me alone! Leave me alone! Dr. Schiller!!"

She has thrown the box of candy to the floor. "I don't want your candy. I don't want anything from you. I'll never go home with you. I hate you! You killed my brother! I know. I found you out. You killed him! You're crying, but inside you don't mean it at all."

"How dare you talk to me that way? How dare you?" cries Mrs. McKay.

Dr. Schiller has come. Seeing the state of Virginia's nerves he tactfully leads the McKays away. In the hall Mrs. McKay is still gesturing volubly.

"Next time it will be better," Dr. Schiller promises, as he comes back to Virginia.

"It'll never be any better," sobs Virginia.

"When you improve a little more . . . You'll get along with them."

"You know that's not true. Let me get out. I want to live again. And I can't in here. Please!"

"Where would you go?"

"The world. Out there."

"You're not equipped for that, Virginia. Adaptation to your parents is child's play compared to the conflicts and the harshness of the world today. Even a normal world would be terribly difficult for a young girl—alone. And today—the world is in transition. New conflicts and problems are piling up. You'd run up against them every day . . . reflected in everybody you'd meet. No, you're not strong enough yet—"

The phone rings. There is a call for Dr. Schiller. An emergency has arisen.

He goes to the hall to call Nurse Regis. While his back is turned Virginia slips a key out of his key wallet and puts it in her bosom. He is back to tell her that she should stay there until Miss Regis comes. "I must see another patient," Dr. Schiller explains. "You mustn't be discouraged. It takes time . . ."

The Doctor has gone out through the side door. "As soon as he is gone Virginia looks about quickly, thinks for a moment, formulating a plan of escape. She goes to the Doctor's coat, searches in the pocket, finds a handful of small change, pipe, pouch, handkerchief, etc. She keeps the change, returns the other articles, puts on the coat. She buttons it up, goes to the door, looks out. The corridor is clear. She slips into the corridor. . . ."

Now she has let herself through the heavy outside door. A burst of sunlight greets her. She notes the song of a bird on the limb of a birch tree. "Then she fills her lungs with air, plunges into the sunlight and out of the hospital."

ACT I

The ground floor of the Sunbright Steam Laundry is divided into three zones. There is a corner of the weighing and marking room, where the wash is received. The "kitchen," where the steaming machines take care of the wash, is on an elevation, and the mangling room, where the rough part of the ironing is done, is just beyond.

A week after Virginia McKay left Greendale Sanitarium she is standing just inside the Sunbright laundry door looking for the boss. She has come to ask for a job. As she stands at the head of a short flight of steps no one pays any attention to her. Both the work and the chatter of the fifteen or twenty employees flows on without interruption.

"The air is thick with heavy clouds of steam and the reek of chemicals; the floor is flooded with slippery suds, the wet heat is almost unbearable, the walls and the ceilings, the machines and the humans, black and white, glisten, constant driblets of sweat streaming off them."

Here the most skilled laborer, the "Washer," in high rubber boots and apron, loads the washing machines. The clothes are macerated in hot and rinsed in cold water and passed on to the "Puller," who lifts them out of the washing machine and carts them over to the "extractor," which whirls them about in a huge drum until they are half dry. From there they are passed on to the mangle room, where the "shakers" and "feeders" and "takers off" put them through the ironing process. This routine, "ironically reminiscent of a Roxy ballet," is going on as Virginia stands at the head of the stairs looking down.

The wash passes from section to section. There is more or less joshing among the workers. Cora, evidently the worse for a drink or two, weaves her way in only to meet Louis, the foreman, and be ordered out of the place—the drunken bum. Cora isn't worried. She can make more in a night— And what she thinks of Louis is plenty—the bastard.

Still they pay no attention to Virginia. Louis, angered by his encounter with Cora, is moving among them now, pushing them to more and greater effort. What do they think this is—a holiday? They pay little attention to Louis, but they hate their jobs. One, Modesto, is tired of dirty, stinkin' clothes. Comes the revolution he is going to get himself a job in a poifume factory. . . .

Virginia has come into the room, still looking for the boss. She is almost run down by a truck of wet wash. John Kehler has pulled her out of the way just in time. She turns on him as she feels his hand on her arm—

"Don't do that!"

"Sorry, sister, you almost got run over," explains John. "What is it? What do you want?"

"I want to see someone about a job."

"You?"

"Yes. . . ."

"It's tough work."

"I don't mind that. I've gone to eight places this morning. The last place a woman on the line told me you needed some girls here. . . . Please. . . . I've got to get a job."

The boss has come out of the kitchen. He is a hard, driving fellow. He follows up where the foreman left off in exhorting the workers to "step on it." Now he sees Virginia and stops to answer her. Yes, he needs "sleevers." Had she ever sleeved? No, Virginia had never sleeved. She had never worked in a laundry before. But she's willing. And she'll work awfully hard—

"Can't use you," says the boss curtly.

"I had to fire Cora this morning. She came in drunk," speaks up Louis, whose appraisal of Virginia has been increasingly intimate.

"Please!" pleads Virginia.

"I'm sorry. Good-by."

"Wait a minute!" objects John. "We got to get that stuff out today. The girl'll have to put in overtime as it is. Why don't you stick one of the shakers on the sleever. One of them should be able to work that now, and you can let this kid be a shaker. That's easy. She'll catch on in a minute."

"That's a good idea," adds the foreman. "We're short on the mangles, too."

"You get 35 cents an hour," says the boss, turning to Virginia. "Your hours are from eight to five-thirty. Half an hour off for lunch. All right?"

"Yes."

Virginia is hired. Her name, she tells them, is Harriet—Harriet Hope. No, she hasn't any union card. John offers to fix that—and John's the shop chairman. O.K.

The boss turns her over to Louis, who would continue the questioning. What is her address? She hasn't any. She has been living with friends, but she's moving.

"See me before you leave tonight," suggests Louis, looking Harriet over. "Maybe I can fix you up. Hang your coat there. . . . Don't leave any money in the coat . . . Bring your pocketbook out with you. . . . Hey, you," he calls to one of the girls at the mangles, "break in the new girl on shakin' out the small pieces. . . . You, you go on the sheets."

Soon Harriet is learning to shake out the small pieces. No one takes much notice of her, except John and his brother, Jim, a rather sensitive, frail worker.

"Did you notice that kid's face?" asks Jim.

"Yeah. She looked as if she was goin' to burst out cryin' any minute," noticed John.

" 'And I a stranger and afraid in a world I never made,' " quotes Jim.

"Is that one of your poems?"

"If I could write like that . . ."

"I like some of yours better. . . ."

"What the hell do you know about poetry?"

"Not a goddam thing." . . .

The other girls would be friendly with Harriet. They are greatly interested in her dress. It's swell. And in her boy friends. But she hasn't any boy friends, she tells them—

"No?" The girl called Ruth is surprised. "Say—my new boy friend's boy friend is a regular Georgie Raft. Maybe Saturday night I can fix it up for you . . . Boys, he's a scream when he gets drunk. He'll go right up to anybody on the street and give her a feel. He's a scream. And if anybody says a word, he slaps 'em down. . . . Hey, Moysh, maybe we can fix you up with the new girl!"

"Me? A girl?" Moysh has had experience. "Yeah. Every time I say to my mother, 'Ma, I'm gone out with a girl,' she begins to cry. 'I want you to be happy, my son. We ain't got enough for rent . . . but don't mind that, Morris. Go on . . . you're a good boy . . . you deserve some pleasure . . . as for me . . . I'll kill myself.' . . . So, I don't sleep all night . . . feelin' like a rat."

"Look at me," comforts the one called Modesto. "And forget it. I felt like a rat, so I got married. Now I'm a mouse."

Harriet goes a little faint in the heat. They suggest slyly that she put up the window. She does. In a moment Louis is roaring to know who raised it, and why. Learning it's "Harriet" he softens. Dirt comes in open windows, he explains, gets on the mangles and stays on the wash.

Louis has another idea, too. He'll shift Harriet to sheets. She'll earn a couple bucks more a week. . . .

"Hey, you, new girl. Louis got a yen for you," calls the one known as Pearl. "If you're smart you'll give Louis a good time."

"She's just beating her gums," warns another. "You better watch out for Louis. . . . He's a mean man."

"Yeah, he's a wolf," adds Rosebud.

Her end of the sheet slips from Harriet's hand. She grabs for it and burns her hand. The girls are understanding if not sympathetic.

"You'll get used to it," says one.

"You might lose a couple of fingernails," adds another.

"But don't worry, they'll grow back. That happens to lots of us. Come on. Faster . . . Faster . . ."

The curtain has fallen to denote a lapse of time. When it rises it is getting dark outside and the lights are on. The workers are near exhaustion. Harriet has kept going on her nerves. In the kitchen John is cleaning up the machines. But the work in the mangles has piled up.

The work has piled up, the Boss explains, because the world insists that it must send its wash in on Monday. Why not Tuesday? Or Wednesday? Or any other day? But, no. Because a hundred years ago Monday was wash day it still has to be wash day. The world's in a rut. Let Louis send the girls home now, and bring them in an hour earlier in the morning.

The girls rush for the time clock, and for hats and coats. Soon the room is emptied, save for "Harriet." She is waiting to see the boss. Louis can't understand why. So far as she is concerned, he is much better than the Boss. Let her wait until he locks up—

The Boss cannot do anything for Harriet. She was hoping he could pay her for her five hours. The best he can do is to give her a dime for carfare. She'll get the rest at the end of the week. How does he know that she will come back?

John has reappeared with Harriet's union card. He finds her sitting on some bundles of wash, her head against the wall, her eyes closed. Why doesn't she go home?

"Hey, John. We're shutting up," calls Louis.

Harriet's face whitens. "Don't leave me alone with him," she pleads.

JOHN—You're waiting for him, aren't you?

HARRIET—He told me to. Do I have to?

JOHN—No, sister. Not unless you want to.

HARRIET—Why do you call me sister?

JOHN—Just an expression.

HARRIET—I'm afraid of him. Something in his eyes . . . as if he wanted to hurt me. The others looked at me that way.

JOHN—Who?

HARRIET—Men who come up to me on the street. . . . They whisper things. They frighten me.

JOHN—Say, how old are you?

HARRIET—Twenty. Then I don't have to stay here . . . even if he asked me to?

JOHN—No.

HARRIET—Where are you going now?

JOHN—Me? (*She nods.*) Grab a bite to eat, then home.
HARRIET—Will you take me with you?
JOHN—Hm?
HARRIET—Please. Last night I tried to sleep in the subway.
There was a drunken man touched me. I ran away. I'm so tired
. . . and I'm hungry.
JOHN—All right. Come on.

The scene changes. John and Harriet have arrived outside the
door of John's apartment in a wretched, cold-water tenement
house. Through a window the narrow court can be seen festooned
with clotheslines. "The squalor of the apartment is emphasized
by the careless disorder, the rubbish and dust that accumulate in
the rooms of a man who works hard all day and lives alone at
night."
Harriet has been ill. "John had bought her dinner, but after
several days of virtual starvation she was unable to retain any of
the food." She is wobbly, now, and he solicitously moves the
furniture out of her way and gets her into a chair.
Harriet's feet are soaked from the sloshing water of the laundry.
A hot bath is what she needs. John goes into the cubicle kitchen,
turns on the water, and gets a small tub from the window sill.
It will take about an hour to heat the water.
The rumble of an elevated train is heard. And a ring at the
doorbell. John has a caller. Two callers. Rocco and his mangy
dog, Pizon. Rocco is an amiable and voluble Italian. He lives,
with the dog, upstairs. He is embarrassed but pleased to find
Miss Hope there. If he had known—he wouldn't have busted in.
But—it's about time John was getting himself a girl.
"I tella John all-a-time, why you no getta dog?" Rocco explains
to Harriet. "He sitta here, smokin' a pipea, all alone, isa not
good. I tella him, get a dog; if you can no getta dog, getta
woman, getta something. A dog isa better, but the woman isa
all right too."
"Rocky" has gone now. He has got some stuff that will fix up
Pizon's fleas and he is hoping they are both going to sleep better
than they had the night before. The way Rocky talks to Pizon
amuses Harriet, or would, if she were not so dead for sleep—
"Yeah, that Kiyoodle's Rocky's wife, sister, son, mother and the
whole damn family," says John, still fussing with the preparations
for Harriet's bath. "When a man lives alone, he's got to have
something."
"You live alone, don't you?"

"Oh, that's different. . . . I got my kid brother and his family
. . . the water's takin' an awful long time . . . Hey . . . you
can hardly keep your eyes open. Would you like to go right to
sleep?"

"Yes. I'm very tired."

"You can undress in there," says John, indicating the kitchen.
He takes a blanket off the bed and spreads it out on the floor.
Harriet timidly takes off her outer dress. "Please . . . will you
look the other way?" she calls, coming to the door of the kitchen.

John does and Harriet climbs wearily into the bed, drawing the
sheet up around her. John has taken a reading lamp and adjusted the plug. He fetches the alarm clock and a book. It is
Dickens' "Old Curiosity Shop."

"Will you set it for six?" asks Harriet. "I have to be there
early."

John—Why don't you sleep late tomorrow?

Harriet—What about my job?

John—You're all worn out.

Harriet—But I need my job. You don't know how hard I
looked before I found it.

John—It isn't gonna do you any good if you cave in . . . Do
you like spaghetti? Italian style? I'm a wizard at it. If you
come back tomorrow I'll fix some for you.

Harriet—Set it for six.

John—All right. (*He sets it.*) If you change your mind in
the morning, don't get up. Make yourself at home. I'll leave
the key on the table. There's some money in the coffee tin, third
shelf. In case you need anything for the ice-box. I think I'm
out of eggs and—whatever you need. I'd like to talk to you some
tomorrow night. Will you come back?

Harriet—I don't know. Maybe.

John—You're welcome if you want to.

Harriet—I'll see. (*He arranges the reading lamp on the floor,
and turns off the overhead light.*)

John—This light bother you?

Harriet—No.

John—I like to read a couple of minutes before I kick off.

Harriet—What are you reading? (*Sits up.*)

John—"Old Curiosity Shop." Ever read it? By a guy named
Charles Dickens. My mother gave me this book when I was
fourteen. I must have read it ten to twenty times. I always get
a kick out of it.

HARRIET—Do you love your mother?

JOHN—My mother is dead.

HARRIET—Did you love her?

JOHN—Very much. She was a wonderful woman.

HARRIET—Did she love you?

JOHN—She worked her fingers to the bone so I could go through high school. That's a lot for a miner's kid.

HARRIET—And your father?

JOHN—Well, he used to beat me and Jim. I run away when I was seventeen. Took Jim with me.

HARRIET—I hated my mother and father.

JOHN—Did they kick you around?

HARRIET—No. (JOHN *looks at her, puzzled, waiting for an explanation, but it doesn't come. She averts her face.*)

JOHN—I never really hated my father. We just didn't understand each other. I met him years later. We were working in the same mine. I was a man then. We became friends. He was changed. That was after my mother died. Half the life goes out of a man when he loses his woman. Sometime later he was killed in a mine cave-in. I guess he didn't care much.

John is enthusiastic about Dickens. She asks him to read some of his book aloud. He has no more than started than she falls asleep. The El roars by. John picks up the clock, ponders for a moment, then sets the alarm. He has turned out the light and rolled himself up in the blanket when there is a racket on the stairs. Harriet sits bolt upright. "The blue light from the window illuminates her terror-stricken face." John laughs—

"Don't be scared!" he says. "That's only Rocky and his mutt. Whenever he feels low he throws a soupbone down the stairs and the dog chases it. It gives him a great kick."

The scramble in the hall continues. John turns over and, with a genial "Good night" is off to sleep. "Harriet is still sitting up, tense, on the verge of hysteria," as the curtain falls.

Next morning Harriet is sleeping soundly. John, rolled in his blanket, is stirring restlessly on the floor. It is early and the tenement is coming slowly to life. There are distant alarm clocks waking their owners. An occasional baby cry is heard. Windows are opened and closed.

John has smothered the alarm clock as Harriet turns and moans in her sleep. As she settles back to sleep John pulls on his trousers and goes to the kitchen. He puts coffee on to boil, rum-

mages among a collection of paper bags, finds a single orange,
which he puts aside, and a loaf of rye bread from which he cuts
a thick slice. When the coffee is ready he pours himself a cup,
grabs his bread and is standing looking down at Harriet when
she stirs again. Hastily he goes back to the kitchen, slices the
orange, leaves it on a plate, scribbles a note and tiptoes out.

The noises of the tenement increase. Suddenly Harriet awakes
with a start. For a moment her surroundings mystify her. Then
she remembers and dresses herself quickly. She is ready to rush
out when she finds John's note. A glance at the clock tells her
it is too late for work. Hesitantly she decides to take a little
breakfast. Finishing this she starts again for the door. The
dirty dishes catch her eye. She returns and washes them. She
would put them on the shelves, but the shelves are too dirty.
She gets a rag and wipes the shelves. Again she would go, but
stops at the window. Across the court she can see other women
going about their morning housekeeping. She would straighten
up the bed. When she slaps the pillow a cloud of dust rises. She
hangs the bedclothes out the window to air. Now, as she opens
the outer door to leave she sees a neighbor, Mrs. Zubriski, down
on her knees scrubbing the floor. Harriet is fascinated. She
closes the door, steps back and inspects the floor of John's apartment. It is filthy. In the kitchen she puts a pan of water on to
heat, finds soap, a brush and a pail. A moment later she, too,
is on her knees, scrubbing the floor, like Mrs. Zubriski. Awkwardly at first. Then she falls into the rhythm of it. "For the
first time she relaxes and is happy. . . . She has become a part
of the life around her." The curtain falls.

ACT II

By the time John gets home that night Harriet has the apartment pretty clean. She is tired but triumphant. Through the
day she has met the Zubriskis from across the hall, made friends
with little Mary Zubriski, who has a doll that wets when you feed
it water, learned that Mr. Zubriski has been out of work so long
that it is beginning to weigh on his mind, and sympathized with
Anna Zubriski, a girl of her own age, who cannot marry her Al
because Al is not making enough to stand two rents. Still, as
Harriet says, if things work out, someday Anna and Al will
marry—

"What do you mean?" Anna wants to know.

"I was just thinking of a girl I know who can never get married," sighs Harriet.

"Is she crippled?"

"Yes. . . . So, you see, you're not so badly off."

"Listen! I got a mirror . . . And I got eyes . . . I'm no Hedy Lamarr. All my life I looked for a nice, home-loving boy like Al. All right, so I found one. But he ain't gonna wait around forever . . . He's only human . . . He's a man. He gets tired and lonely . . . He's got to have a woman . . . If it ain't me it's gonna be somebody else . . . God, what I want is very simple . . . Any human being is entitled to that little . . . but I can't have it. All right . . . so I can't. Only don't sing me a song about how lucky I am. That luck I wouldn't wish on a dog."

"I didn't mean anything."

"I know you didn't. Don't mind me. The Zubriskis are punch drunk. Come over later, huh?" . . .

John is home. He notes the change in the apartment with enthusiasm. However, he had wanted Harriet to rest, not work. He is amused at the bunch of things Harriet has picked up and left for him to sort out. Things he has forgotten he ever had. Most of them might as well be thrown out. He thinks she is right, too, about putting up a new shelf and giving it a coat of paint—

"I'm glad you stayed," says John. "I been thinking about you all day, wondering if you'd still be here."

"You didn't mind my cleaning up?"

"Mind? You don't know what a kick it gives me just to see you fussin' around the place."

"It was fun. It was good for me. I liked doing it. It's strange how much of a person . . ."

She has been standing on a chair and he has taken her arm to help her down. They are staring at each other. He would take her in his arms, but her emotions disturb her. She is confused and frightened and pulls her hand away. He lets her go.

She had been making some spaghetti, she tells him. Mrs. Zubriski had told her how. But it is no good. She can't do anything right—

"O.K. Come on, we'll go out," suggests John.

"No. I'm not hungry."

JOHN—I don't get you . . . You're a funny kid. What's eating you, anyway?

HARRIET (*turns*)—Why did you set the alarm back this morning? You know how much that job meant to me. Why didn't you awaken me?

JOHN (*getting angry*)—Because I knew if you tried to go to the shop you'd fall flat on your face. (*He goes into the kitchen, examines the spaghetti, puts it back on the stove, returns.*) Spaghetti looks fine. There's nothing wrong with that. Keep a slow fire under it . . . And don't worry about the job. It's still there. I spoke to the boss. You can go back tomorrow if you want to. (*He lies down on the bed.*) I'm going to close my eyes a couple of minutes . . . I'm tired.

HARRIET (*standing at the head of the bed, watches him a moment*)—John . . .

JOHN—Yeah?

HARRIET—I didn't mean to be ungrateful. I didn't know the world was so full of people who were confused and lost, too. Don't hate me, John. I don't want you to hate me.

JOHN—What's this hate business? Why should I hate you? I don't hate anybody. I don't believe in it.

HARRIET—You might, if you weren't so strong . . . so sure of yourself.

JOHN—What gave you that idea?

HARRIET—It's as if everything you touch belongs to you . . . Really belongs to you. Yesterday, in the laundry I felt that, even before I heard your voice, before I saw your face . . . when you grabbed my arm. Then this afternoon I went down on the street for a little while and stood in front of the house. I got a little frightened again. The street was dirty and noisy. The old gate downstairs half off . . . the doorway, the stairs, the walls were crumbling . . . I thought the house was going to cave in on top of me. I ran back in here . . . It was all right again . . . It was firm . . . It was safe. I got the feeling it would stand forever. It was your room. You were in it. You see, that's what I mean about you. Things belong to you. You give them your strength. And because you have it you don't know what it is to be without it. Why don't you put the pillow under your head . . . Here! Let me! Lift up! (*She puts the pillow under him. He grasps her arms gently.*)

JOHN—Come here. . . . I can't make you out.

HARRIET—I'm not important . . . I don't matter.

JOHN—Look! Why are you always apologizing for yourself? Why are you always ducking and backing away? Nobody's swinging at you. Tell me! What are you afraid of?

HARRIET—You wouldn't understand.

JOHN—How do you know? Try! What is it? What have you done? I don't care. Is it the police?

HARRIET—No. It's not that.

JOHN—Who are you? Tell me about yourself. Where do you come from? What do you want? What do you expect out of life? What do you pray for at night?

HARRIET—What I want?

JOHN—Yes.

HARRIET—It's not so easy. Things inside pulling you in different directions . . . twisting and turning.

JOHN—You see, you don't even know what you want.

HARRIET—I do . . . I know . . .

JOHN—What?

HARRIET—I want to feel . . . I want to live, I want to be in the world with other people. . . . I want a place that's safe . . . where nothing can get at me.

JOHN—Where would that be?

HARRIET—Here, with you . . . I could . . .

JOHN—You want to live here with me?

HARRIET—Yes . . . Yes.

JOHN—All right! Fine! (*He takes her in his arms. She is rigid and terrified . . . then a fierce wave of response as she returns the embrace.*)

It is three weeks later. Harriet is quite at home now in John's much improved apartment. At the moment she is watering geraniums that she has put in makeshift flower boxes on the fire-escape, and thanking the neighbor on the fire-escape above for the hint she had given her about putting coffee grounds on them. The geraniums have done fine with the help of the coffee grounds, but the nasturtiums aren't so good.

John and his brother, Jim, come noisily up the stairs. There has been a fight at the shop and John is taking Jim to task for having started it. They drop the subject when Harriet greets them. She kisses John affectionately and welcomes Jim. Their talk is of casual things—of a projected boat trip; of Sally and the baby; of the flowers on the fire-escape—until suddenly they discover that Jim has a black eye. That's not so funny. The fight had also shown up the pain in Jim's back, and John had had to take a punch at the truckman to save Jim.

"I guess I lost my temper a little," John confesses to Harriet.

"A little?" explodes Jim. "Ben Adhem here carved the Bill of Rights all over Fritz's puss. Oh, that was beautiful—from the floor."

"Naw, I shouldn't have hit him," protests John. "The hell! He doesn't know any better. You oughta get your pants kicked for starting a rumpus at the place."

That sort of argument excites Jim. He can't understand John. "Can't you see?" he demands of his brother. "Everything that's important to us, those guys want to tear up and throw away." He slaps the newspaper he is carrying. "This isn't happening 3,000 miles away, it's happening here, yeah . . . here. Christ, John, it took all history to get guys like us outa hock. Liberty isn't just a statue in New York Harbor important only because three men can stand in the thumb. I'm for democracy. That's my meat. That's me. Any guy that wants to take it away from me does it over my dead body."

"Yeah? From the way you look it won't be such a hard job. Relax!"

Jim laughs. "The world's going right back to the Dark Ages, and Abou Ben Adhem here wants me to relax! Too much relaxing! Somebody's got to do something about it before it's too late."

"And you're the guys that's goin' to do it?"

"If a house painter can start it, a puller in a laundry can stop it."

Mrs. Zubriski has come out into the hall. John hears her. He has got Mr. Zubriski a job at the shop, he tells Harriet, and Harriet, thrilled with the news, rushes to the door to tell Mrs. Zubriski. A moment later the hall landing is swarming with Zubriskis and foaming with excitement. Mrs. Zubriski is screaming for Mr. Zubriski and trying to kiss "Mrs. Kohler's" hand. Mr. Zubriski is trying to absorb the good news without letting anyone see that he is crying.

"Who cryin'?" demands the excited Zubriski. "Me no cryin'! Mommusha! Me sittin' by window, lookin' it out . . . leely bugs flyin' in face, catchin' in eye . . . eyes gettin' in water."

"For two years he no me call Mommusha," explains Mrs. Zubriski, happily, tearfully, as her husband disappears sobbing into the house. "Mrs. Kohler, God blessin' you!"

"He has already, Mommusha," says Harriet.

To continue the celebration, Harriet is back in the living room throwing her arms around John's neck and calling him angel for the good he's done. When she has gone into the kitchen Jim takes advantage of the moment to suggest that Harriet is a really nice girl. He thinks John should be doing something about her.

He'd like to be eating a hunk of their wedding cake—and he is surprised that John doesn't take a poke at him for suggesting it. But John doesn't. He just changes the subject. . . .

Rocky and Pizon stop by on their way upstairs. Pizon has learned a new trick. He sits up at the count of three—when he wants to. Just now he doesn't want to, which goes to show how smart he is, according to Rocky. . . . The renting agent is in, collecting. Rocky hides in the kitchen until he's gone. . . . In the hall the agent meets Anna, gets his rent and gives her a receipt. . . . Now Harriet and John are alone, and supper's nearly ready.

"What did you do today?" John wants to know, as Harriet brings his pipe and fills it for him.

"I walked, went shopping," says Harriet. "There are so many children in the street. I watched them. They were playing. They're so happy and carefree. They don't worry about the world, do they?"

JOHN—Don't kid yourself. I used to spend hours just watchin' Jim's little bug. Did you ever watch a new born baby?

HARRIET—No.

JOHN—Don't let anybody ever tell you a baby don't feel . . . They sense things. Your heart goes right out to them. Nothin' but that little cry for help between them and a dark world. Funny thing I noticed about that cry, though. Times I wouldn't hear it, Jim wouldn't hear it, but Sally heard it. She would hear that little cry right through thunder. Yeah, that's a fact. (*She gives him his pipe. . . . He kisses her.*) Thanks. (*She smiles.*) Yep. Someday when I can afford 'em I want a whole football team. (*The smile on her face fades,—worry creeps into her face.*)

HARRIET—Johnny?

JOHN—Yeah.

HARRIET—I've been wondering . . .

JOHN—What?

HARRIET—Do you think I'll have a baby?

JOHN—No.

HARRIET—Why not?

JOHN—Well, after that . . . I . . . I've tried to be more careful.

HARRIET—What do you mean? Tell me.

JOHN—Don't you know?

HARRIET—No.

JOHN—Well, there are ways of . . . Why don't you talk to Sally?

HARRIET—All right! Don't say any more.

JOHN—I'm sorry, sweetheart, I . . . (*He reaches for her arm. . . . She pulls away.*)

HARRIET—No . . . Don't touch me.

JOHN—I know it's . . .

HARRIET—Don't talk to me about it . . . It's ugly . . . It's ugly.

JOHN—There are a lot of things in life that are ugly . . .

HARRIET—Then I don't care to be alive.

JOHN—I don't know what you're talking about. Sometimes you act like you were in another world.

HARRIET—Maybe I am.

Harriet has gone quickly into the kitchen, shutting the door after her. . . . Anna Zubriski comes across the hall to confirm the news of her father's job and to add her radiant thanks. She runs into the kitchen to find Harriet. She and Al can get married now, Anna announces, joyfully.

"Do you want to?" asks Harriet.

"Want to? Oh, my God!"

"Aren't you afraid?"

"Afraid? All my life I've been marking time, waiting for this moment. My . . . my whole life is just beginning. What's there to be afraid in that?"

Anna has thrown her arms impulsively around Harriet and kissed her and run from the room.

John has come into the kitchen. He faces a happy but still puzzled Harriet. Why won't she marry him? There are reasons, Harriet insists. He doesn't know anything about her. That he loves her she can believe, and she loves him, but there are other things she can't tell. Finally he drags her reasons from her— She cannot marry him because she is insane!

For a moment John is shocked, then incredulous. She tries desperately to explain. She reminds him of the morning they met in the laundry. She had just escaped from Greendale hospital. He is staring at her open-mouthed. Suddenly his collar is choking him. Harriet says what she can to reassure him—

"Don't worry," she says. "When the sickness comes I just get terribly frightened and lost. It's like an awful dream."

"But you seem all right." John can't understand.

"It lasts a little while. Then I get sick again. It happened when my brother was killed."

JOHN—You had a brother killed?

HARRIET—It was my father's and mother's fault. Their hate killed him. They hated us. (HARRIET *sees the look of anguish on his face. She goes to him.*) It's all right. I'm not really alive, you see. It's as if I died with him. (*She gets coat.*) Thanks, John. You've been so good to me. I should have told you in the beginning, but I just didn't have the courage. I loved you so much. Good-by. (*She goes, shutting the door behind her. JOHN sits there in a stupor for a moment. Suddenly he rises, runs to the door, catches her on the stairs.*)

JOHN—Wait a minute, Harriet. You can't go just like this.

HARRIET—Please, John, let me. For your sake.

JOHN—Come inside. I want to talk to you. I can't let you just walk away like that. You can stay and give me supper, can't you?

HARRIET—You want me to?

JOHN—Yeah. (*He takes off her hat and coat for her. They go back into the apartment. HARRIET goes into the kitchen. JOHN stares after her. She pours out some soup and returns.*) Tell me, if we got a good doctor . . .

HARRIET—I've had the best.

JOHN (*seating her and himself at table*)—What did you mean about their killing your brother?

HARRIET—Their hate killed him. They didn't want us. They hated children. Our house was full of hate. They used to have the most terrible quarrels . . . in front of us . . . in front of the servants . . . it didn't matter who was there. When we got older, they gave us things . . . anything, just to let them alone. We had much. We had nothing . . . except each other. Then, when Tommy was killed . . .

JOHN—How was he killed?

HARRIET—They bought him a car—a very fast car. He was too young. He crashed into a train. They knew it was a death trap. You don't believe me?

JOHN—I once bought Jim's kid a BB air rifle and he shot himself in the hand with it.

HARRIET—That's different.

JOHN—All right . . . Don't get upset.

HARRIET—That's strange. I used to hate anybody who disagreed with me. Even Dr. Schiller. But with you it's different.

You're so much a part of me and I feel part of you.

JOHN—Let's make a bargain. Whenever we talk about this, I'll try to see it your way, but if I can't, you've got to try and see it mine. Is it a bargain?

HARRIET—John . . . you're very kind . . .

JOHN—I'm not being kind . . . I'm being selfish.

HARRIET—It isn't fair to you. You don't know.

JOHN—I know I love you and I can't get along without you. Will you stay?

HARRIET—All right, John. (*She pours the soup.*)

JOHN—Thanks. (*He tastes the soup.*) Say, this is O.K.

HARRIET—Do you really like it?

JOHN—As Rocky would say—son of a witch, he's a pretty goddam gooda swell soup.

"Harriet smiles at John, then laughs, happily, as John sucks up the soup with great noises of appreciation." The curtain falls.

It is three months later. Harriet and John have Jim and Sally, the Zubriskis and Rocco in to supper. The meal is over now. Harriet is in the kitchen fixing a bowl of fruit. Jim is fooling around with the dials of the radio. At the moment he is getting the tailend of a European digest from Columbia, with a Kalten-born analysis.

The talk at the table is of the courageous Poles, who are still holding out, waiting, hoping for French and English aid that has no way of getting through to them. The Zubriskis are depressed, but hopeful. Mr. Zubriski thinks it is all a clever Polish trap. Those Poles, they'll wait until they get the Germans across the line and then—"Polish soldiers comin' out from holes in ground—we gotten 'em in trap," he promises.

"But meantime alla Polish people gonna get killed . . ." protests Rocco.

"They not killa Polish so easy . . ."

"It looks bad," sighs John. "Where's your Russia now, Jim?"

"I don't know . . . I don't understand," admits Jim.

It is time for her baby to be in bed, and Sally would be starting home. But Jim is interested in one more broadcast and is stubborn. . . .

Harriet finds few takers for her fruit. Everybody's filled up. Rocco, he's damn near bust. There's a burst of music from the radio. Harriet is hoping Jim will keep that on. But, no, Jim must have more war news—

". . . Jan Gura, a Warsaw Councilor, described over the radio a visit to the front line . . ." comes from the loud speaker. "There, he said, he talked with boys between 12 and 18 wearing steel helmets. One was toothless, he said, another had his head bandaged and a third was wounded in the legs . . . but all were cheerful and determined. The communiqué went on to tell of widespread destruction from German bombs and shells, of bombs that fell before St. John's Cathedral as worshipers emerged from Mass, of machine gun attacks from the air on the church-goers. . . ."

"This isn't war—it's murder!" cries Jim.

". . . the Parliament building and hundreds of other buildings had been destroyed," continues the announcer. "The Mayor, his speech interrupted by the explosion of bombs, his voice breaking with emotion . . . described the buildings in ruins . . . 'We are wading in blood,' he said. 'The wounded and the dead . . . mostly women and children . . . lying in the streets uncared for. We haven't people enough to bury the dead or attend to the wounded.' "

"Jesus Christ Almighty!" cries Jim.

Harriet has hurried into the kitchen. "When I gotten Hitler here I cracken his head," swears Mr. Zubriski. "Every German people should be killed," adds Mrs. Zubriski.

"No, no . . . that's wrong," protests John. "The awful part is that the German people don't want this. No people want it. That's what makes me so mad I can't see . . . nobody wants war. Their hands are tied. Their minds are tied . . . they get their heads chopped off if they even listen to a radio. They don't know what's happening. They're not allowed to think. They're not allowed to breathe. But it will get through to them. When this war ends, they'll be the ones to end it, by turning on the Nazis and getting rid of them."

Now the war talk is boiling again. Rocco is trying to explain that Mussolini is not a war man. He's just a bad figurer. He tell everybody to have babies, everybody have babies, including Rocco's 80-year-old uncle, then there's no place for the babies to live, and nothing for the babies to eat. So Mussolini has to take pieces of other countries. Just because he's no good at figure.

All right, agrees Mr. Zubriski. He has big family, too. Why shouldn't he move some of them in on Rocco? Because, explodes Rocco, that's different. He doesn't know how, but it's different.

"Don't laugh. It's not so funny," says Jim. "If Governments are going to lie and cheat and kill . . . that's the rule for people, too. So where are we? Who can put his head on a pillow at night? There's no safety—not in your own room. If these fellows aren't stopped . . . Wolves run through the streets . . . the world becomes a screaming, crazy wilderness."

Now Sally is going home. She is not going to stay there and see Jim work himself into a fit. Jim's sick. "His bones are turning to water," she tells John. "You ought to see him at night when he comes home, wringing wet . . . Then he stays up all night worrying about all this. He isn't well. He shouldn't be working—"

Jim would resent this revealing of his weakness. He resents Sally's saying that she will get her old job back again. "If you ever have to go back to work again, it's not going to be to support a guy in a wheelchair," shouts Jim. . . .

Harriet has been sitting in the kitchen alone. John goes to her now. He would help her with the dishes, but she thinks he should stay with the others. She is all right. A little worried because this is September—it was in September that her brother was killed. She tries not to think of it. She has been well for five months, now. Better than ever before—but sometimes— like last night when she cried out in her sleep. John had wakened her then, and shaken her. And she had tried to forget. He has put his arm around her now, protectingly— "Oh, John, hold me tight!" she cries. "Tighter! September is always the worst. The least little thing—"

"All right! All right! . . . Now, let's stop it. I don't want you to think about it any more."

"All right, John."

"Come on inside."

"The roaches . . ."

"Let them have a picnic, too. Come on!"

"I don't want to go inside. I want to get away from all that talk for a minute. That's all you hear. Everywhere you look, the papers, in the movies, you read, you see horrible pictures, building's blown to bits, men—killing, killing. Hate everywhere! Death keeps coming closer! . . . The world is so frightening. I feel I just want to run away."

"Come on inside . . . sit next to me and hold my hand, huh?"

Out in the hallway the Zubriski children are playing. Pretending to be all dressed up and out for a walk in the Park. Pretending to hail a peanut man and buy a nickel's worth. And now they have run into a pretend air raid, with young Danny making noises like airplanes, and bombs as well.

"Oh, my baby is killed! My baby is killed!" shouts Mary, holding her doll close. "My poor baby!"

She is moaning and groveling on the floor. But the boy Janek is even worse. He has been gassed. Look! He can't breathe even! And Danny! Danny's crashed! He is down on the floor, groaning—

The game is too much for Harriet. She is screaming to them to stop. Sally, too, takes a hand. "I wish we could just once in our lifetime go out for an evening and not have the kids on our necks!" sighs Sally.

Harriet is making a valiant effort to control her nerves. She tries desperately to talk of other things. She begs Jim to give up his search for more war stuff on the radio and to play more music. She is shouting now, and John is anxious—

"I'm sick of seeing you all glued to the damned radio, listening to this horror as if it were a baseball game," Harriet shouts, hysterically.

"Boy! What caused that?" John would know.

"She's right. I'm sick of it, too," agrees Sally. And Jim, a little guiltily, turns back to the music.

Mrs. Zubriski is convinced everybody is tired and should be going home. The party breaks up. They are all grateful and Harriet is apologetic for her "blitzkrieg."

"I still love you," says Jim. In the hall he turns to John. "There's a funny feeling in the air," he says. "Do you get it? At the tips of your fingers . . . in the pit of your belly . . . Like it's the end of the world. Do you get it?"

John doesn't get it. "Maybe I got gas," concludes Jim. "So long."

"So long . . . Oh, Jim . . . Come here a minute." Jim comes back. "You look like hell," cautions John. "See another doctor, will you?"

"Aw . . ."

"Will you?"

"Yeah . . . yeah. . . ."

"And look, kid . . . she didn't mean anything."

"Of course she didn't."

"She hasn't been feeling so good lately. You know how women are. Ups and downs."

"Oh, forget it, will you? I know just how she feels."

John can't forget entirely. He can't understand why Harriet should let herself go that way. And then excuse herself by saying she doesn't feel well—that's kid stuff.

"I don't want to talk about it any more. Please, John! Let me alone! Go away now. I want to be alone."

"I'm going out for a walk," announces John, and goes.

For a moment Harriet wanders aimlessly about the room. "Her lips move as if she were talking to someone, but no sound comes out. Her eyes glaze. Jim has left the radio on. It is still playing softly and attracts her attention. She shuts it off—

"Hate . . . hate . . . everywhere! Death . . . kill . . . kill . . . Shut it off! Shut it off!" She moves over to the window and closes it. "You see, Tommy, I was right. They tried to tell me 'no' . . . Hate kills . . . Hate killed you. You? Tommy? My sweet brother . . . lying in the streets . . . your body torn . . . Burning, crying . . . No . . . You were buried! You're not there. Oh, my God, what's the matter with me? This is . . . I mustn't get sick. No! Don't go back! Don't! Stop! Stop thinking . . . Oh, God . . . It's getting all mixed up again!"

From one of the tenement flats across the court comes a burst of laughter. "Everything becomes a blurred jumble of sound. The lights fade out. The El roars by, whipping Harriet's face with its lights. The jumble of chaotic sound increases." The curtain falls.

ACT III

A few days later Harriet is still trying to fight off the thoughts that assail her, still trying to "Stop thinking." When her doorbell rings she pulls herself together and admits Anna.

Anna is animated and interested. She has a secret to tell. She is going to have a baby. It is a thrilling experience for her—but Harriet should see Al. The way Al carries on. "You'd think he was going to have the baby," giggles Anna. "He even throws up in the morning. I'm all right—and he throws up! You'd die laughing!" Anna has a good laugh at the thought of it.

"You're next! It's your turn now," jokes Anna, taking Harriet's hand.

"Johnny wants a baby," admits Harriet. Her lips begin to tremble. She bites back her tears. "Anna—do me a favor. Go down to the drugstore and call Riverdale 7085. Ask for Dr. Schiller. . . . Tell him Miss McKay . . . That's my maiden name. I want him to call for me here. Give him the address . . . Tell him the name—Kohler . . . He'll know what it's about . . ."

With a promise not to say anything to John about the call, Anna has gone. A moment later John is home. Harriet rushes

into his arms. He has had a hard day at the laundry and is dead
on his feet. But he found time to stop and buy something. It's
a lizard-skin pocketbook. He hopes it's her style—

Harriet is in tears. There's nothing to cry about, she admits,
but she just has to. "It's a beautiful bag, Johnny," she says, and
they're laughing when he drops a quarter into the bag for luck.

John submits to being made comfortable; to having his slippers
brought for him and put on his tired feet. But he feels he should
be going over to see how Jim is. Jim had doubled up in the
laundry and had to go home.

"I love your feet, Johnny," Harriet is saying, caressingly. "To
wake up at night and not feel you next to me." There is anguish
in her voice, which startles him.

"What are you talking about?"

"John, if it should happen, and I have to go back to the hospital, you'd be a good boy? You wouldn't let it hurt you too
much?"

"Oh, stop it."

"Would you?"

"Cut it out."

"Would you?"

"I'd dry up and blow away."

"After a while you'd forget."

"In a minute I'm going to get awfully mad at you."

She tells him of Anna's baby, and is quick to notice the look
in his eyes as he tries casually to say he's glad for Anna and Al.
Again she forces a confession from him that he would like to have
a kid—if it were hers.

"A girl will come along someday. She'll be right for you.
She'll be the one, she'll have my baby," she says.

"You want to be slugged?" he demands, waving an ugly fist
under her nose.

"Yes. Hit me! Slap my mouth! Hurt me!" He has caught
her in his arms and is kissing her roughly when the doorbell rings.

Anna is back to report on her errand. Harriet takes her into
the kitchen. Anna had talked with Dr. Schiller. He will be there
that night. He was surprised to hear from Harriet, and more
surprised to learn of her marriage and so forth. . . .

Rocco has brought a bottle of wine for the ailing Jimmy. He
is terribly disgusted to hear that the doctors have barred alcohol
for the patient. "Goddam! How the hell he's gonna get better?
The Doctor's a son of a witch . . . she's adrink plenty, I betcha
my life."

The wine calls for a toast, however. Al has come looking for Anna. He is fearfully worried when he discovers that she has run upstairs and got out of breath. The Zubriskis are called. Everybody is happy to toast Anna—but Al insists she can't have any wine. He gets milk for her from the kitchen. In the midst of their laughter they decide to toast Harriet and what should be her prospects, too. She has no excuse now. She's gotta have a baby.

Harriet's laughter is hearty. Soon she cannot control it. She has thrown herself on the bed and is laughing hysterically when the doorbell rings.

There is a man at the door, asking for John. He is Jim's next door neighbor. Jim's wife had asked him to come for John. Jim's in a bad way.

"They took him to Bellevue Hospital," reports the man.

"My brother?"

"Yeah. He's bleeding from the nose. They got a pipe in. I never saw anything like it. You better hurry. The doctor says he's very bad."

In a dazed way John is starting down the stairs. Harriet stands for a minute staring after him. Then she suddenly shrieks.

"John! Wait for me!"

She is running after him as the curtain falls.

Late that night the Zubriskis, Anna and Al, Rocco and his dog and Dr. Schiller are variously seated around the Kohler apartment waiting for news from the hospital. Al has called four times since John and Harriet left, but has had little satisfaction from the reports of the hospital attendants.

Dr. Schiller has waited about as long as he can, but agrees to wait another ten minutes. Meantime he has gained a good deal of information about Harriet and the new life she has been living. In return he has given of his professional advice to quiet Al's fears that if Anna doesn't come to bed her baby is likely to be marked, and advised Rocco to ask at the drugstore for something that will help Pizon's worms.

They have settled back for another wait when John is heard coming heavily up the stairs. He is crushed with grief. He leans heavily on Harriet as they come into the room.

Jim is dead. His lungs had collapsed—

"The doctors worked over him for hours. He was fighting so hard. He wanted to live. It just wasn't in the cards."

Harriet finds a chair for John. He is too dazed to notice what

THE WORLD WE MAKE

THE WORLD WE MAKE139

is happening. He crosses to the bed and sits there. He doesn't
want the bed made. He doesn't want any coffee. He wants to be
left alone. He receives their expressions of sympathy with little
response. Presently they have all gone.

Dr. Schiller turns to Harriet. She tells him a little of John's
deep grief at the loss of his brother. She is, she is quick to confess, not really married. She wishes Dr. Schiller could help John.
She, he insists, can do that much better than he can. She can't
believe that. He has seen how John has put her off. "It is a
natural reaction for some people in time of grief," Dr. Schiller
explains.

HARRIET—Not if I were really able to help him. You were
right. I've failed. I'm not fit. There's no real place for me
here.

DR. SCHILLER—You've done better than you think, my dear
. . . far better than I ever thought you could. You see, I've
been talking to your neighbors . . . I know all you've accomplished.

HARRIET—What have I accomplished? At a time like this . . .
when he needs me so . . . when I should be strong . . . I'm
afraid again.

DR. SCHILLER—You must know, these days stronger people
than you all over the world have this same feeling . . . a general
sense of helplessness against a great disorder. It expresses itself
in many ways, but it is one universal fear.

HARRIET—How can anyone go on then? What gives us the
courage to go on?

DR. SCHILLER—Faith in people . . . in their good instinct . . .
in a world which after all we make. And a compulsion to help
those who need us. That's a great satisfaction, my dear. Believe
me.

HARRIET—No. You don't understand. You keep the world
away. You don't let anything touch you. If you could only
know how it can cut and tear you.

DR. SCHILLER—Why do you say that? What do you know
of me? Only the doctor. I am a human being as well. You
know in Vienna I had my own hospital. I was doing new work.
"Great! Important!" some said. Perhaps. Then suddenly they
came. Wanted me to subscribe to their inhumanity . . . I
couldn't . . . they took my hospital . . . destroyed my records.
Ten years of work. They didn't destroy me. I came here. I had
to start over again. That's all right. We all have our problems.

We're very lucky to be in a country where the human spirit is free.

HARRIET—All the time you were helping me . . . you were suffering too?

DR. SCHILLER—At this moment my mother is in Poland. I don't know whether she is dead or alive. You called me. I came. I'm doing my job as best I can. That's what we must all do. Never surrender.

HARRIET—Yes . . . I see. For you that's the answer. But what can I do?

DR. SCHILLER—Your job. (*He glances toward the kitchen.*)

HARRIET—If I could . . . but it's no use . . . I can't . . .

DR. SCHILLER—You can.

HARRIET—I can't.

DR. SCHILLER—Go on! You can. If we really want something . . . really want it . . . (HARRIET *goes inside.*)

HARRIET—John . . . (*He stares at her dully.*) Is there anything I can get you?

JOHN—No. (*He chokes back a sob.*) Christ!

HARRIET—Don't try to be so strong, John. . . . Wouldn't it be better just to give in to it?

JOHN—What's there to give in to? He's dead . . . it's over . . . that's all there is to it.

HARRIET—Here, John, drink this. (*She offers him a cup of coffee.*)

JOHN—I don't want it.

HARRIET—Please, darling, you haven't had a thing since noon . . . Just a sip . . . Come!

JOHN—I told you I don't want it. Are you trying to choke me! (*He pushes aside the cup, it falls and breaks. He stares at her resentfully. . . . She looks at him for a moment . . . sighs, bends down, picks up the broken pieces and holds them in her hands.*) Now leave me alone.

HARRIET—John, darling, please don't shut me out. . . . I know how you're suffering . . . I know how badly you feel . . . Let me be a part of it. Don't make me a stranger. Let me try to help you, please . . . my darling . . . please.

JOHN—We were so close . . . We were kids together . . .

HARRIET—I lost a brother, too. . . .

JOHN—He used to follow me around like a puppy. He was only fifteen when I went away . . . he had to come with me. I can see him so clear . . . with his bundle over his shoulder . . . on the road . . . there was a big moon. We slept in the field that night. It was a great adventure for him. He stayed up all night, talking about the beauty of the world . . . And tonight, lying there . . . so white . . . fighting for every single breath . . . to turn to me and say, "I can't quit now. I got too much to do. How do you like that? That little runt couldn't hold his own life in . . . wantin' to go out and save the world. It's almost funny, isn't it?

HARRIET—But that was Jim . . . that's what made him . . .

JOHN—He never stopped taking a licking. Not for a minute. Never had a damn thing out of it. Nothing! Wasted!

HARRIET—That's not true, John. He had a great deal. His life was full. He felt so deeply. He had love, not only for Sally and the baby and you, but for people, for everyone that suffered.

JOHN—To Hell with that . . .

HARRIET—Don't . . . please . . .

JOHN—To Hell with that.

HARRIET—I didn't know you could be so cruel! Perhaps you're strong enough to live without love. But I'm not. That was my sickness, that was my death. And now you're sending me back.

JOHN (*reaches for her hand . . . starts to cry*)—Harriet . . . I . . .

HARRIET—Oh, my darling, cry . . . cry! Let it all come out! All the heartache . . . all the bitterness. I know, my darling, I know. Cry for Jim, but be glad for him, too. It's not dying that's so terrible, Johnny, it's failing to live. My brother's life was wasted. . . . He died empty-poor. Jim went away rich. He carried a dream with him. He was triumphant. He never surrendered. And we won't either, will we, darling. We have so much to live for . . . so much to fight for.

THE CURTAIN FALLS

LIFE WITH FATHER

A Comedy in Three Acts

By Howard Lindsay and Russel Crouse

THE early weeks of the new theatre season of 1939-40 were not encouraging. Through September, which usually ushers in at least two or three theatre hits on Broadway, the World's Fair was still the supreme show attraction in New York. It was not until the second week in October that a real hit was scored and this by Gertrude Lawrence in Samson Raphaelson's "Skylark."

Five days later the Kaufman-Hart comedy, "The Man Who Came to Dinner" set the town laughing and cheering at the same time. The first musical comedy hit of the year, the Rodgers-Hart-Marion "Too Many Girls"; the first William Saroyan success, "The Time of Your Life," followed. And then, the first week in November, came the Lindsay-Crouse "Life with Father." In the Woollcottian phrase, by that time dancing in the streets was pretty general.

The late Clarence Day character sketches of his father, published as "God and My Father," "Life with Father" and "Life with Mother," had attracted the attention of playwrights before Mr. Day died in 1935. He, as his widow, who served as a "family consultant" in the staging of the play recalls, was reluctant to let anyone attempt to make a play of the very intimate family material of which he had made use in the stories. Neither was he at all convinced that a successful comedy could be written from them.

"Men have written books about real people before," Mrs. Day has written in explaining Mr. Day's attitude, "but generally because they have had some strange or phenomenal thing happen to them. They have nurtured a genius, perhaps, or pursued a glamorous life in the world of the theatre, music or the arts.

"But here was a family that owes its very life to the fact that nothing happened to them. Nothing, that is, except to live a warm, rich, quarrelsome and affectionate family life, and to be uninhibitedly themselves within the handsomely paneled walls of an absolutely conventional world in New York of the eighteen eighties."

Yet out of the lives of this family to which nothing ever hap-

142

pened has come one of the great family comedies of the native theatre. It's success has been steadily consistent. For months the only change in the attendance count at the Empire Theatre was in the number of standees, the seats being all sold many weeks in advance.

The play was the better part of two years in the making, after Oscar Serlin, the producer, had agreed with Howard Lindsay and Russel Crouse on its writing. Weeks were spent in clearing the prejudices of living members of the Day family, and in gaining their approval of the script as the playwrights submitted it to them. When it was ready a first draft was tried at a Summer theatre in Lakewood, which is hard by Skowhegan, Me., with Mr. and Mrs. Lindsay (Dorothy Stickney) in the rôles of Clarence and Vinnie Day.

The Clarence Day home which is the scene of the play was at 480 Madison Avenue, New York. In the eighteen eighties this was the center of the better residence section. We meet the family first in what is known as the morning room. Because it was also the most comfortable room in the house the morning room was generally used as a living room as well. There are sliding doors in the arch at back. When closed these doors shut the room off from the entrance hall, the stairs leading to the upper floors and the rest of the house.

This morning the sun is streaming through the eastern windows, lighting up the "somewhat less than comfortable furniture of the period." There is a large mirror in a Victorian frame over the mantel, and "looking down from the walls are the Day ancestors in painted portraits. The room has the warm quality that comes only from having been lived in by a family which enjoys each other's company—a family of considerable means."

At the moment a dining room extension table at one side of the room is being set for breakfast by Annie, a new maid. It being Annie's first day she is naturally a little nervous. Vinnie Day, "a charming, lovable and spirited woman of forty," would re-assure Annie if she could, but the maid is still pretty nervous.

Vinnie's survey of the table finds everything practically in its proper place. There is a slight mix-up of the initialed napkin rings, and, of course, the cream and sugar must always be placed at Mr. Day's end of the table.

"If Mr. Day speaks to you, just say: 'Yes, sir,' " advises Vinnie. "Don't be nervous. You'll get used to him."

Clarence Jr., the eldest son, is the first down for breakfast. "He is a manly, serious, good-looking boy. Because he is starting in at Yale next year he thinks he is grown up." Like all the Days, including Mother and Father, young Clarence is red-headed.

Clarence greets his mother affably and has a look at the newspaper at Father's place. The first page news is disturbing. There has been another wreck on the New Haven, and that is not only likely to affect the market, but it is certain to affect Father.

"I do wish that New Haven would stop having wrecks," sighs Vinnie. "If they knew how it upsets your father—"

A fresh tear in Clarence's suit has caught Vinnie's eye. That, added to the burn in her son's blue suit, means that he simply will have to have new clothes. Imparting this news to Father, it is plainly evident, is not a task that Vinnie relishes. . . .

John, the second son, "about fifteen, gangly and a little awkward," is next to arrive and greet his mother. Then Whitney, thirteen, and active, even for his age, arrives. Finally Harlan, the youngest Day, comes sliding down the banister, and rushes into his mother's arms. "Harlan is a roly-poly, lovable, good-natured youngster of six." His hair may be a shade or two redder than his brothers', but no more than a shade.

There are one or two matters that it were better to have understood before Father arrives. Right after breakfast, Vinnie would have Clarence and John move a small bureau from her room into theirs. This obviously means that someone is coming to visit, though Vinnie will not admit as much—and, anyway, she wants it to be a surprise to Father.

There are also a few minor confusions. Whitney has a ball game to pitch at the big field at Fifty-seventh and Madison (they are building on the old grounds at Fiftieth Street) and he would like to borrow John's glove. Whitney also has his catechism to learn, and if he doesn't learn that he can't be confirmed. Whitney is trying to remember what he has learned of his catechism when Father appears on the stairway. The family stands at attention—

"Father is in his forties, distinguished in appearance, with great charm and vitality, extremely well dressed in a conservative way." His greetings are not unfriendly, but neither is his temper perfect. His clothes are too tight, for one thing, though he had written those fellows in London as long as a year ago that they were making his clothes too tight. And he is *not* putting on weight, as Vinnie suggests. He weighs exactly what he has always weighed.

Clarence, Vinnie takes occasion to mention when the family is settled at table, will have to have new clothes. Father is not interested. When Clarence is ready to start for Yale he will have a thousand dollars to spend for an outfit. Until then he will have to get along with what he has—

"Every suit I own still has plenty of wear in it," Father announces. "I wear my clothes until they're worn out."

"Well, if you want your clothes worn out, Clarence can wear them out much faster than you can," insists Vinnie.

"Yes, and, Father, you don't get a chance to wear them out. Every time you get a new batch of clothes, Mother sends the old ones to the missionary barrel. I guess I'm just as good as any old missionary."

There is, Father is ready to admit, something in what Clarence says. Mother's interest in missionaries doubtless influences the decision. Anyway, Clarence can have Father's black suit cut down. . . .

Father's appraising glance has swept the table. "Whitney, don't eat so fast!" he commands.

"Well, Father, I'm going to pitch today and I promised to get there early, but before I go I have to study my catechism."

"What do you bother with that for?"

"Because," says Vinnie, with spirit, "if he doesn't know his catechism he can't be confirmed!"

"But I'm going to pitch today," pleads Whitney.

"Vinnie, Whitney's going to pitch today and he can be confirmed any old time."

Vinnie is quite distressed. "Clare, sometimes it seems to me that you don't care whether your children get to Heaven or not."

"Oh, Whitney'll get to Heaven all right. (*To* WHITNEY.) I'll be there before you are, Whitney; I'll see that you get in."

"What makes you so sure they'll let you in?" asks Vinnie.

"Well, if they don't I'll certainly raise a devil of a row."

"Clare, I do hope you'll behave when you get to Heaven," sighs Vinnie, a little shocked.

Annie, the maid, quite flustered by the picture of Father's "raising a row at the gates of Heaven," is trying to serve the bacon and eggs. In her confusion she holds the platter pretty high, and this is enough to start another of Father's explosions. Why can't Vinnie find a maid that knows how to serve! Why do they always have to be changing maids anyway? Where's the one they had yesterday?

By which time Annie has finished with the serving and is in tears at the sideboard. And what a damned noise her sniffling makes— Must Father also stand that? And how can it be his fault? He hasn't addressed a word to her. He was talking to Vinnie—not to Annie. . . .

There is quiet again until the mail is distributed and Mother discovers a letter that suggests a change in her social activities for the coming winter. Instead of a series of dinners she will give one big musicale. There is a lovely young girl who whistles— whistles sixteen different pieces for twenty-five dollars. Father is not impressed—

"I won't pay twenty-five dollars to any human peanut-stand," he announces with conviction.

"Clare, I can arrange this so it won't cost you a penny. If I invite fifty people and charge them fifty cents apiece, there's the twenty-five dollars right there!"

"You can't invite people to your own house and charge them admission."

"I can if the money's for the missionary fund."

"Then where will you get the twenty-five dollars to pay that poor girl for her whistling?"

"Now, Clare, let's not cross that bridge until we come to it."

"And if we do cross it, it will cost me twenty-five dollars. Vinnie, I'm putting my foot down about this musicale, just as I've had to put my foot down about your keeping this house full of visiting relatives. Why can't we live here by ourselves in peace and comfort?"

By stamping three times on the floor Father has announced to Margaret, the cook, that she is wanted. Margaret is wanted because whatever it is that she has offered for coffee isn't. "You couldn't possibly take water and coffee beans and arrive at that," protests Father, sending his cup back to the kitchen. . . .

The boys, having finished their breakfasts and been excused, Father settles briefly to reading the paper. Chauncey Depew is having another birthday he discovers, but that's not news. There's that damned New Haven wreck and that is most disturbing news. Margaret, too, is back with something resembling bad news—

"If you please, ma'am, there's a package been delivered with a dollar due on it," reports Margaret. "Some kitchen knives."

VINNIE—Oh, yes, those knives from Lewis & Conger's. (*She gets her purse from the drawer in the console table and gives* MARGARET *a dollar.*) Here, give this dollar to the man, Margaret.

FATHER—Make a memorandum of that, Vinnie. One dollar and whatever it was for.

VINNIE (*looking into purse*)—Clare dear, I'm afraid I'm going to need some more money.

FATHER—What for?

VINNIE—You were complaining of the coffee this morning. Well, that nice French drip coffee pot is broken—and you know how it got broken.

FATHER (*taking out his wallet*)—Never mind that, Vinnie. As I remember, that coffee pot cost five dollars and something. Here's six dollars. And when you get it, enter the exact amount in the ledger downstairs.

VINNIE—Thank you, Clare.

FATHER—We can't go on month after month having the household accounts in such a mess.

VINNIE (*sitting on arm of* FATHER's *chair*)—No, and I've thought of a system that will make my bookkeeping perfect.

FATHER—I'm certainly relieved to hear that. What is it?

VINNIE—Well, Clare dear, you never make half the fuss over how much I've spent as you do over my not being able to remember what I've spent it for.

FATHER—Exactly. This house must be run on a business basis. That's why I insist on your keeping books.

VINNIE—That's the whole point, Clare. All we have to do is open charge accounts everywhere and the stores will do my bookkeeping for me.

FATHER—Wait a minute, Vinnie—

VINNIE—Then when the bills come in you'd know exactly where your money had gone.

FATHER—I certainly would. Vinnie, I get enough bills as it is.

VINNIE—Yes, and those bills always help. They show you just where I spent the money. Now if we had charge accounts everywhere—

FATHER—Now, Vinnie, I don't know about that.

VINNIE—Clare dear, don't you hate those arguments we have every month? I certainly do. Not to have those I should think would be worth something to you.

FATHER—Well, I'll open an account at Lewis & Conger's—and one at McCreery's to start with—we'll see how it works out. (*He shakes his head doubtfully. Her victory gained,* VINNIE *moves away.*)

VINNIE—Thank you, Clare. Oh—the rector's coming to tea today.

FATHER—The rector? I'm glad you warned me. I'll go to the club. Don't expect me home until dinner time.

VINNIE—I do wish you'd take a little more interest in the church.

FATHER—Vinnie, getting me into Heaven's your job. If there's anything wrong with my ticket when I get there, you can fix it up. Everybody loves you so much—I'm sure God must, too.

VINNIE—I'll do my best, Clare. It wouldn't be Heaven without you.

FATHER—If you're there, Vinnie, I'll manage to get in some way, even if I have to climb the fence.

For a second a call from the boys that they have moved the bureau stirs Father's curiosity, but by the time a flustered Vinnie is halfway upstairs something in the paper has completely obliterated all other thought from the master's mind.

"Oh, God!" shouts Father, gesticulating wildly with the paper half crushed in his hand.

"What's the matter, Clare? What's wrong?" Vinnie calls excitedly from the stairs.

"Why did God make so many damned fools and Democrats?" demands Father, addressing the Universe in general.

"Oh, politics," mutters Vinnie and greatly relieved, she continues on her way.

"Yes, but it's taking the bread out of our mouths," Father shouts after her. Now he turns his attack directly on those political enemies of good order with which his imagination peoples the room. "It's robbery, that's what it is, highway robbery! Honest Hugh Grant! Honest! Bah! A fine mayor you've turned out to be.

"If you can't run this city without raising taxes every five minutes," Father continues, addressing Honest Hugh Grant as though he were cowering on the carpet, "you'd better get out and let someone who can. Let me tell you, sir, that the real-estate owners of New York City are not going to tolerate these conditions any longer."

Father has just reached a particularly violent attack upon Tammany graft when Annie starts into the room to clear the table. Assuming that there must be a visitor lurking about somewhere the maid curtsies and retires precipitately, only to be sent back by Vinnie who meets her in the hall. Vinnie knows Father. He is just reading his newspaper. And Father goes on reading—by laying into not only Honest Hugh but the whole Dick Croker Tammany gang.

"Don't forget what happened to William Marcy Tweed—and if you put our taxes up once more, we'll put you in jail!" thunders Father at his invisible hearers.

With this statement ringing through the room Father disappears into the hall, gathers his stick and gloves, adjusts his square derby, and proceeds with dignity through the hall and out the front door.

In great excitement Annie piles her tray full of dishes and starts hurriedly for the kitchen. A moment later there is a deafening crash. An excited Annie has fallen down stairs. Father had threatened to put her in jail, explains Annie. . . .

The visitors have arrived. They are Cousin Cora and a young friend, Mary Skinner. Cousin Cora "is an attractive country cousin of about thirty." Miss Skinner "is a refreshingly pretty small-town girl of sixteen."

Cora has some little trouble separating John and Clarence—boys do grow so fast—but soon has them straightened out and is ready to unreel her family news. There is an item about Aunt Carrie, who broke her hip "the night Robert Ingersoll lectured. Of course she couldn't get there; and it was a good thing for Mr. Ingersoll she didn't." And an item about Grandpa Ebbetts, who hasn't been at all well. And of course there is Mary Skinner—

"This is Mary's first trip to New York. She was so excited when she saw a horse car," Cora reports.

"We'll have to show Mary around. I'll tell you—I'll have Mr. Day take us all to Delmonico's for dinner tonight."

"Delmonico's!"

"Oh, that's marvelous! Think of that, Mary—Delmonico's! And Cousin Clare's such a wonderful host."

"I know you girls want to freshen up. So come upstairs. Clarence, I'll let the girls use your room now, and when they've finished you can move, and bring up their bags. They're out in the hall. (*Starts upstairs with* Cora.) I've given you girls Clarence's room, but he didn't know about it until this morning and he hasn't moved out yet."

Vinnie and Cora have disappeared up the stairs. Mary Skinner is following slowly after. Now she turns on the stairs and faces young Clarence, who has come back from the hall after relaying the bag-carrying job to John. For a moment Mary and John stare at each other—

"Cora didn't tell me about you," says Mary, with a smile that is as devastating as it is meant to be. "I never met a Yale man before."

And then, "with an audible whinny of girlish excitement," Mary runs upstairs. Clarence stares after her for a few seconds and then turns back into the room with a look of "What happened to me just then?" spread over his surprised countenance.

"Suddenly, however, his face breaks into a smile which indicates that, whatever has happened, he likes it." The curtain falls.

Tea time that afternoon finds the Reverend Dr. Lloyd in the Days' living room with Vinnie and the two younger boys, Whitney and Harlan. The Reverend Dr. Lloyd "is a plump, bustling man, very good-hearted and pleasant." He and Vinnie share one point in common, which is "their devotion to the Church and its rituals. Vinnie's devotion comes from her natural piety; Dr. Lloyd's is a little more professional."

The purpose of this tea-time meeting is the matter of Whitney's preparation for confirmation. Whitney has been reciting what he remembers of his catechism, which, to Harlan, at least, is a very good performance. To his mother and Dr. Lloyd it could be better, but it seems probable that by Sunday it will be possible for Dr. Lloyd to send Whitney's name with others to Bishop Potter. . . .

Just before Dr. Lloyd is leaving the subject of the new church comes up. The Doctor really had hoped that Mr. Day would be home, but, as Vinnie explains, Mr. Day probably stopped on his way home from the office to take a gallop in the park—

"Tell me—has he ever been thrown from a horse?" Dr. Lloyd inquires, solicitously.

"Oh, no!" Vinnie is quick to assure him. "No horse would throw Mr. Day!"

"I've wondered," Dr. Lloyd explains. "I thought he might have had an accident. I notice he never kneels in church."

"Oh, that's no accident! But I don't want you to think he doesn't pray. He does. Why, sometimes you can hear him pray all over the house. But he never kneels."

Suddenly Father appears in the archway. He would have disappeared again quite as suddenly if Vinnie had not seen him. Being caught he accepts the situation with as much grace as possible. Dr. Lloyd is delighted. Now he will have a chance to tell Mr. Day of the new church plans. Nor is he deterred by Father's report that he has had a very busy day and is tired out—

"Poor Clare, he must work very hard," Vinnie is saying to Dr. Lloyd. "He always comes home tired. Although how a man can get tired just sitting at his desk all day, I don't know. I suppose Wall Street is just as much a mystery to you as it is to me, Dr. Lloyd."

"No, no, it's all very clear to me. My mind often goes to the business man. The picture I'm most fond of is when I envision him at the close of the day's work. There he sits—this hard-headed man of affairs—surrounded by the ledgers that he has been studying closely and harshly for hours. I see him pausing in his toil—and by chance he raises his eyes and looks out of the window at the light in God's sky and it comes over him that money and ledgers are dross. (FATHER *stares at* DR. LLOYD *with some amazement.*) He realizes that all those figures of profit and loss are without importance or consequence—vanity and dust. And I see this troubled man bow his head and with streaming eyes resolve to devote his life to far higher things."

"Well, I'll be damned!" ejaculates Father.

The arrival of a new maid with fresh tea is helpful, though Father would like to know what has become of the maid they had that morning. She was prettier. Soon Dr. Lloyd has got back to the proposed new edifice—

"Of course, we're going to have to raise a large sum of money," he admits.

"Well, personally, I'm against the church hop-skipping-and-jumping all over the town," announces Father. "And it so happens that during the last year I've suffered heavy losses in the market—damned heavy losses—"

VINNIE—Clare!

FATHER—So any contribution I make will have to be a small one.

VINNIE—But, Clare, for so worthy a cause!

FATHER— —and if your Finance Committee thinks it's too small they can blame the rascals that are running the New Haven Railroad!

DR. LLOYD—The amount everyone is to subscribe has already been decided.

FATHER (*bristling*)—Who decided it?

DR. LLOYD—After considerable thought we've found a formula which we believe is fair and equitable. It apportions the burden lightly on those least able to carry it and justly on those shoulders we know are stronger. We've voted that our supporting members should each contribute a sum equal to the cost of their pews.

FATHER (*his jaw drops*)—I paid five thousand dollars for my pew!

VINNIE—Yes, Clare. That makes our contribution five thousand dollars.

FATHER—That's robbery! Do you know what that pew is worth today? Three thousand dollars. That's what the last one sold for. I've taken a loss of two thousand dollars on that pew already. Frank Baggs sold me that pew when the market was at its peak. He knew when to get out. (*He turns to* VINNIE.) And I'm warning you now that if the market ever goes up I'm going to unload that pew.

VINNIE—Clarence Day! How can you speak of the Lord's temple as though it were something to be bought and sold on Wall Street!

FATHER—Vinnie, this is a matter of dollars and cents, and that's something you don't know anything about!

Vinnie is afraid that Father is coming pretty close to blasphemy, but Dr. Lloyd understands. The business man's approach to such questions must be the practical approach. The Church has tried to be practical, too. He is not quite sure whether the new church is to cost eighty-five thousand dollars, or a hundred and eighty-five, and he is in some doubt as to the amount of the proposed mortgage, but it is all being worked out—

"Dr. Lloyd, you preach that some day we'll all have to answer to God," says Father.

"We shall indeed!"

"Well, I hope God doesn't ask you any questions with figures in them."

Now Cora and Mary are back from their shopping tour and quite wild with the wonder of what they have seen and what they have bought. Dr. Lloyd has left and Father, greeting Cousin Cora and her pretty young friend most cordially, would know all their plans. Why can't they stay to dinner? Of course they will have to take pot luck, but—

"That's all arranged, Clare," Vinnie cuts in, quickly. She would hurry Cora and Mary upstairs with their packages and thus postpone the revelation that Father has house guests. The postponement is not for long. Cousin Cora has just asked Clarence if he minds carrying her packages up to her room—or perhaps she should say his room—when Father's cordiality suffers a quick drop in temperature.

"Vinnie!" he commands, rather than calls.

Vinnie is busily engaged in getting her guests and their purchases upstairs before the gathering storm breaks.

"Vinnie, I wish to speak to you before you go upstairs," announces Father, sternly.

Vinnie manages to get the girls upstairs and has closed the

sliding doors before she returns to Father. "Now, Clare, you know you've always liked Cora," she begins, persuasively.

"What has that got to do with her planking herself down in my house and bringing hordes of strangers with her?" explodes Father.

VINNIE (*reproachfully*)—How can you call that sweet little girl a horde of strangers?

FATHER—Why don't they go to a hotel? New York is full of hotels built for the express purpose of housing such nuisances.

VINNIE—Clare! Two girls alone in a hotel! Who knows what might happen to them?

FATHER—All right. Then put 'em on the next train. If they want to roam—the damned gypsies—lend 'em a hand! Keep 'em roaming!

VINNIE—What have we got a home for if we can't show a little hospitality?

FATHER—I didn't buy this home to show hospitality—I bought it for my own comfort!

VINNIE—Well, how much are they going to interfere with your comfort living in that little room of Clarence's?

FATHER—The trouble is, damn it, they don't live there. They live in the bathroom! Every time I want to take my bath it's full of giggling females—washing their hair. From the time they take, you'd think it was the Seven Sutherland Sisters. I tell you, I won't have it! Send 'em to a hotel. I'll pay the bill gladly, but get them out of here!

CLARENCE (*putting his head through the sliding door*)—Father, I'm afraid they can hear you upstairs.

FATHER—Then keep those doors closed!

VINNIE (*with decision*)—Clarence, you open those doors—open them all the way! (CLARENCE *does so.* VINNIE *lowers her voice but maintains her spirit.*) Now, Clare, you behave yourself! (FATHER *glares at her angrily.*) They're here and they're going to stay here.

FATHER—That's enough, Vinnie! I want no more of this argument. (*He goes to his chair by the window, muttering.*) Damnation!

And now the second blow lands. Clarence asks innocently if he may go with them to Delmonico's to dinner. It is the first Father has heard of the dinner plans. "Oh, God!" he protests with fervor. Again Vinnie is summarily summoned and again she bustles over to close the sliding doors.

"Do I understand that I can't have dinner in my own home?" demands Father.

"It'll do us both good to get out of this house. You need a little change. It'll make you feel better."

"I have a home to have dinner in. Any time I can't have dinner at home this house is for sale!"

"Well, you can't have dinner here tonight because it isn't ordered."

"Let me tell you I'm ready to sell this place this very minute if I can't live here in peace. And we can all go and sit under a palm tree and live on breadfruit and pickles."

"But, Clare, Cora and Mary want to see something of New York."

"Oh, that's it! Well, that's no affair of mine! I am not a guide to Chinatown and the Bowery." With which declaration Father stalks out. . . .

Mary Skinner has come downstairs freshened and smiling. Young Clarence is there, very polite and formal. They have some little difficulty finding a common subject, but are agreed on a few things. They both like red as a color, though, as Clarence points out, green is better out of doors. They're both interested in colleges, too, though—

"Mother wants me to go to Ohio Wesleyan—because it's Methodist," reports Mary reluctantly. "You see, we're Methodists."

"Oh, that's too bad! I don't mean it's too bad that you're a Methodist. Anybody's got a right to be anything they want. But what I mean is—we're Episcopalians."

"Yes, I know. I've known ever since I saw your minister—and his collar. (*She looks pretty sad for a minute and then her face brightens.*) Oh, I just remembered—my father was an Episcopalian. He was baptized an Episcopalian. He was an Episcopalian right up to the time he married my mother. *She* was the Methodist."

"I'll bet your father's a nice man," says Clarence.

Mary's father, it appears, owns the livery stable. That gives them another subject—they both love horses. In fact the horse is Clarence's favorite animal. . . .

Whitney and Harlan, following a bit of superior instruction from Father, have settled to a game of tiddledy winks on the

floor. Cora has gone to dress for the Delmonico dinner and Mary
is following Cora to see that she gets properly hooked up. At
the stairs Mary turns to ask Father a very important question—
"Mr. Day, were you always an Episcopalian?"
"What?"

MARY—Were you always an Episcopalian?

FATHER—I've always gone to the Episcopal church, yes.

MARY—But you weren't baptized a Methodist or anything,
were you? You were baptized an Episcopalian?

FATHER—Come to think of it, I don't believe I was ever baptized at all.

MARY—Oh!

VINNIE—Clare, that's not very funny, joking about a subject
like that.

FATHER—I'm not joking—I remember now—I never was baptized.

VINNIE—Clare, that's ridiculous, everyone's baptized.

FATHER (*sitting down complacently*)—Well, I'm not.

VINNIE—Why, no one would keep a little baby from being
baptized.

FATHER—You know Father and Mother—free-thinkers, both
of them—believed their children should decide those things for
themselves.

VINNIE—But, Clare—

FATHER—I remember when I was ten or twelve years old,
Mother said I ought to give some thought to it. I suppose I
thought about it, but I never got around to having it done to me.
(*The shock to* VINNIE *is as great as if* FATHER *had calmly announced himself guilty of murder. She walks to* FATHER, *staring
at him in horror.* CORA *and* MARY, *sensing the coming battle,
withdraw to the neutral shelter of the hall.*)

VINNIE—Clare, do you know what you're saying?

FATHER—I'm saying I've never been baptized.

VINNIE (*in a sudden panic*)—Then something has to be done
about it right away.

FATHER (*not the least concerned*)—Now, Vinnie, don't get excited over nothing.

VINNIE—Nothing! (*Then as only a woman can ask such a
question.*) Clare, why haven't you ever told me?

FATHER—What difference does it make?

VINNIE (*the panic returning*)—I've never heard of anyone who
wasn't baptized. Even the savages in darkest Africa—

FATHER—It's all right for savages and children. But if an oversight was made in my case it's too late to correct it now.

VINNIE—But if you're not baptized you're not a Christian!

FATHER (*rising in wrath*)—Why, confound it, of course I'm a Christian! A damn good Christian, too! (FATHER's *voice tells* CLARENCE *a major engagement has begun. He hurriedly springs to the sliding doors and closes them, removing himself,* MARY *and* CORA *from the scene of action.*) A lot better Christian than those psalm-singing donkeys in church!

VINNIE—You can't be if you won't be baptized.

FATHER—I won't be baptized and I will be a Christian! I beg to inform you I'll be a Christian in my own way.

VINNIE—Clare, don't you want to meet us all in Heaven?

FATHER—Of course! And I'm going to!

VINNIE—But you can't go to Heaven if you're not baptized!

FATHER—That's a lot of folderol!

VINNIE—Clarence Day, don't you blaspheme like that! You're coming to church with me before you go to the office in the morning and be baptized then and there!

FATHER—Vinnie, don't be ridiculous! If you think I'm going to stand there and have some minister splash water on me at my age, you're mistaken!

VINNIE—But, Clare—

FATHER—That's enough of this, Vinnie. I'm hungry. (*Draws himself up and starts for the door. He does not realize that he and* VINNIE *are now engaged in a battle to the death.*) I'm dressing for dinner. (*Throws open the doors, revealing* WHITNEY *and* HARLAN, *who obviously have been eavesdropping and have heard the awful revelation of* FATHER's *paganism.* FATHER *stalks past them upstairs. The two boys come down into the room staring at their mother, who has been standing, too shocked at* FATHER's *callous impiety to speak or move.*)

WHITNEY—Mother, if Father hasn't been baptized he hasn't any name. In the sight of the Church he hasn't any name.

VINNIE—That's right! (*To herself.*) Maybe we're not even married!

"This awful thought takes possession of Vinnie. Her eyes turn slowly toward the children and she suddenly realizes their doubtful status. Her hand goes to her mouth to cover a quick gasp of horror."

The curtain falls.

ACT II

It is the following Sunday, after church. The Days and their guests are just home from service. Vinnie and Cora are wearing their Sunday best. Father is in his cutaway, silk hat and cane. Even Whitney and Harlan are stiff and proper as they enter the living room. Clarence and Mary, as John reports, have fallen behind—way behind.

Vinnie is not happy. The Rev. Dr. Lloyd's sermon, it appears, was about baptism and seemed, to Father at least, to be directed straight at him. Nevertheless, Father, according to Vinnie, had no right to create the scene he did stamping out of church after service, shouting so loud that now the whole congregation must know that he has never been baptized—

"But he's going to be, Cora," declares Vinnie, with firmness. "You mark my words—he's going to be! I just couldn't go to Heaven without Clare. Why, I get lonesome for him when I go to Ohio." . . .

Father, holding his watch, and also his temper, would like to know why no preparations have been made for Sunday dinner. Vinnie explains that there was not time for both church and an early dinner before Cora and Mary had to leave for their train.

Father could have done without church quite comfortably. And if he did make a scene by shouting his convictions as he marched up the aisle he is glad of it. No Rev. Lloyd is going to preach at him as though he were a damn criminal.

"Clare, you don't seem to understand what the Church is for," pleads Vinnie.

"Vinnie, if there's one place the Church should leave alone, it's a man's soul!" Father answers, haughtily.

"Clare, dear, don't you believe what it says in the Bible?"

"A man has to use his common sense about the Bible, Vinnie, if he has any. For instance, you'd be in a pretty fix if I gave all my money to the poor."

And now, of all times, Father would go over Vinnie's household accounts. Nor will he be put off, even by Vinnie's plea that it isn't fair for him to go over the accounts when he's hungry. Father has gone to his desk and is expecting Vinnie to follow, but before she does there are a few other things that Vinnie has to look after.

For one thing why doesn't Clarence kneel in church? Just because his father doesn't kneel? Or because his father's suit is too tight for him?

The suit isn't too tight, but Clarence just can't seem to make Father's clothes do anything Father wouldn't do. Even the first time he had worn the suit to a party and Dora Wakefield sat in his lap when they were playing musical chairs Clarence had jumped up so fast he nearly upset Dora. Not because Dora was sitting on his lap, but because she was sitting on Father's trousers.

"Mother, I've just got to have a suit of my own!" protests Clarence. And Vinnie agrees with him, though just at the moment—

Mary has finished her packing and is downstairs, which hurries Vinnie away to the kitchen to see about a box lunch they are to take for the train.

Mary would like to tell Clarence how much she has enjoyed their friendship. She is a little self-conscious. Anyway she is going to write him about it—that is, if he writes her first. Clarence will be expecting Mary to write first—about her trip and all —and he won't stand any nonsense about that. To emphasize his authority he has taken her hand and she is happy. Mary insists, however, that he should write first, because that would show that he liked her. Clarence does like her—better than any other girl he ever met. Writing first has nothing to do with that. Still, Mary persists that it does. When she puts her hand on his shoulder to emphasize her point he draws embarrassedly away. She is not to be curbed now—

"But, Clarence! We'll see each other in a month. And we'll be writing each other, too. I hope we will." Mary has got up now and is standing over him. "Oh, Clarence, please write me first, because it will show me how much you like me. Please! I'll show you how much I like you!" With this statement Mary has thrown herself on Clarence's lap and buried her head on his shoulder.

"Get up! Get up!" cries Clarence, hoarsely. "Don't do that, Mary! Please don't do that!"

Mary pulls her head back, looks at him and then springs from his lap and runs away. She has covered her face with her hands and is sobbing. Nor can he quiet her.

"Now you'll think I'm just a bold and forward girl," wails Mary. "Yes, you will—you'll think I'm bold!"

"Oh, no—it's not that."

"Was it because it's Sunday?" Mary asks, hopefully.

"No, it would be the same any day," answers Clarence, in despair. He would explain further, but Mary gives him no chance.

"Oh, it's just because you didn't want me sitting on your lap."

"It was nice of you to do it."

"It was nice of me! So you told me to get up! You just couldn't bear to have me sit there. Well, you needn't write me first. You needn't write me any letters at all, because I'll tear them up without opening them! I guess I know now you don't like me! I never want to see you again. I—I—"

Mary has run toward the stairs, almost bumping into Father, who is coming in with a sheaf of bills and his note-book under his arm. She is sobbing as she runs upstairs and Father is perturbed. He would know what has happened. Clarence is too upset emotionally to be entirely coherent, but one thing he knows: He has got to have a new suit of clothes. "You don't know how important this is to me," protests Clarence and Father senses his son's misery. Women have come into Clarence's emotional life, and something will have to be done about it.

"This comes as quite a shock to me," admits Father.

"What does, Father?"

FATHER—Your being so grown up! Still, I might have known that if you're going to college this Fall—yes, you're at an age when you'll be meeting girls. Clarence, there are things about women that I think you ought to know! (*He closes the doors, then comes and sits beside* CLARENCE, *hesitating for a moment before he speaks.*) Yes, I think it's better for you to hear this from me than to have to learn it for yourself. Clarence, women aren't the angels that you think they are! Well, now—first, let me explain this to you. You see, Clarence, we men have to run this world and it's not an easy job. It takes work, and it takes thinking. A man has to be sure of his facts and figures. He has to reason things out. Now, you take a woman—a woman thinks —no, I'm wrong right there—a woman doesn't think at all! She gets stirred up! And she gets stirred up over the damnedest things! Now, I love my wife just as much as any man, but that doesn't mean I should stand for a lot of folderol! By God! I won't stand for it! (*Looks toward the spot where he had his last clash with* VINNIE.)

CLARENCE—Stand for what, Father?

FATHER (*to himself*)—That's the one thing I will not submit myself to. (*He has ceased explaining women to* CLARENCE *and is now explaining himself.*) Clarence, if a man thinks a certain thing is the wrong thing to do he shouldn't do it. If he thinks a thing is right he should do it. Now that has nothing to do with whether he loves his wife or not.

CLARENCE—Who says it has, Father?

FATHER—They do!

CLARENCE—Who, sir?

FATHER—Women! They get stirred up and then they try to get you stirred up, too. If you can keep reason and logic in the argument, a man can hold his own, of course. But if they can *switch* you—pretty soon the argument's about whether you love them or not. I swear I don't know how they do it! Don't you let 'em, Clarence! Don't you let 'em!

CLARENCE—I see what you mean so far, Father. If you don't watch yourself, love can make you do a lot of things you don't want to do.

FATHER—Exactly!

CLARENCE—But if you do watch out and know just how to handle women—

FATHER—Then you'll be all right. All a man has to do is be firm. You know how sometimes I have to be firm with your mother. Just now about this month's household accounts—

CLARENCE—Yes, but what can you do when they cry?

FATHER (*giving this a moment's thought*)—Well, that's quite a question. You just have to make them understand that what you're doing is for their good.

CLARENCE—I see.

FATHER (*rising*)—Now, Clarence, you know all about women. (*Goes to the table and sits down in front of his account book, opening it.*)

CLARENCE (*rising and looking at him*)—But, Father—

FATHER—Yes, Clarence.

CLARENCE—I thought you were going to tell me about—

FATHER—About what?

CLARENCE—About women.

FATHER (*realizing with some shock that* CLARENCE *expected him to be more specific*)—Clarence, there are some things gentlemen don't discuss! I've told you all you need to know. The thing for you to remember is—be firm!

Clarence tries a moment later to follow his father's advice. He would be firm with Mary, when she comes back for her handkerchief and practically ignores him. Which strengthens his determination to be firm with his father about that new suit of clothes. But Father is going over Vinnie's accounts now and both the volume and character of his cry, the explosive "Oh, God!" of the enraged male, discourages any kind of approach, though it does bring Vinnie quickly into the scene.

The "Oh, God!" it transpires, has been aroused by the discovery of a bill from some person who signs herself "Mademoiselle Mimi." Father will be damned if he will pay any bill submitted by any person who hasn't sense enough to put her name on her bills.

Furthermore there is a matter of six dollars that Father would like cleared up. He had given the six dollars to Vinnie to buy a new coffee pot (never mind who broke the old coffee pot—or why) and he would like to know what she has done with it.

Vinnie tries to explain that she couldn't get another imported coffee pot. Nobody sells them any more because of the tariff and certainly Father has had something to do with that, voting all the time the way he does to raise the tariff. Besides—

"Vinnie, what happened to that six dollars?" Father finally demands, refusing to be put off.

"What six dollars?" Vinnie is still the wide-eyed innocent.

FATHER—I gave you six dollars to buy a new coffee pot and now I find that you apparently got one at Lewis & Conger's and charged it. Here's their bill: "One coffee pot—five dollars."

VINNIE—So you owe me a dollar and you can hand it right over. (*She holds out her hand for it.*)

FATHER—I'll do nothing of the kind! What did you do with that six dollars?

VINNIE—Why, Clare, I can't tell you now, dear. Why didn't you ask me at the time?

FATHER—Oh, my God!

VINNIE—Wait a moment! I spent four dollars and a half for that new umbrella I told you I wanted and you said I didn't need, but I did, very much.

FATHER (*taking his pencil and writing in the account book*)— Now we're getting somewhere. One umbrella—four dollars and a half.

VINNIE—And that must have been the week I paid Mrs. Tobin for two extra days' washing.

FATHER (*entering the item*)—Mrs. Tobin.

VINNIE—So that was two dollars more.

FATHER—Two dollars.

VINNIE—That makes six dollars and fifty cents. And that's another fifty cents you owe me.

FATHER—I don't owe you anything. (*Stung by* VINNIE's

tactics into a determination to pin her butterfly mind down.)
What you owe me is an explanation of where my money's gone!
We're going over this account book item by item. (*Starts to sort
the bills for the purpose of cross-examination, but the butterfly
takes wing again.*)

VINNIE—I do the very best I can to keep down expenses. And
you know yourself that Cousin Phoebe spends twice as much as
we do.

FATHER—Damn Cousin Phoebe!—I don't wish to be told how
she throws her money around.

VINNIE—Oh, Clare, how can you? And I thought you were
so fond of Cousin Phoebe.

FATHER—All right, I am fond of Cousin Phoebe, but I can
get along without hearing so much about her.

VINNIE—You talk about your own relatives enough.

FATHER (*hurt*)—That's not fair, Vinnie. When I talk about
my relatives I criticize them.

VINNIE—If I can't even speak of Cousin Phoebe—

FATHER—You can speak of her all you want to—but I won't
have Cousin Phoebe or anyone else dictating to me how to run
my house. Now this month's total—

VINNIE (*righteously*)—I didn't say a word about her dictating,
Clare—she isn't that kind!

FATHER (*dazed*)—I don't know what you said, now. You
never stick to the point. I endeavor to show you how to run this
house on a business basis and you wind up by jibbering and
jabbering about everything under the sun. If you'll just explain
to me—

VINNIE (*finally cornered, realizes time has come for tears and
quietly turns them on*)—I don't know what you expect of me. I
tire myself out chasing up and down those stairs all day long—
trying to look after your comfort—to bring up our children—I do
the mending and the marketing and as if that isn't enough, you
want me to be an expert bookkeeper, too.

FATHER (*touched where* VINNIE *has hoped to touch him*)—
Vinnie, I want to be reasonable; but can't you understand?—I'm
doing all this for your own good. (VINNIE *rises with a moan.*
FATHER *sighs with resignation.*) I suppose I'll have to go ahead
just paying the bills and hoping I've got money enough in the
bank to meet them. But it's all very discouraging.

VINNIE—I'll try to do better, Clare.

FATHER (*looking up into her tearful face and melting*)—That's all I'm asking. (*She goes to him and puts her arm around his shoulder.*) I'll go down and make out the checks and sign them.

Still Vinnie isn't entirely consoled. Nor does one of Father's intended jokes about his moral right to sign checks, seeing that in the sight of the Lord he hasn't any name, serve to brighten her. It merely reminds her of the neglected baptism and again stirs her determination to see that something is done about it. . . . Now Vinnie has the dollar and a half he "owes" her and has proceeded up the stairs "in a one-woman march of triumph." . . .

There is a good deal of confusion and a little unhappiness attending the departure of Cora and Mary. The confusion is stirred partly by Father's anxiety about the waiting cab. Cabs cost money. Let the women get themselves to the Grand Central Depot and do their waiting there.

The unhappiness is that which comes to Clarence when Mary persists in believing that he does not like her, and in her continual refusal to promise to write unless he writes first. Clarence tries awfully hard to be firm, but Cora and Mary are no sooner out of the house than he has grabbed pen, ink and paper and begun—

"Dear Mary—" The curtain falls.

At breakfast two days later there is still another new maid. This one is Nora, "heavily built and along toward middle age." She, in her turn, must learn from the boys something of the routine that satisfies, even if it doesn't please, Father.

Harlan, Whitney and Clarence are in their places. John has had his breakfast early and gone in search of a job. Clarence would have gone, too, but he is expecting a letter and wanted to wait for the postman. Now the postman has come and there isn't anything for Clarence.

Vinnie has sent word by Nora that she isn't feeling well and doesn't want any breakfast. The announcement disturbs Father. Vinnie knows that it always upsets his day when she doesn't appear at breakfast. She has no right to do this to him. Besides, there is nothing the matter with her, really. Their mother is a perfectly healthy woman, Father assures the boys. "She gets an ache or a twinge, and instead of being firm about it, she gives in to it," explains Father.

Another postman has arrived with a special delivery. It is for Father, or Father thinks it is until he begins reading. Then he is completely mystified—

"This is the damndest nonsense I ever read," protests Father, turning the letter over. "As far as I can make out this woman claims that she sat on my lap and I didn't like it."

Clarence, who has had a glance at the postmark, is disturbed, but hesitant about speaking.

"Why, this gets worse and worse," explodes Father. "It just turns into a lot of sentimental lovey-dovey mush." He has crushed the letter and thrown it into the fireplace. "Is this someone's idea of a practical joke? Why should I be the butt—"

Vinnie has appeared on the stairway. "Her hair is down in two braids over her shoulder. She is wearing a lacy combing jacket over her corset cover and a striped petticoat." Vinnie is not feeling well, but she thought Father might need her. If he doesn't she'll go back to bed. And she doesn't want any breakfast. Certainly not any bacon and eggs.

It isn't just a headache that is bothering Vinnie. She thinks she may have caught some sort of germ. And it isn't all her imagination, either, as Father would like her to believe. She isn't planning to send for the doctor, though she would send for one if she thought she were seriously ill.

"Vinnie, I didn't mean to upset you," Father is saying, contritely, when the boys have gone. He has taken her hand and is stroking it with what he thinks is tenderness. "I was just trying to help. When you take to your bed I have a damned lonely time around here. So when I see you getting it into your head that you're sick, I want to do something about it. (*He continues to pat her hand vigorously with what he thinks is reassurance.*) Just because some of your friends have given in to this is no reason why you should imagine you're sick, Vinnie."

"Oh, stop, Clare!" Vinnie has snatched her hand away. "Get out of this house and go to your office!"

And Father, "a little bewildered and somewhat indignant at this rebuff to his tenderness," gets his hat and cane and marches out of the house, slamming the door after him.

Vinnie has started for the stairs when Clarence comes bustling back to retrieve the letter his father has tossed into the fireplace. He is concerned for his mother's health, and would do anything he could for her, but the letter is of supreme importance. When he has smoothed it out and read it, it is also of great satisfaction to him.

John is back, with the job. A job for him and one for Clarence. They have the agency for "Bartlett's Beneficent Balm—A Boon to Mankind." And what a remedy that is! "Look what it cures!" thrills John. Clarence is reading from the bottle—

"A sovereign cure for colds, coughs, catarrh, asthma, quinsy, and sore throat; poor digestion, summer complaint, colic, dyspepsia, heartburn, and shortness of breath; lumbago, rheumatism, heart disease, giddiness, and women's complaints; nervous prostration, St. Vitus's dance, jaundice, and la grippe; proud flesh, pink eye, seasickness, and pimples."

Clarence is greatly impressed. Anybody who is sick at all ought to need a bottle of medicine like that. The boys are to have the territory of all Manhattan Island and are to get a commission of twenty-five cents on every bottle they sell for a dollar.

They have decided that they should start right in calling on friends of their father and mother, but—

"Suppose they ask us if we use it at our house?" suggests John.

"It would be better if we could say we did," admits Clarence.

At which moment Nora appears with a tray bearing a cup of tea for Mrs. Day. This gives the boys an idea. Clarence will take the tray to his mother. Nora needn't bother.

"Mother wasn't feeling well this morning," Clarence reports, eyeing John questioningly.

"What was the matter with her?"

"I don't know—she was just complaining."

"Well, it says here it's good for women's complaints," says John.

Clarence has taken the cork from the bottle of Bartlett's Beneficent Balm and sniffed the contents inquiringly. John also sniffs. They nod knowingly at each other and Clarence measures out a spoonful of the medicine for Mother's tea. John, wanting to be sure that Mother has enough to cure her, pours in a little more from the bottle as the curtain falls.

Three hours have elapsed when the curtain rises. The breakfast things have been cleared and there is an air of considerable excitement in the Day house.

Nora has brought in a kettle of steaming hot water. The doctor is waiting for that upstairs. Harlan is at the window anxiously waiting some sign of his father, who has been sent for. Margaret has gone to fetch the minister.

Now Father has arrived in a cab and dashed upstairs. He and Whitney had ridden in the cab all the way from Father's office. It had taken them a long time, Whitney explains, because the horse wouldn't go very fast until Father had spoken to him personally.

Presently Father is downstairs again. Mother wouldn't let him stay in the room. Now Dr. Humphreys, who is "the family-doctor type of the period, with just enough whiskers to make him impressive," has followed Father.

"She's a pretty sick woman, Mr. Day," reports Dr. Humphreys. "I had given her a sedative just before you came—and after you left the room I had to give her another."

The doctor is greatly mystified. If Mrs. Day had not eaten any breakfast, as they report, it seems strange that she should have such violent attacks of nausea. "It's almost as though she were poisoned," Dr. Humphreys concludes, and dashes out to the drugstore. (*He could have phoned, if there had been a phone, but* FATHER *doesn't believe in phones.*)

It's always lonesome in the house when Mother stays in bed. Harlan notices that, and Father agrees with him. Whitney, too, is worried about his catechism. Who's going to hear that? And who is going to read to Harlan? Father, of course, will take on these jobs, but they're not easy.

There is a good deal about baptism in the catechism lesson. As well as a few embarrassing questions from Whitney. " 'What is the outward visible sign or form in Baptism?' " reads Father.

" 'Water; wherein the person is baptized, in the name of the Father, and of the Son, and of the Holy Ghost.' You haven't been baptized, Father, have you?"

" 'What is the inward and spiritual grace?' " demands Father, ignoring Whitney.

"If you don't have to be baptized, why do I have to be confirmed?"

" 'What is the inward and spiritual grace?' " repeats Father, firmly.

" 'A death unto sin, and a new birth unto righteousness; for being by nature born in sin, and the children of wrath, we are hereby made the children of grace.' Is that why you get mad so much, Father—because you're a child of wrath?"

"Whitney, mind your manners! You're not supposed to ask questions of your elders! 'What is required of persons to be baptized?' "

" 'Repentance, whereby—whereby—' (*He pauses.*)"

And that is the end of the lesson. There is no use Father hearing more until Whitney has studied more. With relief on both sides the boys are permitted to escape to the back yard on promise that they will not do any pounding or shouting to disturb their mother.

Father tiptoes across the room anxiously. He is worried. And more worried when he discovers that Margaret has been sent to fetch the minister. The sight of Dr. Lloyd irritates him. The ministerial sympathy has an ominous and artificial ring.

Presently Dr. Humphreys is back, and with him a Dr. Somers, whom Dr. Humphreys has taken it upon himself to call in consultation. "Mrs. Day is in good hands now, Mr. Day," advises Dr. Lloyd, reassuringly as the doctors go upstairs. "There's nothing you and I can do at the moment to help."

Father is not so sure, and after a moment's consideration he decides that there is something that can be done.

"Dr. Lloyd, there's something that's troubling Mrs. Day's mind. I think you know what I refer to." Father motions the minister to a seat.

"Yes—you mean the fact that you've never been baptized."

"I gathered you knew about it from your sermon last Sunday. (*Looks at him a second with indignant memory.*) But let's not get angry. I think something had better be done about it."

"Yes, Mr. Day."

"When the doctors get through up there I want you to talk to Mrs. Day. I want you to tell her something."

"Yes, I'll be glad to," answers Dr. Lloyd, eagerly.

"You're just the man to do it! She shouldn't be upset about this—I want you to tell her that my being baptized would just be a lot of damn nonsense."

This is not what Dr. Lloyd expected, and he is plainly upset. Baptism, he explains, is one of the sacraments of the Church. And the solution is very simple—if Mr. Day would only consent to be baptized. But Mr. Day will not. "I'm surprised that a grown man like you would suggest such a thing" is his final word on the subject.

The doctors have come downstairs and retired mysteriously for their consultation. Father would worm from them, if he could, some idea of the seriousness of Vinnie's condition, but they are professionally uncommunicative. Father is plainly frightened.

"This Dr. Somers—I've heard his name often—he's very well thought of, isn't he?" Father asks Dr. Lloyd.

"Oh, yes indeed!"

FATHER—If Vinnie's really—if anyone could help her, he could —don't you think?

DR. LLOYD—A very fine physician. But there's a greater Help, ever present in the hour of need. Let us turn to Him in prayer. Let us kneel and pray. (FATHER *looks at him, straightens, then walks to the other side of the room.*) Let us kneel and pray. (FATHER *finally bows his head.* DR. LLOYD *looks at him and, not kneeling himself, raises his head and speaks simply in prayer.*) Oh, Lord, look down from Heaven—behold, visit, and relieve this thy servant who is grieved with sickness, and extend to her thy accustomed goodness. We know she has sinned against Thee in thought, word, and deed. Have mercy on her, O Lord, have mercy on this miserable sinner. Forgive her—

FATHER—She's not a miserable sinner and you know it! (*Then* FATHER *speaks directly to the Deity.*) O God! You know Vinnie's not a miserable sinner. She's a damn fine woman! She shouldn't be made to suffer. It's got to stop, I tell You, it's got to stop!

VINNIE (*appearing on the stairway in her nightgown*)—What's the matter, Clare? What's wrong?

FATHER (*not hearing her*)—Have mercy, I say, have mercy, damn it!

VINNIE—What's the matter, Clare? What's wrong?

FATHER (*turns, sees* VINNIE, *rushes to her*)—Vinnie, what are you doing down here? You shouldn't be out of bed. You get right back upstairs. (*He now has his arms around her.*)

VINNIE—Oh, Clare, I heard you call. Do you need me?

FATHER (*deeply moved*)—Vinnie—I know now how much I need you. Get well, Vinnie. I'll be baptized. I promise. I'll be baptized.

VINNIE—You will? Oh, Clare!

FATHER—I'll do anything. We'll go to Europe, just we two— you won't have to worry about the children or the household accounts— (VINNIE *faints against* FATHER'S *shoulder.*) Vinnie! (*He stoops to lift her.*)

DR. LLOYD—I'll get the doctor. But don't worry, Mr. Day— she'll be all right now. (FATHER *lifts* VINNIE *up in his arms.*) Bless you for what you've done, Mr. Day.

FATHER—What did I do?

DR. LLOYD—You promised to be baptized!

FATHER (*aghast*)—I did? (*With horror* FATHER *realizes he has been betrayed—and by himself.*) Oh, God!

The curtain falls.

ACT III

It is a month later. The Day living room is unusually tranquil. Vinnie, who has been embroidering petit point, has stopped long enough to confer with Margaret about the meals. Especially about the next morning's breakfast. Vinnie has her reason for wanting to have something that will both surprise and please Mr. Day. Also there are to be two extra—Cousin Cora and her friend are coming up from Springfield again and they are almost sure to get in just before breakfast time.

Now Clarence is home from a shopping errand. He has found in McCreery's exactly what his mother had sent him for—a large china pug dog. It is, Vinnie thinks, the darlingest thing she has ever seen, and she has been hoping it wouldn't be sold all the time she has been ill. Now she has it and is happy.

Vinnie has gone to have a red ribbon pressed for the china dog's neck when John arrives. John has been down to collect his own and Clarence's commission from Dr. Bartlett. The doctor owed them sixteen dollars apiece, and Clarence has been depending on the money. In fact, on the strength of getting that sixteen dollars Clarence had ordered a fifteen dollar suit of clothes at McCreery's when he was getting the china dog.

But, as John explains, Dr. Bartlett has paid them off with "Benificent Balm." And does that put Clarence in a fix! He has already ordered alterations in the suit and he has to have the fifteen dollars that afternoon! He can't offer McCreery fifteen bottles of "Beneficent Balm," because McCreery's doesn't sell medicine. There's only one thing to do. Clarence will have to brace Father.

Father isn't interested. He is rather pleased, in fact, when Clarence repeats that he finds it impossible to do anything in Father's cut-down clothes that Father wouldn't do—not kneel or anything. And he will have to kneel sometime—if he is ever going to get married, or propose, or anything like that. Still, Father isn't interested. And the idea of fifteen dollars for a suit of clothes—"Why, you're beginning to talk as crazy as your mother," insists Father.

Vinnie is glad to find Father home, but he doesn't have to come home early from the office every day now. She is quite well again. And she has some awfully good news for him. She has been talking with that nice Mr. Morley, the young minister who had substituted for Dr. Lloyd one Sunday—the one Father had liked so well—and the Rev. Morley has a parish in Audubon, which is up above Harlem.

"Isn't that wonderful?" chirps Vinnie, with new enthusiasm. "Nobody knows you up there. You'll be perfectly safe!"

FATHER—Safe? Vinnie, what the devil are you talking about?

VINNIE—I've been all over everything with Mr. Morley and he's agreed to baptize you.

FATHER—Oh, he has—the young whippersnapper! Damn nice of him!

VINNIE—We can go up there any morning, Clare—we don't even have to make an appointment.

FATHER—Vinnie, you're just making a lot of plans for nothing. Who said I was going to be baptized at all?

VINNIE (*aghast*)—Why, Clare! *You* did!

FATHER—Now, Vinnie!—

VINNIE—You gave me your promise—your Sacred Promise. You stood right on that spot and said: "I'll be baptized. I promise—I'll be baptized."

FATHER—What if I did?

VINNIE (*amazed, she comes down and faces him*)—Aren't you a man of your word?

FATHER (*rising*)—Vinnie, that was under entirely different circumstances. We all thought you were dying, so naturally I said that to make you feel better. As a matter of fact, the doctor told me that's what cured you. So it seems to me pretty ungrateful of you to press this matter any further.

VINNIE—Clarence Day, you gave me your Sacred Promise!

FATHER (*getting annoyed*)—Vinnie, you were sick when I said that. Now you're well again.

MARGARET (*entering with the pug dog, which now has the freshly pressed ribbon tied around its neck, and putting it on table*)—Is that all right, Mrs. Day?

VINNIE (*dismissingly*)—That's fine, Margaret, thank you. (MARGARET *exits.*) My being well has nothing to do with it. You gave me your word! You gave the Lord your word. If you had seen how eager Mr. Morley was to bring you into the fold. (FATHER, *trying to escape, has been moving toward the arch when suddenly the pug dog catches his eye and he stares at it fascinated.*) And you're going to march yourself up to his church some morning before you go to the office and be christened. If you think for one minute that I'm going to—

FATHER—What in the name of Heaven is that?

VINNIE—If you think I'm going to let you add the sin of breaking your Solemn and Sacred Promise—

FATHER—I demand to know what that repulsive object is!

VINNIE (*exasperated in her turn*)—It's perfectly plain what it is—it's a pug dog!

FATHER—What's it doing in this house?

VINNIE (*defiantly*)—I wanted it and I bought it.

FATHER—You spent good money for that?

VINNIE—Clare, we're not talking about that! We're talking about you. Don't try to change the subject!

FATHER—How much did you pay for that atrocity?

VINNIE—I don't know. I sent Clarence down for it. Listen to me, Clare—

FATHER—Clarence, what did you pay for that?

CLARENCE—I didn't pay anything. I charged it.

FATHER (*looking at* VINNIE)—Charged it! I might have known. (*To* CLARENCE.) How much was it?

CLARENCE—Fifteen dollars.

FATHER—Fifteen dollars for that eyesore?

VINNIE (*to the rescue of the pug dog*)—Don't you call that lovely work of art an eyesore! That will look beautiful sitting on a red cushion by the fireplace in the parlor.

FATHER—If that sits in the parlor, I won't! Furthermore, I don't even want it in the same house with me. Get it out of here! (*He starts for the stairs.*)

VINNIE—You're just using that for an excuse. You're not going to get out of this room until you set a date for your baptism.

FATHER (*turning at the foot of the stairs*)—I'll tell you one thing! I'll never be baptized while that hideous monstrosity is in this house.

VINNIE (*calling after him as he stalks upstairs*)—All right! It goes back this afternoon and he's christened first thing in the morning.

Now Clarence has an idea. If he takes the pug dog back to McCreery's, and they credit the Days with fifteen dollars, why can't that pay for his suit? It can, agrees Vinnie, and then the suit won't cost Father a cent! How bright of Clarence!

But there is still the next morning and the baptism to be arranged for. Let Clarence engage a cab for eight o'clock. They will forget Father's feeling about cabs. Let Clarence engage one of the best—"the kind they use at funerals." And let them stand together on Father's promise to be baptized if the china dog is returned. . . .

Vinnie is happily humming "Sweet Marie" when Father comes back. He is pleased to hear her singing again. And that reminds him—he had stopped in Tiffany's on his way home and bought her a little something. He hands her a box.

"Oh, Clare!" Vinnie has opened the box, put the ring on her finger admiringly.

"Glad if it pleases you," mutters Father, settling down to his newspaper.

"I don't know how to thank you." Vinnie has kissed him and sat down happily beside him.

VINNIE—Clare, this is the loveliest ring you ever bought me. Now that I have this, you needn't buy me any more rings.

FATHER—Well, if you don't want any more.

VINNIE—What I'd really like now is a nice diamond necklace.

FATHER (*alarmed*)—Vinnie, do you know how much a diamond necklace costs?

VINNIE—I know, Clare, but don't you see?—your giving me this ring shows that I mean a little something to you. Now, a diamond necklace—

FATHER—Good God, if you don't know by this time how I feel about you! We've been married for twenty years and I've loved you every minute of it.

VINNIE—What did you say? (*Her eyes well with tears at* FATHER's *definite statement of his love.*)

FATHER—I said we'd been married twenty years and I've loved you every minute of it. But if I have to buy out jewelry stores to prove it—if I haven't shown it to you in my words and actions, I might as well— (*He turns and sees* VINNIE *dabbing her eyes and speaks with resignation.*) What have I done now?

VINNIE—It's all right, Clare—I'm just so happy.

FATHER—Happy!

VINNIE—You said you loved me! And this beautiful ring— that's something else I didn't expect. Oh, Clare, I love surprises. (*She nestles against him.*)

FATHER—That's another thing I can't understand about you, Vinnie. Now, *I* like to know what to expect. Then I'm prepared to meet it.

VINNIE (*putting her head on his shoulder*)—Yes, I know. But, Clare, life would be pretty dull if we always knew what was coming.

FATHER—Well, it's certainly not dull around here. In this house you never know what's going to hit you tomorrow.

VINNIE (*to herself*)—Tomorrow! (*She starts to sing*, FATHER *listening to her happily*.)

> "Every daisy in the dell,
> Knows my secret, knows it well,
> And yet I dare not tell,
> Sweet Marie!"

At breakfast next morning there is still another new maid. Margaret is this one's name, but Father quickly informs her that she can't be Margaret. There is already one Margaret in the house. So this Margaret becomes Maggie.

When Vinnie comes downstairs she is dressed in white. "Somehow she almost has the appearance of a bride going to her wedding." As the boys stand to greet her Father notices that they, too, are dressed in their Sunday best. Something must be going on.

For the moment Father's mind is diverted. He has tasted the kippers and is pleased. He must stamp on the floor and summon Margaret to tell her that the kippers are good. And the hot biscuits, too. Everything's fine—and then Clarence's new suit arrives and Father notices the "charge" mark. If things are being charged to him he wants to know about it.

"Now, Clare, stop your fussing," fusses Vinnie. "It's a new suit of clothes for Clarence and it's not costing you a penny."

FATHER—It's marked "Charge fifteen dollars"—it's costing me fifteen dollars. And I told Clarence—

VINNIE—Clare, can't you take my word it isn't costing you a penny?

FATHER—I'd like to have you explain why it isn't.

VINNIE (*triumphantly*)—Because Clarence took the pug dog back and got the suit instead.

FATHER—Of course, and they'll charge me fifteen dollars for the suit.

VINNIE—Nonsense, Clare. We gave them the pug dog for the suit. Don't you see?

FATHER—Then they'll charge me fifteen dollars for the pug dog.

VINNIE—But, Clare, they can't! We haven't got the pug dog. We sent that back.

FATHER (*bewildered, but not convinced*)—Now wait a minute, Vinnie. There's something wrong with your reasoning.

VINNIE—I'm surprised, Clare, and you're supposed to be so good at figures. Why, it's perfectly clear to me.

FATHER—Vinnie! They're going to charge me for one thing or the other.

VINNIE—Don't you let them!

In deep disgust Father gets up, throws his napkin on the table and stamps over to the window. And what he sees from the window adds to his irritation. Cousin Cora and Mary Skinner have driven up in a cab! With an explosive "Oh, God!" Father would have the house closed and the doors locked. Those damned gypsies are not going to move in on him again! Let them get back in the cab and drive right on to Ohio, if they're extravagant enough to take a cab when there's a street car passing the door! Let—

But Vinnie has hurried to the door and greeted Cora and Mary in her best welcoming tone. A moment later the family greetings are in full swing and an irate Father has settled back gloomily to finishing his kippers and opening his mail.

A second later there is another paternal explosion. Father is yelling loudly for John. From the letter he waves in his hand Father has learned that his son has been going around town selling dog medicine. At least if it isn't dog medicine, as John protests, Mrs. Sprague's little boy had given some to his dog and the dog had died. She wants ten dollars for a new dog!

"Well, he shouldn't have given it to a dog. It's for humans! Why, it's Bartlett's Beneficent Balm—'Made from a secret formula'!"

"Have you been going around among our friends and neighbors selling some damned Dr. Munyon patent nostrum?"

"But it's good medicine, Father. I can prove it by Mother."

"Vinnie, what do you know about this?"

"Nothing, Clare, but I'm sure that John—"

"No, I mean that day Mother—"

"That's enough! You're going to every house where you sold a bottle of that concoction and buy it all back."

Including the ten dollars for a new dog, it will cost Father a hundred and thirty-eight dollars to square John with the community. Father will pay it, but it will all come out of John's allowance, which means, John figures, that he will be practically penniless until he is twenty-one.

Cousin Cora attempts to break through the restraint with a bit of Springfield news and Father buries himself again in his

paper. He stays buried until a moment later when he hears Cora
telling Vinnie that not only have she and Mary had their breakfast, but that they cannot possibly stay even over-night. Then
Father emerges all smiles. He is even quite insistent that they
should at least have a cup of coffee with the family.

And now the great decision cannot be put off any longer.
Maggie is in to announce the arrival of the cab.

"The cab? What cab?" demands Father.

"The cab that's to take us to Audubon," answers Vinnie,
sweetly.

FATHER—Who's going to Audubon?

VINNIE—We all are. Cora, the most wonderful thing has
happened!

CORA—What, Cousin Vinnie?

VINNIE (*happily*)—Clare's going to be baptized this morning.

FATHER (*not believing his ears*)—Vinnie—what are you saying?

VINNIE (*with determination*)—I'm saying you're going to be
baptized this morning!

FATHER—I'm not going to be baptized this morning or any
other morning!

VINNIE—You promised yesterday that as soon as I sent that
pug dog back you'd be baptized.

FATHER—I promised no such thing!

VINNIE—You certainly did!

FATHER—I never said anything remotely like that!

VINNIE—Clarence was right here and heard it. You ask him!

FATHER—Clarence be damned! I know what I said! I don't
remember exactly, but it wasn't that!

VINNIE—Well, I remember. That's why I ordered the cab!

FATHER (*suddenly remembering*)—The cab! Oh, my God,
that cab! (*He rises and glares out the window at the cab, then
turns back and speaks peremptorily.*) Vinnie! You send that
right back!

VINNIE—I'll do nothing of the kind. I'm going to see that you
get to Heaven.

FATHER—I can't go to Heaven in a cab!

VINNIE—Well, you can start in a cab! I'm not sure whether
they'll ever let you into Heaven or not, but I know they won't
unless you're baptized.

FATHER—They can't keep me out of Heaven on a technicality.

VINNIE—Clare, stop quibbling! You might as well face it—
you've got to make your peace with God.

FATHER—I never had any trouble with God until you stirred Him up!

Little by little Father's resistance is broken down. He protests a little peevishly that the children should not be taken along to witness their father's indignity, and though she knows they would be proud of him, Vinnie agrees to this. As a final hope he advances the argument that he must go to the office to get John the money to buy back the medicine he has sold—

"When I think of you going around this town selling dog medicine!" Father has turned back to John with rising anger.

"It wasn't dog medicine, Father," John repeats, insistently.

FATHER—John, we're starting downtown this minute!

VINNIE—You're doing no such thing! You gave me your Sacred Promise that day I almost died—

JOHN—Yes, and she would have died if we hadn't given her some of that medicine. That proves it's a good medicine!

FATHER (*aghast*)—You gave your mother some of that dog medicine!

VINNIE—Oh, no, John, you didn't! (*She sinks weakly into the chair below the fireplace.*)

JOHN—Yes, we did, Mother. We put some in your tea that morning.

FATHER—You did what? Without her knowing it? Do you realize you might have killed your mother? You did kill Mrs. Sprague's dog. (*After a solemn pause.*) John, you've done a very serious thing. I'll have to give considerable thought as to how you're going to be punished for this.

VINNIE—But, Clare—

FATHER—No, Vinnie. When I think of that day—with the house full of doctors—why, Cora, we even sent for the minister. Why, we might have lost you! (*He goes to* VINNIE, *really moved, and puts his hand on her shoulder.*) It's all right now, Vinnie, thank God. You're well again. But what I went through that afternoon—the way I felt—I'll never forget it.

VINNIE—Don't talk that way, Clare. You've forgotten it already.

FATHER—What do you mean?

VINNIE—That was the day you gave me your Sacred Promise.

FATHER—But I wouldn't have promised if I hadn't thought you were dying—and you wouldn't have almost died if John hadn't given you that medicine. Don't you see? The whole thing's illegal!

VINNIE—Suppose I had died! It wouldn't make any difference to you. You don't care whether we meet in Heaven or not—you don't care whether you ever see me and the children again. (*She almost succeeds in crying.* HARLAN *and* WHITNEY *go to her in sympathy, putting their arms around her.*)

FATHER (*distressed*)—Now, Vinnie, you're not being fair to me.

VINNIE—It's all right, Clare. If you don't love us enough there's nothing we can do about it.

FATHER (*hurt, walks away to other side of the room*)—That's got nothing to do with it! I love my family as much as any man. There's nothing within reason I wouldn't do for you, and you know it! All these years I've struggled and worked just to prove— (*He has reached the window and looks out.*) There's that damn cab! Vinnie, you're not well enough to go all the way up to Audubon.

VINNIE (*perkily*)—I'm well enough if we ride.

FATHER—But that trip would take all morning. And those cabs cost a dollar an hour.

VINNIE (*with smug complacence*)—That's one of their best cabs. That costs two dollars an hour.

FATHER (*staring at her a second, horrified—then explodes*)—Then why aren't you ready? Get your hat on! Damn! Damnation! Amen!

Vinnie is stunned for a moment by Father's sudden surrender, but quickly puts on her bonnet and follows him to the hall. Whitney, Harlan and Cousin Cora have gone out to watch them start. John has gone to his mother in the hall.

"Mother, I didn't mean to almost kill you," he says contritely.

"Now don't you worry about what your father said. (*Tenderly.*) It's all right, dear. (*She kisses him.*) It worked out fine!"

"Mary! Here comes Clarence," John calls, as he follows his mother.

Mary has come back from the window and seated herself in Father's chair. Clarence appears on the stairs wearing his new suit. Without a word he goes to Mary and kneels before her. "They are both starry-eyed," and gazing raptly at each other as Father passes through the hall on his way out. "Oh, God!" he exclaims, as his glance falls on his kneeling son.

Clarence springs up in embarrassment as Vinnie comes hurriedly back into the hall.

"What's the matter? What's wrong?"

"Nothing's wrong, Mother—" Clarence assures her. Then, for want of something better to say, he adds: "Going to the office, Father?"

"No! I'm going to be baptized, damn it!"

Father has angrily slammed on his hat and stalked out. "Vinnie gives a triumphant nod and follows him. The curtain starts down, and as it falls Clarence again kneels at Mary's feet."

THE CURTAIN FALLS

THE MAN WHO CAME TO DINNER

A Comedy in Three Acts

By GEORGE S. KAUFMAN AND MOSS HART

THOSE happy collaborators, George S. Kaufman and Moss
Hart, were ready and waiting for the theatre season of 1939-40.
They had been working through the Spring and Summer on a
comedy they had begun with some idea that it might prove an
amusing "vehicle" for their play acting chum, Alexander Woollcott. "The Man Who Came to Dinner" they called it, and its
story was to turn on a typical Woollcottian adventure in which
this popular lecturer, reviewer, town crier and raconteur would be
marooned in the home of a small-town hostess as the result of a
fractured hip.

As the comedy developed it seemed less and less likely that
Mr. Woollcott would really want to play the part of its irascible,
not to say insulting hero, and, following an exchange of conclusions on the subject, it was decided to seek another actor. Monty
Woolley, at the head of the Dramatic Society at Yale during his
college years and a professional stage director and actor on Broadway since his graduation, was finally given the assignment.

"The Man Who Came to Dinner" was brought to Broadway
in October. Its success was immediate and of such proportions
that the only comparison newspaper reviewers could call to mind
was the similar sensation caused by another Kaufman-Hart comedy, "You Can't Take It with You," two years before. Within
a fortnight the sale of seats had extended far past the new year.
A second company was organized for Chicago, with the former
dancer, Clifton Webb, in the titular rôle, and a third company
was projected for a series of Pacific Coast engagements in which
Mr. Woollcott thought he would like to have a chance at playing
the hero for whom he was supposed to have served as model.

There was little doubt in the minds of his friends and former
confreres, the New York drama critics, that this was indeed a
friendly cartoon of the popular writer. Nor were all of them
convinced that many liberties had been taken by the play's
authors.

"There has never been anyone in what he calls 'our time' with
an air of faint monopoly," wrote John Anderson in the *Journal-*

American, "quite like this Falstaffian figure. No one so full of
the carbolic acid of human kindness; no one with the enthusiasm,
the ruthless wit, the wayward taste, disarming prejudice, and relentless sentimentality of the man so carefully undisguised as
the hero of 'The Man Who Came to Dinner.' "

It is into the living room in the home of Mr. and Mrs. Ernest
Stanley in a small Ohio town that we are first ushered in the
play. It is a large, comfortable and tastefully furnished room,
lived in quite evidently by people of means and good taste. As
we enter we find Mrs. Stanley, a slightly fluttery small-town
matron, standing before the closed doors of the library listening
a little timidly to a muffled conversation heard dully from the
other side of the doors. When the doors are suddenly opened a
second later Mrs. Stanley is obliged to step back quickly not to
be caught with her ear to the door.

A nurse in full uniform scurries out of the library, closing the
doors back of her. She has no time to answer Mrs. Stanley, who
would know whether the occupant of the library is or is not about
to emerge.

There is a ringing of the doorbell, and a moment later a ringing of the telephone bell. And, whenever the library doors are
opened, a man's voice raised in bitterness if not in anger can
be heard rumbling inside. Richard Stanley, the good-looking 21-
year-old son of the household, has answered the doorbell and
received two packages—one from New York, the other from
San Francisco. June, the attractive 20-year-old Stanley daughter, at the phone is practically flabbergasted when she is informed
by long-distance that H. G. Wells will be calling back at two
o'clock from London.

Sarah, the cook, having found an excuse for bringing a pitcher
of orange juice to the library, is thrilled when, the doors opening
in response to her knock, she hears the growling voice inside declare with emphasis: "You have the touch of a sex-starved cobra!"

"His voice is just the same as on the radio!" beams Sarah.

Now two friends of Mrs. Stanley's have arrived. They are
Mrs. Dexter and Mrs. McCutcheon and they are at least a-twit-
ter. Particularly after they have heard that H. G. Wells has
called from London, and that the stack of cablegrams and telegrams on the table are literally from all over. It is Mrs. Mc-
Cutcheon who then produces a clipping from a recent copy of
Time, and tremulously reads it aloud.

"Your name's in it, too, Daisy," Mrs. McCutcheon reports.

"It tells all about the whole thing. Listen: 'Portly Sheridan Whiteside, critic, lecturer, wit, radio orator, intimate friend of the great and near great, last week found his celebrated wit no weapon with which to combat a fractured hip. The Falstaffian Mr. Whiteside, trekking across the country on one of his annual lecture tours, met his Waterloo in the shape of a small piece of ice on the doorstep of Mr. and Mrs. Ernest W. Stanley, of Mesalia, Ohio. Result: Canceled lectures and disappointments to thousands of adoring clubwomen in Omaha, Denver and points west. Further result: The idol of the air waves rests until further notice in home of surprised Mr. and Mrs. Stanley. Possibility: Christmas may be postponed this year.' What's *that* mean?"

Mrs. Stanley confirms the truth of *Time's* report. It is all quite regrettable that this should have happened to poor Mr. Whiteside, but quite wonderful that the Stanleys should have been given this chance to have him with them—it will be marvelous to sit around in the evening and discuss books and plays with him, now that he is getting well. Mr. Stanley, however, who has just joined the group, is pretty much upset by the whole business.

"I'm sure it's a great honor, his being in the house," admits Mr. Stanley; "but it *is* a little upsetting—phone going all the time, bells ringing, messenger boys running in and out—"

And now the great moment has arrived. The library doors are pushed back by an extremely personable and business-like young woman. She is about thirty and her name is Margaret Cutler—"Maggie to her friends." Miss Cutler, Mrs. Stanley nervously explains, is Mr. Whitehead's secretary. She has come, as soon appears, to herald the Whiteside approach. Eagerly Mrs. Stanley assembles the family.

Dr. Bradley, a heavy and slightly pompous physician, bag in hand, is first to appear, followed by a wheel chair rolled by the nurse. The chair "is full of pillows, blankets, and Sheridan Whiteside. Sheridan Whiteside is indeed portly and Falstaffian. He is wearing an elaborate velvet smoking jacket and a very loud tie, and he looks like every caricature ever drawn of him. There is a hush as the wheel chair rolls into the room. Welcoming smiles break over every face. The chair comes to a halt; Mr. Whiteside looks slowly around, into each and every beaming face. His fingers drum for a moment on the arm of the chair. He looks slowly around once more. And then he speaks."

"I may vomit," threatens Mr. Whiteside, quietly, to Maggie.

Mrs. Stanley is quick to laugh off the threat with a nervous little catch in her voice. "Good morning, Mr. Whiteside," she says, cheerily. "I'm Mrs. Ernest Stanley—remember? And this is Mr. Stanley."

STANLEY—How do you do, Mr. Whiteside? I hope that you are better.

WHITESIDE—Thank you. I am suing you for a hundred and fifty thousand dollars.

STANLEY—How's that? What?

WHITESIDE—I said I am suing you for a hundred and fifty thousand dollars.

MRS. STANLEY—You mean—because you fell on our steps, Mr. Whiteside?

WHITESIDE—Samuel J. Liebowitz will explain it to you in court . . . Who are those two harpies standing there like the kiss of death?

MRS. McCUTCHEON (*with a gasp, drops the calf's-foot jelly. It smashes to the floor*)—Oh, dear! My calf's-foot jelly!

WHITESIDE—Made from your own foot, I have no doubt. And now, Mrs. Stanley, I have a few small matters to take up with you. Since this corner druggist at my elbow tells me that I shall be confined in this moldy mortuary for at least another ten days, due entirely to your stupidity and negligence, I shall have to carry on my activities as best I can. I shall require the exclusive use of this room, as well as that drafty sewer which you call the library. I want no one to come in or out while I am in this room.

STANLEY—What do you mean, sir?

MRS. STANLEY (*stunned*)—But we have to go up the stairs to get to our rooms, Mr. Whiteside.

WHITESIDE—Isn't there a back entrance?

MRS. STANLEY—Why—yes.

WHITESIDE—Then use that. I shall also require a room for my secretary, Miss Cutler. I shall have a great many incoming and outgoing calls, so please use the telephone as little as possible. I sleep until noon and require quiet through the house until that hour. There will be five for lunch today. Where is the cook?

STANLEY—Mr. Whiteside, if I may interrupt for a moment—

WHITESIDE—You may not, sir. . . . Will you take your clammy hand off my chair? (*This last to the nurse.*) . . . And now will you all leave quietly, or must I ask Miss Cutler to pass among you with a baseball bat?

Mr. Stanley is literally boiling within, but is able to bring his emotions under control for the moment. He promises to get in touch with Mrs. Stanley later as he storms out of the house.

Mrs. Stanley, still stunned, weakly receives Mr. Whiteside's menu for lunch. He is expecting guests. If Mrs. Stanley has already ordered lunch, as it happens she has, she can have it served to her upstairs on a tray.

And now, if Mr. Whiteside can get the cigarettes John Stanley is bringing him—"evidently by ox-cart"—he will be ready to go ahead with the work of the morning. First, however, he must be rid of Dr. Bradley, and the doctor also has a modest request to make. He would be ever so pleased if Mr. Whiteside would glance through a little thing he has written called "Forty Years an Ohio Doctor. The Story of a Humble Practitioner." Another Whiteside explosion is stifled by the narrowest of margins.

"Maggie, will you take 'Forty Years Below the Navel' or whatever it is called?" Whiteside demands, handing Miss Cutler the manuscript the moment Dr. Bradley has left. But Miss Cutler is in no mood for flippancies.

"I must say you have certainly behaved with all of your accustomed grace and charm," she says, surveying him a little contemptuously.

"Look here, Puss—I am in no mood to discuss my behavior, good or bad."

"These people have done everything in their power to make you comfortable. And they happen, God knows why, to look upon you with a certain wonder and admiration."

"If they had looked a little more carefully at their door-step I would not be troubling them now. I did not wish to cross their cheerless threshold. I was hounded and badgered into it. I now find myself, after two weeks of racking pain, accused of behaving without charm. What would you have me do? Kiss them?"

"Very well, Sherry. After ten years I should have known better than to try to do anything about your manners. But when I finally give up this job I may write a book about it all. 'Cavalcade of Insult, or Through the Years with Prince Charming.'"

"Listen, Repulsive, you are tied to me with an umbilical cord made of piano wire. And now if we may dismiss the subject of my charm, for which, incidentally, I receive fifteen hundred dollars per appearance, possibly we can go to work. . . ."

But there is a new interruption. A "wraith-like lady of uncertain years has more or less floated into the room. She is carrying a spray of holly and her whole manner suggests something not quite of this world."

The wraith-like one is Harriet Stanley, Mr. Stanley's sister, and she has brought the holly to Mr. Whiteside because she remembers what he wrote about "Tess" and "Jude the Obscure." With which information she floats out again.

Wonderingly Whiteside follows her with his eyes. For the moment he is startled. There is something familiar about the face—but there is no time now for wondering. He must get at his mail.

It is a strange assortment, this mail. Dozens of letters from young men who want to be dramatic critics. Inquiries from Columbia Broadcasting Company asking about the Christmas Eve broadcast. That will be taken care of at the New York studio, Mr. Whiteside dictates, and his personal guests will include "Jasha Heifetz, Katharine Cornell, Schiaparelli, the Lunts and Dr. Alexas Carrel, with Anthony Eden on short wave from England."

There are telegrams, with accompanying dinner dates, to be sent to Sacha Guitry in Paris, and the Maharajah of Jehraput, Bombay. A wire is to go to Arturo Toscanini reminding him of the annual Whiteside charity concert for the Home for Paroled Convicts at the Met. And then an interruption by long distance from Hollywood. Banjo is on the wire. And Banjo is a card. It is with some difficulty that Mr. Whiteside gets the telephone away from Miss Cutler. He succeeds finally—

"How are you, you fawn's behind?" shouts Whiteside in the phone. "And what are you giving me for Christmas? (*He roars with laughter at* BANJO's *answer.*) What news, Banjo, my boy? How's the picture coming? . . . How are Wacko and Sloppo? . . . No, no, I'm all right. . . . Yes, I'm in very good hands. Dr. Crippen is taking care of me. . . . What about you? Having any fun? . . . Playing any cribbage? . . . What? (*Again he laughs loudly*) . . . Well, don't take all his money —leave a little bit for me . . . You're what? . . . Having your portrait painted? By whom? Milt Gross? . . . No, I'm going back to New York from here. I'll be there for twelve days, and then I go to Dartmouth for the Drama Festival. You wouldn't understand . . . Well, I can't waste my time talking to Holly-wood riffraff. Kiss Louella Parsons for me. Good-by. (*He hangs up and turns to* MAGGIE.)   He took fourteen hundred dollars from Sam Goldwyn last night, and Sam said, 'Banjo, I will never play garbage with you again.' "

They have returned to the correspondence.   There is a sweet and lengthy cable from the actress, Lorraine Sheldon, sympa-thizing with her "poor sweet Sherry" over his accident.   Lorraine reports that she has been in Scotland for the shooting with Lord and Lady Cunard, and in Surrey with Lord Bottomley, but she is about to sail for home on the *Normandie*.   She signs herself "Your blossom girl," and that makes Miss Cutler a little ill.

There is also word from "Destiny's Tot," who would be the one Miss Cutler describes as "England's little Rover Boy."   Bev-erly Carlton is the name and it seems that Beverly has just finished a new play in Pago Pago, and is leaving Honolulu shortly on his way home.   There would have been a tart wire dispatched to Beverly Carlton, too, but just now there is a fur-ther interruption.   A young man named Bert Jefferson, repre-senting the Mesalia *Journal*, has called and will not be denied. The choicest Whiteside insults fail to discourage him.   The Jef-ferson job is important, says Mr. Jefferson; journalism is impor-tant, the future of the Mesalia *Journal* is important, Mr. White-side is news—therefore—

"Young man, that kind of jounalistic trick went out with Rich-ard Harding Davis," announces Whiteside, solemnly.   And then he softens.   "Come over here," he says, invitingly.   "I suppose you've written that novel?"

JEFFERSON—No, I've written that play.

WHITESIDE—Well, I don't want to read it.   But you can send me your paper— I'll take a year's subscription.   Do you write the editorials, too?

JEFFERSON—Every one of them.

WHITESIDE—I know just what they're like.   Ah, me!   I'm afraid you're that noble young newspaper man—crusading, ideal-istic, dull.   (*He looks him up and down.*)   Very good casting, too.

JEFFERSON—You're not bad casting yourself, Mr. Whiteside.

WHITESIDE—We won't discuss it. . . .   Do these old eyes see a box of goodies over there?   Hand them to me on your way out.

JEFFERSON (*as he passes over the candy*)—The trouble is, Mr. Whiteside, that your being in this town comes under the heading of news. Practically the biggest news since the Armistice.

WHITESIDE (*examining the candy*)—Mm. Pecan butternut fudge.

MISS PREEN (*on her way to the kitchen from the library, stops short as she sees* MR. WHITESIDE *with a piece of candy in his hand*)—Oh, my! You mustn't eat candy, Mr. Whiteside. It's very bad for you.

WHITESIDE (*turning*)—My great-aunt Jennifer ate a whole box of candy every day of her life. She lived to be a hundred and two, and when she had been dead three days she looked better than you do now. (*He swings blandly back to his visitor.*) What were you saying, old fellow?

JEFFERSON (*as* MISS PREEN *makes a hasty exit*)—I can at least report to my readers that chivalry is not yet dead.

WHITESIDE—We won't discuss it. . . . Well, now that you have won me with your pretty ways, what do you want?

JEFFERSON—Well, how about a brief talk on famous murders? You're an authority on murder as a fine art.

WHITESIDE—My dear boy, when I talk about murder I get paid for it. I have made more money out of the Snyder-Gray case than the lawyers did. So don't expect to get it for nothing.

JEFFERSON—Well, then, what do you think of Mesalia, how long are you going to be here, where are you going, things like that?

WHITESIDE—Very well. (a) Mesalia is a town of irresistible charm, (b) I cannot wait to get out of it, and (c) I am going from here to Crockfield, for my semi-annual visit to the Crockfield Home for Paroled Convicts, for which I have raised over half a million dollars in the last five years. From there I go to New York. . . . Have you ever been to Crockfield, Jefferson?

JEFFERSON—No, I haven't. I always meant to.

WHITESIDE—As a newspaper man you ought to go, instead of wasting your time with me. It's only about seventy-five miles from here. Did you ever hear how Crockfield started?

JEFFERSON—No, I didn't.

In his most fluent and mellifluous tones Sheridan Whiteside thereupon describes the founding of the Crockfield haven by Elias P. Crockfield, the great humanitarian, himself a paroled convict. Now, twenty-five years later, the haven is being sustained by those who have long had faith in Elias and his work. . . .

Mr. Jefferson has his interview and is duly grateful. Miss Cutler has returned from the library with the mail for Mr. Whiteside to sign. And now the doorbell has announced the arrival of Professor Adolph Metz, another of the Whiteside passions. The professor is probably "the world's greatest authority on insect life," and he has come, first to convey his regret that his friend has been laid low, and then to present him with a souvenir that shall also serve as a source of entertainment during the days of his convalescence. Prof. Metz, with the aid of his boys and girls, has constructed for his famous friend a community of *Periplaneta Americana,* commonly known as the American cockroach. Inside a huge glass case, which is uncovered with a flourish, there are ten thousand of the interesting little fellows—

"Here in Roach City they play, they make love, they mate, they die," explains the Professor. "See, here is the graveyard. They even bury their own dead. . . . You can watch them, Sherry, while they live out their whole lives. It is fascinating. Look! Here is where they store their grain, here is the commissary of the aristocracy, here is the maternity hospital."

"Magnificent! This is my next piece for the London *Mercury.*"

"With these ear-phones, Sherry, you listen to the mating calls. There are the microphones down inside. Listen!"

"Mm," mutters Whiteside in pleased astonishment. "How long has this been going on?"

Mrs. Stanley has started to tiptoe timorously down the stairs. Suddenly she is startled into excited protest at the discovery of the cockroaches. But there is no time to bother with Mrs. Stanley. The doorbell has rung again and the Whiteside luncheon guests from Crockfield have arrived.

There are three of them, two white and one black. Handcuffed together, they are guarded by a uniformed attendant.

"These men, now serving the final months of their prison terms," Whiteside is explaining to Jefferson, "have chosen to enter the ivy-covered walls of Crockfield. They have come here today to learn from me a little of its tradition. . . . Gentlemen, I envy you your great adventure."

John, standing in the dining room doorway, has announced lunch and Mr. Whiteside, wheeling about in his chair, is eager to go right in.

"You're Michaelson, aren't you?" he asks of one of the sturdier convicts. "Butcher-shop murders?"

"Yes, sir."

"Thought I recognized you. . . . After you, Baker. . . . The other fellow, Jefferson—(*He lowers his tone.*)—is Henderson, the hatchet fiend. Always did it in a bathtub—remember? (*His voice rises as he wheels himself into the dining room.*) We're having chicken livers Tetrazzini, and Cherries Jubilee for dessert. I hope every little tummy is a-flutter with gastric juices. Serve the white wine with the fish, John, and close the doors. I don't want a lot of people prying on their betters."

"The doors close. Only Mrs. Stanley is left outside. She collapses quietly into a chair" as the curtain falls.

A week has passed. It is late afternoon and Sheridan White-side is asleep in his wheel chair. On a stand alongside is Roach City. Whiteside has on the ear-phones. "He has apparently dozed off while listening to the mating calls of *Periplaneta Americana.*"

The room is in considerable disorder, having in a week taken on something of the character of its occupant. There are stacks of books on the tables, and perhaps a half dozen volumes, "which apparently did not appeal to the Master," have been tossed on the floor.

For a moment Mr. Whiteside sleeps on. He is aroused by the entrance of Miss Preen, the nurse, with a glass of murky medicine. The experience is not pleasant. "I was dreaming of Lillian Russell, and I awake to find you," growls the patient.

He is further disturbed to learn that Miss Cutler has gone out with Mr. Jefferson. Nor is he more than momentarily mollified by the appearance of Sarah, the cook, with a tray of her latest pastries prepared especially for the great man.

"I have known but three great cooks in my time," Whiteside confesses, deftly pouring his medicine into a nearby vase and helping himself to a handful of Sarah's cakes. "The Khedive of Egypt had one, my great-aunt Jennifer another, and the third, Sarah, is you."

Sarah is practically overcome with pride. When Whiteside goes on to suggest that it would be nice if she and her husband, John, were to come to New York and work for him she might have swooned if Whiteside had not broken the spell by calling loudly for Miss Preen.

He is still perturbed about Miss Cutler's going out with Mr. Jefferson and would have more details. Miss Preen can add nothing to what she has told him. Presently the room is cleared by the appearance on the stairs of Mr. and Mrs. Stanley. Mr.

Stanley, "obviously at the boiling point," is carrying a slip of paper in his hand and Mrs. Stanley, apprehensive and nervous, is following closely after him, begging him from step to step to please have a care.

"Be quiet, Daisy," snaps Mr. Stanley, as he approaches the distinguished guest. "Mr. Whiteside, I want to talk to you. I don't care whether you're busy or not. I have stood all that I'm going to stand."

"Indeed?" blandly inquires Whiteside.

STANLEY—This is the last straw. I have just received a bill from the telephone company for seven hundred and eighty-four dollars. (*He reads from the slip in his hand.*) Oklahoma City, Calcutta, Hollywood, Paris, Brussels, Rome, New York, New York, New York, New York, New York, New York— (*His voice trails off in an endless succession of New Yorks.*) Now I realize, Mr. Whiteside, that you are a distinguished man of letters—

MRS. STANLEY—Yes, of course. We both do.

STANLEY—Please—But in the past week we have not been able to call our souls our own. We have not had a meal in the dining room *once*. I have to tiptoe out of the house in the mornings.

MRS. STANLEY—Now, Ernest—

STANLEY (*waving her away*)—I come home to find convicts sitting at my dinner table—butcher-shop murderers. A man putting cockroaches in the kitchen.

MRS. STANLEY—They just escaped, Ernest.

STANLEY—That's not the point. I don't like coming home to find twenty-two Chinese students using my bathroom. I tell you I won't stand for it, no matter *who* you are.

WHITESIDE—Have you quite finished?

STANLEY—No, I have not. I go down into the cellar this morning and trip over that octopus that William Beebe sent you. I tell you I won't stand it. Mr. Whiteside, I want you to leave this house as soon as you can and go to a hotel. . . . Stop pawing me, Daisy. . . . That's all I've got to say, Mr. Whiteside.

WHITESIDE—And quite enough, I should say. May I remind you again, Mr. Stanley, that I am not a willing guest in this house? I am informed by my doctor that I must remain quiet for another ten days, at which time I shall get out of here so fast that the wind will knock you over, I hope. If, however, you insist on my leaving before that, thereby causing me to suffer a relapse, I shall sue you for every additional day that I am held inactive, which will amount, I assure you, to a tidy sum.

STANLEY (*to his wife*)—This is outrageous. Do we have to—

WHITESIDE—As for the details of your petty complaints, those twenty-two Chinese students came straight from the White House, where I assure you they used the bathroom too.

MRS. STANLEY—Mr. Whiteside, my husband didn't mean—

STANLEY—Yes, I did. I meant every word of it.

WHITESIDE—There is only one point that you make in which I see some slight justice. I do not expect you to pay for my telephone calls, and I shall see to it that restitution is made. Can you provide me with the exact amount?

STANLEY—I certainly can, and I certainly will.

WHITESIDE—Good. I shall instruct my lawyers to deduct it from the hundred and fifty thousand dollars that I am suing you for.

Mr. Stanley is fairly choked with rage as he storms up the stairs again, followed meekly by Mrs. Stanley. Mr. Whiteside enjoys his triumph for a moment, but again his mind is diverted to the newer problem of his secretary and Mr. Jefferson. He phones the Mesalia *Journal*, only to learn that Mr. Jefferson has not returned. For a moment he is diverted by the appearance of the Stanley children. He would, he admits, make friends with them. He has been observing them for a week and is convinced they are quite likable young people. But again there is a suggestion of shock in their report that they have been skating and that they saw Miss Cutler and Mr. Jefferson on the ice.

A moment later the young folks have gone and Miss Cutler has returned. She is radiant as she greets her frowning employer, though filled with protest that he has the room looking like an old parrot-cage. Whiteside merely glowers at her—

"Don't look at me with those great cow-eyes, you sex-ridden hag," he shouts, furiously. "Where have you been all afternoon? Alley-catting around with Bert Jefferson?"

MAGGIE (*her face aglow*)—Sherry—Bert read his play to me this afternoon. It's superb. It isn't just that play written by a newspaper man. It's superb. I want you to read it *tonight*. (*She puts it in his lap.*) It just cries out for Cornell. If you like it, will you send it to her, Sherry? And will you read it tonight?

WHITESIDE—No, I will not read it tonight or any other time. And while we're on the subject of Mr. Jefferson, you might ask him if he wouldn't like to pay your salary, since he takes up all your time.

MAGGIE—Oh, come now, Sherry. It isn't as bad as that.

WHITESIDE—I have not even been able to reach you, not knowing what haylofts you frequent.

MAGGIE—Oh, stop behaving like a spoiled child, Sherry.

WHITESIDE—Don't take that patronizing tone with me, you flea-bitten Cleopatra. I am sick and tired of your sneaking out like some lovesick high-school girl every time my back is turned.

MAGGIE—Well, Sherry—(*She pulls together the library doors and faces* WHITESIDE.)—I'm afraid you've hit the nail on the head. (*With a flourish, she removes her hat.*)

WHITESIDE—Stop acting like Zasu Pitts and explain yourself.

MAGGIE—I'll make it quick, Sherry. I'm in love.

WHITESIDE—Nonsense. This is merely delayed puberty.

MAGGIE—No, Sherry, I'm afraid this is it. You're going to lose a very excellent secretary.

WHITESIDE—You are out of your mind.

MAGGIE—Yes, I think I am, a little. But I'm a girl who's waited a long time for this to happen, and now it has. Mr. Jefferson doesn't know it yet, but I'm going to try my darndest to marry him.

WHITESIDE (*as she pauses*)—Is that all?

MAGGIE—Yes, except that—well—I suppose this is what might be called my resignation—as soon as you've got someone else.

WHITESIDE (*there is a slight pause*)—Now listen to me, Maggie. We have been together for a long time. You are indispensable to me, but I think I am unselfish enough not to let that stand in the way where your happiness is concerned. Because, whether you know it or not, I have a deep affection for you.

MAGGIE—I know that, Sherry.

WHITESIDE—That being the case, I will not stand by and allow you to make a fool of yourself.

MAGGIE—I'm not, Sherry.

WHITESIDE—You are, my dear. You are behaving like a Booth Tarkington heroine. It's—it's incredible. I cannot believe that a girl who for the past ten years has had the great of the world served up on a platter before her—I cannot believe that it is anything but a kind of temporary insanity when you are swept off your feet in seven days by a second-rate, small-town newspaper man.

MAGGIE—Sherry, I can't explain what's happened. I can only tell you that it's so. It's hard for me to believe too, Sherry. Here I am, a hard-bitten old cynic, behaving like *True Story*

Magazine, and liking it. Discovering the moon, and ice-skating
— I keep laughing to myself all the time, but there it is. What
can I do about it, Sherry? I'm in love.

WHITESIDE (*with sudden decision*)—We're leaving here tomorrow. Hip or no hip, we're leaving here tomorrow. I don't
care if I fracture the other one. Get me a train schedule and
start packing. I'll pull you out of this, Miss Stardust. *I'll* get
the ants out of those moonlit pants.

MAGGIE—It's no good, Sherry. I'd be back on the next streamlined train.

Whiteside cannot understand. Maggie's intentions are incredible. Even when she explains that, though she has had ten gay
and exciting years with him, meeting the great of the world, she
has reached the time when she is tired of laughing. When he
answers spiritedly that he intends to do everything in his power
to prevent her from being anesthetized by "this Joan Crawford
fantasy," she turns on him in something of his own temper—

"Now listen to me, Whiteside," she says. "I know you. Lay
off. I know what a devil you can be. I've seen you do it to
other people, but don't you dare do it to me. Don't drug *yourself* into the idea that all you're thinking of is my happiness.
You're thinking of yourself a little bit too, and all those months
of breaking in somebody new. I've seen you in a passion before
when your life has been disrupted, and you couldn't dine in Calcutta on July twelfth with Boo-Boo. Well, that's too bad, but
there it is. I'm going to marry Bert if he'll have me, and don't
you dare try any of your tricks. I'm on to every one of them.
So lay off. That's my message to *you,* Big Lord Fauntleroy."

With a swish Maggie has turned and run up the stairs. For
a moment Mr. Whiteside, "left stewing in his own juice," is in
a perfect fury. Angrily he bangs his hand upon the arm of his
chair. He slaps the play manuscript in his lap. "As he does
so the dawn of an idea comes into his mind." The play's the
thing—

He has wheeled himself to the telephone. A second later he
is putting in a trans-Atlantic call for the *Normandie.* He wants
to talk to Lorraine Sheldon. She had sailed from Southampton
two days ago. He has just hung up the receiver when Dr. Bradley comes bustling in. The doctor is exploding with good news.
He has been looking at the wrong X-rays. Now that he has
found the right ones he discovers that Mr. Whiteside is perfectly and absolutely well.

Curiously the patient does not react with the expected glee. He does not even try to rise from his chair. To the contrary he begs Dr. Bradley to lower his voice and to draw closer. A new thought has come to Mr. Whiteside. He has been reading over the Bradley manuscript, "Forty Years an Ohio Doctor" a second time. He is convinced now much can be done with it. He would like to work on it with the author, touching up a few uneven spots. But— If it were to become generally known, especially to his lecture bureau and his radio sponsors, that he was again a well man he would be forced to leave Mesalia immediately. Therefore, for the present, his healing must be kept a profound secret. Not even Miss Cutler must know.

Dr. Bradley is properly impressed. Not a soul shall be told. Not even Mrs. Bradley. And when can they start work? "I've got just one patient that's dying and then I'll be perfectly free," gleefully announces the doctor. But Mr. Whiteside thinks perhaps the following day will be soon enough. The doctor is disappearing, a very proud and happy man, as the telephone begins a violent ringing. Mr. Whiteside picks up the receiver—

"Yes, yes—this is Mr. Whiteside on the phone. . . . Put them through. . . . Hello. Is this my Blossom Girl?" He is smiling broadly now. "How are you, my lovely? . . . No, no, I'm all right. . . . Yes, still out here. . . . Lorraine, dear, when do you land in New York? . . . Tuesday? That's fine. . . . Now listen closely, my pet. I've great news for you. I've discovered a wonderful play with an enchanting part in it for you. Cornell would give her eye teeth to play it, but I think I can get it for you. . . . Now wait, wait. Let me tell you. The author is a young newspaper man in this town. Of course he wants Cornell, but if you jump on a train and get right out here, I think you could swing it, if you play your cards right. . . . No, he's young, and very attractive, and just your dish, my dear. It just takes a little doing, and you're the girl that can do it. Isn't that exciting, my pet? . . . Yes. . . . Yes, that's right. . . . And look. Don't send me any messages. Just get on a train and arrive. . . . Oh, no, don't thank me, my darling. It's perfectly all right. Have a nice trip and hurry out here. Good-by, my blossom."

He has put down the phone and, "jovial as hell," has turned to an astonished Miss Preen, just entering the room with a glass of forbidding medicine. "My, you're looking radiant this evening," he grins. He reaches for the draught and swallows it in a single gulp. Miss Preen, still in a daze, staggers back into the library.

Down the stairs comes Maggie Cutler. She is dressed for the street, and there is something she wants to get off her mind. "Sherry, I'm sorry for what I said before," she says, pausing on the stairs. "I'm afraid I was a little unjust."

"That's all right, Maggie dear." He is all nobility now. "We all lose our tempers now and then."

"I promised to have dinner with Bert and go to a movie, but we'll come back and play cribbage with you instead."

"Fine."

"See you soon, Sherry dear."

She has kissed him lightly on the brow and gone her way. He looks after her until he hears the door slam. "Then his face lights up and he bursts happily into song as he wheels himself into the library—

> " 'I'se des a 'ittle wabbit in the sunshine,
> I'se des a 'ittle wabbit in the wain—' "

The curtain falls.

ACT II

It is late afternoon of the day before Christmas. For the last week the Stanley family preparations have been carried on more or less privately upstairs. In the Stanley living room Sheridan Whiteside has established a high and luxuriant Christmas tree.

At the moment Sarah and John, under Miss Cutler's direction, are putting the final touches on the tree. From the library they have brought dozens of packages and piled them at its base. Many of these are huge, all of them are interesting. Sarah and John are properly impressed and naturally curious.

"When'll Mr. Whiteside open them, Miss Cutler?" John would know.

"Well, John, you see Christmas is Mr. Whiteside's personal property," explains Maggie. "He invented it and it belongs to him. First thing tomorrow morning, Mr. Whiteside will open each and every present, and there will be the damnedest fuss you ever saw."

"My! Look who he's got presents from!" exclaims Sarah, bending over the packages. "Shirley Temple, William Lyon Phelps, Billy Rose, Ethel Waters, Somerset Maugham—I can hardly wait for tonight."

Bert Jefferson has called. He wants to take Maggie down town to see the Christmas present that, "under the influence of God knows what," he has bought her. They call out their intentions to Whiteside, but before they can get away he has wheeled himself into the room. He isn't very happy, but he is reconciled.

Bert and Maggie have gone, happy as children. Whiteside has checked with the hotel and found that Lorraine Sheldon has not yet arrived. An expressman has arrived with a crate of four live penguins. They are a present from Admiral Richard E. Byrd and quite startling to Miss Preen.

"Directions for feeding right on top," the expressman explains. "These two slats are open."

" 'To be fed only whale blubber, eels and cracked lobster,' " reads John.

"They got Coca-Cola this morning. And liked it," reports the expressman, a little defiantly.

The penguins are taken to the library, where Whiteside expects to find them very companionable. John has loosened the two slats, to give them a bit more room, but this doesn't work out so well. Presently Miss Preen is rushing in to report that the birds are loose and that one of them has a thermometer in its mouth. . . .

Richard Stanley has brought some of his newest candid camera studies to show Mr. Whiteside. Whiteside is frankly quite thrilled with them. They represent, he insists, "the essence of photographic journalism," and he advises Richard not to let his family dissuade him from roaming the world in developing his picture passion. The quicker he gets away the better.

Now comes June Stanley and she, too, is seeking the great man's advice. June is desperately in love with a young labor organizer named Sandy. Sandy has been sent on to organize the men in Mr. Stanley's factory. Naturally Mr. Stanley has not been any too well pleased with the success of Sandy's efforts and, though he loves June better than life, Sandy is inclined to hesitate about taking that matter up with her father.

"He's tried to fire Sandy twice, out at the factory, but he couldn't on account of the Wagner Act, thank God!" says June.

"Yes, he thinks I wrote that, too," adds Sandy.

Now Sandy has just learned that he is to be transferred to Chicago, and he may have to go on to San Francisco. What should they do?

This problem is absurdly easy for Whiteside. (*He is inter-*

rupted briefly by a phone call from Paris. Gertrude Stein wants him to listen to the bells of Notre Dame. It is an annual gesture on Miss Stein's part and makes him quite happy.) As to June and Sandy and their problem: There is nothing for them to do but get married at once. What if it should make the Stanleys unhappy? Unhappiness would be good for them. Help them develop their characters—

"Look at me," demands Whiteside. "I left home at the age of four and haven't been back since. They hear me on the radio and that's enough for them."

So June and Sandy go happily on their way, just in time to avoid Mr. and Mrs. Stanley who can be heard approaching in force down the stairway. The Stanleys are expecting to deliver a few presents in the neighborhood and have no intention of stopping to exchange greetings with their now smiling guest. Mr. Stanley's own Christmas tree has fallen on his head, raising a lump, and this may be one cause of the Whiteside smile.

The Stanleys have gone when Harriet Stanley appears, a little stealthily. She has come to bring dear Mr. Whiteside her Christmas offering—a picture of herself as she used to be—but she is insistent that he shall not open it before the stroke of midnight. . . .

The doorbell has rung. The next moment Lorraine Sheldon is practically in the Whiteside arms. "Lorraine! My Blossom Girl!" and "Sherry! My Sweet!" they exclaim in unison.

Lorraine is known as "the most chic actress on the New York or London stage, and justly so. She glitters as she walks. She is beautiful, and even, God save the word, glamorous. . . . Her rank as one of the Ten Best-Dressed Women of the World is richly deserved. She is, in short, a siren of no mean talents, and knows it."

LORRAINE (*wasting no time*)—Oh, darling, look at that poor tortured face! Let me kiss it! You poor darling, your eyes have a kind of gallant compassion. How drawn you are! Sherry, my sweet, I want to cry.

WHITESIDE—All right, all right. You've made a very nice entrance. Now relax, dear.

LORRAINE—But, Sherry, darling, I've been so worried. And now seeing you in that chair . . .

WHITESIDE—This chair fits my fanny as nothing else ever has. I feel better than I have in years, and my only concern is news of the outside world. So take that skunk off and tell me everything. How are you, my dear?

LORRAINE (*removing a cascade of silver fox from her shoulders*)—Darling, I'm so relieved. You look perfectly wonderful —I never saw you look better. My dear, do I look a wreck? I just dashed through New York. Didn't do a thing about Christmas. Hattie Carnegie and had my hair done, and got right on the train. And the *Normandie* coming back was simply hectic. Fun, you know, but simply exhausting. Jock Whitney, and Cary Grant, and Dorothy di Frasso—it was *too* exhausting. And of course London before that was so magnificent, my dear—well, I simply never got to bed at all. Darling, I've so much to tell you I don't know where to start.

WHITESIDE—Well, start with the dirt first, dear—that's what I want to hear.

LORRAINE—Let me see. . . . Well, Sybil Cartwright got thrown right out of Ciro's—it was the night before I sailed. She was wearing one of those new cellophane dresses, and you could absolutely see Trafalgar Square. And, oh, yes—Sir Harry Montrose—the painter, *you* know—is suing his mother for disorderly conduct. It's just shocked, *every*one. Oh, and before I forget— Anthony Eden told me he's going to be on your New Year's broadcast, and he gave me a message for you. He said for God's sake not to introduce him again as the English Grover Whalen.

WHITESIDE—Nonsense. . . . Now come, dear, what about *you?* What about your love life? I don't believe for one moment that you never got to bed at all, if you'll pardon the expression.

LORRAINE—Sherry dear, you're dreadful.

WHITESIDE—What about that splendid bit of English mutton, Lord Bottomley? Haven't you hooked him yet?

LORRAINE—Sherry, please. Cedric is a very dear friend of mine.

WHITESIDE—Now, Blossom Girl, this is Sherry. Don't try to pull the bed clothes over *my* eyes. Don't tell *me* you wouldn't like to be Lady Bottomley, with a hundred thousand pounds a year and twelve castles. By the way, has he had his teeth fixed yet? Every time I order Roquefort cheese I think of those teeth.

LORRAINE—Sherry, really! . . . Cedric may not be brilliant, but he's rather sweet, poor lamb, and he's very fond of me, and he does represent a kind of English way of living that I like. Surrey, and London for the season—shooting box in Scotland— that lovely old castle in Wales. You were there, Sherry—you know what I mean.

Whiteside—Mm. I do indeed.

Lorraine—Well, really, Sherry, why not? If I can marry
Cedric I don't know why I shouldn't. Shall I tell you something, Sherry? I think, from something he said just before I
sailed, that he's finally coming around to it. It wasn't definite,
mind you, but—don't be surprised if I *am* Lady Bottomley before very long.

Whiteside—Lady Bottomley! Won't Kansas City be surprised! However, I shall be a flower girl and give the groom an
iron toothpick as a wedding present. Come ahead, my Blossom
—let's hear some more of your skullduggery.

But Lorraine is eager to know about the play Whiteside has
found for her. The details of that conspiracy are soon related.
Young Mr. Jefferson, who is most attractive, had brought him
the play, Mr. Whiteside explains, with the understanding that
he send it on to Kit Cornell. Despite a feeling of disloyalty
toward Kit, Whiteside determined to give Lorraine a chance at
it first. And that is how it has happened. The rest is up to her.
Let her run back to the hotel and get into her working clothes.
Then let her meet Bert Jefferson and the rest will be up to her.
Incidentally, Whiteside would have Lorraine know that their mutual friend, and her fellow actor, Beverly Carlton, whom Whiteside has spoken of as "the greatest single talent in the English
theatre today," is coming this evening to pay them a flying
visit. Lorraine is not pleased with the news. Nor is it because
she is jealous. When they were together Beverly may have got
the better notices, as Whiteside charges. Lorraine wouldn't
know about that. She never reads notices. . . .

And now Maggie Cutler has come rushing through the door
with an exclamatory greeting on her lips—"Sherry, what do
you think? I've just been given the most beautiful . . ."

At sight of Lorraine the words die on her lips. Her greeting
is icily formal. A second later Bert Jefferson has appeared and
been introduced. Lorraine loses no time—

"Why, Mr. Jefferson, you don't look like a newspaper man.
You don't look like a newspaper man at all."

"Really? I thought it was written all over me in neon lights."

"Oh, no, not at all. I should have said you were—oh, I don't
know—an aviator or an explorer or something. They have that
same kind of dash about them. I'm simply enchanted with your
town, Mr. Jefferson. It gives one such a warm, gracious feeling. Tell me—have you lived here all your life?"

"Practically."

"If you wish to hear the story of his life, Lorraine, kindly do so on your own time," interrupts Whiteside. "Maggie and I have work to do. Get out of here, Jefferson. On your way, Blossom."

"He's the world's rudest man, isn't he?" chirrups Lorraine.

She would take Mr. Jefferson in her taxi, but Bert has his own car and gallantly offers to take Miss Sheldon back to the Mansion House. In a moment they are gone.

Maggie can't understand it. How does it happen that Lorraine, "snug as a bug in somebody's bed" on the *Normandie*, should suddenly appear on the Mesalia front? Whiteside pretends to be so busy trying to cut four minutes out of his radio address that he cannot talk with her. Before she is able to settle this point there is another ring at the doorbell and Beverly Carlton is with them.

Beverly is "very confident, very British, very Beverly Carlton," and quite rapturously conversational. For the next several minutes he regales them with the Carlton adventures glittering "through the South Seas like a silver scimitar," and frolicking "through Zambesia, raping the Major General's daughter and finishing a three-act play at the same time."

He thinks he may have caught a glimpse of "La Sheldon" as he came in, and, learning that he did, the subject is quickly turned to Lorraine and the most recent dirt concerning her and Lord Bottomley in London. Beverly has it in a letter he has just received and which he proceeds to read to them with gusto—

"It is the latest report from London on the winter maneuvers of Miss Lorraine Sheldon against the left flank—in fact, all flanks—of Lord Cedric Bottomley," Beverly reports. "Listen: 'Lorraine has just left us in a cloud of Chanel Number Five. Since September, in her relentless pursuit of His Lordship, she has paused only to change girdles and check her oil. She has chased him, panting, from castle to castle, till he finally took refuge, for several week-ends, in the gentlemen's lavatory of the House of Lords. Practically no one is betting on the Derby this year; we are all making book on Lorraine. She is sailing tomorrow on the *Normandie*, but would return on the *Yankee Clipper* if Bottomley so much as belches in her direction.' Have you ever met Lord Bottomley, Magpie dear?"

Maggie indicates that she has not met His Lordship and Beverly goes immediately into an extravagant impersonation of that worthy, "very British, very full of teeth, stuttering"—

" 'No v-v-very good shooting today, blast it.   Only s-s-six
partridges, f-f-four grouse, and the D-D-Duke of Sutherland.' "
      "My God, that's Bottomley to the very bottom," chuckles
Whiteside.
      " 'R-r-ripping debate in the House today,' " Beverly continues,
still in character.   " 'Old Basil spoke for th-th-three hours.
D-d-dropped dead at the end of it.   Ripping.' "
      "You're making it up, Beverly," laughs Maggie.   "No one
sounds like that."
      "It's so good it's uncanny," reiterates Whiteside.   "Damn it,
Beverly, why must you race right out of here?   I never see enough
of you, you ungrateful moppet."
      "Sherry darling, I can only tell you that my love for you is
so great that I changed trains at Chicago to spend ten minutes
with you and wish you a Merry Christmas.   Merry Christmas,
my lad.   My little Magpie."
      Beverly does have time, however, to sing them one song from
his newest revue, and might have sung another if at that moment three radio men had not arrived.   They have come to arrange for the hook-up that will carry the Whiteside Christmas
greetings over the world and there is no time for delay.   Whiteside still has four minutes to cut from his manuscript and Maggie proceeds to wheel him into the library that he may set about
the cutting even while he is shouting his farewells to Beverly.
      Alone with Beverly for a moment Maggie is quick to tell him
her trouble and solicit his aid.
      "I've fallen in love," Maggie confesses.   "For the first time
in my life.   Beverly, I'm in love.   I can't tell you about it—
there isn't time.   But Sherry is trying to break it up.   In his
own fiendish way he's doing everything he can to break it up."
      "Why, the old devil!   What's he doing?"
      "Lorraine.   He's brought Lorraine here to smash it."
      "Oh, it's somebody *here*?   In this town?"
      "He's a newspaper man—the one you're going to see at the
station—and he's written a play, and I know Sherry must be
using that as bait.   You know Lorraine—she'll eat him up alive.
You've got to help me, Beverly."
      "Of course I will, Magpie.   What do you want me to do?"
      "I've got to get Lorraine out of here—the farther away the
better—and you can do it for me."
      "But how?   How can I?   I'm leaving."
      The radio men have come back into the room to set up their
equipment.   Maggie and Beverly move into the hall and carry

on their conversation in whispers. Suddenly Beverly is doubled with laughter. "I'd love it," he shouts. "I'd absolutely love it . . . It's simply enchanting, and bitches Sherry and Lorraine at the same time. It's pure heaven! I adore it, and I shall do it up brown."

"Darling, the first baby will be named Beverly," exclaims Maggie, embracing him. "You're wonderful."

"Of course I am. Come to Chislewick for your honeymoon and I'll put you up. Good-by, my lovely. I adore you."

Maggie is very happy as she comes back into the room after seeing Beverly to the door. She is even humming a bit of Beverly's song and enters gaily into helping John straighten up the room. She has gone into the library when first June, then Richard Stanley come down the stairs. June is carrying a suitcase and John has a light bag with two cameras slung over his shoulder. June and Richard have stopped a minute to speak to Mr. Whiteside, but just then the door bell rings and they scurry out through the dining room.

It is Lorraine Sheldon who now arrives, resplendently arrayed in evening gown and wrap. She is in a lightly patronizing mood, so far as Maggie is concerned, but gains no advantage in the exchange of subtle digs. Suddenly Lorraine remembers Beverly and is relieved to learn that he has come and gone—

"When I finished acting with him I was a perfect wreck," Lorraine is saying. "All during that tender love scene that the critics thought was so magnificent he kept dropping peanut shells down my dress. I wouldn't act with him again if I were starving."

"Tell me, Lorraine, have you found a new play yet?"

"No. No, I haven't. There was a pile of manuscripts waiting in New York for me, but I hurried right out here to Sherry."

"Yes, it was wonderful of you, Lorraine—to drop everything that way and rush to Sherry's wheel chair."

"Well, after all, Maggie dear, what else has one in this world but friends? . . . How long will Sherry be in there, I wonder?"

"Not long. . . . Did you know that Mr. Jefferson has written quite a good play? The young man that drove you to the hotel."

"Really? No, I didn't. Isn't that interesting?"

"Yes, isn't it?"

The telephone has rung. Maggie at the receiver takes the message; perhaps a little too casually—

"Hello. . . . Yes. . . . Yes . . . Miss Lorraine Sheldon? Yes, she's here . . . There's a trans-Atlantic call coming through for you, Lorraine."

MAGGIE (*as she hands over the receiver*)—It's London.
LORRAINE—London? . . . Hello. (*Then in a louder tone.*) Hello . . . Cedric! . . . Cedric, is this you? . . . Why, Cedric, you darling! Why, what a surprise! How'd you know I was here? . . . Darling, don't talk so fast and you won't stutter so . . . That's better . . . Yes, now I can hear you . . . Yes, very clearly. It's as though you were just around the corner . . . I see . . . What? . . . Darling! Cedric, dearest, would you wait just a moment? (*She turns to* MAGGIE.) Maggie, would you mind? It's Lord Bottomley—a *very* personal call. Would you mind?
MAGGIE—Oh, not at all. (*She goes into the dining room; almost does a little waltz step as she goes.*)
LORRAINE—Yes, my dearest—now tell me . . . Cedric, please don't stutter so. Don't be nervous. (*She listens for a moment again.*) Oh, my darling. Oh, my sweet. You don't know how I've prayed for this, every night on the boat . . . Darling, yes! Yes, a thousand times Yes! . . . I'll take a plane right out of here and catch the next boat. Oh, my sweet, we're going to be the happiest people in the world. I wish I were there now in your arms, Cedric . . . What? . . . Cedric, don't stutter so . . . Yes, and I love *you*, my darling—oh, so much! . . . Oh, my dear sweet. My darling, my darling. . . . Yes, yes! I will, I will, darling. I'll be thinking of you every moment . . . You've made me the happiest girl in the world . . . Good-by, good-by, darling. Good-by. (*Bursting with her news, she throws open the library doors.*) Sherry, Sherry! Do you know what's happened? Cedric just called from London— He's asked me to marry him. Sherry, think of it! At last! I've got to get right out of here and catch the next boat. How far are we from Chicago? I can get a plane from there.
MAGGIE (*emerging, mouse-like, from the dining room*)—May I come in?
LORRAINE—Maggie dear, can I get a plane out of here right away? Or I'll even take a train to Chicago and fly from there. I've simply got to get the next boat for England. When is it— do you know? Is there a newspaper here?
MAGGIE—The *Queen Mary* sails Friday. Why, what's all the excitement, Lorraine? What's happened?
LORRAINE—Maggie, the most wonderful thing in the world has

happened. Lord Bottomley has asked me to marry him . . .
Oh, Maggie! (*And in her exuberance she throws her arms around
her.*)

MAGGIE—Really? Well, what do you know?

LORRAINE—Isn't it wonderful? I'm so excited I can hardly
think. Maggie dear, you must help me get out of here.

MAGGIE—I'd be delighted to, Lorraine.

Sheridan Whiteside has wheeled himself into the room and has
been sitting through the last of the conversation "like a thunder cloud." He doesn't like the situation, nor the thought of
Lorraine's tossing her career "into the ashcan." Such acts help
to explain, however, why Cornell remains the first lady of the
American theatre.

"Oh, this is wonderful," exclaims Maggie, who has been busy
with her time-tables. "We're in luck, Lorraine. You can get a
plane out of Toledo at ten-three. It takes about an hour to get
there. Why, it all works out wonderfully, doesn't it, Sherry?"

Now Lorraine, all excitement, must call the hotel and talk
with Cosette, her maid. Such a wonderful maid, too. Hurriedly
Cosette is given her instructions about the immediate packing,
and the sending of cables to Lady Cunard, and Lady Astor, to
Lord Beaverbrook and the Duchess of Sutherland, telling them
of Lorraine's immediate return and her approaching marriage.
And a cable to Cartier, in Paris, to bring over the triple string
of pearls Lorraine had looked at. . . .

Bert Jefferson has come in. Certainly, he will be very glad
to drive Lorraine and Maggie over to Toledo, so she can catch
an early plane. He would also be glad to mix a Jefferson Special cocktail, so they may all drink to Lorraine's health.

"By the way, I got a two-minute interview with Beverly Carlton at the station," Bert suddenly recalls. "You were right, Mr.
Whiteside— He's quite something."

"Go ahead, Bert—mix the drinks," interjects Maggie, uneasily.

BERT—I was lucky to get even two minutes. He was in a
telephone booth most of the time. Couldn't hear what he was
saying, but from the faces he was making it looked like a scene
from one of his plays.

MAGGIE (*hiding her frenzy*)—Bert, mix those drinks, will you?

WHITESIDE (*suddenly galvanized*)—Just a minute, if you

please, Jefferson. Mr. Carlton was in a telephone booth at the station?

BERT—Certainly was—I thought he'd never come out. Kept talking and making the damnedest faces for about five minutes.

MAGGIE (*tensely*)—Bert, for goodness' sake, will you—

WHITESIDE (*ever so sweetly*)—Bert, my boy, I have an idea I shall love the Jefferson Special. Make me a double one, will you? My headache has gone with the wind.

BERT—Okay. (*He goes.*)

WHITESIDE (*his eyes gleaming, immediately whirls his wheel chair across the room to the telephone—a finger to his lips*)— Sssh! Philo Vance is now at work.

LORRAINE—What?

WHITESIDE—Sssh! (*He picks up telephone. His voice is absolutely musical.*) Operator! Has there been a call from England over this telephone within the past half hour? . . . Yes, I'll wait.

LORRAINE—Sherry, what *is* all this?

WHITESIDE—What's that? There have been no calls from England for the past three days? Thank you . . . Now, will you repeat that, please? . . . Blossom Girl. (*He beckons to* LORRAINE, *then puts the receiver to her ear.*) Hear it, dear? (*Then again to the operator.*) Thank you and a Merry Christmas. (*He hangs up.*) Yes, indeed, it seems we're going to have a real old-fashioned Christmas.

LORRAINE (*stunned*)—Sherry, what is all this? What's going on? What does this mean?

WHITESIDE—My dear, you have just played the greatest love scene of your career with your old friend, Beverly Carlton.

LORRAINE—Why—why, that's not true. I was talking to Cedric. What do you mean?

WHITESIDE—I mean, my blossom, that that was Beverly you poured out your girlish heart to, not Lord Bottomley. Ah, me, who'd have thought five minutes ago that you would not be going to London!

LORRAINE—Sherry, stop it! What is this? I want this explained.

WHITESIDE—Explained? You heard the operator, my dear. All I can tell you is that Beverly was indulging in one of his famous bits of mimicry, that's all. You've heard him do Lord Bottomley before, haven't you?

LORRAINE (*as it dawns on her*)—Yes . . . Yes, of course . . .

But—but why would he want to do such a thing! This is one of
the most dreadful— Oh, my God! Those cables!

In a single bound Lorraine has reached the telephone. Soon
she has Cosette on the wire again and, in great excitement, has
canceled all her previous instructions. Cosette, it is to be gathered from Lorraine's conversation, is a trifle confused. Whiteside would caution Lorraine. It would be wiser for her to take
things easy. But Lorraine is in no mood to take anything easy.
Why this thing has happened to her; why Beverly Carlton would
be so unutterably low as to play her a trick like that, she cannot understand.

Suddenly a light begins to break. Lorraine glances toward the
dining room into which Bert Jefferson has disappeared. The
next second her glance has shifted to Maggie's bracelet. Now
she begins to understand—

"Of course," Lorraine exclaims, exultantly. "It makes complete sense now. And to think that I nearly—well! Wild horses
couldn't get me out of here now, Maggie! And if I were you
I'd hang onto the bracelet, dear. It'll be something to remember him by!"

The radio men have come in from the library and are com-
pleting their hook-up. Sheridan Whiteside will be on the air
in another couple of minutes. Bert has come from the dining
room with a tray full of "Jefferson Specials." Noting the radio
preparations he is afraid there will not be time to serve them,
but Lorraine is reassuring. She is not leaving after all. Her
plans have all been changed.

"And I hear you've written a simply marvelous play, Mr. Jefferson," adds Lorraine warmly. "I want you to read it to me—
tonight. Will you? We'll go back to the Mansion House right
after dinner, and you'll read me your play."

BERT—Why—why, I should say so. I'd be delighted. . . .
Maggie, did you hear that? Say! I'll bet *you* did this. You
arranged the whole thing. Well, it's the finest Christmas present you could have given me. (MAGGIE *looks at him for one
anguished moment. Then without a word, she dashes into the
hall, grabs her coat and flings herself out of the house.* BERT,
bewildered, stands looking after her.)

STANLEY (*coming pellmell down the stairs with* MRS. STAN-
LEY, *each clutching a letter*)—Mr. Whiteside! My son has run
off on a freighter and my daughter is marrying an anarchist!

They say *you* told them to do it!

Mrs. Stanley—My poor June! My poor Richard! This is the most awful—

Westcott (*raising his voice*)—Please! *Please!* Quiet! We're going on the air. (Stanley *chokes and looks with fury.* Mrs. Stanley *is softly crying.*)

Dr. Bradley (*emerging from the dining room*)—Oh! I see you're still busy.

Stanley (*bursting forth*)—Mr. Whiteside, you are the—

Westcott (*yelling*)—*Quiet!* For God's sake, quiet! QUIET! . . . All right, boys! (*From the hallway come six Choir Boys, dressed in their robes. They take their places by the microphone as the voice of the technician completes the hook-up.*)

Technician—O.K., New York. (*He raises his arm, waiting to give the signal.* Westcott *is watching him. There is a dead pause of about five seconds.* John *and* Sarah *are on tiptoe in the dining room. Then the arm drops.*)

Westcott (*into the microphone*)—Good evening, everybody. Cream of Mush brings you Sheridan Whiteside. (*The Leader gestures to the Choir Boys, and they raise their lovely voices in "Heilige Nacht." Another gesture from* Westcott, *and* Whiteside *begins to speak, with the boys singing as a background.*)

Whiteside—This is Whiteside speaking. On this eve of eves, when my own heart is overflowing with peace and kindness, I think it is most fitting to tell once again the story of that still and lustrous night, nigh onto two thousand years ago, when first the star of Bethlehem was glimpsed in a wondrous sky . . .

"The famous Whiteside voice goes out over the air to the listening millions as—"

The curtain falls.

ACT III

It is Christmas morning. The bright December sun is pouring into the Stanley library and Sheridan Whiteside is roaring lustily for Miss Preen from the other side of the library doors. Once the nurse arrives and opens the doors Mr. Whiteside rolls himself into the living room. He is quite angry with his "Lady Nausea."

He is even more upset when Maggie Cutler comes down the stairs wearing a traveling suit and carrying a suitcase. She is taking the one o'clock train. She has brought him his keys and his driving license. He will know where to find his other things when he gets back to his New York apartment. But Mr. Whiteside is not accepting Miss Cutler's resignation without protest—

WHITESIDE—Just a moment, Mrs. Siddons! Where *were* you until three o'clock this morning? I sat up half the night in the station wagon, worrying about you. You heard me calling to you when you came in. Why didn't you answer me?

MAGGIE—Look, Sherry, it's over, and you've won. I don't want to talk about it.

WHITESIDE—Oh, come, come, come, come, come. What are you trying to do—make me feel like a naughty, naughty boy? Honestly, Maggie, sometimes you can be very annoying.

MAGGIE (*looking at him in wonder*)—You know, you're quite wonderful, Sherry, in a way. *You're* annoyed. I wish there was a laugh left in me. Shall I tell you something, Sherry? I think you are a selfish, petty egomaniac who would see his mother burned at the stake if that was the only way he could light his cigarette. I think you'd sacrifice your best friend without a moment's hesitation if he disturbed the sacred routine of your self-centered, paltry little life. I think you are incapable of any human emotion that goes higher up than your stomach, and I was the fool of the world for ever thinking I could trust you.

WHITESIDE (*pretty indignant at this*)—Well, as long as I live, I shall never do anyone a good turn again. I won't ask you to apologize, Maggie, but six months from now you will be thanking me instead of berating me.

MAGGIE—In six months, Sherry, I expect to be so far away from you— (*She is halted by a loud voice from the hallway, as the door bangs.*)

BERT (*entering, full of Christmas cheer with "Hello—hello—hello!"*)—Merry Christmas, everybody! Merry Christmas! I'm a little high, but I can explain everything. Hi, Maggie! Hi, Mr. Whiteside! Shake hands with a successful playwright. Maggie, why'd you run away last night? Where were you? Miss Sheldon thinks the play is wonderful. I read her the play and she thinks it's wonderful. Isn't that wonderful?

MAGGIE—Yes, that's fine, Bert.

BERT—Isn't that wonderful, Mr. Whiteside?

WHITESIDE—Jefferson, I think you ought to go home, don't you?

BERT—What? No—biggest day of my life. I know I'm a

little drunk, but this is a big day. We've been sitting over in
Billy's Tavern all night. Never realized it was daylight until
it was daylight. . . . Listen, Maggie—Miss Sheldon says the
play needs just a little bit of fixing—do it in three weeks. She's
going to take me to a little place she's got in Lake Placid—just
for three weeks. Going to work on the play together. Isn't it
wonderful? Why don't you say something, Maggie?

WHITESIDE—Look, Bert, I suggest you tell us all about this
later.

Bert is agreeable to almost any plan. When Whiteside suggests that Dr. Bradley, who also has stopped in, take him to
breakfast and a cup of black coffee he accepts the suggestion
with enthusiasm. The sight of Bert on his way reduces Maggie
to tears. She is going to find it hard to forgive Whiteside for
what he has done. . . .

Harriet Stanley comes creeping mouselike down the stairs.
She would know the Whiteside reaction to her Christmas gift.
It happens that the great man has not yet opened it, but when
he does he is interested to find that it is an old photograph of
Miss Stanley when she was twenty-two and wearing her favorite
dress. Again he is struck with her resemblance to someone he
vaguely remembers. "What—what is it about that woman?" A
ring at the door bell and Miss Stanley has bolted up the stairs.

Miss Preen answers the bell and now there is a commotion in
the hall. A male voice can be heard inquiring if this is "Polly
Adler's?" And the next moment a protesting Miss Preen is carried bodily into the room in the arms of "a pixie-like gentleman
who is kissing her over and over."

The gentleman, it transpires, is Banjo, and Banjo has come to
spend Christmas with his old friend Whiteside. Banjo, to hear
him tell it, has just finished a picture for Darryl Zanuck and is
on his way to Nova Scotia. He wants to see Maggie, too.

Now the whole story comes out—the story of Maggie's defec-
tion, of Lorraine Sheldon's arrival and the kidnaping of Bert
Jefferson. Something obviously has to be done. Having brought
Lorraine on, Whiteside now must think of some way to be rid of
her. That's where he needs Banjo's help.

Now Miss Preen appears, also in street clothes and with a
suitcase. She, also, is leaving.

"You realize, Miss Preen, that this is completely unprofes-
sional?" glowers Whiteside.

"I do indeed," answers Miss Preen, with firmness. "I am not

only walking out on this case, Mr. Whiteside—I am leaving the nursing profession. I became a nurse because all my life, ever since I was a little girl, I was filled with the idea of serving a suffering humanity. After one month with you, Mr. Whiteside, I am going to work in a munitions factory. From now on anything that I can do to help exterminate the human race will fill me with the greatest of pleasure. If Florence Nightingale had ever nursed *you*, Mr. Whiteside, she would have married Jack the Ripper instead of founding the Red Cross. Good day."

Mr. Whiteside has not quite recovered from this blow before Mrs. Stanley has rushed down the stairs with the news that Mr. Stanley is back and is bringing his daughter June with him. June is very depressed. Mr. Stanley is exceedingly stern, and very angry. With a wave of his arm he sends June upstairs with her mother and turns to give Mr. Whiteside the verbal currying he feels that obnoxious interferer in the Stanley affairs deserves.

Not only has he saved his daughter from the labor agitator to whom she might have been married, thanks to Mr. Whiteside, snaps Stanley, but his son, Richard, has also been apprehended in Toledo and is on his way home in the custody of the law. Furthermore Mr. Stanley has provided himself with a warrant for Mr. Whiteside's ejection, and two burly deputy sheriffs to see that it is properly served. Fifteen minutes is all he will allow Mr. Whiteside to pack up and get started—

"Fifteen minutes, Mr. Whiteside—and that means bag, baggage, wheel chair, penguins, octopus and cockroaches. I am now going upstairs to smash our radio, so that not even accidentally will I ever hear your voice again."

"Sure you don't want my autograph, old fellow?" blandly inquires Whiteside.

Banjo, still fondling the remains of a breakfast Sarah has given him, is also still pondering his friend's dilemma, but without results. There are just ten minutes left, as Mr. Stanley announces from the top of the stair.

And then Lorraine Sheldon comes. She is fairly radiant this Christmas morning. Everything is working out beautifully. She has been practically swept off her feet by Bert Jefferson's play and he is such an attractive man she is deliriously happy in contemplating the Lake Placid sojourn.

Maggie has come from the library with a sheaf of papers. They contain a list of all the things of which Whiteside will want to be reminded—except the New Year's Eve broadcast, and there is a schedule of that somewhere.

"New Year's Eve?" coos Lorraine. "Oh, Bert and I'll hear it in Lake Placid. You were at my cottage up there once, weren't you, Sherry? It's lovely, isn't it? Away from everything. Just snow and clear, cold nights. (*The door bell rings.*) Oh, that's probably Bert. I told him to meet me here. (MAGGIE, *as though she had not heard a word, goes quietly into the library.* LOR- RAINE *relaxes.*) You know, I'm looking forward to Lake Placid. Bert's the kind of man who will do all winter sports beautifully."

"Will he get time?" Banjo asks, gently.

And now there is a further commotion at the door. A moment later three American Express men have brought in an Egyptian mummy case which has been sent as a little Christmas offering to Sheridan Whiteside by his old friend, the Khedive of Egypt. Rather elaborate and quite heavy. The men stand it in the center of the room and go—just as Mr. Stanley appears again at the head of the stairs—

"*Five* minutes, Mr. Whiteside," he calls, and adds, with a shaking finger pointed at the mummy case, "including *that!*"

Lorraine, depressed a little because Bert has not appeared and because her beloved Sherry is not at all his old Christmasy self, turns to the mummy case with interest—

"You know, I think it is rather beautiful," she is saying. "I must go to Egypt some day—I really must. I know I'd love it. The first time I went to Pompeii I cried all night. All those people—all those lives. Where are they now? Sherry! Don't you ever think about that? I do. Here was a woman—like myself—a woman who once lived and loved, full of the same passions, fears, jealousies, hates. And what remains of any of it now? Just this, and nothing more. (*She opens the case, then, with a sudden impulse, steps into it and folds her arms, mummy-fashion.*) A span of four thousand years—a mere atom in the eternity of time—and here am I, another woman living out her life. I want to cry."

She closes her eyes and as she stands there the eyes of White- side and Banjo meet. "The same idea has leaped into their minds." Casually Banjo walks toward the case. Just as he reaches it Lorraine steps blandly out. She must put such serious thoughts out of her mind this glorious Christmas Day. White- side has been greatly impressed.

"Lorraine dear, have you ever played Saint Joan?" he asks.

LORRAINE—No, I haven't, Sherry. What makes you ask that?

WHITESIDE—There was something about your expression as you stood in that case—there was an absolute halo about you.

LORRAINE—Why, Sherry, how sweet!

WHITESIDE—It transcended any mortal expression I've ever seen. Step into it again, dear.

LORRAINE—Sherry, you're joshing me—aren't you?

WHITESIDE—My dear, I don't make light of these things. I was deeply moved. There was a strange beauty about you, Lorraine—pure da Vinci. Please do it again.

LORRAINE—Well, I don't know exactly what it was that I did, but I'll— (*She starts to step into the case again, then changes her mind.*) Oh, I feel too silly, Sherry. (BANJO's *eyes are fixed somewhere on the ceiling, but he is somewhat less innocent than he seems.*)

WHITESIDE (*returning to the battle*)—Lorraine dear, in that single moment you approached the epitome of your art, and you should not be ashamed of it. You asked me a little while ago what I wanted for a Christmas present. All I want, Lorraine, is the memory of you in that mummy case.

LORRAINE—Why, darling, I'm—all choked up. (*Crossing her arms, she takes a moment or two to throw herself in the mood, then steps reverently into the case.*) "Dust thou art, and dust to dust—"

WHITESIDE (*leaping out of the chair as* BANJO *closes and fastens the case*)—Eureka!

BANJO—There's service for you!

WHITESIDE—Will she be all right in there?

BANJO—Sure—She can breathe easy. I'll let her out as soon as we get on the plane. . . . What are we going to do now? How do we get this out of here?

WHITESIDE—One thing at a time—that's the next step.

BANJO—Think fast, Captain. Think fast.

Maggie is in from the library again with still another sheaf of Whiteside papers. She has put everything in order and would know what Whiteside would like to keep and what she should throw out. She is about to dispose of Harriet Stanley's picture when Whiteside reaches for it. Suddenly the flash of recollection for which he has been seeking comes to him. A look of triumph gleams in the master's eye, but he contrives to smother his excitement until Maggie has gone back to the library. Then he is on his feet in an instant, shouting to a startled Banjo: "I knew I'd seen this face before! I knew it! Now I know how to get this out of here." He has tapped the mummy case knowingly. At which instant a thoroughly satisfied Mr. Stanley comes down the stairs. "The time is up, Mr. Whiteside," he calls. "Fifteen minutes."

WHITESIDE—Ah, yes, Mr. Stanley. Fifteen minutes. But just one favor before I go. I would like you to summon those two officers and ask them to help this gentleman down to the airport with this mummy case. Would you be good enough to do that, Mr. Stanley?

STANLEY—I will do nothing of the kind.

WHITESIDE (*ever so sweetly*)—Oh, I think you will, Mr. Stanley. Or shall I inform my radio audience, on my next broadcast, that your sister, Harriet Stanley, is none other than the famous Harriet Sedley, who murdered her mother and father with an ax twenty-five years ago in Gloucester, Massachusetts. . . . (*At which* MR. STANLEY *quietly collapses into a chair*.) Come, Mr. Stanley, it's a very small favor. Or would you rather have the good folk of Mesalia repeating at your very doorstep that once popular little jingle:

> "Harriet Sedley took an ax
> And gave her mother forty whacks,
> And when the job was nicely done,
> She gave her father forty-one."

Remember, Mr. Stanley, I too am giving up something. It would make a hell of a broadcast. . . . Well?

STANLEY (*licked at last*)—Mr. Whiteside, you are the damnedest person I have ever met.

WHITESIDE—I often think so myself, old fellow. . . . Officers, will you come in here, please?

BANJO—Whiteside, you're a great man. (*He places a reverent kiss on the mummy case.*)

WHITESIDE (*as the deputies enter*)—Come right in, officers. Mr. Stanley would like you to help this gentleman down to the airport with this mummy case. He is sending it to a friend in Nova Scotia.

BANJO—Collect.

WHITESIDE—Right, Mr. Stanley?

STANLEY (*weakly*)—Yes. . . . Yes.

WHITESIDE—Thank you, gentlemen—handle it carefully. . . . Banjo, my love, you're wonderful and I may write a book about you.

BANJO—Don't bother—I can't read. (*To* MAGGIE *as she enters from the library.*) Good-by, Maggie—love conquers all. . . . Don't drop that case, boys—it contains an antique. (*And he goes out with the mummy case, to say nothing of* MISS LORRAINE SHELDON.)

MAGGIE (*catching on to what has happened*)—Sherry! Sherry, was that—?

WHITESIDE—It was indeed. The field is clear and you have my blessing.

MAGGIE—Sherry! Sherry, you old reprobate!

WHITESIDE—Just send me a necktie some time. My hat and coat, Maggie, and also your railroad ticket. I am leaving for New York.

MAGGIE—You're leaving, Sherry?

WHITESIDE—Don't argue, Rat Girl— Do as you're told.

MAGGIE—Yes, Mr. Whiteside. (*She goes happily into the library, just as* BERT *returns.*)

BERT—Mr. Whiteside, I want to apologize for—

WHITESIDE—Don't give it a thought, Bert. There's been a slight change of plan. Miss Sheldon is off on a world cruise— I am taking your play to Katharine Cornell. Miss Cutler will explain everything. (MAGGIE *brings* WHITESIDE'S *coat, hat, cane.*) Oh, thank you, Maggie, my darling.

DR. BRADLEY (*coming out of the library. Still trying*)—Mr. Whiteside, are you very busy?

WHITESIDE—Ah, yes, Doctor. *Very* busy. But if you ever get to New York, Doctor, try and find me. (*He takes* MAGGIE *in his arms.*) Good-by, my lamb. I love you very much.

MAGGIE—Sherry, you're wonderful.

WHITESIDE—Nonsense. . . . Good-by, Jefferson. You'll never know the trouble you've caused.

BERT—Good-by, Mr. Whiteside.

WHITESIDE—Good-by, Mr. Stanley. I would like to hear, in the near future, that your daughter has married her young man and that your son has been permitted to follow his own bent. OR ELSE. . . . Merry Christmas, everybody!

"And out he strolls. But the worst is yet to come. There is a loud crash on the porch, followed by an anguished yell. Maggie gives a little shriek and rushes out. Bert and the Doctor rush after her. Down the stairs come Mrs. Stanley, June and Richard. From the dining room John and Sarah come running. 'What's

happened?' 'What is it?' And then we see. Into view come
Bert and the Doctor, carrying Mr. Whiteside between them. He
is screaming his head off: 'Miss Preen! Miss Preen! I want
Miss Preen back! . . . Mr. Stanley, I am suing you for *three*
hundred and fifty thousand dollars!' Mr. Stanley throws up his
hands in despair. Mrs. Stanley simply faints away."

THE CURTAIN FALLS

THE MALE ANIMAL
A Comedy in Three Acts

By James Thurber and Elliott Nugent

SHORTLY after the first of the year, on January 9, 1940, to be exact, "The Male Animal" scored the third knockout comedy success of the 1939-40 theatre season in New York. Broadway had, previous to the holidays, welcomed two wildly successful comedy hits with open mouths and slightly hysterical guffaws—in greeting the Kaufman-Hart "The Man Who Came to Dinner" and the Lindsay-Crouse "Life with Father." It looked very much like a comedy year.

James Thurber and Elliott Nugent, authors of this gay college comedy, were fellow undergraduates at Ohio State in the class of 1920. They were also fellow editors of the college paper, "The Lantern," and they were even then determined to collaborate one day in the writing of a play. It took them nearly twenty years to get around to it.

Meantime young Mr. Nugent had followed a successful acting career, first with his family and then on his own, by becoming a director of motion pictures in Hollywood, and Mr. Thurber had tried a variety of things, starting with a State Department clerkship and ending up as a cartoonist and editorial contributor to the *New Yorker* magazine.

It is recorded that after the collaborators finally got "The Male Animal" sketched out, both as to story and characters, it took them only three months to get it into rehearsal. They tried it out first on the Pacific Coast and were so encouraged by its reception there that they brought it to Broadway direct. Its success was immediate and was generously sustained through the Winter.

It is a Friday afternoon in the late Fall when we first meet Professor "Tommy" Turner and Ellen, his wife, of "The Male Animal." They have been preparing for a small and early cocktail party in the living room of their modest home on the campus of Midwestern University in a small college town.

The Turner household budget is limited, but Mrs. Turner has been able to make the Turner living room attractive. "There are some good prints on the walls. The hangings are cheerful, and the furniture, picked up through various bargains and in-

215

heritances, goes together to make a pleasing, informal atmosphere." Two small sofas and a variety of occasional chairs and end tables add to the comfort of the room.

Cleota, a colored maid, has come to answer a telephone that has been ringing insistently. Cleota is a little dumb, and it may be a little deaf, but she manages to let the caller know that Mr. Turner is not at home at the moment. He is out buying "likkah."

A moment later she is able to recall for Mrs. Turner that a Dr. Damon had called and was either coming over to see Mr. Turner or would like Mr. Turner to come to see him—"or sumpin'."

Ellen Turner "is an extremely pretty young woman about twenty-nine or thirty. Quick of speech and movement, she has a ready smile and a sweetness of personality that warms the room. She is completely feminine and acts always from an emotional, not an intellectual stimulus."

Now Prof. Turner has arrived. He carries flowers for Ellen and two wrapped bottles of liquor for the party. "Tommy" Turner is "a young associate professor, thirty-three years old. He wears glasses, is rather more charming than handsome. His clothes are a little baggy. He has a way of disarranging his hair with his hands, so that he looks like a puzzled spaniel at times."

Before Ellen has finished placing the flowers in a vase of water there is a rush of youth through the door. Patricia Stanley, Ellen's young and vivacious sister, has arrived with Wally Myers, a large and somewhat awkward fullback. These two come with news of the arrival at the Beta House of one Joe Ferguson, a Midwestern hero of other days, and an old friend of Ellen's. Patricia is mildly excited by the arrival of Mr. Ferguson because she knows something of Ellen's one-time romantic interest in him, but Wally is completely thrilled at the very thought of meeting this "all-time all-American" hero.

"Does he mean that Joe now belongs to the ages—like Lincoln?" Tommy would know.

"Um-hum, in a way," Ellen answers, casually.

"Well, I suppose he has passed into legend. I used to admire him myself—almost," admits Tommy.

Another expected guest is Ed Keller. It is a little more difficult for Tommy to take Mr. Keller. But Ed, as Ellen explains, has been asked so Joe Ferguson would have someone to talk football to. "Besides, Ed's his closest friend here. He practically paid Joe's way through college. You can stand the Kellers one night."

"Just barely. I don't know how to entertain trustees."

Tommy is rather pleased to hear that Dean Damon has phoned. He thinks probably the Dean wants to see him about a promotion that has practically been confirmed. The promotion means $500 a year more for Tommy—and a fur coat next Winter for Ellen! Tommy gets a little kiss for this thought, but he is in trouble the next minute when Ellen discovers all the match boxes missing from the ash trays.

"I haven't seen any match boxes," Tommy is protesting, as Ellen proceeds to search his pockets. "What's going on here? Say, you look very pretty tonight. That's a new dress, isn't it?"

ELLEN—No. It's my hair that's bothering you. It's done a new way.

TOMMY—Doesn't bother me. I like it.

ELLEN (*who has found two match boxes*)—One more.

TOMMY—Oh, you exaggerate this match-box thing. Oh. (*Hands her one.*) I ought to take you out to dinner more and show you off.

ELLEN—Well, we're going out tonight after the rally.

TOMMY—I mean just the two of us. Tonight will be just like old times. Remember how Joe was always horning in on our dinner dates? I don't believe we ever had one that he didn't come over and diagram the Washington Monument play or something on the tablecloth with a pencil.

ELLEN—Statue of Liberty play, darling.

TOMMY—He was always coming. I never saw him going.

ELLEN—There's still one missing.

TOMMY—I haven't got it. (*He finds it.*) I'll bet Joe does something to get his wife down. Probably cleans his guns with doilies. Clumsy guy. Always knocking knives and forks on the floor.

ELLEN—He wasn't clumsy. He was very graceful. He was a swell dancer. (*She puts away some books.*)

TOMMY—I remember he got the first and the last dance with you the last time we all went to a dance together.

ELLEN—Phi Psi Christmas dance, wasn't it?

TOMMY—No, the May dance. Out at the Trowbridge Farm. Remember how it rained?

ELLEN—I remember I had the last dance with Joe because you disappeared somewhere.

TOMMY—No, I was watching—from behind some ferns.

ELLEN—They played "Three O'Clock in the Morning" and

"Who?" It was a lovely night, wasn't it?

TOMMY—No, it poured down. You and Joe were dancing out on the terrace when it started. You both got soaked, but you kept right on dancing.

ELLEN—Oh, yes, I remember. My dress was ruined.

TOMMY—You were shining wet—like Venus and Triton.

ELLEN—Why didn't you cut in?

TOMMY—I had a cold. Besides, my feet hurt.

The ringing of the doorbell sends Tommy scurrying upstairs to dress. The visitors are Dean Damon and Michael Barnes. Dean Damon is at the head of the English department of Midwestern. "He is a tall, thin, distinguished-looking man of some sixty-five years. . . . He talks slowly . . . often hesitates, peers over his glasses before saying the last word of a phrase or sentence." Michael Barnes, a senior in the Arts College, "is an intensely serious young man and a fine literary student."

Dr. Damon has dropped in, unofficially, before the party to speak to Prof. Turner about a new problem of which young Mr. Barnes is the center. As editor of *The Lit* Michael has written what Dr. Damon characterizes as "another of his fiery editorials," and which he proceeds to read aloud.

"When this so-called University forces such men out of its faculty as Professor Kennedy, Professor Sykes, and Professor Chapman, because they have been ignorantly called Reds, it surrenders its right to be called a seat of learning," Michael has written. "It admits that it is nothing more nor less than a training school for bond salesmen, farmers, real estate dealers and ambulance chasers. It announces to the world that its faculty is subservient . . ." Damon peers over his glasses at Michael.

MICHAEL—Oh, I didn't mean you, of course, Dr. Damon.

DAMON— ". . . That its faculty is subservient to its trustees, and that its trustees represent a political viewpoint which must finally emerge under its proper name, which is—Fascism."

PATRICIA—Oh, Michael! There you go again!

DAMON—Wait till you hear where he has actually gone.

PATRICIA—Isn't that all?

DAMON—Unhappily, there is more.

PATRICIA—Oh, Lord! (TOMMY *sits down.*)

DAMON (*continuing*)—"These professors were not Reds. They were distinguished liberals. Let us thank God that we still have one man left who is going ahead teaching what he believes should be taught."

TOMMY—Who's that?

DAMON—Sh! "He is not afraid to bring up even the Sacco-Vanzetti case. He has read to his classes on the same day Vanzetti's last statement and Lincoln's letter to Mrs. Bixby." I hope we are not alienating the many friends of Abraham Lincoln. (TOMMY *rises and glances at* MICHAEL *questioningly.*) "The hounds of bigotry and reaction will, of course, be set upon the trail of this courageous teacher, but, if they think they are merely on the spoor of a lamb they are destined to the same disappointment as the hunters who, in chasing the wild boar, came accidentally upon a tigress and her cubs. Our hats are off to Professor Thomas Turner of the English Department." That's all.

ELLEN—Tommy?

TOMMY—Michael, I think you might have consulted me about this.

PATRICIA—Michael, you fool! They'll kick you out of school for this—and Tommy, too!

ELLEN—You never told me you had brought up the Sacco-Vanzetti case in your classes, Tommy.

DAMON—Yes, just what is this Vanzetti letter you have read?

TOMMY—I haven't read it yet.

MICHAEL—When you told me the other day you were going to read it, I thought you meant that day.

TOMMY—No, Michael, I just meant some day. But I was talking to you as a friend, I was not giving an interview to an editor.

ELLEN—But why were you going to read this letter, Tommy?

TOMMY—Because it's a fine piece of English composition and I'm teaching a class in English composition. An obscure little class. I don't want any publicity, Michael. I just want to be let alone.

ELLEN—But, Tommy, nobody thinks of Vanzetti as a writer.

TOMMY—It happens that he developed into an extraordinary writer. I don't think you could help being interested in the letter yourself, Dr. Damon.

DAMON—You would be surprised at my strength of will in these matters, Thomas. What I am interested in is preserving some air of academic calm here at Midwestern—and also in retaining my chair in the English Department.

PATRICIA—You don't want to get Tommy kicked out of school, do you, Michael?

MICHAEL—No. I didn't think of that. I thought Mr. Turner

was about the only man we had left who would read whatever he
wanted to to his classes.   I thought he was the one man who
would stand up to these stadium builders.

TOMMY—I'm not standing up to anyone, Michael.   I'm not
challenging anyone.   This is just an innocent little piece I wanted
to read.   (MICHAEL *turns away*.)

ELLEN (*rises*)—I know it must be all right, Tommy, but you
can't read it now.   Keller and the other trustees kicked Don
Chapman out last month for doing things just as harmless as this.
(*Turning to* MICHAEL.)   You'll have to change that editorial,
Michael.

MICHAEL—I can't.   The magazines were run off the presses
last night.   They've already been delivered to the newsstands.

DAMON—They go on sale in the morning.   (*To* ELLEN.)   I
think that our—er—tigress here may have to issue a denial tomorrow.   After all, he hasn't read it.

Dr. Damon is not too reassuring when Patricia would know if
he thinks Michael will be kicked out of school.   He quite understands how Michael intended the editorial, but he is afraid Ed
Keller won't understand, and the Keller influence "rolls like the
juggernaut over the careers of young professors."

They have left now, Patricia dismissing young Michael a little
snippily.   Tommy has gone to change to his gray suit, explaining
to Ellen as he goes that he probably can put off reading the
Vanzetti piece for awhile.   Tommy is no tiger, he knows that, but
he doesn't like to be thought a pussycat, either.   He is singing
a snatch of "Who's Afraid of the Big Bad Wolf?" as he disappears. . . .

Now Ed Ferguson has arrived, trailed by the adoring Wally.
Joe bursts through the door as soon as Ellen opens it and explodes
with enthusiasm—

"Ellen!   How are you, baby?   God, you look great!   Why,
you're younger and prettier than ever!   If I were a braver man
I'd kiss you.   Doggone it, I will kiss you!"

With which declaration he kisses Ellen on the cheek, hugs her,
lifts her off the floor and whirls her around.   Joe "is all we have
been led to expect—big, dynamic, well dressed, prosperous.   He
is full of good nature and a boundless enthusiasm for everything."

"It's terribly nice to see you again, Joe," declares Ellen, catching something of his ebullience.   "If I were a younger woman,
I'd say it's been all of ten years."

"Gosh, this is swell!   Where's the great Thomas?"

"Tommy will be right down. I see Wally found you—so you've met?"

"Yeh. We joined forces outside."

Football having been suggested, there are a couple of points that Joe would have settled. Is Stalenkiwiecz going in at the other half tomorrow? No, Wierasocka has been picked for that honor, Wally explains. "Stalenkiwiecz is laid up. They think he's got whooping cough."

The information is not pleasing to Joe. "I've got a thousand fish on that game," he confesses. . . .

Joe's greeting of Tommy is friendly, though a shade formal. It is wonderful to find the Turners looking so well—which reminds him that he has brought Ellen a few "flowering weeds" for her birthday. He recovers a box of orchids from the hall. Ellen is naturally delighted. Tommy had given her some "flowering weeds" too—also for her birthday—she lies.

"Boy, it's sure great to be here!" enthuses Joe.

"It's nice to have you. . . . Staying long?" Tommy would know.

"Got to be in Washington next week. Well, Tommy, I see you've still got a lot of books."

"Oh, yes."

"You know I never get a chance to read books."

"Say, you must have a swell job!" ejaculates the wide-eyed Wally.

"By the time I get through at night, I'm lucky if I can keep up with what's going on in the world. Way things are changing, you gotta do that. I take fifteen magazines. That keeps me busy."

"Tommy's had several articles in *Harper's* and the *Atlantic*."

"No! Say, that's fine! But you'll have to boil them down to *The Reader's Digest* to reach me, Tommy. You know, that's a great little magazine."

It is while Tommy is mixing drinks that Joe confesses a family problem. He and his wife are being divorced, but they are both taking it in their stride. Joe had even had Mrs. Ferguson and her new boy friend out to lunch. That, to Tommy, would seem rather complicated—

"Oh, you're not up to date, Tommy," chides Ellen. "That's the modern way of doing things."

"Sure. Take it in your stride," repeats Joe. "Gosh, Ellen, I can't take my eyes off you!"

With the arrival of the Damons the party begins to get under way. Patricia comes downstairs to help with the serving. There are cocktails and sherry and a lot of conversation. Then Ed and Myrtle Keller arrive. Keller "is a big, loud, slightly bald man of about thirty-eight, heavy around the middle." Myrtle, his wife, "also in her late thirties, dresses well and is not bad-looking, was once pretty, but is now a slightly faded blonde."

Now Ed, passing the Turners by with a "Hi!" and a "Hello!" has discovered his old pal Joe and the air is filled with gurgles of satisfaction mixed with an assortment of "Hiya, you old rascal!" "Hahya, boy!" "Hello, you old son-of-a-gun!" "Gosh, I'm glad to see you!" "Gee, you're looking swell, Ed, old boy!" and so on. The acompanying backslaps are also impressively enthusiastic.

Gradually the party settles. Joe, remembering Ellen's birthday again, is all for drinking a toast. Which they do with song. Tommy, serving the cocktails, is not neglecting his own glass. He tries valiantly to keep up with the small talk. He would talk business with Joe, if he could remember whether Joe's business was in Detroit or Pittsburgh. And he would exchange views on real estate with Ed, if Ed were interested. Ed is just plain disgusted with business. "What can you expect, with that man in the White House?" demands Ed, and promptly answers himself. "You know what I think? I think he's crazy!"

The women, by themselves, are having a grand time discussing operations, consultations and such. Ellen, sitting by Tommy on the couch, is gently trying to get Tommy's drink away from him.

"Well, Dr. Damon, we men on the Board of Trustees are certainly glad that this Red scare is over," Ed Keller is saying.

"No doubt you are," agrees Dr. Damon.

ED—Now maybe the new stadium project will get somewhere.
DAMON (*eagerly moving toward* ED)—And the Endowment Fund?
ED—Yeh, sure—that's important too. I'm working to convince the substantial alumni that we've got all this Parlor-Pink business over and done with. Got 'em all weeded out.
JOE—Yeah—all that newspaper stuff was pretty bad.
ED—Sure. Nobody felt like coming through for anything when they read about men like Kennedy and Sykes and Chapman being on the faculty. That Chapman was nothing but a damn Red. (DAMON *covers his disgust and turns to* ELLEN.)
TOMMY—No, he wasn't, Mr. Keller. Don Chapman was a humanist.

ELLEN (*laying a quieting hand on* TOMMY's *arm*)—We knew him very well.

JOE—How do you know he wasn't a Red, Tommy?

ED—He went to Soviet Russia for his vacation once, didn't he?

TOMMY—He just went to see the Drama Festival.

ED (*suspiciously*)—Well, it's a mighty long way to go to see a show.

Cleota has announced supper and the movement is toward the dining room. Presently, one by one, two by two, the guests are back with loaded plates. Out of the scattered buzz of conversation pops the name of Michael Barnes, followed by references to a remarkable editorial. At least Dr. Damon has told Mrs. Damon that it is remarkable. Just now, however, Dr. Damon is very much concerned with a change of subject, but the curiosity of Mr. Keller has been aroused. He wants to know what it is that this young fellow Barnes has done—

"Oh, it's really nothing," insists Ellen.

"Well, since it's come up, Ellen, we might as well tell Mr. Keller," says Tommy. "He'll read about it tomorrow . . . (ELLEN *rises.*) I told Michael I was going to read something to one of my English classes, and he got a mistaken idea about it and wrote a sort of—"

ELLEN (*breaking in quickly*)—Just a silly little editorial—that's all.

ED—I see.

PATRICIA—Because Tommy isn't really going to read it at all.

ED—What was it this kid said you were going to read? Anything important?

TOMMY (*after a moment*)—It's a short, but beautifully written piece of English by Bartolomeo Vanzetti.

ED—Never heard of him. (*Then, as the name registers.*) Hey, you don't mean Vanzetti of Sacco and Vanzetti?

TOMMY—Yes, the same man.

ED—You mean you're going to read something he wrote?

TOMMY—Yes, I was going to.

ELLEN (*quickly*)—But now he's not—Michael didn't understand.

ED—Why would you ever think of such a dumb thing in the first place? (TOMMY *has lost any appetite he may have had. He rises and puts his plate and cup on the table.*)

TOMMY—It's part of a series. I read many such letters to my

class.

E<small>D</small>—You mean letters by anarchists?

T<small>OMMY</small> (*restrains himself*)—No, letters by men who were not professional writers—like Lincoln, General Sherman . . .

E<small>D</small>—Well, it's a damn good thing you changed your mind. Putting Lincoln and General Sherman in a class with Vanzetti! Wouldn't look very good.

J<small>OE</small>—What's this?

E<small>D</small>—Wait a minute. (*To* T<small>OMMY</small>.) Is this thing going to be printed? This editorial?

D<small>AMON</small>—We discovered it too late to stop it.

E<small>D</small>—And this kid didn't submit it to the publications committee?

D<small>AMON</small>—Unfortunately, he did not. Ellen, dear, Mrs. Damon and I must be running along.

E<small>LLEN</small>—Oh, I'm sorry.

D<small>AMON</small>—I have a committee meeting.

B<small>LANCHE</small> (*astonished*)—What committee?

D<small>AMON</small>—Come, Blanche.

B<small>LANCHE</small> (*rising*)—Oh, yes, that little committee.

E<small>D</small>—Well, I hope this thing's not too bad. You better deny it quick, Turner. I tell you! I'll call the papers in the morning.

T<small>OMMY</small>—No, I'll take care of it.

Ed's attention is temporarily diverted when Myrtle appears with a dish of sherbet for him, but he is still inclined to repeat his convictions that they don't want any more of this Red—or even Pink—business around there. Americanism is what they want to teach—

"But how can you define Americanism?" quietly demands Tommy.

"Why—er—everybody knows what Americanism is! What do you believe in?"

"I believe that a college should be concerned with ideas. Not just your ideas . . . or my ideas, but all ideas."

"No, sir! That's the *trouble* . . . too damn many ideas floating around. . . . You put ideas of any kind into young people's heads, and the first thing you know, they start believing them."

"On the contrary," interjects Dean Damon. "I have been putting ideas into young people's heads for forty-two years with no —visible—results whatever."

Blanche laughs a little dubiously and would get her husband started home. Before they can get away Mr. Keller has declared himself:

"Turner, you'd better think twice before you read anything," he says. "I can promise you the trustees will clamp down on any professor who tries anything funny! I'm telling you that for your own good."

The next minute Joe Ferguson has broken into the group with a demand for a little music and more fun. Soon the parade to the dining room has started again.

With the room cleared Ellen thinks she will have a chance to check on Tommy. Has he been drinking too much? There is a funny look in his eyes.

"Did you hear what Mr. Keller said to me?" Tommy demands. "I don't like to be talked to like that."

"Just because he was nasty and you've had a few drinks . . . Tommy, you're not going to go ahead and read that letter?"

TOMMY—Yes, Ellen, I think I have to.

ELLEN—Tommy, try to be practical for once. At least wait until you're not so mad. Try to think of this the way any other man would think of it.

TOMMY—I'm not any other man.

ELLEN—Well, try to be. Do you think Joe would do something that would get him in trouble just because somebody irritated him?

TOMMY—Joe! I don't see why you don't try to understand how *I* feel about this.

ELLEN—I'm simply trying to keep you out of a lot of trouble. I don't see why—

TOMMY—But you see how Joe would feel. That's very plain to you, isn't it?

ELLEN—Yes, it is. Joe wouldn't get all mixed up.

TOMMY—I'm not mixed up. I'm trying to understand what goes on in your mind. It *can't* be like Joe Ferguson's mind!

ELLEN—Oh, you and your mind! (*Turns away, exasperated.*) I have to go through such a lot with your mind!

TOMMY—Maybe you wouldn't if you understood it better.

ELLEN—Oh, I know, I know! I'm too dumb for you!

TOMMY—Now, Ellen, I didn't say that.

ELLEN—You said Joe and I were stupid.

TOMMY—I said he was.

ELLEN—But he isn't. He's a big man. In some ways he's smarter than you.

TOMMY—Well, you ought to know. (*He turns away from her.*)

ELLEN (*catching his arm*)—Oh, look, Tommy—what are we fighting about?

TOMMY (*turns*)—You said I was dumb.

ELLEN—Tommy, you've had too many drinks or you wouldn't say that.

TOMMY—No, I haven't, but I don't feel very well. I feel very unhappy and slightly sick.

ELLEN—I'll get you some bicarbonate of soda.

Tommy has started slowly up the stairs. Suddenly he decides he had better hurry and makes a dash. Noting his distress, Ellen would follow Tommy, but just then Joe Ferguson comes back from the dining room. Ellen explains that there's really nothing the matter. Tommy is feeling a little sick. He isn't used to drinking anything.

Joe is mildly sympathetic, but the Victrola has caught his eye and his interest. He hunts out a new record. And what does he find but the very tune they were playing at that May dance— "Who?"—

> "Who-o-o stole my heart away?
> Who-o-o makes me dream all day?
> Dreams I know can never come true.
> Seems as though I'd ever be blue.
> Who-o-o means my happiness . . ."

As naturally as if they had always danced to that song they begin dancing again. It certainly takes them both back. Ellen can remember that it was raining the night of the dance, and Joe recalls that Ellen had said she didn't know it. He is holding her closer now. Gradually they slow down to a stop and for a second stand looking at each other, "he ardently, she caught up in the music. Joe kisses her and she kisses back for a long moment, then tries to pull away." Joe tries to kiss Ellen again, but she protests—

"Oh, no, Joe, please, I . . . Say, how many cocktails did *I* have?"

They have started dancing again as the rumble of voices from the dining room rises. Tommy, "a little pale and disheveled, comes down the stairs and sees them dancing." Myrtle and Ed Keller come from the dining room.

"Look, Ed! Just like the old days, isn't it? Seeing them dancing together?"

"I'll say! They make a darn' handsome couple, don't they?"

"She dances like a dream," Joe tosses over his shoulder.

"Like a 'dream can never come true,' eh, Joe?" chuckles Ed. "You look mighty sweet in there, boy."

Ellen's eye catches Tommy on the stairs. She stops dancing and would go to him. Tommy's all right. He just thought he needed a little air. In the distance a band is heard. That excites everybody and there is a rush for the doors. From the kitchen Patricia brings a glass of bicarbonate of soda. That's for Tommy—

"Just—just put it by for a moment," says Tommy, turning to Ellen. "I'm going to walk around out here—until I feel better. Good night, everybody . . . You're coming to lunch tomorrow, aren't you, Joe?"

"Yes, sir!"

"That's what I thought."

Tommy has gone into the garden. The band music grows louder. The team and a lot of kids are headed for the Neil Avenue gate. Ed and Myrtle and Joe are all for getting over to the rally as soon as possible. And after the rally? Joe would like to take them all to the Dixie Club. Ellen would love that, but she remembers Tommy—

"No, I'm not going," she says to Joe, and then, raising her voice, she calls: "I'm going to stay here with you, Tommy."

"No, I'd rather you didn't, really," answers Tommy from the garden.

The band has stopped in front of the Turner house. Nutsy Miller, dressed in a band leader's uniform, is in to invite Joe Ferguson to ride in a carriage.

"Okay, fellas! Whatta ya say, Ellen—you ride with me. Some fun, huh!"

"Oh—all right! Hurray!" Ellen has caught the spirit of the celebration.

Now they are parading toward the door singing lustily—

> "And if we win the game,
> We'll buy a keg of booze,
> And we'll drink to old Midwestern
> Till we wobble in our shoes."

Outside the appearance of Joe Ferguson is greeted with cheers and a rah-rah-rah for the returned hero.

Tommy comes in from the garden. The shouting and the band

music fade into the distance. He has found the glass of soda and frowns at it. With a weak "Rah-rah-rah!" he crosses to the Victrola and starts the record. "Dreams I know can never come true . . ." trickles from the instrument—

"Tommy listens for a moment, then makes awkwardly, solemnly, a couple of dance steps, frowns, shakes his head, and drops onto a settee, giving it up. He drinks the bitter cup of soda as the music ends."

The curtain falls.

ACT II

It is just after lunch the following day. Ellen Turner is seated in the center of the Turner living room finishing her coffee. Joe Ferguson is demonstrating a football play to Patricia, who sits on the floor amid a scattered array of cups, plates, salt cellars, glasses, knives, saucers and forks.

"Now here—it's a balanced line. Move those two men out a little more," Joe is saying. Patricia follows instructions. "This is a wonderful play! The coach gave it to me in the strictest confidence!"

Ellen stops the demonstration long enough to inquire about Tommy. He has been away a long time and does not answer his office phone. Patricia had seen Tommy about an hour before. He was walking along the road back of the "Ag" buildings and he did not hear her when she called.

Joe is sure everything will work out all right, but his real interest is in his demonstration. With great particularity he explains the expected plays, executes a couple of fancy Notre Dame shifts, and finally, with the admitted aid of Lindstrom and Wiersocka, completely crushes the whole Michigan team with a smartly executed touchdown.

"It's a fake fake," Joe explains to his wondering audience. "It's an old play, so corny only a football genius like Coach Sprague would use it. With no interference at all, Wally cuts over and goes straight down the right side of the field. He stiff-arms the safety man . . . (Joe *is running with the cream pitcher now.*) . . . Touchdown!"

"Whoopee!" shouts Patricia, knocking over the jam pot in her excitement. "Oh, God! There goes Wupperman!" she exclaims. But even without Wupperman the game is already won.

"You can take the teams to the showers now, Cleota," Ellen instructs the maid.

Joe is still playing. He is holding the cream pitcher as the ball and backs over near the garden door to get a good start. "Did I ever tell you about how we used the Statue of Liberty play?" Joe asks, holding the cream pitcher back of him. "I would go back for a pass, and Jonesy would take it out of my hand and cut around to the left . . ."

Tommy, coming back from the garden, quietly lifts the cream pitcher from Joe's hand and returns to the garden. Joe, having lost himself in the play, is unconscious of the theft but suddenly realizes that both the imaginary ball and the cream pitcher are missing. He is vastly puzzled. The doorbell rings and the others forget the Statue of Liberty play—but Joe still can't find the cream pitcher. He looks to see if he has dropped it, slyly shakes the door drapes to be sure. His expression is that "of a prize bloodhound who has lost a scent."

Dr. Damon is at the door. He has brought a copy of *The Literary Magazine* containing Michael Barnes' editorial. "It is a powder magazine. The bombs are bursting all around," he explains.

The telephone rings. It is Ed Keller's office announcing that Mr. Keller is on his way over. Joe Ferguson has read the editorial and is properly shocked. "Calls the trustees Fascists! This kid's dangerous—un-American!" says Joe. "This is bad stuff for the university. I'm afraid all hell's going to break loose."

A moment later Ed Keller appears. He wants to see Turner before the game, and he is looking for President Cartwright of the college. Finding Dean Damon he takes the matter up with him.

"I thought Turner was going to deny this story," says Keller. "Papers keep calling *me*—they say he hasn't. Here I am, bearing the brunt of this damn disgraceful attack. 'Fascists!' You oughtta heard Si McMillan! And do you know Kressinger's in town from Detroit?"

"Is he a trustee, too?" asks Ellen.

"Oh, yes, young Michael has exploded his dynamite at a moment when the concentration of trustees is at its thickest."

"Yeh. There goes the new stadium. There goes your Endowment Fund! Unless something is done, and done quick! (*He turns on* ELLEN, *with a roar.*) Ellen, you tell your husband what I said!"

"Look, Ed, it isn't Ellen's fault."

"It isn't my fault, either," insists Keller, nearly breaking down. "I kept this whole week end free. I got my office full of eighteen-year-old Bourbon so we fellows could cut loose a little. And look what happens! All we need now is for Wiersocka to fumble a punt."

Keller has stomped out the door followed by Joe. Patricia, too, is preparing to rush from the house. She tried to talk to Michael on the phone but he hung up on her, and she is ready to "knock his ears off." Meantime she slips the bolt on the door—

"There, I've bolted that young genius out!" she announces. "Oh, Ellen! Give me a football player any time. (*She crosses to her sister for comfort.*) Give me a guy without so much intellect or whatever it is. Somebody that doesn't want to be bawling the world out all the time—always doing something brave or fine or something."

Michael has gone around the house and now comes through the garden door. He is greatly upset, but Patricia will have none of him.

"She won't listen to me, Mrs. Turner," protests Michael. "I'm not trying to ruin your husband's life or my life or anybody's life. It's the principle of the thing she won't see."

"Oh, the principle! (*She stomps over to him.*) I'll bet nobody else would make a fool of himself and his friends and—my brother-in-law—over a principle."

"All right, Pat," Michael answers, with the enormous gravity of the young man in love. "I'm very glad to know the qualities you admire in a man. They are certainly the noble virtues, and I'm sure Wally is lousy with them."

"Oh, make up your mind who you're imitating, Ralph Waldo Emerson or Hemingway! You—you *writer!*"

"*Now* who's imitating Hemingway?"

"I wish you'd go away!"

"I'm going! I'm going for good! I'm going out of your life!"

Michael has rushed to the door and jerked the knob, intending to make a dramatic exit. But the knob comes off in his hand.

"It's bolted, you dope!" Patricia flings over her shoulder as she disappears into the garden.

Michael adjusts the knob and gets the door open finally, whereupon in walks Tommy Turner with the knob from the other side of the door in his hand. He is vastly puzzled by this, but Michael's explanation is helpful. Patricia, concludes Michael, prefers a "handsome, half-witted half-back."

"You can't get anywhere with a woman who doesn't understand what you have to do," complains Michael. To which Tommy agrees.

Michael goes, but he is to come back later so that Prof. Turner can give him a piece of his mind.

And now Ellen finds Tommy. She is pleased to note that he had remembered where he lived. She is pleased, too, to tell him what has happened—that Ed Keller and Dr. Damon both have been there and that the promises to be a lot of trouble if Tommy doesn't hurry and deny Michael's story. As to that Tommy has his own ideas. He hasn't denied the story but he has thought a lot about what he wants to say. Among other decisions that have influenced him is one that he is now seeing Ellen and himself clearly for the first time.

Ellen can understand Tommy's jealousy if it has been stirred by his seeing Joe kiss her. She admits the kiss and she admits that she wanted to have a good time, which Tommy spoiled. But if he is going to be jealous she wishes he would make a job of it.

"If you're going to be jealous *be* jealous, rave or throw things, but don't act like the lead in a senior-class play!" demands Ellen.

"I'm trying to tell you that I don't care what you and Joe do! I'm trying to tell you that it's fine! It's very lucky that he came back just now."

ELLEN—Why, what do you mean?

TOMMY—I mean on the money *I* make, I can go on fine alone, reading whatever I want to to my classes! That's what I want! And that's what I'm going to do.

ELLEN—Oh, that's what you want! Suddenly that's what you want. More than me?

TOMMY—It isn't so sudden. Not any more sudden than your feeling for Joe. It's logical. We get in each other's way. You wear yourself out picking up after me. Taking matches out of my pockets. Disarranging my whole way of life. (*She follows him as he moves away from her.*)

ELLEN—Why haven't you said all this before?

TOMMY—I couldn't very well.

ELLEN—Why couldn't you? If you felt this way?

TOMMY—Well, we hadn't split up on this letter issue, for one thing—and then there was no place for you to go. (*He sits on a sofa.*) I didn't want you to have to go back to Cleveland, or to work in some tea shoppe!

ELLEN—Oh, I see. Some tea shoppe! That's what you think I'd have to do! Well, you needn't have spared my feelings. I can make as much money as you!

TOMMY—You don't have to, now.

ELLEN (*whirling*)—Oh, you mean you waited to tell me all this till Joe came along! I thought you were jealous of Joe. I could understand that. You aren't the least bit aroused at the idea of his kissing me—*out in the dark—for hours!*

TOMMY—No, I'm not.

ELLEN (*full of exclamation points*)—So that's why you've been wandering around! That's what you've been figuring out! How nice it would be if he would take me off your hands, so you could be left alone with your books and match boxes and *litter!* I suppose any man would do as well as Joe!

TOMMY (*rises to face her as she rushes up to him*)—He's not just any man, and you know that! He's always been in love with you, and you've always been in love with him! (*He is angry and jealous now and brings up his own exclamation points.*)

ELLEN—That's ridiculous!

TOMMY (*moving toward her*)—I felt it when I saw you dancing together. It was unmistakable. You've just admitted it.

ELLEN—Oh, you can't do that *now!* You can't be jealous *now*, just because you think I want you to be!

TOMMY (*rising to his big denunciation*)—I saw you dancing together—like angels! I saw you go out in that goddam carriage together! I saw you together years ago, when I was young enough and dumb enough to believe that I really took you away from him. There's something that happens when you two dance together that doesn't happen when *we* dance together!

ELLEN (*worried, angry and tired*)—All right—have it your way. If you want to be free, then I want to be free—and I've gone around for ten years mooning about Joe. . . . Well, maybe I have—maybe I have, because I'm certainly sick of you right now!

They are still shouting at each other when Joe Ferguson arrives with a bottle of rum for the party. Ellen thinks she could do with a little rum right now. Tommy goes for glasses and when the liquor is poured they drink a toast, proposed by Ellen, to Tommy's happiness. And then Ellen tells Joe what it is all about: Tommy wants to live alone. So, she and Tommy are breaking up.

This announcement is a little startling to Joe. And a little embarrassing. He thinks perhaps he had better go, but Tommy insists he should stay. After all, Joe has known Ellen as long as he has—

"I knew her a long time before you did," snaps Joe, getting

into the spirit of the quarrel, "and this is a hell of a way to be treating her."

"I was just saying I barged in and took her away from you."

"Oh, no, you didn't! You had nothing to do with it. She got sore at me on account of another girl."

"Oh, *that's* where I came in?"

"Sure. If you think you took her away from me, you're crazy. Here, you better have some rum."

Tommy doesn't need any rum. Joe goes on with the story of the quarrel that broke up his and Ellen's affair. Ellen had been jealous of another girl—a girl she insisted Joe had been friendly with and liked to boast about. So she had said she never wanted to see Joe again and he took her seriously. But Brenda (that's Joe's wife) says it only showed that Ellen really liked him.

Brenda, it seems, has always been jealous of Ellen—ever since she had found a picture Ellen had given him. It was the one with a floppy blue hat that went down over one eye. "She looks nice in hats like that," Tommy admits, remembering an old lovely hat.

That is too much for Ellen. She is crying now, and has thrown herself on the sofa. They are both of a mind to go to her, but Tommy isn't going to have any interference from anybody in this matter. And Joe is going to see to it that Ellen gets away from all this sort of thing.

Ellen wishes they would both please go away and quit their quarreling. "Nobody has said a word about what I want to do. You're going to settle that between yourselves. Bandying me back and forth!"

"Nobody's bandying you, Ellen," protests Tommy.

"I know when I'm being bandied! I don't want either of you! You can both go to hell!"

With this Ellen runs up the stairs and leaves her two knights facing each other. They cannot quite decide to which of them Ellen is referring. Joe is sorry for what has happened and a little puzzled as to how they got into it. "You're not sorry it happened. You're sorry I found it out," counters Tommy.

It is Tommy's notion that Joe has let himself in for something. He will have to devote a good deal of thought to Ellen from now on. Women are like that.

"This thing is too deep for jealousy or for anything but honesty," says Tommy. "A woman must not go on living with a man when she dances better with another man."

Furthermore Tommy is convinced that Joe had better go up-

stairs and comfort Ellen. She will need comforting and he is the
one she will expect. Joe, for his part, doesn't believe any such
thing. In fact, he doesn't feel at all right even about the thought
of going upstairs. But, when Tommy insists, up he goes. . . .

Michael is back, as Prof. Turner told him to be, but he doesn't
think he should be expected to take much more, after all that he
has been through—with Patricia and everything. Michael has
practically put Patricia out of his mind, though it is hard for him
to forget that she is the kind of a girl who knows something about
Shelley; the kind of a girl who would remember odd things like
"A Sonnet on Political Greatness"—

"Yes, but when an issue comes up and a man has to be himself
alone," continues Michael, "she reveals the true stature of her
character and goes off to Hennick's with that football player. I
saw them—right in the front window—drinking Seven-Up. He
uses a straw."

"Yes, but he's handsome. What is more, he whirls. He's a
hunter. He comes home at night with meat slung over his shoulders, and you sit there drawing pictures on the wall of your cave."

"I see. Maybe I ought to sock him with a ball-bat."

"No. You are a civilized man, Michael. If the male animal
in you doesn't like the full implications of that, he must nevertheless be swayed by Reason. You are not living in the days of
King Arthur when you fought for your woman. Nowadays, the
man and his wife and the other man talk it over. Quietly and
calmly. They all go out to dinner together."

"Intellectually, Patricia is sleeping with that guy. I feel like
going out tonight with the Hot Garters."

"With the what?"

"It's a girl. They call her that. What if she was kicked out
of the Pi Phi House? She's honest! She does what she believes
in! And—well, Hot Garters doesn't argue all the time anyway."

"Look, hasn't she got a name? You don't call her *that*, do
you?"

"Marcia Gardner. They just call her . . ."

"Yes, you told me what they call her."

"Patricia's not coming to class when you read that letter. She's
gone over to the Philistines. . . . Oh, God, Mr. Turner, I wish
I were like you! Middle-aged, settled down, happily married—
and through with all this hell you feel when you're young and in
love."

"Middle-aged?"

"Yes, you know what Rupert Brooke says:

'That time when all is over . . .
And love has turned to kindliness.'

Is kindliness peaceful?"

"Don't ask *me*."

From upstairs comes the sound of two quick crashes. A moment later Joe Ferguson, "worn and worried, his hair slightly disarranged," hurries down. Joe admits that he has every reason to be ruffled, but he refuses to discuss the matter before Michael.

With Michael gone Joe confesses that Ellen's actions when he tried to comfort her indicated that she was still pretty bitter. She had taken something Tommy had given her and smashed it against the wall. Every time Joe had mentioned Tommy's name Ellen had thrown something at him. Which might be significant—

"When Ellen and I had that fight about the girl," says Joe, "she threw things on account of me, and Brenda thinks that meant she was in love with me. Now she throws things on account of *you*."

"In both instances, she threw them at *you*, didn't she?"

"Yeh, I guess so."

"Well, there you are. What did she say when you left? What was she doing?"

"She was in a terrible state. I don't think she'll be able to go to the game. She may have a sick headache for days. What do you do then?"

Ellen is not that low. Presently she comes down the stairs, with no sign of tears or hysterics, and ready for the game. She is going with Joe, and if they don't hurry they'll be missing some of the fun. Tommy is not going to the game, but he would like to be sure that Ellen takes a warm wrap and a thermos of hot coffee.

"You'd better make a note of this, Joe," warns Tommy. "It gets cold in stadiums late in the afternoon. Ellen gets chilly sometimes, so she likes hot coffee."

He would hand the thermos to Ellen, but she grabs it out of his hand, throws it on the floor and rushes out the door.

"Did you slap her?" angrily demands Joe.

"No, I kicked her," answers Tommy.

"Well, you did something. Here I get her all calmed down and you make her cry again. I see now what kind of a life she has here. I'm going to take her away from this and keep her away!"

"All right! Why don't you get started?" Tommy is shouting

at the top of his voice.

"Because I've got a few more things to say to you," Joe shouts back. "First!—"

Before he can continue the voice of an announcer over the radio has caught his ear: "Well, here we are on Midwestern's field on a mighty fine afternoon for a football game . . . It looks like the Big Day of the year, folks. Neither one of these great teams has lost a game. The Michigan squad is out on the field warming up. They look even bigger than last year. . . . Here comes the Scarlet Stampede now!"

"My God, they're coming out on the field! We'll miss the kick-off! *God damn it!*"

With this exclamation Joe dashes out the front door. Tommy stands looking after him as the band blares and the curtain falls.

Two hours later, when it is growing dark outside, Tommy and Michael are sprawled in a couple of chairs in the Turner living room. Each has a glass in his hand and "the room shows indications of quite a bout: a bottle here, a few magazines flung there, a cushion on the floor."

Tommy takes up a bottle that had held Scotch and pours what is left of the liquor in Michael's glass. When he finds he has none left for himself he takes back a part of what he has given Michael. They are both obviously uncertain as to the time—and many other things.

"Do you know the first law of human nature?" Tommy is demanding, resuming a discussion that evidently has been going on for some time.

"Yes. Self-propagation," answers Michael.

TOMMY—Not any more. That's gone with last year's nightingale.

MICHAEL—Gone with last year's rose. (*Slight pause.*)

TOMMY—Yes . . . Defense of the home. . . . Against prowlers and predatory—prowlers . . . Do you know what the tiger does when the sanctity of his home is jeopardized?

MICHAEL—I know. You told me. He talks it over with the other man, quietly and calmly.

TOMMY—He does not. I'm ashamed of you.

MICHAEL—I think we must have another drink—possibly.

TOMMY—All right. Hey! Hey! (*He is pleased with this shouting.*) That's the way to talk to 'em. (*He puts back his head and yells.*) Heyyy!!

CLEOTA (*entering and turning on the lights*)—Mistuh Turner, what is it?

TOMMY—What do you want?   Oh, we should like to have something more to drink.

CLEOTA—They ain' any more to drink.   I'll make you some black coffee. (*She goes out.*)

TOMMY (*pause*)—What'd she say?

MICHAEL—Nothing.

TOMMY—Where was I?

MICHAEL—Let's see—you were talking about tigers.

TOMMY—Oh, yes.   But let us take the wolf.   What does he do?   I mean, when they come for his mate.   He tears 'em to pieces.

MICHAEL—But we are civilized men.   Aren't we?

TOMMY—And so does the leopard, and the lion and the hawk. They tear 'em to pieces.   Without a word.

MICHAEL—You had it figured out the other way around a while ago.   You said we should give up our women. (TOMMY *stands, falters.*)   It's better sitting down. (TOMMY *sits.*)

TOMMY—Let us say that the tiger wakes up one morning and finds that the wolf has come down on the fold.   What does he—? Before I tell you what he does, I will tell you what he does not do.

MICHAEL—Yes, sir.

TOMMY—He does not expose everyone to a humiliating intellectual analysis.   He comes out of his corner like this— (*Rises, assuming an awkward fighting pose, fists up, then sits quickly again.*)   The bull elephant in him is aroused.

MICHAEL (*plaintively*)—Can't you stick to one animal?

TOMMY—No, that's my point.   All animals are the same, including the human being.   We are male animals, too. (MICHAEL *stares at him, bewildered.*)

MICHAEL—You said . . .

TOMMY—Even the penguin. (*His voice shows some emotion as he thinks of the penguin.*)   He stands for no monkey-business where his mate is concerned.   Swans have been known to drown scotties who threatened their nests.

MICHAEL—I don't think so.

TOMMY—There it is, in us always, though it may be asleep. The male animal.   The mate.   When you are married long enough, you become a mate. . . . Think of the sea-lion for a minute.

MICHAEL—All right.

TOMMY—His mate is lying there in a corner of the cave on

a bed of tender boughs or something. (*Turns to* MICHAEL *for confirmation.*)   Is that right, "tender boughs"?

MICHAEL—Yeah!

TOMMY (*illustrating by a gesture, a great seal, or eel*)—Now, who comes swimming quietly in through the early morning mist, sleek and powerful, dancing and whirling and throwing kisses?

MICHAEL—Joe Ferguson.

TOMMY—And what do I do?

MICHAEL—You say, "Hello."

TOMMY (*in self-disgust*)—The sea-lion knows better. He snarls. He gores. He roars with his antlers. He knows that love is a thing you do something about. He knows it is a thing that words can kill. You do something. You don't just sit there. (MICHAEL *rises.*) I don't mean you. (MICHAEL *sits.*) A woman likes a man who does something. All the male animals fight for the female, from the land crab to the bird of paradise. They don't just sit and talk. They act. (*He removes his glasses and blinks owlishly around.*) I hope I have made all this clear to you. Are there any questions?

MICHAEL—No, sir.

Ellen and Joe are back from the game. Ellen is a little surprised at what she finds. What has Tommy been doing? Tommy has been drinking. And celebrating. Tommy has at last found himself. He knows now what he has to do. He thinks perhaps Ellen had better go away for a little while. Ellen obliges by going upstairs.

Now Tommy would turn his attention to Joe, who is full of conversation about the game. First Tommy and Michael must clear the furniture from the center of the room to give the male animal room to work in. They pay very little attention to what Joe is saying. For his part, Joe is convinced that they are both pie-eyed.

"What's the idea of moving all the furniture around like this?" Joe demands.

"I don't want you to break anything when you fall," explains Tommy, with confidence.

"I'm not going to fall," replies Joe.

"Yes, you are. I am going to knock you cold."

Tommy has rolled up his sleeves and Michael has taken a seat on the arm of the settee to watch the show. Still Joe refuses to take them seriously. He would have them sit down and talk things over. But he gets no more than a sneer for his suggestion.

"Talk, he says, to a man of action. Sit down, he says, to a tigress and her cubs!" Tommy is disgusted. And it will do Joe no good to call for Cleota. She can't help him.

"You crept into this house to take Ellen away, didn't you? You thought it was the house of a professor who would talk and *talk* and TALK . . ."

"And by God you have! I came here to see a football game—"

But Tommy will have no excuses. Now he has assumed the position of a fighter and is advancing as menacingly as possible. Joe takes hold of his outstretched arm and whirls him about, but Tommy is not discouraged. He thinks perhaps he could knock Joe further if he had him in the back yard and tries to drag him there.

Ellen is on the stairs. She is surprised at the attitude of the men, and a little hopeful when Tommy tells her they are fighting. Her hope dies, however, when Joe assures her that she is not involved. Tommy is sore about a lot of other things.

The band and the cheering crowd are approaching outside. The Midwestern celebrants are looking for Joe Ferguson. They want him to ride in the parade. Ellen is ready for the celebration.

"You're getting me in deeper and deeper," wails Joe. Ellen calls to him to follow her. "I shoulda taken a poke at you when I had the chance!"

"Fine! Come out in the back yard!" challenges Tommy. With Michael's aid he has edged the reluctant Joe toward the garden door. Suddenly Tommy, overcome by his impatience, stops and hits Joe a crack in the nose.

"Ow-w-w! Now you've started my sinus trouble!" wails Joe, getting pretty mad. "By God, if you want a fight you've got a fight!" With that he spreads his hand over Tommy's face and forces him through the door. Tommy's arms flail the air impotently. Outside the fight continues noisily. Michael gets a chair and plants it in front of the door, giving him a vantage point from which he shouts instructions and encouragement to Prof. Turner.

Now Patricia and Wally Myers have rushed in from outside. And Cleota has come from the dining room. The excitement is boiling. Presently Ellen reappears, looking for Joe. The sound of carnage attracts her to the garden. A moment later Joe and Wally carry the unconscious professor in and deposit him on the sofa.

"Tommy!" screams Ellen.

The phone is ringing insistently. Cleota goes to answer it. "Professah Turner's res-i-dence," she is shouting imperturbably into the phone as the curtain falls.

ACT III

About noon the following Monday the Turner living room has been stripped of its signs of festivity. At the moment both telephone and doorbells are ringing and a confused Cleota is having a good deal of trouble trying to answer them.

When she finds out who they are, both the young man at the door and the young man on the phone turn out to be reporters eager to get in touch with Prof. Turner. But, as Cleota explains with some spirit Prof. Turner "ain' talkin' to nobody 'cause his haid hurts." "He jus' ain' talkin' 'cause he cain' talk," insists Cleota. She would slam the door shut and keep it shut, but this time it is Patricia who wants to get in.

Ellen is downstairs to report that Tommy is doing a good deal of tossing around and muttering, but is really better. The doctor is going to let him up later in the afternoon. There has only been a little concussion.

"I guess when anybody's as crazy as Tommy or Michael, a little concussion doesn't make any difference," ventures Patricia.

Ellen is still a little vague as to what she is going to do about the situation. She is convinced Tommy doesn't think she is smart enough to understand what he is thinking about.

"I'm all mixed up," confesses Ellen. "I want to go away some place where I can think."

"Look: this is a new century," insists Patricia. "You're not Diana-of-the-Crossways or somebody."

"Well, what do you want me to do—stay here when he doesn't want me?"

"No, but if you're going away, go away with Joe. Tommy's certainly been throwing you at him. Why don't you take him up on it? See what happens."

"Is this advice to the lovelorn? Do you think he would come running after me?"

"Well, you've got to quit moping around and do something. I thought we Stanley women were supposed to have some resources. (Rises and faces ELLEN.) Look, your great-grandmother chased her man all the way to Nebraska in a covered wagon."

"Well, I'm not going to chase anybody anywhere! I'm going to talk this over with Tommy, fairly and squarely, face to face."

" 'Fairly and squarely!' How did your generation ever get through the 1920's?"

"We didn't."

Ellen has gone on an errand when Tommy comes slowly down the stairs. He is wearing a terry-cloth bathrobe and has a wet Turkish towel twisted about his head. He thinks it is all right for him to be up, but the next minute he is ready to sit down and remain pretty quiet. Patricia's news that Ellen has gone out to get the transfer man for her trunk does not add greatly to Tommy's peace of mind.

The phone rings. Patricia answers. It is a call for Michael Barnes and it is that Hot Garters Gardner person! She had heard that Michael was on his way over and she would like to have him call her. So that's where Michael was Saturday night—

A moment later Michael arrives. Tommy tries to warn him of the telephone call, but his pantomime is too cryptic. Michael gets the idea a moment later, however, when Patricia gives him The Garter's number and, flouncing out of the room, advises him to call back.

"Did The Garters call here?" Michael is horrified.

"That's what I was trying to tell you," explains Tommy. "Patricia answered the phone. The—elastics—snapped right in her face."

"And I didn't even *do* anything. I hope."

Michael has just come from President Cartwright's office. The President had flayed him alive and then suspended him.

"Michael, tell me . . . Are you really a Communist?" asks Tommy.

"Me? No. I only know one guy who is," answers Michael. "I'm—well, I guess I'm an unconfused liberal. . . ."

As soon as she is alone with Tommy, Ellen tries to inaugurate her "fair and square" talk, but not with complete success.

"I know you think I'm not very bright or something," she begins. "But you must realize that you got me all mixed up Friday, and that you were even less helpful Saturday."

"That wasn't me Saturday. That was a drunken sea-lion."

"I rather liked you as a sea-lion."

"Yes, I must have been very funny. Did you ever read Hodgson's poem, 'The Bull'?"

"Oh, Tommy!"

"It's the story of the defeated male. There is no defeat that can be quite so complete."

"You wouldn't admit that this defeat was on account of— No, it has to be something out of a book."

" 'When the bull's head is in the dust, life goes on and leaves him there'; it's a psychological fact. The poets understand these things."

"And all the cows react the same way? As if they were reading instructions from a blackboard? Oh, Tommy, listen to me . . ."

"The point is, I don't want any pity."

Joe Ferguson has arrived. He is both curious and apologetic. He is sure he had not hit Tommy very hard. Tommy had fallen and struck his head on a bench. Also he is nursing a sore hand. "You kinda bit me," he explains to Tommy.

Joe would like to know where they all stand. As to that Tommy advises him to let it work itself out.

Ellen has a plan. She thinks perhaps she and Joe could start out by spending a few days at a little inn at Granville. That worries Joe. He really has to be in Washington Monday. It worries Tommy, too. But not Ellen—

"I'll try to make it as clear as I can for both of you," she says. "I simply have to make a fresh start now, Tommy. You understand women; you must see that. I can't stay here now. You've made your plans, and now I have to make mine."

"Yes—but not like this—not running off to Granville," protests Tommy.

"All right, if you're afraid of a scandal, we'll go farther away. Put Granville out of your mind, then. We'll go directly to Pittsburgh."

Joe doesn't like that idea, either. Besides his mother isn't very well. "You're not being very gallant, Joe," protests Ellen.

"No, but I come from a long line of married people! And besides, I'm not going to Pittsburgh directly. I've got to go to Washington, and that's one place I couldn't take you, Ellen!"

"You'll take her any place she wants to go, but she's not going any place!"

"Oh, yes, I am."

Before this can be settled Ed Keller barges in. Ed has been sitting out in the car waiting for Joe and he is tired of waiting. He would like to talk to Tommy, if Tommy is able to talk. He would like to report that there has been a meeting of the trustees, that Michael Barnes is out and that Tommy will be asked to resign tonight—

"There's just one thing you can do; come out with a statement to the papers, quick," advises Ed. "Say you were sick. Say you didn't know anything about Barnes' editorial. You think it's an outrage. You're not going to read this Vanzetti thing, and you think Barnes is getting what he deserves. That's the only thing that'll save your neck."

"Tommy wouldn't say that about Michael, Ed, and you shouldn't ask him to," flares Ellen.

"Thank you!" mutters Tommy.

Just the same Ellen would like to know just what the reading of the letter really does mean to Tommy. Knowing that much she might understand a lot of other things.

Tommy would try to explain. He isn't fighting about himself and Ellen any longer. He is fighting for something that is bigger than either of them.

He is ready to read the Vanzetti letter to them if they will listen. Even to Ed, who hasn't the least notion what it is all about. At which moment Dr. Damon steps in.

"I'm just going to read the Inquisition a letter from one of its victims," Tommy explains.

"That's about enough of that," protests Ed Keller, threateningly.

"Gentlemen, gentlemen!" Dr. Damon is worried. "This may not be wise, Thomas."

TOMMY—It may not be wise, but it's necessary. I think you'll have to take a stand, too, Dr. Damon.

DAMON—I hope not. (*Sits on settee;* JOE *seats himself on the fireplace bench;* ELLEN *sits at opposite side of room.*)

TOMMY—So did I hope not. I didn't start out to lead a crusade. I simply mentioned one day that I meant one day to read to my class three letters by men whose profession was not literature, but who had something sincere to say. Once I had declared that very harmless intention the world began to shake, great institutions trembled, and football players descended upon me and my wife! I realized then that I was doing something important.

ED (*sarcastically*)—You make it sound mighty innocent. Reading Lincoln and General Sherman—and Vanzetti. What was the reason you gave for picking out Vanzetti?

TOMMY (*to* ED)—*Originally* I chose him to show that what we call broken English can sometimes be very moving and eloquent, but now—

Ed—We wouldn't object if this was just a case of broken Eng-·
lish—it's more than that.

Tommy—Yes, you've made it more than that.

Ed—Vanzetti was an anarchist! He was executed for murder.

Tommy—He was accused of murder, but thousands of people
believe he was executed simply because of the ideas he believed
in.

Ed—That's a dangerous thing to bring up.

Tommy (*getting really mad*)—No, it's a dangerous thing to
keep down. I'm fighting for a teacher's rights, but if you want
to make it political, all right! You can't suppress ideas because
you don't like them—not in this country—not yet. This is a
university! (*To* Damon.) It's our business to bring what
light we can into this muddled world—to try to follow truth!

Damon—You are quite right, Thomas, but I wish you would
make an effort not to—uh—uh—intone.

Tommy—I'm not intoning—I'm yelling! And for God's sake,
sir, put away that umbrella! (Damon *covers his umbrella with
his hat.*) Don't you see: this isn't about Vanzetta; this is about
us! If I can't read this letter today, tomorrow none of us will
be able to teach anything except what Mr. Keller here and the
legislature permit us to teach. Can't you see what that leads
to—what it has led to in other places? We're holding the last
fortress of free thought, and if we surrender to prejudice and
dictation, we're cowards! (*He strides across the room.*)

Ellen—Tommy, no matter how deeply you feel about this,
what can you *do?* What can any one man do? Except to lose
everything . . .

Tommy—Ellen, I have very little more to lose. And I can't
tell you what I hope to gain. I can't answer that. I only know
that I have to do it. (Patricia *appears in the doorway, stops
and listens.*)

Damon—May we hear the letter—in a slightly calmer mood,
perhaps?

Tommy—Yes, sir . . . This may disappoint you a little, Mr.
Keller. It isn't inflammatory, so it may make you feel a little
silly. At least, I hope so. . . . (*He holds up the book, pauses.*
Ed *and* Joe *get set in their chairs.*) Vanzetti wrote this in April,
1927, after he was sentenced to die. It has been printed in many
newspapers. It appears in this book. You could destroy every
printed copy of it, but it would not die out of the language,
because a great many people know it by heart. (*He reads,*

hardly referring to the book, watching them.) "If it had not been for these thing, I might have live out my life talking at street corners to scorning men. I might have die, unmarked, unknown, a failure. Now we are not a failure. Never in our full life could we hope to do so much work for tolerance, for Justice, for man's understanding of man, as now we do by accident. Our words—our lives—our pain—nothing! The taking of our lives—the lives of a good shoe-maker and a poor fish-peddler—all! That last moment belongs to us—that agony is our triumph!" . . . Well, that's it!

He closes the book amidst a complete and slightly strained silence. Keller is plainly puzzled. Ellen, moved by the letter, looks up in surprise to meet Tommy's eyes. Joe fidgets uncomfortably. When he speaks it is to admit that the letter is not so bad. Reading it to the class couldn't do much harm.

Ed Keller, however, strives to maintain his position. "Yes, it will," he insists. "If he reads this letter to his class he'll get a lot of those kids worried about that man. Make socialists out of 'em."

"It's got me worried already," says Tommy.

"No—I won't have it. You fellows are trying to defy the authority of the trustees. You say you're going to take a stand. Well, we've *taken* a stand. I wouldn't care if that letter were by Alexander Hamilton."

"Neither would I! The principle is exactly the same."

Joe thinks perhaps if Tommy were to substitute something by Hoover it might help. Ellen, too, has an idea, but Tommy will not let her state it. He prefers to fight his own battles. Ellen had only wanted to say, it turns out, that she is no longer Tommy's wife. That she is going to Pittsburgh to live with Joe.

This is much too much for Ed Keller. "Why, you can't do that," he protests, in great excitement. "The newspapers would make Midwestern University look like some kind of a honky-tonk or something! Why, this is worse than that god-damn letter!"

Ellen stands firm. She certainly can't stay there now. It is all very disturbing to Mr. Keller.

"Well, I've got this much straight—if we can keep sex out of this for a minute!" says Ed. "I came here to say to you that if you read this letter today you're out of this university tomorrow! You take this stand and you stand alone!"

And now Dean Damon has taken a hand. "Mr. Keller," he says, walking deliberately over to face Ed, "for forty-two years

I have followed a policy of appeasement. I might say I have been kicked around in this institution by one Edward K. Keller after another . . ."

"There is only one Edward K. Keller."

"There has always been at least one. But there is an increasing element in the faculty which resents your attitude toward any teacher who raises his voice or so much as clears his throat. I warn you that if you persist in persecuting Thomas Turner, you will have a fight on your hands, my friend."

"Do you think that Bryson and Kressinger and I are afraid of a few dissatisfied book-worms who work for twenty-five hundred dollars a year?"

"These men are not malcontents! Some of them are distinguished scholars who have made this university what it is!" objects Dr. Damon.

"They've made it what it is! What about me? Who's getting this new stadium? Who brought Coach Sprague here from Southern Methodist?"

"He means that this thing is bigger than stadiums and coaches, Ed," explains Joe.

"Nothing's bigger than the new stadium," insists Ed.

Then a second surprise strikes them. Michael Barnes and Nutsy Miller have been circulating petitions for Prof. Turner. Already they have nearly four hundred names, including those of Stalenkiwiecz and Wierasocka! Ed Keller just can't believe his eyes. "They can't do this to me!" wails Ed. "Two of the biggest men in the university signing the red petition! You, the greatest halfback we ever had, running away with a woman! Why— *they'll never ask us to the Rose Bowl now!*"

He is ready to rush from the house, defiantly shouting that, even if he should resign from the Board of Trustees, he will kick Tommy out of the university if it's the last thing he does. And just to make it even Tommy is ready to kick Ed out of his house. . . .

When Ellen, Tommy and Joe are alone Ellen again would talk with Tommy, but Tommy is in no mood to listen to her. It isn't a declaration of loyalty he wants to hear. Nor does he want to have Ellen standing around like a Red Cross nurse because she knows he is in trouble.

Joe would serve as a well-meaning referee, but that doesn't work either. Ellen is getting madder by the minute. Suddenly, when Tommy suggests that they settle things quietly and calmly, she picks up a large ash tray from the table and smashes it on the floor. That gives Tommy an idea. He can throw things, too. He grabs up his teacup and hurls it into the fireplace. He is reaching for the saucer when Joe interferes—

"Now, wait—let me handle this. *I don't throw things,*" says Joe. "I just want to say that I came to this city to see a football game . . ."

"Oh, no, you didn't!" shouts Ellen, right in Joe's face. "You came for me. You haven't been here for a ball game in ten years. You wait till Brenda and you are separated, then you come for me!"

"Oh, hell!" explodes Joe, and tosses a saucer into the fireplace on his own account.

"That's very smart, Ellen," agrees Tommy, desperately insisting upon his doom. "That's very penetrating. That's all I wanted to know. (*To* Joe.) Subconsciously, you came here for Ellen, so don't try to deny it."

"I don't do things subconsciously!" shrills Joe. "You're full of childish explanations of every goddamn thing that comes up!"

"And you're full of psychological evasions!"

This is too much for Ellen. With a shriek she runs upstairs. She is not going to listen any more. And this time, Joe announces, he is not going upstairs to comfort her. A moment later Ellen is back with her suitcase. Tommy and Ed are still shouting at each other.

Ellen, it appears, has been packed for three days. Still, Tommy does not think she should go with only one suitcase. Surely she will want to take some of her books. He is having a hard time to keep his voice from breaking, but manages to hold out.

Michael has stuck his head in the door to warn Prof. Turner that he has but five minutes before class.

"Well, so long, Joe," Tommy is saying. "I know you'll get her a place of her own for a while anyway. You can take that four-poster money with you, Ellen. I'll have one more check coming, too."

Joe—What's "four-poster money"?
Ellen (*her voice trembling pathetically*)—We were saving up to buy a new bed. (*She cries, and collapses on settee.*)
Joe—Oh, God, here we go again!
Tommy (*comes back again, desperately*)—*Why* did you have to ask what four-poster money is? (*To* Ellen.) Ellen, please.
Ellen (*hysterically*)—Oh, go on! Go on! Put on your coat. If you're going to be kicked out of school, you can't go over there

looking like a tramp.

TOMMY (*balefully*)—All right! (*He clumps upstairs like King Lear.*)

JOE—Look, Ellen, everything's gonna be all right.

ELLEN—Is it?

JOE (*looking after* TOMMY)—I wouldn't worry about that guy.

ELLEN—I don't.

JOE—I mean he's sure to get another job. He's had more publicity than Wally Myers.

ELLEN—I don't care what becomes of him. (JOE *studies her drooping figure narrowly.*)

JOE—Come here. (*He pulls her to her feet, facing him.*) You're still crazy about that guy, aren't you?

ELLEN—I'm kind of scared of him. He used to be just—nice, but now he's wonderful! (TOMMY *appears on stairs in time to catch the end of this. Very slowly light begins to dawn upon him.* JOE *sees him, but* ELLEN *doesn't.*)

JOE—I don't think he's so wonderful.

ELLEN—Yes, he is! That letter's wonderful. What he's trying to do is wonderful. He wouldn't let me or you or anyone stop him. Even Ed.

JOE—He's a scrapper, all right, but he can't dance. (*He crosses to the Victrola, pulling her along. He has an idea and does everything for* TOMMY's *benefit.* TOMMY *comes down slowly.* JOE *turns on the Victrola, which plays "Who?"*)

ELLEN—Oh, who wants to dance now?

JOE (*making her dance, keeping her back to* TOMMY)—This is important. It's all in the light you give off.

ELLEN—Light! What are you talking about?

JOE (*with intensity*)—The important thing about dancing is that the man has got to lead. (*He beckons to* TOMMY; *with one stride,* TOMMY *turns her away from* JOE.)

TOMMY—May I cut in?

ELLEN—Tommy! Let me go!

TOMMY (*shouting*)—No, I think you're wonderful, too!

ELLEN—You think I'm dumb! Were you listening?

TOMMY—No, I wasn't.

JOE (*up near the door*)—Hey—don't start that again!

TOMMY (*puts on his hat, still dancing feverishly*)—Joe—why don't you go back to your wife? We can send her a wire.

JOE—Don't worry about me, brother. I sent her a wire this morning. (*He goes out into the fresh air, a happy man.* TOMMY *still dances with* ELLEN—*they are almost in tears.*)

TOMMY—Quit leading!

ELLEN—I'm not leading!   You *were* listening!

TOMMY—You were yelling.   Well, turn!

ELLEN—Make me turn!   (*He does.*)   Don't be so rough—
and put your hat on straight!   You look terrible!   (*Half-cry-
ing, she throws her arms around* TOMMY.   *They are kissing each
other very, very hard.*)

THE CURTAIN FALLS

THE TIME OF YOUR LIFE

A Drama in Three Acts

By William Saroyan

WILLIAM SAROYAN'S first experience with the theatre, so far as available records go, was that associated with the production of a curious one-act drama of his called "My Heart's in the Highlands." This play was produced experimentally by the Group Theatre in New York in the Spring of 1939 and, after an uncertain première, was adopted by the Theatre Guild for a series of subscription performances.

The reviews of "My Heart's in the Highlands" ranged from Wolcott Gibbs' statement in the *New Yorker* magazine which read: "This collision between the most completely undisciplined talent in American letters and the actors of the Group Theatre bored me nearly to distraction and I would advise you to stay away from it unless you are especially fond of being badgered in the name of the experimental drama," to the rather more or less ecstatic confessions of John Mason Brown in the New York *Evening Post*, who wrote: "Far be it from me to pretend that i understand precisely what Mr. Saroyan is up to. But what he is saying with deliberate vagueness . . . interested and moved me more than most of the productions I have seen this Winter."

"My Heart's in the Highlands" was repeated for forty-four performances and withdrawn. The author was greatly heartened by his experiences, gaily thanked even his bitterest critics for the help their critiques provided, and set about the writing of another play. This one, as Mr. Saroyan reports in the published version, was written in six days and was to have had six acts, each act to represent a day of any worker's week. Mr. Saroyan, however, ended with five acts, it may be out of deference to the five-day week, and these five acts in the process of being fitted to the conventions of the theatre, were afterward reduced to three by the directors of the Theatre Guild and Eddie Dowling, who were the play's associated producers. The play's first title was "The Light Fantastic," its second, suggested by George Jean Nathan, "Sunset Sonata." Its third the current "The Time of Your Life."

Mr. Saroyan also planned, with the first production, to have the play's theme announced over a loud speaker before the curtain rose. "In the time of your life, live—so that in that good time there shall be no ugliness or death for yourself or for any life your life touches," he had wanted to say. "Seek goodness everywhere, and when it is found, bring it out of its hiding place and let it be free and unashamed. Place in matter and in flesh the least of the values, for these are the things that hold death and must pass away. . . . In the time of your life, live—so that in that wondrous time you shall not add to the misery and sorrow of the world, but shall smile to the infinite delight and mystery of it." This pre-statement of theme was afterward abandoned.

Many changes were made in the original Saroyan script before "The Time of Your Life" reached a Broadway production, but the author worked with his producers and was amenable to their advice. The play was most favorably received and with few critical reservations. The Saroyan originality, active imagination and literary artistry were duly accepted and praised as the freshest and most promising that the native theatre had recently revealed. Public response proved an endorsement of the critical evaluations and "The Time of Your Life," though hardly one of the major successes of the season, played successfully through several months.

At the opening of the play the time is the present. The place is "Nick's Pacific Street Saloon, Restaurant and Entertainment Palace at the foot of Embarcadero, in San Francisco." It is about 11.30 in the morning of a clear October day. We enter and look about.

Nick himself is back of the bar. He is "a big red-headed Italian-American with an enormous naked woman tattooed in red on the inside of his right arm." Near the center of the Palace of Entertainment Joe, a youngish, good-looking fellow, is sitting at a table, thinking. Joe is "always calm, always quiet, always thinking, always eager, always bored, always superior. His expensive clothes are casually and youthfully worn and give him an almost boyish appearance." At the end of the bar is "The Arab, . . . a lean old man with a rather ferocious old-country mustache, with the ends twisted up."

The routine is what might be expected at 11.30 in the morning in Nick's place . . . A sailor, finishing his drink at the bar, leaves. . . . A boy called Sam, having swept the place out, disappears through a door leading to the kitchen. . . . A newsboy comes shuffling down the stairs, expectant but not too hopeful.

He has five papers left. Joe buys them all, glances at the headlines and throws them on the floor . . . The Arab picks up a
paper, also looks at the headlines and shakes his head solemnly,
muttering: "No foundation. All the way down the line."

A drunk comes shuffling down the stairs, makes a bee line for
the telephone, looks for a nickel in the return chute and would
sit down with Joe. Nick, however, promptly administers the
bum's rush. The drunk is out for a moment and then right back
to proclaim loudly and with gestures that this, bygod, is a free
country.

Willie, a marble-game fanatic, "explodes through the swinging doors," orders a beer by a sign language with which Nick
is familiar, drinks it, sighs with satisfaction and starts to leave.
At the door he hesitates. His eyes turn fondly to the marble
game and rest affectionately on all its lights and gadgets. A
second later he has dug up a nickel and is at the lever that sends
the marbles bumping past obstacles and falling into pockets.
This, to Willie, "is the beginning of great drama—Himself vs.
the machine. Willie vs. Destiny. His skill and daring vs. the
cunning and trickery of the novelty industry of America, and
the whole challenging world." . . . The nickel-in-the-slot phonograph, which has been playing "The Missouri Waltz," stops with
a click. . . . The play is on—

Joe has, for the moment, stopped thinking and is calling for
Tom, quietly at first and then with a shout. Presently Tom
appears. He "is a great big man of about thirty . . . handsome,
dumb, innocent, troubled and a little bewildered by everything."

Joe has an errand for Tom, but first he would impress certain
facts upon his mind. Who was it saved his (Tom's) life? It
was Joe. And how did Joe save Tom's life? By making him
eat a lot of chicken soup when he was sick and hungry; by taking him to a doctor; by giving him money for food and clothes
and paying his rent.

"You in good health now?" demands Joe. "You got clothes?
You eat three times a day? Sometimes four?"

"Yeah, Joe. Sometimes five," agrees Tom.

"Then where the hell have you been?"

TOM (*humbly*)—Joe, I was out in the street listening to the
boys. They're talking about the trouble down here on the water-
front.

JOE (*sharply*)—I want you to be around when I need you.

TOM (*pleased that the bawling-out is over*)—I won't do it

again. Joe, one guy out there says there's got to be a revolution before anything will ever be all right.

JOE (*impatient*)—I know all about it. Now, here. Take this money. Go up to the Emporium. You know where the Emporium is?

TOM—Yeah, sure, Joe.

JOE—All right. Take the elevator and go up to the fourth floor. Walk around to the back, to the toy department? Buy me a couple of dollars' worth of toys and bring them here.

TOM (*amazed*)—Toys? What kind of toys, Joe?

JOE—Any kind of toys. Little ones that I can put on this table.

TOM—What do you want toys for, Joe?

JOE (*mildly angry*)—What?

TOM—All right, all right. You don't have to get sore at everything. What'll people think, a big guy like me buying toys?

JOE—What people?

TOM—Aw, Joe, you're always making me do crazy things for you, and *I'm* the guy that gets embarrassed. You just sit in this place and make me do all the dirty work.

JOE (*looking away*)—Do what I tell you.

TOM—O.K., but I wish I knew why.

JOE (*as* TOM *makes to go*)—Wait a minute. Here's a nickel. Put it in the phonograph. Number seven. I want to hear that waltz again.

TOM—Boy, I'm glad *I* don't have to stay and listen to it. Joe, what do you hear in that song anyway? We listen to that song ten times a day. Why can't we hear number six, or two, or nine? There are a lot of other numbers.

JOE (*emphatically*)—Put the nickel in the phonograph. (*Pause.*) Sit down and wait till the music's over. Then go get me some toys.

TOM—O.K. O.K.

JOE (*loudly*)—Never mind being a martyr about it either. The cause isn't worth it.

Kitty Duval, "who lives in a room in the New York Hotel around the corner, comes beyond the swinging doors quietly, and walks slowly to the bar, her reality and rhythm a perfect accompaniment to the sorrowful American music, which is her music, as it is Tom's." . . . "She is a small powerful girl, with that kind of delicate and rugged beauty which no circumstance of evil or ugly reality can destroy." . . . "There is an angry purity and a fierce pride in her."

As Kitty goes to the bar, and accepts a glass of beer from Nick, both Joe and Tom turn to look at her. Joe "recognizes her as a great person immediately." Tom is practically struck dumb by the sight of her. "He stands like a lump, fascinated and undone by his almost religious adoration for her." Tom moves, as one dazed, toward the girl, but Joe's voice, calling roughly to him, stirs him out of his reverie. A moment later he has curtly been sent on the errand to buy Joe two dollars' worth of toys that can be set on a table.

Joe has turned to Kitty. With "great compassion" he tries to change her thought, to arouse her, from the dream that seems to have settled over her. He would buy her champagne if she would sit at table with him. Kitty is suspicious. She has seen the way Joe has shouted at Tom, and is resentful. Even Joe's "I have only the noblest thoughts for both your person and your spirit" does not entirely convince her. But when Nick, the bar-keeper, derisively applies the name of her profession to her she is put suddenly on the defensive.

"Don't you call me names," answers Kitty, furiously. "I used to be in burlesque."

"If you were ever in burlesque, I used to be Charlie Chaplin," sneers Nick.

"I was in burlesque. I played the burlesque circuit from coast to coast. I've had flowers sent to me by European royalty. I've had dinner with young men of wealth and social position."

Joe and Kitty sit at table drinking the champagne Nick has brought, a little reluctantly and with explanations. Nick wouldn't have Kitty think that she is being especially honored. The only reason he has champagne in stock is because Joe buys it and feeds it to a lot of people. Joe's "crazy, or something."

"To the spirit, Kitty Duval." Joe has raised his glass, and Kitty, partly convinced now of his sincerity, gratefully drinks with him.

Again Nick takes orders. At Joe's request he puts a nickel in the phonograph, even though he personally isn't a lover of music. Among other things Nick is convinced that Tschaikowsky is a dope.

"I like champagne, and everything that goes with it," Kitty is saying to Joe. "Big houses with big porches, and big rooms with big windows, and big lawns, and big trees, and flowers growing everywhere, and big shepherd dogs sleeping in the shade."

It is Dudley R. Bostwick who next breaks through the swinging doors. "Dudley is a young man of about twenty-four or twenty-five . . . neatly dressed in bargain clothes, overworked and irritated by the routine and dullness and monotony of his life . . . The swindled young man. Educated, but without the least real understanding. . . . He is a great personality because against all these handicaps what he wants is simple and basic: a woman. . . . His face is ridiculous. His personal rhythm is tense and jittery. His speech is shrill and violent. His gestures are wild. His ego is disjointed and epileptic. And yet deeply he possesses the same wholeness of spirit, and directness of energy, that is in all species of animals. . . . He is a young man who has been taught that he has a chance, as a person, and believes it. As a matter of fact, he hasn't a chance in the world, and should have been told by somebody, or should not have had his natural and valuable ignorance spoiled by education, ruining an otherwise perfectly good and charming member of the human race."

While Dudley is at the phone dialing feverishly in an effort to contact Miss Elsie Mandelspiegel, a second young man arrives. This is Harry. Harry's clothes don't fit, being a little too large in both the coat and the pants. "He is a dumb young fellow, but he has ideas. A philosophy, in fact. His philosophy is simple and beautiful. The world is sorrowful. The world needs laughter. Harry is funny. The world needs Harry. Harry will make the world laugh."

While Dudley is still at the phone, Harry reveals his needs to Nick. Harry is a great comedian. He can sing and dance and tell gags. He offers a few samples. The dancing is good, the comedy is static. Nick is not impressed. . . .

Dudley has finally found someone on the phone. If this is Elsie he would tell her that he is about to jump in the bay unless she agrees to marry him. "I can't think of anything but you," Dudley is shrilly protesting. "All the time. Day and night and night and day. Elsie, I love you. I love you. What?"

Dudley has a wrong number, but that doesn't stop him. The girl he is speaking to is Lorene Smith and Lorene is interested. Sure, she'd like to meet him? Where? At Nick's. No. 3 Pacific Street. . . .

Harry is still working desperately at being funny. He has reached the tag of a supposedly humorous monologue about the fellow who didn't want to go to war. Nick has had enough—

"All right, Comedian. Lay off a minute!"

"Nobody's got a sense of humor any more," sighs the broken-hearted Harry. "The world's dying for comedy like never before, but nobody knows how to laugh." . . .

Wesley, an emaciated colored boy, has drifted up to the bar. Wesley wants a job, too. He ain't hungry, but he wants a job. Does he belong to a union? Wesley doesn't know anything about unions. Yet he expects to get a job! Nick is disgusted. The disappointment, plus his half-starved condition, are too much for Wesley. He would have fainted if Nick and the Arab hadn't caught him. They carry him into the kitchen.

Harry is still at his dancing. Dudley is moaning about his lost Elsie and already regretting his date with the new Lorene. Joe and Kitty drinking silently at their table again become conscious of each other—

"What's the dream now, Kitty Duval?" asks Joe.

KITTY (*dreaming the words and pictures*)—I dream of home. Christ, I always dream of home. I've no home. I've no place. But I always dream of all of us together again. We had a farm in Ohio. There was nothing good about it. It was always sad. There was always trouble. But I always dream about it as if I could go back and Papa would be there and Mamma and Louie and my little brother Stephen and my sister Mary. I'm Polish. Duval! My name isn't Duval, it's Koranovsky. Katerina Koranovsky. We lost everything. The house, the farm, the trees, the horses, the cows, the chickens. Papa died. He was old. He was thirteen years older than Mamma. We moved to Chicago. We tried to work. We tried to stay together. Louie got in trouble. The fellows he was with killed him for something. I don't know what. Stephen ran away from home. Seventeen years old. I don't know where he is. Then Mamma died. (*Pause.*) What's the dream? I dream of home.

NICK (*coming out of the kitchen with* WESLEY)—Here. Sit down here and rest. That'll hold you for a while. Why didn't you tell me you were hungry? You all right now?

WESLEY (*sitting down in the chair at the piano*)—Yes, I am. Thank you. I didn't know I was *that* hungry.

NICK—Fine. (*To* HARRY *who is dancing.*) Hey. What the hell do you think you're doing?

HARRY (*stopping*)—That's my own idea. I'm a natural-born dancer and comedian. (WESLEY *begins slowly, one note, one chord at a time, to play the piano.*)

NICK—You're no good. Why don't you try some other kind

of work? Why don't you get a job in a store, selling something? What do you want to be a comedian for?

HARRY—I've got something for the world and they haven't got sense enough to let me give it to them. Nobody knows me.

DUDLEY—Elsie. Now I'm waiting for some dame I've never seen before. Lorene Smith. Never saw her in my life. Just happened to get the wrong number. She turns on the personality, and I'm a cooked Indian. Give me a beer, please.

HARRY—Nick, you've got to see my act. It's the greatest thing of its kind in America. All I want is a chance. No salary to begin. Let me try it out tonight. If I don't wow 'em, O.K. I'll go home. If vaudeville wasn't dead, a guy like me would have a chance.

NICK—You're not funny. You're a sad young punk. What the hell do you want to try to be funny for? You'll break everybody's heart. What's there for you to be funny about? You've been poor all your life, haven't you?

HARRY—I've been poor all right, but don't forget that some things count more than some other things.

NICK—What counts more, for instance, than what else, for instance?

HARRY—Talent, for instance, counts more than money, for instance, that's what, and I've got talent. I get new ideas night and day. Everything comes natural to me. I've got style, but it'll take me a little time to round it out. That's all. (*By now* WESLEY *is playing something of his own which is very good and out of the world. He plays about half a minute, after which* HARRY *begins to dance.*)

NICK (*watching*)—I run the lousiest dive in Frisco, and a guy arrives and makes me stock up with champagne. The whores come in and holler at me that they're ladies. Talent comes in and begs me for a chance to show itself. Even society people come here once in a while. I don't know what for. Maybe it's liquor. Maybe it's the location. Maybe it's my personality. Maybe it's the crazy personality of the joint. The old honky-tonk. (*Pause.*) Maybe they can't feel at home anywhere else.

At the piano Wesley is playing with increasing confidence. The rhythm is infectious. Harry is fitting his dance steps to the music. Kitty has heard and responded, too. She would have Joe dance with her, but Joe never learned to dance. Nor will he try.

When Tom returns with the toys, however, and immediately

goes ga-ga again at sight of Kitty, Joe finds a partner for "the queen of the world burlesque." He hands Tom five dollars and appoints him a substitute. With this encouragement Tom and Kitty melt into a dance.

Lorene Smith has come looking for the young man she talked with on the telephone. Lorene "is about thirty-seven, very over-bearing and funny-looking." Dudley R. Bostwick takes one look at her and then announces that the Dudley Bostwick who talked to her over the phone hobbled out of the place on crutches ten minutes ago. Lorene is suspicious, but as she only came to help save the young man from suicide, it doesn't matter.

"Be of help? What kind of help could she be, of?" demands Dudley, when Lorene has left. Now he has returned to the phone, mumbling to himself. "She'll come to the phone one of these days," he mutters, defiantly. "If there's anything to true love at all. She'll come to the phone. Sunset 7349." He spins the dials impatiently. . . .

Tom and Kitty have stopped dancing. Joe is unwrapping and inspecting his toys. He looks up to hear Tom declare his im-passioned love for Kitty and hears her answering invitation to come to her room. There is a wild look in Tom's eyes as he and Kitty go out. Joe, smiling, returns to the toys. . . .

Again there is excitement at the phone. Elsie Mandelspiegel has answered! Dudley can hardly believe his ears. Excitedly he calls to Elsie for help! She must come to him! She must come to Nick's on Pacific Street! She— But Elsie has either hung up or they were disconnected. . . .

Harry, the dancer comedian, with Wesley improvising at the piano, have worked into an act. Harry is enthusiastic about it. Nick is also impressed. They can try it that night, if they want to, if Wesley can remember what he has been playing. Harry can stay and wait table. . . .

Nick has gone back of the bar. "The atmosphere is now one of warm, natural, American ease; every man innocent and good; each doing what he believes he should do, or what he must do. There is deep American naïveté and faith in the behavior of each person. . . . Each man is following his destiny as he feels it should be followed; or is abandoning it as he feels it must, by now, be abandoned; or is forgetting it for the moment as he feels he should forget it. . . . Each person belongs to the environment, in his own person, as himself; Wesley is playing better than ever. Harry is hoofing better than ever. Nick is behind the bar shining glasses. Joe is smiling at the toy and studying it. Dudley, although still troubled, is at least calm now and full of melancholy poise. Willie, at the marble game, is happy. The Arab is deep in his memories, where he wants to be."

Into this scene and atmosphere comes Blick. "Blick is the sort of human being you dislike at sight. . . . There is nothing obviously wrong with him, and yet you know that it is impossible . . . to accept him as a human being. He is the strong man without strength—strong only among the weak—the weakling who uses force on the weaker."

BLICK (*entering casually*)—Hello, Nick.

NICK (*stopping his work and leaning across the bar*)—What do you want to come here for? You're too big a man for a little honky-tonk.

BLICK (*flattered*)—Now, Nick.

NICK—Important people never come here. *Here.* Have a drink. (*Whiskey bottle.*)

BLICK—Thanks. I don't drink.

NICK (*drinking the drink himself*)—Well, why don't you?

BLICK—I have responsibilities.

NICK—You're head of the lousy Vice Squad. There's no vice here.

BLICK (*sharply*)—Street-walkers are working out of this place.

NICK (*angry*)—What do you want?

BLICK (*loudly*)—I just want you to know that it's got to stop.

NICK—Don't look at me. I can't tell a street-walker from a lady. You married?

BLICK—You're not asking me questions. I'm telling you.

NICK (*interrupting*)—You're a man of about forty-five or so. You ought to know better.

BLICK (*angry*)—Street-walkers are working out of this place.

NICK (*beginning to shout*)—Now, don't start any trouble with me. People come here to drink and loaf around. I don't care who they are.

BLICK—Well, I do.

NICK—The only way to find out if a lady is a street-walker is to walk the streets with her, go to bed, and make sure. You wouldn't want to do that. You'd *like* to, of course.

BLICK—Any more of it, and I'll have your joint closed.

NICK (*very casually, without ill-will*)—Listen. I've got no use for you, or anybody like you. You're out to change the world from something bad to something worse. Something like yourself.

BLICK (*furious pause, and contempt*)—I'll be back tonight. (*He begins to go.*)

NICK (*very angry but very calm*)—Do yourself a big favor and don't come back tonight. Send somebody else. I don't like your personality.

BLICK (*casually, but with contempt*)—Don't break any laws. I don't like yours, either.

There is a moment of silence after Blick has disappeared. Gradually the normal activities are resumed. But Nick is unhappy. "What's a punk like that want to go out and try to change the world for? He's sick."

"I guess he wants to change the world at that," agrees Joe, soberly.

"So I go to work and hate him," says Nick.

"It's not him, Nick. It's everything."

"Yeah, I know. But I've still got no use for him. He's no good. You know what I mean? He hurts little people. (*Confused.*) One of the girls tried to commit suicide on account of him. (*Furiously.*) I'll break his head if he hurts anybody around here. This is my joint. (*Afterthought.*) Or anybody's feelings, either."

"He may not be so bad, deep down underneath."

"I know all about him. He's no good. . . . I've got a good joint. There's nothing wrong here. . . ."

Joe has set one of the mechanical toys performing. One by one the others gather around the table to watch the toy. "Nick, this is a toy," Joe is saying. "A contraption devised by the cunning of man to drive boredom, or grief, or anger out of children. A noble gadget. A gadget, I might say, infinitely nobler than any other I can think of at the moment."

Wesley is playing the toy's music box theme on the piano and Harry is giving an imitation of its movements in the dance. The lights dim as the curtain falls.

ACT II

An hour later the scene in Nick's place has changed but slightly. At his table Joe is shuffling a deck of cards. At a neighboring table sits a young woman who has drifted in and ordered a glass of beer. The handbag she lays on the table is marked with the letters "M. L." She and Joe have been regarding each other from time to time with mild curiosity. Now

Joe would guess her name from the initials.

Is it Madge Laubowitz?   Or Mabel Lepescu?   Or Margie Longworthy?   It is none of these the young woman assures him. Nor Midge Laurie, either.

This is becoming a sort of quiz game, and is played in deadly seriousness, both Joe and the young woman being a little high. "J. T." are his initials, Joe confesses.   No, the "J." is not for John.   It's for Joseph—though everybody calls him Joe.   And he's Irish.

The "M." is for Mary in her name, Mary admits.   And she's Irish, too.   At least on her father's side.   Her mother was English—

JOE—I'm Irish on both sides.   Mary's one of my favorite names.   I guess that's why I didn't think of it.   I met a girl in Mexico City named Mary once.   She was an American from Philadelphia.   She got married there.   In Mexico City, I mean. While I was there.   We were in love, too.   At least *I* was.   You never know about anyone else.   They were engaged, you see, and her mother was with her, so they went through with it. Must have been six or seven years ago.   She's probably got three or four children by this time.

MARY—Are you still in love with her?

JOE—Well—no.   To tell you the truth, I'm not sure.   I guess I am.   I didn't even know she was engaged until a couple of days before they got married.   I thought *I* was going to marry her.   I kept thinking all the time about the kind of kids we would be likely to have.   My favorite was the third one.   The first two were fine.   Handsome and fine and intelligent, but that third one was different.   Dumb and goofy-looking.   I liked *him* a lot.   When she told me she was going to be married, I didn't feel so bad about the first two, it was that dumb one.

MARY (*after a pause of some few seconds*)—What do you do?

JOE—Do?   To tell you the truth, nothing.

MARY—Do you always drink a great deal?

JOE (*scientifically*)—Not always.   Only when I'm awake.   I sleep seven or eight hours every night, you know.

MARY—How nice.   I mean to drink when you're awake.

JOE (*thoughtfully*)—It's a privilege.

MARY—Do you really *like* to drink?

JOE (*positively*)—As much as I like to breathe.

MARY (*beautifully*)—Why?

JOE (*dramatically*)—Why do I like to drink?   (*Pause.*)   Because I don't like to be gypped. Because I don't like to be dead most of the time and just a little alive every once in a long while. (*Pause.*) If I don't drink, I become fascinated by unimportant things—like everybody else. I get busy. Do things. All kinds of little stupid things, for all kinds of little stupid reasons. Proud, selfish, ordinary things. I've done them. Now I don't do anything. I live all the time. Then I go to sleep.

Mary is still a little mystified. She would like to know more about Joe. What are his plans? He hasn't any. Why does he drink? Well, that takes a bit of pondering, but Joe finally has the answer. Every day has twenty-four hours. "Out of the twenty-four hours at least twenty-three and a half are—my God, I don't know why—dull, dead, boring, empty, and murderous," Joe insists, seriously. "Minutes on the clock, *not time of living*. It doesn't make any difference who you are or what you do, twenty-three and a half hours of the twenty-four are spent waiting."

"Waiting?"

"And the more you wait, the less there is to wait for." Joe's voice has grown loud and his gestures are a little wild.

"Oh?"

"That goes on for days and days, and weeks and months and years and years, and the first thing you know *all* the years are dead. All the minutes are dead. You yourself are dead. There's nothing to wait for any more. Nothing except minutes on the clock. No time of life. Nothing but minutes, and idiocy. Beautiful, bright, intelligent idiocy. (*Pause.*) Does that answer your question?"

"I'm afraid it does. Thank you. You shouldn't have gone to all the trouble."

Mary, it appears, as the confessions proceed, is married and the mother of a son and daughter. Sad? Mary has always been sad. For whom is Mary waiting? She isn't waiting for anyone. Neither is Joe. Of course there is Mary's husband. He's a lawyer. Joe thinks he likes Mary's husband. He must be a great guy. How about Joe's responsibilities? Joe has one—and thousands. "As a matter of fact I feel responsible to everybody," confesses Joe. "At least to everybody I meet. I've been trying for three years to find out if it's possible to live what I think is a civilized life. I mean a life that can't hurt any other life."

"You're famous?"

"Very. Utterly unknown, but very famous. Would you like to dance?"

"All right."

"I'm sorry. I don't dance. I didn't think you'd like to."

"To tell you the truth, I don't like to dance at all."

Presently a silence has come upon them and they are looking steadily at each other, and with great charm.

"Are you really in love with me?" asks Mary.

"Yes."

"Is it the champagne?"

"Yes. Partly, at least."

"If you don't see me again, will you be very unhappy?"

"Very."

"I'm so pleased."

Mary has risen and is preparing to go. Joe is deeply grieved as he, too, gets to his feet. "I must go now," says Mary. "Please don't get up. Good-by."

"Good-by."

For a moment they stand looking at each other. Then Mary turns and goes and Joe stares after her for a long time. . . .

The newsboy is back. This time he has eleven papers left. Joe buys them all, only to glance at the headlines and throw the papers away. The newsboy can't understand this gesture, and doesn't try to. He has lost interest in being a newsboy, anyway. He wants Nick to give him a job. He might be a great lyric tenor. To prove this he breaks into a somewhat uncertain rendering of "When Irish Eyes Are Smiling." Any Greek from Salonica who can sing like that means something to Nick.

"Joe, people are so wonderful. Look at that kid," says Nick.

"Of course they're wonderful," agrees Joe. "Every one of them is wonderful. . . . A nation like this can't go wrong." . . .

McCarthy and Krupp have come through the doors and swung around to the bar. "McCarthy is a big man in work clothes, which make him seem very young. . . . He has broad shoulders, a lean intelligent face, thick black hair. . . . His speech is clear and full of warmth. . . . He enjoys the world, in spite of the mess it is, and he is fond of people, in spite of the mess they are."

Krupp, also tall and broad-shouldered, "is physically encumbered by his uniform, club, pistol, belt, and cap. And he is plainly not at home in the rôle of a policeman. . . . His understanding is less than McCarthy's, but he is honest and he doesn't try to bluff."

These two are in the midst of a somewhat heated discussion. Nick serves them beer and they go on with their argument. "You don't understand what I mean," the policeman is saying. "All I do is carry out orders, carry out orders. I don't know what the idea is behind the order. Who it's for, or who it's against, or why. All I do is carry it out."

The order for the moment is for Krupp to preserve the peace at the waterfront. For whom? How is Krupp to know? For the citizens, he suspects. McCarthy doubts it. McCarthy is a citizen, but if he happened to be on the other side from Krupp, Krupp would be preserving the peace by hitting him over the head with a club. . . . It's McCarthy's idea that Krupp doesn't read enough. And it's Krupp's idea that McCarthy doesn't know what he's fighting for.

McCarthy's fighting for the rights of the inferior—"For the world full of Mahoneys who haven't got what it takes to make monkeys out of everybody else, near by. The men who were created equal. Remember?"

"Mac, you're not inferior," insists Krupp.

"I'm a longshoreman. And an idealist. I'm a man with too much brawn to be an intellectual, exclusively. I married a small, sensitive, cultured woman so that my kids would be sissies instead of suckers. A strong man with any sensibility has no choice in this world but to be a heel, or a worker. I haven't the heart to be a heel, so I'm a worker. I've got a son in high school who's already thinking of being a writer."

"I wanted to be a writer once," admits Krupp.

"They *all* wanted to be writers," insists McCarthy. "Every maniac in the world that ever brought about the murder of people through war started out in an attic or a basement writing poetry. It stank. So they got even by becoming important heels. And it's still going on. . . . Right now on Telegraph Hill is some punk who is trying to be Shakespeare. Ten years from now he'll be a senator. Or a communist."

What the country needs is more magazines, McCarthy is convinced. Thousands of magazines, so every writer could get his stuff printed. That would make them believe that they are immortal and keep them from going haywire.

"The lousiest people in the world are writers," concludes McCarthy. "Language is all right. It's the people who use language that are lousy."

The Arab with the mouth organ has been listening intently. He shuffles a little closer to McCarthy. "What do you think,

Brother?" asks Mac. The Arab ponders deeply and answers cryptically: "No foundation. All the way down the line. What. What-not. Nothing. I go walk and look at the sky." Presumably he does.

Harry has developed a new dance. He thinks he has something this time. He is showing it to Nick, and to the others, when the phone rings. This time, of all people, it is Dudley Bostwick's Elsie. She's coming down. And is Dudley Bostwick pleased? "He hangs up, looks about him strangely, as if he were just born, walks around touching things, putting chairs in place, and so on." . . .

Harry, having convinced McCarthy that he is a great dancer, would also try another comedy monologue on him. And does. A sad muddled monologue proving that *"everybody's* behind the eight-ball." But again results are not what he expected. Krupp has a notion that perhaps he should take Harry in. McCarthy would stop that. Mac isn't laughing, that's true, but he doesn't know just why. "There are *kinds* of laughter, son," he says to Harry, comfortingly. "I must say, in all truth, that I *am* laughing, although not out loud."

"I want to *hear* people laugh. *Out loud.* That's why I keep thinking of funny things to say."

"Well. They may catch on in time," says McCarthy. He and Krupp go into the street together. . . .

Tom is back. He still has his five dollars. He is very unhappy about Kitty. He has left her crying in her room. She wouldn't stop crying. Wanted to tell him about her home. And the garden. The collie dog and the flowers. Tom can't stand Kitty crying. Tom loves Kitty. She's not like those other streetwalkers. Tom wants to marry Kitty. And why not? Joe sees no reason. But Nick does.

"She's been in burlesque," says Nick. "She's had flowers sent to her by European royalty. She's dined with young men of quality and social position. She's above Tom." . . .

Joe has sent Tom on another errand. He is to buy the biggest Rand-McNally map of the nations of Europe he can find in Schwabacher-Frey's. And on his way back he is to stop in a pawnshop on Third Street and get Joe a good revolver and some cartridges.

"What are you going to do?" Nick would know; "study the map and then go out and shoot somebody?"

"I want to read the names of some European towns and rivers

and valleys and mountains."

"What do you want with the revolver?"

"I want to study it. I'm interested in things."

Joe has another idea, too. Let Tom take the toys up to Kitty. They might stop her crying. "You get curious about the way they work and you forget whatever it is you're remembering that's making you cry. That's what they're for." Joe remembers. When his mother died he stopped crying when they gave him toys.

A newcomer has joined the group. "An old man who looks as if he might have been Kit Carson at one time walks in importantly, moves about, and finally stands at Joe's table."

KIT CARSON—Murphy's the name. Just an old trapper. Mind if I sit down?

JOE—Be delighted. What'll you drink?

KIT CARSON (*sitting down*)—Beer. Same as I've been drinking. And thanks.

JOE (*to* NICK)—Glass of beer, Nick. (NICK *brings beer to table.* KIT CARSON *swallows it in one swig, wipes his big white mustache with the back of his right hand.*)

KIT CARSON (*moving in*)—I don't suppose you ever fell in love with a midget weighing thirty-nine pounds?

JOE (*studying the man*)—Can't say I have, but have another beer.

KIT CARSON (*intimately*)—Thanks, thanks. Down in Gallup, twenty years ago. Fellow by the name of Rufus Jenkins came to town with six white horses and two black ones. Said he wanted a man to break the horses for him because his left leg was wood and he couldn't do it. Had a meeting at Parker's Mercantile Store and finally came to blows, me and Henry Walpal. Bashed his head with a brass cuspidor and ran away to Mexico, but he didn't die. Couldn't speak a word. Took up with a cattle-breeder named Diego, educated in California. Spoke the language better than you and me. Said, Your job, Murph, is to feed them prize bulls. I said, Fine, what'll I feed them? He said, Hay, lettuce, salt, beer, and aspirin. Came to blows two days later over an accordion he claimed I stole. I had *borrowed* it. During the fight I busted it over his head; ruined one of the finest accordions I ever saw. Grabbed a horse and rode back across the border. Texas. Got to talking with a fellow who looked honest. Turned out to be a Ranger who was looking for me.

JOE—Yeah. You were saying, a thirty-nine-pound midget.

KIT CARSON—Will I ever forget that lady? Will I ever get over that amazon of small proportions?

JOE—Will you?

KIT CARSON—If I live to be sixty.

JOE—Sixty? You look more than sixty now.

KIT CARSON—That's trouble showing in my face. Trouble and complications. I was fifty-eight three months ago.

JOE—That accounts for it, then. Go ahead, tell me more.

KIT CARSON—Told the Texas Ranger my name was Rothstein, mining engineer from Pennsylvania, looking for something worth while. Mentioned two places in Houston. Nearly lost an eye early one morning, going down the stairs. Ran into a six-footer with an iron-claw where his right hand was supposed to be. Said, You broke up my home. Told him I was a stranger in Houston. The girls gathered at the top of the stairs to see a fight. Seven of them. Six feet and an iron-claw. That's bad on the nerves. Kicked him in the mouth when he swung for my head with the claw. Would have lost an eye except for quick thinking. He rolled into the gutter and pulled a gun. Fired seven times. I was back upstairs. Left the place an hour later, dressed in silk and feathers, with a hat swung around over my face. Saw him standing on the corner, waiting. Said, Care for a wiggle? Said he didn't. I went on down the street and left town. I don't suppose you ever had to put a dress on to save your skin, did you?

JOE—No, and I never fell in love with a midget weighing thirty-nine pounds. Have another beer?

KIT CARSON—Thanks.

There are other tall stories that Kit Carson knows—and tells —with the slightest encouragement. One about herding cattle on a bicycle is good, though the story of the Toledo hurricane of 1918 may be a little more adventuresome. Carson is still going strong when Tom gets back with a Rand-McNally Atlas, a revolver and a box of cartridges. Seeing Tom and Joe are interested in other things Kit retires to the bar. . . .

Tom had taken the toys to Kitty, he reports, but they had not stopped her crying. Started her harder than ever, in fact. Tom is worried. He's afraid he and Joe will never have enough money so he can marry Kitty—

"Joe, I got to marry Kitty," Tom protests, seriously. "You ought to see the crazy room she lives in."

Joe—What kind of a room is it?

Tom—It's little. It crowds you in. It's bad, Joe. Kitty don't belong in a place like that.

Joe—You want to take her away from there?

Tom—Yeah. I want her to live in a house where there's room enough to live. Kitty ought to have a garden, or something.

Joe—You want to take care of her?

Tom—Yeah, sure, Joe. I ought to take care of somebody good that makes me feel like *I'm* somebody.

Joe—That means you'll have to get a job. What can you do?

Tom—I finished high school, but I don't know what I can do.

Joe—Sometimes when you think about it, what do you think you'd like to do?

Tom—Just sit around like you, Joe, and have somebody run errands for me and drink champagne and take things easy and never be broke and never worry about money.

Joe—That's a noble ambition.

Nick (*to* Joe)—How do you do it?

Joe—I really don't know, but I think you've got to have the full co-operation of the Good Lord.

Nick—I can't understand the way you talk.

Tom—Joe, shall I go back and see if I can get her to stop crying?

Joe—Give me a hand and I'll go with you.

Tom (*amazed*)—What! You're going to get up already?

Joe—She's crying, isn't she?

Tom—She's crying. Worse than ever now.

Joe—I thought the toys would stop her.

Tom—I've seen you sit in one place from four in the morning till two the next morning.

Joe—At my best, Tom, I don't travel by foot. That's all. Come on. Give me a hand. I'll find some way to stop her from crying.

Tom (*helping* Joe)—Joe, I never did tell you. You're a different kind of guy.

Joe (*swiftly, a little angry*)—Don't be silly. I don't understand things. I'm trying to understand them.

"Joe is a little drunk. They go out together. The lights go down slowly, while Wesley plays the piano.

When the lights are up again, Kitty's bed in a corner of a small room is seen. Kitty, "in a dress she has carried around with her from the early days in Ohio, is seated on the bed tying a ribbon in her hair." She is deeply grieved at the change she sees in her hand mirror. She tries to read, but cannot. The sight of an old picture taken in her youth sets her sobbing again.

Tom and Joe have arrived, but are not greatly successful as comforters. Joe is carrying a rather large toy carrousel which he sets going. The tinkling tune and the whirling toy slowly stir Kitty's interest. She sits on the edge of the bed and watches.

Tom has found the picture of Kitty as a girl. She wanted to be a great actress then, Kitty confesses. She is still beautiful, Tom insists.

"Do you remember when you were a little boy?" Kitty asks Tom.

"Yeah, I remember sometimes, Kitty," answers Tom, thoughtfully.

TOM (*looking steadily at* JOE)—Sometimes I wanted to be a locomotive engineer. Sometimes I wanted to be a policeman.

KITTY—I wanted to be a great actress. (*She looks up into* TOM's *face.*) Tom, didn't you ever want to be a doctor?

TOM (*looks at* JOE. JOE *holds* TOM's *eyes again, encouraging* TOM *by his serious expression to go on talking*)—Yeah, now I remember. Sure, Kitty. I wanted to be a doctor—once.

KITTY (*smiling sadly*)—I'm so glad. Because I wanted to be an actress and have a young doctor come to the theatre and see me and fall in love with me and send me flowers. (JOE *pantomimes to* TOM, *demanding that he go on talking.*)

TOM—I would do that, Kitty.

KITTY—I wouldn't know who it was, and then one day I'd see him in the street and fall in love with him. I wouldn't know he was the one who was in love with me. I'd think about him all the time. I'd dream about him. I'd dream of being near him the rest of my life. I'd dream of having children that looked like him. I wouldn't be an actress all the time. Only until I found him and fell in love with him. After that we'd take a train and go to beautiful cities and see the wonderful people everywhere and give money to the poor and whenever people were sick he'd go to them and make them well again. (TOM *looks at* JOE, *bewildered, confused, and full of sorrow.* KITTY *is deep in memory, almost in a trance.*)

JOE (*gently*)—Talk to her, Tom. Be the wonderful young

doctor she dreamed about and never found. Go ahead. Correct the errors of the world.

TOM (*pathetically*)—Joe. I don't know what to say.

There is a commotion in the hall. A mellow-voiced sailor is looking for Kitty Duval. Nor will he be stopped by any of those other women who are getting in his way. Tom is distressed. Kitty is sitting bolt upright, frightened, when the sailor, drunk and lonely, finds the door to Kitty's room. He is singing sadly as he comes to Kitty's bed. And then he stops— "Hi-ya, Kitty. . . . Oh, visitors! . . . Sorry. . . . A thousand apologies. . . . I'll come back later."

"If you do, I'll kill you," thunders Tom, grabbing the boy by the shoulders.

Joe has taken hold of Tom to stop him, and shoves the sailor away. He manages finally to get Tom's attention.

"Tom. You stay here with Kitty," says Joe, "I'm going down to Union Square to hire an automobile. I'll be back in a few minutes. We'll ride out to the ocean and watch the sun go down. Then we'll ride down the Great Highway to Half Moon Bay. We'll have supper down there, and you and Kitty can dance."

"Joe, you mean you're going to go on an errand for me? You mean you're not going to send me?" Tom is quite unable to express his amazement and gratitude.

"That's right," says Joe.

As Tom studies Kitty, his face becomes childlike and somber. "He sets the carrousel into motion, listens, watching Kitty, who lifts herself slowly, looking only at Tom. Tom lifts the turning carrousel and moves it slowly toward Kitty, as though the toy were his heart. The piano music comes up loudly and the lights go down, while Harry is heard dancing swiftly. The lights are out.

The scene changes back to Nick's place. When the lights come up Wesley, the colored boy, is at the piano. Harry is dancing on the stage. Nick is back of the bar. The Arab is where he was and Kit Carson is asleep, his head resting on his folded arms.

The optimistic drunk of the first scene comes barging in again through the doors and makes straight for the telephone, hoping to find a stray nickel in the return chute. Nick, as usual, comes from the bar to throw the drunk out, but this time he is stopped.

The drunk flashes a half dollar. For the half dollar he buys
himself a half dozen drinks, and tosses them off to a selection
of toasts: "To the old, God bless them." "To the new, God
love them." "To—children and small animals, like little dogs
that don't bite." "To reforestation!" And, in conclusion, "To
—President Taft."

The ring of the telephone awakens Kit Carson with a start.
He jumps to his feet, expecting, even inviting a fight. It
takes Kit a minute to get the lay of the situation. But his offer
still holds.

"If there is anything I can do, name it," Kit tells Nick. "I'm
fifty-eight years old; been through three wars; married four
times; the father of countless children whose names I don't even
know. I've got no money. I live from hand to mouth. But if
there's anything I can do, name it. I'll do it."

"Listen, Pop. For a moment, please sit down and go back
to sleep—for me," pleads Nick.

"I can do that, too," agrees Kit. And does. But not for
long.

Nick, at the phone, is protesting to someone in authority about
the vice squad agent, Blick. "I know his brother-in-law is important, but I don't want him to come down here," Nick is saying. "He looks for trouble everywhere, and he always finds it.
I don't break any laws. I've got a dive in the lousiest part of
town. Five years nobody's been robbed, murdered, or gypped.
I leave people alone. Your swanky joints uptown make trouble
for you every night." . . .

The doors swing in and Elsie Mandelspiegel comes down the
steps. "She is a beautiful dark girl, with a sorrowful, wise,
dreaming face, almost on the verge of tears, and full of pity.
There is an aura of dream about her." . . . Dudley doesn't notice her for a moment or two. When he does finally see her, he
is so amazed he can barely move or speak."

"Hello, Dudley," calls Elsie, looking at him.

"Elsie."

ELSIE—I'm sorry. (*Explaining.*) So many people are sick.
Last night a little boy died. I love you, but— (*She gestures,
trying to indicate how hopeless love is. They sit down.*)

DUDLEY (*staring at her, stunned and quieted*)—Elsie. You'll
never know how glad I am to see you. Just to see you. (*Pathetically.*) I was afraid I'd never see you again. It was driving
me crazy. I didn't want to live. Honest. (*He shakes his head*

mournfully, with dumb and beautiful affection.) I know. You
told me before, but I can't help it, Elsie. I love you.

ELSIE (*quietly, somberly, gently, with great compassion*)—I
know you love me, and I love you, but don't you see love is impossible in this world?

DUDLEY—Maybe it isn't, Elsie.

ELSIE—Love is for birds. They have wings to fly away on
when it's time for flying. For tigers in the jungle because they
don't know their end. We know our end. Every night I watch
over poor, dying men. I hear them breathing, crying, talking in
their sleep. Crying for air and water and love, for mother and
field and sunlight. We can never know love or greatness. We
should know both.

DUDLEY (*deeply moved by her words*)—Elsie, I love you.

ELSIE—You want to live. *I* want to live, too, but where?
Where can we escape our poor world?

DUDLEY—Elsie, we'll find a place.

ELSIE (*smiling at him*)—All right. We'll try again. We'll
go together to a room in a cheap hotel, and dream that the world
is beautiful, and that living is full of love and greatness. But in
the morning, can we forget debts, and duties, and the cost of
ridiculous things?

DUDLEY (*with blind faith*)—Sure, we can, Elsie.

ELSIE—All right, Dudley. Of course. Come on. The time
for the new pathetic war has come. Let's hurry, before they
dress you, stand you in line, hand you a gun, and have you kill
and be killed.

Elsie has taken Dudley's hand. He embraces her shyly, "as
if he might hurt her." They go, "as if they were a couple of
animals."

Two street-walkers who have come in and gone to the bar burst
out laughing. "It's floosies like her that raise hell with our
racket," sneers one of them.

Policeman Krupp has stopped in. The street-walkers pass him
gingerly on their way out. Krupp is worried again. Tonight
McCarthy is to be one of the longshoremen detailed to prevent
the unloading of the *Mary Luckenbach*—

"Why the hell McCarthy ever became a longshoreman instead
of a professor of some kind is something I'll never know," wails
Krupp.

"Cowboys and Indians, cops and robbers, longshoremen and
finks," ventures Nick.

"They're all guys who are trying to be happy; trying to make a living; support a family; bring up children; enjoy sleep. Go to a movie; take a drive on Sunday. They're all good guys, so out of nowhere, comes trouble. All they want is a chance to get out of debt and relax in front of a radio while Amos and Andy go through their act. What the hell do they always want to make trouble for?"

It is Krupp's conclusion that we're all crazy, the lot of us. "Here we are in this wonderful world, full of all the wonderful things—here we are—all of us, and look at us. Just look at us. We're crazy. We're nuts. We've got everything, but we always feel lousy and dissatisfied just the same."

"Of course we're crazy. Even so, we've got to go on living together."

"There's no hope," says Krupp, waving his hand at the people in Nick's. "I don't suppose it's right for an officer of the law to feel the way I feel, but, by God, right or not right, that's how I feel. Why are we all so lousy? This is a good world. . . . This is a nice world. So why do they make all the trouble?"

"I don't know. Why?"

"We're crazy, that's why. We're no good any more. All the corruption everywhere. The poor kids selling themselves. A couple of years ago they were in grammar school. Everybody trying to get a lot of money in a hurry. Everybody betting the horses. Nobody going quietly for a little walk to the ocean. Nobody taking things easy and not wanting to make some kind of killing. Nick, I'm going to quit being a cop. Let somebody else keep law and order. The stuff I hear about at headquarters. I'm thirty-seven years old, and I still can't get used to it. The only trouble is, the wife'll raise hell."

"Ah, the wife."

"She's a wonderful woman, Nick. We've got two of the swellest boys in the world. Twelve and seven years old."

The Arab has lifted himself out of his chair and moved closer. Krupp goes on with his explanation. For seven years he has wanted to quit, but if he quits, where's the money coming from? And that, agrees Nick, is one of the reasons we're all crazy.

"Every once in awhile I catch myself being mean, hating people just because they're down and out, broke and hungry, sick or drunk," Krupp confesses. "And then when I'm with the stuffed shirts at headquarters, all of a sudden I'm nice to them, trying to make an impression. On who? People I don't like. And I feel disgusted. (*With finality.*) I'm going to quit. That's

all. Quit. Out. I'm going to give them back the uniform and
the gadgets that go with it. I don't want any part of it. This
is a good world. What do they want to make all the trouble
for all the time?"

The Arab has an answer for that. "No foundation," he ventures. "All the way down the line."

"Is that all he ever says?" Krupp asks Nick.

"That's all he's been saying *this* week."

"What'd he say last week?"

"Didn't say anything. Played the harmonica."

That's a suggestion. The Arab gets out his harmonica again
to play an old country song. A moment later they are all listening quietly. Wesley has quit playing the piano. Harry has
stopped dancing.

"That's something," agrees Harry, solemnly.

"That's crying. That's crying," insists Wesley.

"I want to make people laugh," says Harry.

"That's deep, deep crying. That's crying a long time ago.
That's crying a thousand years ago. Some place five thousand
miles away."

Now Wesley has gone to the piano and is accompanying the
weird and lightly mournful harmonica solo. Harry goes back
to the stage and starts to dance, softly. For a few moments
they all listen. Then Krupp speaks—

"Well, anyhow, Nick . . . What I said, forget it."

"Sure."

"It gets me down once in awhile."

"No harm in talking."

Krupp has swung around, straightened his belt and squared his
shoulders. He is a policeman again. "Keep the girls out of
here," he warns, loudly.

"Take it easy," Nick shouts back, giving the bar a vicious
wiping.

The music and dancing have increased as the curtain falls.

ACT III

That evening, in Nick's, Willie is still at his marble game and
Kit Carson is looking on. Joe has the revolver and cartridges
that Tom brought beside him at his table. Nick is behind the
bar and Tom is leaning against the bar "dreaming of love and
Kitty."

A man in evening clothes and top hat, with a woman, also in

evening clothes, obviously slumming, are unexpected guests. They
sit at table and Nick offers them a menu. In Pacific Street a
Salvation Army band is playing and a loud but uncertain rendering of "The Blood of the Lamb" comes through the doors. Following the song the confession of a hoarse-voiced sinner, probably
the drunkard, can be heard.

Now Tom has left the bar and come over to Joe. He would
talk about Kitty Duval and thank Joe again for the ride to
Half Moon Bay and the dinner and champagne they had had.
But there is something else that has been troubling Tom—

"Joe, where do you get all that money?" he asks. "You paid
for the automobile. You paid for supper and the two bottles of
champagne at the Half Moon Bay Restaurant. You moved Kitty
out of the New York Hotel around the corner to the St. Francis
Hotel on Powell Street. I saw you pay her rent. I saw you give
her money for new clothes. Where do you get all that money,
Joe? Three years now and I've never asked."

Joe looks up at Tom, sorrowfully. He is "a little irritated, not
so much with Tom as with the world and himself, his own superiority." When he speaks it is "clearly, slowly and solemnly."

"Now don't be a fool, Tom," says Joe. "Listen carefully. If
anybody's got any money—to hoard or to throw away—you can
be sure he stole it from other people. Not from rich people who
can spare it, but from poor people who can't. From their lives
and from their dreams. I'm no exception. I *earned* the money
I throw away. I stole it like everybody else does. I hurt people
to get it. Loafing around this way, I *still* earn money. The
money itself earns more. I *still* hurt people. I don't know who
they are, or where they are. If I did, I'd feel worse than I do.
I've got a Christian conscience in a world that's got no conscience
at all. The world's trying to get some sort of a *social* conscience,
but it's having a devil of a time trying to do that. I've got money.
I'll always have money, as long as this world stays the way it is.
I don't work. I don't make anything. (*He sips.*) I drink. I
worked when I was a kid. I worked *hard*. I mean hard, Tom.
People are supposed to enjoy living. I got tired. (*He lifts the
gun and looks at it while he talks.*) I decided to get even on the
world. Well, you can't enjoy living unless you work. Unless you
do something. I don't do anything. I don't *want* to do anything
any more. There isn't anything I can do that won't make me
feel embarrassed. Because I can't do simple, good things. I
haven't the patience. And I'm too smart. Money is the guiltiest
thing in the world. It stinks. Now don't ever bother me about

it again."

"I didn't mean to make you feel bad, Joe," meekly says Tom.

Now Joe has another idea. He would have Tom take the revolver and the cartridges out and give them to some worthy hold-up man. At this the society lady and her escort are both curious and disturbed. The man is disgusted as well.

"You wanted to visit a honky-tonk," he growls. "Well, this is a honky-tonk." And then he adds, addressing the world: "Married twenty-eight years and she's still looking for adventure!"

Joe is determined the gun shall go to someone who needs a gun, but he decides to attend to that himself. Meantime let Tom go out and get him a lot of other things—copies of *Life, Liberty* and *Time;* all the kinds of chewing gum there are, several colors of jelly beans and six panatela cigars. While he's about it let him give a dollar to a news kid, a dollar to an old man and two dollars to the Salvation Army. Finally, let him ask the Salvation Army to sing the one that goes: "Let the lower lights be burning, send a gleam across the wave—" He breaks hoarsely and loudly into this hymn by way of making identification perfect.

"He's absolutely insane," ventures the society lady.

"You asked me to take you to a honky-tonk instead of to the Mark Hopkins," growls her man. "You're *here* in a honky-tonk. I can't help it if he's crazy."

Kit Carson has left Willie and the marble game, lured by Joe's singing. Kit who has also been to a Presbyterian Sunday School, likes to sing, too. He sits down with Joe and when the Salvation Army starts "Let the lower lights be burning" Kit and Joe join in lustily. So does the society lady—until her husband stops her.

"Know anything about guns?" Joe asks Kit, who at the moment is busily flirting with the society lady.

"All there is to know," Kit answers, wisely. "Didn't fight the Ojibways for nothing. Up there in the Lake Takalooca Country, in Michigan. (*Remembering.*) Along about in 1881 or two. Fought 'em right up to the shore of the lake. Made 'em swim for Canada. One fellow in particular, an Indian named Harry Daisy."

At Joe's invitation, Kit cocks an expert eye at the gun and pronounces it a "pretty nice hunk of shooting iron." He becomes increasingly important as he awkwardly takes the gun apart and explains its workings. He has the barrel out and loaded with cartridges finally, and as he puts it back is playfully pointing it at the society pair when these two jump screaming to their feet. The scream scares Kit more than the gun scares society. Not until Joe has recovered and unloaded it is the quiet of Nick's place restored.

It is, however, not quiet for long. Willie has hit the jack-pot, or lucky total, and the marble game is groaning and lighting up like a circus wagon. A loud bell rings. An American flag pops out. From the depths of the machine come the strains of "America." The delighted Willie stands at salute. Joe, Kit and the society lady stand and join in the singing.

Presently the machine has quieted. The flag is back in place and only Willie's enthusiasm is still at its peak. With an air of triumph he collects his winnings—six nickels—from Nick—

"Took me a little while, but I finally did it," Willie relates proudly. "It's scientific, really. With a little skill a man can make a modest living beating the marble games. Not that that's what I want to do. I just don't like the idea of anything getting the best of me. A machine or anything else. Myself, I'm the kind of a guy who makes up his mind to do something, and then goes to work and does it. There's no other way a man can be a success at anything."

Tom is back with his purchases, his arms filled with magazines, chewing gum, jelly beans, etc. Shortly Joe and Tom have started a gum chewing contest to see which of them can get the most gum in the mouth at one time. Kit is the referee.

The contestants can still talk, however, and Tom would have further knowledge of Kitty Duval. Why had Joe moved her from the New York Hotel to the St. Francis Hotel, and bought her all those new clothes? Joe had his reasons. A nice room, good clothes and good food will work a great change with Kitty. A change in which Joe expects Tom to figure.

"By the grace of God you're the other half of that girl," says Joe. "Not the angry woman that swaggers into this water-front dive and shouts because the world has kicked her around. *Any*-body can have *her*. You belong to the little kid in Ohio who once dreamed of living. Not with her carcass, for money, so she can have food and clothes, and pay rent. With *all* of her. I put her in that hotel, so she can have a chance to gather herself together again. She can't do that in the New York Hotel. You saw what happens there. There's nobody anywhere for her to talk to, except you. They all make her talk like a whore. After a while, she'll *believe* them. Then she won't be able to remember. She'll get lonely. Sure. People can get lonely for *misery*, even. I want her to go on being lonely for you, so she can come together again the way she was meant to be from the beginning. Loneli-

ness is good for people. Right now it's the only thing for
Kitty. . . . You really want to marry her, don't you?"

"Honest to God, Joe. Only, I haven't got any money."

This is a problem Joe thinks may be overcome. Tom will have
to have a job of some kind. He might try prize-fighting, except
that he could never hit a man he didn't hate. He might try
driving a truck. Why not? Tom loves travel and he can drive
anything with wheels and a motor. Another minute and Joe is
talking to a friend on the phone and Tom has a job. Tom hasn't
got a driver's license and he doesn't belong to a union—but those
things can be taken care of later. Let the trucker have a look at
Tom, suggests Joe. Sure, he'd be ready to start for San Diego
anytime.

Tom is ready and excited. The only thing he worries about
is Kitty, and Joe agrees to look after her. . . .

Wesley and Harry are back. They have been over to the
docks watching the longshoremen's strike. Watching the cops
beat up the strikers, too. Nick gets them back to work. Let
Harry tend bar while he goes over to the dock and has a look for
himself. And let Wesley do a little work at the piano.

The society pair has ordered and been served a bottle of champagne and everything has settled down for the moment when
Kitty Duval comes in. She is looking very beautiful in her new
clothes, but she seems a little embarrassed. Everybody in the
room is greatly impressed, except Joe. He accepts Kitty as she is,
quite naturally. Has her sit by him, and has Harry bring another
glass for her.

"Where is Tom?" asks Kitty, sorrowfully.

"He's getting a job tonight driving a truck. He'll be back in
a couple of days."

KITTY (*sadly*)—I told him I'd marry him.

JOE—He wanted to see you and say good-by.

KITTY—He's too good for me. He's like a little boy. (*Wearily.*) I'm— Too many things have happened to me.

JOE—Kitty Duval, you're one of the few truly innocent people
I have ever known. He'll be back in a couple of days. Go back
to the hotel and wait for him.

KITTY—That's what I mean. I can't stand being alone. I'm
no good. I tried very hard. I don't know what it is. I miss—
(*She gestures.*)

JOE (*gently*)—Do you really want to come back here, Kitty?

KITTY—I don't know. I'm not sure. Everything smells different. I don't know how to feel, or what to think. (*Gesturing pathetically.*) I know I don't belong there. It's what I've wanted all my life, but it's too late. I try to be happy about it, but all I can do is remember everything and cry.

JOE—I don't know what to tell you, Kitty. I didn't mean to hurt you.

KITTY—You haven't hurt me. You're the only person who's ever been good to me. I've never known anybody like you. I'm not sure about love any more, but I know I love you, and I know I love Tom.

JOE—I love you too, Kitty Duval.

KITTY—He'll want babies. I know he will. I know I will, too. Of course I will. I can't— (*She shakes her head.*)

JOE—Tom's a baby himself. You'll be very happy together. He wants you to ride with him in the truck. Tom's good for you. You're good for Tom.

KITTY (*like a child*)—Do you want me to go back and wait for him?

JOE—I can't tell you what to do. I think it would be a good idea, though.

KITTY—I wish I could tell you how it makes me feel to be alone. It's almost worse.

JOE—It might take a whole week, Kitty. (*He looks at her sharply, at the arrival of an idea.*) Didn't you speak of reading a book? A book of poems?

KITTY—I didn't know what I was saying.

JOE (*trying to get up*)—Of course you knew. I think you'll like poetry. Wait here a minute, Kitty. I'll go see if I can find some books.

KITTY—All right, Joe.

Joe has gone when Blick of the vice squad comes in. He is accompanied by two policemen. Blick is looking for Nick and anything he can find to complain about. He barks at Harry and commands Wesley to shut off the music. He sees Kitty and begins a vicious cross-questioning of her and her right to be there. What's her name? Where does she live? Where does she work? What does she do?

As Blick's manner becomes rough Kit Carson objects. No man can talk to a lady like that in his presence. The cops start to move in on Kit. Blick waves them back.

"It's all right, boys. I'll take care of this," he says, turning to Kit: "What'd you say?"

"You got no right to hurt people. Who are you?"

For an answer Blick grabs Kit and hustles him out the door. There is the sound of a blow and a groan. Blick is back, breathing hard. Again he turns on Kitty. The society man thinks to interfere, too, but changes his mind before the glowering threats of Blick. Disgustedly the visitor takes his wife by the arm and hustles her out of the place.

Blick is standing menacingly above Kitty, hurling his questions at her, sneering at her answers. She tells him again that her name is Kitty Duval; that she has recently moved from the New York Hotel to the St. Francis; that she is looking for work; that she is an actress, that she has worked in burlesque—

"You're a liar!" shouts Blick.

"It's the truth," answers Kitty, pathetically.

BLICK—What are you doing here?

KITTY—I came to see if I could get a job here.

BLICK—Doing what?

KITTY—Singing—and—dancing.

BLICK—You can't sing or dance. What are you lying for?

KITTY—I can. I sang and danced in burlesque all over the country.

BLICK—You're a liar.

KITTY—I said lines, too.

BLICK—So you danced in burlesque?

KITTY—Yes.

BLICK—All right. Let's see what you did.

KITTY—I can't. There's no music, and I haven't got the right clothes.

BLICK—There's music. (*To* WESLEY.) Put a nickel in that phonograph. (WESLEY *can't move.*) Come on. Put a nickel in that phonograph. (WESLEY *does so. To* KITTY.) All right. Get up on that stage and do a hot little burlesque number. (KITTY *stands. Walks slowly to the stage, but is unable to move.* JOE *comes in holding three books.*) Get going, now. Let's see you dance the way you did in burlesque, all over the country. (KITTY *tries to do a burlesque dance. It is beautiful in a tragic way.*) All right, start taking them off! (KITTY *removes her hat and starts to remove her jacket.*)

JOE (*moving closer to the stage, amazed—hurrying to* KITTY) —Get down from there. (*He takes* KITTY *into his arms. She is crying. To* BLICK.) What the hell do you think you're doing!

WESLEY (*like a little boy, very angry*)—It's that man, Blick. He made her take off her clothes. He beat up the old man, too.

Blick turns angrily on Wesley and pushes him into the kitchen. The boy's groans follow the sound of blows.

Tom comes through the doors. His truck is outside. Joe gives him his orders quickly. Let him take Kitty with him to San Diego. She can dress in the truck. He hands Tom money, and Kitty the books he has brought. As Wesley's cries grow louder Joe pushes Tom and Kitty toward the door—

"Get out of here!" he shouts. "Get married in San Diego. I'll see you when you get back."

Tom and Kitty have gone. Joe takes the revolver out of his pocket and walks toward the kitchen door.

"I've always wanted to kill somebody, but I never knew who it should be," he mutters.

At the door Joe stands for a second watching Blick. He aims very carefully and pulls the trigger. There is no report.

Nick has come through the doors, noted what is happening and makes a rush to disarm Joe.

"That dumb Tom," Joe protests. "Buys a six-shooter that won't even shoot once!" He sinks into a chair, dead to the world.

Blick backs out of the kitchen. Nick turns on him—

"Blick! I told you to stay out of here!" He has taken the vice squad agent by the collar and started him for the door. "Now get out of here! If you come back again I'm going to take you in that room where you've been beating up that colored boy, and I'm going to murder you—slowly—with my hands. Beat it!"

Harry has been sent to look after Wesley. Willie comes from the street without sensing that anything is changed. He has another nickel for the marble game. He puts it in and the machine, stopped at the winning cog, again throws up the American flag and begins to play "America." Willie stands again at attention, but as the flag disappears he shakes his head thoughtfully—

"As far as I'm concerned this is the only country in the world," he announces. "If you ask me, nuts to Europe!"

The machine is still going. The flag keeps coming up and going down. Willie gives the machine a whack on the side, and it runs faster than before. Finally he tries a new nickel and that stops it.

Outside in the distance two shots are heard.

Joe is still apparently unconscious at his table. The newsboy speaks to him. No answer. He starts the phonograph playing Joe's favorite "Missouri Waltz."

Nick bursts through the swinging doors. He is delighted. "Joe, Blick's dead," Nick shouts, exultantly. "Somebody just shot him and none of the cops are trying to find out who!"

Joe doesn't hear. Nick shouts the news a second time.

JOE (*coming to*)—Blick? Dead? Good! That God damn gun wouldn't go off. I *told* Tom to get a good one.

NICK—Joe, you wanted to kill that guy! (HARRY *returns.*) I'm going to buy you a bottle of champagne. (NICK *goes to the bar.* JOE *rises, takes his hat from rack, puts coat on. The newsboy jumps up, helps* JOE *with coat.*) What's the matter, Joe?

JOE—Nothing. Nothing.

NICK—How about the champagne?

JOE—Thanks. (*Going.*)

NICK—It's not eleven yet. Where you going, Joe?

JOE—I don't know. Nowhere.

NICK—Will I see you tomorrow?

JOE—I don't know. I don't think so. (KIT CARSON *enters, walks to* JOE. JOE *and* KIT *look at one another knowingly.*) Somebody just shot a man. How are you feeling?

KIT—Never felt better in my life. (*Loudly, bragging, but somber.*) I shot a man once. In San Francisco. Shot him two times. In 1939, I think it was. In October. Fellow named Blick or Glick or something like that. Couldn't stand the way he talked to ladies. Went up to my room and got my old pearl-handled revolver and waited for him on Pacific Street. Saw him walking, and let him have it. Two times. Had to throw the beautiful revolver into the Bay. (HARRY, NICK, *the* ARAB *and the* DRUNKARD *close in around him.*)

JOE (*searching his pockets, brings out the revolver, puts it in* KIT'S *hand, looks at him with great admiration and affection, loudly.*) Kit, did I ever tell you about the time I fell in love with a midget weighing thirty-nine pounds?

KIT (*amazed*)—Now, son.

"Joe walks slowly to the stairs leading to the street, turns and waves. Kit, and then one by one everybody else, waves, and the marble game goes into its beautiful American routine again. The play ends."

THE CURTAIN FALLS

SKYLARK

A Comedy in Three Acts

By Samson Raphaelson

"SKYLARK," which was the first popular success of the 1939-40 theatre season, is the type of comedy that frequently confounds the critics and establishes the most friendly and satisfactory relations with its audiences. The story is not in any sense novel, the situations have at least been frequently suggested, if not actually duplicated in the theatre, and the results finally achieved in the resolving of plot and theme are definitely and conventionally foreshadowed.

Still the play is a success. In this instance the presence of Miss Gertrude Lawrence in the star rôle was admittedly greatly in the play's favor. But it probably will be found when "Skylark" reaches the Summer theatres and such Winter stock companies as remain active that its essential dramatic and comedy values will prove as dependably serviceable in the country as they did on Broadway. Which is another way of saying that they are the same human and sympathetically acceptable values that have accounted for the popular success of a great many thousand successes on the stage and on the screen over a long period of time.

Miss Lawrence, Mr. Raphaelson, her author, and John Golden, the producer, had some little difficulty extracting a play from the Raphaelson magazine story that served as its inspiration. They tried a first version in Boston, but with no better than fair success. They worked out a second version for a trial spin at a Summer theatre in Dennis, Mass., and took it later to Chicago, where it was more generously approved. Finally they brought the play to Broadway and there it was played prosperously the season through.

The first view we have of the country house of the Tony Kenyons, near New York, finds it set for a party. The living room, opening onto a garden terrace and flanked by the main hall, is furnished "in sparkling form." The time is a Saturday evening in late Summer.

"The guests were invited for eight o'clock, but it's only a quarter to, and naturally we don't expect anybody till nine," Theodore, the butler, is telling a delayed guest over the phone at curtain rise.

George Gorell, neighbor and member of Tony Kenyon's advertising firm, is an early arrival. He has stopped in before going home to dress because he is bringing Tony's present to Lydia Kenyon. It is the Kenyons' tenth anniversary. That is what the party has been organized to celebrate.

Tony's present is a wrist watch from Cartiers. He probably would have selected it himself, but he has been working day and night on a new Baby Malt campaign and has had no time for anything, not even anniversaries. Tonight he is hoping for an okay on the account from Harley Valentine, head of the Baby Malt syndicate, who is to be a guest.

"When you're a kid you go to parties for ice cream," Tony explains to Gorell, whose eyebrows have risen at the suggestion of mixing business with an anniversary. "When you're a young fellow, you go to find romance. But when you get on in years, like us, how dull a party can be if you don't close at least one deal."

There is also a Mrs. Valentine who wields considerable influence in the Valentine family, but Tony has not had to play politics with her up to now.

"She's quite a gal," Gorell remembers. "When I used to take her out she was only in the chorus—but she certainly knew what she wanted."

"She scares me a little," admits Tony.

"Oh, she's not so bad. If you can get her interested, you'll get your okay in five minutes. Myrtle Valentine knows as little about advertising as she does about virtue, but she knows which side of the bed her husband sleeps on."

"I'd rather concentrate on her husband. It's much simpler to handle the half-witted sons of self-made men than the smart girls who marry them."

Tony has slipped Lydia's anniversary gift into his pocket. George Gorell has gone his way to dress for the party. Theodore has brought in the evening papers and put them on a small table. Lydia Kenyon comes down the stairs for a final check-up. "She is an attractive, spirited woman. She wears a dressing robe. Obviously all she needs to do is to change from it into her party dress."

Theodore has been careful about the arrangements. He has hidden all the Lucky Strikes, Chesterfields and Camel cigarettes. He has put Abercrombie's Sunshine Soap in the bathrooms. He has brought out the new pinch bottles of Dillingham's Whiskey.

Certainly no advertising agency executive could ask for more. But—what can they do with Baby Malt? "If we just put a can of it on the piano in the music room it might look a little obvious, don't you think?" asks Lydia. Theodore is afraid it might.

There is also the problem of Lydia's anniversary gift for Tony. This turns out to be a large, leather-bound scrapbook, and she would like to put it where Tony will be most likely to pick it up accidentally. On top of the evening papers seems a good place. Lydia barely has time to get it there before Tony is back.

Tony is still stirred up about his Baby Malt account, and none of Lydia's obvious subterfuges can get him anywhere near the easy chair, the evening papers or the scrapbook. What he is interested in is the Valentines and Lydia's contacts with them. Does Lydia know that Myrtle Valentine was once in the chorus? Lydia does. She also knows that Myrtle was once Miss Broadway, and then Miss New York, and then Miss America. After which she became Mrs. Valentine.

How does Lydia get along with Mrs. Valentine? Oh, not badly at all. And with Mr. Valentine, too. It was Mr. Valentine who had once said to her: "My dear Mrs. Kenyon, you have a wonderful cook—" and asked for the bicarbonate of soda. Proving, to Tony, that Mr. Valentine is an epicure. Something might be made out of that.

Still the scrapbook remains unnoticed. Even when he is looking for an evening paper Tony slips one out from under Lydia's gift and does not see it. When Lydia playfully balances the scrapbook on her head and calls attention to it as a newfangled hat Tony is not surprised. She will probably be wearing something like that one of these days. In complete disgust Lydia finally drops the book on the floor with a thud. Then Tony comes to.

They are both on the floor now turning the pages and smiling at the recollections they inspire. A picture of old "Jedge" Parker who had married them. A picture of a Fifth Avenue bus, vintage of eleven years ago, which is very like the one on which they had picked each other up—

"Gee, that was a hot day—and you were wearing a kind of, a sort of flowery dress. . . . Am I right?"

"Oh, Tony!" At least this is some show of interest and Lydia is encouraged.

Tony (*innocently rambling*)—Don't you wish sometimes for the good old days? . . . You know, when we were young, Maggie, honeysuckle climbin' round yo' doah?

LYDIA—Nah—this is good enough for me.

TONY (*waking up a little*)—I don't like the way you said that.

LYDIA—So all right. So I'm one of these unhappy wives.

TONY—I'm not kidding—I'm half serious . . . Did you like it better when you were a college graduate, learning the department store business from the bottom?

LYDIA—Of course not. It only took me one second to give up my career for the man I love.

TONY—What do you do with yourself all day, anyway?

LYDIA—Tony, dear, if I told you, it would sound so boring that I'd stop doing it myself.

TONY—But you like it, huh?

LYDIA—So long as I don't talk about it. (*Her hand has been on the page ready to turn, and now she turns the page over. On the next page is glued a sheet of paper.* TONY *glances at it—and then looks closer with real interest.*)

TONY—Now where in blazes did you ever get that!

LYDIA—From your own trembling hand, darling.

TONY (*reading*)—"Dear Sir: We regret that we are compelled to dispense with your services as of today. Please consider this our official two-weeks' notice. Copy department. . . ." (*He looks up at the top of the sheet and reads the date.*) "December 7, 1930." Nine years ago. Swell Christmas present, wasn't it?

LYDIA—Terrific.

TONY—Wasn't that the Christmas you were going to have a baby—and then . . .

LYDIA (*quietly*)—Yes, that was the Christmas.

TONY (*soberly*)—I know a thing like that must be an awful blow to a woman—to realize she can never have a baby. I think about it every once in a while. . . . I often wonder how much you think about it.

LYDIA—Do you?

TONY—It must have been tough on you.

LYDIA—It was, but in other ways it was one of the loveliest Christmases I ever had.

TONY—How come?

LYDIA—It was, that's all.

TONY—Me out of a job, thoroughly licked, not a dollar in the house, hanging around you like a kid grabbing his mother's apron strings—practically weeping on your bosom . . .

LYDIA—I liked it. (*She turns another page quickly.*) Just for a belly-laugh, how would you like to read some of your own love

letters?
TONY (*uncomfortably*)—Are they really funny?
LYDIA—They're beautiful.
TONY (*impressed*)—No kiddin'?
LYDIA—No kiddin'.

Tony is a little embarrassed by the love letters, and uncomfortable. He covers by begging off from reading more of them.
He hadn't realized how tired he really is. What he needs is a
vacation. Hasn't had one for three—maybe four—years. Six,
to be exact, Lydia is quick to remind him.
And now Tony is off on a dream trip that soon has them both
enthused. He deserves a vacation. He will take it up with the
firm. They'll go to South America. Buenos Aires! Rio de
Janeiro! They'll take a one-cabin boat and make it a long trip.
They'll—
"Tony Kenyon, I love you, I adore you, I worship you," thrills
Lydia.
"Live!" exclaims Tony, exultantly.
"Love!"
"Jeehosophat, I'm thirty-five."
"Dammit, I'm thirty."
"Are you really?"
"Going on *forty*."
"You don't look it."
"Tony, may I ask a favor?"
"Go right ahead."
"How about a little kiss?"
"And why not?" He kisses her—"an affectionate, husbandly
kiss."
"I'm not the girl to ask for passion just before a party—"
admits Lydia. "But try again, will you?"
Tony has carefully arranged his trousers so the knees won't
crease, taken Lydia in his arms and is "about to deliver a classic
kiss," when a new thought assails him. He could open a branch
office in Buenos Aires while he's there! And that thought leads
to others. The risk he's taking in staying away from the office
for three months. The competition is pretty terrible. And you
can't blame the boys for wanting to push themselves whenever a
chance offers—
"Maybe we'd better not go," suggests Lydia, a little painfully.
"It was a nice impulse," admits Tony. There is a pause.
"I had a wonderful trip!" declares Lydia, though not too good-

naturedly.

Theodore has come to make a confession. He could not help overhearing Mr. Kenyon when he and Mr. Gorell were discussing Mrs. Valentine and he feels that it is his duty to report what he knows of Mrs. Valentine's attempts to acquire Mattie, the Kenyon cook. On the word of Mrs. Valentine's butler, that is Mrs. Valentine's intention.

Lydia is not at all surprised, but the situation is news to Tony. Welcome news, too. Certainly something can be done about this. Lydia, however, has not the slightest intention of letting Mrs. Valentine have Mattie, if that is what Tony is thinking of doing.

"Listen!" commands Tony, with spirit. "One—Baby Malt is my account. Two—there's an additional million in advertising which I may get tonight. Three—that means an additional one hundred and fifty thousand to the agency in commissions. Four— *that* means I'm sitting prettier than ever."

"One—I've had Mattie for five years. Two—I'm very fond of her."

Tony can't understand. Lydia, he recalls, has been acting strangely for the last week or two. Lydia can't understand how he knew that, seeing he hadn't been paying her the least attention. No, she is not trying to start a fight. She is perfectly willing to drop the subject right now— But—she refuses to reconsider the cook problem—

"If you want a drink, I'll pour it for you. If you want a joke, I'll try to amuse you. And if you want a kiss—I still have thousands in storage." But further than that Lydia refuses to budge.

TONY—Darling, this is our anniversary party—how can you talk like that?

LYDIA—This party isn't yours and mine. Our guests are a Who's Who of the advertising business. It's a super-conference.

TONY (*angrily*)—You're certainly bubbling over with romance!

LYDIA (*rising and beginning to straighten the room*)—To mention romance in the same breath with this party would be a social error—or should I say a business error?

TONY (*following her*)—I'll be damned! Married ten years, and everything runs smoothly, and—what's eating you all of a sudden, anyway?

LYDIA—It isn't all of a sudden. It's been going on for six years.

TONY—That's a fine how-do-you-do! Six years! And in all those years couldn't you find a more appropriate time than tonight to—to . . .

LYDIA—As a matter of fact, no. You're too busy Saturdays and Sundays having conferences. Besides, I didn't want to nag at you.

TONY—What the hell do you think you're doing right now?

LYDIA—Answering questions.

TONY—And what do you mean, six years? In the last six years you've had anything any woman could ask for.

LYDIA—No. I had that in the first four years.

TONY—I suppose you hate this house, and the clothes you have on, and the wrist watch I gave you for your anniversary. (LYDIA *stares at him.*) Good Lord—I nearly forgot! (*He fishes out the jewel case with an embarrassed grin, and gives it to her.*) Happy anniversary! (LYDIA *looks at him a moment with growing tenderness and amusement. Then she opens the case. Her face lights up as she sees the wrist watch.*)

LYDIA—Oh, it's gorgeous! (*She turns it over.*) What a beautiful inscription—"From Tony, to Lydia, with love!" . . . (*She rises and flings her arms around him.*) Oh, thank you, darling!

TONY (*embracing her*)—Do you really like it?

LYDIA—I adore it.

TONY—Love me?

LYDIA—I love you very much. In fact, I married you for love.

TONY (*breaking angrily out of the embrace and striding away*)—What do you think I married *you* for?

LYDIA (*following him, also angry*)—I've often wondered! Apparently to entertain all your business contacts, most of whom I dislike—and you dislike too, if you stop to think about it.

Tony is still at a loss to understand Lydia's attitude. All he has asked her to do is to appease his biggest client. But Lydia is through with appeasement. This is the point at which appeasement is going to stop—

"You'll have to keep your clients out of my kitchen," she warns him. "The living room is as far as they go."

"All right," thunders Tony, losing his temper. "Now get this. If you don't give that cook to Mrs. Valentine and do it with good grace . . ."

"What do you expect me to do—put Mattie on a platter and deliver her to the Valentine house with an apple in her mouth?"

"Well, I'll tell you what *I'll* do. I'm going to fire Mattie tomorrow and send her over myself with a bonus."

"You wouldn't do that! Tony Kenyon, if you dared to do such a thing, I'd never talk to you again as long as I lived!"

Theodore has come to announce the arrival of the first guests—
Ned and Charlotte Franklin. Tony and Lydia are still boiling,
but automatically slip back into their rôles of host and hostess.

Tony and Ned go to the library to look at the Baby Malt draw-
ings. Lydia and Charlotte have a moment for mutual commisera-
tions. Neither of them is exactly happy. It is natural they
should think again of the days of their independence, when they
both had good jobs and good times. Perhaps they might again
do something about their living problems that would give them
a greater satisfaction than they are now enjoying. Lydia might
go in for interior decoration. Charlotte might take a chance at
acting.

"What do you suppose we'll be like ten years from now?"
Lydia demands.

"I can't imagine."

"I can. We'll be ten pounds heavier. Charlotte, is that all
marriage is—anniversaries and starches and fats?"

She is half way up the stairs before Charlotte has any chance
to answer. It is time for the party to assemble and there is a
job of dressing to be done.

Charlotte is alone when Bill Blake enters. Bill "is hard-bitten,
rugged, but with a potent dream in him somewhere. He might
be any age. At the moment he has had a few drinks, but this
affects only the tangent of his mind, not of his body. He is in
evening clothes, black tie . . . Bill always walks slowly, almost
scuffling; rarely looks at anyone directly, seeming most of the
time to be in a world of his own; doesn't smile or get excited,
and yet is anything but an unfriendly fellow."

Bill's concern for the moment is liquor. He is, to trust his
slightly incoherent explanation, a guest at the home of Mr. and
Mrs. Valentine. They have included him in their invitation to
the Kenyons'. Mrs. Valentine has an idea that he is "too sweet
on the bottle," so such drinking as he does during the evening
he hopes to keep a secret between himself and Theodore.

Presently Lydia is back. Her evening gown is "a very smart
and expensive one, as is becoming the wife of a figure in the
advertising world." She is puzzled by the presence of Bill Blake,
even after Charlotte has tried to explain his being a guest of the
Valentines. Bill decides that perhaps they should play Twenty
Questions and that Charlotte should be It. Then she can go
clear down to the end of the garden and stay there until she is
called.

Charlotte accepts her dismissal with a gay little laugh and

leaves Lydia to study Bill and make what she can of him. Lydia begins by suggesting that Bill have another drink. Bill thinks he will be needing one, because "there's nothing so sad as a wedding anniversary." Lydia decides she is glad to meet Bill. As to that, Bill is doubtful.

"Any woman that's been married ten years doesn't really want to meet me," insists Bill. "Meeting me is meeting life. You just want to play at meeting me. You want to go slumming with life. You want to shoot the chutes with a happy little frightened squeak, then you want to nibble at some popcorn, climb into your car, go home and shiver gratefully about what you almost did."

"Now look here, Mister—what are you selling? The sanctity of the home, or fun on the side?"

"I'm for either one of them—so long as it rings the bell."

Lydia considers this for a moment and then decides in Bill's favor. "What's your name?" she asks, moving toward him.

"Bill Blake."

"How do you do, Mr. Blake!"

They are shaking hands when the Valentines arrive. Tony follows them in from the hall. "Myrtle Valentine is young, beautiful, hard and obvious. Her figure is particularly good, and she dresses it carefully. She wears a good deal of jewelry, mostly diamonds. Harley is middle-aged, well-fed—a friendly fellow, trying vaguely to be the son of his rugged pioneering father but failing for the rather pathetic reason that he is a fool."

Mrs. Valentine is quick to see that Bill Blake has made himself known and that Lydia is interested. She would, if she could, take over the situation and is active in both formally introducing and explaining Bill. Mr. Blake, it appears, is one of the best court-room lawyers in New York, *the* William Blake who is so often in the newspapers. It was Bill, Harley Valentine recalls, who, in addressing the court about corporations on one occasion, "said that big corporations have as much right to steal as big gangsters —ha, ha, ha!"

"Yes, Mr. Blake has great possibilities—but he needs to be guided," adds Myrtle.

"Listen, Mrs. V.," counters Bill, who has been sitting expressionless through all the chatter, "don't talk so loud, see?—because I can overhear every word, get me?"

It is Harley Valentine who takes charge now. The evening belongs to the Kenyons, as Harley figures it, and he is prepared to offer a toast—

"To the Kenyons! Here before us stands a couple who are

young, healthy, successful, with a charming home, and the most
wonderful cook this side of the Rocky Mountains—"

"How right you are!" interrupts Myrtle Valentine. "Do you
know, Mrs. Kenyon, we've been coveting and *coveting* your cook."

"Really?"

"I've often said to Harley, 'Poochie, the—c-cuisine at the Kenyons' is so much more divine than poor me seems able to provide.' "

"You flatter me." The atmosphere is at something of a tension.

"Darling—may I make a suggestion?" Tony asks, quickly.

"I know just what you are going to say, dear," quickly replies
Lydia, with deadly urbanity. "We *must* ask Mr. and Mrs. Valentine to dinner more frequently."

This is not at all what either Tony or Mrs. Valentine had in
mind. At Lydia's suggestion Tony tries to explain—

"Mrs. Valentine, we were discussing our cook a while ago. Then
we remembered how you enjoyed Mattie's, er, cuisine—and my
wife said to me, 'Why not ask Mrs. Valentine if she would like
to have Mattie?' Well, that's what we're doing right now."

"Now, isn't that lovely?" babbles Harley, innocently.

"I don't know what to say! It's such a generous offer—I
couldn't possibly think of it! And yet— (MRS. VALENTINE *has
leaned toward* LYDIA.) "Well, only on one condition—*you* must
have dinner with *us* one of these days."

"Yes, yes, you really must," echoes Harley.

At which moment Charlotte, still playing Twenty Questions,
bursts in from the garden. She finds the party anything but
ready. Bill welcomes her genially with the announcement that
they are all about to drink a toast to the Kenyons. Charlotte
rounds up her husband, George Gorell arrives and everything is
set. The guests are standing, with raised glasses, Lydia expressionless, Tony stiff and smiling, as Harley speaks—

"Well—to the Kenyons! An ideal couple! A magnificent example of the highest type American husband and wife! May the
next ten years bring them even more health, prosperity and—and
wealth! May they . . ."

"Well, anyway—to the Kenyons!"

Bill and Lydia are looking at each other intently as the curtain
falls.

A little after four o'clock that same morning the Kenyons' living room is showing the usual party ravages. Chairs have been

huddled where groups were sitting near the fireplace. "Half-empty highball and wine glasses are on the mantel, on the table, and on the floor. Ash trays are thick with cigarette butts."

Tony Kenyon and George Gorell, the agency executives, have settled to a perfect understanding with Harley Valentine, their client. All three are in agreement that Tony and his associates have done an outstanding job with the Baby Malt account. George and Tony are particularly pleased that Mrs. Valentine has also given her approval of the campaign. "There's certainly nothing like Mrs. Valentine's instinct," agrees Tony.

"Yes, she has both feet on the ground," admits the pleased Mr. Valentine. "She takes a great interest in everything I do, and when she disapproves—well, ha, ha, she doesn't exactly scold me, you know, but one little frown from that expressive face . . ."

"That's just the word—expressive."

"I wouldn't know what to do without her. When my father died and left me with more than eleven corporations—well, frankly, I didn't know which way to turn."

A moment later Myrtle Valentine comes from the garden, "a slightly ominous frown on her face." She is pleased that her husband and his friends have been approving her feminine instinct, because she has just been putting it to use herself.

"I don't seem to be able to find Mr. Blake," reports Myrtle. "I understand that he and Mrs. Kenyon wandered away more than an hour ago. I can assure you, after consulting my feminine intuition, that they're not picking daisies."

This announcement is a little startling to the boys, and becomes something more than that when Mrs. Valentine calmly announces that now her feminine instinct inclines her to doubt the enthusiasm of her first feeling toward the Baby Malt campaign—

"You know how it is with those things—they either grow on you or they don't," says Myrtle. And she is glad that her husband has not yet formally okayed the campaign.

"Of course, I might change my mind tomorrow," adds Myrtle. "Mr. Kenyon might be able to explain it to me in the light of the morning after—and, who knows, he might convince me. (*To* TONY *in farewell.*) Will you give our apologies to Mrs. Kenyon? And I think Mr. Blake will understand our not waiting for him any longer. Come, poochie. Good night, Mr. Kenyon. It's been a lovely party."

The Valentines have swept out of the house, leaving Tony at least a little baffled. Not George, however. He thinks he knows, even if Tony doesn't, "what's eating" Mrs. Valentine.

"Do you think this fellow Blake is merely the house guest of the Valentines?"

"Do you mean he's her boy friend?"

GEORGE—What did you think he was—her godfather?

TONY (*exploding*)—I'll be damned! Who the hell does that guy think my wife is—and why does she let him think so! Where do you suppose they are right now? . . . On the night of our anniversary, can you imagine? It's supposed to be the happiest—that's when a woman is supposed to—who *is* this heel Blake, anyway? It's her fault more than his—any woman in her right mind, and a louse like that comes within ten feet of her, she ought to know it . . . I'm going to tear the roof off when she gets home. She'll remember this anniversary, all right! . . . Ten years of marriage—and to do a thing like that! Doesn't she think I have any *feelings?*

GEORGE—Keep your shirt on.

TONY (*sinking into the sofa, injured, weary, and with the air of a ruined monarch*)—A million dollars, that's all—a hundred and fifty thousand in commissions to us! Oh, Lord, after the way I worked—after the way *all* of us worked. . . .

GEORGE—Listen—do you want a little advice? Be a nice guy when she comes in.

TONY—Be a nice guy!

GEORGE—I know more about it than you do—you've only been married once, and I'm a bachelor.

TONY—What do you expect me to do—pat the heel on the back, and invite him to be *our* house guest?

GEORGE—You never can predict how a woman will react. I know a girl who will retaliate by giving you something to be mad about—in fact, I know five girls like that.

TONY (*after thinking a moment*)—Maybe you're right. No use having a scene. Hell, I know Lydia is okay. I wouldn't be surprised if she's still sore about the cook! Or maybe she took a little ride and didn't realize how time was passing. The heel probably showed her his best side—people do with Lydia.

GEORGE—Now you're talking sense.

The boys have gone when Lydia Kenyon and Bill Blake come drifting in from the garden. Lydia is wearing a sports coat over her evening dress, and is feeling grand. All her life she has wanted to walk out on a party and now she's done it.

LYDIA—The ride in the night air was lovely, the view from the hill was enchanting, and the ride back was lovelier. Two rides, one hill, one dawn. What does it add up to? I'm not very good at figures.

BILL (*indicating the room*)—What does *this* add up to?

LYDIA—Why, bless my soul, if it isn't the remains of the party —the dregs of my anniversary.

BILL (*as he goes over and pours himself a drink*)—I'm a fortune teller—it's the history of your life.

LYDIA (*sharply*)—No, it isn't.

BILL—What are you going to do about it?

LYDIA—Fight.

BILL—No, you won't. You can't lick the twentieth century— not when you're married to it. You won't fight. You'll drink a little, and you'll flirt a little . . .

LYDIA—That sounds nasty.

BILL—You drank a little tonight, didn't you?

LYDIA—Yes.

BILL—And you flirted—that's all this amounts to. Well, you'll drink a little more next time; you'll flirt a little more. And you won't be so particular. And on your twentieth anniversary . . .

LYDIA—Don't. Please don't.

BILL—You'll become like me. Without the bottle I'm nothing. And with the bottle—well, the next move is somebody like Myrtle.

LYDIA (*puzzled*)—You mean Mrs. Valentine?

BILL—I'm trying to put my cards on the table.

LYDIA—So *she's* your moonlight.

BILL—She's fireworks, which is better than total darkness. She's the Empress Catherine, get me? All the other boys are afraid of her, because if the Emperor caught them, why, they wouldn't be eating any more. Well, there was a little excitement in that. Then it began to bore me, and I was going to chuck her, when I remembered Collins, Wilkinson, Cohen and Blake. Blake, that's me, see? The firm gets half its business from *Mr.* Myrtle. Well, I don't really care, but the boys are awfully nice. When the bottle and I go away on a trip, Collins and Wilkinson and Cohen, why, they sit with a lamp shining in the window, and they wait. Nothing could be prettier than that, could it? So every time I want to tell her "Farewell, and to hell with you," I take three drinks, one to Collins, one to Wilkinson, and one to Cohen. And then she doesn't look any worse to me than any other tramp . . .

LYDIA—And that's the story of *your* life.

BILL—Until tonight . . .

LYDIA (*studying him*)—What do you want?

BILL—I'd pin a good-by note to Collins and Wilkinson and Cohen's pillow for you. I love you. . . . We walked out on a party tonight. It wasn't so hard. Why can't we walk out on a world this morning? . . . I've got a boat on the Sound. Sixty feet at the waterline, with a Diesel auxiliary. A sloop with a fifteen-foot beam. A woman could go on that boat, couldn't she?

LYDIA—What kind of a woman?

BILL—Well, she'd have beauty, otherwise I wouldn't want her. And she'd have bitterness and pain, otherwise she wouldn't want me. And she'd have courage—she'd be crazy enough to do what she needed to do.

LYDIA—What would such a woman find on your boat? Now don't tell me the sky and the sea, because they're not enough. One can get seasick, and one can also get sky-sick. I found that out.

BILL—The boat would stop at places, wouldn't it? And there'd be people in those places, wouldn't there? People scrambling for bread, and people scrambling for words, and all of them scrambling for each other, different people in each place you stop—and maybe, maybe the day suddenly comes when you find one place where you want to stay. (*Pause.*)

LYDIA—Have you had many passengers on your boat?

BILL—None.

LYDIA—I'm beginning to feel very sorry for you.

BILL—I'm sorry for myself. I was in a war, and it had no beauty. I've been hungry, and there's no charm in that. I've basked in electric lights, and they hurt my eyes. So I quit. I'm yellow, see?

LYDIA—*I'm* not.

BILL—How do you know? Why, you haven't even tried.

LYDIA (*desperately*)—What do you think I'm doing right now? . . . Let's not talk any more! I know what I want. I've always known. Please don't talk any more—just let me be . . . I'd like you to go now.

Without a word, Bill walks out through the French doors. For a moment Lydia sits still, "the meaning of the whole night crowd-ing in on her." Then Tony comes.

Tony is not angry, but very incisive. With a surge of feeling
Lydia suddenly goes to him. "Darling, forgive me," she is saying,
holding him as she talks. "I've behaved atrociously. I was furious about the cook, and I went off with this man whom I hardly
know—who means nothing to me—nothing, I tell you!"

TONY (*irritated*)—I'm not worrying about that, for Heaven's
sake!

LYDIA (*hurtling on*)—I wanted our anniversary to be something
beautiful. Is that being romantic? Is that being sentimental?
I would have forgotten all these last years, if you had only made
tonight something that belonged to us—don't you understand,
darling? . . . Well, you made it ugly and I—I made it ugly, too.
What terrible things people do to each other! We punish each
other and hurt each other when so little could heal everything. . . . I love you. Don't you see how much I love you?
It's not too late yet. It's still tonight—it's still our anniversary.
Let's salvage something out of it!

TONY (*impatiently*)—Lydia, do you know who this Blake is?

LYDIA—I think I do.

TONY—Do you know about him and Myrtle Valentine?

LYDIA (*staring at him*)—Yes.

TONY—Then what are you handing me all that applesauce for?
I'm in a spot, don't you realize that? Did you think you could
meander away for an hour with Myrtle's sweetie without her finding out?

LYDIA (*slowly*)—Tony, you don't know what you're doing . . . !

TONY (*frantically*)—*I* don't know what *I'm* doing? That's the
prize remark of the night! Well, I'll tell you what I'm doing.
I'm ordering you to get on that phone before that female gets
into bed with her husband. I don't know what you can say to
her. That's up to you. But you're going to get there fast, and
you're going to think fast, and you're going to talk fast. And
this is the beginning and the end of all the high-falutin' discon-
tented-wife business, too. I want this whole mess straightened
out!

There is a dead silence for a few moments. Then Lydia rises
slowly and obediently goes to the phone. She dials Myrtle Valentine's number and is soon explaining the innocence and completely
accidental nature of her ride in the night with Mr. Blake. Mrs.
Valentine receives the information graciously, is glad to hear Bill

is at last on his way back to the Valentines and Tony is greatly relieved.

"Thank God you didn't ruin our anniversary!" he exclaims. "Let's forget the whole thing, shall we? I'm sorry, you're sorry, we're both tired . . . Let's forget it."

"Oh, that's all right," agrees Lydia, again with a little smile.

They are standing close together now. Tony would put his arms around Lydia, and Lydia is wondering just what she will do if he does. Then Theodore appears with the *Times* and Tony's mind is suddenly and completely diverted. He must see the *Times*. Will Lydia excuse him? Lydia will, and does. At the door of the library Tony turns, a little sheepishly. "Good night, dear," he calls. "Good night, Tony," she answers over her shoulder.

"Good night, madam," echoes Theodore. "Many happy returns of the day."

For a second Lydia stands, lost in her thoughts, smiling again as she realizes the irony of Theodore's congratulations. "Thank you, Theodore," she calls. Now, her mind suddenly made up, she picks up her coat from the chair and goes to the phone and dials a number.

"Taxi? . . . This is Mrs. Kenyon. Will you please send over a cab right away? . . . Thank you."

The morning sun has come blazing into the room. Lydia puts on her coat and is gone. The slam of the front door echoes through the house as the curtain falls.

ACT II

The following evening, about 9, we find the advertising trio, Tony, George and Ned, in the Kenyons' living room. Tony is serving whiskey and soda. There has been a conference, or should have been. Tony, however, cannot get his mind back to business. His wife has left him and he has spent a terrible day trying to find her. He has phoned all the hotels, asking for Lydia under both her married and her maiden names, but without result.

Ned and George are sympathetic, and try to be understanding. Of course it is the familiar problem of the neglected wife. Every man has to face that sooner or later. Every married man, at least. George doesn't. "The worst I ever had was a neglected ootsie-wootsie," confesses George.

Lydia's special delivery letter had been specific. " 'Nor is this a sudden impulse,' " Tony reads to them. " 'I've watched you

falling more deeply in love with your business each year.' " . . .
" 'Marriage to you isn't unbearable; it's simply too, too ridiculous.' " . . . " 'You're not happy, but you seem to like it. Well,
I'm not happy, and I *don't* like it.' " . . . " 'If I had anything to
give you, I'd stay. Or if I could offer something big enough to
challenge your work, I'd put up a fight.' "

"Reverse the reasoning and you get your answer," concludes
Tony. "If I want her, I quit my job."

Again George and Ned try to think of something for Tony to
do. Has he ever thought of adopting a baby? "A baby is an
anchor to a woman—it ties her down, makes her happy," says
Ned. Tony thinks the problem has got beyond the baby stage.

It is while Tony is changing his coat, to go over to George's
apartment where he thinks he may be able to work, that the boys
get an idea. Why shouldn't they consider Tony's problem as an
advertising problem? How would they tackle it? Why not give
it a merchandising angle? Their product would be Love. Their
consumer Mrs. X. Their manufacturer Mr. X—although it's a
kind of sideline with him. Now, the quality of Mr. X's product
is tops, a class product, but the price is high. Still Mr. X is
hopeful of keeping Mrs. X away from the chain stores. So—
No, it wouldn't work. Unless— Unless Mr. X, not being worried about any pure food laws, should try misrepresenting his
product—

"I do! I lie to my wife all the time!" cheerfully admits Ned.

"Ned, I think you've got something there!" agrees George.

They are ready for Tony when he re-appears. Lying is the
thing for him to try. "It's the safest, most reliable thing a red-
blooded man can do," announces George. Let Tony promise
Lydia anything that will make her happy. Promises, promises
and more promises—

Before they can outline a lying campaign, Bill Blake is announced. Tony decides to see him alone.

Blake has come in answer to a call from Tony. No, he doesn't
want a drink. No, he doesn't know where Lydia is. He would
be very glad to help Tony find her, because he is worried himself.
Where had Lydia gone the night before? Bill can't remember.
What had Lydia talked about?

"Pal, she was having a look at the horizon," reports Bill.

"What horizon?"

BILL—There's only one. She examined it with great care. She
was interested. But she decided to wait till she could get it at a

bargain price. Then she thought maybe it could be done on the installment plan. Then she came in and tried on the apron again. She didn't think it looked very pretty. So she threw it away. Well, the wind was blowing awfully hard, and there she was in that No Man's Land between the apron and the horizon . . . Now, I had a banjo, see? It was a little out of tune, get me?

Tony (*on edge*)—I don't know what you're talking about.

Bill (*adding it up patiently*)—The lady seemed to be unhappy. She didn't like the cigarettes, the whiskey, and the soap.

Tony—What else? Did she consult you about a divorce?

Bill—No, but it's a simple matter. I wouldn't get it in New York—that's messy. Reno is the best, and you have your choice of mental cruelty, desertion, nonsupport, incompatibility . . .

Tony—Incompatibility, in your hat! See here, Blake, there's going to be no divorce—is that clear? She can't prove a damn thing—and, if necessary, I'll fight it through forty-eight states, and I'll bring her back every time.

Bill—Well, you're sitting pretty. According to the law, sleeping with your business doesn't constitute adultery.

Tony—And now, before I ask you to go—if there's anything else she said, you'll be good enough to lay it on the table. And stick to the words—leave out the music.

Bill (*honestly trying*)—Well, let me see . . . She didn't like your friends.

Tony—She didn't! Well, that's too bad! Did she perhaps suggest, in so many words, that I quit my job?

Bill (*softly*)—You wouldn't do that, would you?

Tony—Think I'm crazy?

Bill—Spit in your boss's eye, take your woman by the hand, climb to the top of a hill. Look us over, moon. She's a woman, she's life itself—she makes the grass grow, see? I've got hold of her hand, and I'm not letting go . . . She's a skylark . . . (*Pause.*)

Tony—Blake, just how do you fit into this picture, anyway?

Bill—I'm a Mister Nobody, see? And you're a Mister Somebody. All a woman can love is what she might have if there was a Mister Somebody to give it to her. Well, she starts out by picking her man—but if he can't play the part, the words are still there, aren't they? Maybe Mister Nobody can say them—and mean them.

Tony (*advancing on him*)—You seem to make a specialty of other men's wives, don't you?

BILL (*rising—mildly*)—I don't want to fight with you.
TONY (*dangerously*)—You'd better be going.
BILL—Just as you say, pal.
TONY—Don't call me pal!

They are still pretty tense as Lydia comes in through the hall.
She is dressed in a tailored suit and hat. She greets them pleasantly, casually. She is surprised to find Mr. Blake there, and
pleased. She wants to consult him on a legal matter. Will he
please wait at the station for her? He will.
Where has she been? Tony wants to know. She has been
visiting Joe Leslie and Jean Martin. They are living on West
Eleventh Street and they have a small house with a garden. And
an eight-year-old boy. It had been a wonderful visit. It was
Jean who had lent her the tailored suit.
Lydia is a little tired. Tony would have her go upstairs, take
a nice hot bath and get some rest. They can go into their affairs
tomorrow.
"I won't be here tomorrow," says Lydia, quietly. "I'm not
staying here tonight. I came to pack some more things—and
to tell you I want a divorce."
Tony is not submitting to any such plan as that. He has no
intention of letting her go. To impress the idea upon her he has
grabbed her by the arms and is holding her rather violently.
"Please, Tony—let's not have a scene," Lydia pleads. "I ask
nothing of you—I have no right to. You were supporting me.
You weren't mistreating me. . . ."

TONY (*bitterly*)—Thanks for the reference!
LYDIA—I have only one right—the right to leave you.
TONY—What'll you do—go to work at two-bits a week?
LYDIA—Yes—because after I've worked a while, when I've
saved a little, I can go away and live a little—and you can't do
that in the upper brackets.
TONY—Oh, rats.
LYDIA—All this is very painful. That's why I put it in a letter.
I didn't want to say over and over things that we both know.
TONY—I don't know anything.
LYDIA—Oh, Tony, it was so clear—last night. There it was—
our marriage—like an old calendar. You just don't need me any
more.
TONY—Let me decide that.
LYDIA—Life's too short. I was heading in a different direction

when we met on that Fifth Avenue bus. Now you're going your way—and I'm going right back to that day on the bus, back to the minute before I ever saw you.

TONY—Back to Joe Leslie, and Jean, and Phil What's-his-name—a lot of mediocrities that have stood still for ten years!

LYDIA—That's where I'm going!

TONY (*nastily*)—I wish you luck. I hope you meet the right fellow this time.

LYDIA—It's not impossible.

TONY—Mr. Blake, for instance. A drunkard might be an interesting change.

LYDIA—I'm concerned with Mr. Blake only as a lawyer. (*She picks up her bag.*) Good-by, Tony.

TONY (*coming close to her*)—I love you.

LYDIA—I love you, too. (*His arms go around her. She stands unresisting, strong.*) It's no use, Tony. You know it, and I know it. Please let me go. (*His arms drop slowly.*)

TONY (*crushed*)—Aren't you going upstairs for your things?

LYDIA (*after a moment*)—All right. I'll pack a suitcase. (*Starting.*) And maybe a few other little things—I won't need much.

With Lydia gone to pack, Tony makes his report to Ned and George. Again they assure him that "the old baloney" is the only way out of such messes. And it isn't as hard as he might think—

"Suppose a client behaved like that—you'd have to lie then, wouldn't you?" George demands. "Imagine she's on the other side of a conference table. You're no longer a husband. You're a man."

By the time Lydia comes downstairs Tony has made his decision, fortified by a good drink of whiskey.

"Did you get everything so quickly?" Tony asks cordially, as Lydia appears, carrying a small overnight bag. "Come in! Don't stand out here in the hall."

LYDIA (*advancing a hesitant step*)—I have all I need.

TONY (*in the ring now, ruthlessly sparring for an opening*)—And now you're going—back to that bus?

LYDIA—Please, Tony—don't joke about it.

TONY—I'm quite serious. (*Coming closer to her.*) You know, that bus belongs to me, too. I was once on it, same as you. . . . (*Gently.*) Sit down a minute. (*Puzzled and studying him, LYDIA*) *sits.*) When I saw you on that bus, I knew just one thing—that I wanted to be near you. (*He sits down by her, carefully putting her bag out of the way.*) And I still want to be near you, no matter how much it costs.

LYDIA—Don't be silly, Tony. You couldn't afford the price —and I'd never ask you to pay it. You couldn't serve your job and me at the same time, and I know where your heart is.

TONY—Then I quit my job. How's that?

LYDIA—It hurts me to see you like this. I know you couldn't possibly quit, even if you *did* think you meant it—but it's touching to see you in such a mood.

TONY (*feeling his way*)—Half-time—wouldn't do, would it?

LYDIA—Half-time—what do you mean?

TONY—Come home early—no work in the evening—no conferences on Sunday—vacation every year . . .

LYDIA—It would be wonderful. But can you look me in the face and say it would be possible?

TONY—No, I guess not . . . The only thing is quit.

LYDIA (*still puzzled, and moved*)—Tony, what's happened to you? You don't sound like yourself.

TONY—It's a little difficult to explain. I've been thinking a lot since I got your letter. And in my heart I knew you were right. But I was fighting it. You know, it's not easy to give in.

LYDIA (*sympathetically*)—I can understand that, dear.

TONY—When you walked into the house tonight—Blake comes in first and acts as if you were his property, and then you march in and treat me like the party of the second part— Well, all the things I was going to say just flew out of my head. I got sore.

LYDIA—Oh, Tony! . . .

TONY—Look—what you want is: Chuck the high living—to hell with money, security, two cars in the garage and all that. Am I right?

LYDIA—Well—it isn't what I *want,* Tony. It's the only alternative. Either you're successful and a slave to everything and everybody, including the Myrtle Valentines of the world, or you have a little freedom, a little self-respect, the way it was with us in the beginning.

TONY—Listen—I agree with you absolutely. You're right— one hundred per cent.

LYDIA—Tony, I just can't believe my ears!

Tony hasn't a very definite plan. He only knows that he is ready to go back to the bus—and start all over. All right. He never has heard of the advertising business. He isn't sure of what he hopes to be. He only knows that he is crazy about Lydia. At that time they just wanted each other—

"Why, sweetheart—you were so beautiful," Tony is saying. "Not beautiful the way pretty girls are pretty—you were just all mine—too wonderful for me, too glorious—and yet only for me. One look at you, and I had life insurance out in your name. I was fighting gangsters to rescue you from them. We had a back yard with a kid playing around— (*Suddenly remembering.*) I'm sorry, darling—"

"That's all right, dear." There are tears of happiness in Lydia's eyes.

"I loved you then almost as much as I love you now," Tony goes on, moving closer to Lydia. "Take your hat off, dear, will you, please?"

Everything looks like an easy victory for Tony until they are interrupted by the phone's ringing. Blake is calling. Is Lydia in? Certainly she is in. And at the phone. But her monosyllabic replies to Blake are cryptic. Tony takes the phone from her.

"My wife isn't getting a divorce, if that's what you want to know!" he shouts.

"*Maybe* I'm not," Lydia corrects him, when she recovers the phone. Tony persists that everything is going to be all right. Lydia repeats the promise to Blake. The lawyer wants to know if he is willing to put that in writing.

". . . No, Bill—he says he's willing to start all over, if necessary—as if he'd never even heard of the advertising business . . ." Lydia is repeating to Bill. There is a long pause while she is getting Bill's answer, and Tony is pretty frantic. Then she turns to report—

". . . He says that if you quit your job, you'd freeze to death on the mountain top. That you don't know the moon from a street lamp. That you wouldn't be Romeo; you'd just be unemployed."

"Will you do me one favor? Will you hang up on that heel and give me a chance to talk to you?"

LYDIA—No, I won't. I'm *glad* we're not alone. I'm *glad* Bill's here. I was just in danger of being swept off my feet! (*Into the telephone.*) Just a minute, Bill—no, everything's all right. Where are you—in a booth? . . . Are you comfortable? . . . Yes, of *course* I'm thinking . . . Yes . . . That's true, too

. . . (*To* Tony.) He says I'm entitled to a definite picture of what you're going to do after you quit your job. He feels, as my representative, that I shouldn't commit myself without a program.

Tony—Tell him— (*Slowly, thinking hard.*) Tell him we'll take a year to ourselves—that I'm going to take you by the hand and let you lead me. Tell him we'll travel, find out what the world is like . . . go to the theatre and concerts, read books . . . Tell him we'll have a look at the horizon.

Lydia (*taking this in with a look of growing wonder, into the telephone*)—Oh, Bill—he *has* a program. It's what? . . . Yes . . . Yes . . . Yes—that's practically what he said! (*To* Tony, *amused and slightly skeptical.*) He says you're just repeating the words he put into your mouth!

Tony (*angrily*)—When you're through, *I'd* like to talk to him.

Lydia—You can talk to him now. (*She hands him the telephone.*)

Tony—Hello, Blake. You bet I'm taking the words out of your mouth. What of it? I *mean* them—isn't that enough? . . . What? . . . You've got a hell of a nerve, asking me a question like that!

Lydia—What does he want to know?

Tony (*outraged*)—He wants to know how we're going to do all this, how much money I've got!

Lydia (*calmly*)—*I* think that's an excellent question.

Tony—But—but—just a minute, dear. (*Into the telephone.*) What? Oh, sure. (*He puts down the telephone.*) He's going out to get some more nickels.

Lydia—Now, let's see. In the checking account last Wednesday we had four thousand. How much have we in the savings account?

Tony (*sitting beside her*)—About seven.

Lydia—Is that all we have in the world?

Tony—We've got the house—in six years the mortgage will be paid.

Lydia—Tony, it's disgraceful! Do you suppose it's my fault?

Tony (*moving close to her*)—Of course not! Now look, darling . . .

Lydia (*moving away*)—Don't you think Bill is back by now? (*See picks up the telephone.*) Hello—are you back?

Tony (*angrily*)—You're not going to tell him how much money we have—that's our private business.

LYDIA—Bill, our finances are our own business. I don't think you should ask such questions. After all, Tony is my own husband . . . I've known him almost eleven years . . . What? . . . Now, see here, Bill . . . *What!* . . . Now that's going too far—I won't let anyone talk to me like that, lawyer or no lawyer! . . . Good-by! (*She hangs up, amused and annoyed.*) The nerve of him!

TONY—What did he say, anyway?

LYDIA—He said you were a liar—a fantastic and unprincipled liar. The man is an idiot.

TONY (*quickly*)—Oh, let's forget him.

LYDIA—He's already forgotten.

Tony thinks he can wind up things at the office in four or five weeks. Well, it may take six or seven. Anyway, what are a few weeks when they have a whole lifetime before them? They are happy now and gaily starting a footrace for the stairs when they bump smack into Theodore. The butler has come to report that Mrs. Valentine is calling.

In their new happiness Tony and Lydia decide they may as well see Mrs. Valentine. She has probably come about the cook. They might as well give her Mattie, seeing they will not be wanting her much longer anyway.

But it isn't Mattie that Mrs. Valentine has come to see about. It is something about which she would like to talk with Mrs. Kenyon alone. So Tony is dismissed.

It is Mr. Blake who is worrying Myrtle Valentine, and she is pretty sore about him. Nor is she to be put off by Lydia's assurance that she has no intention of seeing Mr. Blake again.

It appears that Mr. Blake had not shown up at the Valentines' at all the night before. And if Lydia didn't know that, why was Blake at her house again this afternoon? And why did he telephone her from the station after he left?

"Just what did you come here for, anyway?" Lydia finally demands, her resentment rising.

"To tell you what I think of you," snaps Mrs. Valentine. "You put on a lot of airs for a woman in your position. Just because I've been patient with you, it's gone to your head. Well, it's the last time I'll be broadminded. The perfect wife and the perfect hostess—for crying out loud!"

"You certainly answered my question!"

"Who are you, anyway? A nobody from a squirt college in Boston, whose husband doesn't make in a year what mine makes in a week. And there's nothing you can do that I can't do better —how do you like that? I'm a better wife in one minute than you'll be in a lifetime. I gave my husband a baby at the end of one year, which is more than you've been able to do in ten!"

"Oh, get out of here!"

"Not until I'm ready—*I'm* giving the orders, see? Hands off Bill Blake—or maybe you think it'll be easy for your husband to get another job."

That is a little too much for Lydia to take. The idea of Mrs. Valentine's assuming that anything she can do or say will affect Tony's standing with his agency is preposterous. And yet, before Mrs. Valentine is through, Lydia is partly convinced that what she threatens may be possible. Perhaps that is business. But she doesn't care greatly. Tony was going to quit anyway. Maybe she should thank Mrs. Valentine for that. Perhaps she should really say something sweet to her. But on second thought she decides not to. It might ruin everything.

"Good-by," Lydia is saying, with a sweet smile, as she extends her hand. "Good-by—*you bitch!*"

With a murderous look, Myrtle has yanked her hand away and stormed out through the hall. With a smile of triumph Lydia dances to the door of the bar and flings it open. "Tony! Tony!" she calls.

"Is she gone?" queries Tony, coming in with a tray of drinks.

LYDIA—Yes, she's gone.

TONY—I thought she might stay, so I went to the bar and rigged this up.

LYDIA—Darling, I have exciting news for you.

TONY—Have you?

LYDIA (*blissfully*)—You don't have to wait seven weeks, or six—or even one week. You're fired! Isn't it wonderful?

TONY (*panic-stricken, setting down the tray*)—What happened?

LYDIA (*coming to him*)—Tony, she was impossible. I tried— God knows I tried—I was determined to be nice to that woman if it killed me.

TONY (*gripping her arm*)—Give it to me word for word.

LYDIA—Oh, Tony, she played right into our hands, and I couldn't resist it. I said just exactly the things that would get you fired as of Monday morning. And that's what you wanted, isn't it?

TONY (*in agony, but hiding it*)—That's right—that's what I

wanted.

LYDIA—And it doesn't really matter whether you walked out or whether you were kicked out, does it?

TONY—No—of course not.

LYDIA (*exulting*)—Oh, darling, we're free! Right now—*this minute*—we're free!

TONY (*dying, but smiling*)—Can you imagine!

LYDIA (*in heaven*)—Oh, Tony, I'm so proud of myself! Why, only fifteen minutes ago you had an office, a desk, a telephone, a thousand things to do—and in one easy stroke I wiped it all out! That's what I'd call genius—wouldn't you?

TONY—That's right, darling—that's what I'd call it!

The curtain falls.

ACT III

It is the following Saturday afternoon. Theodore is just showing Ned and Charlotte Franklin into the Kenyons' living room. The Franklins are plainly ill at ease and trying to map out some sort of greeting program before they meet the Kenyons. Charlotte is half convinced they should not have come at all.

"Listen. It's a week since Tony was fired and I've been promoted into his job," Ned is saying. "I can't help that, can I? The least I can do is drop in like a good fellow and act as if we were equals. Sit *down*, will you?"

"All right. Now just how much am I supposed to know? Am I supposed to know Tony has been lying to Lydia? Am I supposed to know how he happened to get fired?"

"Well, Tony told me all about it last Monday, and he knows you worm everything out of me."

The Franklins are on their way to the Valentines, and that also is a little embarrassing—in this house.

The situation clears rapidly when Tony arrives. He is relaxed and cheerful, the picture of contentment. He knows all about Ned's having his job and is a little sorry—for Ned. And Charlotte. She'll never see anything of him now. Tony really feels like offering his condolences. Which Charlotte doesn't like at all.

"You needn't be so smug!" Charlotte advances. "We know the spot you're in!"

"Listen—I've stepped off the express train," Tony answers, earnestly. "I'm in the woods by a rippling brook, and I love it."

"Now, Tony, Lydia isn't around, so you don't have to talk

to *us* like that."

"I really mean it. On my word of honor. I want you to know Lydia has done the greatest thing in the world for me. And it's so great that I've become a missionary. I want to pass it along."

Before they can stop him he has edged into a place beside them on the sofa and started a recital of the wonderful things he and Lydia have been doing the last week. A day at Coney Island. Three nights at the theatre! Golf! Time to read a book! And tomorrow— But Ned and Charlotte are going. They are afraid they are a little late already. They hope Tony will not be offended—

"Offended?" repeats Tony. "I'm *sorry* for you. Look at yourselves—two people in the prime of life, edging away from your oldest friend for fear of getting in bad with your boss! When I think of you ten years ago, Ned—and you, Charlotte! Wait a minute. (*He goes to the album, starts turning pages.*) I want you to see yourselves when you had spirit, courage, enthusiasm—" As he opens the album he finds three photographs of a baby. For a moment he is puzzled, and then he remembers. "I'll be damned!" he mutters, half to himself. "She must have fallen for it! Can you imagine?"

Now the truth must out. It was Ned who had started it by saying something about adopting a baby. With this as an inspiration Tony had gone to a foundling asylum, picked out a baby, and "finagled it into Lydia's life."

"The theory was that if a woman has a baby she'd want her husband to have a job, wouldn't she?" he demands.

But later Tony had changed and decided against this plan. He had a report from the doctor that Lydia had seen the baby and hadn't even "batted an eyelash." He felt that he had failed.

"Oh, pooh! If Lydia had fallen for that baby, you'd be reading the help wanted ads right now," declares Charlotte.

Before they can go Lydia has come from the garden. She, too, is in great spirits and a little sorry for Ned and Charlotte. If they would listen she, also, would like to tell them about the lovely week the Kenyons have had, but she is afraid it might depress them.

Had Tony told them about the rumba lessons they had been taking? And have they noticed the cigarettes?

"Look, Charlotte—Lucky Strikes! And we have Haig and Haig Whiskey! And I had a bath this morning with Ivory Soap!"

"Congratulations—and good-by!" calls the exasperated Charlotte, hurrying her husband toward the door.

"Good-by!" echoes Lydia, too dazed to follow. "What do you suppose is the matter with them?"

"Well, they came here to feel sorry for us because I'm out of a job."

"And then they found we're sorry for them because they *have* a job—and they couldn't take it!"

"I guess that's it."

"Oh, Tony, I'm frightened. Everything is too perfect. I go around frightened to death that it won't last. And when I look at the faces of people on the streets, I feel ashamed of myself for being so lucky . . . Happiness is a painful thing. I never realized that before . . . Aren't I an idiot—I'm crying!"

"Don't—or you'll have me crying, too. I feel pretty good myself."

"Oh, darling, let's be careful—be careful not to get killed slipping in the bathtub." She is clinging desperately to him now. "And when you cross the street—ask the policeman to help you!"

"I promise!" agrees Tony.

And now Lydia is ready to confess a few other misgivings. She thought she wanted to sell the house, but now that someone wants to buy she hates to think of it. Of course this is their only chance of taking that trip—

All right, when shall they start? Tony would be getting busy. Next Monday? To Lydia that does seem awfully soon. Perhaps in the Fall— Tony thinks maybe a bust on the nose would help her decide.

Then Bill Blake telephones from the Valentines. Exultantly Tony tells him of the plans for the South American trip. And they are sailing Monday morning. Bill would like to come over. He has some thought of kicking Myrtle Valentine in the pants, but that can wait.

The next caller is George Gorell. George is glad to know that Tony and Lydia are so enthusiastic about their new-found freedom and their trip. Otherwise he would be inclined to tell Tony of a new job he has heard about. It seems that a certain Mr. Sonny Sheldon, president of Sheldon Motors, has been talking to George about Tony and wondering if he (Sheldon) could induce Tony to take over the job of advertising and sales manager of his firm. Sheldon Motors, of course, doesn't knock at anybody's front door more than once.

Even Lydia is interested in what George has to say. Not, of course, that it will make the least difference in their plans, but just because it is flattering to anybody to hear that he is wanted.

Sheldon Motors is so desperately in need of someone, George reports, that Mr. Sheldon is willing to give such an executive as he thinks Tony would make a contract with *carte blanche*.

"Boy, if this were only a month ago!" ejaculates Tony, suddenly waking up. "George, the man who wants to buy a medium-priced car doesn't want to see a picture of Madame Pompadour —he wants to see the car. And he doesn't want to read about the exquisite rustle of silk in front of the Opéra Comique in Paris. He wants to read about brakes, and gear shifts, and is there a place to put the gasoline."

"Sheldon told me he'd even let you dictate the design of the car."

"Say, he's no fool," insists Tony, thoughtfully pacing the floor. "That car *needs* redesigning. . . ."

Before he knows it Tony is wondering what has been the matter with him all these days. How could he have believed all the stuff he has been telling himself—and Lydia?

"Five minutes ago I meant every word I said," insists Tony.

"Five minutes ago you didn't have a job," suggests the none too subtle George.

Lydia is back and George is leaving. "Why don't you have a drink with me at the Advertising Club, say, at six," suggests Tony, casually.

"Six? I'll be there," agrees George. "So long, Lydia."

"Not 'So long!'—Bon voyage!"

"Oh, my goodness, I forgot—Bon voyage! (*Maliciously.*) Bon voyage, Tony!"

George leaves. Now it is Tony who suggests that perhaps Lydia was right about their not being in too great a hurry to sell the house. Perhaps, too, they would be rushing the trip a little too much if they tried to get started by Monday. It might even be possible that Lydia would like to hear a little more about the Sheldon proposition—

Lydia is working on a list of things to be done to expedite their packing and their departure. She is concentrating on this task when Tony drifts over to the side table where the album is. Suddenly he "discovers" the baby pictures.

"Lydia, what are these?"

"Those?" Lydia is a little disconcerted by the discovery. "Oh, those are pictures of a boy friend of mine. Do you like them."

"I think they're beautiful. Whose baby is it?"

"It's an orphan."

And then the story is told. It happened the day Lydia had gone to see Dr. Standish for her annual check-up. There was a baby doctor across the hall and he had Fuzzy (that's what Lydia calls her boy friend) and brought him in for Dr. Standish to look at. Think of it! They were going to send *that* baby to the Foundling's Home—

"Where did you expect them to send it?"

"I diapered it . . ."

TONY—Is that any reason for not sending it to the Foundling's Home?

LYDIA (*offended—putting down the pictures*)—Oh, I was afraid you were going to be like this. I just knew it. That's why I never mentioned it.

TONY (*quickly—and very tenderly*)—Darling—am I being stupid? Because I don't mean to be. I'm terribly interested—except that I don't fully understand. I'm dying to hear about it, honestly.

LYDIA—Well, it seems this child comes of very good stock—they don't tell you; it's against the rules; but they know, and it was obvious to *me* at a glance. He's just past the age where they're meaningless and meaty, and just at the age where they're —heavenly. His eyes are hazel green with little flecks of gray and blue in them, and you can see already how wonderful his hands are and his ears—and there's definite character in his mouth. Can you imagine that—in a child less than a year old? I asked if all babies in the Foundling's Home were as glorious as this one and they said oh, no, this is something very special.

TONY—You mean—you were considering adopting this baby?

LYDIA—Oh, I knew it was impossible in every way. The doctor kept urging me—it seems he has influence with the Foundling's Home and he could reserve the child for me. But naturally, the minute I stopped to think about it, I let the whole thing drop.

TONY—Why? I don't hate babies.

LYDIA—Darling—a baby is a responsibility. One has to think ahead. I'd want to give a baby the best of everything—you'd want your son to go to college, wouldn't you? How could you do all that and be free the way you are now?

TONY—I see what you mean.

LYDIA—Tony, your happiness has been such a wonderful thing for me to watch—I couldn't let *ten* babies interfere with it.

TONY—Maybe that's why you were so reluctant about the

trip . . .

LYDIA—Suppose I were? What's the difference? Once we're on that boat, I'll get over it. It can't be love—I only saw him twice. At best, it's only infatuation. And you yourself said I'd forget the *house* in a week.

TONY—Umm—yes—I suppose so . . .

LYDIA—Anyway, children don't solve everything. Look at Charlotte. She has two, and they're her own. Would you call her a happy woman?

TONY (*going back to the pictures*)—Let's have another look at those pictures.

LYDIA (*joining him as he looks at them*)—They're not very good, I'm afraid. I took them myself. You know how it is with indoor pictures—and they didn't enlarge very well. He wouldn't lie still, either.

TONY—Nice smile.

LYDIA—Do you get the impression of unusual vitality?

TONY—Yes—yes, I do.

LYDIA—He has a—a kind of football player's face, wouldn't you say?

TONY (*laying the pictures aside*)—Darling, you obviously worship that child.

LYDIA—Don't be silly. I worship only one person in the world.

TONY—Look—suppose we don't go to Mexico. After all, I've had a gorgeous week. This Sheldon job might not be so awful.

LYDIA (*putting her hand across his mouth*)—Don't say another word. Oh, Tony, I'll never forget this moment.

TONY—Why?

LYDIA (*deeply moved*)—Do you realize that in six years you never gave a thought to me, and now, after one week of being human, you're about to sacrifice your whole new life—aren't you?

TONY—Well, not exactly . . . You see, this man Sheldon wants me badly . . .

LYDIA—Oh, Tony—I couldn't do that to you. You shall have your trip! And I'll get over this baby.

Lydia has started to put the pictures away when Bill Blake appears in the French doors. Lydia would show him the baby pictures. Tony would rather introduce a new subject if he could, but Lydia is much too interested in the baby now to be easily diverted. She can see that Tony is irritated. But, she explains to Bill, there is good reason for that. Tony thinks, because she came across this baby in the doctor's office that she ought to adopt it.

In a second Lawyer Blake has them figuratively on the witness stand and is on the scent of the truth. Was it Lydia's idea to go to the doctor? Didn't Tony suggest it? Was she sick?

"As a lawyer," Bill explains to the protesting Tony, "I am always a little suspicious of coincidences."

"What are you trying to say, Bill?" Lydia demands.

"He's trying to say that I deliberately placed this baby in your arms, darling. Shall I kick him out, or will you?"

Lydia is not pleased. She thinks Bill is going too far, but a moment later when he threatens to phone Dr. Standish she is convinced that Tony has been lying.

"You didn't mean a word of it when you said you'd quit your job," she says, facing her husband.

"I didn't."

Lydia—And when Mrs. Valentine walked out of our house, you weren't glad at all—you were hating it.

Tony—I was.

Lydia—And all this week you were lying to me.

Tony—No, I wasn't.

Lydia—I don't believe that.

Tony—All right. Then I was.

Lydia—The trip, selling the house, selling the cars—you didn't intend to go through with any of it. You intended to work for Sheldon.

Tony—That's right.

Bill—Your reservations on my boat are still good.

Lydia (to Bill)—Oh, shut up!

Tony—And get the hell out of here!

Lydia—No—don't go. I want you to stay.

Tony—Then *I'm* going.

Lydia (looking at him inscrutably)—No, Tony—you're not going. Not before I've told you what I think of you.

Tony (sinking into a chair)—Go ahead—I suppose I've got it coming to me.

Lydia—You bet you have! (Slowly thinking it out, she moves away from him.) Anybody who gets himself into such a *mess* —sneaking off to doctors' offices, picking babies from a Foundling's home . . . playing golf, reading books, and going to the theatre—all for a woman! (Turning to him.) Tony, it's a miracle you didn't crack up!

Tony—Don't you think you've said enough?

LYDIA—Not half enough. (*Looking at him with growing realization.*) Why, you're the man Bill has been describing all his life! You're the great lover. You worked twenty-four hours a day to deceive me—so that you wouldn't lose me. You worked harder for me than you ever worked for Baby Malt! Why, you did everything but steal and kill—you actually learned to dance the rumba—for me! . . . Do you know what I think? (*Adoringly.*) I think you're wonderful!

TONY (*dazed*)—I don't get this.

BILL—The lady is kidding you, pal.

LYDIA—No, I'm not kidding you. And I'm not kidding myself, either. And I'm not kidding Bill. (*To* BILL.) You said he wouldn't be Romeo, that he'd just be unemployed. Well, you were wrong. Romeo had only one love—but Tony had two. He wanted to have his cake and eat it so badly that he lost it and choked on it at the same time! Oh, Tony, when I think of all the things I've done to you—and instead of taking me over your knee and spanking me, you smiled and you drank a toast to the future! What would you call that, Mr. Blake—incompatibility?

BILL (*beginning to leave*)—My error. I should never have come to your party.

LYDIA (*going to him*)—No, I'm glad you came. I want to thank you for coming . . . I want to thank everybody. (*Turning to* TONY.) I want to thank Tony, too—for consenting to be the father of my child.

TONY (*still puzzled, but getting the general idea*)—Don't wait for me—I'm still catching up.

LYDIA (*going to him*)—Darling, have you accepted that job yet?

TONY—I'm meeting Sheldon at the Advertising Club at six. (*Taking her hand.*) And you're coming with me.

LYDIA—Who's going to stop me? I've just found out that I have a husband, and you and Mr. Sheldon might as well find out right now that you have a wife. (*They look at each other. They have both, for the moment, forgotten that they are not alone, until* BILL *reminds them.*)

BILL—Well . . . (*They turn to him.*) I leave you both, without any compliments. (*To* LYDIA.) You had the moon. You really knew what I was talking about. You knew the world was out there somewhere. But you're trading it in for twin beds, and an armchair by the fire, and a baby. Well, I don't wish you any harm. It's not better than nothing, but you'll never find out. Good luck to you! (*He starts to go.*)

LYDIA—Bill— (*He stops. She goes quickly over to him, looking at him affectionately. She kisses him on the cheek.*) Bon voyage, pal!

"Bill's expression doesn't change as he gives her a bored salute, turns and goes. She and Tony look after him."

THE CURTAIN FALLS

MARGIN FOR ERROR
A Drama in Two Acts

By Clare Boothe

WHEN "Margin for Error" was produced in early November, it was generally conceded by the play's reviewers that Clare Boothe, the author, had at last found a proper vent for her keenest satire and a perfect target for those barbed shafts of wit which she had so successfully tipped with venom in her former successes, "The Women" and "Kiss the Boys Good-bye." It was also as freely admitted that this was the first successful anti-Nazi play to reach the stage, a rare combination of melodrama and comedy. "It takes a murder to bring out the jovial streak in Miss Clare Boothe, writer of acid plays," wrote Richard Lockridge in the New York Evening *Sun*.

"Where all others have so far failed, Miss Boothe has half succeeded," Henry R. Luce has, with the frankness of a husband, written in the introduction to the published play. "But her peculiar success does not really lie in having got National Socialism on stage. Her success—or rather what will later be defined as her half success—is her success in dramatizing the democrat's rebuttal to National Socialism. For in all these years of failure the difficulty has not in fact been to get National Socialism on stage. The real difficulty has been to get on stage a convincing *rebuttal* to National Socialism. It is in this that Miss Boothe has half succeeded. She succeeded with her character of Moe Finkelstein, the Jewish policeman. Her success is glorious, a heart-warming triumph. She failed with Thomas S. Denny, the just-an-American. Her failure is a dull thump—a failure of some significance because symptomatic of a failure in contemporary American life."

However Miss Boothe's critics may have been divided in their analyses of the reason, or excuse, for the success of "Margin for Error," the play-supporting public was both frankly outspoken and liberal in its endorsement. The "comedy-melodrama" ran through till early Spring at the regular theatre tariffs, and through an additional several weeks when a popular-priced supplemental season was inaugurated.

The library in the home of the German Consul General, which

is the scene of the play, is on the second floor of a house of the brownstone era in a large American city. "It is a large room paneled in clumsily carved stained oak" and is particularly noticeable because looking across the room, one sees a "deep-mullioned, book-lined bay window which forms an alcove" and practically divides the library in two. By drawing a pair of heavy, mustard-colored brocade curtains across this alcove it can be completely shut off from the rest of the room.

The alcove is furnished with a heavy square desk, before which is placed a high-backed leather swivel chair. There is a small wall-safe behind the desk, disguised as a panel of books. In front of the alcove, at one side, stands a bust of Adolf Hitler on a pedestal, and at the other a standard containing the American and Nazi flags. A large map of Germany is on the right wall over the fireplace. There are etchings of the Wagnerian operas on the side walls and a cellarette-bar-cabinet, as well as a cabinet-victrola-and-radio in the room's furnishings.

As we enter the library we discover Otto Horst, the American Bund leader, "a fat, forty-year-old ex-elocution teacher, with a pasty, intra-mural complexion." A vain, humorless, conceited "pushover for flattery," Horst is wearing a tight-fitting Nazi-brown military uniform. He is standing on the alcove step reading a speech to Baron Max von Alvenstor, the Consul's secretary, who sits with his back to the reader, listening and smoking but not paying too close attention. Von Alvenstor "is a German of the spiritual stamp who sincerely believes that the Treaty of Versailles is the one great crime of history. To him the word 'Kultur' really represents German poetry, philosophy and music, and not the guns, which he is nevertheless willing to see used to defend them. He is blond, blue-eyed, well bred and well tailored; in short, he is the exact opposite of all his own leaders. Having studied at Oxford, he speaks faultless English, and in his conversation with Horst simply cannot control an attitude of superiority and boredom."

Horst is just drawing toward the close of his speech. ". . . that the American-Germanic peoples' Bunds stand for peace, for jobs, for freedom. But not jobs for Communists, traitors and war-mongers! Some say we are not American. Is it un-American to say that all Jews are Communists?"

"No, but it's inaccurate," interrupts Max, coolly.

"Please, Baron! . . . And that all Jews who are not Communists are Capitalists? They either congregate in secret cellars, plotting to undermine law and order, or they live on the fat of the land, while the down-trodden Aryan toils!"

The appearance at the door of Officer Moe Finkelstein interrupts the speech. Officer Moe "is in his late twenties, small, slender and almost handsome in a rather wistful, Jewish way. . . . In common with most of the people of his race he has the gifts of ready sympathy, loquacity and inquisitiveness. Born in some sub-human crevice of a large American city, he has kept intact his allegiance to his family and to his God. It is the passionate conviction of his life that the nationals of all other countries are misguided and unfortunate."

Officer Finkelstein has come to relieve Officer Kapinski as consul guard. He will be on the front door from 4 till 7. The thought of Jewish policemen guarding the German Consulate is almost too much for Horst. "If I were Hitler, I'd break off diplomatic relations," he explodes.

Now Horst has finished his speech and seeks Von Alvenstor's endorsement. He doesn't get it. To Max the speech harps too much on the race issue. But to Horst it is entirely in line with what he is trying to do. "My best bet is to create conflict among creeds and colors," he says. "Then step in, when they're exhausted, and take the whole country over—*bang!* Next week I attack the Catholics, Masons, Negroes, and Café Society."

"Perhaps you'd better just purge Elsa Maxwell, and leave the rest to Hitler," suggests Max.

Horst has handed in his report of activities, including an advance copy of the final Dies report, snitched right off the Congressman's desk. "The Congressman finds great Nazi strength everywhere," notes Horst. "You just must send that on to Berlin! In fact, um—it's the only encouraging report we *could* send."

There is also an item of Bund expenses. Horst will have to have more money. As for the ten thousand the Consul is supposed to have given him last month—he didn't get it. Which is rather surprising news to Max. What money Horst has been given, he reports, he has cautiously banked under twenty different names in twenty different banks.

Officer Moe Finkelstein is back. There are a couple of things that are worrying him. One is, this Otto Horst who has just left. He's headed for trouble, according to Moe, and he advises Max to be wary of him—

"When a guy like Otto stands on his Constitutional rights to preach murder—there oughta be some Constitutional way to give *him* a military funeral!" says Moe. ". . . I'm telling you—

Das Otto is headed for der Clink. You just wanna look out when his time comes you don't get mugged and finger-printed with him. But why should I tip you guys off? I'm too democratic."

Moe has heard that there is somebody dead in the Consul's house. And there it is. Mrs. Baumer's pet parrot, Winston Churchill, had died that morning after eating poisoned grapes left by an anonymous admirer of Consul Baumer.

"A guy like the Consul, which ain't exactly popular oughta watch his diet," cautions Moe.

Frieda, a "well-cushioned, trim little blonde" has come to announce Dr. Jennings. Her contempt for Officer Moe is ostentatious, but Moe is able to take it. Dr. Jennings "is a fine-looking, middle-aged practitioner," whose "generally gentle and efficient bedside manner" has for the moment deserted him.

The Doctor has made innumerable calls at the Consulate, hoping to have news of his friend, Prof. Norberg, who has been held for two years in a concentration camp in Germany. So far he has been unable to learn anything, though Consul Baumer is presumed to have been working in Prof. Norberg's interest.

"The Norbergs are now in Concentration Camp 39," Max reports. "That means their release is imminent—"

"Baron, it's unthinkable that a German citizen as useful as Prof. Norberg has been held for two years in a concentration camp because of lecture notes found in his scrap basket!"

"In Germany, Doctor, political lectures are dangerous."

"But the man wasn't a politician—he was a scientist. He merely quoted another Aryan, Professor Earnest Hooton of Harvard: that the Jews are a biologically sound and superior race, because persecution has bred out their physical and mental weaklings."

"Yes, but what did he say about our Fuehrer?"

"All he said was that your Fuehrer is the victim of an aggravated psycho-neurosis—with obsessional paranoid trends and delusions of grandeur!" . . . And as a medical man I find the opinion conservative." The Doctor has gone to the door. "I have a call to make. I'll be back in an hour—"

"Doctor, the Fuehrer is broadcasting at five. The Consul has canceled all appointments—"

"Then I will be back at 4:30. (Firmly.) It'll be my last visit. I want a definite answer about Prof. Norberg, or I'll take up this whole matter with the State Department in Washington. Good afternoon, Baron."

"Good afternoon, Doctor."

Sophie Baumer, the Consul's wife, has apparently been listening. As Dr. Jennings leaves she enters hurriedly. "Sophie is a dark, pretty, vaguely foreign-looking woman in her early thirties. Her brown troubled eyes emphasize the dramatic pallor of her face." She is deeply concerned for Dr. Jennings and plainly suspicious of the help that her husband has promised to give, not only Dr. Jennings, but many others—

"He hasn't really tried to help them," she says. "He takes their money, and never even writes a word to Berlin about their relatives."

Sophie is bitter. She is more than suspicious that her husband had deliberately poisoned her parrot. It may be, as Max suggests, because he was furious about certain things that had appeared in a column written by an American newspaper man, Tom Denny—

"Sophie, you gave that story to Tom Denny for his paper," Max charges, openly—

"No, Max!"

MAX—Yes. And you also gave him the story last week that Otto Horst reports directly here for Berlin orders. Sophie, I know how you feel about Germany now, but it's got to stop! (*Gently.*) You know I am very fond of you—

SOPHIE (*reassured*)—I know that—

MAX—But if there's going to be any conflict between my friendship and my duty—

SOPHIE—Of course, Max! (*Frightened again.*) Does Karl know I told Tom Denny?

MAX—I hope not!

SOPHIE—Max, thank you for warning me. It is—just a warning?

MAX—That's all. (*Patting her hand.*) Now forget it.

SOPHIE (*rebellious*)—But why is it patriotism when you and Karl spy on America—and treason when I spy on Germany?

MAX—You're a German citizen—

SOPHIE—No! My father's a Czech. My mother was an American—

MAX—You're still the Consul's wife.

SOPHIE—I don't want to be any longer! But he won't give me a divorce. (*In despair.*) Oh, Max, what am I going to do?

MAX—Why don't you leave him?

SOPHIE—My father is still . . . in Prague, Max.

Max (*smiling*)—Oh, Karl wouldn't take it out on your father.
Sophie—You're so sensitive about most people. But you really don't know Karl, do you?
Max—He hasn't had an easy job in this post. He has plenty to worry about. I quite understand how *you* feel, but my relation to him is different. He's my chief. (*Uneasily.*) I've got to give him the benefit of every doubt.

There is the sound of a heavy step in the hall, followed by a loud, angry voice—
"Warum öffnen sie die türe nicht schneller?"
"Entschuldigen Sie, Herr Konsul—"
"You haven't seen me," whispers Sophie, excitedly. She is out one door a split second before Consul Karl Baumer enters another at the opposite side of the room. He "is the type of German who makes caricaturists lives easy and pro-German propaganda difficult. He is a type, moreover, by no means uncommon in official Germany. He has a completely shaven, glistening bullet head, he is tough, pallid and fleshy, though despite his flabby awkwardness, he can move, when the occasion requires, with alarming alacrity." . . . "A born sycophant, he is therefore unrelentingly arrogant to his dependents. Something of a sadist, and a good deal of a glutton, he fancies himself as a bon-vivant and man of the world. He wears a bat-wing collar, pin-stripe morning trousers and a monocle."
With business-like efficiency the Consul takes up the office routine. He is surprised to hear that Otto Horst is coming back for more money, after the ten thousand he had been given last month, but suddenly admits that he had held up that payment. He cannot quite understand how the Fuehrer ever appointed "this Dummkopf" as the American Fuehrer and has a suspicion that orders will be coming shortly suggesting that Horst be "liquidated"—
"What a shame that Stalin, and not Hitler, invented a beautiful word like that," sighs the Consul.
"Thomas Denny predicts they will soon share it," says Max.
"That's possible."
"A Communist-Nazi Alliance?"
"Why not? Hitler could bring out a new edition of 'Mein Kampf'—for one hundred and eighty million new customers. *If* he could collect the rubles."
"Well, if that day ever comes, I cease to be a Nazi."
"You're so sure of everything, Max." The Consul has fixed

his monocle cynically.

"I am sure of that, sir, or I haven't understood my Fuehrer," answers Max, heatedly.

"Let's hope nobody understands him. Peace is a static state of misunderstanding. When nations understand each other clearly, war is inevitable."

"That's too cynical a philosophy for me, sir. . . . Horst likes his job. He wouldn't be so easy to liquidate."

"Still, a nice little plan is working in me."

"Another of your inspirations?"

"Yes." The Consul taps his brow in unconscious humor. "My inspirations come to me as they come to Hitler—out of nothing."

Max would like to know more of the Consul's inspiration, but, says the Consul, Max is sometimes *too* curious. Which may be a trait handed down to him by his English grandmother.

Max is in no mood to accept gracefully the Consul's sly implications. He knows that his English grandmother was lowly born, but he had inherited nothing from her. His father was a Prussian nobleman. If the Consul is intimating anything different—

They are both pretty touchy this morning. It may have been the parrot— The Consul bridles at this suggestion. Having been sent poisoned grapes in the mail, why shouldn't he have tried them on the parrot?

"I am daily threatened to be shot at in the street," protests the Consul. "What stands between me and death? *Two Jewish policemen!* You are on edge, Max. I am on a precipice."

They have turned to the examination of papers in a dispatch box, the key to which the Consul wears upon his watch chain. There is a short memo in the box which, when Max decodes it, informs them that Dr. Jennings' friend, Prof. Norberg, has been released from Concentration Camp 39. This will permit the Consul to dispose of Dr. Jennings who has been getting on his nerves. But— There is an added note—"Norberg's in a hospital at Düsseldorf. His wife died in the concentration camp—in childbirth . . ." The Consul would dismiss this information curtly—

"Sir, I rather like the old Doctor," says Max. "This is bad news for him. Let me tell him—"

CONSUL—I said *I* will see him. Anything else?

MAX (*showing a big package of bills*)—The money. Fifty thousand dollars.

CONSUL—Fifty thousand—! (*Pacing, horribly irritated.*)

What am I to do with fifty thousand!? Start a hundred more camps! Get a broadcasting station! Buy up American journalists! Next Berlin will order me to corrupt Dorothy Thompson with an autographed picture of Hitler. (*Grabs newspaper from low table.*) I can't get even one good word from this second-rate columnist, Thomas Denny.

MAX (*appalled*)—You didn't make *him* an offer?

CONSUL—Max, am I a Dummkopf? I opened the doors of this Consulate—I offered him my friendship. I answered all his impertinent questions. I even let him make love to my wife!

MAX (*nervously*)—I say, you *are* imagining things—

CONSUL—There are certain precise facts in Mr. Denny's column— (*Viciously.*) Haven't *you* noticed?

MAX—Of course I have. But you can't accuse Sophie—

CONSUL—Now go decode that report, put the money in the safe, and stop gossiping about my wife!

MAX—Well, that's the limit! (*He goes to safe abruptly, controlling, no doubt, an impulse to sock his superior on the jaw.*)

CONSUL—Exactly! And my patience is exhausted.

MAX (*coldly*)—So is mine, sir. (*Returning from the safe where he has deposited the money.*) Now, let's be frank. I do feel, lately, that you doubt—my loyalty.

CONSUL (*unctuously*)—If I doubt your loyalty, perhaps it is because you doubt mine. Suspicion breeds suspicion.

MAX—I'm not suspicious, sir. I'm worried. I've told you— it's the books—I just *can't* make them balance.

CONSUL—You are not supposed to keep books. (*Furious.*) Books are dangerous!

MAX—I keep the figures in my head. That's why Berlin sent me. We received over a million dollars from Berlin this year. We just haven't *spent* a million.

CONSUL—And what do you think we've done with it?

MAX—I hope I've made a mistake. But I make a shortage of two hundred and fifty thousand. Those funds belonged to our country. You must help me straighten things out.

CONSUL—How can I straighten out books you keep in your head?

MAX—You will have to try, sir. (*Firmly.*) I can't delay sending my report to Berlin any longer—

CONSUL (*turning his back on* MAX, *and in a placating voice*) —I'll do what I can, Max—

MAX—When?

CONSUL—Tomorrow.

MAX—No, tonight, sir. The dispatch goes back at midnight—
CONSUL—Very well, Max.

There is also an unopened letter in the dispatch box which, as
Max would open it, the Consul grabs from him. Even though
it might be in code it is addressed to the Consul and marked
"Strictly Personal." The letter is from one Schroeder in London and has been a long time coming. It is the report of a certain investigation—

"Lately, sir, anybody you don't like—you suspect of being
Jewish," says Max. "Forgive me, but it's become rather an obsession."

"This can be a useful obsession for a smart Nazi. It often
solves many *personal* as well as political problems—"

The Consul's list of appointments had included many refugees. Max has canceled them all so the time will be free for the
Fuehrer's broadcast at 5. He would like to refer the refugees to
the Embassy, but the Consul insists on seeing them—

"Sir, you do take money from these people, don't you?" suddenly charges Max.

"My private income is none of your affair, Max."

"I'm sorry, it is! Now, look here, sir. I'm tired of dropping
gentle hints. We've got to straighten out both the finances and
ethics of this Consulate."

The Consul has put a record on the Victrola and suggests point-
edly that he would like to be alone—with his letter—

"Sir, does that letter concern me?" demands Max, abruptly.
The Consul evades an answer.

As Max leaves the room the Consul starts to put the letter in
his desk. Something he sees through the window attracts his
attention. He takes up a pair of binoculars, and is back of the
curtain confirming his suspicions when Sophie, his wife, comes
quietly into the room and starts to cross to the outer door. Her
hand is on the doorknob when the Consul stops her. He would
know where she is going. She is going shopping. He would have
her come and look through the binoculars. Who is the large
man she can see standing in the doorway? It is Tom Denny.
And what is Mr. Denny doing there? The Consul had better ask
Tom, suggests Sophie.

"I gave Mr. Denny my full co-operation," says the Consul,
with pointed emphasis. "And how does he repay me? He spies
on me. He publishes dirty articles about me and my work. Also
a few facts, which are true. And I did not give them to him.

Who did, Sophie?" Sophie doesn't know. . . .

Policeman Moe Finkelstein has arrived in answer to the Consul's summons. He is "breezy, but braced." He would be amiable, even friendly. He will call the Consul "Sir" if he has to. He will stand with his hat in his hand if that is one of the rules. He has been sent there by the Mayor to keep the Consul happy. No, he doesn't like the assignment particularly. Neither does his mother. But his mother is sentimental—

"I say it's got its merits. Imagine me being responsible for your health!" Moe is grinning happily. "Now where could a cockeyed thing like this happen, except in a Democracy?"

"Absolutely nowhere," agrees the Consul.

Moe—Yeah. Ain't it *swell?* I mean—this is the kind of a country where you gotta defend the other guy's life and liberty with your own life, even though you *know* he ain't feeling so sweet toward your person.

Consul—Democracy is a good word for that. Stupidity is better.

Moe—Well, so long as I was a minority—which is what *you* are in my country, sir—I'd be for it.

Consul—Oh, I am for it—until I and what I stand for become the majority.

Moe—That I should only live so long as that will take you!

Max—Please try to treat the Consul with respect.

Moe—We got free speech in this country. That's quite a handicap—in this instance.

Consul—I am annoyed that you put your solicitude for my welfare on such altruistic grounds. This is a matter of life and death for you.

Moe (*puzzled*)—How do you dope that one?

Consul—Do you realize what will happen to you if anything happens to me?

Moe—Sure, I get sacked off the force, if a hair of your head gets touched— (*Twinkling as he surveys the bullet, baby-bald head of the* Consul.) So I got to be extra careful.

Consul—Shut up!

Moe—Just holding up my end of the conversation.

Consul—You are a Jew!

Max—Sir, this man is an American national!

Consul (*to* Max)—Schweigen Sie! (*To* Moe.) I wish to remind you of something your breed of American nationals is apt to forget. If anything happens to me, International Jewry will be held responsible. Have you any relatives in Germany?

MOE—Nope. I come of a smart family. They left long before Hitler.

CONSUL—Then all your other co-religionists everywhere in Germany will be hostages for my safety. You remember what happened to them when Grynszpan shot our Secretary in Paris? Max, you tell him the colorful details—

MAX—You tell him. You enjoy it. (*Exits into his office, slamming that door, too.*)

MOE (*controlling himself*)—I know the colorful details. In this country Dillinger and Capone used to pull stunts like that. You know where they wound up. I'm hoping for the best in your case. Can I go now?

CONSUL—No. We both agree you are responsible for my safety.

MOE—Yes, sir.

CONSUL—Still you let suspicious characters hang around my house.

MOE—Kindly blueprint that.

CONSUL (*going toward alcove*)—There is a man in a slouch hat—out there.

MOE (*nodding pleasantly to* SOPHIE *who suddenly turns as if to warn him not to speak*)—Oh, the big guy? I asked Officer Solomon about him. Sol says he's a friend of yours—

CONSUL—Why should a friend of mine wait on the sidewalk?

MOE—Maybe that's as close as a friend of yours wants to get.

CONSUL (*furious*)—Officer Fogelstein!

MOE—Finkelstein—Moe Finkelstein.

CONSUL—Moe—huh—Moses!

MOE—Yeah, Moses. Great guy. The original Fuehrer. (*Wistfully, to himself.*) Wish he was around now with that Big Stick and a Red Sea handy—

CONSUL—Shut up! Tell this man I want to see him. His name is Thomas Denny.

MOE—No kidding! Gee, next to Winchell he's getting to be my favorite reading. Say! He's no friend of *yours*, sir!

CONSUL—Tell him Mr. and Mrs. Baumer want to see him.

SOPHIE (*distressed*)—No, Officer, tell him to go away.

CONSUL—You take orders from me.

MOE—Sorry, lady, my instructions are, I gotta do what he says.

CONSUL—Ya, you "gotta do what I says"!

MOE—Sir, your English ain't out of Shakespeare either.

CONSUL—In one minute I'll slap your face.

MOE—Listen, I've got on a uniform—

CONSUL—You should be ashamed to wear it.

MOE (*angry and unable to control himself any longer*)—I ain't! I wanted to wear this uniform. Ain't nobody stuffed me into it against my will—

CONSUL (*thrusting his face into* MOE'S)—I'll report you for insolence—

MOE (*with heroic restraint, as he realizes his situation is delicate and his official responsibility grave*)—Listen, sir, I don't want to start nothing. A *personal* grudge against you, I ain't got. (*Letting himself go a little.*) You done me a favor. You've made me see the difference between being in a land of the free and a land run by a screwball gangster. (*He turns to the door.*)

CONSUL—Hitler is a genius!

MOE—Yeah, but he's a *stupid* genius! (*The* CONSUL *moves angrily toward him.* MOE *retreats to the door.*) O.K. Hitler's united Germany! But he's united everybody else's country, too. And against him.

CONSUL (*charging on him, raging*)—You parasite! You lousy, illiterate, poverty-stricken spawn of the Ghetto—

MOE—Sa-a-y! You got me wrong. I'm really a smart intellectual and an international banker!

Moe has left quickly. The Consul returns to the subject of Tom Denny. Sophie is quite frank. She loves Tom Denny. She wants a divorce. She had married the Consul only because she wanted to get back to her mother's country and had no money. They have now ceased to be of the slightest use to each other. Why will he not let her go?

Max has rushed back with another decoded message. This one is bad news. Berlin is recalling Herr Baumer—

"They give me twenty-four hours." The Consul is reading the paper he has grabbed from Max. "Twenty-four hours to get rid of Horst, establish more favorable relations with the press . . ."

"And clear up the finances of this office!" adds Max.

"What, no order to overthrow the government at Washington?" Sophie is surprised.

"Sophie, this is serious for all of us—" The Consul is explaining ominously. "You know what'll happen to me if I go back? The Third Reich allows no margin for error!"

With Max gone the Consul tries to think of a way out. He

believes he can manage Horst. The shortage in funds he can put against Max. With the word that he has had from London, he tells Sophie that Max's grandmother was a full-blooded Jewess—no one in Berlin will take his word.

Sophie is horrified at both the news about Max, and at her husband's plans. She will do nothing to help him. If she doesn't, the Consul warns, he will see that Berlin deports her. She will have to help. She will have to tell Mr. Denny of her situation and beg him to help her by influencing the press to give Consul Baumer a good report until the tragic affair of Max is forgotten. If she refuses— Well, she is an informer. And Berlin knows what to do with traitors. In addition to this, let Sophie remember that her father is still in Prague—

"So, don't try any tricks," warns the Consul. "Don't run away with your romantic reporter. It might save you, but it won't save Max and it certainly won't be so nice for your dear papa."

Sophie has flung herself, sobbing, on the settee. Max is back to announce the arrival of Dr. Jennings. Sophie would warn Max. "He's got to have a scapegoat, but we can beat him!" she cries. When the Consul grabs hold of her wrists to restrain her, she breaks away and rushes out the door into the arms of Dr. Jennings, calling wildly to him, to anybody, for help.

Dr. Jennings, astounded to find Mrs. Baumer in this hysterical condition, sends her to her room. He will bring her a sedative. From Herr Baumer he would have some explanation of her hysteria. It is, the Consul explains, the result of the tension under which they are living. Two days now he has received deadly poisons through the mails. The deadly cyanide, "the suicide's poison," which can be bought in any photographer's store.

Dr. Jennings has gone to Mrs. Baumer's room. Max has turned to face the Consul. "What did she mean that you needed a scapegoat?" he demands.

"You tell *me*, Max," grins the Consul.

"Very well. Now what have you done with that two hundred fifty thousand?"

"The stock market. Max, the Third Reich allows no margin for error—but Wall St. requires a very big one. I was sold out."

"What damn stupidity! Why, even Americans have stopped playing the market—"

"Max, when I came to this country and saw how rich it was, I said—How much richer will it be under National Socialism. So I played the market long. But Democracies are perverse. Every time our Fuehrer opened his mouth—down this market tumbled!"

You can draw your report for Berlin now."

Max is not ready to do that. After all, Consul Baumer is his friend, and there are such things as human relationships. Perhaps, suggests Baumer, it is Max who is frightened— Perhaps his blood has begun to question—

"There is no answer in my blood that says I do not belong to Germany, that Germany does not belong to me," cries Max, hysterically. "For God's sake, sir! You know I love Germany. I love all *he* has done for it. He gave us back our honor, our belief in the beauty of our own traditions—"

"Please, Max, this is *not* a Nuremberg rally—"

"It's not true! It can't be. (*His whole person seems to be warding off a horrible physical assault.*) I couldn't bear it!"

"Of course not. Life would be intolerable—"

The Consul has taken out the letter and shown it to Max. The gleam of expectancy in his eye suggests to the excited Max that the whole thing is a trick; that this is how the Consul expects to find his scapegoat. With a rush Max is at the Consul's throat, demanding the letter. The men are struggling as Horst comes amazedly upon them.

"Heil Hitler!" the American Fuehrer cries. "Come, boys, what goes on here?"

The Consul and Max break apart, straightening their collars. Max, explains the Consul, has had bad news about his grandmother and is overwrought. The Consul will not need Horst's help in adjusting the matter.

Max has gone to his office. Horst would know if there are orders for him from Berlin? And money? His expenses have been high. Not only for uniforms, but also for four thousand knives, like the sample he is carrying—knives with cork handles that will not show fingerprints. He also has a new revolver, but no permit.

The Consul is not pleased. Why must Horst go on being a Dummkopf? Once he was almost taken up for drunken driving. Again he had nearly been convicted of perjury. It is the Consul's conviction that Horst is finished.

"At first you made a convincing noise," says Baumer. "But now you are obscuring our great Nazi truths— You have become a national comic strip!"

"When I come to power, Karl Baumer, I shall purge you," shouts Horst, furiously.

There is, thinks Baumer, little cause for Horst to take his situation personally. They all must take orders from Berlin. What

Horst should do is to find a martyr. If he could contrive to get himself "rubbed out by a Jew" it might help. The Consul has a feeling that that could be arranged—

"You're trying to mouder me!" screams Horst. "I won't have it! If Berlin's so hard up for a martyr, let them send one over! And they'd better send someone to kill him—"

"Is the American Fuehrer not prepared to die for his Nazi principles?"

Horst is terrified. He isn't ready. He hasn't finished his memoirs. And, if there must be a martyr, why not the Consul? He is much more important. His house, too, is surrounded by Jews. The Consul is also a real German. The American Fuehrer was born in Milwaukee—

The Consul is firm. He thinks it can be arranged for Horst to be found late at night in the hallway of the Consulate with one of the cork-handled knives in his back. And who could be more safely relied upon to do the job than the Consul himself?

"When you were discovered I should simply say you had a quarrel this afternoon with my Jewish policeman—"

"But suppose you couldn't prove the policeman did it?" demands the desperate Horst. "Suppose they suspect you?"

"Why should anyone suspect me of murdering you any more than they would suspect you of murdering me?" calmly inquires the Consul, plainly indicating that the interview is over.

"There's something *in* that thought, Baumer—" Horst is staring thoughtfully at the Consul's back as the latter goes to the door.

"The Fuehrer broadcasts in ten minutes," the Consul is saying. "That always gives me further inspiration. Afterward, we will discuss my inspiration—"

"And mine too," adds Horst, saluting with vigorous confidence. "Heil Hitler!"

Horst has gone. Consul Baumer has summoned Tom Denny, who has been brought in by Officer Finkelstein. Denny is inclined to kid the Consul, but the kidding soon takes on the more serious aspects of argument. Denny would stop this—

"Baumer, we can't argue," he says. "We begin from opposite premises. You believe the citizen was born to serve the state. We believe the citizen is the state—"

"Our belief has created a great Germany—"

DENNY—All the returns on Germany are not in yet. Don't forget. America's still the richest and freest nation.

Consul—I hope you can defend this fat Eden.

Denny—Any time you don't think so, just try to come and get it!

Consul—Then it may be too late. By that time America may have caught the disease which has weakened its sister democracies. The little disease they picked up in Munich—

Denny—Oh, we're thinking about that too, Baumer.

Consul—Fortunately, that's all you Americans do, is think!

Denny—Well, we've had the habit for a couple of centuries. We've got the biggest Brain Trust in the world, one hundred and thirty million people who can all do their *own* thinking.

Consul—Such a wasted effort, when your President Rosenfeld is determined to do it for them.

Denny—O.K. But who checks even the President's thinking? (*Kidding his way out of a tense, trite and fruitless discussion.*) The most fearless and uncensored journalists, who, I am proud to say, all violently and publicly disagree with one another. But there's one thing we don't disagree about— (*Seriously.*) We just don't like *you*. Now, the officer said Mrs. Baumer also wanted to see me.

Consul—Yes. But she's not well now. She's had a slight shock. Or, should I say I have had a slight shock? Berlin is about to recall me.

Denny (*his mouth relaxing in a happy grin*)—That's dandy.

Consul—Thanks to your articles.

Denny—May I quote you?

Consul—Still, there's an "out" for me which might be acceptable to Berlin.

Denny (*cheerfully*)—Right now I'm having no part in it.

Consul—You're afraid you would lose your job if you changed your views?

Denny (*laughing*)—Oh, yes. That has me terrified.

Consul—Let me be frank. Headline news may burst out of this office before midnight. I'd like you to cover it—with sympathy. Mr. Denny, there's $50,000 in that safe. Let me conclude this talk by giving it to you.

Denny—You know how I'm going to head off my Sunday column? "Berlin offers its entire gold reserve for a few kind words from your correspondent."

The Consul's next statement finds Denny visibly unprepared. It is to the effect that Sophie Baumer is in love with him. How far their love has gone the Consul does not pretend to know, nor,

being a gentleman, will he inquire. In any event Mrs. Baumer
is sailing on the *Bremen*. If she does not sail the Consul will
have her deported—

"Mr. Denny, Berlin is recalling me because certain facts have
leaked out of my office," continues the Consul. "Now, in self-
defense I will have to explain that my wife was your informer.
And Berlin has such a brutal custom. They use *axes* on little
ladies' necks in Berlin—"

The cold, determined expression of the Consul convinces Denny
that he means what he says.

"Well, Baumer, you've found my price," he says, grimly.
"But I've got to think it over. I have a feeling now I'd rather
shoot you than deliver."

Dr. Jennings is back. He reports Mrs. Baumer suffering from
a "compulsion neurosis," and he advises Consul Baumer against
leaving loaded weapons handy, for fear of what Mrs. Baumer
might do to herself. Nor would it be wise for Tom to see her at
this time.

Alone with the Consul, Dr. Jennings demands news of the Norbergs. Professor Norberg, he is told, has been released and is on
his way to America. The Doctor's relief is great. Max is called
to prepare the affidavits. Of course there still is the question of
Norberg's passage money. But the Doctor has already given the
Consul $5,000 and refuses to give more—

"Listen, Baumer, it was very difficult for me to raise that
$5,000," the Doctor is protesting. "I only did it because—Nor-
berg's my son-in-law—Mrs. Norberg is my daughter—"

"Your daughter."

"Yes. My only daughter."

"Why didn't you tell me this before?"

"I'm a good judge of human nature. I knew if this was a
racket—the fact she was my daughter would make it more
costly—"

"You are too hard on me. (*Magnanimously.*) We will waive
the question of the passage money!"

The Doctor's smile is lightly, but briefly, triumphant. Max,
in answer to the Consul's demand that he give the Doctor the
memo on Norberg that they had received that morning, is trying to evade compliance with that order. He makes several excuses, including that of the imminence of the Fuehrer's broadcast.
Dr. Jennings' suspicions are aroused. There is a threat in his
voice as the Consul would hurry him toward the reception room—

"By God, Baumer, if this *is* a trick—if any harm comes to my girl—"

The radio announcer has given warning. Adolf Hitler is about to speak from Berlin—

"Max, break it to him gently," suggests the Consul, as Dr. Jennings disappears.

"It's the last piece of dirty work I do for you," Max exclaims, furiously. "Baumer, you can forget appeasement. You can't buy my loyalty to Germany. No matter what's in that letter, I send my report at midnight."

"Max, this patriotism will undo you," smiles the Consul, as he goes out the door.

It is growing dark. Frieda comes to snap on the lights. Officer Finkelstein drifts in, looking for the Consul. He is not averse to having a few words with the pretty Frieda. Already he is beginning to understand German. Already Frieda is beginning to understand America as a land of opportunity. "You're beautiful!" insists Moe. "Meinen Sie?" queries Frieda, smiling cutely. "Aw, you dames understand *that* in any language!" protests Moe. "Listen, your eyes—Dietrich!" Moe is pantomiming excitedly. "Your shape—Hedy Lamarr! Your lips—Loretta Young—" "Nein. Greta Garbo!" corrects Frieda, pouting prettily.

Before the Consul is back to find them waltzing gaily about the room, Moe has made a Saturday night date with Frieda. It is to include the movies, chop suey, dancing and anything else that Frieda may agree to. "Why does anybody learn to talk?" chuckles Moe. "It ain't really necessary."

Moe has waltzed Frieda out of the room. Tom Denny is back, followed by Sophie. The Consul is smiling at them cheerfully. He even offers them the next minute and a half, before the Fuehrer's broadcast, for a final tête-à-tête, and leaves them.

Sophie is tremulous with fear as Denny takes her in his arms reassuringly. The worst things that she imagines will happen—her deportation and the killing of her father—Tom assures Sophie will never happen.

"Before I let him ship you off, I'll kill him!" swears Tom.

"And I'd help you!" adds Sophie, fiercely. . . .

The first thing for them to do, insists Tom, is to get away from there. Sophie doesn't think she should abandon Max. The Consul, she explains, having found out that Max is partly Jewish, is planning to make him take the rap for the missing money—

The waltz music that has been coming from the radio ends abruptly. "We are now on the air for an international broadcast," the announcer is saying—

"Oh, boy! Now we're in for a dose of Mr. Shicklegruber!" promises Denny, turning off the radio in disgust.

"Schicklegruber?" Sophie doesn't understand.

"Schicklegruber, that's Adolf's real name," Denny explains. "His mother's name. His father never gave him one, as everyone realizes intuitively. Just think, history might have been different if he hadn't changed it to Hitler!"

"Why?"

"Heil Schicklegruber!"

"How silly!"

"Whenever you're frightened, darling, of all that Hitler stands for, just *think* Heil Schicklegruber!"

There has been a slight delay in the broadcast. Outside in the street a crowd has been collecting. The Consul doesn't like this. Moe agrees to send for more police if the crowd gets bigger.

Now Horst has rushed in to report the assembling of the mob. "When the Fuehrer speaks the dogs always gather to howl at him out there," sneers the Consul.

The crowd has taken up a sort of chant. "A tisket, a tasket, put Baumer in a casket!" Which convinces Horst that it is Baumer they want for a martyr.

Moe has sent for a squad of police. He advises closing the curtains. The mob is threatening to hurl things. But the Consul is not afraid. Furthermore he would like Officer Finkelstein to know that a loaded revolver has been brought into the Consulate by an uninvited guest, as Horst will testify. The gun had been used to threaten him—

"Finkelstein, you've allowed someone armed, without a permit, to enter my house. I am preferring charges against you—for dereliction of duty."

"Aw—you can't do that, sir. It'd reflect on the whole force. Jeez, they'd break me—"

"I hope so." The idea pleases the Consul.

"Say, even you wouldn't do that to a family man. (*Pleading.*) Listen, I got a *mother*. I got Momma's family. Listen, I'm in a jam like everybody else—"

"Horst, throw this fellow out!" commands the Consul.

"Who, me?"

"A frame-up, if I ever saw one! Listen, I'm a neutral and I'm going to stay a neutral until I face you across a trench, and will I put six inches of steel right through your swastika—"

"Horst, thrash him!"

"Baumer, you're the one he threatened!" Horst is very jittery.

"Listen, sweetheart," says Moe, turning belligerently to Horst, "if you wanna fight, come around tomorrow morning, when I won't be wearing this uniform—"

The Consul is sitting at his desk, "complacent, grinning, immobile." He has turned his back on everybody. There is a further delay in the broadcast. Suddenly Dr. Jennings bursts excitedly into the room, "a bewildered and broken man." He refuses to believe the translation Max has given him—that Norberg is in a German hospital, his mind gone; that his daughter had died in the concentration camp—

"If you'd told me sooner she was your daughter—" the Consul is saying.

"You—you could have gotten her out long ago—" interrupts the Doctor, fiercely.

"Doctor, you *must* go home—" Sophie has taken the Doctor's arm and is urging him toward the door.

"Yes, I must have self-control. I'll kill that man if I don't get out of here. I'll kill him!"

"That makes three of us now who'd like to see you laid out with candles," Denny reminds the Consul.

"The list is growing." The Consul is not at all disturbed.

Moe advises against anyone leaving the house. Sophie has forced Dr. Jennings into a chair. The Consul is threatening to read the letter revealing Max's ancestry aloud when Max grabs it from his hand and throws it into the fire.

"Karl, he ought to kill you for that!" exclaims Sophie.

"That makes four, Baumer," counts Denny.

The Consul, his mock sympathy rebuffed by Max, goes to the bar and pours a glass of Scotch which he places before Max. The radio announcer is setting the stage for the broadcast. The Consul has returned to the bar and poured himself a drink of brandy—

"All at once the field is a blaze of floodlights. It is the signal! The Fuehrer has arrived!" reports the radio announcer.

The Consul goes to the bust of Hitler and raises his glass. "Der Fuehrer!"

From outside the Consulate there comes a blare of motorcycle sirens. "A well-aimed brick crashes through the window, missing the Consul so narrowly he staggers back to the table and puts his glass down." There is the screech of other sirens. "And now the Awful, Awful Voice of Hitler, the man who talked a nation and perhaps a civilization to its doom begins, hysterical, guttural, hideously sure and hard and loud—"

Denny is standing in front of the fireplace. Dr. Jennings is slumped down in a wing chair. Horst is at the bar drinking beer. Sophie is leaning against the window. Max, "rigid and white," has sunk into an easy chair. The Awful Voice beats on. Denny has moved over to stand beside Sophie, his arm around her.

The Consul, coming from in back of the curtains, looks at them all triumphantly and sinks into his swivel chair. His back is to them as he picks up his brandy glass. Their backs are all to him. The Awful Voice is saying something about Jews. Suddenly Horst moves toward the Consul's chair. Denny turns from the window and starts for the bar. Horst drops down to the table and reaches for a cigarette. He turns again to the radio.

Max has also risen suddenly and walked toward the desk. He is back of the Consul when he reaches for something on the desk and draws back quickly as the Consul moves as though to take his hand. Sophie, turning, sees Max, and walks up as though to comfort him. She leans forward to plead with the Consul. Something he says causes her to stiffen and draw away. Denny comes from the bar to support her. They both talk to the Consul, who has deliberately moved the chair with its back to them and turns his head away from them. The Awful Voice goes on.

Sophie and Denny have moved over to a sofa and sat down. "Sophie, we can't argue with a madman!" Denny is saying. Horst has turned up the radio. "And now the yammer gives way to the thunderous, sea-surge of the mob, the 'Sieg Heil! Sieg Heil!'"

Now Dr. Jennings rises slowly, "totally unperceived by anybody," and goes to the Consul's desk. From its top he whips the gun, holds it around the chair to the Consul's head and fires. "The shot is lost in a last bestial howl from the radio. The Consul's body falls abruptly forward, face down, on the desk."

Dr. Jennings turns, the gun in his hand, as though to speak, to accuse himself. No one hears him. He carefully wipes the handle of the gun on his coat, lays it by the Consul's right hand, and returns to his chair. . . .

Moe Finkelstein is at the door trying to shout down the radio. "Hey! Mr. Baumer! Solomon's grabbed the guy which flung that brick. They got him at the station house. You wanna prefer charges?"

"Sssh!" cautions Horst.

"They gotta know," Moe persists, leaning over the Consul. "Listen, sir. I said . . . Jeez!"

The Consul is dead. Quickly Moe makes a hurried examination of the windows, the desk, etc. He turns to shout the news to the others. They are sitting, their backs to him, "with magnificent dead-pans."

"Something about this inimical array of backs causes him to shut his mouth. And it is at that moment he remembers, what it may have seemed impossible he should ever forget, that he is a Jew, and that in this horrid circumstance he bears a curious responsibility. He whistles softly through his teeth and, wiping his forehead, looks Jehovahward imploringly as the curtain falls."

ACT II

The scene is the same. No one has moved from the position he was in at the curtain's fall. The Awful Voice is still screaming on. Moe Finkelstein has clapped his cap on his head, made a second inspection of the alcove windows and returned to face the others.

His first order is for Horst to shut off the radio. His second that none of them shall move. Baumer's dead. There's no doubt about that. "An autopsy's the only future Mr. Baumer's got," Moe assures them.

Dr. Jennings ventures an opinion that it probably is a thrombosis. But it wasn't anything like a "thrombis," as Moe sees it. Nor a suicide. At least the Consul had not shot himself, as Denny and Horst, and even the Doctor, would like to believe. Nobody heard a shot.

Yet Baumer had reason for wanting to take his life: He had been a failure, as Denny points out. He had been taking Nazi funds, Sophie remembers. And he had been recalled to Germany—

"Now, get this fast, everybody! This wasn't no suicide. This was murder!" announces Moe. ". . . This guy's been bumped off, and one of you is guilty."

"But that's impossible," suggests Dr. Jennings, very reasonably. "We were all sitting here quietly listening to the radio. Somebody must have come through the window. The last thing we heard him say was that he was going to open the window."

"Then somebody from the street must have climbed through the window," suggests Max.

"But nobody didn't. Because the window is locked inside. How do you like that?"

"But they may have shot him through it?"

"No. There ain't no holes in the window. The only hole's in him," explains Moe, with an apology to Mrs. Baumer when she shrinks from the picture. Tactfully Moe now draws the curtains across the alcove, thereafter concealing the Consul's body.

Continuing his investigations, Moe discovers that the servants are all in the kitchen listening to the broadcast. Anyway, they would have had to come through the hall, and Moe has been in the hall the whole time.

"Now if the guy who done it will come clean, I'll call for the Homicide, and the rest of you can go about your business," continues Moe, moving expectantly toward the telephone.

Dr. Jennings—Well, we're naturally shocked, but none of us is behaving at all like a man with a murder on his conscience.

Moe—Listen, I ain't no Sherlock Holmes, but the party, or parties, that did this pulled one boner.

Dr. Jennings—He left a clue perhaps? (*Feeling his own breast pocket as he talks.*) He dropped a handkerchief, a fountain pen—

Moe—I ain't saying what it is. But any dope would know it spelt murder.

Denny—Then you'd better call the Homicide now. You're not in a position to investigate this alleged crime. If it's not suicide, there's some simple explanation of how the criminal got in.

Max—A trained mind will find it.

Denny—By this delay you may be helping a dangerous criminal in making his getaway.

Dr. Jennings—Precisely.

Max—Officer, I agree with these gentlemen.

Horst—But I agree with the officer! (*He confronts Moe, his nostrils twitching with excitement.*) Yes, one of us in this room is a mad dog, a killer! Proceed, Finkelstein. It's interesting to see your mind work.

Moe—Listen, Otto, if my mind can't work now, I may as well swop it for yours, God forbid . . . Look, everybody, *I'm* in a very unusual situation—

Dr. Jennings—The Chinese say a wise man never finds a dead one.

Moe—I wish to hell this had all happened in China.

Denny (*going to telephone*)—If you won't phone for the Homicide, I will!

Moe—For God's sake, Mister, wait! (*With bitter urgency.*) *I* was responsible for that guy's safety.

Dr. Jennings (*puzzled*)—No one can hold you responsible for what happened in this room, if you were not in it.

Horst—*If* he was not in it. Ha!

Moe—*My name is Moe Finkelstein.*

Horst—Exactly!

Denny—Don't get the connection—

Dr. Jennings—Nor I.

Moe (*points to* Horst)—He got it. Right away *he* got it!

Max (*dully*)—Yes—and I think I get it, too.

Sophie—But *you* had no motive—

Moe—Lady, for a lot of people, the shape of my noise is *plenty* of motive.

Denny (*indignantly*)—But hell, man, you're in America!

Moe—Likewise I'm an American. So I ain't worried much about myself. But there's still a lot of people with noses like mine in Germany. Look, the squad gets here, and reporters— and there ain't nobody obliging 'em with no snap confession. So coroner's inquests take hours. (*Looks at* Horst.) But cables to Germany go fast!

Max (*sharply*)—I remember what happened in Berlin when Grynszpan shot the Secretary of our Paris Embassy.

Dr. Jennings is willing to provide Moe with an alibi. He (Jennings) had been sitting where he could see the hall door and he is willing to swear that Moe came in but once—and that once but five minutes before. But, counters Horst, suppose Moe had tiptoed in from the other side of the room, then no one would have seen him. In fact Horst is willing to swear that that is what actually occurred—until he is reminded that if he knows that much, and failed to report it, he is guilty as an accessory to the murder.

Still, Officer Finkelstein is in a spot. He would plead with them all to help him. They all want to help—except Horst.

"What is the matter with all you Dummkopfs?" shrieks Horst. "He had a quarrel with Baumer. We all heard him. He threatened to kill him. You probably destroyed the real evidence against you just now when you went behind that curtain. But the evidence that you can't destroy is that you had a motive and absolutely no alibi—unless you can make one of these blind fools give it to you."

"Horst, you're deliberately trying to pin this thing on this boy!" charges the Doctor.

"But obviously. We are Aryans. Why, if he's not guilty,

then one of us is. That would be a pretty kettle of gefüllte fish!"

Moe is now convinced that an alibi will not be enough. He will have to produce the murderer. To find the murderer he is going to do a little questioning. He's seen enough movies, Moe explains, to know the ropes. First, there must be a motive.

Horst is convinced Moe had the only good motive, but Dr. Jennings is free to confess that he also had one. So had Tom Denny, who admits his love for Mrs. Baumer. Max doesn't believe he had a motive, though the Doctor is a little skeptical. And Horst is sure he had none.

"Sooner or later Baumer would supply a motive to anybody who worked with him, gratis," declares Denny.

"I'm sure of it," checks Dr. Jennings. "As Prof. Norberg put it in his study of Criminality, the solution of any crime lies in the personality of the murdered man himself."

Three of them, Moe decides, had motives. So who owned the gun?

They had all seen the gun. They all knew it was loaded. It will be easy to trace where it was bought by its serial number—

"Not where I bought this one!" boasts Horst, without intending to. Which settles the ownership of the gun.

"O.K. Now, folks, we got a weapon," announces Moe, professionally. "Likewise all the motives we'll get till this brace of goose-steppers starts squealing. (*To* HORST *and* MAX.) Now let's straighten out the chronic of events leading up to this murder."

"Well, it all began in 1923 with a beer-hall putsch in Munich," says Denny.

"I get you. But if we start going back that far, we're sure to wind up in the Garden of Eden, cross-examining the snake. O.K. We'll begin with the putsch at 5:07 o'clock on this block."

"Why?"

"On account of at that hour we was all in this room. And one of us had the opportunity for murder some time after that. So it's 5:07 o'clock, and in I breezes, and tells Baumer he's gotta close them drapes or he's gonna get conked. (*Shrugging.*) And was Finkelstein a prophet! So Baumer tells me to scram, and I makes a mellerdramatic exit—"

"Vowing vengeance on Baumer."

"Nope. I just wished him he should grow like an onion, with his head in the ground forever. Which is nothing compared to what Momma's going to wish Otto. O.K. Exit copper—enter brick. That's one minute later—5:08 o'clock."

Denny remembers that when the brick nearly hit Baumer he was standing by the bust toasting Hitler. After a moment's confusion the Consul had started back to open the windows, so the crowd outside could hear the Fuehrer. The Consul disappeared back of the curtains and they all sat down to listen to the broadcast. No one had seen the Consul come back and sit down.

Moe puts them all back in the positions they say they were in when Baumer was Heiling Hitler. He turns to Sophie—

"Now, lady, with your kind permission I'm going to impersonate your dear departed husband. . . . Momma should see me —O.K. (*On step, striking a stance.*) So I'm Baumer, and I says 'Heil Hitler!' (*Salutes, raises his eyes to ceiling.*) God forgive me! And Hitler's a great guy, and he's gonna mop up the world, and baloney and baloney and baloney, and people ain't got enough on their minds, so I'll just open the windows for it. (*Half steps behind the curtain.*) Now go and park yourselves where you went after I said that— (Sophie *sits down on sofa at right.* Denny *goes directly to sit with* Sophie. Horst *sits on settee left. Neither the* Doctor *nor* Max *needs to move.* Moe *looks at them critically.*) Say! This is exactly the way I found you when I come in by the hall door and stumbles across the stiff."

"Ha! Exactly! Why not?" Horst wants to know.

"Officer, if you were on duty in the hall, can't Officer Solomon give you an alibi?" demands Dr. Jennings, nervously.

"Sol took the German who tossed the confetti through the window to the station house. When that brick came in, my alibi went out."

When they try to remember how long a time elapsed between the time they started listening to the radio and the time Moe came into the room there is a wide divergence of opinion. Dr. Jennings, especially, is confused. He thinks it might have been "a minute, an hour, or an eternity." "I was so stunned I must have lost track of time," says the Doctor.

But if they are all satisfied that nobody moved after they sat down it proves either that somebody is lying or that Moe must have sneaked in by the office door and done the murder. Such a confession would greatly satisfy Horst.

Now Dr. Jennings decides that he must tell more. That one of them is lying he admits to be obvious. "I was sitting in this chair, where you must realize I was in a unique position to commit this murder," the Doctor points out.

"Yeah, I realize it," admits Moe.

DR. JENNINGS—But I didn't do it!

MOE (*leans over the* DOCTOR *and says kindly*)—Doc, you look like a good guy. If you say you didn't, I'll try to believe you.

DR. JENNINGS—Thank you. But I was also in a unique position to see the actions of everyone else in this room.

HORST—If you saw all of us, we all have alibis now. You said in the beginning none of us moved.

DR. JENNINGS—No, Horst. I said none of you moved *after* we were all in the positions in which the officer found us. But before—while Hitler was speaking—

MOE—Now take it easy, Doc. Folks, I wanna make an announcement. (*He turns to the others.*) After you all heard Baumer say he was gonna open the window, one of you did move. Now how do I know that? Because I was in the hall when you turned up the radio. After Hitler turns the juice on, I went into the Baron's office—

HORST—Why?

MOE (*patiently*)—Otto, them Heil Hitlers don't relax me. Now, when I was in the office, I looked through that door once. (*Points to open office door.*) And I saw somebody in here moving.

ALL—Who?

MOE—I ain't saying who yet.

HORST (*nervously*)—You mean the person you saw moving is the one you're going to accuse of murder?

MOE—I'm saying, any guy who ain't willing to admit he got an attack of wanderlust during that speech is a pretty suspicious character. And will the D.A. get a load of it. O.K. Now everybody go back to the Heil Hitler positions.

They resume their original positions, and then, under Moe's prodding, try to recall their next moves. Sophie and Denny go back to the sofa. Horst tries to demonstrate how he got to the easy chair, and Dr. Jennings insists he would have seen such a move and has no recollection of it. Both the Doctor and Denny now remember seeing Horst move both toward and away from the Consul's desk, a little stealthily. Max admits he had moved, but had changed his mind about leaving and stopped in the office door.

So far everything checks with what Moe saw when he peeked

in the door. On a general check-up it looks both to Moe and the Doctor as though Horst is the one who had been provided with an excellent opportunity to commit murder. But the evidence is all circumstantial. Horst, excited in his denials, suddenly recalls an alibi. It was he who had turned up the radio at the Consul's request. Yes, they all remember that. At least Denny remembers standing at the bar and seeing Sophie turn from the window and go to Baumer's desk—

"So I went right after her. She started to argue with Baumer. I told her it was useless, the man was a maniac. He said: 'Turn the radio up louder.' "

"Yes. So I did it! Like this—" cries Horst, exultantly, as he again turns on the radio. Hitler is still talking. "Coming to you by courtesy of David Sarnoff," comments Moe, as he turns it off. "O.K. Now where are we? After Baumer went to his desk, the Doctor never moved at no time. The Baron here moved first. He could have done it. Otto moved next. Otto could have done it. Then Mrs. Baumer and Mr. Denny goes to the desk. But when they was up there, Baumer was still living because he tells them to turn the radio up louder. And then they both goes and parks themselves on that sofa. After that the Doc says nobody moved. O.K. So everybody but me and the Doc has got alibis. Maybe they ain't good ones, but all everybody's gotta do is stick to them. Because there ain't no witnesses. Nobody saw nobody commit no murder. It's the perfect crime, folks. Which leaves me where I started—the perfect scapegoat. (*Wearily.*) I guess I never had much of a chance to unravel this one. I kinda hoped if the guy who done it had any sense of justice—which leaves you out, Otto—he'd say so. But I got too much faith in human nature. O.K. So there ain't nothing much going to happen to me. But a lot of innocent people is going for a hell of a bloody sleigh-ride—"

DR. JENNINGS (*rising and stretching out a detaining hand toward* MOE)—Officer.

MOE (*stops dialing*)—Doc?

DR. JENNINGS—You know I shot him. You guessed it when I made that slip about the one minute. I had been sitting in this chair just one minute after I obeyed that delightful impulse. I wiped the gun on my coat. It was so simple.

MOE (*relieved*)—O.K. So you shot him.

SOPHIE (*runs toward the* DOCTOR)—Doctor, you didn't, you couldn't have—

Dr. Jennings—Please, Mrs. Baumer. A jury will find, I hope, extenuating circumstances. I'm sorry, too, that we've played this ugly game so long. But I was so hoping that we'd find some way to pin it on dear Otto—for at least the morning editions.

Horst—Ha! But I'm not a Dummkopf! I foresaw your strategy. The first thing I made you say was, I never moved *after* I came to the radio!

Dr. Jennings—Yes, that was my error. Now, Officer, let's get going. I'm ready. (Horst *obligingly goes to open the door for* Moe *and* Dr. Jennings.)

Moe—But I ain't, Doc. Sit down. (*Presses* Dr. Jennings *gently into wing chair, and walks toward the center of the room and confronts them all fiercely.*) Now let's everybody stop yammering about guns. That's what's been confusing me.

Dr. Jennings—I don't understand—

Moe—Nobody said anything about a knife. Somebody else stabbed him! (Sophie *buries her shocked face on* Denny's *ever-obliging shirt front.*) I'm sorry, lady. But holy Jeez, a guy that's been stabbed first don't shoot himself after. And after a guy has been shot he ain't in no shape to tickle himself with a knife. (*Pleased.*) That's how I deducted a double murder.

Horst (*white*)—Stabbed? With what kind of a knife?

Moe—With a cork-handled knife which had some foreign words on it.

Max—That was yours, Horst!

Moe (*to* Horst)—Say, you sure travel with an arsenal! Don't happen to have a time bomb on you?

Horst (*livid*)—You won't find any fingerprints on that knife! Cork doesn't hold them!

Moe—If you knew that, we'll hold it as evidence against you!

For a moment the burden of guilt shifts from Denny and Sophie to Horst. Denny admits that he and Sophie had noticed the knife. It was then that Denny, to avert suspicion, had moved the body and muttered the order to turn the radio up. But Horst had been seen at the Consul's chair just before them. Also, as Max now relates, Horst had a motive. He was to have been liquidated.

"You were told to get yourself killed and make it look as though a Jew had done it," Max reminds him. "Oh, I know the mind of a Nazi."

For proof of what he says Max refers them to the papers in Baumer's safe. But the safe is German property and can't be touched, exults Horst. Furthermore, in that same safe is equally strong circumstantial evidence pointing to the Baron, evidence contained in the letter over which Max and the Consul were fighting when Horst had come upon them.

With a dash to the fireplace Horst has recovered the half-burned letter and Max is on him trying to take it from him. Now Moe has the letter and, though he cannot read the German text, he does recognize the word "Jude." "I know that word in any language," grimly admits Moe.

"Yes, I wanted to kill him when I first found out about that letter," Max admits. "But later I only wanted to die myself. Yes, I went to the desk, but I went there to kill myself—"

"So you took the gun and stabbed him! I mean—the knife!" sneers Horst.

"O.K., Mr. Goebbels!" shouts Moe, to quiet them. "So where do we go from here? I'll tell you. Still nowhere. The Baron and Otto say he was alive. (*To* DENNY.) You and Mrs. Baumer say he was dead. Now all you still gotta do is stick to them stories. The only thing that's different now is there's two Jews in it. And still a lot of helpless people four thousand miles away from where we're sitting who are going to take the rap for *both* of us."

Moe is about to call the Homicide Squad when Stophie stops him. It was she who had stabbed the Consul. Nor will she let Denny take the blame.

This time Moe is convinced he has the truth. "Women use knives mostly," he says. "That's what comes from hanging around the kitchen." He is at the phone again when Dr. Jennings interposes another doubt. He questions whether a woman has the strength to reach a man's heart with a knife and is still convinced it was his bullet that caused the Consul's death. He asks permission to examine the body before the Coroner arrives. Moe grants the permission, against his better judgment, but he calls Mulrooney of the Homicide Squad just the same.

Suddenly Dr. Jennings reappears from in back of the curtains in a state of excitement. Mrs. Baumer's knife had not killed Baumer. Neither had his (Jennings') bullet. The Consul had been poisoned! With cyanide potassium!

"He was quite dead when Mrs. Baumer got to him. He drank it from a glass on his desk. . . . Cyanide drains all oxygen from the blood instantly. It is over in less than a minute. But he must have had spasms, short but very ugly spasms. Now, if he drank after he sat in that chair, he would have fallen out of it.

It is safe to assume that he drank while he was on his feet—and fell into it!"

"Listen, he had them spasms while you all thought he was opening the windows," suggests Moe.

"Then whoever put the poison in his glass did it *before* he went to the desk?"

"Most certainly."

"This puts everybody right back in the picture!"

The search is on again. Sophie can explain the poison. She had found it in the medicine chest after accusing her husband of having poisoned her parrot. She had taken it to him and he had put it in his desk. But where is it now?

Moe decides they should all be searched. He will take Horst. He will let Denny and the Doctor search each other. The Doctor manages to whisper a secret to Denny. He had found Baumer's safe open and had taken not only the Horst records, but the $50,000 in Nazi funds as well—"to buy myself assorted political refugees," explains the Doctor looking at Sophie; "one in particular from Czechoslovakia."

"The Doctor's pockets are empty," announces Denny, loudly, slipping the money back.

On Horst Officer Finkelstein finds an assortment of bank books as well as a bank roll. Also a shiny bullet-proof vest.

Suddenly the poison is found. It is in Max's pocket. How it came there Max doesn't know. He didn't put it there.

"I *know* you didn't," agrees Moe. "You wouldn't poison no guy and then sit around like a dumb cluck for two hours hatching the evidence in your pocket."

"Why wouldn't he?"

"On account of the brains he inherited from his grandmother!"

"Then how did the poison get in his pocket? I suppose I planted it?"

"That's a damned good suggestion. If we can find out when you did it!"

Again Moe puts them back where they were just before the brick came through the window. Now he is acting the Consul again and has gone to the bar to pour Max's drink of Scotch and the Consul's drink of brandy—"his own *brandy!*" But, Dr. Jennings is quick to point out, the glass from which the Consul had been drinking had *whiskey* in it!

It is plain, now. Sophie recalls that the Consul had told her that he knew Max was going to commit suicide. Max remembers the Consul coming over and standing by him to console him.

Then came the brick! In the confusion the Consul had put down his glass of brandy—and when he reached for it a moment later he had taken up the glass of whiskey into which he had slipped the poison for Max.

Max is ecstatic now. "Oh, put it on his tombstone!" he is shouting: "The Third Reich allows no margin for error!"

"Well, the Dummkopf!" snorts Horst, disgustedly. Then he makes one last try: "But you can't prove that Baumer switched those glasses accidentally before the reporters get here!"

Moe—Listen, boys. How we gonna prove it definitely so this schmutz can't possibly smear it?

Dr. Jennings—Listen! I was sitting in that chair—

Moe—You're telling me!

Dr. Jennings—When the brick sailed in. Naturally I turned. I saw Baumer set his brandy down. Then—I attached no significance to it at the time—I quite definitely saw him pick up Max's whiskey!

Sophie—Why, I did too! I very definitely recall it!

Denny—why, hell, so did I see that!

Max—So did I.

Horst—But I didn't!

Moe—Now, Otto, who's gonna take your word against the word of a couple of Jewish boys in this city? (*The sirens give way to the clanging of the police wagon outside.*) That's the pie-wagon.

Sophie—But, Officer! The Doctor and I did stab and shoot him.

Dr. Jennings—Mrs. Baumer, there are no penalties attached to such delicate attentions to a corpse.

Denny—You are murderers emotionally, but not legally.

Moe—Yeah. But das Otto is headed for der Clink. (*With a swift, happy, practiced gesture he puts handcuffs on* Horst.)

Horst—Handcuffs? On me? Why, I'm the only one in this room who didn't try to murder the Consul—

Denny—Maybe that's an offense in itself, Otto.

Horst (*struggling*)—You can't hold me on anything!

Moe—Carrying concealed weapons—pending income-tax charges. (*Showing* Horst *to the door.*) What'd you say your lawyer's name is?

Horst—Ouch—Benjamin Rosenblatt.

Moe—If he gets you off this, you oughta make him an honorary Aryan. (*The door bursts open and* Captain Mulrooney *enters. He is six feet of powerful, red-faced, exasperated authority.*)

MULROONEY (*bellowing*)—Now, Finkelstein, what the hell's happened!

MOE (*sheepishly*)—Well, Captain Mulrooney, it seems the Consul was shot, stabbed and poisoned.

MULROONEY—Well, the son of a bitch— Did it kill him?

THE CURTAIN FALLS

MORNING'S AT SEVEN

A Comedy in Three Acts

By PAUL OSBORN

BY the time Paul Osborn's comedy, "Morning's at Seven," reached Broadway—which was December 1—the town had been thrown into mild hysterics by two other laugh plays—"Life with Father" and "The Man Who Came to Dinner." These were fairly robustious character comedies, and the Osborn play, which is placid to a degree, and practically without anything resembling a stirring episode until it is well into its second act, was immediately subjected to comparisons of contrast that were definitely against it.

The quiet Osborn humor, however, plus the author's gift for the projection of highly sensitized and incisively human character, did find a small public of delighted playgoers, and stock company productions of the comedy have since justified their faith in the play.

"Morning's at Seven" is concerned with the simple lives of a family group in which the "juveniles" are a romantic pair aged 40 and 39 respectively. Their immediate friends and relatives are all in their late sixties and early seventies. Interest in the comedy would naturally be confined to mature playgoers who doubtless have had their fill of the more exciting younger generation plays. These elders, we feel, have also a considerable claim upon the theatre, having supported it for a generation or more. Hence "Morning's at Seven" is offered in these pages especially for their enjoyment.

For fifty years the Swansons and the Boltons have lived in adjoining houses in a mid-western town. Cora Swanson and Ida Bolton are sisters. A third sister, Aaronetta Gibbs, lives with the Swansons and always has. There are three Boltons, Carl, Ida and their 40-year-old son, Homer.

We meet the Swansons and the Boltons first in the back yards of their respective homes. The rear elevations of the two houses are much alike, and the back yards are practically duplicates, save that the Swansons' grass is neater, the hedge more evenly trimmed and the general upkeep of the place a grade above that of the Boltons'. A path leading to the street separates the two houses.

350

This late afternoon in the early Fall Theodore and Cora Swanson are sitting in their back yard, and "Arry" is on the back porch facing the path. "Thor" has been recounting his experience with a doctor who had made a most careful examination of him, took his blood pressure and all, and still could not find anything wrong. He's just a lousy doctor, that's all. "By God, I don't know how a doctor like that gets the reputation he has," says Thor. "Didn't even say I had to give up smoking!"

"Well, that's silly," agrees Cora. "Everybody knows you ought to give up smoking."

"Of course they do! I smoke much too much. It stands to reason that when a man gets along in his late sixties he's got to cut down on things like that. Well, I'll see old Doc Brooks to-morrow. He may be old, but I'll bet he knows enough to tell me to quit smoking."

It soon appears that Aaronetta's vigil is focused on the expected arrival of Homer Bolton and his girl, Myrtle Brown. And wouldn't it be awful if they shouldn't come after all! Everybody being so excited and everything. And Ida having got the Allen girl in to help her with the work—

"Do you think we'll meet her? Myrtle, I mean?" wonders Arry.

"Meet her? I guess Homer won't be bringing any girl of his home without introducing her to his old aunts and uncle," says Thor.

ARRY—Well, there's something awful funny about it, if you ask me. How long has Homer been engaged to Myrtle now, Cora?

CORA—It must be nearly seven years. Of course they were going together four or five years before that.

ARRY—Well, don't you think it's funny, Homer's going with a girl for twelve years and none of us has ever seen her? Not even his own mother?

THOR—Well, Homer's shy. He can't be rushed into anything. Anyway, he's bringing her home now.

ARRY—Well, that's just because of that movie Ida saw the other day about the old bachelor. She said she felt so sorry for that old bachelor she came right home and gave Homer a terrible talking to. Said if he didn't bring Myrtle home she'd make him eat his dinners down town for a whole month.

CORA—Oh, she didn't either, Arry!

ARRY (to CORA)—She told me she did! (To THOR.) She said she wasn't going to have any son of hers end up the way that old bachelor in the movie did.

THOR—Why? How'd he end up?

ARRY—He shot himself. (*They all giggle.*) Anyway, Ida's right about that old bachelor business. Homer's forty years old his last birthday, remember. If he's going to marry Myrtle he'd better do it pretty soon.

THOR—Well, I don't think Ida ought to rush him. You got to let a man work out those things for himself.

CORA—Homer likes his *home.* He likes it here with his mother.

ARRY—Well, I just wonder what Myrtle thinks. I see myself waiting twelve years for any man.

THOR—You been waiting sixty-five years for one! (*He laughs heartily.*)

ARRY (*flaring up*)—Don't you worry, Theodore Swanson! I could have had plenty of men if I'd wanted them!

THOR—Sure you could, Arry.

ARRY—And they're plenty I could have right now too! If I just put my mind to it.

THOR—Sure there are.

ARRY—Don't think I don't see the way men look at me on the street. I know what they're thinking. I could have a home of my own in two minutes if I wanted one.

THOR—Don't doubt it for a second, Arry.

ARRY—I was the prettiest of all us four sisters, wasn't I, Cora?

CORA—No. You weren't as pretty as Esty.

ARRY—Well, I was prettier than you or Ida. And look at what Esty got! Do you think I'd be married to a man like David?

THOR—Of course you wouldn't, Arry.

ARRY—Trouble with me is I never saw a man who was worth the powder to blow him up with. Pretty poor specimens on the whole.

Aaronetta's suspicions of the male sex extend definitely to Homer, too. At least she has been wondering a lot if there isn't something going on between Homer and Myrtle. Something could be going on every night, for all they knew. But Thor is inclined to dispute this conclusion. Not every night. Not with Myrtle living in North Lyons. They don't see each other every night. Still, Arry insists, it could be true.

"If it was anybody but Homer I'd be inclined to say it could be," admits Thor. "But Homer—I don't know."

"Well, I know it isn't," snaps Cora. "Homer has never spent a night away from his home in his whole life as far as I know. He's always here in the mornings."

"Well, my goodness, he wouldn't have to spend the whole night, would he?" demands Arry.

Ida Bolton has appeared on her back porch and called Cora. Together they step inside the Bolton kitchen and are seen gesticulating a little wildly as they talk. This conference is not pleasing to Arry at all. They are always yapping, Cora and Ida—like a couple of old hens.

And there is another thing Arry doesn't like. It's this business about her getting a man and having a home of her own. If Cora says much more about that there's going to be trouble. Theodore is plainly upset by this attitude on Arry's part.

"Now your home's right here with us, Arry. Just as long as you want it," says Thor.

"Well, don't you forget it either. I guess I'm entitled to some consideration around here." . . .

Cora is back from Ida's and the mystery of the excited conference is explained. It's Carl. Carl is threatening to have another of his fits. At the moment he is standing with his forehead leaned up against the kitchen wall and everybody has to walk around him. Looks like a fit all right. It's all because of this visit of Homer's and Myrtle's, too. That's Arry's opinion.

"Don't you see? He can't face her. That's the way it always used to be. Any new person he wanted to make an impression on— Oh, I bet he's going to have a terrible spell! I'd better go over and see what I can do!"

But Cora puts an end to that. Arry will do no such thing. The next minute Homer and Myrtle have driven up in front of the house. Arry can see them down the path and is dancing with excitement. Cora and Thor are up on the porch trying to get a look at the arrivals without exposing themselves.

Now Homer is helping Myrtle out of the car—and the way he's got hold of her arm is proof to Arry that there certainly is something going on there.

Now Homer and Myrtle have gone in the front door of the Boltons', and Carl Bolton has come out the back door. Thor sees him first and tries quietly to attract the attention of the others. Now they have all seen him and are pretty embarrassed at having been caught peeking. Carl, however, is too preoccupied to have noticed. He answers their greetings perfunctorily but he really doesn't hear anything they say. And now he has crossed the yard and leaned his head upon his hand against the tree.

"By God, he's having a spell all right!" announces Thor in an awed whisper.

"Poor Ida! I'd better telephone her he's out of the kitchen," suggests Cora.

"I think we ought to 'phone Esty about it all, too," thinks Arry. "It's only fair. Goodness knows she doesn't have much in her life any more. Come on, Thor. . . ."

Ida has found Carl leaning against the tree and taken him to task. This is no time for him to have a spell. He's gotta come out of it before it takes hold of him. Homer and Myrtle are there and want to see him. Myrtle especially.

"Why should anyone want to meet a failure like me?" sighs Carl.

"Oh, Carl, you're just giving in to it," protests Ida, firmly. "Now stop it. You've got to help entertain her. You know how hard it is for Homer to talk in front of strangers. You're the host, Carl. You just can't have a spell now."

CARL (*straightening up*)—I never asked much out of life! Never made many demands! All I wanted to be was just a dentist!

IDA—Oh, my goodness! Never mind about that now, Carl!

CARL—That's not so much to ask! Just to be a dentist. Charlie Watson went on and became a dentist! But I wasn't up to it!

IDA—Of course you were, Carl! It just didn't work out that way.

CARL—I had a lofty ideal but I never achieved it.

IDA—You're just as good as anybody else, Carl.

CARL—I failed. (*He leans on the tree again.* HOMER *and* MYRTLE *come out onto the porch.*)

HOMER—This's the back yard.

IDA (*pushing* CARL *off*)—Oh, my goodness! They're coming out! Carl! Carl!

MYRTLE—The back yard! Oh, isn't it lovely!

HOMER—That's the garage.

MYRTLE—Oh, yes! Isn't it nice!

HOMER—That one's my father's and mine and that one's Uncle Thor's. My father built them both.

MYRTLE—He must be terribly clever.

HOMER—He's a good builder. (*Pause.*) That's the hedge.

MYRTLE—Oh, yes.

HOMER—That's where Aunt Cora thinks she heard a man hid‧ing a couple of times.

MYRTLE—Oh, that's right. I remember.

HOMER—She says she heard him cough once just about dark.

MYRTLE—Well, does she think it's somebody watching the house?

HOMER—I guess so. Guess she just imagined it, though.

MYRTLE—Oh!

HOMER—Uncle Thor says it's probably just one of Aunt Arry's men hanging around to check up on her.

MYRTLE—Oh, maybe that's it.

HOMER—No, that's a joke.

MYRTLE—Oh, I see.

Myrtle, who is a little on the baby-talk order, sees the joke, laughing nervously to prove it. A moment later she sees Ida Bolton backing into the yard without Carl. Ida thinks Carl probably has gone for a little walk. Myrtle is ever so anxious that Mr. Bolton will come back soon. She does so want to meet him. Meantime she is eager that Mrs. Bolton should know how greatly she appreciates the back yard. It's simply heavenly. So cool, with the trees and all. So kind of wild, too. It's simply heavenly.

Homer, inclined to plumpness and a slow mind, deprecatingly admits that there are mosquitoes occasionally, but his mother is quick to add that there doesn't seem to have been as many this year as there were last year. Which reminds Myrtle that that is the way things go sometimes. One year there will be a lot of mosquitoes—and caterpillars, too—and the next year not nearly so many. It certainly is interesting. And probably it all has some purpose, or mosquitoes and caterpillars would not have been put here. "It's all a part of some big plan," Myrtle is convinced. "Some big—plan of some kind."

Conversation sort of lags after that. Mrs. Bolton thinks perhaps she had better be seeing about supper. She shouldn't sit down for even a minute. But she does. For a split minute. And then she gets right up again.

"I'll leave you two youngsters out here by yourselves," she says. "I guess you can attend to yourselves all right."

"Well, maybe we can," giggles Myrtle.

Myrtle is still interested in the back yard and the family. She thinks Homer's mother is just too wonderful—so *friendly*, just as a mother should be—and so—so *human*. She has gone over to stand by Homer, who is still pretty solemn.

"And that's where your Uncle Thor and Aunt Cora live," Myrtle is saying.

"And Aunt Arry."

MYRTLE—Oh, yes. She's the maiden aunt, isn't she?

HOMER—She's the old maid.

MYRTLE (*giving a little nervous laugh*)—How long has she been living with them.

HOMER—About forty-five to fifty years.

MYRTLE—My goodness, that must be pretty hard on your Aunt Cora.

HOMER—Why? They're sisters.

MYRTLE (*sitting*)—Yes, but wouldn't you think a woman would want to live alone—I mean just alone with her husband?

HOMER—Aunt Arry didn't have any other place to go when her mother died, so Aunt Cora took her in.

MYRTLE—Aunt Cora must be pretty nice, I think, to share her home like that.

HOMER—Aunt Cora's nice. Not as nice as Mother.

MYRTLE—Oh, of course not! Of course not. My goodness— Anyway it must be awfully pleasant for all of them to live so close together now that they're getting older. They must be a lot of company for each other.

HOMER—Then there's Aunt Esther, too.

MYRTLE—Oh, yes, Aunt Esther.

HOMER (*pointing*)—She lives up the street about a block and a half.

MYRTLE—And she's married to—?

HOMER—Uncle David.

MYRTLE—That's right. He's the one who studies all the time.

HOMER—He's a very highly educated man. He doesn't like us.

MYRTLE—Why not?

HOMER—He thinks we're morons.

MYRTLE—Morons? Why does he think that?

HOMER—I don't know. He says we don't think about important enough things.

MYRTLE—Does he think about important things?

HOMER—Practically all of the time.

MYRTLE—What does he do?

HOMER—Doesn't do anything now. He used to be a college professor. But he couldn't get along with the president.

MYRTLE—Oh.

HOMER—He said the president was a moron too!

MYRTLE—Well, he doesn't think *you're* a moron, Homer?

HOMER—He thinks we all are except my father.

MYRTLE—Why, what's the matter with your father?

HOMER—He says my father has something more than the rest of us. Something that makes him question life sometimes.

MYRTLE—Oh, I see.

HOMER—But the rest of us are all morons. That's why he never comes down here and never lets any of us come up there.

MYRTLE—He sounds awfully odd to me.

HOMER—He doesn't let Aunt Esther come down either. He's afraid we'll pull her down to our level.

MYRTLE—So she never comes down?

HOMER—Just when he doesn't know it. She hasn't been down now for over a week though.

MYRTLE (*rises—takes off hat and leaves it on porch*)—I'm afraid I wouldn't like your Uncle David very well.

HOMER—Oh, I think you would. He's awfully nice. I've always sort of liked Uncle David.

Myrtle's tone takes on a greater intimacy. She would talk with Homer about their own affairs. She is awfully hopeful that she has made a good impression on Homer's mother. She had tried hard. Of course she is naturally a little curious as to why she has been brought to meet the Boltons after all these years. There have been plenty of other invitations, but Homer has never brought her before. Naturally she is curious about what has happened to change Homer's mind.

It was a movie, Homer explains, that gave his mother the idea. As for what his mother might think if she knew all about them, Homer doesn't see any reason why she should know.

"Older people don't understand things like that very well," explains Homer, nervously. "Maybe we'd better not talk about it here."

"Oh, all right," agrees Myrtle. "Of course your mother must think it's rather funny about you and me, though. Being engaged so long. Hasn't she ever asked you anything about it? About when we're going to get married, I mean?"

"Uh-huh."

"What did you say to her?"

"I told her you had a job."

"Oh!—Well, I was thinking about my job the other day. I was wondering whether I oughtn't to give it up."

"I thought you liked it."

"Oh, I do! It's a good job. But— Well, I get awfully sick

of it sometimes. And, after all, I am thirty-nine years old, you know."

Homer would change the subject if he could, but Myrtle is persistent. She has taken his arm and snuggled up to him, which fusses him even more, because he fears they may be seen from the other house. Myrtle draws away from him and is standing by a tree, gazing ruminatively into the distance.

"I get awfully lonesome sometimes about this time of day," she says. "Or maybe a little later. I guess it's really not so bad at the office. I'm usually pretty busy. But when I get through and have to go to my room.—And then, when it starts getting dark.— Often when I know you're not going to be coming down I don't bother to get myself any supper. I just go right to bed." They both laugh embarrassedly at this. "Sometimes I wonder how I ever happened to get stuck with that job," Myrtle goes on. "It doesn't seem natural. I guess when you come right down to it what a woman really wants is a home of her own."

Aunt Arry has come out of the Swanson house and walked into the Swanson back yard. Homer knows that she has seen him and Myrtle, though she pretends to be oblivious of their presence. Arry fans herself energetically, pauses to pick a weed from the lawn and then suddenly discovers that she is not alone. There is an exchange of "Hellos" with Homer, but Myrtle is formally overlooked until the situation becomes a little embarrassing. Then Homer suddenly remembers to introduce Myrtle to his aunt. Of course Myrtle remembers Aunt Arry. It was she who had sent Myrtle that lovely handsome linen luncheon set, with flowers on it, for her hope chest. Appliquéd flowers, they were, Arry confirms, and they looked almost real. Myrtle could never forget that luncheon set.

Cora is passing the screen door as she hears Arry inquiring of Homer about his father. The family skeleton is about to be exposed. Cora is quick to stop the exposure. Her call to Arry to help with the supper is a good deal of a hiss, but it is effective. "I wasn't going to tell her a thing," insists Arry in an undertone as she passes Cora.

"How do you do, Myrtle," Cora calls, cheerfully.

"How do you do?" answers Myrtle.

"I expect we'll meet each other after supper."

"I expect so."

"Well, excuse me. I've got to go in now."

"All right."

"I'm Aunt Cora," Cora calls back, lest there be some misunderstanding.

"Yes, I know," admits Myrtle. And that having been attended to, Myrtle tells Homer and his mother, who have come from the house, that she thinks she will be getting cleaned up for supper.

"Just ask the Allen girl in there and she'll show you where to go," says Mrs. Bolton. "The little towel with the escalloped border is for you."

It is the first time Homer and his mother have had a chance to talk. Homer is still terribly worried about his father and the threatened spell. Homer is especially worried for fear it may be one of Father's "fork" spells. If he should begin talking about going back to the fork, that will be terrible. But so long as he just has a dentist spell, that may not be so bad.

Mrs. Bolton is ever so pleased with Myrtle. She wants Homer to know. Homer, however, is far from pleased, and he especially doesn't want his mother to keep leaving him alone with Myrtle. Myrtle gets entirely too personal when she is alone with him. Wants to know too many things—why he brought her home and things like that.

There are some things about which Homer has not yet made up his mind, and he doesn't like being rushed. He likes living at home. Even though he was to move into the Sycamore Drive home his father has built and furnished for him and Myrtle, it wouldn't be the same. Homer has all his things at home, and he doesn't relish the thought of having his routines disturbed. Of course he hasn't seen the movie his mother saw, but he has a feeling that she would get awfully lonesome, too.

"Oh, I don't say it's going to be easy for me, either," admits Ida. "Of course it isn't."

IDA—It'll seem strange not to have you coming home after your day's work. But I've had you a long time. Longer than most mothers.

HOMER—I don't know what you'd do with my little room up there.

IDA—I've thought of that, too. I think I'll keep it just as it is. And you'll know that it'll be ready for you any time you want it. Perhaps you'll want to spend a night down here sometime—you and Myrtle.

HOMER (*gloomily*)—My room's too small for two people.

IDA—We might move in a double bed.

HOMER (*embarrassed*)—Oh, Mother! (*Pause.*) And Myrtle gets so personal sometimes.

IDA—What do you mean?

HOMER—Oh, she wants to know all sorts of things. The other day she asked me what size underwear I wore.

IDA—She did? What for?

HOMER—I guess she wanted to buy me some.

IDA—Well, that does seem odd.

HOMER—She wrote it down in a little book she's got. (*Pause. They are both depressed.*)

IDA—Of course after you're married she'll be buying your underwear. (*Pause.*)

HOMER—There's something awful nice about Myrtle though.

IDA—Of course there is.

HOMER—She's awfully good-hearted and she does nice little things for you all the time.

IDA—Does she?

HOMER—She's awfully lonesome down there in North Lyons too. It isn't that I'm not awfully fond of her, Mother.

IDA—Do you love her, Homer?

HOMER—Well, I wouldn't want never to see her again. (*Pause.*) Mother.

IDA—Yes, Homer?

HOMER—If I was to marry Myrtle do you think I'd—get used to it?

IDA (*faintly*)—I guess so—

HOMER—I don't know. Maybe I would. And you want me to do it so bad— (IDA *is crying.*) Mother, what's the matter!

IDA—Never mind me, Homer!

HOMER—Mother, you're crying!

IDA—I never thought of that! That she'd be buying your underwear! (*She has a fresh burst of crying and starts toward the house.*)

HOMER—Mother—

IDA—Never mind me, Homer. I'll be all right. I'm just a silly old goose!

The whole thing is getting to be a little too much for Homer. He is pacing the back yard, mumbling his disgust at having upset his mother, kicking the ground viciously as he walks. Now he stops by the tree and for a minute leans his head against the tree, as his father had done. At that moment Thor Swanson appears on the other porch. In the gathering twilight he sees what he sees and a soft but exclamatory "Jesus!" escapes him. The next moment he has stuck his head in the door and called excitedly to

Arry and Cora.

Homer is startled, but his mood persists. When Cora and Arry
come rushing out to add their stares to those of Thor, Homer
mumbles his way past them and goes into the house. There is
nothing the matter with him, Homer insists.

The others are not sure. To Thor, Homer was certainly having
a spell just like his father. "Heredity, by God!" That's what
it is. "He was standing just like this—" Thor is giving a realistic
demonstration by leaning against the house when Esther Crampton comes down the path. Esther is the eldest, and the daintiest,
of the sisters. Her hair is very white, her expression gentle and
pleasant and there is a twinkle in her eyes.

They all try to tell her at once of their discovery of Homer and
his indicated spell. Arry is particularly vehement and excited.
She doesn't like it when Esther would laugh their fears away.
Esther doesn't think Homer has the gumption to have a spell.
He's too lazy. Cora and Thor are inclined to agree with her, now
they come to think of it. But Arry is disgusted with them. With
Thor, especially, for not standing by his first conviction. She is
so angry, as she flounces into the house, that Thor feels he must
go in and comfort her— "The way Arry can always take Thor
in—" It's disgusting to Cora.

Esty has come, at Ida's telephoned request, to have a talk with
Carl if he's acting bad. She feels she must be home before David
gets back from his walk. Cora doesn't think Carl is bad. It's
just one of those dentist spells—

"Well, I've seen those dentist spells when they got pretty bad
sometimes," recalls Esty. "It's only one step from a dentist spell
to a 'Where am I?' spell, you know. . . . Well, we can't do anything until he gets back. I'll talk to him. Maybe if he isn't too
far gone it might help some— Now, tell me. Have you met
Myrtle yet?"

"I haven't really met her. I just talked to her a second."

ESTHER (*controlling a giggle*)—What's she like?

CORA (*giggling nervously*)—Now, Esty! She's very nice! Not
the way we imagined at all!

ESTHER—She has got teeth like this though, hasn't she?

CORA—Now, Esty, she has no such thing!

ESTHER—And she talks like this to Homer. (*They both giggle.*)

CORA—She doesn't either! She's perfectly all right! And we
shouldn't sit here and giggle about it!

ESTHER—I can't help it! Somehow the idea of Homer's having

a girl—

CORA—You know what Arry thinks? Well, Arry thinks that maybe everything isn't as straight there as it might be.

ESTHER—Well, maybe it isn't. Wonderful things can happen.

CORA—Esty! (*This sets them off into a mild case of hysterics.*)

ESTHER (*wiping her eyes*)—My goodness, I haven't laughed so much for a long time.

CORA—That's right. How *is* David behaving?

ESTHER—Oh, I don't know, Cora. This last week I've hardly been out of the house.

CORA—I think it's a shame.

ESTHER—He made me promise I'd never come down again without his permission.

CORA—You didn't promise him—?

ESTHER—Well—I—I really had to. He said— (*She gives a nervous giggle.*) He said if I ever came down again I'd—I'd have to live on the second floor the rest of my life.

CORA—Live on the second floor?

ESTHER—Upstairs. And he'd live downstairs.

CORA—But that's silly, Esty! You couldn't live on the second floor.

ESTHER—I guess I'd have to. The house divided, you know.

CORA—How would you get your meals?

ESTHER—He says I can come down the backstairs and use the kitchen when I want it.

CORA—If that isn't just like David! Why doesn't *he* live on the second floor?

ESTHER—He thought it would be easier for me on account of the bathroom.

CORA—Oh! Well, what would *he* do for a bathroom?

ESTHER—He'd have another put in. In that little closet off the kitchen.

CORA—But that would cost money, Esty!

ESTHER—I know it would. That's the one thing that worries me. Of course he'd only put in a seat and a basin. He says maybe I'd let him use the bath now and then.

CORA (*sharply*)—Well, *I* wouldn't!

ESTHER—Oh, I'd have to. He says he'll put up a bell that will ring when he wants to use it. So we wouldn't bump into each other.

CORA—And you wouldn't see each other at all?

ESTHER—I guess not. He says if we're going to be independent we might as well be independent. Of course if we should meet in the hall we'd bow to each other, like two acquaintances.

CORA—Well, he's just trying to scare you, Esty. And I think you ought to take a stand against him! You ought to be able to come down here any time you want to. David's just jealous!

ESTHER—I know it, Cora. He gets more so all the time. If he'd only stop talking about his Crystal Fortress.

CORA—You know, Esty, I always thought that Crystal Fortress was rather a lovely idea.

ESTHER—You wouldn't if you'd lived in it fifty-five years.

CORA—No, I think it's lovely. Your friends or anybody can come up to the fortress and look in through the door—and you can see them and talk to them and everything—but no one can ever really come into it except just the two of you. Just you two all alone there by yourselves. It must be nice sometimes to be all alone with—the person you live with.

It is Cora's secret hope, she admits to Esther, that Homer will not marry Myrtle. If he doesn't Carl has promised to let Cora lease the Sycamore Drive house. Then she and Thor can move up there and let Arry have the house they live in now—let her have it, and everything that's in it. Cora isn't sure Thor would agree—but she certainly hopes he would.

Carl Bolton has appeared in the other yard. Esther and Cora watch curiously to see what he will do. Carl doesn't do anything but stand staring at the house, as though he might be a little afraid to go in. Esther thinks perhaps she had better go over and speak to him, which she does.

Carl is a little startled, but pleasant. Asks about David and is glad to hear that David is well. David, insists Carl, is a wonderful man. Yes, Myrtle is there. Carl hasn't met her, but expects to. He thinks for a moment that he will go in now, with Esther, as Esther suggests, but on second thought this doesn't seem to be just the right time. He is a little afraid of another spell coming on him.

"You seem all right, Carl," says Esther, comfortingly.

"Yes. All right now— It's just that—! Just that—! I'm not a stupid man, Esty!"

ESTHER—I know you're not, Carl.

CARL—I'm not an educated man like David, but I'm not a stupid one!

ESTHER—Of course you're not.

CARL (*rising*)—Then *where am I*, Esty? *Where am I?*

ESTHER (*rising—sharply*)—Now, Carl!

CARL (*excited*)—That's what I say, "Where am I in life." I'm caught, Esty.

ESTHER—Now listen to me, Carl—

CARL—I'm not where I should be at all! There's some other place in life where I should be! I'm *Carl Bolton,* Esty!

ESTHER—Yes, yes, now be quiet—

CARL—The same Carl Bolton I was when I was a boy!

ESTHER—Yes, Carl, but—

CARL—But now I'm sixty-eight years old and WHERE AM I?

ESTHER—Now stop this, Carl!

CARL—Maybe I'm not Carl Bolton any more at all!

ESTHER—Well, maybe you're not!

CARL (*staring at her*)—What's that, Esty?

ESTHER—I say maybe you're not Carl Bolton any more.

CARL—I don't understand. How could that be?

ESTHER (*patting his arm reassuringly*)—Carl, you don't think you're the only one who feels this way about things, do you?

CARL—Why—I don't know, Esty—

ESTHER—Well, I think lots of people feel exactly the same way as you do, only they don't go around having spells about it. You know, Carl, I don't think it's been any harder on you than on any of the others. Just think of all that Cora's been through. Never having a real home of her own. And Thor.—Arry having the whip hand over him all these years! I bet sometimes he wishes he were somewhere else in life, too.

CARL—Yes, that's true, Esty, but—

ESTHER—Even if it only meant living alone with Cora in another house.

CARL—Did Cora tell you about that?

ESTHER—Yes. She said you might lease her the house.

CARL—Well, I—I did promise her, Esty. She kept at me so about it—I guess I shouldn't have, though—

ESTHER—Why not? If Homer isn't going to use it there's no reason to just go on keeping it empty.

CARL—But, there's another thing about letting Cora have the house, though, you know, Esty— I mean— Well, what do you think?

ESTHER—You mean—Arry?

CARL (*nods*)—What do you think? Do you think Arry would —let Thor go?

ESTHER—Well, we've never been sure about Arry and Thor, Carl.

CARL—You girls have always been pretty sure. Gee, Esty, I'd hate for Arry to start anything.

ESTHER—I know. I thought of that when Cora was telling me. But I think you ought to do it, Carl. I think you ought to do it.

CARL—All right, Esty. (*Pause.*) I wonder if Cora ever knew about Arry and Thor?

ESTHER—If she did she's kept it to herself pretty well— Oh, well, I think Arry really loved Thor. I think she probably still does. Anyway, it's the closest thing to a husband she'll ever know. Come to think of it, Carl, I guess Arry doesn't quite know where she is either.

CARL—Well, things get tangled up, don't they, Esty?

ESTHER—Don't they, though.

CARL—For everybody, I guess. (*Pause.*) I feel better. Lots better.

ESTHER—That's good. Shall we go in and see Myrtle then?

CARL—All right. (*They start toward the house.*) I always feel better talking to you, Esty.

ESTHER—Well, I'm the oldest.

They have gone into the house. Both yards are empty for a moment. It is getting dark. Suddenly a man appears coming through the Swanson hedge. He is a small man, well groomed and rather studious in appearance. He makes his way cautiously across the Swanson yard and is peering through one of the Boltons' lighted windows.

From the Swanson dining room Cora, setting the table, has seen the man through the window. Immediately she is excited. She calls to Thor and Arry. Thor comes out on the porch to demand what the intruder wants. As he switches on the porch light he recognizes Esther's husband, David Crampton.

Now the women begin calling excitedly to Esther, advising her to make a run for it out the front door. Meantime Thor is busy denying that Esther is even there. Anyway, if she is there, or was there, it was only for a minute and she's gone now.

Esther stops all this by appearing quite calmly on the Bolton porch. She faces David and explains that she had come down because Myrtle is there, and, besides, Cora phoned that Carl was about to have a spell.

David does not move. He appears to be surveying them, individually and as a group. Suddenly he throws his head back in a puzzled way, and mutters to himself: "And God created them in his own image; male and female created he them."

He greets them now, each by name. Homer introduces Myrtle, and Myrtle rates a formal bow from David. Now he has resumed his survey of them—

"Well, well, here we all are together again," says David. "Our own little circle. I must say you all seem to me very much the same as you always did."

He is beaming now and there is a rustling in the group as they exchange bewildered expressions.

"That's very nice of you, David," admits Thor.

"Yes, just about the same," David goes on. "A little older, perhaps. Grayer. Pulses all a trifle slower, probably. But I can still see the same bright, intelligent expressions on your faces that I remember so well. . . . And now, before I leave you, there is just one thing more. You have all been in my home at one time or another. You all know how the entry hall leads into the living room and so is the entrance to the lower floor. And from the entry hall the staircase leads to the second floor. Well, now since Esther has decided it will be better for us to live apart from each other . . . from now on I'll be living on the lower floor; Esther on the second—"

There is great consternation among them as David pauses. What does he mean, and why is he doing this? And what d'ye know—

"Esther is a free agent now," David continues, raising a hand to silence them. "She has a perfect right to come and go as she pleases and to have anyone she wishes visit her. Doubtless you will be there a great deal. Now none of you would come into the lower floor of course. But may I suggest that as you pass through the entry hall and on up the stairs to try to be as silent as possible?"

"But, David, you don't really mean it?" protests Esther.

"That was our understanding, was it not, Esther? It seems to me it was."

"But, David, these are my *sisters!* They're all I have! I've got to have something in my life!"

"And now you have your sisters. Who am I to deprive you of that?"

Arry is the only one to make any spirited reply to David. She doesn't think he has any right to treat Esty that way and says so. Esty, too, rises in her own defense to say that all she wants is to see her sisters occasionally. All they do is to talk. "I have a good time with my sisters," insists Esther. "I don't care how ignorant they are!" Practically in one voice the sisters back Esther up in this decision.

David is unmoved. He is bidding them good-night now, with easy formality. When he comes to Carl he has an idea. Carl is a builder. Perhaps he could install a bit of plumbing in David's house—making a bathroom of the first floor closet. Carl thinks probably he could. Anyway he would like to have a look at the closet in the morning. With a further reminder that they should be quiet when they call on Esther, David has left them.

The reaction of the group is varied. The sisters are angered, but Thor thinks David can be awfully nice when he wants to be, and Carl is convinced that David is no fool. The tone of Carl's voice arouses them. It has an ominous pitch. "David lives straight ahead the way he was meant to," Carl is saying. "*He* knows where he is. *He* didn't branch off."

Ida and Homer both hurry to Carl. They recognize the spell sign. If they can only get him into the house— But it is too late—

"David thought it all out way back there at the crossroads. Then he went straight ahead," intones Carl. "He lived his life just as he planned it. But *I* branched off."

"Come on now, Carl," pleads Ida, taking his arm.

"Don't you see? I took the wrong turn. I got lost."

"Now, get hold of yourself, Father," demands Homer.

"I've got to go back to the fork!" Conviction settles on Carl.

"Oh, Carl, Carl! Don't say that!" cries Ida.

"I've got to take the other way. I've got to go back to the fork."

"Don't say that, Carl," wails Ida.

"Father, stop it! You're hurting my mother! You stop it now," orders Homer, taking his father by the shoulders and shaking him. This seems to bring Carl to. He looks about the group wonderingly. He didn't mean anything, he protests. He just meant that he would have to go back to the fork. Whether the fork is beyond the hedge or not, that is where Carl goes. Ida calls piteously after him, but he does not come back and Homer helps his weeping mother into the house.

All this is pretty bewildering to Myrtle. More so when, after Homer and Ida disappear in the house, Homer switches off the porch light and leaves Myrtle outside. The family turns to watch her. It is Arry who comes to the rescue. She will take Myrtle up to her room and show her the luncheon set she is making. It was to have been a surprise, Arry says, but she really intended it for Myrtle all the time. . . .

Cora has persuaded Esther to stay the night with her. They are pretty depressed. It doesn't look as though Homer would ever marry Myrtle now.

Arry has left Myrtle lying down in her room and come back to Thor. She would like to talk, but Thor isn't very responsive.

"Well, guess we'd better go in," says Arry, finally giving up.

"Yup," yups Thor.

" 'S going to be a nice night, Thor."

"Yup."

"Remember how bright it was the night we took the boat to—"

"Shh! Arry!"

"All right." Arry is quieted. But not for long. "I get awful sick of having to keep still all the time!" she suddenly bursts out. "Sometimes I wish Cora would die!"

"Arry!"

"I didn't mean that, Thor! I didn't mean that!" Arry is frightened now.

"I should hope not," protests Thor, crossing to the porch.

"I really didn't, Thor!"

"I don't like that, Arry."

Thor has gone abruptly into the house. Arry stands a moment alone, frightened. She looks up at the sky—

"I didn't mean that! Honest!" she repeats, and hurries in as the curtain falls.

ACT II

At 7 o'clock next morning the Swanson-Bolton back yards are flooded with sunlight. Thor Swanson is the first to appear. He is eating his breakfast—an apple—and he hates apples. Esther Crampton is the next one down. Apparently no one has slept very well. Thor couldn't sleep at all—the way Cora was kicking— "you'd thought she had the measles or something."

It seems that after Esther went to bed Ida had come over to report that Homer had broken off with Myrtle. Told her he couldn't leave his mother now that his father was having spells again. Myrtle is still around. She can't get a train back to North Lyons until afternoon. . . .

Aaronetta is the first one to make something of the fact that Cora has disappeared. She isn't in bed and she isn't at Ida's, and to Arry that means she is up to something. More than that, Carl Bolton had not been home all night. Ida is nearly frantic. She would, if she could, call on the Boy Scouts to start out a searching party, but Homer won't let her. Homer's afraid it might cause talk.

As for Cora and Carl, Arry knows that Cora had been wanting to talk with Carl. What about? That's what Arry would like to know. "Cora's up to something, you mark my words," warns Arry. "Last night when she found out that Homer wasn't going to marry Myrtle she got as nervous as a monkey. She's got some bee in her bonnet, and if it's what I think it is—"

Arry has seen Esther suddenly put her hand to her mouth and eyes her suspiciously. "What do *you* think she wants to see Carl about, Esty?" she demands.

"Me?" asks Esther, innocently.

"Yes—me," mimics Arry.

"How would I know, Arry?"

"Oh, you make me sick. But I'll tell you one thing! If Cora's up to something—and if it's what I think it is—well, some people around here had just better watch out, that's all I say." She is looking significantly at Thor, and Thor is squirming uneasily.

Ida is back with her worry about poor Carl. Surely something should be done. Perhaps they should drag the river. Perhaps they should, Esther agrees, but there doesn't happen to be a river anywhere around there.

Perhaps he should notify the police, Thor suggests. When Ida is horrified at that suggestion Thor tries to convince her that he could do it very quietly, through an officer friend, without letting the police know anything much—even about Carl. Ida agrees to risk the police being notified, discreetly, but if it all comes out in the papers she is going to be distressed. . . .

Cora is back. She is still looking for Carl, and she isn't going to tell anyone what she wants to see Carl for, especially Arry. Which is enough to send Arry flouncing out of the yard. She certainly wouldn't want Cora to tell her anything she didn't want to.

To Esther Cora is willing to admit that she is fearfully upset. She has the lease for the Sycamore Drive house all made out, ready to sign, and she can't find Carl. Esther is of a mind to caution Cora. How does she know Thor is going to take to the plan? "Remember, it isn't so easy to pick up and leave a house you've lived in so long—leave all the furniture and everything you're used to," says Esther. "Do you know what I think?"

"What?"

"I think it might be a good idea to talk it over first with—Arry."

"Arry!" Cora is suspicious.

"Yes."

"Why? What business is it of hers?" Cora's voice is hard.

"It is her business in a way."

"I don't see how."

"Well, she's always lived with you. You're the only home she's ever known. You can't say she's not concerned."

"I don't care if she is concerned. Thor is *my* husband, Esty."

"Of course, Cora. I just thought—"

"You just thought nothing—" There is a suspicion of a sneer in Cora's voice.

"But, Cora—"

Before Esther can go on Thor and Ida have come from the Boltons'. Cora has quickly slipped the lease into her waist, and a part of it still shows.

Thor and Ida have not been able to agree on what to tell the police about Carl. Ida refused to let them have a description of him, and how can they look for a man without knowing what he looks like? Also Thor would like to know what Cora has been doing all morning. So would Arry, who has come from the house. Arry would also like to know what that paper is Cora has in her waist, and gets her hands slapped when she reaches for it. The paper is none of Arry's business, snaps Cora.

Now Ida is agreed that perhaps if they could give the police a description of Carl, without giving them his name, it would be all right. Carl is sixty-six— No, sixty-eight— No, he can't be— But he is. Well, Thor would never have thought it. And he has blue eyes. They're agreed on that. And he's bald— Well, not exactly bald. He still has a fringe— Ida remembers that, even if the others don't— And quite a bit of hair in back—

"Really?" The back hair is a great surprise to Thor. "Well, that just goes to show. You look at a thing and you look at it and still you don't see it. I'm going to get a good square look at Carl the next time I see him," says Thor.

"If you ever get a chance to see him," Ida reminds him, tearfully.

Arry has been circling closer and closer to Cora. Now she makes a sudden snatch at the paper and has it, and a chase is on. Arry runs from one yard to the other, around chairs, dodging the pursuing Cora, and trying desperately to get the envelope she has grabbed open. "Catch her, Ida," screams Cora. "Hurry! Head her off that way!"

"Give her back that paper!" commands Esther.

"What the hell's going on here?" demands Thor.

"You dare read that paper and I'll fix you, Aaronetta Gibbs!" shrieks Cora.

Arry can't dodge them all. She finally is cornered by Ida, Esther and Cora. They are all shrieking and pulling at each other when David walks in. Immediately the scuffling and the noise is quieted.

"Playing tag?" asks David, pleasantly.

"No, no— We were just—" Esther is trying to explain.

DAVID—Don't apologize, Esther. You are a free agent now. You can amuse yourself any way you wish.

ESTHER—But you don't understand, David—

DAVID—Please go on with the game. Don't let me interrupt you—

ESTHER—But we weren't playing a game. We were—

DAVID (*calling*)—I'll go in and wait for you in your room, Carl. (*Starts up steps of house.*)

CARL (*off stage*)—All right, David.

EVERYBODY—Carl!

ESTHER—David! (*She follows him into house.* CARL, *loaded down with tools, enters.* IDA *crosses to him.*)

IDA—Carl.

CARL (*putting down bags*)—Oh, Ida— I hope you haven't been worried, Ida.

IDA—Worried! My goodness, Carl. I've been nearly frantic. Where have you been? What's the matter? Are you all right? Are you hurt?

CARL (*surprised*)—Hurt?

IDA—But where have you been, Carl? You stayed out all night. I've been nearly frantic. We even called the police.

CARL—Police?

IDA—We thought you might be dead!

CARL—Dead? No.

IDA—You didn't come home all night. I've been nearly frantic. Where have you been, Carl?

CARL (*surprised she doesn't know*)—Why, I've been up at David's.

IDA—But where did you sleep?

CARL—Well, we didn't sleep, Ida— We talked. David's going to help me find out where I am. We're right in the middle of it now. We just stopped long enough to come down and get my tools and pack my clothes—

IDA—Pack your clothes?

CARL—Yes, I— (*Realizes she doesn't understand.*) Oh! You see, I'm moving, Ida.

IDA—What do you mean?

CARL—Well, David has invited me to live with him. He wants me to.

IDA—Live with David?

CARL—Yes. You see, we're going to live on the lower floor. We're going to put in a real bath instead of just a seat and a basin and we're going to use the side entrance and—

IDA—What are you talking about, Carl?

CARL (*turning to her—as to a child*)—I'm going to live with David for a while.

IDA—But what about *me?*

CARL (*blankly*)—You?

IDA—Yes, *me*, Carl.

CARL—Oh, that's right. Well, you can live here just the way you do now.

IDA—You don't mean you're going to leave me, Carl?

CARL—But, I've lived here a long time, Ida. I want to live somewhere else for a while. You'll be all right. You've got Homer.

IDA—I just don't understand—

CARL (*crossing to pick up tools*)—I'll explain it to you sometime, Ida. I'll come down and see you—

DAVID (*calling from inside house*)—We're wasting valuable time, Carl.

CARL (*briskly*)—Be right there, David. Be right there.

IDA—Carl! I've got to talk to you, Carl— (*Follows him—* ARRY, THOR *and* CORA *are watching.*)

THOR—Well, what the hell do you know about that?

ARRY—I always knew that marriage wouldn't last— Anyway, Carl *has* got hair on the back of his head. Quite a bit of it.

THOR—There you are! Damn it all, I forgot to look again!

Cora has started again for the Boltons' back door to see Carl, and Arry has stopped her again. The struggle for the paper is about to be resumed. Thor is pretty irritated at the whole business, but they pay little heed to him. Cora's got a paper and Arry wants to know what's in it. And now Cora suddenly changes her mind and hands Arry the paper. Let her read it if she wants to.

Arry reads the lease and passes it to Thor. Thor reads it and is

completely dumfounded. A twenty-year-lease on Homer's house?
Made out to Cora? What's the big idea?

Cora is ready to explain. She is going to rent Homer's house
for them. For just the two of them. They haven't got many
years left, and Cora is determined that they shall spend them
together in a real home of their own. Thor is completely confused.

"I've thought it all out, Thor," explains Cora, her voice entirely
steady. "We can give this house to Arry. We can make out
some kind of transfer and she can own it in her own name. She
won't be lonesome with Ida and Esty here. And we can have
what's left of the years together—alone—as we should always have
had them in the past."

"Cora!" Thor is horrified. Arry turns quickly and runs into
the house. "Arry!" Thor takes a step toward the house and then
turns back. "By God, Cora, how could you say a thing like that?"

"It's the truth, ain't it?" demands Cora.

"But right in front of Arry!"

"She had it coming to her."

Thor continues to be deeply concerned for Arry's feelings, but
Cora stands firm. She has made her plans. Is Thor for them
or against them? "Poor Arry! She's all alone in the world!"
protests Thor. "So am I," answers Cora. "You can be alone a
lot of different ways, Thor." Is there anything that Thor is afraid
of? Thor doesn't even know what she means. In that case Cora
thinks he had better be thinking her plan over while she goes to
find Carl and to sign the lease.

Now Arry has come from the house to face Thor. Thor's terribly sorry. He is sure Cora didn't mean anything. She was just
mad. Arry knows what Cora meant. What she wants to know
is what Thor is going to do. If Cora gets Homer's house, is Thor
going to move up there? Of course not. Then, how will he get
out of it? Thor will find a way.

"You listened to Cora. Now you listen to me, Thor." Arry is
very positive. "Cora can talk about having what is left of her
life alone with you. Well, what about me? How many years do
you think I've got left?"

"I know, Arry. I know—"

ARRY—And whose fault is it that *I* haven't a home of my own?
THOR—All right, Arry. Now your home's right here with us—
ARRY—I've got just as much right here as Cora.
THOR—Now be quiet, Arry. I'll think of something.
ARRY—You'd better. Because I'm not going to spend the rest

of my life alone. After all I've given up.

THOR—I don't think Carl'll give her the house anyway.

ARRY—Well, if he does, and you leave me now, Thor, don't think I won't tell what's happened. I'm not ashamed. I'd *like* to have Cora know.

THOR (*sharply*)—Now keep still, Arry.

ARRY—All right. But don't think Cora's going to make it easy for you. You'd better think up something pretty good, Thor. (*She starts in—stops on top step.*) You didn't have much breakfast this morning, did you?

THOR (*abused*)—I had an apple.

ARRY—Well, come in, I'll fix you something. (*She goes in.*)

THOR—Doggone it all! (*As he starts in,* HOMER *comes out furious; slams the porch door; sees* THOR.) 'Morning, Homer.

HOMER (*stops pacing*)—'Morning, Uncle Thor. (*Continues pacing—suddenly stops and looks up, furious.*) Aunt Cora got my house away from me!

THOR (*quickly*)—What's that?

HOMER—While I was shaving!

THOR—What do you mean, Homer?

HOMER—I was upstairs shaving and when I came down my father had rented my house to Aunt Cora.

THOR—You mean he signed the lease?

HOMER—Just as I was coming downstairs.

THOR—Oh, my God! (*He goes in.*)

Homer has resumed his pacing the back yard when his mother joins him. Ida is terribly upset, too, about Homer having lost his house, but, after all, he wasn't going to use it, since he and Myrtle were not going to marry. That doesn't make any difference to Homer. He and Myrtle are still engaged, aren't they? And they talk to each other about the house. What are they going to talk about now?

"What I'm going to say to Myrtle when she gets up I don't know," protests Homer. "It'll just about break her heart. She makes plans about that house all the time. She's told all her friends down in North Lyons about her beautiful house. Well, now she hasn't got one any more. We just took it away from her. Pretty small business, I must say! Invite a girl to stay overnight and then take her house away from her when she is asleep. Pretty small business. *I* don't know what the world's coming to."

Ida promises to talk to Carl as soon as he and David come out of the bedroom, where they have locked themselves in to pack, but Homer is not encouraged. Homer, in fact, is sunk. He can't understand what it's all about. "Why hasn't Myrtle a home and been living up there in my house all this time? What's it all about that I'm forty years old and still living here and not having a home of my own?"

"But that's what you've always wanted, Homer," his mother reminds him.

"*Why* have I wanted it?" demands Homer, accusingly. "I'm a man."

"Of course, Homer."

"Then what's it all about? Myrtle cried half the night last night. I heard her. And then my father leaves home. And then they take our beautiful house away from us. So, what's it all about?"

"I'm so sorry, Homer."

"I've got to think these things out. That's what I've got to do. I've got to think these things out."

"Oh, dear! Oh, dear!"

Ida is assailed by another problem as she follows Homer out of the yard. A moment later Carl and David come from the house. They are loaded with suitcases, tools, etc., and are in the midst of a discussion. At least David is. Carl is listening eagerly.

It is a supposititious case that David is presenting to Carl. Carl is already a dentist. He has his office, his instruments, every-thing—including, Carl is quick to add, an x-ray machine. And now he is working on a patient. Suddenly he stops. And what does he say to himself? "What?" asks Carl.

"WHERE AM I?" answers David. "What am I doing here? I'm caught! I'm *Carl Bolton!* Where am I? Just as you do now—And how are you going to answer yourself? You can't say: Where am I? I'm a dentist. *What* am I, yes. But that's not what you ask yourself, Carl. You ask yourself: *Where* am I? Where am I in *life?* What's the meaning of it? And that's a very natural question, Carl. It's a question that a man like you must inevitably ask himself. The only reason that you think it strange, that anyone thinks it's strange, is because the people you have been in contact with have never let that problem worry them. They are content to answer the question: 'Where am I?' by: 'I'm a dentist.' And why shouldn't they? After all it doesn't much matter where they are, does it?"

"But the answer, David. What's the answer?"

"Ah, that's another thing. That's what we must find out."

"If I could only find out that answer—"

"We'll talk about it, Carl. We'll talk about it."

They are loaded and starting away when Ida and Esther appear. Ida is tearful and distressed. She has been a good wife to Carl for years— She can't understand. Esther, on the other hand, understands perfectly and is content. If these men want to leave them let them go. "For heaven's sakes let them go and find out where they are once and for all," advises Esther. "If they got to be as old as they are without knowing, the Lord knows it's high time for them to find out."

"You see, Carl, as I was saying, there are some people who never ask themselves the question: Where am I?" says David.

"There's some people who don't have to," answers Esther. "I *know* where *I* am. I'm on the second floor. And to tell the truth, I'm beginning to like the idea pretty well."

DAVID—Well, I'm glad if the arrangement pleases you, Esther.

ESTHER—It does. I've had more fun last night and today than I've had for a long time.

DAVID—Ah, yes. Your games and so forth—

ESTHER—That's right. I like games. With lots of people on both sides.

DAVID—Ah, yes. Well, you're a free agent now, Esther.

ESTHER—I know I am. When I sat outside that locked door a few minutes ago waiting for you two to come out, I suddenly said to myself: "There's no fool like an old fool," and I was thinking of you and Carl. And then I said it again and it suddenly meant *me*. For fifty years I've washed and cooked and brought up children and now suddenly I've got a chance to be free. I can come down here any time I want to, can go to the movies with the girls —do anything. (*She stretches.*) It's nice! (*Pause.* DAVID *stands looking at her. Suddenly he turns to* CARL.)

DAVID—Well, Carl, we'd better get back to the bathroom.

CARL—All right, David. (*Picking up tools.*) I'll come down and see you, Ida. (*Starts up.*)

IDA (*following*)—I never thought you'd leave me, Carl.

CARL—I never thought I would either, Ida, but— (*They exit.*)

DAVID (*starting out—then turning back to* ESTHER)—You'll be occupying the second floor tonight?

ESTHER—I haven't decided yet. I may stay down here. Thor says I can stay as long as I like.

DAVID—Ah!

ESTHER—But I'll be quiet if I come in late.

DAVID (*standing looking at her for a second*)—Well, pleasant dreams, Esther.

ESTHER—Thank you.

DAVID (*starts out—stops and turns*)—I meant to say, if you prefer the lower floor to the upper—

ESTHER—No, I think I prefer the upper.

DAVID—I thought perhaps the stairs—

ESTHER—The stairs won't bother me any.

DAVID—That's fine. (*He hesitates a minute.*) If there is any rearrangement of furniture you wish done, Carl and I will be glad to help you.

ESTHER—Thank you, David.

DAVID—There's no use straining yourself.

ESTHER—No.

DAVID—Well, good morning, Esther.

ESTHER—Good morning, David.

Esther watches David disappear up the path. There is an amused smile on her face. Suddenly she begins to sing, softly. "O sole mio— Ti-di-di-di-di—"

Cora comes from Ida's house waving the lease triumphantly. It is all signed. Cora is going now to see Harold Blake, the truckman. She thinks perhaps Esther is right about the furniture, so she has decided to take Thor's chair and a couple of other things to keep him contented. Arry won't miss them—not with the whole house to live in.

"Well, good-by, Esty," calls Cora, as she starts out between the houses; "and if anybody wants to make trouble, they can."

Esther is worried. She takes up the matter with Ida. Cora evidently is determined to go through with the Sycamore house move and Arry is likely to stir up a lot of trouble. Arry's pretty mad. Now if they were to tell Arry that they already knew about her and Thor that might stop her. She wouldn't have anything to tell.

They have started in search of Arry when Myrtle appears on the Bolton porch. She's an awful laggard, Myrtle confesses. But she isn't always that way. Is Homer anywhere around, she wonders.

Homer is. He comes now, a little depressed, but quite willing to take a walk with Myrtle, which is what she suggests. They might even walk up and look at their new house. That idea is a little disturbing, but Homer accepts it. As soon as Ida has followed Esther into the Swansons', Myrtle is quick to assure Homer that he shouldn't feel bad about anything. Myrtle understands— about Homer's mother and everything. They (she and Homer) can go right along as they have been. After all it has been rather wonderful—

But there is something else that Homer must tell Myrtle. It's about the loss of their house. It isn't easy, but finally Homer has broken the bad news. Myrtle takes it standing, but the shock is pretty hard. After a time she recovers her poise. Homer is awfully proud of her.

"It's all right," Myrtle agrees, in a dazed voice. "Of course it's all right— It really wasn't our house, was it? Not really. It was your father's house. You couldn't expect him to just keep it empty until— He has kept it empty for five years— You couldn't expect—"

She has turned away from him, trying to keep back the tears.

HOMER (*stepping toward her*)—I'll build you one myself, Myrtle. I'll build you a house that'll make that house look like a garage.

MYRTLE—Don't be silly.

HOMER—Myrtle—I've been thinking things out.

MYRTLE (*wearily*)—Yes, you said you had.

HOMER—Not just last night. Today, too. I ought to have got married and had a home of my own a long time ago. I ought to have done it.

MYRTLE (*faintly*)—Why didn't you, Homer?

HOMER—I got caught. Somehow or other I got caught. But I'd do it now, Myrtle. I'd do it now except—

MYRTLE—Except what?

HOMER—Except now I really have to stay here with my mother.

MYRTLE—What do you mean?

HOMER—My father's going away. He said to my mother, "You'll be all right. You've got Homer."

MYRTLE—What did he mean?

HOMER—He meant she had me to take care of her. She didn't need him.

MYRTLE (*slightly bitter*)—She's always depended on you, Homer. You told me that last night.

HOMER—Yes, that's what I mean. She's always had me to take care of her. Maybe that's the trouble.

MYRTLE (*turning to him after a pause*)—Homer! Do you mean you really want to marry me now—? Because if you do—

if you really want to— It doesn't matter about our house—and
you could be with your mother too. I could come and live here
with you in this house. And we could have your little room. It's
a darling little room. I looked at it on the way down. And we
could all be together. (*Pause.*) That is, if you *wanted* to, of
course.

HOMER—You mean, you'd live here—with everybody?

MYRTLE—Of course I would. I'd just love it.

HOMER—You always said a woman wanted a home of her own.

MYRTLE—Well, I'd be having it. It'd be even nicer in one
way than being up there on Sycamore Drive. We'd never be
lonesome here.

HOMER—I'm awfully fond of you, Myrtle.

MYRTLE—Are you, Homer?

HOMER—I'm fonder of you than anything I could think of.
(*Pause. He stands looking at her.*) I think you're wonderful.

MYRTLE—Thank you, Homer. (MYRTLE *looks away a minute—starts to say something—then changes her mind.*) Shall
we take our walk?

After a moment's hesitancy, and with a defiant glance at the
house, Homer puts his arm around Myrtle and they disappear
up the path.

Now the door of the Swanson house has opened and Esther
is revealed pulling Arry out on to the porch. When Arry holds
back Ida gets behind her and pushes. Arry is mad, but also
curious. After a short tussle, in which she has finally broken
away from her sisters, she is ready to listen to what they have
to say.

What they have to say is that they think it will be a good
thing for Cora and Thor to move up to the Sycamore Drive
house. Arry doesn't. Nor does Arry think Thor wants to move.
She hasn't talked with him—much. But that is what she thinks.

"Cora wants to live alone with Thor," Esther is saying.

"Well, she's not going to," snaps Arry, viciously.

"Oh, isn't she!"

"Over my dead body she is. If they try anything there's a
few things I can tell!"

"You've made that threat a lot of times, Arry—"

"I mean it."

"What could you tell, Arry?"

"Plenty."

"What could you tell that all of us don't already know? That we haven't all known for years?"

There is a sudden pause. Arry looks up at Esther, startled. "What do you mean, Esty?" She turns to Ida, frightened. "What do you mean?"

"Do you think we're all blind, Arry?" asks Ida.

"Don't you think all of us know, by this time, about you and Thor?" adds Esther.

"No—no—Esty—" Arry is frightened.

"We've all known for years. All of us."

"No—no—"

"But we've all kept our mouths shut for Cora's sake. If you want to make a nasty business out of it go on and do it. But it won't get you anywhere, Arry. And you won't look so nice, carrying on for years with the husband of your own sister right under her very nose—"

"Esty! Esty, what do you mean?" Arry is shocked. "You don't think—Ida, you don't think—that Thor and me—all this time— Oh, my God!" She has buried her face in her hands and is moaning distressfully. Suddenly she has turned toward the house and is yelling for Thor. When Thor, puzzled by the excitement, comes hurriedly from the house Arry faces him.

"They say that— They think that—"

She cannot go on. Between the houses Cora has appeared. Arry hesitates a moment, looks at Cora, and then suddenly runs into the house weeping. Neither Cora nor Thor can understand. Esty would explain if she could. She and Arry had just had a little fuss. She will tell Cora about it later, she says, as she follows Arry into the house.

"Thor! I wonder what she could have said to Arry?" wonders Cora. She is looking at him intently.

"I don't know, Cora. Maybe she said something Arry didn't like so much."

"Yes, she must have. I wonder what it could have been."

But Cora has other things to think of. She has made all arrangements for their moving the day after tomorrow and must go now to look after some packing cases. She thinks they are in Ida's house; and she and Ida go to look for them, leaving Thor bewildered and muttering to himself—

"Day after tomorrow! The day after tomorrow! Good God!"

Thor is sitting on the ledge of the porch, visibly distressed when Myrtle and Homer come down the path. Myrtle goes quickly into the Bolton house. Homer, with repressed excitement, approaches Thor—

HOMER—I've got to talk to you, Uncle Thor.
THOR—Well, go ahead, Homer.
HOMER—It's about my house. I've got to have it back.
THOR—Well, by God, Homer, nobody wishes you had it back more than I do.
HOMER—But I've *got* to have it back.
THOR—Well, there's no use talking to me about it. You'll have to talk to your Aunt Cora.
HOMER—No, I've got to talk to you about it. You see, last night when I thought my father was going to start having spells again—I felt I shouldn't leave my mother—and I told that to Myrtle and—
THOR—Yeah, I see the predicament, Homer, but—
HOMER—But this morning Myrtle said we could get married and live here with my mother and—
THOR—I know, Homer. That's kinda tough but—
HOMER—It isn't that so much, but, you see— Myrtle just told me. She's going to have a—baby. (*Pause. There is a complete, dead silence.* THOR *looks at* HOMER *in complete and utter bewilderment.*)
THOR (*in a ghostly whisper*)—What?
HOMER—Uh-huh.
THOR—A—baby?
HOMER—Uh-huh.
THOR—You mean—a—(*He gestures with his hands.*)—baby—
HOMER—Uh-huh.
THOR (*in a whisper, slowly looking* HOMER *over*)—Well, for God's sakes! (*He rises and walks around* HOMER, *staring at him from all angles.*) (HOMER *stands, head down in embarrassment.*) Well, what the hell do you know about that! (HOMER's *head sinks lower.*) Well, I'll be God damned! (*Suddenly* THOR's *face lights up with a great glow. He beams at* HOMER. *He shouts—*) Well! Well! (*He rubs his hands together, beaming at* HOMER.) Well! Well! Well! Well! What the hell do you know about that! (*Slaps* HOMER *on the back.*) That's a pretty good one! Yes, sir, by God, you certainly had your old Uncle Thor fooled!
HOMER (*suddenly smiling, modestly*)—Just one of those things, you know.
THOR—Sure, sure!

HOMER—Don't really know how it happened.

THOR—By God, ain't it the truth.

HOMER—Kinda lose your head sometimes—

THOR (*clapping him on the back*)—Ain't it the truth. By God!
Well, what the hell do you know about that!

The curtain falls.

ACT III

A short time later Cora and Esther are sitting on the steps
of the Swanson house. Cora has evidently just finished imparting the great secret to Esther, and is eagerly watching the expression on Esther's face, which is one of sheer blankness.

Esther simply cannot understand. Not Homer! It just isn't
possible. Not a baby!

"Shh! For goodness' sakes, Esty, don't keep saying it," cautions Cora, nervously. "If Arry ever got hold of it Ida would
find out in a minute!"

"But I just don't understand. How did it happen?"

"How does it usually happen?"

"But Homer must have—must have—"

"Of course he must have. That's the point."

"Must have been all this time—"

"Seven years—"

"Well. I give up. I've seen a lot of things in my time, Cora.
First the telephone. Everybody said it wouldn't work."

"Now stop it, Esty." Cora is giggling nervously. "Somebody'll
hear you. Besides it's an awful thing."

Esther is prepared to admit that much. She wonders what
they are going to do about it. Of course Homer and Myrtle will
have to take a trip when the time comes. Meantime, above
everything, Esther must not let on to Thor that she knows. Nobody knows. The only reason Homer told Thor was because he
wants his house back. Thor thinks Cora will have to give it
back. That thought doesn't please Cora. She knows it isn't
because of the baby that Thor doesn't want to take the house.
He's just afraid to move up there with her.

Esther would change this mood if she could. Cora admits that
she is sure Thor loves her—and always has, from the first. She
knows that she always has come first—which is something to be
able to say after fifty years. "Yes. It's something. It's a *lot.*
If that's all you can get," admits Cora.

Cora has started in the house when Thor comes out of the

Boltons', followed by Ida, Myrtle and Homer. What Homer wants to do, Thor is telling him, is to take a nice, long honeymoon. "To hell with these picky little two, three week affairs," says Thor, expansively. "Months, I say, even if you have to wait a few months before you can get away."

"That sounds like a good idea, Uncle Thor," admits Homer.

"You bet it's a good idea. Pick some nice, quiet place and just settle down and live there awhile. Get to know each other. Come on, we'll dig up that atlas and have a look— Oop—" They have started down the steps and Myrtle trips a little. "Watch out there," warns Thor, solicitously taking Myrtle by the arm. "Take it easy. Bad step there— Well, Esty, old girl, have you heard the news?"

"Why—I—I thought it was a se—" Esther is startled.

"Homer and Myrtle are going to be married," says Cora, quickly, saving the situation.

"Congratulations, Homer . . . I'm sure you'll be very happy, Myrtle."

"Well, I just guess I will be," thrills Myrtle. "My goodness, I'm about as happy right now as a girl has any right to be. Everybody's being so nice it just—hurts."

At Thor's prompting Cora also adds her congratulations, and her feeling that Myrtle is going to be very happy. Again Myrtle admits that she is just about as happy as any girl can be. "It isn't every day that a girl gets a proposal of marriage," Myrtle admits. "I just guess we'll be happy, won't we, Homer?"

"Might be happy if we had a house to live in," mutters Homer.

"Now you stop talking about that, Homer," says Myrtle. "My goodness, we can get along without that house. We'll be so happy right here in this house that you'll be astounded."

"I don't want to live in this house."

"Well, we're going to. Now you stop striking discordant notes, Homer. We're just going to change the subject, and not revert to it again. We'll just change the subject—er—"

They wait while Myrtle thinks up a change. She finally remembers what Mother Ida had said when she heard of Homer's intentions. "She said she didn't feel so much as if she was losing a son, but more like she was gaining a daughter," Myrtle reports.

Mother Ida is still inclined to be a little on the sad side at the thought of Homer's change, but now Homer is determined. He and Myrtle are going to be married and they are going to live alone. Furthermore, if Homer should ever have a son he isn't going to let him stay around the house after he's nineteen.

"You don't see an animal hanging around home after it's grown up, do you?" Homer demands.

A grown male dog isn't hesitant about leaving his mother. And look at pigs. A mother pushes them right out—and that's the way it ought to be.

A few more such discordant notes from Homer and his mother has burst into tears and run into the house. Myrtle is quite angry with Homer. . . .

Arry has come back. She has brought a letter which she hands to Esther. She wants Esther to read the letter sometime. To Cora she promises that she (Cora) will not be bothered with her any more. Cora senses the situation—

"Arry wants to talk to Thor, Esty," she says. "Would you take a little walk with me?"

After they have gone Arry does talk with Thor. Talks with him about getting old and what it means to a person. "I always thought of getting old sort of like going to bed when you're nice and drowsy—and yet you know you won't fall to sleep for a little while yet—and you just sort of lie there sort of comfortably— and enjoy it— But it isn't like that at all."

Arry has been thinking. She wants Thor to know that she appreciates all that he has done for her, having her in his home all these years. No, it wasn't ever Arry's home. Arry hasn't got a home—

"That's what I mean about getting old," she says. "I guess it's nice and peaceful if you've got a home. If you got a husband. If you've got somebody to get old with. But I haven't."

So Arry has made up her mind to go away. She will leave Thor and Cora to have a home together. She should have done it years ago, but she didn't. Now she is going to try to forget Thor. When she dies she is hoping they will put on her stone—

> "Home is the sailor, home from the sea,
> And the hunter, home from the hills."

Arry isn't sorry—for anything. She wants Thor to know that. When she goes back to the house Thor looks after her sadly. "Poor Arry! All alone in the world!" he mutters.

Carl and David are back, loaded down with Carl's tools and luggage. Carl still doesn't know exactly where he is, but David has given him a great deal of food for thought, including the germ of an idea as to how a man can find out where he stands. He is sure Carl will eventually be able to pin this thought down.

Esther has come in. She greets them casually. They have come back because Carl has discovered that making a bathroom out of the first floor closet would cost approximately three hundred dollars, and as they haven't got three hundred dollars the idea didn't seem very practical.

Carl has taken his tools into the house now. Esther and David are facing each other. He would follow Carl, when she stops him.

"David, I'd like to read you something," she says.

"Well, Esty, I—"

ESTHER—You know what we've all suspected about Arry and Thor all these years, don't you, David?

DAVID (*turning*)—Oh, I've heard the talk, Esther. I never paid much attention to it.

ESTHER—Arry just gave me this letter. (*Shows the letter.* DAVID *puts down bags, crosses to stump and sits.*) Do you remember— Oh, it must have been all of forty years ago—after Arry had been living with them about a year—Cora had to go to the hospital for a couple of weeks?

DAVID—I think I do—vaguely—

ESTHER—Thor and Arry were alone. She was about seventeen. She didn't know much about anything. Right off the farm. She was pretty, full of life. You remember how Arry was. And— (*She reads.*) ". . . and I don't know how it happened, Esty. I just don't. I loved Thor so much. I didn't realize it. I should have gone away but I couldn't. We were both so miserable and scared. We didn't know what to do. But never after that time, Esty. Never. If Cora should ever know I'd just die." (ESTHER *puts the letter down. They both sit thinking a moment.*) And so she just went on—living with them—because there wasn't any other place for her to go after that. (*Pause.*) Well, I feel kind of sorry for Arry. I guess she feels her life hasn't been to much purpose. (*She reads.*) "When you and Ida told me what all of you had been thinking all this time—it seems to me I'd never be able to hold up my head again. It doesn't much matter about the years ahead—but it suddenly seemed as if all the years I've already lived didn't make much sense. I might just as well not have lived them." (*Pause. She puts the letter down.*)

DAVID (*rising*)—In the eyes of the world—I'm a failure—but we've kept our lives clear, Esther, and intelligent.

ESTHER—Yes, David, we have, haven't we?

DAVID—We've never let that other third element come in.

We've kept ourselves to ourselves.

ESTHER (*smiling*)—Yes, I know what you mean by a Crystal Fortress, David. (*He turns away. There is a moment's pause. ESTHER watches him, smiling.*)

DAVID—It's a tragic line Aaronetta says about the years behind her. "I might just as well not have lived them."

ESTHER—Yes.

DAVID (*turning to her, hesitating*)—Did you ever feel like that, Esther?

ESTHER—No, David.

DAVID (*eagerly*)—That's good.

ESTHER—But, you see, I always had you, David.

DAVID (*touched and embarrassed*)—Thank you, Esther. (*He turns to her with a smile and a short bow.*) Thank you. I'll take these in.

David has disappeared in the house when Cora comes down the path. Esther has put Arry's letter away and turns to meet her. Cora has come to a decision. She is going to give Homer's house back to him. She has decided that, after all, living in the other house alone with Thor isn't what she is after. There is something else. Cora hates Arry—

"I hate her," she repeats over Esther's protest. "But she can go on living with us. There's no other place for her. But she's not going on living with us the way she has been. Because I'm going to find out where I stand, Esty. And I'm going to live alone with Thor in that very house—even with Arry there. . . . You remember that poem Papa used to say about us girls, Esty?

" 'Esty's smartest,
Arry's wildest,
Ida's slowest,
Cora's mildest.'

"And then he always used to look at me and say, 'Poor Cora!' You remember that?"

"Yes."

"Well, I'm not 'Poor Cora' any more. There's such a thing as being too mild."

Carl has come from the house. Before he has a chance to ask her Cora tells him she is giving the house back to Homer, and that pleases Carl.

Now Thor, Myrtle and Homer have come out, having fully agreed on a place for the honeymoon. "And wait until you see

that water coming down," Thor is saying. "And there's a little
boat that goes right out under the falls. Cora and I spent a
whole week there once."

Homer is pleased and Myrtle delighted. And now David has
come to add his congratulations. "I hope you're not being too
impetuous," he says to Homer. "Myrtle, I hope—"

"My goodness, I just guess I will be," anticipates Myrtle. "I'm
just about as happy this minute as any girl has a right to be—"

To cap their happiness Cora comes now to tell Homer and
Myrtle that their house is their own again. By now Myrtle is
so happy she just feels like crying. At which moment Arry
appears on the porch of the Swanson house carrying a hatbox
and a suitcase. She has on a large picture hat and looks very
pretty. Thor says she does, as Cora stiffens and looks the other
way.

Arry is moving out, she explains, which surprises them all into
little protests of surprise. Yes, Arry is leaving. She realizes now
that she should have left years ago. It is a little upsetting, says
Arry, to find out at her age that she isn't wanted any more—
"That all the years you thought you were a part of a home you
were really just sort of a—servant in it—and you could be dismissed when your services were no longer needed—"

"By God, don't say that, Arry. You don't have to go anywhere." Esther has moved nearer to Cora.

"But, Thor, I'm not wanted here."

"You are, too. By God, this is your home, Arry. Isn't that
so, Cora?"

"Oh, don't ask Cora, Thor. Cora wants to live alone— She
doesn't want any sister of hers—"

Cora has moved in at this, prepared to give battle. Esther
holds her back, handing her Arry's letter and motioning her to
read it, which Cora does. Now Arry has turned to Myrtle—

ARRY—I haven't had the opportunity to felicitate you on
your approaching nuptials, Myrtle. I know you'll be very happy.

MYRTLE—Thank you, Aunt Arry.

ARRY—Homer too, of course.

HOMER—Thank you, Aunt Arry.

ARRY—But when you come right down to it, it's the woman
that ought to be the happiest.

MYRTLE—I just guess that's the truth.

ARRY—She's the one who makes the home and looks after
things and keeps it together.

MYRTLE—That's just the woman's function, I should think. (CORA *has finished half the letter. She turns swiftly to* ESTHER— ESTY *motions her to finish the letter.*)

ARRY—And marriage gives a woman dignity, Myrtle. It gives her dignity and companionship and a place to be when she gets old. I know you'll be very happy, Myrtle.

MYRTLE—I know I will be.

ARRY—That's right. (*She turns.* CORA *has finished the letter and you see it has softened her.* ARRY *and she look at each other.* ARRY *is terrified and looks accusingly at* ESTY.) Esty! (ESTY *nods admittal that she gave* CORA *the letter. A moment's pause.* CORA *rises slowly. Crumples the letter and goes to* ARRY.)

CORA—You're going away, Arry?

ARRY—Yes, Cora.

CORA (*touched*)—I'll—I'll miss you, Arry— (ARRY *looks at her slowly.*)

THOR—By God, you don't have to go, Arry.

ARRY—Yes, Thor, I must go. We'll see each other now and then but I'm not going to live here any more.

THOR—But where are you going to go?

ARRY—Well, I'm going to move over to Ida's—Ida told me years ago if I ever wanted to move over to her I could. Didn't you, Ida?

IDA—Of course, Arry.

CARL—Any time you want to, Arry.

ARRY—Well, now I want to. I want to spend the rest of the years with you.

HOMER (*after a pause*)—Well, if we're going to see our house we'd better go.

MYRTLE—Our house! My goodness! I've just never had so many people so nice to me all at once—

THOR—By God, Myrtle, if anybody isn't nice to you just come to your old Uncle Thor.

MYRTLE—Well, I certainly will. I'll just look on you as— well, as my—protector. (*They laugh together.*)

HOMER (*taking hold of* MYRTLE, *gruffly*)—All right. That's enough. We better go now.

MYRTLE—Yes, Homer.

"Arry hands Carl her bags and starts towards Ida's house" as

THE CURTAIN FALLS

THE PLAYS AND THEIR AUTHORS

"There Shall Be No Night," a drama in three acts by Robert
E. Sherwood. Copyright, 1940, by the author. Copyright
and published, 1940, by Charles Scribner's Sons, New York
and London.

Robert E. Sherwood is an old and valued contributor to "The
Best Plays," as our regular readers know. This is, in fact, his
seventh appearance as one of the theatre's outstanding dramatists
whose plays have won unusual distinction. Last season he headed
the list with "Abe Lincoln in Illinois." This year it is his fine
drama, "There Shall Be No Night." Previously he has been
represented by such favorites as "The Road to Rome," "Reunion
in Vienna," "Idiot's Delight," "The Petrified Forest" and the
popular adaptation he made of Jacques Deval's "Tovarich."
Mr. Sherwood was born in New Rochelle, N. Y., served with
Canada's Black Watch in the first World War, and has had
an active literary career since then.

"Key Largo," a drama in three acts by Maxwell Anderson.
Copyright, 1939, by the author. Copyright and published,
1939, by Anderson House, Washington, D. C. Distributed
by Dodd, Mead & Co., New York.

Maxwell Anderson's last appearance as a Best Plays dramatist was in the 1937-38 volume, when his "The Star-Wagon" won
him a place. He has been writing plays since 1923, and during
that time has been represented in the yearbook ten times,
beginning with his co-authorship with Laurence Stallings of
"What Price Glory?" the season of 1924-25. His historical
dramas, which brought him particular renown, have included
"Elizabeth the Queen," "Mary of Scotland" and "Valley Forge."
He won a Pulitzer prize with "Both Your Houses" and two Dramatic Critics' Circle awards with "Winterset" and "High Tor."
He was born in Atlantic, Pa., has done a bit of teaching, some
newspaper work and a good deal of writing.

"The World We Make," a drama in three acts by Sidney Kingsley, taken from a novel, "The Outward Room," by Millen Brand. Copyright, 1939, by the author. Copyright and published, 1940, by Samuel French, New York.

Sidney Kingsley has been writing for the stage ever since he was a member of the Cornell Dramatic Club during his college years. His first play to be produced was the "Men in White" which won him a Pulitzer prize the season of 1933-34 and was included in the yearbook of the drama of that year. Two years later he scored again with "Dead End," which brought him several minor theatre club awards. He has had some experience acting in both amateur and professional companies. Mr. Kingsley was born in New York City.

"Life with Father," a comedy in three acts by Howard Lindsay and Russel Crouse. Copyright 1939, 1940, by Howard Lindsay, Russel Crouse and Katherine B. Day. Copyright and published, 1940, by Alfred A. Knopf, New York.

Howard Lindsay and Russel Crouse specialized in musical comedy librettos during the first years of their joint labors. Three were staged, "Anything Goes," "Red Hot and Blue" and "Hurray for What?" "Anything Goes," was the hit of its season. "Life with Father," which they fashioned from various newspaper and magazine sketches written by the late Clarence Day, is their first comedy without music. Mr. Lindsay has been fussing around the theatre all his life, and has had considerable experience as author, actor, director and producer. He wrote the farcical "She Loves Me Not," which was a comedy sensation some years ago. He also was co-author with Bertrand Robinson of "Tommy," "Your Uncle Dudley" and "Oh, Promise Me." He was born in Waterford, N. Y.—the youngest of a family of six.

Mr. Crouse leaped, not too abruptly, from newspaper work to playwriting. In 1931 he was doing a New York Evening *Post* column which left him with a good deal of time on his hands. Part of this he devoted to fashioning the book of a musical comedy which was produced as "The Gang's All Here." Its reception was not encouraging. He wrote "Hold Your Horses" for Joe Cook, with Corey Ford as a collaborator, and that was better. Then he went to work with Howard Lindsay, and their success has been pretty steady. Mr. Crouse was born in Findlay, Ohio, in 1893.

"The Man Who Came to Dinner," a comedy in three acts by
    George S. Kaufman and Moss Hart. Copyright, 1939, by
    the authors. Copyright and published, 1939, by Random
    House, New York.

The Kaufman-Hart combination is another familiar of these
pages. Only last season they were represented by the long-running "The American Way." Before that they gave us "You
Can't Take It with You," the comedy success of its season;
"Merrily We Roll Along," and, as far back as the season of
1930-31, "Once in a Lifetime." Of the seventeen volumes of
"The Best Plays" that have been published since Mr. Kaufman
began writing for the stage in 1921 he has been represented in
fifteen of them. Mr. Kaufman was born in Pittsburgh, Pa., and
Mr. Hart in New York. Mr. Kaufman approached the stage
by way of journalism, Mr. Hart through the offices of a play
producer.

"The Male Animal," a comedy in three acts by James Thurber
    and Elliott Nugent. Copyright, 1940, by the authors.
    Copyright and published, 1940, by Random House, New
    York. Published in Canada by the Macmillan Co., New
    York.

James Thurber and Elliott Nugent are new members of the
Best Plays Authors' Fraternity, their entry with "The Male Animal" being a first appearance for both. It is also Mr. Thurber's
first try at playwriting, but Mr. Nugent has been at it practically all his conscious life. He was a co-author, with his father,
J. C. Nugent, of a comedy called "Kempy" back in 1922, and
has a dozen or more similar achievements to his credit, including a popular success, "The Poor Nut," which ran a couple of
seasons in the middle nineteen-twenties. Mr. Thurber and Mr.
Nugent were classmates at Ohio State University in 1920, and
both nursed literary ambitions. Mr. Thurber edited the college
magazine, "The Sun Dial," with Nugent as an assistant, and together they practically wrote the campus daily, called "The Lantern." Out of college their paths parted but their friendship
held firm. Thurber went into newspaper work, Nugent turned

naturally to acting and writing for the stage. Thurber became managing editor of the *New Yorker* magazine and achieved fame as a cartoonist and author as well. Nugent eventually found himself in Hollywood, doubling as author, director and actor. Last Summer they were both in Hollywood working on "The Male Animal." When the comedy was tried out on the coast and made a lot of friends it was decided to bring it to New York, where it was the first hit of 1940. Thurber was born in Columbus, Ohio, and Nugent in Dover, Ohio. Thurber married Helen Wismer, magazine editor. Nugent married Norma Lee, actress.

"Skylark," a comedy in three acts by Samson Raphaelson. Copyright, 1939, by the author. Copyright, and published, 1939, by Random House, New York.

Either journalism or the advertising business lost a good man when Samson Raphaelson, born New York, 1896, decided to be a dramatist, which he did in the middle nineteen-twenties. His first play was "The Jazz Singer," which George Jessel played successfully for months. His first big success in the theatre was scored with "Accent on Youth," which was a feature of the 1934-35 collection of "Best Plays." His other plays have included "Young Love" and "The Wooden Slipper." Mr. Raphaelson lived and worked for some years in Chicago. Recently he has been active also as a scenarist in Hollywood.

"The Time of Your Life," a comedy in three acts by William Saroyan. Copyright, 1939, by the author. Copyright and published, 1939, by Harcourt, Brace & Co., New York.

William Saroyan, the newest of dramatists to arrive on Broadway, had two plays produced the season of 1939-40. One was "The Time of Your Life," which won him both the New York Critics' Circle plaque and the Pulitzer award of $1,000, as the best play by an American author to be shown that season. The other, "My Heart's in the Highlands," won no more than a battery of mixed reviews. Mr. Saroyan was not too greatly impressed with either of these experiences. He accepted with formal graciousness the Critics' award and refused the Pulitzer $1,000, saying that he would feel he was debasing art by its acceptance. A compromise of sorts was worked out. Mr. Saroyan is the son of Armenian immigrant parents, was born near Fresno, Calif., thirty-two years ago, does most of his writing in San Francisco and won his first fame as a writer of short stories, notably "The Daring Young Man on the Flying Trapeze."

"Margin for Error," a comedy melodrama in three acts by Clare Boothe. Copyright, 1939, by the author. Copyright and published, 1940, by Random House, New York.

This is Clare Boothe's third appearance as a Best Plays author. She made her bow with "The Women," a sensationally successful satire of the 1936-37 season. She followed the year after that with a fairly riotous satire called "Kiss the Boys Good-Bye," aimed at the international ballyhoo worked up over the selection of an actress to play the heroine in the picture version of "Gone with the Wind." This season she scored successfully with the satirical melodrama aimed at the Nazi menace, "Margin for Error." Miss Boothe, for long a brilliant magazine editor and novelist, is married to Henry R. Luce, editor of *Time, Life,* and *Fortune,* who has written an interesting analytical review of his wife's anti-Nazi play for the book version published by Random House. Miss Boothe was prominent in New York society before she took to literature as an escape. She was born in New York City in 1902.

"Morning's at Seven," a comedy in three acts by Paul Osborn. Copyright, 1939, by the author.

Paul Osborn came to prominence in the theatre in 1930, when Mary Boland played a comedy of his called "The Vinegar Tree" and scored a considerable success with it. It was seven years before he earned a second Best Plays rating with his adaptation of Lawrence Edward Watkin's novel, "On Borrowed Time." He was born in Evansville, Ind., in 1901, was given his A.B. and M.A. by the University of Michigan and studied playwriting with Prof. George Pierce Baker at Harvard. He has made his home the last several years in Brattleboro, Vt.

PLAYS PRODUCED IN NEW YORK

June 18, 1939—June 18, 1940

(Plays marked with asterisk were still playing June 18, 1940)

STREETS OF PARIS

(274 performances)

A musical revue in two acts with contributions by Charles Sherman, Tom McKnight, Mitchell Hodges, S. Jay Kaufman, Edward Duryea Dowling, James LaVer, Frank Eyton and Lee Brody; lyrics by Harold J. Rome and Al Dubin; music by James McHugh. Produced by Messrs. Shubert in association with Olsen and Johnson at the Broadhurst Theatre, New York, June 19, 1939.

Principals engaged—

Luella Gear	Bobby Clark
Carmen Miranda	Bud Abbott
Jeanne Tyler	Gower Champion
Della Lind	Lou Costello
Yvonne Bouvier	Jean Sablon
Gloria Gilbert	Ramon Vinay
Margaret Irving	John McCauley
Barbara Beech	Michael Moore
Frances O'Day	Frederic Nay
Maxine Martin	Hugh Ellsworth
Mildred Hughes	Billy Branch
Aina Constant	Edward Wells
Magda Kari	Ben Dova
Bernice Smith	Mons Hoffman
Lillian Lillemy	Lincoln Wilderton
Nancy Lewis	Buddy Roberts
Mary Ann	Charles La Torre

Jo and Jeanne Readinger
Margo, Kate and Evelyn Hylton
Ward and Van

Staged by Edward Duryea and Dennis Murray; dances by Robert Alton; settings by Lawrence L. Goldwasser; costumes by Irene Sharaff.

(Closed February 10, 1940)

FROM VIENNA

(79 performances)

A musical revue by Lothar Metzl, Werner Michel, Hans Weigel, Jura Soyfer, Peter Hammerschlag and David Gregory; adaptations by John La Touche, Eva Frankin and Hugo Hauff;

music by Werner Michel, Walter Drix, Otto Andreas and Jimmy Berg. Produced by The Refugee Artists Group at the Music Box, New York, June 20, 1939.

Principals engaged—

Illa Roden
Elizabeth Neumann
Nelly Franck
Maria Pichler
Hedy Pitt
Katherine Mattern
Fred Essler
Karl Mueller
Hans Herberth

Paul Lindenberg
Fred Lorenz
Henry Werbeck
Kurt Reichert
Walter Martin
John Banner
Lothar Rewalt
Louis Ebers
Henry Vanicelli

Staged by Herbert Berghof; supervised by Charles Friedman, settings by Donald Oenslager; costumes by Irene Sharaff; lighting by Hassard Short.

(Closed August 26, 1939)

YOKEL BOY

(208 performances)

A musical comedy in two acts by Lew Brown, Charles Tobias and Samuel H. Stept. Produced by Lew Brown at the Majestic Theatre, New York, July 6, 1939.

Cast of characters—

Elmer Whipple....................................Buddy Ebsen
Judy...Judy Canova
Tiny...Dixie Dunbar
"Punko" Parks.....................................Phil Silvers
Spud..Jackie Heller
Mary Hawkins......................................Lois January
Cliff Hawkins......................................Ralph Riggs
Blacksmith...Mark Plant
Mr. Rubbish..Lew Hearn
Grandpa Hawkins, Mayor.........................Charles Althoff
Mrs. Hawkins....................................Almira Sessions
Annie ....Ann Canova
Hank ....Zeke Canova
Jimmy Powell......................................Ralph Holmes
Sheriff...Ben Roberts
Angelina Bouchet..............................Helene Standish
Gateman..Sidney Salzer
Another Gateman..................................Jack Richards
Assistant to "Punko" Parks.........................Ray Clarke
Doorman..Dick Langdon
Marie...Ruth Rathbun

Ladies of the Ensemble: Lorraine Belore, June Blake, Helen Cole, Marguerite De Coursey, Glorianna King, Maxine Moore, Helene Standish.

Yokel Girls: Irene Austin, Kalli Barton, Jeanne Bergersen, Pamela Clifford, Muriel Cole, Helen Dell, Jane Everett, Margaret Fitz-Patrick, Miriam Franklyn, Marjorie Johnstone, Grace Kaye, Katheryn Lazell, Jeanette Lee, Velma Lord, Marion Lulling, Alice Malteur, Joan Mann, Gloria Martin, Mary Joan Martin, Dorothy Matthews, Frances Rands, Ruth Rathbun, Tina Rigat, Renee Russell, Natalie Wynn.

Minute Men from Lexington: James Burrell, Charles Clarke, Philip Crosbie, Roy Johnston, F. Richard Moors, Joseph Peterson, Louis Salmon, Donald Showalter, Turnley Walker, Harold Woodward.

Yokel Boys: Bob Beh, Dick Langdon, Eddie Murray, Mortimer O'Brien, Jack Richards, Sidney Salzer, Phil Shaw.

Acts I and II.—Around the Hawkins Farm, Town of Lexington, Mass., and in Hollywood, Calif.

Staged by Lew Brown; dances by Gene Snyder; settings by Walter Jagemann; costumes by Frances Feist and Veronica.

(Closed January 6, 1940)

THE AMERICAN WAY

(Return engagement 80 performances)

A play in two acts by George Kaufman and Moss Hart; music by Oscar Levant. Produced by Sam H. Harris and Max Gordon at the Center Theatre, New York, July 17, 1940.

Cast of characters—

Martin Gunther	Fredric March
Irma Gunther	Florence Eldridge
Immigration Official	James MacDonald
Lisa Gunther as a child	{ Janet Regan / Norma Clerc / Virginia Lodge }
A Boy	Bobby Barron
Another Boy	Bob White
Judge Hewitt	Bradford Hunt
Mrs. Kennedy	Jeanne Wardley
Mrs. White	Grace Valentine
Dr. Squires	Sydney Grant
Otto Heinrich	Maurice Wells
Clara Heinrich	Elsa Ersi
Samuel Brockton	McKay Morris
A Political Speaker	Robert Rhodes
Another Political Speaker	James Moore
Winifred Baxter	Ruth Weston
A School Teacher	Mary Murray
Antonio Coletti	John Long
Alex Hewitt as a child	{ Buddy Buehler / Robert Cushman }
Karl Gunther as a child	{ Teddy Casey / Buddy Irving }
Bobby	Tommy Lewis
Anna	Janet Fox

Factory Workers: Jerome Thor, Sidney Stone, Brant Gorman, James Russo.

Mrs. Brockton	Eileen Burns
Mrs. Hewitt	Jeanne Shelby
The Chairman	John Lorenz
Mayor McEvoy	Hugh Cameron
Dr. MacFarlane	Le Roi Operti
Jeff	Allen Kearns
Mrs. Squires	Mary Brandon

Tennis Girls: Mona Moray, Gerry Carr, Katherine Duncan.

Lisa Gunther	Adrienne Marden
Alex Hewitt	Alan Hewitt
Karl Gunther	David Wayne
Tommy	Walter Kelly
Mandolin Player	Stephen Sandes
Helen	Dora Sayers
Tommy Nelson	Alex Courtney
Another Young Man	Edward Elliott
Karl Gunther, Age 9	Dickie Van Patten
Julia Hewitt, Age 11	Elinor Pittis
Mary Hewitt, Age 10	Claire Howard
A Political Speaker	Richard Lloyd
A Minister	Walter Beck

Julia, Age 21.....................................Barbara Wooddell
Mary, Age 20.....................................Gretchen Davidson
Karl, Age 21......................................Whittner Bissell
Ruth...Marian Edwards
Ed Lorenz..Jack Arnold
John Williams....................................George Herndon
Henry Courtney....................................Ward Tallmon
 Opening scene—Ellis Island, 1896. Other scenes—Small American
Town.
 Staged by George S. Kaufman; lighting and technical direction
by Hassard Short; settings by Donald Oenslager; costumes by Irene
Sharaff.

A first engagement of "The American Way" included 164
performances running from January 21 to June 10, 1939. July
17, 1939, the play reopened and ran through September 23,
1939, with 80 performances.

August 31, 1939, at the Center Theatre a matinee perform-
ance was presented by the cast of "The American Way." Act II
of "Girls in Uniform," by Christa Winsloe, directed by Barbara
Adams; Act I, Scene 1 of "Merrily We Roll Along" by George
S. Kaufman and Moss Hart, directed by John Kennedy; "The
Last Mile" by John Wesley, directed by James Russo and Act III
of "When Ladies Meet" by Rachel Crothers, directed by Le Roi
Operti, were given.

(Closed September 23, 1939)

GEORGE WHITE'S SCANDALS

(120 performances)

A revue with lyrics by Jack Yellen, music by Sammy Fain,
sketches by Matt Brooks, Eddie Davis and George White. Produced by Mr. White at the Alvin Theatre, New York, August
28, 1939.

Principals engaged—

Willie Howard   Ella Logan
Eugene Howard   Dorothy Koster
Jack Williams   Ann Miller
Ben Blue   Collette Lyons
Raymond Middleton   Betty Allen
Craig Mathues   June Mann
Billy Rayes   Lois Andrew
Fred Manatt   Martha Burnett
Harry Stockwell   Christine Forsythe
Ross Wyse, Jr.   Florette Du Elk
Harold Whalen   Frances Neal
James French   Rose Marie Magrill
Barbara Lenton   Kay Buckley
Kim Loo Sisters   Knight Sisters
 The Three Stooges: Moe and Curly Howard and Larry Fine;
 Victor Arden and His Orchestra.
 Staged by George White; dialogue directed by William K. Wells;
settings by Albert Johnson; costumes by Charles Le Maire.

(Closed December 9, 1939)

LEAVE IT TO ME!

(Return engagement 16 performances)

A musical comedy in two acts by Bella and Samuel Spewack; music and lyrics by Cole Porter. Returned by Vinton Freedley to the Imperial Theatre, New York, September 4, 1939.

Cast of characters—

First Secretary	Ruth Bond
Second Secretary	Beverly Hosier
Buckley Joyce Thomas	William Gaxton
First Reporter	William Lilling
Second Reporter	Walter Monroe
Dolly Winslow	Mildred Fenton
J. H. Brody	Edward H. Robins
Mrs. Goodhue	Sophie Tucker

Mrs. Goodhue's Daughters: April, Mildred Chenaval, Ruth Daye, Audrey Palmer, Kay Picture.

Reporter	Chet Bree
Photographer	George E. Mack
French Conductor	Walter Armin
Chauffeur	James W. Carr
Alonzo P. Goodhue	Victor Moore

Secretaries to Mr. Goodhue: Joel Friend, Maurice Kelly, Roy Ross, Jack Seymour, Jack Stanton, Paul Bartels

Prince Alexander Tomofsky	Eugene Sigaloff
Jerry Granger	Dean Carlton
Colette	Tamara
Kostya	Joseph Kallini
Peasant	Peter Lopouhin
Sozanoff	Alexander Asro
Military Attache	John Eliot
Naval Attache	John Panter
Secretaries	Roy Ross / Jack Seymour
Decorators	Michael Forbes / Thomas Jafollo
Waiter	Don Cortez
German Ambassador	Hans Hansen
French Ambassador	Walter Armin
Latvian Minister	Peter Lopouhin
British Ambassador	J. Colville Dunn
Italian Ambassador	Thomas Jafolla
Japanese Ambassador	George E. Mack
Mackenzie	Charles Campbell
Graustein	Walter Armin
Folkin	Ivan Izmailov
Secretary	Stanton Bier
Foreign Minister	Alexis Bolan
Stalin	Walter Armin

Act I.—Scene 1—City Room of Paris and Chicago *World-Tribune.* 2—Gare de l'Est, Paris. 3—Park in Moscow. 4—Anteroom. American Embassy, Moscow. 5—Goodhue's Bedroom in Embassy. 6—Thomas' Hotel Suite, Moscow. 7—Red Square. Act II.—Scene 1—Red Square. 2—A Droshka. 3—Anteroom. 4—A Steppe. 5—Embassy Drawing Room. 6—Park. 7—Moscow Railroad Station.

Staged by Samuel Spewack; dances and ensembles by Robert Alton; music directed by Max Meth; settings by Albert Johnson; costumes by Raoul Pene Du Bois.

"Leave It to Me" was first produced at the Imperial Theatre, New York, November 9, 1938, and continued there until July 15, 1939, 291 performances. The above is the original cast with a few substitutions, notably that of Mildred Fenton who took the part of Dolly Winslow formerly played by Mary Martin.

(Closed September 16, 1939)

JOURNEY'S END

(16 performances)

A drama in three acts by R. C. Sherriff. Revived by Leonard Sillman at the Empire Theatre, New York, September 18, 1939.

Cast of characters—

Captain Hardy	Hugh Rennie
Lieutenant Osborne	Reginald Mason
Private Mason	Victor Beecroft
2nd Lieutenant Raleigh	Jack Merivale
Captain Stanhope	Colin Keith-Johnston
2nd Lieutenant Trotter	A. P. Kaye
2nd Lieutenant Hibbert	Glenn Hunter
Company Sergeant-Major	Ralph Sumpter
The Colonel	Richard Temple
German Soldier	Everett Ripley
Private Broughton	Philip Huston
Bert	Houseley Stevens, Jr.

Acts I, II and III.—Dugout in the British Trench before St. Quentin, March, 1918.

Staged by Leonard Sillman; setting by Lemuel Ayers.

A revival of the R. C. Sherriff drama which was a hit of the 1928-29 season on Broadway. (See "Best Plays of 1928-29.") In the original cast Colin Keith-Johnson was the Captain Stanhope, Derek Williams the Lieutenant Raleigh and Leon Quartermaine the Lieutenant Osborne.

(Closed September 30, 1939)

SEE MY LAWYER

(224 performances)

A comedy in three acts by Richard Maibaum and Harry Clork. Produced by George Abbott at the Biltmore Theatre, New York, September 27, 1939.

Cast of characters—

Fay Frankel	Mary Rolfe
Arthur Lee	Milton Berle
Joseph O'Rourke	Millard Mitchell
Peter Russo	Gary Merrill
Morris Schneerer	Teddy Hart
Seymore Tyler	David Hoffman
Irving Frankel	Norman Tokar
Charlie	Robert Griffith
Telephone Linesman	Ralph Bell
Robert Carlin	Eddie Nugent

```
Ichiro Kato.......................................George Hirose
S. B. Jameson....................................Fleming Ward
Western Union Boy................................Richard Lee
Shoeshine Boy....................................Walter Wagner
Blossom Le Verne.................................Robin Raymond
A Man............................................John Shellie
Police Officer...................................Carroll Ashburn
```
    Acts I, II and III.—Law Offices of Lee, Russo and O'Rourke,
Mid-Manhattan.
    Staged by Ezra Hunt; setting by Cirker and Robbins.

Arthur Lee, Joseph O'Rourke and Peter Russo are three young
lawyers newly started in business and down to their last borrowed dollar. Into their offices drifts Robert Carlin, eccentric
playboy. His car has knocked down the law firm's office boy
and Carlin seeks a settlement. The firm fastens to him with
avidity as his counsel and is thereafter kept busy for the rest
of the evening getting him out of scrapes the playwright gets
him into.

(Closed April 6, 1940)

THE STRAW HAT REVUE

(75 performances)

A revue in two acts conceived and assembled by Max Liebman;
music and lyrics by Sylvia Fine and James Shelton; special music
by Glenn Bacon; sketches by Max Liebman and Samuel Locke.
Produced by The Straw Hat Company at the Ambassador Theatre, New York, September 29, 1939.

Principals engaged—

Imogene Coca	Danny Kaye
Lee Brody	James Shelton
Dorothy Bird	Alfred Drake
Lilli Sandan	Herbert Shepard
Albia Kavan	Jerome Andrews
Gertrude Goldsmith	Robert Burton
Ruthanna Boris	Jerome Robbins
Dolores Grenafei	Pancho Scordi
Meta Mata	Otto Hari
Nana Matisse	Leon Barte
Vera Volkenau	William Bales
Maude Davis	Richard Reed
Nan Rae	Bronson Dudley
Marjorie Moffett	Henriette Henning

    Staged by Max Liebman; settings by Edward Gilbert; choreography
by Jerome Andrews.

A superior Summer theatre revue discovered by Harry Kaufman at Camp Temamint, Bushkill, Pa., and reorganized for a
Broadway showing under the sponsorship of Mr. Kaufman and
the Messrs. Shubert.

(Closed December 2, 1939)

THEY KNEW WHAT THEY WANTED

(24 performances)

A comedy in three acts by Sidney Howard. Revived by Leonard
Sillman at the Empire Theatre, New York, October 2, 1939.

Cast of characters—

Joe	Douglass Montgomery
Father McKee	Charles Kennedy
Ah Gee	Peter Chong
Tony	Giuseppe Sterni
The R.F.D.	Philip Huston
Amy	June Walker
Angelo	Joseph Conway
Giorgio	Everett Ripley
The Doctor	Charles Maxwell
First Italian Mother	Dolores Baladoni
Her Daughter	Marylin Wahl
Second Italian Mother	Miriam Battista
Her Son	Edward Mayor

Farm Hands: Marvis Butler, Norma Green, Nanon Kiam, Shirley
Osborne, Elena Salvatore; David Beale, Walter Black, Robert
Carr, Ralph Constantino, Joseph M. De Villard, Vito Scotti.

Singer and Guitarist	Rosito Anthony
Concertina Player	Boris Matusewitch

Acts I, II and III.—Tony's Farmhouse in Napa Valley, California.
Staged by Robert Ross; setting by Lemuel Ayers.

A revival of the 1924-25 Pulitzer Prize play. In the original
production (see "Best Plays of 1924-25") Pauline Lord played
Amy, Richard Bennett was the Tony and Glenn Anders the Joe.

(Closed October 21, 1939)

SKYLARK

(256 performances)

A comedy in three acts by Samson Raphaelson. Produced by
John Golden at the Morosco Theatre, New York, October 11, 1939.

Cast of characters—

George Gorell	Walter Gilbert
Theodore	Horace Sinclair
Tony Kenyon	Donald Cook
Lydia Kenyon	Gertrude Lawrence
Ned Franklin	William David
Charlotte Franklin	Gertrude Bryan
A Maid	Ann Driscoll
Bill Blake	Glenn Anders
Myrtle Valentine	Vivian Vance
Harley Valentine	Robert Burton

Acts I, II and III.—Living Room of Tony Kenyon's Country House
near New York City.
Staged by Samson Raphaelson; setting by Donald Oenslager.

See page 283.

(Closed May 25, 1940)

THREE SISTERS

(9 performances)

A play in four acts by Anton Chekhov; translated by Bernard
Guilbert Guerney; acting version by Samuel Rosen. Revived by
The Surry Theatre under the sponsorship of Dwight Deere Wiman
at the Longacre Theatre, New York, October 14, 1939.

Cast of characters—

The Sisters Prozoroff:
Olga Sergeievna.................................Helen Wynn
Irina Sergeievna..............................Katherine Emery
Maria Sergeievna (Masha).......................Anne Revere
Baron Nikolai Lvovitch Tusenbach.....................John Boruff
Ivan Romanovitch Tchebutikin........................Jabez Gray
Capt. Vassily Vassilievitch Solyony.................Thomas Speidel
Anfisa...Ann Garrett
Ferapont...George Cotton
Lieut.-Col. Alexander Vershinin...............Shepperd Strudwick
Andrei Sergeievitch Prozoroff.......................Hume Cronyn
Kuligin..Robert Allen
Natasha.......................................Dorothy Mathews
Fedotik ....Carl Gose
Rode ....Maurice Manson
Maid..Alexandra Taran
   Acts I and II.—Living Room in Home of the Prozoroffs in a Pro-
vincial Town near Moscow. Act III.—Bedroom of Olga and Irina.
Act IV.—The Garden.
   Staged by Samuel Rosen; settings by Johannes Larsen; costumes
by Lucinda Ballard.

Olga, Irina and Maria Sergeievna, trapped in a small garrison
town near Moscow, denied social contact with their kind and reduced to a contemplation of their boresome and frustrated lives,
seek such release as they can find. Maria manages to extract
some pleasure from a restrained but sympathetic affair with Lieut.-
Col. Vershinin, but Olga and Irina are less fortunate. When the
regiment is ordered away the lives of the three sisters sink back
into the former dullness.

(Closed October 21, 1939)

* THE MAN WHO CAME TO DINNER

(288 performances)

A comedy in three acts by Moss Hart and George Kaufman.
Produced by Sam H. Harris at the Music Box, New York, October 16, 1939.

Cast of characters—

Mrs. Ernest W. Stanley.......................Virginia Hammond
Miss Preen...Mary Wickes

Richard Stanley...............................Gordon Merrick
June Stanley..................................Barbara Wooddell
John..George Probert
Sarah.................................Mrs. Priestley Morrison
Mrs. Dexter...................................Barbara Adams
Mrs. McCutcheon...............................Edmonia Nolley
Mr. Stanley...................................George Lessey
Maggie Cutler.................................Edith Atwater
Dr. Bradley...................................Dudley Clements
Sheridan Whiteside............................Monty Woolley
Harriet Stanley...............................Ruth Vivian
Bert Jefferson................................Theodore Newton
Professor Metz................................LeRoi Operti
Mr. Baker.....................................Carl Johnson
Expressman....................................Harold Woolf
Lorraine Sheldon..............................Carol Goodner
Sandy...Michael Harvey
Beverly Carlton...............................John Hoysradt
Wescott.......................................Edward Fisher
Radio Technicians............................ { Rodney Stewart
                                               { Carl Johnson
Banjo...David Burns
Deputies..................................... { Curtis Karpe
                                               { Phil Sheridan
Plainclothes Man..............................William Postance
  Luncheon Guests: Phil Sheridan, Charles Washington, William
    Postance.
  Six Young Boys: Daniel Leone, Jack Whitman, Daniel Landon,
    Donald Landon, DeWitt Purdue, Robert Rea.
  Acts I, II and III.—Home of Mr. and Mrs. Stanley in a Small
Town in Ohio.
  Staged by George S. Kaufman; setting by Donald Oenslager.

See page 179.

LADIES AND GENTLEMEN

(105 performances)

A play in two acts by Charles MacArthur and Ben Hecht from
a play by L. Bush-Fekete. Produced by Gilbert Miller at the
Martin Beck Theatre, New York, October 17, 1939.

Cast of characters—

A Bailiff.....................................Harry Antrim
Purdey..Frank Conlan
Van Duren.....................................James Seeley
Pettijohn.....................................George Watts
Herz..Martin Wolfson
The Sheriff...................................William Lynn
Patullo.......................................Pat Harrington
Butterworth...................................Joseph Sweeney
Ward..Roy Roberts
Reynolds......................................Robert Keith
Mrs. Wolfe....................................Edna West
Mrs. Bradford.................................Evelyn Varden
Mrs. Moore....................................Jacqueline Paige
Miss Scott....................................Helen Hayes
Mrs. Rudd.....................................Connie Gilchrist
Campbell......................................Philip Merivale
Hutchinson....................................Donald Mackenzie
George..Guy Monypenny
  Act I.—Scene 1—Hotel Sitting Room in Los Angeles. 2—Bedroom.
3—Balcony. Act II.—Scene 1—A Mountain Top. 2 and 3—The
Jury Room.

Staged by Charles MacArthur and Lewis Allen; settings by Boris Aronson.

Miss Scott, secretary to a motion picture magnate in Hollywood, is drawn on a jury that is to try a popular novelist for the murder of his wife. The wife had been pushed off a cliff on Mount Wilson. The prosecution contends the novelist wanted to marry his secretary. Miss Scott does not believe the novelist, being the writer he is, could have committed the crime. The other jurors are pretty much against her, including the middle-aged foreman, Campbell. During the course of the trial Miss Scott wins the opposing jurors over, one by one, and falls in love with Campbell and he with her. Campbell is married and the father of two children. In the end Miss Scott sends him back to his family.

(Closed January 13, 1940)

TOO MANY GIRLS

(249 performances)

A musical comedy in two acts by George Marion, Jr.; lyrics by Lorenz Hart; music by Richard Rodgers. Produced by George Abbott at the Imperial Theatre, New York, October 18, 1939.

Cast of characters—

First Robin Hood	Robert Arnold
Second Robin Hood	James Wilkinson
Third Robin Hood	Romolo Di Spirito
Fourth Robin Hood	William Mende
Clint Kelley	Richard Kollmar
Mrs. Tewksbury	Ivy Scott
Manuelito	Desi Arnaz
First Co-Ed	Mildred Law
Second Co-Ed	Leonor Sola
Third Co-Ed	La Verne Lupton
Fourth Co-Ed	Diane Sinclair
Fifth Co-Ed	Key Taylor
Sixth Co-Ed	Vera Fern
Jojo Jordan	Eddie Bracken
Al Terwilliger	Hal LeRoy
Harvey Casey	Clyde Fillmore
Mr. Lister	Hans Robert
Consuelo Casey	Marcy Wescott
Sheriff Andaluz	Byron Shores
Eileen Eilers	Mary Jane Walsh
Talullah Lou	Leila Ernst
Student	Van Johnson
Pepe	Diosa Costello
Beverly Waverly	James MacColl
Deputy Sheriff	Willis Duncan
Cowboy	Edison Rice
Hawker	Harry Jackson

Act I.—Prologue—The Road to the Hunted Stag. Scene 1—The Hunted Stag, an Old Colonial Tavern near Skowhegan, Maine. 2—Gate in Front of Pottawatomie College, Stop Gap, New Mexico. Before Term Begins. 3 and 4—Campus of Pottawatomie College. Act II.—Scene 1—A Road near the College. 2—A Belfry of Pot-

tawatomie College. 3—A Rock in the Desert. 4 and 5—The Campus.
Staged by George Abbott; settings by Jo Mielziner; dances by Robert Alton; costumes by Raoul Pene Du Bois.

Harvey Casey, big business tycoon, decides to send his rebellious daughter, Consuelo, to Pottawatomie College at Stop Gap,
N. M. To guarantee her protection he engages four former All-
American football players to go along and, unknown to Consuelo,
serve her as a sort of bodyguard. At Pottawatomie the football
players get mixed up with the college eleven and Consuelo falls
in love with one of them. The day of the big game she discovers
that she has been watched and orders the boys back East. Compromise and kisses.

(Closed May 18, 1940)

THE POSSESSED

(14 performances)

A drama in fifteen scenes by George Shdanoff, based on ideas
from writings of Fyodor Dostoyevsky, translated by Elizabeth
Reynolds Hapgood. Produced by Chekhov Theatre Productions,
Inc., at the Lyceum Theatre, New York, October 24, 1939.

Cast of characters—

Nicholas Stavrogin	John Flynn
Peter Verkhovenski	Woodrow Chambliss
The Governor	Burke Clarke
Lisa	Beatrice Straight
Lieutenant Drosdov	Peter Tunnard
Shatov	Blair Cutting
Mrs. Stavrogin	Ellen Van Volkenburg
Martha	Mary Lou Taylor
A Servant at Mrs. Stavrogin's	Thomas J. Hughes, Jr.
Kirilov	Hugh Hatfield
Fedka	Sam Schatz

People at the Meeting:

Presiding Officer	Ronald Bennett
A Theorist	Sam Schatz
A Teacher	Thomas J. Hughes, Jr.

Other Members of Verkhovenski's Organization:

Erika Chambliss	J. P. Corr
Louis Dowdney	Eugene Langston
Jeanne Elgart	Ford Rainey
Mary Haynsworth	Allen Reeves
Dierdre Hurst	James Taylor
Donald Bouche	

Governor's Secretary	Bert Griscom
Officer	Alonzo Hinkley
The Stranger	Reginald Pole

Part I.—Scene 1—Outskirts of Industrial Town, Somewhere
Abroad. 2—Drawing Room in Stavrogin's Home. 3—Room of
Shatov and Kirilov. 4, 7 and 8—Stavrogin's Study. 5—Martha's
Room. 6—On a Bridge. Part II.—Scene 9—A Meeting Room.
10—Governor's Office. 11—Stavrogin's Country House. 12—Room
of Shatov and Kirilov., 13—Stavrogin's Study. 14—The Stranger's
Room. 15—A Deserted Part of Town.
Staged by Michael Chekhov; settings by M. Dobujinsky.

Nicholas Stavrogin, a moderate revolutionary, would take things slowly in plunging the world into a fight for the overthrow of organized government. His friend and sinister counselor, Peter Verkhovenski, would urge him to take a more direct and dangerous course. Between them they inspire a general discussion of revolutionary theories as they are found in the works of Fyodor Dostoyevsky.

(Closed November 4, 1939)

CURE FOR MATRIMONY

(27 performances)

A comedy in three acts by Paul F. Treichler. Produced by Producers Theatre, Inc. (from Antioch College, Antioch, Ohio), at the Provincetown Playhouse, New York, October 25, 1939.

Cast of characters—

Anthony	Marshall Jamison
Paula	Priscilla Jamison
Maxine	Jemison McBride
Louis	Cleveland Thomas
Mona	Audrey Benton
Timothy	Arthur Lithgow
George	David Dempsey
Benjamin	Edward Fitzpatrick
Flora	Rita Benson
Millikan	Paul H. Rohmann
Miss Peikenpepper	Evelyn Evers
First Seaman	Junes Eddy
Second Seaman	Walter Dewey
Archbishop Castlebridge	Richard Cahill

Acts I, II and III.—An Island Off the Coast of Maine.
Staged by Ad Karns; setting by Melville Bernstein; costumes by Dolaro Belasco.

A psychiatrist husband, seeking to discover by experiment whether man is by nature a monogamous or polygamous animal, hypnotizes three of his male acquaintances to observe their behavior toward his wife and three of his wife's girl friends to study their actions toward himself. He all but loses his wife, not to mention his honor, and is content in the end to return to a conventional married life.

(Closed November 25, 1939)

THE TIME OF YOUR LIFE

(185 performances)

A comedy in three acts by William Saroyan. Produced by the Theatre Guild, Inc., in association with Eddie Dowling at the Booth Theatre, New York, October 25, 1939.

Cast of characters—

Newsboy	Ross Bagdasarian
Drunk	John Farrell
Willie	Will Lee
Joe	Eddie Dowling
Nick	Charles De Sheim
Tom	Edward Andrews
Kitty Duval	Julie Haydon
Dudley	Curt Conway
Harry	Gene Kelly
Wesley	Reginald Beane
Lorene	Nene Vibber
Blick	Grover Burgess
Arab	Houseley Stevens, Sr.
Mary L.	Celeste Holme
Krupp	William Bendix
McCarthy	Tom Tully
Kit Carson	Len Doyle
Nick's Ma	Michelette Burani
Sailor	Randolph Wade
Elsie	Cathie Bailey
A Killer	Evelyn Geller
Her Side Kick	Mary Cheffey
A Society Lady	Eva Leonard Boyne
A Society Gentleman	Ainsworth Arnold
First Cop	Randolph Wade
Second Cop	John Farrell

Acts I and III.—Nick's Pacific Street Saloon, Restaurant and Entertainment Place at Foot of the Embracadero, San Francisco. Act II.—Scenes 1 and 3—Nick's Saloon. 2—Room in New York Hotel, San Francisco.

Staged by Eddie Dowling and William Saroyan under supervision of Theresa Helburn and Lawrence Langner; settings by Watson Barratt.

See page 250.

(Closed April 6, 1940)

PASTORAL

(14 performances)

A comedy in three acts by Victor Wolfson. Produced by Bonfils and Somnes at the Henry Miller Theatre, New York, November 1, 1939.

Cast of characters—

Wonderful Glory	Georgette Harvey
Sam Ten Brock	Charles Lang
Larry	John Philliber
Ingeborg	Ruth Weston
Genko	John Banner
Keena	Virginia Campbell
Brink	William Nichols
Angela	Judy Parrish
Reef Tabanian	Cornel Wilde
Father Blodgett	Morton L. Stevens
Dick	Dick Wade
Ella May	Elnora Blum
Jimmie	James Waters
Sara Ten Brock	Frieda Altman
Mr. Grewsome	Wallace Acton
Willie	Wilton Graff

Acts I, II and III.—Living Room at Ingeborg's and Genko's Farmhouse in Foothills of the Catskills.

Staged by George Somnes; setting by John Root.

For nine years Ingeborg and Genko, she the mother of a grown son and daughter, he the captain of a Bulgarian gunboat she met in Europe, have been living in "beautiful sin," mostly on the allowances Ingeborg's husband sends for the care of the children. Now they are trying to start a chicken farm in the Catskills. Some of the neighbors are shocked. Others are amused. Ingeborg and Genko don't care. When Ingeborg's husband arrives with the news that he had divorced Ingeborg five years before in Paris it looks as though the lovers would have to marry.

(Closed November 11, 1939)

SUMMER NIGHT

(4 performances)

A drama in two acts by Vicki Baum and Benjamin Glazer. Produced by Lewis E. Gensler at the St. James Theatre, New York, November 2, 1939.

Cast of characters—

The Roving Reporter	Martin Blaine
Barker	Sidney Stone
The Biggest Girl	Wilna Hervey
The Littlest Man	Herman Ergotti
Melvyn Lockhart	Wesley Addy
Speed	Howard Da Silva
Photographer	Leonard Bremen
Jake	Lionel Stander
George Cooper	Gage Clarke
Blanche Cooper	Helen Flint
John B. Bingham	Louis Calhern
Marion Bingham	Violet Heming
Mona	Rita Rhoni
First Picket	Harold Bolton
Second Picket	Charles Furcolowe
Mama Rosario	Josephine Victor
Ginger	Susan Fox
Pat	Boyd Crawford
Pinkey	Lewis Charles
Dance Judge	Peter Cusanelli
Doctor	Lyle Bettger
Nurses	{ Marion O'Brien { Virginia Stevens
Croupier	Guy Standing
Manager	Edmund Dorsey
Bartender	Clancy Cooper
Interne	Stephen Roberts
Policeman	Robert Rhodes
Detective	Tony Kraber

Marathon Couples: Polly Smiley, Peter Leeds, Dortha Brinsfield, Eric Efron, Adele Jerome, Archie King, Rebecca Rowen, Martin Greene.

Act I.—Scene 1—Pacific Park. 2—Mama Rosario's. 3—The Corridor. 4—The Dormitory. 5—The Marathon. Act II.—Scene 1—The Dormitory. 2—The Pier. 3—The Gambling Ship. 4—Pacific Park.

Staged by Lee Strasberg; settings and lighting by Robert Edmond Jones.

Ginger and Pat have been trying to win a marathon dance so they can marry, but Pat collapses. Ginger thinks to take on a movie star temporarily to help her into the movies. The movie star, Melvyn Lockhart, is willing, because of the publicity, but he is also involved with a society lady named Blanche Cooper, whose husband, a banker, is about to embrace bankruptcy. Also suicide. At the river's edge Cooper meets Pat, who is also thinking of ending it all. They call off the suicide and go to a gambling ship where another of Ginger's former friends, an ex-convict, shoots the movie actor. The banker's wife decides to go back to the banker and give him her jewels toward a new start. Ginger and Pat get a break.

(Closed November 4, 1939)

MARGIN FOR ERROR

(264 performances)

A drama in two acts by Clare Boothe. Produced by Richard Aldrich and Richard Myers at the Plymouth Theatre, New York, November 3, 1939.

Cast of characters—

```
Baron Max von Alvenstor.......................Bramwell Fletcher
Officer Finkelstein.................................. Sam Levene
Frieda .............................................Evelyn Wahle
Dr. Jennings.......................................Bert Lytell
Sophie Baumer......................................Elspeth Eric
Karl Baumer.................................Otto L. Preminger
Otto Horst........................................Matt Briggs
Thomas Denny....................................Leif Erickson
Captain Mulrooney............................Edward McNamara
      Acts I and II.—Library of German Consul in American City Prior
to 1939.
      Staged by Otto Preminger; setting by Donald Oenslager.
```

See page 317.

(Closed June 15, 1940)

SEA DOGS

(16 performances)

A melodrama in three acts by Wilson Starbuck. Produced by Clarence Taylor at the Maxine Elliott Theatre, New York, November 6, 1939.

Cast of characters—

```
Macarthur, Second Mate.........................Robert Williams
Johnson, Able Bodied Seaman......................Sandy Strouse
```

Smith, Able Bodied Seaman...........................John Gage
Daily, Chief Mate..................................Russell Hardie
Stevens, Wireless Operator........................Barton Hepburn
Captain Wickford...............................Joseph Macaulay
Thomas, Ordinary Seaman.......................James McCallion
Bosun...Roderick Maybee
Jojo, Officers' Messman...........................Richard Wang
Mickey Walsh, Able Bodied Seaman.................Ben Lackland
Gus, Able Bodied Seaman........................Aage Steenshorne
Third Assistant Engineer............................Grant Mills
First Assistant Engineer........................Robert J. Mulligan
Brewster, Third Mate...........................William Mowry
Chief Engineer.......................................John Robb
Captain Knowles..................................Stanley Jessup
Edward Bingham..................................James Todd
Gibson ....Jack Gilchrist
    Sailors: Carl Boyden, Lawrence Cosby, Brandon Kealeigh, Philip
    Beeche.
    Act I.—Deck of S.S. *Bellmead*. Act II.—Scene 1—Radio Shack.
2—Dining Salon. Act III.—Scene 1—Deck. 2—Dining Salon.
    Staged by Melville Burke; settings by John Root.

The one time good ship *Bellmead* is on her way north from
Capetown. There is a fire in the hold. There is a reform school
fugitive aboard with an infected hand. The captain is drunk and
the crew is on the point of mutiny. Daily, chief mate, decides
on action. He will operate on the infected hand, even though he
has to knock out the captain to do it. He will summon help if
necessary. And he does. The *Bellmead* limps into the last act,
the captain is arrested as a smuggler of narcotics, the fugitive
dies and Daily marries the fugitive's sister, to whom he was engaged all the time.

(Closed November 18, 1939)

*LIFE WITH FATHER

(257 performances)

A comedy in three acts adapted by Howard Lindsay and Russel
Crouse from a book and essays by Clarence Day. Produced by
Oscar Serlin at the Empire Theatre, New York, November 8, 1939.

Cast of characters—

Vinnie...Dorothy Stickney
Annie..Katherine Bard
Clarence..................................John Drew Devereaux
John ....Richard Simon
Whitney...Raymond Roe
Harlan..Larry Robinson
Father..Howard Lindsay
Margaret.......................................Dorothy Bernard
Cora ....Ruth Hammond
Mary..Teresa Wright
The Rev. Dr. Lloyd............................Richard Sterling
Delia...Portia Morrow
Nora...Nellie Burt
Dr. Humphreys..................................A. H. Van Buren
Dr. Sommers.....................................John C. King

Maggie..Timothy Kearse
    Acts I, II and III.—Morning Room of Day House on Madison
Avenue, New York City, 1880.
    Staged by Bretaigne Windust; setting and costumes by Stewart
Chaney.

See page 142.

THUNDER ROCK

(23 performances)

A drama in three acts by Robert Ardrey. Produced by the
Group Theatre, Inc., at the Mansfield Theatre, New York, November 14, 1939.

Cast of characters—

Streeter......................................Myron McCormick
Nonny..Harry Bratsburg
Inspector Flanning.............................Roman Bohnen
Charleston.......................................Luther Adler
Captain Joshua..............................Morris Carnovsky
Briggs...Art Smith
Dr. Stefan Kurtz................................Lee J. Cobb
Melanie......................................Frances Farmer
Miss Kirby.......................................Ruth Nelson
Anne Marie......................................Mary Fowler
Chang..Robert Lewis
Cassidy..Phil Brown
    Acts I, II and III.—Interior Room of Lighthouse on Thunder Rock,
a speck of an Island in Northern Lake Michigan.
    Staged by Elia Kazan; setting by Mordecai Gorelik; lighting by
Michael Gordon; costumes by Paul Morrison.

Out of college Charleston, grown radical, determines to retire
from a messy world and go to work as a lighthouse attendant on
Thunder Rock, where he will see no one from month's end to
month's end. In his solitude he creates a ghost world of his own,
bringing back to life several of the passengers and crew of a ship
that had foundered on Thunder Rock in 1849. Living with them
in his imagination, following them through their crises, Charleston
discovers that the world of 1849 was little more satisfactory than
that of 1939. There had been great improvement in the condition
of the people in the ninety years intervening, and there promises
to be greater improvement in the ninety years to follow. It is his
place, he decides, to come out of his solitude and take up the fight
for liberty and democracy.

(Closed December 2, 1939)

THE BEST PLAYS OF 1939-40

VERY WARM FOR MAY

(59 performances)

A musical comedy in two acts by Jerome Kern and Oscar Hammerstein 2nd. Produced by Max Gordon at the Alvin Theatre, New York, November 17, 1939.

Cast of characters—

William Graham	Donald Brian
Jackson	Avon Long
May Graham	Grace McDonald
Johnny Graham	Jack Whiting
Kenny	Ray Mayer
Raymond Sibley	Robert Shackelton
Sonny Spofford	Richard Quine
Liz Spofford	Frances Mercer
Lowell Pennyfeather	Max Showalter
Ogdon Quiler	Hiram Sherman
Jethro Hancock	William Torpey
Winnie Spofford	Eve Arden
Beamish	Len Mence
Schlessinger	Seldon Bennett
Electrician	Bruce Evans

Members of the Ogdon Quiler Progressive Workshop: Susan, Vera Ellen; Smoothy, Don Loper; Honey, Maxine Barrat; Mr. Pratt, Frank Egan; Jane, Evelyn Thawl; Sylvia, Kate Friedlich; Mr. Magee, Peter Chambers; Miss Wasserman, Virginia Card; Miss Hyde, Kay Picture; Walter, Walter Long; Carroll, Hollace Shaw; Charles, Ralph Magalssen; Pam, Pamela Randell; Alice, Marie Louise Quevli; Helen, Helena Bliss; Dolores, Dolores Anderson; Beulah, Beulah Blake; Andre, Andre Charise; Louis, Louis Hightower; Sally, Sally Craven; Jack, Jack Seymour; Webb, Webb Tilton; Peter, Jack Wilson; Bill, William Collins; Eleanor, Eleanor Eberle; Helen, Helen Donovan; Rudy, Rudy Miller; Ethel, Ethel Lynn; June, June Allyson; Claire, Caire Harvey; Billie, Billie Wirth; Miriam, Miriam Franklyn.

Matty Malneck's Orchestra: Alvin, Matty Malneck; O'Cedar, Milton Delugg; Homer, Charles Marlowe; Marshal, Marshal Fisher; Ralph, Ralph Hansell; Joseph, Joseph Quintile; Jean, Jean Plummer; Russ, Russ Morhoff.

Act I.—Scene 1—The Graham Home, Great Neck, Long Island. 2—Winnie's Barn. Act II.—Scene 1—Terrace of Winnie's Home. 2 and 4—Corner of Winnie's Barn Theatre. 3 and 5—Stage of Winnie's Barn Theatre.

Staged by Oscar Hammerstein 2nd and Vincente Minnelli; dances by Albertina Rasch; settings by Minnelli; music directed by Robert Emmett Dolan.

May Graham, the singing and dancing daughter of showfolk, wants to leave school and go on the stage. Her father, a retired comedian, and her brother, a playwright and producer, say she can't. May runs away and joins a barn theatre enterprise. Her family finds her and she is forgiven in time for the finale.

(Closed January 6, 1940)

THE WORLD WE MAKE

(80 performances)

A drama in three acts by Sidney Kingsley based on Millen Brand's novel, "The Outward Room." Produced by Sidney Kingsley at the Guild Theatre, New York, November 20, 1939.

Cast of characters—

Dr. Schiller	Rudolph Forster
Head Nurse	Louise Huntington
Nurse Regis	Dagmar Hampf
Virginia McKay	Margo
Mrs. McKay	Zolya Talma
Mr. McKay	Carroll Ashburn
First Laundry Truckman	Frank Richards
Second Laundry Truckman	Erwin Edwards
Third Laundry Truckman	Jerome Thor
Modesto	Nick Dennis
Morris, the Marker	Solen Burry
Cora	Bonnie Roberts
Jim Kohler	Joseph Pevney
John Kohler	Herbert Rudley
Louis, the Foreman	Harold Gary
Boss	Albert Vees
Ruth	Ruth Sherrill
Rosebud	Billie Haywood
Pearl	Katherine Murphy
Rocco	Tito Vuolo
Mary	Daga Hammond
Mrs. Zubriski	Kasia Orzaweski
Mr. Zubriski	Harold Stone
Anna	Thelma Schnee
Neighbor	Louise Huntington
Renting Agent	Lee Harrett
Sally	Eve March
Danny	Buddy Swan
Janch	Eric Roberts
Al	James O'Rear
Neighbor	Randolph Preston

Laundry Workers: Florence Redd, Eloise Bouldin, Mildred Truppo, May King, Dagmar Hampf.

Prologue.—Greendale Sanitarium. Act I.—Scene 1—World-Wide Laundry. 2 and 3—John Kohler's Flat. Acts II and III.—John Kohler's Flat.

Staged by Sidney Kingsley; settings by Harry Horner.

See page 110.

(Closed January 27, 1940)

ARIES IS RISING

(7 performances)

A comedy in three acts by Caroline North and Earl Blackwell. Produced by Harry R. Irving and Michael Dolan at the Golden Theatre, New York, November 21, 1939.

Cast of characters—

Aunt Lou	Frances Smith
Delivery Man	Arthur West
Madame Bernardi	Constance Collier
Martha Wood Baugh	Blanche Sweet
Roland Harris	John Craven
Mattie Kate Baugh	Mary Mason
Gladys Gay	Bernadine Hayes
Bruce Prince	George Carleton
Sammy	Edmund Dorsay
Miss Pritchard	Victoria Horne
Maxine	Evelyn Barrows
Denise	Ariane Allen
Nick Mikalos	Charles La Torre
Mrs. Baxter	Aileen Poe
Shirley Baxter	Carmina Cansino
Ted	Cledge Roberts
Bill Cask	Frederick Howard
Gus	Lathrop Mitchell
Charlie	Edmond Le Comte
A Waiter	Sam Elberton
Jerry Walker	Ruth Holden
Jake	Clifford Dunstan
The Hon. Emery Howlett	Morton L. Stevens

Act I.—Living Room of Apartment in Converted Brownstone House in West Fifties, New York City. Act II.—Scene 1—Offices of Acropolis and Banner Picture Companies, Radio City. 2—Living Room of Brownstone House. Act III.—Living Room in Villa of Garden of Allah, Hollywood, California.

Staged by Robert Ross; settings by Nicholas Yellenti.

Martha Wood Baugh and her daughter, Mattie Kate Baugh, come up from the South, hoping to get a screen test for Mattie in New York. To help with a little publicity Roland Harris, a reporter in love with Mattie, prints a story that Mattie, disguised, has been serving as a page boy in the senate at Washington. In the resulting excitement Mattie is screen-tested and accepted. When she gets to Hollywood it is discovered that she is dumber than expected and it is her mother, Martha, who is the real desire of the screen executives. Madame Bernardi, astrologist and seer, floats in and out of the plot with prophecies.

(Closed November 25, 1939)

RING TWO

(5 performances)

A comedy in three acts by Gladys Hurlbut. Produced by George Abbott at the Henry Miller Theatre, New York, November 22, 1939.

Cast of characters—

Maggie Brown	Edith Van Cleve
Grant	William Swetland
Nellie	Maxine Stuart
Mary Carr	June Walker
Michael Carr	Paul McGrath

THE BEST PLAYS OF 1939-40   415

```
Peggy Carr.........................................Gene  Tierney
Durward  Nesbitt...................................Tom  Powers
Rosa Romero.......................................Betty  Field
White ............................................Richard  Gregg
Emma.............................................Marietta  Canty
Butch  Martin.....................................James  Corner
Dopey  Clark......................................William  Blees
Julian............................................Louis  Smith
The Two Chocolate Drops..................  { William  Stapleton
                                          { Willamae  Stapleton
```
Acts I, II and III.—Living Room of Mary Carr's Renovated
Farmhouse in Connecticut Hills.
Staged by George Abbott; setting by John Root.

Mary Carr is a popular actress now retired and divorced. She
buys a place in the country in the hope of achieving peace of mind.
Immediately she is overrun with guests, including her ex-husband,
her ex-leading man, her husband's daughter, her leading man's
newest affair, her booking agent and an assortment of here-today-
but-gone-tomorrow servants. In a week-end crisis there is a
blizzard, the ex-husband gets lost in the snow and Mary discovers that she still loves him. A reconciliation follows.

(Closed November 25, 1939)

I KNOW WHAT I LIKE

(11 performances)

A comedy in three acts by Justin Sturm. Produced by T. Edward
Hambleton and Richard Skinner at the Hudson Theatre, New
York, November 24, 1939.

Cast of characters—
```
Thurston........................................Doe Doe Green
Miss Steel...................................Virginia Chauvenet
Mr. Holden.......................................Gage  Clarke
Sir Arthur Keswick............................Reynolds  Evans
Karl Hedstrom......................................John  Beal
Sandra Page.......................................Helen  Claire
Heming...........................................Frank  Brown
Larner .........................................William  Hansen
Rita .............................................Haila  Stoddard
Harvey Van Ingen.............................Edmund  George
Charles........................................Edward  Broadley
```
Act I.—Scene 1—Holden's Art Gallery. 2—Karl's Studio. Act
II.—Karl's Studio. Act III.—Sandra's Home.
Staged by Auriol Lee; settings by Donald Oenslager.

Karl Hedstrom is a struggling young artist with a great talent
but little patience. Meeting the richly favored Sandra Page, and
needing money to court her, Karl agrees to copy an El Greco for
$1,500, which a crooked broker tries to pass off on Sandra as
genuine. When it comes down to cases Karl confesses the hoax
and is miserable, but Sandra throws over her banker lover and
marries Karl.
(Closed December 2, 1939)

KEY LARGO

(105 performances)

A drama in prologue and two acts by Maxwell Anderson. Produced by The Playwrights' Company at the Ethel Barrymore Theatre, New York, November 27, 1939.

Cast of characters—

Victor d'Alcala	Jose Ferrer
Nimmo	Charles Ellis
Jerry	James Gregory
Monte	Alfred Etcheverry
King McCloud	Paul Muni
Sheriff Gash	Ralph Theodore
D'Alcala	Harold Johnsrud
Alegre d'Alcala	Uta Hagen
Gage	Crahan Denton
Corky	Richard Cowdery
Murillo	Frederic Tozere
Hunk	Carl Malden
Priscilla	Eve Abbott
Killarney	Ruth March
Mrs. Aaronson	Goldie Hannelin
Mr. Aaronson	Richard Bishop
Mrs. Wheeler	Ethel Jackson
Mr. Wheeler	Richard Barbee
Osceola Horn	William Challee
First Man Tourist	John Fearnley
First Woman Tourist	Norma Millay
Second Woman Tourist	Helen Carroll
John Horn	Averell Harris
Sam	Hudson Shotwell

Prologue.—A Hilltop in Spain, January, 1939. Act I.—A Wharf on Key Largo, Florida. Act II.—The Interior of D'Alcala's House.
Staged by Guthrie McClintic; settings by Jo Mielsiner.

See page 67.

(Closed February 24, 1940)

FARM OF THREE ECHOES

(48 performances)

A drama in three acts by Noel Langley. Produced by Victor Payne-Jennings and Arthur Hopkins at the Cort Theatre, New York, November 28, 1939.

Cast of characters—

Ouma Gerart	Ethel Barrymore
Lisha Gerart	Ann Dere
Jan Gerart	Dean Jagger
Isaac Gerart	McKay Morris
Saul Portenaar	Eduard Franz
Logenhoofen	Victor Esker
Naomi deMeer	Priscilla Newton
Dyke Hesse	John Griggs
Marie Hesse	Nancy Sheridan

Acts I, II and III.—Living Room of the Farmhouse, Orange Free State, South Africa.
Staged by Arthur Hopkins; setting by Cirker and Robbins.

Ouma Gerart, who has lived all her life on a South African farm, is 97 years old and still alert. When she was younger and could no longer stand the brutal treatment of her husband she slipped a loaded shell into a gun he was cleaning and he blew his head off. Now her daughter-in-law, Lisha, is having husband trouble with her brutal mate, Isaac Gerart. She cuts his saddle girth, his horse pitches him off and he breaks his neck. Comes Jan Gerart, Ouma's grandson, and, knowing what he knows, he is reluctant to marry the orphaned Naomi deMeer for fear, if he becomes cruel, she will also do away with him. It takes considerable drama to bring Jan and Naomi together.

(Closed January 6, 1940)

SWINGIN' THE DREAM

(13 performances)

A musical variation of Shakespeare's "A Midsummer Night's Dream" by Gilbert Seldes and Erik Charell; music by Jimmy Van Heusen; lyrics by Eddie de Lange. Produced by Erik Charell at the Center Theatre, New York, November 29, 1939.

Cast of characters—

Majordomo	Herman Green
Theodore, Governor of Louisiana	Joseph Holland
Polly	Ruth Ford
Crimson	Catheryn Laughlin
Egbert	George LeSoir
Gloria	Eleanor Lynn
	(Courtesy of the Group Theatre)
Cornelius	Thomas Coley
Alexander	Boyd Crawford
Helena	Dorothy McGuire
Starveling	Nicodemus
Quince	Jackie Mabley
Snug	Gerald de la Fontaine
Snout	Troy Brown
Flute	Oscar Polk
Bottom	Louis Armstrong
Peaceful Pearl	Alberta Perkins
Puck	Butterfly McQueen
First Pixie	Vivian Danbridge
Second Pixie	Dorothy Danbridge
Third Pixie	Etta Danbridge
Titania	Maxine Sullivan
Drummer Boy	Sunny Payne
Oberon	Juan Hernandez

Players in the Opera "Pyramus and Thisbe"

Prologue (Quince)	Jackie Mabley
Pyramus (Bottom)	Louis Armstrong
Thisbe (Flute)	Oscar Polk
Wall (Snout)	Troy Brown
Moon (Starveling)	Nicodemus
Lion (Snug)	Gerald de la Fontaine
Cupid	Bill Bailey

The Benny Goodman Sextet: Benny Goodman, Clarinet; Lionel Hampton, Vibraharp; Fletcher Henderson, Piano; Charles Chris-

tian, Guitar; Arthur Bernstein, Bass; Nick Fatool, Drums.
Bud Freeman & the Summa Cum Laude: Bud Freeman, Saxo-
phone; Max Kaminsky, Cornet; Peewee Russell, Clarinet; Eddie
Condon, Guitar; Brad Gowan, Valve Trombone; Dave Bowman,
Piano; Sidney Catlett, Drums.
Specialties: Bill Bailey: Dancer. The Danbridge Sisters: Dorothy,
Etta and Vivian. The Rhythmettes: Alberta Perkins, Cora Parks,
Anna Mae Fritz. The Deep River Boys: George Lawson, Harry
Douglas, Vernon Gardner, Edward Ware.
Act I.—The Governor's Summer Residence, New Orleans, 1890.
Act II.—Scene 1—Voodoo Wood. 2—Governor's Summer Residence.
Staged by Erik Charell; dialogue directed by Philip Loeb; dances
by Agnes de Mille; jitterbugs by Herbert White; swing choir by Lyn
Murray; settings after Walt Disney cartoons by Herbert Andrews
and Walter Jageman; music supervised by Benny Goodman and Don
Voorhees.

In the "swing" version of "A Midsummer Night's Dream" it is
the Governor of Louisiana, living in New Orleans in 1890, for
whom the revels are staged by Bully Bottom and his crew of
simple artisans. The lovers are put under the fairies' spell in a
voodoo wood and a colored Puck circles the world and brings back
a flit gun with which to work Titania's magic.

(Closed December 9, 1939)

MORNING'S AT SEVEN

(44 performances)

A comedy in three acts by Paul Osborn. Produced by Dwight
Deere Wiman at the Longacre Theatre, New York, November 30,
1939.

Cast of characters—

Theodore Swanson..............................Thomas Chalmers
Cora Swanson......................................Jean Adair
Aaronetta Gibbs...................................Dorothy Gish
Ida Bolton.......................................Kate McComb
Carl Bolton.....................................Russell Collins
Homer Bolton....................................John Alexander
Myrtle Brown......................................Enid Markey
Esther Crampton..................................Effie Shannon
David Crampton...................................Herbert Yost
    Acts I, II and III.—Two Backyards in an American Town.
    Staged by Joshua Logan; setting by Jo Mielziner.

See page 350.

(Closed January 6, 1940)

HAMLET

(40 performances)

A tragedy in three acts (in its entirety) by William Shakespeare.
(Incidental music by Lehman Engel.) Revived by Maurice Evans
at the 44th Street Theatre, New York, December 4, 1939.

Cast of characters—

Francisco	Lauren Gilbert
Bernardo	John McQuade
Marcellus	Donald Cameron
Horatio	Donald Randolph
Claudius, King of Denmark	Henry Edwards
Gertrude, Queen of Denmark	Mady Christians
Hamlet	Maurice Evans
Polonius, Lord Chamberlain	Raymond Johnson
Laertes	Sidney Smith
Voltimand	Walter Williams
Cornelius	Frederic Carney
A Page	Kurt Richards
Ophelia	Katherine Locke
Ghost of Hamlet's Father	John Barclay
Reynaldo	Henry Jones
Rosencrantz	Lauren Gilbert
Guildenstern	Emmett Rogers
Player King	Rhys Williams
Player Queen	Kurt Richards
Third Player	John McQuade
Fourth Player	Howard Wierum
A Lady in Waiting	Jackson Perkins
Fortinbras, Prince of Norway	John Barclay
A Captain	Alfred Paschall
A Gentleman	George Keane
Two Sailors	Alfred Paschall / John McQuade
A Grave-Digger	Rhys Williams
Second Grave-Digger	Henry Jones
A Priest	Walter Williams
Osric	Maury Tuckerman
Ambassadors, from England	George Keane / Emmett Rogers

Lords, Ladies, Soldiers and Attendants: Constance Friend, Jackson Perkins, June Brown, Jess Dimond, Frederic Carney, George Keane, Alfred Paschall, Melvin Parks, John McQuade, Alexander Nicol and Howard Wierum.

Act I.—Scenes 1, 4 and 5—Platform before the Castle of Elsinore, Denmark. 2—Room of State in Castle. 3 and 6—Polonius' House. 7 and 8—Rooms in the Castle. Act II.—Scene 1—Courtyard in Castle. 2—King's Apartments. 3—Queen's Apartments. 4—Room in Castle. 5—Corridor in Castle. 6—Frontiers of Denmark. Act III.—Scenes 1 and 5—Corridor in Castle. 3—Polonius' House. 4—A Churchyard. 6—Courtyard.

Staged by Margaret Webster; costumes and scenery by David Ffolkes.

Maurice Evans' first revival of the full-length "Hamlet" was staged at the St. James Theatre in New York, Oct. 12, 1938. In the Fall of 1939 he played in several mid-western cities before starting a return engagement at the 46th Street Theatre. Principal changes in cast were those of Raymond Johnson, playing Polonius, and Rhys Williams as the First Grave-Digger.

(Closed January 6, 1940)

FOREIGNERS

(7 performances)

A comedy in three acts by Frederick Lonsdale. Produced by Messrs. Shubert in association with Arch Selwyn at the Belasco Theatre, New York, December 5, 1939.

Cast of characters—

William..Harold de Becker
George...Leon Janney
Captain..J. Malcom Dunn
Spaniard......................................George Beban, Jr.
Bernstey..Richard Ainley
German.......................................George Macready
American.......................................Bertram Thorne
Russian..Ivan Triesault
Frenchman ....Guy De Vestel
Italian...............................Aristides Carlos de Leon
Irishman..Damian O'Flynn
Englishman ....Robert Craven
Jap ....Yoshiwara
The Girl...Martha Scott
Dutch Captain......................................John Cherry
    Act I.—Lounge Room of Small Steamer. Acts II and III.—An
Island.
    Staged by Reginald Bach; settings by Watson Barratt.

Bernstey, a Jew, finds himself a passenger on a small steamer, together with nine representatives of the leading nations of the world. There is much argument engendering hatreds and many threatened breaches of peace until the Captain of the steamer demands a complete disarming of the warring passengers. When the steamer strikes a rock and is wrecked on the shores of a small tropical island Bernstey recovers two of the guns and becomes dictator. A beautiful girl stowaway adds to the complications. Making her choice of a companion among them she favors the Irishman until a rescue is effected. Then she decides to stay on the island with the Jew.

(Closed December 9, 1939)

*DU BARRY WAS A LADY

(224 performances)

A musical comedy in two acts by B. G. De Sylva and Herbert Fields; music and lyrics by Cole Porter. Produced by B. G. De Sylva at the 46th Street Theatre, New York, December 6, 1939.

Cast of characters—

Jones ....Hugh Cameron
Bill Kelly...Walter Armin
Harry Norton..................................Charles Walters
Alice Barton......................................Betty Grable
Florian...Harold Cromer
Louis Blore..Bert Lahr
Vi Hennessey..................................Jean Moorehead
May Daly...Ethel Merman
Alex Barton.....................................Ronald Graham
Ann Barton..Kay Sutton
Manuel Gomez......................................Tito Renaldo
Charley ....Benny Baker

Four Internationals: Douglas Hawkins, Peter Holliday, Robert Herring, Carl Nicholas; Jack Stanton and Roy Ross.
Starlets of the Club Petite: Ann Todd, Geraldine Spreckels; Molly Wincor, Betty Allen; Sigana Sigan, Ann Graham; Ruth Frederic, Janice Carter; Peggy Brown, Jacqueline Franc; Mary Gray, Marguerite Benton.
Act I.—Scene 1—The Club Petite, New York. 2—Washroom at Club Petite. 3—Gardens of Petite Trianon. 4—Du Barry's Bed Chamber. 5—Outer Hall. 6—Salon at Petite Trianon. Act II.—Scene 1—Pavilion, Petite Trianon. 2—Outer Hall. 3—Room in Royal Apartment. 4—Club Petite, New York.
Staged by Edgar McGregor; dances by Robert Alton; settings and costumes by Raoul Pene Du Bois.

Louis Blore, attendant in the men's washroom of the Club Petite in New York, wins $75,000 in the Irish sweeps. Having long had his eye on the star of the floor show, May Daly, Louis seeks to win her away from Alex Barton, the young man to whom she is engaged. He thinks to put Alex away with knock-out drops, but gets his glasses mixed and takes the potion himself. During his delirium Louis dreams that he is Louis XIV and that May Daly is Du Barry, his mistress. His unsuccessful pursuit of May continues through the gardens and boudoirs of Versailles, but unsuccessfully.

THE WOMAN BROWN

(11 performances)

A drama in two acts by Dorothy Cumming. Produced by Margaret Hewes at the Biltmore Theatre, New York, December 8, 1939.

Cast of characters—

Reverend Mr. Shell	Oswald Marshall
Nurse Turnbull	Helen Trenholme
Lizzie Piggott	Daisy Belmore
Johnnie Smith	Buddy Buehler
Mrs. Goodberry	Jessamine Newcombe
Ken Sutter	Colin Keith-Johnston
Mary Brown	Franciska Gaal
Policeman Smith	Ralph Sumpter
Doctor Moore	John McKee
Pete Brown	{ Dickie Van Patten { Ronald Reiss
Allen Child	Natalie Chilvers
Mrs. Mitchmore	Claire Nolte
Usher of the Court	Edmond Stevens
Deputy Clerk	Edward Lester
Attorney General	Harold Young
Judge	Len Mence
Sir Patrick	Cecil Humphreys
Sergeant	Ross Chetwynd
Foreman of the Jury	Lionel Ince
Chaplain	John Clarke
Porter	Harold DeBecker
Alderman	Frank Howson
Sheriff	Charles Wellesley
Clerk	James Corbett
Warden	Avery Graves
Clerk of Court	Eric Walz

Solicitors: Jack Bishop, Lewis McMichael.
Reporters: Jack Hasler, William Topham, David Powell, William
  Short, Richard Rider, Jack Gould, Hugh Fettis.
Act I.—Scenes 1, 3, 4 and 5—Browns' Kitchen, Village of Strong-
oak, England. 2—Kenneth Sutter's Office. Act II.—Scenes 1, 2, 3,
4, 5 and 6—Number 1 Court, "The Old Bailey," London. 7—Cell,
Halloway Prison. 8—Room in Charity Institution.
Staged by Dorothy Cumming; settings by Raymond Sovey.

Mary Brown, married to a drunken sailmaker in a small English
town, is in love with Ken Sutter, the foreman of her husband's
factory. The husband, ill, is reported by his doctor to be slowly
dying. Mary Brown thereupon promises to run away with the
foreman. The nurse attending the sick man is also in love with
the foreman and determined Mary shall not have him. The nurse
doubles the sleeping potion she thinks she is giving to Mary, but
Mary unwittingly passes it on to her husband. Husband dies.
Mary is tried and convicted of murder on circumstantial evidence.
As she goes to the gallows Ken Sutter takes over the care of her
young son.

(Closed December 16, 1939)

STEEL

(9 performances)

A tragedy in two acts by Harold Igo. Produced by Producers
Theatre, Inc., at the Provincetown Playhouse, New York, December 19, 1939.

Cast of characters—

O'Toole...Richard Cahill
Davies...Arthur Lithgow
Hunky..Donald DeFore
Shorty..Ad Karns
Stan ....Paul Rohmann
Joe...Vito Scotti
Pete...Allan Frank
Mike Shine..................................Edward Fitzpatrick
Boy..Allan Vaughan
Yanez.... ....Kenneth Cooper Sloan
Pit Boss...Jay Putney
Foreman...Paul Weaver
First Shoveler..................................Richard Cahill
Second Shoveler..................................John Manners
Third Shoveler..............................Donald Campbell
Butch Mullins.....................................Will Kuluva
First Neighbor.....................................Oma Hagar
Second Neighbor...............................Evelyn Evers
Third Neighbor..............................Helen Kanapielka
Marya...Priscilla Jamison
Fourth Neighbor.............................Bertha Van Zee
Old Peter...Paul Weaver
Gateman ....Donald Campbell
Guard..Allan Frank
Bill the Riveter...............................Richard Cahill
   Act I.—Scenes 1 and 2—Open Hearth Floor of Mammoth Steel
Company, Steelton, Ohio. 3—Open Hearth Furnaces. 4—Hunky's

Home on Company Row. Act II.—Scene 1—Hunky's Home. 2—
Entrance to Mammoth Steel Co. Plant. 3—Top Beam of Skeleton
Skyscraper. 4—The Pit.
    Staged by Ad Karns; settings by Melville Bernstein; costumes by
Margaret Karns.

Hunky, a huge Polish immigrant, goes to work in the steel mills
of Steelton, Ohio, and becomes obsessed with the might and
power of steel as a driving force in the creation of a new world.
When, as the result of a cruel joke by his fellows, the religious
medal he wears about his neck fails to protect him from a serious
burn, he puts steel above religion as the god of his idolatry.
When he is suspected of union sympathies and loses his job he
goes to a sacrificial death in the molten metal.

(Closed December 30, 1939)

ONCE UPON A TIME

(1 performance)

A fantasy in two acts by Lawrence Joseph Dugan. Produced
by Hal A. Salzman at Labor Stage, New York, December 20, 1939.

Cast of characters—

Olaf..Alan Fleming
Miles...Robert Busch
Wolf ....Charles Powers
Rose ....Miriam Stone
Mr. Moon...................................,..A. Courtney White
Ditty..Jewel Hart
General A..Leslie Gorall
General B.......................................Charles Brodsky
General C ....Perry Burton
General D ....Johnny Lynn
General E ....Walter Ward
General F...John Foster
    Act I.—A Mountain Side in a Mythical Land. Act II.—Small
House.
    Staged by Richard Z. Segal; settings by Cirker and Robbins;
lighting by Bolton Wilder.

A "satirical fantasy" in which three young boys climb mountains in search of their heart's desire. One wants to kill and
control. One wants to live in idleness and let the world support
him. One meets a girl and discovers love. The killer organizes
an army to control the others. The author was a drama student
at Yale.

(Closed December 21, 1939)

BILLY DRAWS A HORSE

(13 performances)

A comedy in three acts by Lesley Storm. Produced by Lee Shubert and William A. Brady at The Playhouse, New York, December 21, 1939.

Cast of characters—

Mrs. Smith	Florence Edney
Tim Shields	Douglas Walton
Clare Fleming	Hayley Bell
Dr. Howard Fleming	Arthur Margetson
Grace	Edna Bennett
Grandpapa	Harry Plimmer
Elise Parsons	Elizabeth Inglis
Mrs. Parsons	Grace George
Alfred Parsons	Lumsden Hare
Agnes	Carol Curtis Brown
Pschenschynoff	Leo Bulgakov
Waiter	Jules Epailly
A Customer	William Chambers
Miss Burchill	Marion Sittler

Act I.—Scene 1—Drawing Room in Dr. Fleming's House, London. 2—A Room in Alfred Parsons' House, Chiselfield. Act II.—Room in Alfred Parsons' House. Act III.—Scene 1—A Café in Dieppe. 2—Room in Alfred Parsons' House.

Staged by Harry Wagstaff Gribble; settings by Watson Barratt.

Billy Fleming, a precocious lad of six, has drawn a horse on the wall of the hall opposite his father's consulting room. Billy's art is nothing to excite onlookers, but his uninhibited realism is. Dr. Fleming insists Billy should be disciplined. Clare Fleming, Billy's mother, objects to punishing a boy for daring to be honest. There is a quarrel. Clare goes on a bit of a bender with a young man friend. A family breakup is threatened, but avoided when what is known as wiser council prevails.

(Closed December 31, 1939)

WHEN WE ARE MARRIED

(156 performances)

A comedy in three acts by J. B. Priestley. Produced by Robert Henderson at the Lyceum Theatre, New York, December 25, 1939.

Cast of characters—

Ruby Birtle	Sally O'Neil
Gerald Forbes	Winston O'Keefe
Mrs. Northup	Alison Skipworth
Nancy Holmes	Jane Sterling
Fred Dyson	Lee Parry
Henry Ormonroyd	J. C. Nugent
Alderman Joseph Helliwell	Tom Powers
Maria Helliwell	Alice Fleming

THE BEST PLAYS OF 1939-40   425

Councilor Albert Parker.............................A. P. Kaye
Annie Parker...................................Estelle Winwood
Herbert Soppitt...................................Philip Tonge
Clara Soppitt.....................................Ann Andrews
Lottie Grady.....................................Leona Powers
The Rev. Clement Mercer.......................Henry Mowbray
    Acts I, II and III.—Sitting Room of Alderman Helliwell's House
in Clecklewyke, a Town in the North of England.
    Staged by Robert Henderson; setting by Karle Amend.

The Parkers, the Soppitts and the Helliwells were all married
the same year and for twenty-five years have celebrated their wedding anniversaries together. At their Silver Wedding anniversary
they discover that the parson who married them was not a properly
authorized parson. For twenty-five years, before the law, they
have been living in sin. Very startling. Some of them are worried, some are pleased, all are disturbed. It all comes right at
11 P.M.

(Closed May 4, 1940)

FOLIES BERGERE

(121 performances)

A vaudeville-revue in one act and sixteen scenes. Produced by
Clifford C. Fischer at the Broadway Theatre, New York, December 25, 1939.

Principals engaged—

Joyce Claxton	Gil Lamb
Michele Magnin	Malcia
Florence Spencer	Iris Wayne
Betty Brite	Karin Zoska
Leopold	Juliette
Andree Lorrain	Malo
Harald	Lola
Roberton	Andre
Barsley	Lalage
Lucienne	Ashour
Nita Carol	Fahy
Tino Crisa	Steve Geray
Fred Sanborn	Charles Laurence
The Robinis	The Menciassis
Les Shyrettos	Lime Trio

Little Fred and his Football Dogs.
    Dances directed by George Moro; settings by Raymond Deshays,
Bertin, Lavignac & Pellegry and Grosvois & Lambert.

A French vaudeville running for an hour and a half, presented
twice nightly with matinees added Wednesday and Saturday.

(Closed February 11, 1940)

KINDRED

(16 performances)

A drama in prologue and two acts by Paul Vincent Carroll. Produced by Edward Choate and Arthur Shields at the Maxine Elliott Theatre, New York, December 26, 1939.

Cast of characters—

IN THE PROLOGUE
(The Last Generation)

Mary Griffin	Aline MacMahon
Dermot O'Regan	Wallace Ford
Primrose Carr	Wauna Paul
"Roderick O'Regan"	Charles Kennedy
"Jerome O'Regan"	Hale Norcross

IN THE PLAY
(The Present Generation)

Robert Fenet	Barry Fitzgerald
J. K. Keefe	Thomas Findlay
Mary Fenet, formerly Mary Griffin	Aline MacMahon
Michael Fenet	Harry Young
Agnes Keefe	Haila Stoddard
Alice	Aideen O'Connor
Dermot O'Regan	Arthur Shields
Sergeant Hannigan	Byron Russell

Prologue.—A Shanty on the Outskirts of Altmoran, a Small Town on the Irish Coast, near Dundalk.   Acts I and II.—(A generation later.)   Private Sitting Room Above Robert Fenet's Grocery Shop in Altmoran.

Staged and designed by Robert Edmond Jones.

Dermot O'Regan, a half-mad poet, denies his love for Mary Griffin because of his fear of continuing the unbalanced O'Regan line. When Dermot has refused to marry Mary he is visited by the shades of two O'Regan ancestors. They warn him that the creative artists of the world must carry on the fight against the materialists who have brought the world to the brink of despair. Women are but instruments of the Creator in the fulfillment of the artist's progress. Dermot thereupon seduces his serving woman. When she announces her pregnancy he kills himself. The son illegitimately born becomes a wandering fiddler preaching the gospel of truth in the cause of world reform. Mary Griffin, marrying the village grocer, becomes the mother of a son who goes into politics and denies his mother's idealism. Mary's spiritual kindred with the fiddler son of her dead lover is the stronger bond of the two.

(Closed January 6, 1940)

CHRISTMAS EVE

(6 performances)

A drama in three acts by Gustav Eckstein. Produced by Guthrie McClintic at the Henry Miller Theatre, New York, December 27, 1939.

Cast of characters—

Hanka, the Mother	Beth Merrill
Leo, the Third Child	Sidney Lumet
Peter Tor	Kent Smith
Julia, the Second Child	Katherine Locke
Mother McGlory, the Grandmother	Mildred Natwick
Joe McGlory, the Father	James Rennie
Ignace, the Fourth Child	Michael Macready
Tim, the First Child	Vincent Donehue
Two Italian Boys	John Dione / Peter Palmieri
Doctor Harris	Robert Ross
A Delivery Boy	Peter Scott
Father Flynn	Anthony Blair
Limpy	Himself

Acts I, II and III.—The McGlorys' Apartment in the Somewhat Foreign Quarter of a Good-Sized American City.
Staged by Guthrie McClintic; setting by Jo Mielziner.

Julia McGlory is sex conscious and sex inhibited. When the honest ironworker, Peter Tor, who loves her, visits her in her home and finds her mother, Hanka, with child and daily expectant, Julia is thrown off-balance and is very unhappy. Within the course of a few hours Hanka's baby arrives unexpectedly. At its delivery Julia becomes conscious of the miracle of birth and of her own potentialities as a mother of men.

(Closed December 30, 1939)

* THE MALE ANIMAL

(187 performances)

A comedy in three acts by James Thurber and Elliott Nugent. Produced by Herman Shumlin at the Cort Theatre, New York, January 9, 1940.

Cast of characters—

Cleota	Amanda Randolph
Wally Myers	Don De Fore
Tommy Turner	Elliott Nugent
Ellen Turner	Ruth Matteson
Patricia Stanley	Gene Tierney
Dean Frederick Damon	Ivan Simpson
Michael Barnes	Robert Scott
Joe Ferguson	Leon Ames
Mrs. Blanche Damon	Minna Phillips
Ed Keller	Matt Briggs

Myrtle Keller.....................................Regina Wallace
"Nutsy" Miller...............................Richard Beckhard
Newspaper Reporter...............................John Boruff
    Acts I, II and III.—Living Room in the House of Professor
Thomas Turner in a Mid-Western University Town.
    Staged by Herman Shumlin; setting by Aline Bernstein.

See page 215.

JOHN HENRY

(7 performances)

A music drama in three acts by Roark Bradford; music by
Jacques Wolfe. Produced by Sam Byrd in association with Fred
Mitchell at the 44th Street Theatre, New York, January 10, 1940.

Cast of characters—

Blind Lemon.....................................Joshua White
Julie Anne's Mamma.........................Henrietta Lovelace
Julie Anne's Papa............................George Jones, Jr.
Man Named Sam....................................Joe Attles
Hell Buster.....................................Robert Harvey
Mate ....Alexander Gray
Walking Boss.................................Kenneth Spencer
Old Aunt Dinah...................................Minto Cato
Ruby ....Musa Williams
Julie Anne..Ruby Elzy
John Henry's Papa............................James Lightfoot
John Henry's Mamma...........................Maude Simmons
John Henry.......................................Paul Robeson
Rucker ....George Dickson
Rucker's Wife....................................Sadie McGill
Poor Selma.......................................Myra Johnson
    Pimps' Quartette: Merritt Smith, Wyer Owens Handy, Louis Gil-
bert, William Woolfolk
    Fancy Ladies' Octette: Eva Vaughan, Alyce Carter, Mattie Wash-
ington, Benveneta Washington, Alice White, Ruth Gibbs, Marie
Fraser, Mildred Lassiter
Bad Stacker Lee.....................................Joe Attles
Billie Bob Russell.............................Alexander Gray
Carrie ....Benveneta Washington
Lead Heaver......................................Ray Yeates
Reader ....Merritt Smith
First Caller.....................................Louis Gilbert
Second Caller................................William Woolfolk
Mink Eye....................................J. De Witt Spencer
Roustabout ....C. W. Scott
    Workers, Their Wives, Etc.: James Armstrong, Leona Avery, Er-
nest Baskette, Ella Belle Davis, Oscar Brooks, Maudina Brown,
Jonathan Brice, Alyce Carter, George Dickson, John Diggs, Nora
Evans, Marie Fraser, Samuel A. Floyd, Ruth Gibbs, Louis Gil-
bert, Samuel Gary, James B. Gordon, Edgar Hall, Claudia Hall,
Kate Hall, Wyer Owens Handy, Lloyd Howlett, George Kennedy,
Mildred Lassiter, James Lightfoot, Sadie McGill, Massie Patter-
son, Bayard Rustin, C. W. Scott, Ernest Shaw, Anne Simmons,
Maude Simmons, Randall Steplight, Eva Vaughan, Charles
Welch, Benveneta Washington, Mattie Washington, Alice White,
Frederick Wilkerson, William Woolfolk, Ray Yeates.
    Act I.—Scenes 1 and 2—Steamboat Landing in Black River Coun-
try. 3—Corner of Bird and Third Streets, Argenta, Arkansas. Act
II.—Scene 1—Yaller Dog Railroad Construction Camp. 2—A Mov-
ing Steamboat on the Mississippi River. Act III.—Scene 1—Mink
Eye's Saloon, Back of Town in New Orleans. 2—Steamboat Landing
in Black River Country.
    Staged by Anthony Brown and Charles Friedman; choral direction

by Leonard de Paur; music directed by Don Voorhees; settings by
Albert Johnson; costumes by John Hambleton.

John Henry, the strongest black man in forty-seven states,
roams the Deep South pitting his strength against the forces of
nature. He totes huge bales of cotton, builds railroads and defies
wicked women. But John Henry gets his final come-uppence when
he thinks the only woman he ever loved, the innocent Julie Anne,
has been untrue to him. In his misery he takes to drink, and in
his boastfulness tries to compete with a steam hoist as a cotton
toter. They lay John Henry out on a couple of cotton bales, and
Julie Anne, dead of grief, beside him.

(Closed January 15, 1940)

EARL CARROLL VANITIES

(25 performances)

A revue in two acts assembled by Earl Carroll; lyrics by Dorcas
Cochran and Mitchell Parrish; music by Charles Rosoff and Peter
de Rose. Produced by Earl Carroll at the St. James Theatre,
New York, January 13, 1940.

Principals engaged—

Norman Lawrence	Susan Miller
Puddy Smith	Patricia Lee
Jerry Lester	Beryl Wallace
Prof. Lamberti	Nirska
Gary Stone	Marlyn Stewart
Johnny Woods	Muriel Barr
Don Milheim	Lela Moore
Clarence Low	Babe Westerland
Herbert Adams	Dorothy Barrett
Cass-Owen	Topsy
Walter Norris	Jeanne Carroll
Harriet Bennett	Mary Daniels
Jean Francis	Rose Heitner
Virginia Maples	Bebe Porter
Marna Stansell	Betty Stewart
Barbara Walters	Ygor and Tanya
The Four Hot Shots	The Three Nonchalants

Staged by Earl Carroll; dances by Eddie Prinz; settings and costumes by Jean Le Seyeux.

Earl Carroll, having been successful with his restaurant theatre
in Hollywood, brought the prettiest of his girls and the best of his
specialties to New York in the shape of a revue. New York was
not hospitable.

(Closed February 3, 1940)

JUNO AND THE PAYCOCK

(105 performances)

A drama in three acts by Sean O'Casey. Revived by Edward
Choate and Arthur Shields in association with Robert Edmond
Jones at the Mansfield Theatre, New York, January 16, 1940.

Cast of characters—

Mary Boyle	Aideen O'Connor
Juno Boyle	Sara Allgood
Johnny Boyle	Harry Young
Jerry Devine	Thomas Dillon
"Captain" Jack Boyle	Barry Fitzgerald
"Joxer" Daly	Arthur Shields
A Sewing Machine Vendor	Iris Whitney
A Coal Block Vendor	William Stone
Charlie Bentham, N.T	Lucian Self
Mrs. Maisie Madigan	Grania O'Malley
Mrs. Tancred	Effie Shannon
"Needle" Nugent	Hale Norcross
An Irregular Mobilizer	Charles Keenan
Furniture Removal Man	Byron Russell
Assis't Furniture Removal Man	Jack Graham

Neighbors: Nancy O'Grady, George O'Regan and Harry Selby.
Acts I, II and III.—Living Room of Two-Roomed Tenancy of the
Boyle Family in a Tenement House in Dublin.
Staged by Arthur Shields; setting by Robert Edmond Jones.

"Juno and the Paycock," first produced in New York in March,
1926, has been frequently revived. Its most recent performance
was by the Abbey Players at the Ambassador Theatre December 6,
1937. The current revival was co-operatively arranged by Edward
Choate and Arthur Shields with Sara Allgood and Barry Fitzgerald, Abbey Theatre veterans, in the leading rôles.

(Closed April 13, 1939)

THE MAN WHO KILLED LINCOLN

(5 performances)

A drama in three acts by Elmer Harris, dramatized from a book
by Philip Van Doren Stern. Produced by Joseph M. Gaites at
the Longacre Theatre, New York, January 17, 1940.

Cast of characters—

John Wilkes Booth	Richard Waring
Lewis Paine	John Morny
1st Soldier	Pendleton Harrison
2nd Soldier	Clancy Cooper
Officer	Howard Ferguson
Deery	John L. Kearney
Senator Talbot	Joseph Kramm
1st Congressman	Robert Pitkin
2nd Congressman	Willard Foster
Henry Davis Somers	William Jeffery

```
A Waiter....................................Horace McNally
Louise .........................................Lily Brent
Davy Herold....................................Sam Byrd
George Atzerodt................................Paul Varro
John Surratt...............................Martin Blaine
Murphy......................................John L. Kearney
President Lincoln..........................Charles Keane
Mrs. Lincoln..................................Mary Dorne
Major Rathbone..............................Blaine Harris
Miss Clara Harris...........................Gloria Washburn
Parker ......................................William Hitch
Carland ...................................Franc Bendtsen
Ned Spangler................................Clancy Cooper
Lloyd ...................................Frank McCormack
Samuel Cox..................................Whitford Kane
Henry .......................................Billy Demont
Thomas Jones..................................Edwin Vail
Col. Lafayette C. Baker......................Robert Pitkin
Lieut. Baker..............................Howard Ferguson
Colonel Conger..............................William Hitch
Willie Jett.................................Gene Francis
Garrett ....................................Willard Foster
Mrs. Garrett.................................Mary Dorne
Lieut. Doherty.........................L. Lawrence Weber
Bill Garrett................................Henry Hull, Jr.
Sergeant Boston Corbett..............Pendleton Harrison
```
    Soldiers, Civilians, Dance Hall Girls, Congressmen and Their
    Wives, Etc.: Jill Abbott, Annabelle Brooks, Robert Delaney,
    Elaine Kent, Ellen Morgan, Douglas Stark, Robert Reamer,
    Evelyn Price, George Repp, Molly Sherman, Garry Simpson,
    Louise Swanson.
    Act I.—Scene 1—Terrace Overlooking Washington, April 11,
1865. 2—Deery's Saloon. 3—Booth's Room in the National Hotel.
Act. II.—Scene 1—President's Box in Ford's Theatre. 2—Surratts-
ville Tavern, Maryland. 3—Living Room of Samuel Cox's Home
in Maryland. Act III.—Scene 1—Entrance to East Room of White
House. 2—Maryland Shore of Potomac River. 3—Garrett Farm
near Port Royal, Virginia. 4—Tobacco Barn on Garrett Farm.
    Staged by Felix Brentano; settings by Eugene Dunkel.

John Wilkes Booth, following the surrender of Gen. Robert E.
Lee, decides that if President Lincoln, General Grant and Secretary Seward can be taken off simultaneously, Lee will have a
chance to withdraw his surrender and continue fighting. Booth
shoots Lincoln, escapes with a broken leg, spends an act trying to
get back to Confederate territory, is captured and shot by one
of his pursuers. The author's purpose is to expose the workings
of a fanatic's mind.

(Closed January 20, 1940)

TWO ON AN ISLAND

(96 performances)

A comedy in eleven scenes by Elmer Rice. Produced by The
Playwrights' Company (Maxwell Anderson, S. N. Behrman, Robert
E. Sherwood and Elmer Rice) at the Broadhurst Theatre, New
York, January 22, 1940.

Cast of characters—

William Flynn...............................Robert Williams
Samuel Brodsky ....Martin Ritt
A Red-Cap..Earl Sydnor
Mary Ward..Betty Field
John Thompson...................................John Craven
A Policeman...................................Edward Downes
Clifton Ross....................................Earl McDonald
The Sightseeing Guide..........................Howard da Silva
The Driver.....................................Robert O'Brien
Mrs. Dora Levy...............................Dora Weissman
Dixie Bushby...............................Arthur L. Sachs
Middle-Western Man...........................Roderick Maybee
Middle-Western Woman........................Roberta Bellinger
Frederic Winthrop..............................Whitner Bissell
Lawrence Ormont.................................Luther Adler
Martha Johnson...................................Terry Harris
An Actor......................................Charles Polacheck
Heinz Kaltbart................................Rudolf Weiss
Dorothy Clark...................................Martha Hodge
Katherine Winthrop Holmes......................Joan Wetmore
Martin Blake..................................Herschel Bentley
A Cashier..Norma Green
Gracie Mullen....................................Ann Thomas
A Married Couple..............................{ Sara Peyton
                                              { John Philliber
Helen Ormont...............................Harriet MacGibbon
Sonia Taranova.................................Eva Langbord
Mrs. Ballinger.................................Frederica Going
A Museum Attendant.............................Charles La Torre
Another Married Couple........................{ John Triggs
                                              { Dorothy Darling
Ruth Ormont......................................Helen Renee
A Hindu...Larri Lauria
A Waiter....................................Aage Steenshorne
Another Married Couple........................{ Sellwyn Myers
                                              { Lucille Sears
Fred ....Don Shelton
Dolly ....Adele Longmire
Mrs. Williams...................................Mary Michael
   New Yorkers and Out-of-Towners: Roberta Bellinger, Alvin Chil-
   dress, Dorothy Darling, Evelyn Davis, Virginia Girvin, Frederica
   Going, Terry Harris, Eva Langbord, Charles La Torre, Larri
   Lauria, Adele Longmire, Assotta Marshall, Roderick Maybee,
   Sellwyn Myers, Mary Michael, Robert O'Brien, Sara Peyton,
   John Philliber, Hilary Phillips, Arthur L. Sachs, Lucille Sears,
   Don Shelton, Aage Steenshorne, Earl Sydnor, Joan Wetmore,
   Robert Williams.
   Scene 1—En Route. 2—All Around the Town. 3—Broadway.
4—Underground. 5—The Village. 6—The Coffee Pot. 7—The Met.
8—The Pavement. 9—The Little Lady Herself. 10—Chelsea. 11—
En Route.
   Staged by Elmer Rice; settings by Jo Mielziner; costumes by
Helene Pons.

Mary Ward of New Hampshire and John Thompson of Ohio
arrive in New York the same day and with similar hope of conquering the big city. John wants to write plays, but can make but
little headway. Mary wants to act, but has no better luck. John
is forced to compromise with a variety of jobs. Mary takes to
modeling and clerking. Both meet and fight temptation. Finally,
when they are about to give up and go home, they meet accidentally in the head of the Statue of Liberty and confess their failure.

Falling in love with John, Mary is able to strengthen his determination to make another try, and they both find jobs.

(Closed April 13, 1940)

YOUNG COUPLE WANTED

(13 performances)

A comedy in three acts by Arthur Wilmurt. Produced by Jerome Mayer in association with Carly Wharton and Martin Gabel at the Maxine Elliott Theatre, New York, January 24, 1940.

Cast of characters—

```
Mrs. Fitch.......................................Ethel Intropidi
Mrs. Daly.....................................Zamah Cunningham
Mr. Daly...............................................John Adair
Jed Jones........................................Hugh Marlowe
Betty Monkline....................................Juliet Forbes
Cora Bedell......................................Helen Shields
Lewis Champion...................................Lloyd Gough
Catherine Daly...................................Arlene Francis
Donald Thompson................................Richard Clark
Miss Muhlen...........................Ruth Thane McDevitt
George Jones..................................J. Richard Jones
```
    Act I.—Catherine Daly's Apartment, New York City. Acts II and III.—Apartment in Old New Amsterdam, a Federal Housing Project. Staged by Martin Gabel; settings by Donald Oenslager.

Catherine Daly, a Newark schoolteacher sworn to spinsterhood for five years, and Jed Jones, an eager college graduate who cannot find a job, decide to live together while awaiting a change in their fortunes. Hearing of this unconventional arrangement the parents of Miss Daly are so loud in their criticism that the young people do marry and the schoolteacher loses her job. Jones tries a variety of selling schemes, none of which succeed. Discouraged but game the young couple decide to give up the battle of New York and return to the country, where they will take on the exploitation and sale of a new brand of grape jelly.

(Closed February 3, 1940)

GENEVA

(15 performances)

A satirical comedy in two acts by George Bernard Shaw. Produced by Gilbert Miller in association with Maurice Colbourne and Barry Jones at the Henry Miller Theatre, New York, January 30, 1940.

Cast of characters—

Begonia Brown	Norah Howard
Jew	Beckett Bould
Newcomer	Harvey Braban
Widow	Susan Turner
Journalist	Jack Brown
Bishop	T. Renaud Lockwood
Commissar Posky	Earle Grey
Secretary of the League of Nations	Cyril Gardiner
Usher	Gerald Vane
Sir Orpheus Midlander	Lawrence Hanray
The Judge	Barry Jones
The Betrothed	Patrick Ludlow
Bombardone	Ernest Borrow
Battler	Maurice Colbourne
Soldier	Patrick Crean
Deaconess	Jessica Tandy
General Flanco De Fortinbras	John Turnbull

Act I.—Scene 1—Office of International Committee for Intellectual Co-operation at Geneva. 2—Office of Secretary of League of Nations. Act. II.—The Hague. Salon in the Old Palace.
Staged by Maurice Colbourne.

Begonia Brown, a clerk in the offices of the International Committee for Intellectual Co-operation in Geneva, files with the League of Nations charges of criminal actions against Germany, Italy and Russia. To answer these charges Battler (Hitler), Bombardone (Mussolini) and Commissar Posky are summoned to the League to submit their defense. Seated at the sidelines of the investigation are Sir Orpheus Midlander, British Foreign Minister; General Flanco De Fortinbras of Spain, and a German Jew. Resulting statements and arguments provide a satirical review of European problems of the moment.

(Closed February 10, 1940)

MY DEAR CHILDREN

(117 performances)

A comedy in three acts by Catherine Turney and Jerry Horwin. Produced by Richard Aldrich and Richard Myers at the Belasco Theatre, New York, January 31, 1940.

Cast of characters—

Kleinbach	Arnold Korff
Reed Hanson	Otto Hulett
Portia Trent	Patricia Waters
Titcomb	George Reynolds
Felice, Countess De Britonne	Tala Birell
Allan Manville	John Barrymore
Albert	Roland Hogue
Miranda Burton	Lois Hall
Cordelia Clark	Doris Dudley
Lee Stevenson	Kenneth Treseder
Willard Nelson	Philip Reed
Jacques Korbi	Stiano Braggiotti
Ernst Van Betke	Leo Chalzel

Acts I, II and III.—Château in Swiss Alps near Basle—1938.
Staged by Otto L. Preminger; setting by Donald Oenslager.

Allan Manville, an aging American matinee idol, has begun an
affair with his patron's wife, fleeing with her to a Swiss château.
There he is followed by three of his daughters, Portia, Miranda
and Cordelia, each born of a different mother. As an amateur
father Manville attempts to straighten out their respective ro-
mances, and with some success. "My Dear Children" developed
an astounding popularity because of the star's frequent ad-libbing,
remaining for thirty-three weeks in Chicago.

(Closed May 18, 1940)

THE TAMING OF THE SHREW

(8 performances)

A comedy in two parts by William Shakespeare. Revived by
the Theatre Guild, Inc., in association with John C. Wilson at the
Alvin Theatre, New York, February 5, 1940.

Cast of characters—

(IN THE INDUCTION)

Christopher Sly	Richard Whorf
A Lord	Philip Bourneuf
First Huntsman	Gilmore Bush
Second Huntsman	Cameron Mitchell
Third Huntsman	Brooks West
Bartholomew, a Page	Donald Buka

(IN THE PLAY)

Lucentio	Alan Hewitt
Tranio	Norman Stuart
Two Townswomen	Sharon Curran / Grace Coppin
Pantaloon	Charles Bowden
Baptista	Sydney Greenstreet
Gremio	Francis Compton
Hortensio	Byron McGrath
Bianca	Fay Baker
Katherine	Lynn Fontanne
Biondello	Alex Courtney
Petruchio	Alfred Lunt
Grumio	S. Thomas Gomez
Widow	Edith King
Maid	Grace Coppin
Curtis	Edith King
Servants to Petruchio:	
Nathaniel	Gilmore Bush
Joseph	Ralph Nelson
Gregory	Robert Downing
Philip	Brooks West
Cook	Gordon Mills
Haberdasher	Cameron Mitchell
Tailor	Charles Bowden
A Pedant	Wm. Le Massena
Vincentio	Victor Thorley
Officer	Ralph Nelson
A Prisoner	Cameron Mitchell
Horses	Harry Be Gar / Don Morrell

A Singer...Alex Courtney
A Dancer...Sharon Curran
Choir Boy..Ralph Nelson
   Acrobats: Harry Be Gar, Don Morrell, Eddo Porto.
   Dwarfs: Freddie Goodrow, Ray Holgate, Thomas J. Keenan,
    Charles Silvers.
   Parts 1 and 2—House of a Noble Lord.
   Staged by Harry Wagstaff Gribble; setting by Carolyn Hancock;
costumes by Claggett Wilson.

This was a week of special benefit performances which added
$25,000 to the Finnish Relief Fund being collected by the Herbert
Hoover committee. The Lunts had, during the two previous seasons, traveled 30,000 miles with a repertory including "The Taming of the Shrew," "Idiot's Delight" and "The Sea Gull."

(Closed February 10, 1940)

TWO FOR THE SHOW

(124 performances)

A revue in two acts by Nancy Hamilton; music by Morgan
Lewis. Produced by Gertrude Macy and Stanley Gilkey at the
Booth Theatre, New York, February 8, 1940.

Principals engaged—

Eve Arden	Keenan Wynn
Brenda Forbes	Richard Haydn
Kathryn Kimber	Richard Smart
Frances Comstock	Alfred Drake
Eunice Healey	Tommy Wonder
Betty Hutton	Robert Smith
Nadine Gae	William Archibald
Austine McDonnell	Willard Gary

Norton Dean

   Staged by John Murray Anderson; sketches directed by Joshua Logan;
dances by Robert Alton; music by Ray Kavanagh; settings and costumes
by Raoul Pene Du Bois.

(Closed May 25, 1940)

THE UNCONQUERED

(6 performances)

A drama in three acts by Ayn Rand adapted from the author's
novel, "We the Living." Produced by George Abbott at the Biltmore Theatre, New York, February 13, 1940.

Cast of characters—

A Soldier...John Parrish
Leo Kovalensky ....John Emery
Upravdom..Cliff Dunstan
Kira Argounova....................................Helen Craig
A Student...Paul Ballantyne
Comrade Sonia.....................................Georgiana Brand

```
Pavel Syerov....................................Arthur Pierson
Older Examiner.................................J. Ascher Smith
Andrei Taganov...................................Dean Jagger
Malashkin.......................................Edwin Philips
Comrade Bitiuk....................................Ellen Hall
Girl Clerk....................................Virginia Dunning
Boy Clerk.......................................William Blees
Comrade Voronov...............................Horace Cooper
Stephan Timoshenko............................George Cotton
Karp Morozov.................................Howard Freeman
Antonina Pavlovna................................Lea Penman
G.P.U. Chief................................Marshall Bradford
Assistant G.P.U. Chief.........................Frank O'Connor
Party Club Attendant............................George Smith
Neighbor....................................Ludmilla Toretzka
```

Act I.—Scene 1—Leo's Home in Petrograd, 1924. 2—Technological Institute. 3—Railroad Office. Act. II.—Scenes 1 and 2—Railroad Office. 3—Andrei's Home. 4—Office of the G.P.U. 5—Leo's Home. Act III.—Scene 1—Party Club. 2—Leo's Home.
Staged by George Abbott; settings by Boris Aronson.

Kira Argounova and Leo Kovalensky are Russian aristocrats doing the best they can to readjust their lives to meet the situation in the Stalin Russia of 1924. Leo and Kira cannot marry because of Leo's health. To help him to the Crimea for a rest Kira gives herself to Andrei Taganov, an agent of the secret police. When Leo returns, a well man, and discovers Kira's relations with the OGPU agent, he decides to hire himself out as gigolo to a rich parvenu. Andrei, having fallen in love with Kira, kills himself. Kira goes on living, determined to conquer in the name of individual freedom.

(Closed February 17, 1940)

REUNION IN NEW YORK

(89 performances)

A revue conceived by Lothar Metzl and Werner Michel; sketches by Carl Don, Richard Alma, Richard Holden and Hans Lefebre; lyrics by David Greggory, Peter Barry, and Stewart Arthur; music by André Singer, Bert Silving, Berenece Kazounoff and M. Cooper Paul. Produced by The American Viennese Group, Inc., at the Little Theatre, New York, February 21, 1940.

Principals engaged—

Lotte Goslar	Herbert Berghof
Marie Pichler	Paul Lindenberg
Nell Hyrt	Klaus Brill
Vilma Kurer	Henry Peever
Katherine Mattern	Walter Martin
Annie Desser	Anthony Scott
Charlotte Krauss	Fred Lorenz
Maria Temple	Henry Peever
Nelly Franck	Edgar Vincent
Elisabeth Neumann	Lothar Rewalt
Leo Weith	Liesl Paul

Herman Walter   Bert Silving
Peter Koch   Lothar Metzl
                    Emery Gondor
    Staged by Herbert Berghof and Ezra Stone; settings by Harry
Horner; costumes by Lester Polakov; choreography arranged by
Lotte Gosler; production supervised by Ezra Stone and Marc Daniels.

This was a revised version of a first revue, "From Vienna," presented by a similar company of refugees in New York in June,
1939.
                    (Closed May 4, 1940)

NIGHT MUSIC

(20 performances)

A drama in three acts by Clifford Odets; incidental music by
Hanns Eisler. Produced by Group Theatre at the Broadhurst
Theatre, New York, February 22, 1940.

Cast of characters—

Lieutenant...Tom Tully
Murph...Clancy Cooper
Policeman...John Rustad
Steve Takis...Elia Kazan
A. L. Rosenberger...................................Morris Carnovsky
Fay Tucker..Jane Wyatt
Mrs. Scott..Virginia Stevens
Stagehand...Harry M. Cooke
Beggar..Charles Thompson
Gus-the-Hurrying Salesman...........................Sanford Meisner
Sailor..Harry Bratsburg
Mr. George..Roman Bohnen
Teddy...Lou Polan
Marty...Charles Mendick
Dot...Ruth Nelson
Mr. Nichols ....Harry M. Cooke
Lily..Katherine Allen
Sleeping Man..David Opatoshu
Roy...Phil Brown
Little Man..William Hansen
Blind Man...David Opatoshu
Al..Philip Loeb
Mr. Tucker..Art Smith
Waiter..Will Lee
Eddie Bellows.......................................Walter Coy
Drunken Man...Fred Stewart
Mr. Gilbert...Sanford Meisner
Arnold..John Stearns
Attendant...Bert Conway
    Policemen, Passers-by, Stagehands, Actors, Actresses, et al.: Lydia
    Perera, Florence Odets, Nick Conte, Charles Thompson, Bette
    Grayson, John Stearns, Fred Stewart, Clancy Cooper, Tony Kra-
    ber, Bert Conway.
    Act I.—Scene 1—Police Station. 2—Stage Door of Dover Thea-
tre. 3—Hotel Algiers Lobby. 4—Rooms 212 and 214. 5—Central
Park. Act. II.—Scene 1—Central Park. 2—Hotel Algiers Lobby.
3—Restaurant. 4—The World's Fair. 5—Rooms 212 and 214.
Act. III.—Scene 1—Police Station. 2—Airport.
    Staged by Harold Clurman; settings by Mordecai Gorelik; light-
ing by Michael Gordon.

Steve Takis, errand boy for a Hollywood motion picture company, is sent to New York to bring back to the Hollywood studio

a pair of trained monkeys.   While chaperoning the monkeys one grabs the purse of a passing actress, the other takes Steve's wallet from his pocket and scatters its contents on the sidewalk.   Steve is arrested on suspicion of being a pickpocket with animal confederates.   The officer making the arrest, a philosophical Rosenberger, and the actress, Fay Tucker, become interested in Steve. Over the week-end Fay falls in love with him.   Steve, a would-be social rebel, would push their sympathy aside, but is finally influenced to give up Hollywood and make his way in New York.

(Closed March 9, 1940)

ANOTHER SUN

(11 performances)

A drama in three acts by Dorothy Thompson and Fritz Kortner. Produced by Cheryl Crawford at the National Theatre, New York, February 23, 1940.

Cast of characters—

George Berndt	Hans Jaray
Maria	Celeste Holm
Sergei Volkonsky	Leo Bulgakov
Guglielmo Benedetto	Marshall Bradford
Susan Van Ryn	Kate Warriner
Cliff Jackson	Herbert Rudley
Christina Lenz	Johanna Hofer
Pastor Reisinger	McKay Morris
Professor Friedman	Erwin Kalser
Franzie	Adrienne Gessner
Von Bendow	Arnold Korff

Acts I, II and III.—Living room of New York furnished apartment.

Staged by Fritz Kortner; setting by Ben Edwards, costumes by Paul du Pont.

George Berndt, a famous actor in Germany and on the Continent, and his actress wife, Maria, are driven to America by Der Fuehrer's attitude when Berndt refuses to abandon the play of his friend, a Jew.   In America the Berndts make common cause with other refugees until after the fall of Austria.   After that Maria decides to return to Berlin on invitation from Herr Hitler. George, more passionately devoted to liberty than ever, elects to stay on in America and fight his way through to a new career.

(Closed March 2, 1940)

LEAVE HER TO HEAVEN

(15 performances)

A drama in three acts by John Van Druten. Produced by Dwight Deere Wiman at the Longacre Theatre, New York, February 27, 1940.

Cast of characters—

Madge Monckton	Ruth Chatterton
Robert Ewen	Edmond O'Brien
Mr. Monckton	Reynolds Denniston
Dr. Collins	Francis Compton
Mr. Henstridge	A. G. Andrews
Mrs. Henstridge	Esther Mitchell
Grace Henstridge	Hilda Plowright
Morgan	Edmond Stevens
Davis	Guy Spaull
Martin Reardo	Neil Fitzgerald
Mrs. Lake	Bettina Cerf
David	Eldon Gorst
First Officer	J. Malcom Dunn
Second Officer	William Packer
Mr. Rolleston	Franklyn Fox
Mrs. Williams	Margaret Moffat
Mr. Williams	Harry Sothern
Rogers	Lowell Gilmore

Acts I and III.—London. Act II.—Westcliff-on-Sea.
Staged by Auriol Lee; settings by Watson Barratt.

Madge Monckton, married to a man many years her senior, is carrying on an affair with her chauffeur, Robert Ewen. Ewen, growing jealous of the husband, bashes in his head with a mallet. In the trial for murder that follows Madge tries to take the blame for the killing to save her lover, but the law is not fooled.

(Closed March 9, 1940)

THE BURNING DECK

(3 performances)

A comedy in three acts by Andrew Rosenthal; special music by Lillian Wood Krob. Produced by Jack Small at the Maxine Elliott Theatre, New York, March 1, 1940.

Cast of characters—

Captain Applegate	Dennis Hoey
Nicholas	Ivan Triesault
Don Juan	Alfred Hesse
Jeffrey Brandt	Russell Hardie
Baroness Maude De Rossi	Marion Mill
Niki De Vobourg	Gregory Gaye
Rex Wolfson	Onslow Stevens
Margaret Eaves	Edith King
Cornelia Lauren	Vera Allen
Roby Lauren	George Lloyd

```
Nina Brandt.......................................Zita  Johann
Raphael..........................................Frank  Downing
Ava  Andrus......................................Mary  Howes
A Native Boy.....................................George  Calvert
    Acts I, II and III.—Veranda of Small Hotel on Island in the
Mediterranean.
    Staged by Robert Milton; setting by Harry Horner.
```

Rex Wolfson, popular London novelist, is one of a group of gossiping and world-weary travelers vacationing on an island in the Mediterranean. New arrivals include Cornelia Lauren, the wife who had divorced him when their son, Rody, was an infant. Without knowing their relationship the boy is drawn to his father, who in turn protects him from his mother, she insisting that he (Rody) should give up writing and go into the furniture business. When the others depart Rody and Ava Andrus, a young and ambitious musician, are left on the island to work out their destinies.

(Closed March 2, 1940)

THE WEAK LINK

(32 performances)

A comedy in three acts by Allan Wood. Produced by Chester Erskin in association with Philip Adler at the Golden Theatre, New York, March 4, 1940.

Cast of characters—

```
Matt King........................................Lloyd  Gough
Rosseti..........................................Don  Costello
Mr. Franklin.....................................Hugh  Rennie
Doc Morin........................................Edmund  Dorsay
Swede  Larsen....................................Ray  Mayer
Peter Mason......................................Hume  Cronyn
Gale Roberts.....................................Peggy  French
Red Connelly.....................................Grant  Mills
State Policeman..................................Selden  Bennett
Policeman........................................Albert  West
    Acts I, II and III.—Offices of the Bankers' Protective Association
in Mid-Western City.
    Staged by Chester Erskin; setting by Harry Horner.
```

Peter Mason is an expert at puzzle solving, a chess and checker wizard and a genius at ferreting out the weak link in the burglary protective schemes of big business houses—especially banks. He applies for a job at the headquarters of the Bankers' Protective Association, which happens to be a cover for a gang of bank robbers. The robbers kidnap Peter, together with his fiancée, Gale Roberts, and hold them incommunicado until Peter works out a perfect robbery plan. The robbers overlook the weak link in Peter's own setup, bringing victory rather than defeat to Peter and Gale.

(Closed March 30, 1940)

THE FIFTH COLUMN

(87 performances)

A drama in two acts adapted by Benjamin Glazer from a published play by Ernest Hemingway. Produced by the Theatre Guild, Inc., at the Alvin Theatre, New York, March 6, 1940.

Cast of characters—

Anita	Lenore Ulric
Philip Rawlings	Franchot Tone
Max	Lee J. Cobb
Antonio	Arnold Moss
A Soldier from New York	Wendell K. Phillips
Another Soldier	Henry Levin
Hotel Manager	Emile Boreo
Dorothy Bridges	Katherine Locke
Preston	A. J. Herbert
Petra	Hilda Bruce
A Signaler	Henry Levin
A Sentry	Raoul Henry
Another Sentry	Michael Sage
A Thin Officer	John Gerard
A Man in Civilian Clothes	David Leonard
A General from Germany	William F. Schoeller
A Prowler	John Gerard
Holt	Philip Lewis
Doyle	Charles Jordan
Hotel Electrician	Sid Cassel
An Assault Guard	Michael Sage
Private Wilkinson	Kendall Clark
Another Assault Guard	Raoul Henry
The Butterfly Man	Harry Davis
First Waiter	Sid Cassel
Second Waiter	John Gerard
An Artilleryman	Michael Sage
Two Assault Guards	Fred Catania, Peter Knego

Act I.—Scenes 1, 4 and 5—Rooms 109 and 110, Hotel Florida near Madrid. Winter of 1938. 2—Artillery Post, Top of Extramadura Road. 3 and 6—Seguridad Headquarters. Act II.—Scene 1—A Café. 2—Rooms 109 and 110, Hotel Florida, Madrid.

Staged by Lee Strasberg; settings by Howard Bay; costumes by Paul du Pont; production under personal supervision of Theresa Helburn and Lawrence Langner.

Philip Rawlings, newspaper correspondent, is working with the counter-espionage forces in Madrid in 1938, in the service of the Loyalist army. Rawlings and Max, his Nazi-hating partner, have enlisted in the cause of liberty for the duration of all wars. During a bombardment Rawlings, in liquor, flies to the assistance of Dorothy Bridges, occupying an adjoining room in the Hotel Florida. When Dorothy would be rid of him he refuses to leave. Following the violation of the girl Rawlings is stricken with contrition and would run away to Paris and matrimony with her. Max calls him back to his job as an enlisted liberator.

(Closed May 18, 1940)

A PASSENGER TO BALI

(4 performances)

A drama in three acts by Ellis St. Joseph. Produced by Montgomery Ford at the Ethel Barrymore Theatre, New York, March 14, 1940.

Cast of characters—

Mr. Slaughter	William Harrigan
Kali	Kaie Deei
Mr. Wrangle	Victor Beecroft
Chew	Harry Lowe
Captain English	Colin Keith-Johnson
Rev. Mr. Walkes	Walter Huston
Minheer Van Matsys	Edgar Stehli
Hon. Mr. Chisholm	Cecil Humphreys

Act. I.—Scene 1—Shanghai. 2—At Sea. 3—Bali. Act II.—Scene 1—Bangkok. 2—Shanghai. Act III.—At Sea.

Staged by John Huston; settings by Lawrence Goldwasser; lighting by Feder.

Rev. Mr. Walkes, who was not a reverend at all, but a malicious trouble maker in the South Seas, sneaks a passage aboard the English freighter, *Roundabout*, by pulling the wool over the eyes of her Captain English. Once aboard the freighter the Rev. Walkes gradually reveals his true colors by inciting the crew to threatened mutiny and generally raising several kinds of hell. No port will permit the Rev. Walkes to land. Captain English's only way of being rid of him is to abandon him with the ship when the *Roundabout* is stricken in a typhoon.

(Closed March 16, 1940)

GOODBYE IN THE NIGHT

(8 performances)

A melodrama in a prologue and three acts by Jerome Mayer. Produced by George Abbott at the Biltmore Theatre, New York, March 18, 1940.

Cast of characters—

The Characters in the Prologue Include Dr. Josephs, Inmates of the Asylum, and several guards.

Dr. Josephs	Ernest Rowan
Kitchen Maid	Peggy Gould
Minka	Jean Adair
Joe	Owen Martin
Ollie	James Bell
Jessie Sawyer	Natalie Schafer
Cece Sawyer	Mary Mason
Kurt	Paul Ballantyne
Maude	Edith Van Cleve
A Female Boarder	Ruth McDevitt

```
Pop...........................................John  Carmody
Gertie.........................................Marilyn  Erskine
Chief  O'Malley................................Millard  Mitchell
Rufus..........................................William  Swetland
Syd............................................Marion  Willis
Policemen......................................{ Ralph  Morehouse
                                               { Richard  Kelly
```

Prologue—An Asylum Somewhere in Upper Pennsylvania. Acts I and III.—Farmhouse. Act II.—Scene 1—Rooming House. 2—Filling Station.

Staged by George Abbott; settings by Cirker and Robbins.

Ollie has been an inmate of an insane asylum for some months. During that time he has developed a homicidal tendency based in his belief that his brother-in-law, Joe, is responsible for his mental condition, Joe having started a fire in which Ollie was badly burned. Ollie escapes from the asylum, hunts Joe out and slays him. Interrupted in his disposal of the body he impresses Cece Sawyer and her fiancé, Kurt, tourists, who have begged a night's lodging, into service; takes them, with the body of Joe, in their car, to a filling station and, when discovered by the state police, tries to put the murder on them. Asylum guards finally catch up with Ollie.

(Closed March 23, 1940)

ONE-ACT VARIETY THEATRE

(38 performances)

A program of three short plays: "What D' You Call It" by E. P. Conkle, "According to Law" by Noel Houston and "The Devil is a Good Man" by William Kozlenko. Presented by Eugene Endrey at the Provincetown Theatre, New York, March 19, 1940.

WHAT D' YOU CALL IT

Cast of characters—

```
Andy  Revision................................Jay  Barney
Wert  Harmand.................................William  Keene
One-Eye  Diggins..............................Tom  McGivern,  Jr.
Cass  Hughes..................................Tadeus  Kowal
Ben  Noble....................................Richard  O'Connor
Emmy  Swan....................................Wanda  Rogers
Ham  Oglethorpe...............................Charles  Newman,  Jr.
Bellinger.....................................Martin  K.  Sara
Verne  Harrap.................................Edmund  Le  Comte
Bill  Jordan..................................Jon  David
Soody  Revision...............................Paul  Brandon
```

Scene—Revisionville, a Small Town.

Staged by Coby Ruskin; setting by Edwin H. Vandernoot.

A group of shiftless cracker barrel yokels in a small town sit around criticizing the WPA and the Government's spending plan.

ACCORDING TO LAW

Cast of characters—

Ben Staggs (a lawyer)..............................Don Appell
Henry Terry (district judge).........................Jay Barney
Jim Nailey (county attorney)....................Henry Walden
Senator Lawrence (an attorney).............Charles Newman, Jr.
Charlie Teague.....................................P. Jay Sidney
Henry Yancey (a deputy sheriff)...............Richard O'Connor
Luke (a bailiff)................................Edmund Le Comte
George Randall (a deputy sheriff)..............Tom McGivern, Jr.
Harvey (a court reporter).............................Jon David
    Scene—Courtroom, County Seat.
    Staged by Eugene Endrey; setting by Edwin H. Vandernoot.

A Negro is charged with the rape of a white woman. Ben Staggs, a lawyer taken to liquor, is appointed to his defense. Staggs practically proves that the Negro has been framed by the false testimony of a wife who sought to shield her own guilt. A prejudiced court and jury sentence the victim to the chair.

THE DEVIL IS A GOOD MAN

Cast of characters—

Interlocutor...Jay Barney
Ma Clovenhoof.................................Kathryn Westfall
Pa Clovenhoof....................................Richard Barr
Johnny Clovenhoof................................Paul Brandon
Sardanapulos.................................Edmund Le Comte
Adolph Schukelgruber................................Don Appell
General Gobbleup....................................Martin Sara
Frank..Jon David
Joe...William Keene
Reverend Obidias Monday........................Gregory Morton
Girl on Park Bench.............................Wanda Rogers
Police Sergeant...............................Tom McGivern, Jr.
Hoyle...Ray O'Brien
1st Girl..Suzanne Endrey
2nd Girl...Janice Holter
Boy Picket...Martin Sara
Katy..Kiko Karmi
Amy Monday.....................................Elaine Melchior
    Scene 1—In Hell. 2—Adolph's Sanctum Sanctorum. 3—A Park
    4—Mercey City Police Court. 5—Amy Monday's Apartment.
    Staged by Stephen Moore; settings by Edwin H. Vandernoot.

The Devil is a worthy family man living contentedly in Hell. His son visits the Earth, carrying a special rabbit's foot for luck. He meets a Hitler and a Billy Sunday type of evangelist and is arraigned in police court as a pickpocket.

"Many Things" an intimate revue including one-act plays and sketches was the introductory production of the One-Act Variety Theatre at the Provincetown Playhouse, February 2, 1940. This was followed by the three one-act plays starting March 19, the casts of which are listed above. The third bill, April 25, consisted of "The Last Christmas," a melodrama by Noel Houston; "Pocket Edition," a revue by Alfred D. Geto, Jess Kruger and Robert Weil, music by Buddy Marsh; "This Earth is Ours" a melodrama by William Kozlenko, directed by Stephen Moore. Edwin H. Vandernoot designed the settings. Mr. Endrey also presented "Fireworks on the James," a play in three acts adapted to an American southern locale by Elizabeth McCormick from a translation by John Cournos of Anton Chekhov's "That Worthless Fellow Platonov." Donald Wetmore staged the play. (May 14 through May 23, 1940.)

A CASE OF YOUTH

(5 performances)

A comedy in three acts by Wesley Towner, based on a play by Ludwig Hirshfeld and Eugene Wolf. Produced by Courtney Burr at the National Theatre, New York, March 23, 1940.

Cast of characters—

Dobbs	Frank McCormack
Mrs. Watts	Mary Sargent
Carlo	Bertram Thorn
Diana	Valerie Cossart
Mr. Mayflower	Arthur Margetson
Peter	Richard Kendrick
Midge	Ellen Schwanneke
Boomer	Herbert Duffy
Bessie	Dorothy O'Hanlon
Mrs. Rosenkranz	Babette Feist
Kline	Guy J. Sampsel
Fish	William Rees
Mrs. Marrow	Lalive Brownell
Clark	J. Ascher Smith
Politto	Sey Bockner
Mrs. Finkle	Anne Gerlette
Swithers	Bert Wilcox
Waiter	Auguste Aramini

Acts I and III.—Mr. Mayflower's House in New York. Act II.—Scene 1—Mr. Mayflower's House. 2—Living Room of Peter Ross's Suite at St. Pierre Hotel, New York.
Staged by Arthur Sircom; settings by A. A. Ostrander.

Midge Mayflower is a fixer. When her father carelessly uses certain securities which he should have left alone in the raising of $10,000, and is facing trouble with his creditors and the courts, Midge sends him on a trip and then proceeds to satisfy the creditors by selling the household furniture and to take care of the notes by wangling endorsements out of susceptible males.

(Closed March 27, 1940)

THE BEST PLAYS OF 1939-40447

MAMBA'S DAUGHTERS

(17 performances)

A drama in two acts by Dorothy and DuBose Heyward, dramatized from DuBose Heyward's novel of the same name. Revived by Guthrie McClintic at the Broadway Theatre, New York, March 23, 1940.

Cast of characters—

```
Mamba (Hagar's Mother)........................Georgia Burke
Policeman.......................................Vincent Copeland
Clerk of the Court...............................John Kerr
The Prosecuting Attorney.........................John O'Connor
St. Julien DeC. Wentworth (Saint)...............Robert Thomsen
The Judge........................................Barry Kelley
Hagar...........................................Ethel Waters
Davey...........................................Al Stokes
Ned.............................................Wilson Bradley
Mingo...........................................Louis Sharp
Drayton.........................................Canada Lee
Maum Vina (The Island Matriarch)................Ethel Purnello
Eva.............................................Edna Waters
Willie May......................................Laura Vaughns
The Reverend Quintus Whaley.....................J. Rosamond Johnson
Gilley Bluton...................................Willie Bryant
Dolly...........................................Alberta Hunter
Lissa (as a Child)..............................Joyce Miller
Martha..........................................Rena Mitchell
Gardenia........................................Maude Russell
Tony............................................Jimmy Wright
Lissa...........................................Fredi Washington
```
    Act I.—Scene 1—The Courtroom. Charleston, S. C. 2—The Commissary of Brick House Plantation on Ediwander Island. 3—The Church. 4—Mamba's Room on the Charleston Waterfront. Act II.—Scenes 1, 3 and 5—The Commissary. 2 and 4—Gilly's Cabin, Ediwander Island.
    Staged by Guthrie McClintic; settings by Perry Watkins.
    The Song, "Lonesome Walls" from the lyric by DuBose Heyward sung by Anne Brown for the Radio Broadcast in the play.

"Mamba's Daughters" was first produced at the Empire Theatre, New York, January 3, 1939, and ran for 162 performances. See "Best Plays of 1938-39."

(Closed April 6, 1940)

* SEPARATE ROOMS

(98 performances)

A comedy in three acts by Joseph Carole and Alan Dinehart in collaboration with Alex Gottlieb and Edmund Joseph. Produced by Bobby Crawford at the Maxine Elliott Theatre, New York, March 23, 1940.

Cast of characters—

```
Taggert.........................................Jack Smart
Gary Bryce......................................Austin Fairman
```

```
Don Stackhouse.................................Lyle Talbot
Linda.........................................Mozelle Britton
Scoop Davis...................................James Robbins
Pam...........................................Glenda Farrell
Jim Stackhouse................................Alan Dinehart
Leona Sharpe..................................Madora Keene
```
    Acts I, II and III.—Penthouse Apartment of Jim and Don Stack-
house in New York City.
    Staged by William B. Friedlander.

Jim Stackhouse is a keyhole columnist, specializing in gossip.
Don Stackhouse, his brother, is a playwright who marries the
chilly star of his first success. The actress prefers her Chihuahua
pup as a bedroom companion, a situation brother Jim determines
to correct. He thereupon blackmails Pam, the actress, into ful-
filling her marital obligations and is later caught in the love press
himself.

LILIOM

(56 performances)

A play in a prologue and two acts by Ferenc Molnar, adapted
by Benjamin Glazer; incidental music by Deems Taylor. Produced by Vinton Freedley at the 44th Street Theatre, New York,
March 25, 1940.

Cast of characters—

```
Marie.........................................Helen Shields
Julie.........................................Ingrid Bergman
Mrs. Muskat...................................Ann Mason
"Liliom"......................................Burgess Meredith
Four Servant Girls......Ann Holahan, Elaine Perry, Evelyn Moser,
                                                       Jane Amar
Policemen.......................Joseph Macauley, Howard Freeman
Mother Hollunder .............................Margaret Wycherly
"The Sparrow".................................Elia Kazan
Suburban Policeman............................Frank Vincent
Young Hollunder...............................Kenneth Bates
Wolf Beifeld..................................John Emery
Linzman.......................................Joseph Kramm
First Mounted Police..........................Francis De Sales
Second Mounted Police.........................Lee Berkman
The Doctor....................................Chet Bree
The Carpenter.................................Gibb Penrose
First Policeman of the Beyond.................Joseph Macauley
Second Policeman of the Beyond................Francis De Sales
The Richly Dressed Man........................Howard Freeman
The Poorly Dressed Man........................Richard MacKay
The Old Guard.................................R. Henry Handon
The Magistrate................................Arnold Korff
Louise........................................Joan Tetzel
```
    Peasants, Townspeople, Etc.: The Sword Swallower, Ajax; The
    Juggler, Edwin George; The Strong Man, Richard Vimtour.
    Florence Earle, Mary Gildea, James Russo, Constance Dowling,
    Eleanor Prentiss, Gail Drexel, Patricia Harris, Gigi Gilpin, Bea-
    trice Pearson, Sonny Wright, Joyce Haywood, William Rob-
    ertson.
    Children: Eileen Murphy, Haldor de Becker, John Cushman, Peggy
    Romano, Marilyn Jolie.
    Prologue.—An Amusement Park on the Outskirts of Budapest,
1910. Act I.—Scene 1—A Lonely Place in the Park. Scenes 2 and

3—The Photographic Studio of the Hollunders. Act II.—Scene 1
—A Railroad Track on the Outskirts of the City. 2—The Hollun-
ders' Studio. 3—A Courtroom in the Beyond. 4—Before Julie's
Door.
    Staged by Benno Schneider; settings by Nat Karson.

"Liliom" was first produced by the Theatre Guild in New York
the season of 1920-21. It was revived in 1932 by Eva Le Gallienne
at the Civic Repertory Theatre, New York. See "The Best Plays
of 1920-21."
                    (Closed May 11, 1940)

*LADIES IN RETIREMENT

(95 performances)

A drama in three acts by Reginald Denham and Edward Percy.
Produced by Gilbert Miller at the Henry Miller Theatre, New
York, March 26, 1940.

Cast of characters—

Lucy Gilham.....................................Evelyn Ankers
Leonora Fiske....................................Isobel Elsom
Ellen Creed.......................................Flora Robson
Albert Feather.................................Patrick O'Moore
Louisa Creed...................................Estelle Winwood
Emily Creed................................Jessamine Newcombe
Sister Theresa...................................Florence Edney
    Acts I, II and III.—Living Room of an Old House on the Marshes
of the Thames Estuary Some Ten Miles to the East of Gravesend,
1885.
    Staged by Reginald Denham; setting by Raymond Sovey; cos-
tumes by Helene Pons.

Ellen Creed, living as housekeeper and companion to Leonora
Fiske, retired actress on the Thames marshes, asks her employer
to invite her under-privileged sisters for a week in the country.
The sisters arrive, are discovered to be slightly balmy, and refuse,
after stretching their stay to four weeks, to be put out. When
Miss Fiske orders them back to London, Ellen calmly strangles
her employer and turns the house over to her kin. The Fiske body
is walled up in an old bake oven and for months Ellen explains
the disappearance by reporting Miss Fiske on a world tour. Albert
Feather, her nephew, being suspicious, finally breaks down her
defenses and her exposure threatens.

LADY IN WAITING

(87 performances)

A comedy in three acts by Margery Sharp, based on her novel
"The Nutmeg Tree." Produced by Brock Pemberton at the
Martin Beck Theatre, New York, March 27, 1940.

Cast of characters—

Anthelmine.....................................Michelette Burani
Susan Packett..............................Carol Curtis-Brown
Bryan Relton.............................Stephen Ker Appleby
Mrs. Packett................................Lenore Chippendale
Julia Packett....................................Gladys George
Griffin...Anita Bolster
Burns...Paul A. Foley
Rogers...Guy Spaull
Sir William Warring.............................Alan Napier
Esme Bellingham..............................Mary Heberden
Willie Genocchio.................................Walter Moore
Fred Genocchio.................................Leonard Penn
"Ma" Genocchio................................Ethel Morrison
Bert Genocchio...................................Albert Allen
Joe Genocchio.....................................James Decker

Act I.—Scenes 1 and 4—Mrs. Packett's Living Room, Muzin,
France. 2—Julia's Bathroom, London. 3—Bar-Salon of a Channel
Boat. Act II.—Mrs. Packett's Living Room. Act III.—Julia's Bed-
room at Mrs. Packett's.
Staged by Antoinette Perry; settings by John Root.

Julia Packett, a chorus girl when the First World War was
organized, was in love with a young officer of the British expedi-
tionary force. They were married before he left for the front.
When her baby was born she gave it into the keeping of her husband's people. The child, reared a lady when her own marriage
plans are interfered with, sends for Julia to ask her advice. Julia
flies to her daughter's side and, being rather on the rough diamond
side, has many amusing experiences. In the end she not only
straightens out daughter's affairs, but also gets herself a titled husband.

(Closed June 8, 1940)

THE SCENE OF THE CRIME

(12 performances)

A drama in three acts by Frank Gould. Produced by Harry
Howard at the Fulton Theatre, New York, March 28, 1940.

Cast of characters—

Arthur Hanley...............................Halliam Bosworth
Tobias Rosenfeld...................................Louis Sorin
Edith Hanley.......................................Elaine Kent
Stella Hanley.....................................Kittie Cosgriff
David Hanley..................................Chester Stratton
Jean..Louise Latimer
Katherine...Sheila Trent
Marion Hanley..............................Margaret Callahan
Larry Pearson.................................Robert Morrow
Jimmy Hanley......................................David Wayne
Spence..Howard Lane
Bob Hanley...Allan Hale
Dr. William Hood.................................King Calder

Acts I, II and III.—The Hanley Apartment, New York City.
Staged by Frank Merlin; setting by Cirker and Robbins.

David Hanley, one of a youthful trio that stages a holdup and murders the victim, is convicted and sentenced to the chair. David's parents and his brothers and sisters suffer greatly from the tragedy. Following the execution David's spirit returns to his home and seeks to comfort his family. He has as much trouble getting the message across as Peter Grimm had in the David Belasco era.

(Closed April 4, 1940)

KING RICHARD II

(32 performances)

A tragedy by William Shakespeare with incidental music by Herbert Menges. Revived by Maurice Evans at the St. James Theatre, New York, April 1, 1940.

Cast of characters—

King Richard, the Second	Maurice Evans
John of Gaunt, Duke of Lancaster	John Barclay
Edmund of Langley, Duke of York	Franz Bendtsen
Henry, Surnamed Bolingbroke, Duke of Hereford, Son of Gaunt, Afterwards King Henry IV	Donald Randolph
Thomas Mowbray, Duke of Norfolk	Sydney Smith
Duke of Aumerle	Lauren Gilbert
Bushy	Kurt Richards
Bagot	Everett Ripley
Green	Alexander Scourby
Earl of Northumberland	Charles Dalton
Lord Ross	George Keane
Lord Willoughby	Anthony Ross
The Lord Marshal	Rhys Williams
Mowbray's Herald	Walter Williams
Bolingbroke's Herald	Alfred Paschall
Henry Percy, Surnamed Hotspur	Emmett Rogers
Earl of Salisbury	Howard Wierum
Captain of a Band of Welshmen	Rhys Williams
Bishop of Carlisle	Donald Cameron
Sir Stephen Scroop	Sydney Smith
Gardener	Rhys Williams
Second Gardener	John McQuade
Earl of Surrey	Alfred Paschall
Sir Pierce of Exton	Alexander Scourby
Servant to Exton	John McQuade
A Groom	Donald Cameron
A Keeper	Anthony Ross
Queen to Richard	Carmen Mathews
Duchess of Gloucester	Jackson Perkins
Ladies Attending on Queen	{ June Brown { Jackson Perkins

Lords, Ladies, Officers, Soldiers, Monks, Messenger and Other Attendants: Jessie Dimond, Evelyn Hope, Frederic Carney, Alexander Nicol, Melvin Parks, Alfred Paschall, Walter Williams, John McQuade and Howard Wierum.
Act. I.—Scene 1—King Richard's Palace. 2—Duke of Lancaster's Palace. 3—Lists at Coventry. 4—Windsor Castle. 5—Ely House. Act II.—Scene 1—Windsor Castle. 2—Wilds of Gloucestershire. 3—Camp in Wales. 4—Bristol before the Castle. 5—Coast of Wales. 6—Wales before Flint Castle. Act III.—Scene 1—Duke of York's Garden. 2 and 6—Westminster Hall. 3—London Street. 4—Windsor Castle. 5—Pomfret Castle.
Staged by Margaret Webster; settings by David Ffolkes.

Largely a new cast, but virtually the same production with
which Mr. Evans began his American starring adventure in 1937.
See "The Best Plays of 1936-37."

(Closed April 27, 1940)

AN INTERNATIONAL INCIDENT

(15 performances)

A comedy in three acts by Vincent Sheean.   Produced by Guthrie
McClintic at the Ethel Barrymore Theatre, New York, April 2,
1940.

Cast of characters—

```
Smithers...........................................Arthur  Kennedy
McClosky...........................................Ben  Lackland
Ninette............................................Regina  Valdy
Reggiani...........................................Sidney  Stone
Photographers.........Richard S. Bishop, Peter Scott, John Gage
Mrs. John Wuthering Blackett......................Josephine Hull
"Hank"  Rogers.....................................Kent  Smith
Mrs. Charles Rochester..........................Ethel  Barrymore
Miss Evadne Martin.............................Lea  Penman
Mrs. Thrush....................................Eda  Heinemann
                        IN DETROIT
Mrs. G. Hiram Tracy............................Josephine Hull
Mrs. Burlingame................................Lea  Penman
Mrs. August  Schultz...........................Eda  Heinemann
Riley..........................................Arthur  Kennedy
Jaeger.........................................Sidney  Stone
Witherspoon....................................Ben  Lackland
Photographers.........Richard S. Bishop, Peter Scott, John Gage
The Right Honorable Charles Albert Clarke-Bates,
                       C.B., etc......Cecil Humphreys
    Acts I and III.—A Sitting Room in an Hotel de Luxe in New
York.  Act II.—Scene 1—Sitting Room in an Hotel de Luxe in
Chicago.  2—Sitting Room in an Hotel de Luxe in Detroit.
    Staged by Guthrie McClintic; settings by Stewart Chaney.
```

Mrs. Charles Rochester, American-born, has become famous as
an English novelist.   She returns to America for a lecture tour.
In each city she visits she meets practically the same sample
citizens representing women's clubs and newspapers.   Among the
reporters is one Hank Rogers, a distant relative.   Hank is much
younger than Mrs. Rochester, something of a liberal.   Fearful that
his distinguished relative plans to spread war propaganda during
her tour, he follows her from New York to Chicago and Detroit.
In Detroit he introduces her to a picket line during a strike.   Interfering with a brutal strikebreaker, Mrs. Rochester is struck on
the head by a policeman.   This serves to clarify her opinions in
the class struggle.

(Closed April 13, 1940)

HIGHER AND HIGHER

(84 performances)

A musical comedy in two acts by Gladys Hurlbut and Joshua Logan, based on an idea by Irvin Pincus; lyrics by Lorenz Hart; music by Richard Rodgers; orchestration by Hans Spialek. Produced by Dwight Deere Wiman at the Shubert Theatre, New York, April 4, 1940.

Cast of characters—

Hilda O'Brien	Eva Condon
Byng	Robert Chisholm
Dottie	Billie Worth
Miss Whiffen	Hilda Spong
Sandy Moore	Shirley Ross
Zachary Ash	Jack Haley
Mike O'Brien	Lee Dixon
Minnie Sorenson	Marta Eggert
Scullery Maid	Mary Louise Quevli
Three Nursemaids	Gloria Hope / Hollace Shaw / Jane Richardson
Soda Jerker	Robert Rounsville
Ladies' Maid	Marie Nash
First Cop	Robert Shanley
Cops	Joe Scandur / Richard Moore
Footman	Carl Trees
Patrick O'Toole	Leif Erickson
Ellen	Janet Fox
Truckmen	Robert Rounsville / Joe Scandur
Snorri	Fin Olsen
Sharkey	Himself
The Handyman	Frederic Nay
The Cat	Ted Adair
The Frog	Lyda Sue
The Bat	Sigrid Dagnie
Coachman	Frederic Nay
The Gorilla	Joseph Granville
Purity	Jane Ball

Singing Girls: Kay Duncan, Gloria Hope, Marie Louise Quevli, Jane Richardson, Hollace Shaw.

Singing Boys: William Geery, Joseph Granville, Richard Moore, Robert Rounsville, Joe Scandur, Robert Shanley.

Higher and Higher Specialty Girls: June Allyson, Irene Austin, Jane Ball, Ronnie Cunningham, Sigrid Dagnie, Eleanor Eberle, Vera Ellen, Miriam Franklin, Marguerite James, Kay Picture, Lyda Sue.

Higher and Higher Specialty Boys: Ted Adair, Cliff Ferre, Bunnie Hightower, Louis Hightower, Michael Moore, Frederic Nay, Burton Pierce, Harry Rogue, Jack Seymour, Billy Skipper, Jr., Carl Trees.

Act I.—Scene 1—Section of Ballroom, New York Hotel. 2 and 4—Kitchen, Drake Mansion. 3—Deborah Drake's Bedroom. Act II. —Scene 1—The Kitchen. 2—Zach's Room. 3—The Old Carriage House. 4—Section of Ballroom, New York Hotel.

Staged by Joshua Logan; dances by Robert Alton; settings by Jo Mielziner; costumes by Lucinda Ballard.

Zachary Ash and a houseful of other servants are facing the loss of their wages and their jobs because their employer has embraced bankruptcy. They decide to incorporate one of the maids, Minnie Sorenson, an Icelandic beauty, as a society debutante, marry her to a wealthy Stork club playboy, and share the profits. At a party one of Minnie's old friends, a trained seal from Iceland, bites Mr. Ash in the pants and that brings things to a laughing climax.

(Closed June 15, 1940)

SUSPECT

(31 performances)

A drama in three acts by Edward Percy and Reginald Denham. Produced by Douglas MacLean and Arthur J. Beckhard at the Playhouse, New York, April 9, 1940.

Cast of characters—

```
Robert  Smith..................................Barton  Hepburn
Janet  Rendle....................................Jane  Lauren
Goudie  MacIntyre.............................Grayce  Hampton
Mrs.  Smith......................................Pauline  Lord
Dr.  Rendle.......................................Wallis  Clark
The  Rev.  Alfred  Combermere...................Robert  DeBruce
Sir  Hugo  Const...............................Frederic  Worlock
Lady  Const.....................................Mary  Servoss
```
    Acts I, II and III.—Garden Lounge of Mrs. Smith's Home in Polcurn, Cornwall.
    Staged by Arthur J. Beckhard; setting by Ernest Glover.

For twenty years Mrs. Smith has been living with her son, Robert, and a faithful old servant in an obscure part of Cornwall, England. No one has paid much attention to the Smiths, but now Robert is engaged to be married and both his fiancée, Janet Rendle, and her father, Dr. Rendle, have come to have a look at them. Also Janet's godfather, Sir Hugo Const, a great newspaper publisher who had been a crime reporter as a young man. Sir Hugo recognizes the old servant, Goudie MacIntyre, as a witness in a celebrated murder case in which an embittered daughter who had hacked her father and mother to death escaped conviction because the court held her guilt had not been proved. Sir Hugo and Dr. Rendle suspect Mrs. Smith, but even their crafty cross questioning fails to break her down. She is gleefully hacking away at a chopping block when they leave her.

(Closed May 4, 1940)

MEDICINE SHOW

(35 performances)

A Living Newspaper play in two acts by Oscar Saul and H. R. Hays, with music by Hanns Eisler. Produced by Carly Wharton and Martin Gabel at the New Yorker Theatre, New York, April 12, 1940.

Cast of characters—

Statistician	Martin Gabel
Hall	Coburn Goodwin
Dora	Dorothy McGuire
Mac	John Randolph
Jackson	Philip Bourneuf
Mrs. Jackson	Grace Coppin
Mrs. Sullivan	Isabel Bonner
Joe	Harry Lessin
Clinic Doctor	J. Richard Jones
Dr. Young	Alfred Ryder
Mrs. Young	Zamah Cunningham
Dr. White	Bram Nossen
Kennedy	Richard Clark
Rose	Olive Deering
Quack	Norman Lloyd
Chorines	Linda Lee / Virginia Campbell
Andrew	Joseph M. Dixon
Johnny	Ronald Reiss
Dr. Mackenzie	William Hansen
Ben	Perry Bruskin
Ellie	Sara Floyd
John	Melbourne Ford
Pete	Peter Frye
Sarah	Pearl Gaines
Mary	Norma Green
Bill	Ben Ross
Eli	Leigh Whipper

Staged by Jules Dassin; designed and lighted by Samuel Leve.

The Statistician is there to explain the needs of the many who cannot afford adequate medical protection. And to buttress with documented evidence the statement that 250,000 preventable deaths occur in the United States every year. Due to the opposition of certain Medical Associations organized for the selfish protection of their own memberships thousands of willing young physicians are led to a virtual violation of their Hippocratic oaths. The plea is for socialized medicine and the passage of a public health bill with a generous appropriation attached.

(Closed May 11, 1940)

MORNING STAR

(63 performances)

A comedy in three acts by Sylvia Regan; incidental music by Lee Wainer and Robert Sour. Produced by George Kondolf at the Longacre Theatre, New York, April 16, 1940.

Cast of characters—

Fanny ....Jeanne Greene
Becky Felderman....................................Molly Picon
Aaron Greenspan...................................Joseph Buloff
Esther...Cecilia Evans
Hymie (as a Boy)..............................Kenneth LeRoy
Harry Engel.......................................Martin Blaine
Sadie...Ruth Yorke
Irving Tashman...................................David Morris
Benjamin Brownstein...........................Harold J. Stone
Myron Engel.......................................Henry Sharp
Hymie (as a Young Man)..........................Ross Elliott
Pansy...Georgette Harvey
Hymie Tashman..................................Sidney Lumet
     Acts I, II and III.—Becky Felderman's Home, Lower East Side, New York.
     Staged by Charles K. Freeman; setting by Howard Bay; costumes by Alexander Jones.

Becky Felderman is the mother of four. Her family is living on the East Side in 1910 and is still there in 1931. Her daughter, Esther, was burned to death in the Triangle Shirt Waist Factory fire. Her son, Hymie, was killed in the World War. Her daughter, Fanny, married a song writer, acquiring a fur coat and marital worries. Her daughter, Sadie, married a schoolteacher and ruined his life trying to force him into business. Becky preserves her sweetness and her good nature through it all and finally marries Aaron, the faithful star boarder.

(Closed June 8, 1940)

HEAVENLY EXPRESS

(20 performances)

A fantasy in three acts by Albert Bein; incidental music by Lehman Engel. Produced by Kermit Bloomgarden at the National Theatre, New York, April 18, 1940.

Cast of characters—

Tommy..Phil Brown
Stumpy...William Sands
Methuselah Mike...................................Art Smith
The Overland Kid...............................John Garfield
The Melancholy Bo..............................Curt Conway
"Bullhead" Anderson...........................Harry Bratsburg

```
Ed Peeto...........................................Harry Carey
Dan..............................................Randolph Wade
"Shorty" Rucker......................................Will Lee
Rocky Mountain Red.................................Philip Loeb
Fred Norman....................................Russell Collins
Night Telegraph Operator.........................James O'Rear
Julio............................................Nicholas Conte
Betsy Graham..................................Aline MacMahon
Pat Borlie............................................Burl Ives
Andy Cameron..................................John O'Malley
Steve Corrigan...................................Jack Lambert
Scotty Thompson............................Charles Thompson
```
    Act I.—Scene 1—Railroad Trestle near Ash Fork, Arizona. 2—
Betsy Graham's Boarding House for Railroad Men. Acts II and
III.—Betsy Graham's Boarding House.
    Staged by Robert Lewis; settings by Boris Aronson.

The Overland Kid, according to the legends that follow the
Knights of the Road, died nineteen years ago when he was chased
over the icy roofs of a freight train, slipped and fell down a steep
embankment.   Therefore it must have been the spirit of the
Overland Kid that appeared to the Melancholy Bo one night and
summoned him aboard the Heavenly Express that was even then
swishing over the tracks and disrupting schedules on the whole
Santa Fe system.   He was the Advance Ticket Taker representing
the Almighty Vagabond, he said.   He went on from there to the
home of Betsy Graham, the Melancholy Bo's mother, and summoned her aboard the Express.   And probably clambered aboard
himself after the curtain fell and went back to his Heavenly Home.

(Closed May 4, 1940)

* THERE SHALL BE NO NIGHT

(56 performances)

A drama in three acts by Robert E. Sherwood.   Produced by
The Playwrights Company in association with The Theatre Guild
at the Alvin Theatre, New York, April 29, 1940.

Cast of characters—
```
Dr. Kaarlo Valkonen..............................Alfred Lunt
Miranda Valkonen..............................Lynn Fontanne
Dave Corween..................................Richard Whorf
Uncle Waldemar............................Sydney Greenstreet
Gus Shuman.......................................Brooks West
Erik Valkonen................................Montgomery Clift
Kaatri Alquist................................Elisabeth Fraser
Dr. Ziemssen................................Maurice Colbourne
Major Rutkowski.............................Edward Raquello
Joe Burnett.......................................Charles Ansley
Ben Gichner....................................Thomas Gomez
Frank Olmstead.........................William Le Massena
Sergeant Gosden...............................Claude Horton
Lempi .........................................Phyllis Thaxter
Ilma............................................Charva Chester
Photographer.....................................Ralph Nelson
Photographer.................................Robert Downing
```

Acts I and II.—Living Room of the Valkonens' House in Helsinki.
Act III.—Scene 1—Dave Corween's Rooms, Hotel Kamp, Helsinki.
2—Classroom in School House near Viipuri Bay. 3—The Valkonens'
Living Room, 1940.
Staged by Alfred Lunt; settings by Richard Whorf; costumes by
Valentina.

See page 29.

LOVE'S OLD SWEET SONG

(44 performances)

A comedy in three acts by William Saroyan; music by Paul
Bowles. Produced by The Theatre Guild in association with
Eddie Dowling at the Plymouth Theatre, New York, May 2, 1940.

Cast of characters—

Ann Hamilton, 44	Jessie Royce Landis
Georgie Americanos	Peter Fernandez
Barnaby Gaul, 51 ("old Doc Goodheart")	Walter Huston
Tom Fiora	James S. Elliott
Demetrios	Angi O. Poulos
Cabot Yearling	Arthur Hunnicutt
Leona Yearling, 44	Doro Merande
Newton Yearling, 19	Eugene Fitts
Velma Yearling } Twins	Barbara Hastings
Selma Yearling }	Ardele Hastings
Al Yearling	Thomas Jordan
Henry Yearling	Eric Roberts
Jesse Yearling	Jackie Ayers
Lucy Yearling	Patsy O'Shea
Ella Yearling	Mae Grimes
Susan Yearling	Patricia Roe
Maud Yearling	Carol Esa
Lemmie Yearling	Bob White
Mae Yearling	Eleanor Drexler
Harry Yearling	Michael Artist
Wilbur Yearling	Gerald Matthews
Richard Oliver	Lloyd Gough
Elsa Wax	Beatrice Newport
David F. Windmore	Alan Hewitt
Daniel Hough	John A. Regan
Mr. Smith	Nick Dennis
Mr. Harris	George Travell
Sheriff	Howard Freeman
Stylianos Americanos, 41	Alan Reed
Pericles Americanos, 61	John Economides

Acts I and II.—Yard of Ann Hamilton's California Home. Act
III.—Interior of the Americanos Home.
Staged by Eddie Dowling and William Saroyan. Production under
supervision of Lawrence Langner, Theresa Helburn and Armina
Marshall; settings by Watson Barratt.

Ann Hamilton, 44, receiving a phony love message from one
who signs himself Barnaby Gaul, mistakes a passing pitchman,
good old Dr. Goodheart of the carnivals, for her approaching lover.
Dr. Goodheart is not loathe to play the experiment through, though
it is briefly complicated by the arrival of a family of Pa, Ma and
sixteen little Yearlings, from Oklahoma. The Yearlings settle on
Ann, rifle her home and finally set fire to it. With the help of

Georgie Americanos, a Postal Telegraph messenger, who brought Ann the original message, love finally conquers all.

(Closed June 8, 1940)

GREY FARM

(35 performances)

A melodrama in three acts by Hector Bolitho and Terence Rattigan. Produced by Irving Cooper at the Hudson Theatre, New York, May 3, 1940.

Cast of characters—

Mrs. Iron	Evelyn Varden
Stephen Grantham	John Cromwell
Judith Weaver	Jane Sterling
James Grantham	Oscar Homolka
Mavis	Maria Temple
Lady Weaver	Adrienne Morrison
Ellen	Vera Mellish

Acts I, II and III.—Drawing Room in home of James Grantham, Cambridgeshire.

Staged by Berthold; setting by Raymond Sovey.

James Grantham's wife had died in childbirth. Her son lived on. James Grantham thereupon transferred the great love he had borne the wife to the boy, Stephen. When Stephen wanted to marry Judith Weaver his father was torn with jealousy and resentment. Cursed with the strangler urge, indicated by the fact that both his thumbs were turned up, James Grantham fought against the urge to strangle his son, his son's fiancée and a couple of others. He finally strangled a maid who had tried to blackmail him and then shot himself.

(Closed June 1, 1940)

OUT FROM UNDER

(9 performances)

A comedy in three acts by John Walter Kelly. Produced by Brock Pemberton at the Biltmore Theatre, New York, May 4, 1940.

Cast of characters—

Bessie Gedge	Margaret Douglass
Amy	Viola Dean
Helen Parker	Ruth Weston
Marian Parker	Tina Thayer
Joe Parker	John Alexander
The Reverend Dr. Chester	G. Albert Smith
Humphrey Williams	Philip Ober

```
Lawrence Thomas....................................James Corner
Claire James.......................................Vivian Vance
     Acts I, II and III.—The Parkers' Living Room, Haverford,
Indiana.
     Staged by Antoinette Perry; setting by John Root.
```

Joe Parker, to relieve the boredom of editing a small town paper, writes a sexy novel under a fancy name, putting ideas in the heads of many restless wives. The book proves a best seller; Joe's wife nearly runs away with a cad as a result of her reading it; the publishers send an alluring blonde to woo Joe out of his determined anonymity and onto the lecture platform and there is considerable confusion in the Parker home.

(Closed May 11, 1940)

THE STRANGLER FIG

(8 performances)

A mystery melodrama in a prologue and three acts adapted by Edith Meiser from a book by John Stephen Strange. Produced by William Herz at the Lyceum Theatre, New York, May 6, 1940.

Cast of characters—

```
Maman Chloe....................................Musa Williams
Mrs. Stella Drew..............................Paula MacLean
Jacob Grass......................................Royal Beal
John Stuart........................................James Todd
Daniel Lane....................................William Roselle
Lydia Vaughn....................................Edith Meiser
Solomon Jura....................................John Lorenz
Madeleine Huntington..........................Madeleine Clive
Adele Huntington..............................Margaret Curtis
Franklin.......................................Dooley Wilson
Bolivar Brown....................................Eddie Nugent
     Prologue and Acts I, II and III.—World's End—An Island Off
the Coast of Florida.
     Staged by Frank Coletti; setting by Frederick Fox.
```

Madeleine Huntington, widow of Stephen Huntington, who was strangled mysteriously on an island off the Florida coast years before the play opens, invites all the suspects who had been with Harold back to the island for purposes of investigation. While they are there a couple more are taken off, one being hung up on a closet door and the other picked off by mysterious hands and a bathrobe cord while he was reading quietly. "Good God, what a mess!" mutters one who is close enough to know what he is talking about.

(Closed May 11, 1940)

ROMEO AND JULIET

(36 performances)

A tragedy in three acts by William Shakespeare; music by Alexander Steinert and Laurence Olivier. Revived by Laurence Olivier at the 51st Street Theatre, New York, May 9, 1940.

Cast of characters—

Chorus, Prince Escalus	Wilton Graff
Watchman	Morton L. Stevens
A Friar	Earle Grey
Two Church-Going Women	Clara Speer / Nan Merriman
A Collier	Oliver Cliff
Sampson	William Barrows
Gregory	Joseph Tomes
Abraham	Robert Busch
Balthasar	Jack Merivale
Chief Officer of the Town	Walter Brooke
Tybalt	Cornel Wilde
Page to Tybalt	Ralph Brooke
Benvolio	Wesley Addy
Page to Benvolio	Ralph Grayson
A Third Woman	Patricia Knight
A Fourth Woman	Mary Kane
A Cook	Nancie B. Marsland
A Child	Virginia Burchfield
1st Peace Officer	Charles Prescott
2nd Peace Officer	Howard T. Stark
Capulet	Halliwell Hobbes
Lady Capulet	Katharine Warren
Peter	Raymond Johnson
Montague	Ben Webster
Lady Montague	Barbara Horder
Four Soldiers	John Straub / Charles Martin / Tileston Perry / H. Robert Edwards
Mercutio	Edmond O'Brien
Paris	Frank Downing
Romeo	Laurence Olivier
Nurse	Dame May Whitty
Juliet	Vivien Leigh
Page to Mercutio	Ted Huish
Page to Paris	Brant Gorman
Rosaline	Hazel Brown
Old Capulet	Morton L. Stevens
Friar Laurence	Alexander Knox
Surgeon	Oliver Cliff
Apothecary	Earle Grey
Friar John	Morton L. Stevens

Act I.—Scenes 1, 3 and 8—Street in Verona. 2 and 4—Capulet's Hall. 5—Lane by Wall of Capulet's Orchard. 6 and 9—Capulet's Orchard. 7 and 10—Friar Laurence's Cell. Act II.—Scene 1—Street in Verona. 2—Capulet's Orchard. 3 and 6—Friar Laurence's Cell. 4 and 7—Capulet's Hall. 5—Juliet's Balcony. 8—Juliet's Room. Act III.—Scene 1—Street in Mantua. 2—Friar Laurence's Cell, Verona. 3—Churchyard and Capulet Monument, Verona.

Staged by Laurence Olivier and Robert Ross; dances by Ernst and Maria Matray; settings by Motley; lighting by Robert Edmond Jones.

This is a somewhat expanded version of the Shakespearean tragedy employed by Laurence Olivier at the Old Vic Theatre in London.

(Closed June 8, 1940)

THE RETURN OF THE VAGABOND

(7 performances)

A melodramatic satire in an introductory and two acts by
George M. Cohan. Produced by George M. Cohan at the National Theatre, New York, May 17, 1940.

Cast of characters—

```
The Vagabond...................................George M. Cohan
The Governor...................................McKay Morris
His Wife.......................................Marie Louise Dana
His Daughter...................................Celeste Holm
His Son-in-Law.................................John Morny
The Tavern Keeper..............................E. J. Blunkall
His Son........................................Fred Herrick
His Daughter-in-Law............................Gretchen Davidson
The Italian....................................Joe Verdi
The Doctor.....................................John Cherry
The Banker.....................................Florenz Ames
The Sheriff....................................Edward McNamara
The Captain....................................Len Hollister
His Assistant..................................George Leach
A Stranger.....................................Dona McClelland
A Little Stranger..............................George Thornton
Another Stranger...............................Marshall Bradford
The Coachman...................................Henry Sherwood
The Cop........................................George W. Smith
         Acts I and II.—The Tavern.
      Staged by Sam Forrest; setting by Oden Waller.
```

After twenty years the Vagabond of "The Tavern" returns to
the site of his former adventures, which is an old New England Inn
frequently visited by the Governor of the state and his family.
On this occasion the blithesome Vagabond ushers in a variety of
rain and lightning storms, uncovers a pair of bank robbers, sees
the Governor's daughter married to the frail young man to whom
she was engaged in the earlier play and goes merrily, and a little
messily, on his way.

(Closed May 18, 1940)

AT THE STROKE OF EIGHT

(8 performances)

A drama in a prologue and three acts by Percy Robinson. Produced by Joseph M. Gaites and Albert de Courville at the Belasco
Theatre, New York, May 20, 1940.

Cast of characters—

```
Mrs. Ellis.....................................Margaret Moffat
Inspector Jackson..............................Reynolds Denniston
Constable Hicks................................Ralph Sumpter
Mrs. Nolan.....................................Sara Allgood
```

Tim Nolan..Frank Maxwell
Michael Allen....................................Harry Young
Harold Fairfield................................Richard Waring
Nichols..J. C. Dunn
Dr. Barton.......................................Edward Harvey
Thomas Fairfield................................Reginald Mason
George Hope.....................................Wallis Clark
Madge Barton....................................Valerie Cossart
Sergeant Brown..................................Byron Russell
Father Collins..............................Laurence C. O'Brien
Mrs. Driscoll...................................Grania O'Malley
Old Ryan..Hale Norcross

Prologue—Bedroom in a Kensington flat. Act I.—Scene 1—Parlor at Mrs. Nolan's, Foley St., Lambeth. 2—Smoking Room at the Fairfield's Hindhead. Act II.—Scene 1—Smoking Room at the Fairfield's. 2—Witness Room at the "Old Bailey." Act III.—Scene 1—Smoking Room at the Fairfield's. 2—Parlor at Mrs. Nolan's.

Staged by Albert de Courville; settings by L. L. Goldwasser.

Harold Fairfield, the son of well-born and well-to-do parents, suffers emotional lapses of memory during which he is not accountable for his acts. During one of these he visits the room of a girl of the streets and strangles her in her bed. Tim Nolan, the honest son of the widowed Mrs. Nolan, a good friend of the victim, had also visited her the night of the murder. Tim is arrested, tried and convicted on circumstantial evidence and sentenced to be hanged. Harold, the guilty one, suffers from a tortured conscience until the day of the execution when he summons the strength to write a confession and shoot himself through the head.

(Closed May 25, 1940)

* KEEP OFF THE GRASS

(28 performances)

A musical comedy in two acts; lyrics by Al Dubin and Howard Dietz; sketches by Mort Lewis, Parke Levy, Alan Lipscott, S. J. Kaufman, Reginald Beckwith and Panama and Frank; music by James McHugh. Produced by the Messrs. Shubert at the Broadhurst Theatre, New York, May 23, 1940.

Principals engaged—

Jimmy Durante   The Morelli Singers
Ray Bolger   Jane Froman
Jose Limon   Ilka Chase
Larry Adler   Betty Bruce
John McCauley   Nan Rae
Jack Gleason   Maude Davis
Robert Shackleton   Sunny O'Dea
Emmet Kelly   Virginia O'Brien
Hal Neiman   Margery Moore
Sid Walker   Daphne Vane
Peanuts Bohn   Joanna de Tuscan
Bela de Tuscan   The Toreadors
Dodson's Monkeys

Staged by Fred de Cordova; book directed by Edward Duryea
Dowling; production under supervision of Harry Alvin Kaufman;
settings and costumes by Nat Karson; choreography by George
Balanchine.

RUSSIAN BANK

(11 performances)

A comedy in three acts by Theodore Komisarjevsky and Stuart
Mims, based on an idea of Boris Said. Produced by Theodore
Komisarjevsky at the St. James Theatre, New York, May 24, 1940.

Cast of characters—

Masha	Natasha Boleslavsky
Serov	Mikhail Rasumny
Serova	Natalie Harris
Natasha	Josephine Houston
Butienko	James Rennie
Patterson	Ralph Morehouse
Madame La Generale Denisova	Jeanne Palmer
Valeria	Ernestine Stodelle
Lisa	Jay Mannering
Baron Oeberg	Roger Plowden
Count Malsky	Gerald Kean
Grand Duke Nikita	Tonio Selwart
Shubina	Elena Karam
Koulnis	George Andre
Cameron	John Adair
Stark	Paul Belanger
The Lame Commissar	Mikhail Rasumny
Petrova	Geena Goodwin

Revolutionaries: Alexis Bolan, Michel Michon, Michel Greben,
Arcady Stoyanovsky, Ivan Triesault, Boris Belostozky.

Gypsy Man	Michel Michon
Gypsy Girl	Marjorie Tas

Gypsies: Ara Shvedova, Elena Arafelova, Natasha Boleslavsky,
Gedda Petry, Evelyn Marsh, Arcady Stoyanovsky, Boris Belostozky, Alexis Bolan, Michel Greben.

Cleopatra	Marjorie Tas
Mrs. Cameron	Effie Shannon
Katie	Natalie Harris
Poushnoff	Arcady Stoyanovsky
Tipoff	Alexis Bolan
Schnizel	Mikhail Rasumny

Act I.—Scene 1—Imperial Opera House, St. Petersburg, 1917.
2—Private Waiting Room and Manager's Office at National Security
Bank, Petersburg. Act II.—Scene 1—Madame la Generale's Sitting
Room, 1918. 2—Private Waiting Room and Manager's Office,
National Security Bank, Petersburg. Act III.—Mrs. Cameron's Sit-
ting Room, Long Island, 1933.

Staged by Theodore Komisarjevsky; settings by Louis Bromberg.

Natasha, a handsome prima-donna, being hard pressed in St.
Petersburg before the revolution, undertakes to save her royal
lover, the Grand Duke Nikita, by being nice to a dashing Commissar, Butienko. Comes the revolution and the comrades take
Natasha's funds, the Commissar takes Natasha and practically
everybody takes passage for America. In America Natasha again
meets the Grand Duke at Effie Shannon's place on Long Island.

Meantime she has learned to love her Commissar. The Grand
Duke doesn't care much, either.

(Closed June 1, 1940)

* LOUISIANA PURCHASE

(23 performances)

A musical comedy in two acts by Morrie Ryskind based on a
story by B. G. De Sylva; music and lyrics by Irving Berlin. Produced by B. G. De Sylva at the Imperial Theatre, New York,
May 28, 1940.

Cast of characters—

Secretary	Georgia Carroll
Sam Liebowitz	John Eliot
Col. Davis D. Davis, Sr.	Robert Pitkin
Abner	Nicodemus
Col. Davis D. Davis, Jr.	Ray Mayer
Dean Manning	Ralph Riggs
Police Captain Whitfield	Edward H. Robins
Jim Taylor	William Gaxton
Lee Davis	Nick Long, Jr.
Emmy-Lou	April Ames
Beatrice	Carol Bruce
Marina Van Linden	Vera Zorina
Madame Bordelaise	Irene Bordoni
Senator Oliver P. Loganberry	Victor Moore
Alphonse	Charles La Torre

The Martins: Hugh Martin, Ralph Blane, Jo Jean Rogers, Phyllis
Rogers.

The Buccaneers: John Panter, John Eliot, Don Cortez, James
Phillips.

Premier Danseur	Charles Laskey

Act I.—Scene 1—Lawyer's Office. 2—Library of Jefferson Davis
Club. 3 and 7—Street Scene. 4—Madame Bordelaise's Café. 6—
Private Room, Madame Bordelaise's Café. 8—Mardi Gras Ball.
Act II.—Scene 1—Mardi Gras Ball. 2—A Wood. 3 and 5—Street
Scene. 4—Senator Loganberry's Hotel Apartment. 6—Near the
Capitol. 7—The State Capitol, Baton Rouge.
Staged by Edgar MacGregor; ballets by George Balanchine; dances
by Carl Randall; costumes and settings by Tom Lee.

Jim Taylor is attorney for the Louisiana Purchase Co., Inc.,
which is running things with a high hand in Louisiana. The
United States Senate decides to send Senator Oliver P. Loganberry to investigate. Lawyer Taylor would nullify the Senator's
investigation by involving him in a scandal. He tempts Senator
Loganberry with Zorina, the dancer, and Bordoni, the flirt, but
the Senator eludes both the ladies and the Taylor schemes.

LOVE FOR LOVE

(8 performances)

A comedy in four acts by William Congreve; prologue and epilogue by Charles Hanson Towne; music by Macklin Marrow. Revived by The Players at the Hudson Theatre, New York, June 3, 1940.

Cast of characters—

Sir Sampson Legend..........................Thomas H. Chalmers
Valentine ....Barry Jones
Scandal...Leo G. Carroll
Tattle...Edgar Stehli
Ben...Bobby Clark
Foresight ....Dudley Digges
Jeremy ....Romney Brent
Trapland ....Herbert Ranson
Buckram...A. G. Andrews
Snap ....Paul Parks
Angelica ....Cornelia Otis Skinner
Mrs. Foresight......................................Peggy Wood
Mrs. Frail...Violet Heming
Miss Prue..Dorothy Gish
Nurse to Miss Prue.............................Daisy Belmore
Stewart to Sir Sampson...........................Jack Prescott
Servant to Foresight.............................J. Ascher Smith
    Sailors: John Seymour, Neil Skinner, Richard Ellington, Jack Benwell.
    Singer: Evan Evans.
    Prologue: Walter Hampden.
    Epilogue: Cornelia Otis Skinner.
    Address during intermission: Otis Skinner.
    Act I.—Valentine's Lodgings and Foresight's House. London, 1695.
Acts II and IV.—Foresight's House. Act III.—Valentine's Lodgings.
    Staged and designed by Robert Edmond Jones; costumes by Millia Davenport.

The Congreve comedy was revived by Kenneth Macgowan, Robert Edmond Jones and Eugene O'Neill at the Greenwich Village Theatre, New York, in March, 1925, and repeated at Daly's Theatre the following September. It was given for forty-seven performances during the first engagement and for sixteen during the second. The Players' revival of 1940 was for a week.

(Closed June 8, 1940)

*WALK WITH MUSIC

(15 performances)

A musical comedy in two acts by Guy Bolton, Parke Levy and Alan Lipscott, based on the comedy "Three Blind Mice" by Stephen Powys; lyrics by Johnny Mercer; music by Hoagy Carmichael. Produced by Ruth Selwyn in association with the Messrs. Shubert at the Ethel Barrymore Theatre, New York, June 4, 1940.

Cast of characters—

```
Pamela Gibson....................................Kitty Carlisle
Rhoda Gibson.....................................Mitzi Greene
Carrie Gibson...................................Betty Lawford
Chesterfield ....................................Stepin Fetchit
Henry Trowbridge................................Lee Sullivan
Wing D'Hautville................................Jack Whiting
Steve Harrington................................Art Jarrett
Polly Van Zile...............................Frances Williams
Conrad Harrington................................Marty May
Bellboy...............................................Ted Gary
House Detective..............................Barrie O'Daniels
Stuart Hobson.................................William Castle
```

Modernaires: Ralph Brewster, Bill Conway, Harold Dickinson and
Chuck Goldstein.

Glamour Girls: Connie Constant, Althea Gary, Linda Lee Griffith,
Betty Lynn, Jane Manners, Maxine Martin and Renee Russell.

Dancing Girls: Nancy Chaplin, Muriel Cole, Nona Feid, Christie
Gillespie, Georgia Jarvis, Ruth Morehouse, Eleanor Parr, Sylvia
di Salvo, Lorraine Todd, Terry Kelly, Jean Trybon and Rose
Tyrrell.

Dancing Boys: Larry Baker, Ray Clarke, Frank Gagen, Phil King,
Zoli Parks, Bob Pitts, Jack Richards and Sid Salzer.

Act I.—Scene 1—The Ethel Barrymore Theatre. 2—Gibson Farmhouse. 3—Modiste Shop, New York. 4—Station Platform, Jackson-
ville, Florida. 5—Gibson Patio, Hotel Alcazar, Palm Beach. 6—
Pathway Along Lake Worth, Palm Beach. 7—Pam Gibson's Bedroom. 8—Palm Beach Night Club, New Year's Eve. Act II.—
Scene 1—Gibson Patio. 2—Airport, Miami. 3—Outside the Hotel
Rio, near Havana.

Staged by R. H. Burnside; production under supervision of Row-
land Leigh; dances by Anton Dolin and Herbert Harper; settings by
Watson Barratt; costumes by Tom Lee.

The three Gibson girls, Pamela, Rhoda and Carrie, take what
capital they can salvage from a New Hampshire chicken farm and
invest it in a scheme. Pamela, being the prettiest, will pose as an
heiress in Florida and angle for a rich playboy. Rhoda will pretend to be her maid and Carrie will act as a chaperon. But Pamela
falls in love with a poor dancer, the rich playboy takes to Rhoda,
the maid, and Carrie is at least nonplused.

FEDERAL THEATRE ACTIVITIES

The final curtain of the Federal Theatre Project of the W.P.A.
in New York fell on June 30, 1939, when the three plays which
had continued into the 1939-40 season closed their runs. These
plays were: "Pinocchio," 197 performances; "Sing for Your Supper," 60 performances and "Life and Death of an American," 38
performances.

OFF BROADWAY

A one act musical by Alfred Hayes, George Kleinsinger and Jay Williams called "A Life in the Day of a Secretary" and Marc Blitzstein's "I've Got a Tune" were presented at the Theresa L. Kaufman Auditorium under the auspices of the New Theatre League, June 24, 1939. "A Life in the Day of a Secretary" was the recipient of prizes offered by the New Theatre League and the United Office and Professional Workers of America.

The Manning Productions revived "Night Must Fall" by Emlyn Williams for two weeks at the Cherry Lane Theatre July 3, 1939. The play was staged by Gregory Deane and in the cast were Margaret Draper, James Reach and Edmund Haggarty.

The Promenaders produced "Two for Tonight," an intimate revue at the Cherry Lane Theatre, New York, December 28, 1939. The sketches were written by Ralph Berton and Mitchell Hodges and the lyrics and music by Eugene and Ralph Berton, Bernice Kazounoff and John LaTouche.

The Barter Theatre of Abingdon, Virginia, produced "Everywhere I Roam" by Arnold Sundgaard in the original version, for one performance at the Heckscher Theatre, New York, September 19, 1939. The play in a revised form with Marc Connelly as collaborator had run for 13 performances in December of 1938 at the National Theatre, New York. The Barter Group opened their brief season on September 17 with "Lady Baltimore," an American operetta by Fred Stewart based on Sidney Nyburg's story.

"She Gave Him All She Had with Free Beer and Pretzels," a travesty based on "The Lost Sister" was produced by Harry Bannister at Uncle Sam's Music Hall, New York, November 16, 1939. The play on which the travesty was based was written by Arthur James Peglar and Charles S. Washburn.

Robert Breen's version of Goethe's "Faust" under the name of "Speak of the Devil," its prolog, epilog and three acts edited by Dr. Justus Schifferes, Dr. Van V. Alderman and Henry Cody, was presented by Everyman Theatre at the Nora Bayes Theatre, New York, October 6, 1939. Leonard de Paur wrote the music and Feder directed the lighting. Robert Breen was Mephistopheles; John Morny, Faust; Betty Caine, Gretchen and Stuart Cottman, Maximilian.

"Alternate Current," a drama in three acts by Syd Porcelain was produced by C.P.S. Productions and staged by Paul Stewart at Daly's Theatre, New York, December 22, 1939.

The New York City Chapter of the National Lawyers Guild presented a comedy in three acts called "Court Street" at the Heckscher Theatre, October 20, 1939. The comedy was written by Harry T. Thurschwell and directed by Julius Cohen. The settings were by Jacques Schurre. The play was repeated at the Nora Bayes Theatre, November 25, 1939.

At the Grand Street Playhouse the East Side Dramatic Group presented Arthur Smith's "Boom-Boom Clopper" January 5. Leonard Schwartz directed the performance and the settings were by August Sack.

The Balfour Players produced "Trial" by Shoshanah Bat Dori, staged by Benno Frank and designed by Heinz A. Condell, at the Heckscher Theatre, New York, November 22, 1939.

At the Cherry Lane Theatre, New York, February 19, 1940, the Light Opera Theatre started a season of Gilbert and Sullivan revivals with the production of "Trial by Jury" and "Iolanthe." John F. Grahame did the staging and the music was directed by Alexander Maissel.

The Snarks produced "Short Story," a comedy by Robert Morley at the Heckscher Theatre, New York, March 13, 1940.

"A Man and His Gods," by Tarquiny C. Pironti, formerly produced as "Idiots A La Mode" was produced by the T. and W. Production Company at the Heckscher Theatre, New York, March 26, 1940. It was staged by W. Kneale Morgan.

Merely Players, a co-operative group at the Irving Place Theatre, New York, started a repertory of classic drama with "Othello," February 19, 1940. Erich Hardt staged the play and portrayed Iago. John C. Webb played Othello and Nadra Wells, Desdemona. March 4, 1940, the group under the direction of Eric Arthur and Ruth Aldrich produced "Lysistrata" (a new translation from Aristophanes by Eric Arthur) at the same theatre.

"Flight 13," by Lyman White and staged by Leslie Roush was produced by Jess Goodman at the Heckscher Theatre, New York, March 19, 1940.

The Actors Ensemble produced "Death Sounds the Trumpet" an anti-war play written by Louis Sack at the Cherry Lane Theatre, New York, April 5, 1940. Ad Karns directed the play which had previously had four tryout performances at the Master Theatre under the direction of J. J. Robbins.

The Davenport Free Theatre celebrated its 25th anniversary in

New York with a three and a half hour show on April 2, 1940. The show included revivals of "A Woman's Way," the dream scene from "The Bells," the death scene from "Louis XI."

The Blackfriars, New York Chapter, produced "The Years of the Locusts" by Constance O'Hara at the Heckscher Theatre, New York, April 10, 1940. The Carroll Players produced Philip Barry's "The Joyous Season" at the same theatre, April 7, 1940.

The Cecile Howard Stock Company revived Ayn Rand's "The Night of January 16" at the Cherry Lane Theatre, New York, April 24, 1940. The play was staged by Harry Gabel.

The Comedy Club, headed by Melvin W. Sawin, produced "French without Tears" at the Heckscher Theatre, New York, with Nancy Mae Woodbury in the leading rôle and the Blue Hill Troupe presented Gilbert and Sullivan's "Gondoliers" at the same theatre with John Clarkson Jay as the Grand Inquisitor in April of 1940.

"The Bargain," by Ben Levinson, was staged and produced by the author at the Provincetown Theatre for eight performances starting May 24, 1940. At the same theatre "Mary's Little Lamb," by Aristide d'Angelo and his wife Mary McGowan, staged by Mr. D'Angelo and designed by Gene Johnson ran from June 5 through June 9, 1940.

"This Proud Pilgrimage," a poetic drama by Norman Rosten and staged by Edward Jurist, was produced by Flatbush Arts Theatre at the Heckscher Theatre, New York.

The Lighthouse Players presented a mystery drama, "The Mystery at Greenfingers," by J. B. Priestley, at the Little Theatre of the New York Association for the Blind, December 8 and 9, 1939. In March this group presented "Her Majesty the King," by C. C. Clements; "Murder at Mrs. Loring's," by S. Sylvan Simon and "Miss Marlowe at Play," by A. A. Milne.

DANCE DRAMA

The Ballet Russe de Monte Carlo, sponsored by Universal Art, Inc., was presented by Sol Hurok at the Metropolitan Opera House, New York, from October 26, 1939, through November 19, 1939. In the Spring, after a tour to California and back another three weeks' engagement was presented beginning March 26, 1940. Leonide Massine directed the dancing, Efrem Kurtz and Franz Allers the music and the régisseur général was Jean Yazvinsky. During the engagement three world premières were danced: "Bacchanale," a surrealist ballet by Salvador Dali to Wagner's "Venus-berg" music; "Ghost Town," an American folk ballet based on Mark Twain's "Roughing It," and George D. Lyman's "Sage of the Comstock Lode" with sets and costumes by Raoul Pene du Bois, music by Richard Rodgers and choreography by Marc Platoff; "Devil's Holiday," a comedy on Paginini themes with choreography by Frederick Ashton, décor and costumes by Eugene Berman.

The newly organized, locally sponsored Ballet Theatre opened its first season in New York at the Center Theatre, New York, January 11, 1940. The engagement started with the world première of "The Great American Goof," by William Saroyan; choreography by Eugene Loring; music by Henry Bryant; décor and costumes by Boris Aronson. The principals were Miriam Golden, Eugene Loring and Anthony Tudor who was making his American debut. Other premières offered were "Peter the Wolf," choreography by Adolph Bolm, music by Serge Prokofieff, décor and costumes by Lucinda Ballard; Raymond Scott's "Quintet," costumes and setting by Lucinda Ballard, who also collaborated with Raymond Scott and Anton Dolan on the scenario; "Dark Elegies" by Anthony Tudor; "Ode to Glory" by Yurek Shabelevski, music the "Polonaise Militaire" by Frederic Chopin, with Sonia Wojcikowsha and Shabelevski in the chief rôles; Anthony Tudor's "Jardin aux Lilas" and "Judgement of Paris"; "Goyescas" with choreography by Jose Fernandez, to music of Granados and settings by Nicholas de Molas; Andrée Howard's "Death and the Maiden"; Bronislava Nijinska's version of "La Fille Mal Gardée," with Patricia Bowman in the title rôle; "Black Ritual," subtitled "Obeah" by Agnes de Mille and performed by 16 Negro girls to the music of Darius Milhaud's "Creation of the World and settings by Nicholas de Molas; "Lady into Fox," Andrée Howard's choreographic arrangement of David Garnett's novel with music by Arthur Honegger. Sponsors were greatly heartened by the success of the first season.

The American Ballet Caravan gave a holiday Dance Festival at the St. James Theatre beginning December 27, 1939, in dance dramas of the Far East with Martha Graham, Sai Shoki and Carmalita Maracci taking the principal rôles. Argentinita and her Spanish Ensemble were presented at the Hollywood Theatre by S. Hurok in early January.

MONODRAMA

Helen Howe, in a program of characters and caricatures of her own authorship called "Washington, All Change," was presented by Actor-Managers, Inc., at Labor Stage for one week starting November 13, 1939.

Angna Enters, who authors all her dance playlets, appeared at the Alvin Theatre, New York, in early December, 1939. Her new compositions included "Hurry Up, It's Time," "Confirmation," "Women without Men," "Crackpot Americana," "Weiner Blut, Vienna 1939," "Folies Bergère," "I Got a Right to Sing the Blues," "Homage to Isadora," "The International Flag" and "American Indian-Post Cigar Store." Madeleine Marshall assisted as pianist.

PUPPETS

Sue Hastings' Marionettes at the McMillan Academic Theatre were presented under the auspices of the Children's Theatre of the Columbia University in a series of performances starting October 21, 1939, and continuing until Spring.

A marionette version of "Pinocchio" by Gilbert Josephson was produced by Mr. Josephson at the Waldorf Theatre, from December 26 to December 31, 1939. The program also included Uncle Don and Walt Disney movie cartoons. These same Suzari Marionettes were shown at the Waldorf Theatre by Arnold Van Leer, March 23, 1940, in Yasha Frank's version of "Pinocchio."

Vittorio Podrecca's "Theatre of the Piccoli" was produced by Cheryl Crawford at the Majestic Theatre, March 21, 1940, celebrating the 25th anniversary of the Podrecca marionettes.

COLLEGE PLAYS IN NEW YORK

The Mask and Wig Club of the University of Pennsylvania opened a three-performance engagement at the 46th Street Theatre, New York, December 1, 1939, with "Great Guns," a two-act musical comedy. The book was written by Louis deV. Day, Jr.; music by Clay A. Boland; lyrics by S. Bickley Reichner. G. Elliott Hess staged the show and Walter F. Keenan, Jr., directed the dances.

Princeton University's fifty-first annual Triangle Club show called "Any Moment Now" was produced December 15 and 16, 1939, at the Hollywood Theatre, New York. The book, music and lyrics were by Henry M. Hughes, Carl E. Davis, Mark Frelinghaus and Mark Laurence. It was staged by Karl B. Norton, the settings were by W. Danford Compton and the costumes by Simon Hyde, Jr.

Hunter College's thirteenth annual varsity show, "Girls in Uniform," by Christa Winsloe was presented at the Heckscher Theatre, New York, January 5, 1940. The play was directed by Miss Nancy M. Ferguson.

"Who Ride on White Horses," a three-act play by Richard Breen and Harry Schnibble, was produced and acted by Mimes and Mummers of the Fordham University at the Heckscher Theatre, New York, January 10, 11, 12 and 13, 1940. Robert Speaight, English actor, played the leading rôle and Emmet Lavery, Broadway playwright, working with Albert McCleery directed the play.

"Life Begins in '40," a musical burlesque, was presented by the Columbia Players at the Astor, New York, April 4 and 5, 1940. The book was by Isadore A. L. Diamond, music by Lee Wainer. Paul Winkopp directed and Frank Gagen staged the dances. H. H. Riddleberger designed the settings.

Wigs and Cues, the Barnard College dramatic club, presented three original one-act plays at the Brinckerhoff Theatre, New York, April 6, 1940. The curtain raiser was "Soap," a satire on advertising written by Ninetta di Benedetto and directed by June Amsden. The other plays were "The Law of Tayhol," a South Sea island tragedy by Roberta Hadley, directed by Jane Kass; "Scoutcraft," a farce by Patricia Spollen, directed by Jean Sauer; "The Unknown Soldier," a tragic fantasy by Janice Hoerr, directed by Gertrude Leighton.

The Hasty Pudding Club of Harvard University presented "Assorted Nuts," a musical comedy in two acts (94th edition of their annual revue), at the Waldorf, New York, April 6, 1940. The book was written by Lemuel Bannister, William B. D. Putnam and Bancroft G. Davis; music by Sherwood Rollins, Franklin Tyler, David Burt and Philip Kadison; lyrics by Rollins and Tyler, Robert Bacon, Bayard Clark, W. R. Bowie and Edward C. K. Read. The production was staged by Arthur Pierson, the dances directed by William R. Holbrook and the music by Al Zimmerman.

FOREIGN LANGUAGE PLAYS

There was a noticeable absence of foreign language plays in New York during the season of 1939-40, due to the war. The Yiddish theatre, however, was active.

At the Yiddish Art Theatre Maurice Schwartz presented and staged a drama in two acts called "Salvation" (which Mr. Schwartz had adapted from the novel of the same name by Sholem Asch), September 28, 1939. Music was by Sholem Secunda, settings by Alex Chertov and dances by Lillian Shapiro. In the cast were Mr. Schwartz, Leo Fuchs, Julius Adler, Miriam Riselle, Bertha Gersten, Mark Schweld and Anna Appel. "Salvation" had more than one hundred performances and was succeeded by "If I Were Rothschild," a musical fantasy by Mr. Schwartz with music by Sholom Secunda, based on a story by the late humorist, Sholem Aleichem. Two newcomers to the Yiddish Art Company were Miriam Kressyn and Abe Lax.

The Yiddish Folk Players presented a comedy by Nuchim Stutchkoff, "In a Jewish Grocery," at the Second Avenue Theatre, September 30, 1939. Incidental music was by Maurice Rauch; Michael Gordon of the Group Theatre directed and Howard Bay designed the setting. The leading players of this group were Judah Bleich, Michael Rosenberg and Wolf Barzell. In November they produced "Three Daughters," a comedy in three acts by Abraham Blum; music by Alexander Olshanetsky; lyrics by Michael Rosenberg; settings by Michael Saltzman. Later in the season, January 19, 1940, they produced Leo Robbins' melodrama, "Her Great Mistake." A new player added to the group for this play was J. Mylong Mintz, recently of the German stage.

At the Downtown National Theatre, Jacob Ben-Ami presented and staged "Chaver Nachman," by I. J. Singer, September 30, 1939. This was a dramatization from Mr. Singer's novel "East of Eden." Jacob Ben-Ami, Celia Adler and Ludwig Satz were featured players. Music was by Joseph Rumshinsky and settings by Samuel Leve. Mr. Ben-Ami's second drama of the season was "Life Marches On" by H. Kalmanowich at the same theatre, December 29, 1939.

At the Mercury Theatre, October 12, 1939, the Dramatic Art Theatrical Association presented the Artef Players in "Clinton Street," a Yiddish dramatization in three acts by Louis Miller of Chaver Paver's novel which won the Artef-Icor play contest award in 1938. It was staged by Lem Ward and the settings and lighting were by Sam Leve and Moe Hack. This opening marked the twelfth season of the Artef Players. The principals in the cast were Luba Rymer, Zelda Lerner, Israel Welichansky, Abraham Hirshbein, Louis Freilich, Michael Goldstein, Abraham Shapiro, Jules Dassin and Benny Jacons. Another play presented by this company at the Mercury Theatre was "Uriel Acosta," written by

Karl Gutzkow about one hundred years ago. A Yiddish version by David Hoffstein with music by Maurice Rauch and directed by Benno Schneider was presented December 29, 1939. The settings were by Sam Leve and the costumes by Penny Grotham. Outstanding players were Michael Goldstein, Helen Beverly, Sol Eisikoff, Morris Friedman and Avrum Horowitz. This play was last produced by the Habima Players at the Savoy Theatre, London, in 1937.

STATISTICAL SUMMARY

(LAST SEASON PLAYS WHICH ENDED RUNS AFTER JUNE 15, 1939)

Plays	Number Performances	
Abe Lincoln in Illinois....	472	(Closed November 25, 1939)
I Must Love Someone....	191	(Closed July 22, 1939)
Leave It to Me.........	307	(Closed September 16, 1939)
(Including return engagement, 16)		
No Time for Comedy.....	185	(Closed September 30, 1939)
Outward Bound.........	255	(Closed July 22, 1939)
The Little Foxes.........	410	(Closed February 3, 1940)
The Philadelphia Story...	417	(Closed March 30, 1940)
What a Life............	538	(Closed July 8, 1939)

LONG RUNS ON BROADWAY

To June 15, 1940

(Plays marked with asterisk were still playing June 15, 1940)

Plays	Number Performances	Plays	Number Performances
*Tobacco Road	2,777	Broadway	603
Abie's Irish Rose	2,327	Adonis	603
Lightnin'	1,291	Street Scene	601
*Pins and Needles	1,100	Kiki	600
The Bat	867	Blossom Time	592
White Cargo	864	Brother Rat	577
You Can't Take It with		Show Boat	572
You	837	The Show-Off	571
Three Men on a Horse	835	Sally	570
The Ladder	789	Rose Marie	557
The First Year	760	Strictly Dishonorable	557
*Hellzapoppin	759	Good News	551
Seventh Heaven	704	The Music Master	540
Peg o' My Heart	692	*What a Life	538
The Children's Hour	691	The Boomerang	522
Dead End	687	Blackbirds	518
East Is West	680	Sunny	517
Irene	670	Victoria Regina	517
Boy Meets Girl	669	The Vagabond King	511
The Women	657	The New Moon	509
A Trip to Chinatown	657	Shuffle Along	504
Rain	648	Personal Appearance	501
The Green Pastures	640	Bird in Hand	500
Is Zat So	618	Sailor, Beware!	500
Student Prince	608	Room Service	500

DRAMA CRITICS' CIRCLE AWARD

For three years, following its organization in 1935, the New York Drama Critics' Circle had comparatively little trouble agreeing upon the best play of American authorship produced during the season in New York, even though the selection, according to the Circle's constitution, had to be made by a three-fourths vote of the membership. The season of 1938-39, however, no agreement was reached and the vote was divided between Robert Sherwood's "Abe Lincoln in Illinois" (5) and Lillian Hellman's "The Little Foxes" (6). Clifford Odets' "Rocket to the Moon" and William Saroyan's "My Heart's in the Highlands" received two votes each. To avoid a second similar deadlock the Circle amended its constitution to permit a simple majority vote if, after five ballots, there was no selection on the three-fourths vote basis. In the voting for a 1939-40 selection five ballots were taken without a choice. A majority vote being agreed upon, William Saroyan's "The Time of Your Life" was chosen on the seventh ballot, having received eleven votes to four for Robert Sherwood's "There Shall Be No Night," two for Maxwell Anderson's "Key Largo" and one for George Kaufman's and Moss Hart's "The Man Who Came to Dinner." The Circle decided that no play of foreign authorship of sufficient distinction to warrant a citation had been imported.

The Circle's previous awards have been as follows:

1935-36—Winterset, by Maxwell Anderson
1936-37—High Tor, by Maxwell Anderson
1937-38—Of Mice and Men, by John Steinbeck
1938-39—No decision. (See above.)
1939-40—The Time of Your Life, by William Saroyan

PULITZER PRIZE WINNERS

"For the original American play performed in New York which shall best represent the educational value and power of the stage in raising the standard of good morals, good taste and good manners."—The Will of Joseph Pulitzer, dated April 16, 1904.

In 1929 the advisory board, which, according to the terms of the will, "shall have the power in its discretion to suspend or to change any subject or subjects . . . if in the judgment of the board such suspension, changes or substitutions shall be conducive to the public good," decided to eliminate from the above paragraph relating to the prize-winning play the words "in raising the standard of good morals, good taste and good manners."

The committee awards to date have been:

1917-18—Why Marry? by Jesse Lynch Williams
1918-19—None
1919-20—Beyond the Horizon, by Eugene O'Neill
1920-21—Miss Lulu Bett, by Zona Gale
1921-22—Anna Christie, by Eugene O'Neill
1922-23—Icebound, by Owen Davis
1923-24—Hell-bent fer Heaven, by Hatcher Hughes
1924-25—They Knew What They Wanted, by Sidney Howard
1925-26—Craig's Wife, by George Kelly
1926-27—In Abraham's Bosom, by Paul Green
1927-28—Strange Interlude, by Eugene O'Neill
1928-29—Street Scene, by Elmer Rice
1929-30—The Green Pastures, by Marc Connelly
1930-31—Alison's House, by Susan Glaspell
1931-32—Of Thee I Sing, by George S. Kaufman, Morrie Ryskind, Ira and George Gershwin
1932-33—Both Your Houses, by Maxwell Anderson
1933-34—Men in White, by Sidney Kingsley
1934-35—The Old Maid, by Zoe Akins
1935-36—Idiot's Delight, by Robert E. Sherwood
1936-37—You Can't Take It with You, by Moss Hart and George S. Kaufman
1937-38—Our Town, by Thornton Wilder
1938-39—Abe Lincoln in Illinois, by Robert E. Sherwood
1939-40—The Time of Your Life, by William Saroyan

PREVIOUS VOLUMES OF BEST PLAYS

Plays chosen to represent the theatre seasons from 1909 to 1939 are as follows:

1909-1919

"The Easiest Way," by Eugene Walter. Published by G. W. Dillingham, New York; Houghton Mifflin Co., Boston.

"Mrs. Bumpstead-Leigh," by Harry James Smith. Published by Samuel French, New York.

"Disraeli," by Louis N. Parker. Published by Dodd, Mead and Co., New York.

"Romance," by Edward Sheldon. Published by the Macmillan Co., New York.

"Seven Keys to Baldpate," by George M. Cohan. Published by Bobbs-Merrill Co., Indianapolis, as a novel by Earl Derr Biggers; as a play by Samuel French, New York.

"On Trial," by Elmer Reizenstein. Published by Samuel French, New York.

"The Unchastened Woman," by Louis Kaufman Anspacher. Published by Harcourt, Brace and Howe, Inc., New York.

"Good Gracious Annabelle," by Clare Kummer. Published by Samuel French, New York.

"Why Marry?" by Jesse Lynch Williams. Published by Charles Scribner's Sons, New York.

"John Ferguson," by St. John Ervine. Published by the Macmillan Co., New York.

1919-1920

"Abraham Lincoln," by John Drinkwater. Published by Houghton Mifflin Co., Boston.

"Clarence," by Booth Tarkington. Published by Samuel French, New York.

"Beyond the Horizon," by Eugene G. O'Neill. Published by Boni & Liveright, Inc., New York.

"Déclassée," by Zoe Akins. Published by Liveright, Inc., New York.

"The Famous Mrs. Fair," by James Forbes. Published by Samuel French, New York.

"The Jest," by Sem Benelli. (American adaptation by Edward Sheldon.)

"Jane Clegg," by St. John Ervine. Published by Henry Holt & Co., New York.

"Mamma's Affair," by Rachel Barton Butler. Published by Samuel French, New York.

"Wedding Bells," by Salisbury Field. Published by Samuel French, New York.

"Adam and Eva," by George Middleton and Guy Bolton. Published by Samuel French, New York.

1920-1921

"Deburau," adapted from the French of Sacha Guitry by H. Granville Barker. Published by G. P. Putnam's Sons, New York.

"The First Year," by Frank Craven. Published by Samuel French, New York.

"Enter Madame," by Gilda Varesi and Dolly Byrne. Published by G. P. Putnam's Sons, New York.

"The Green Goddess," by William Archer. Published by Alfred A. Knopf, New York.

"Liliom," by Ferenc Molnar. Published by Boni & Liveright, New York.

"Mary Rose," by James M. Barrie. Published by Charles Scribner's Sons, New York.

"Nice People," by Rachel Crothers. Published by Charles Scribner's Sons, New York.

"The Bad Man," by Porter Emerson Browne. Published by G. P. Putnam's Sons, New York.

"The Emperor Jones," by Eugene G. O'Neill. Published by Boni & Liveright, New York.

"The Skin Game," by John Galsworthy. Published by Charles Scribner's Sons, New York.

1921-1922

"Anna Christie," by Eugene G. O'Neill. Published by Boni & Liveright, New York.

"A Bill of Divorcement," by Clemence Dane. Published by the Macmillan Company, New York.

"Dulcy," by George S. Kaufman and Marc Connelly. Published by G. P. Putnam's Sons, New York.

"He Who Gets Slapped," adapted from the Russian of Leonid Andreyev by Gregory Zilboorg. Published by Brentano's, New York.

"Six Cylinder Love," by William Anthony McGuire.

"The Hero," by Gilbert Emery.

"The Dover Road," by Alan Alexander Milne. Published by Samuel French, New York.

"Ambush," by Arthur Richman.

"The Circle," by William Somerset Maugham.

"The Nest," by Paul Geraldy and Grace George.

1922-1923

"Rain," by John Colton and Clemence Randolph. Published by Liveright, Inc., New York.

"Loyalties," by John Galsworthy. Published by Charles Scribner's Sons, New York.

"Icebound," by Owen Davis. Published by Little, Brown & Company, Boston.

"You and I," by Philip Barry. Published by Brentano's, New York.

"The Fool," by Channing Pollock. Published by Brentano's, New York.

"Merton of the Movies," by George Kaufman and Marc Connelly, based on the novel of the same name by Harry Leon Wilson.

"Why Not?" by Jesse Lynch Williams. Published by Walter H. Baker Co., Boston.

"The Old Soak," by Don Marquis. Published by Doubleday, Page & Company, New York.

"R.U.R.," by Karel Capek. Translated by Paul Selver. Published by Doubleday, Page & Company.

"Mary the 3d," by Rachel Crothers. Published by Brentano's, New York.

1923-1924

"The Swan," translated from the Hungarian of Ferenc Molnar by Melville Baker. Published by Boni & Liveright, New York.

"Outward Bound," by Sutton Vane. Published by Boni & Liveright, New York.

"The Show-off," by George Kelly. Published by Little, Brown & Company, Boston.

"The Changelings," by Lee Wilson Dodd. Published by E. P. Dutton & Company, New York.

"Chicken Feed," by Guy Bolton. Published by Samuel French,

New York and London.

"Sun-Up," by Lula Vollmer. Published by Brentano's, New York.

"Beggar on Horseback," by George Kaufman and Marc Connelly. Published by Boni & Liveright, New York.

"Tarnish," by Gilbert Emery. Published by Brentano's, New York.

"The Goose Hangs High," by Lewis Beach. Published by Little, Brown & Company, Boston.

"Hell-bent fer Heaven," by Hatcher Hughes. Published by Harper Bros., New York.

1924-1925

"What Price Glory?" by Laurence Stallings and Maxwell Anderson. Published by Harcourt, Brace & Co., New York.

"They Knew What They Wanted," by Sidney Howard. Published by Doubleday, Page & Company, New York.

"Desire Under the Elms," by Eugene G. O'Neill. Published by Boni & Liveright, New York.

"The Firebrand," by Edwin Justus Mayer. Published by Boni & Liveright, New York.

"Dancing Mothers," by Edgar Selwyn and Edmund Goulding.

"Mrs. Partridge Presents," by Mary Kennedy and Ruth Warren. Published by Samuel French, New York.

"The Fall Guy," by James Gleason and George Abbott. Published by Samuel French, New York.

"The Youngest," by Philip Barry. Published by Samuel French, New York.

"Minick," by Edna Ferber and George S. Kaufman. Published by Doubleday, Page & Company, New York.

"Wild Birds," by Dan Totheroh. Published by Doubleday, Page & Company, New York.

1925-1926

"Craig's Wife," by George Kelly. Published by Little, Brown & Company, Boston.

"The Great God Brown," by Eugene G. O'Neill. Published by Boni & Liveright, New York.

"The Green Hat," by Michael Arlen.

"The Dybbuk," by S. Ansky, Henry G. Alsberg-Winifred Katzin translation. Published by Boni & Liveright, New York.

"The Enemy," by Channing Pollock. Published by Brentano's,

New York.

"The Last of Mrs. Cheyney," by Frederick Lonsdale. Published by Samuel French, New York.

"Bride of the Lamb," by William Hurlbut. Published by Boni & Liveright, New York.

"The Wisdom Tooth," by Marc Connelly. Published by George H. Doran & Company, New York.

"The Butter and Egg Man," by George Kaufman. Published by Boni & Liveright, New York.

"Young Woodley," by John Van Druten. Published by Simon and Schuster, New York.

1926-1927

"Broadway," by Philip Dunning and George Abbott. Published by George H. Doran Company, New York.

"Saturday's Children," by Maxwell Anderson. Published by Longmans, Green & Company, New York.

"Chicago," by Maurine Watkins. Published by Alfred A. Knopf, Inc., New York.

"The Constant Wife," by William Somerset Maugham. Published by George H. Doran Company, New York.

"The Play's the Thing," by Ferenc Molnar and P. G. Wodehouse. Published by Brentano's, New York.

"The Road to Rome," by Robert Emmet Sherwood. Published by Charles Scribner's Sons, New York.

"The Silver Cord," by Sidney Howard. Published by Charles Scribner's Sons, New York.

"The Cradle Song," translated from the Spanish of G. Martinez Sierra by John Garrett Underhill. Published by E. P. Dutton & Company, New York.

"Daisy Mayme," by George Kelly. Published by Little, Brown & Company, Boston.

"In Abraham's Bosom," by Paul Green. Published by Robert M. McBride & Company, New York.

1927-1928

"Strange Interlude," by Eugene G. O'Neill. Published by Boni & Liveright, New York.

"The Royal Family," by Edna Ferber and George Kaufman. Published by Doubleday, Doran & Company, New York.

"Burlesque," by George Manker Watters. Published by Doubleday, Doran & Company, New York.

"Coquette," by George Abbott and Ann Bridgers. Published by Longmans, Green & Company, New York, London, Toronto.

"Behold the Bridegroom," by George Kelly. Published by Little, Brown & Company, Boston.

"Porgy," by DuBose Heyward. Published by Doubleday, Doran & Company, New York.

"Paris Bound," by Philip Barry. Published by Samuel French, New York.

"Escape," by John Galsworthy. Published by Charles Scribner's Sons, New York.

"The Racket," by Bartlett Cormack. Published by Samuel French, New York.

"The Plough and the Stars," by Sean O'Casey. Published by the Macmillan Company, New York.

1928-1929

"Street Scene," by Elmer Rice. Published by Samuel French, New York.

"Journey's End," by R. C. Sherriff. Published by Brentano's, New York.

"Wings Over Europe," by Robert Nichols and Maurice Browne. Published by Covici-Friede, New York.

"Holiday," by Philip Barry. Published by Samuel French, New York.

"The Front Page," by Ben Hecht and Charles MacArthur. Published by Covici-Friede, New York.

"Let Us Be Gay," by Rachel Crothers. Published by Samuel French, New York.

"Machinal," by Sophie Treadwell.

"Little Accident," by Floyd Dell and Thomas Mitchell.

"Gypsy," by Maxwell Anderson.

"The Kingdom of God," by G. Martinez Sierra; English version by Helen and Harley Granville-Barker. Published by E. P. Dutton & Company, New York.

1929-1930

"The Green Pastures," by Marc Connelly (adapted from "Ol' Man Adam and His Chillun," by Roark Bradford). Published by Farrar & Rinehart, Inc., New York.

"The Criminal Code," by Martin Flavin. Published by Horace Liveright, New York.

"Berkeley Square," by John Balderston. Published by the Macmillan Company, New York.

"Strictly Dishonorable," by Preston Sturges. Published by Horace Liveright, New York.

"The First Mrs. Fraser," by St. John Ervine. Published by the Macmillan Company, New York.

"The Last Mile," by John Wexley. Published by Samuel French, New York.

"June Moon," by Ring W. Lardner and George S. Kaufman. Published by Charles Scribner's Sons, New York.

"Michael and Mary," by A. A. Milne. Published by Chatto & Windus, London.

"Death Takes a Holiday," by Walter Ferris (adapted from the Italian of Alberto Casella). Published by Samuel French, New York.

"Rebound," by Donald Ogden Stewart. Published by Samuel French, New York.

1930-1931

"Elizabeth the Queen," by Maxwell Anderson. Published by Longmans, Green & Co., New York.

"Tomorrow and Tomorrow," by Philip Barry. Published by Samuel French, New York.

"Once in a Lifetime," by George S. Kaufman and Moss Hart. Published by Farrar and Rinehart, New York.

"Green Grow the Lilacs," by Lynn Riggs. Published by Samuel French, New York and London.

"As Husbands Go," by Rachel Crothers. Published by Samuel French, New York.

"Alison's House," by Susan Glasgow. Published by Samuel French, New York.

"Five-Star Final," by Louis Weitzenkorn. Published by Samuel French, New York.

"Overture," by William Bolitho. Published by Simon & Schuster, New York.

"The Barretts of Wimpole Street," by Rudolf Besier. Published by Little, Brown & Company, Boston.

"Grand Hotel," adapted from the German of Vicki Baum by W. A. Drake.

1931-1932

"Of Thee I Sing," by George S. Kaufman and Morrie Ryskind; music and lyrics by George and Ira Gershwin. Published by Alfred Knopf, New York.

"Mourning Becomes Electra," by Eugene G. O'Neill. Published by Horace Liveright, Inc., New York.

"Reunion in Vienna," by Robert Emmet Sherwood. Published

by Charles Scribner's Sons, New York.

"The House of Connelly," by Paul Green. Published by Samuel French, New York.

"The Animal Kingdom," by Philip Barry. Published by Samuel French, New York.

"The Left Bank," by Elmer Rice. Published by Samuel French, New York.

"Another Language," by Rose Franken. Published by Samuel French, New York.

"Brief Moment," by S. N. Behrman. Published by Farrar & Rinehart, New York.

"The Devil Passes," by Benn W. Levy. Published by Martin Secker, London.

"Cynara," by H. M. Harwood and R. F. Gore-Browne. Published by Samuel French, New York.

1932-1933

"Both Your Houses," by Maxwell Anderson. Published by Samuel French, New York.

"Dinner at Eight," by George S. Kaufman and Edna Ferber. Published by Doubleday, Doran & Co., Inc., Garden City, New York.

"When Ladies Meet," by Rachel Crothers. Published by Samuel French, New York.

"Design for Living," by Noel Coward. Published by Doubleday, Doran & Co., Inc., Garden City, New York.

"Biography," by S. N. Behrman. Published by Farrar & Rinehart, Inc., New York.

"Alien Corn," by Sidney Howard. Published by Charles Scribner's Sons, New York.

"The Late Christopher Bean," adapted from the French of René Fauchois by Sidney Howard. Published by Samuel French, New York.

"We, the People," by Elmer Rice. Published by Coward-McCann, Inc., New York.

"Pigeons and People," by George M. Cohan.

"One Sunday Afternoon," by James Hagan. Published by Samuel French, New York.

1933-1934

"Mary of Scotland," by Maxwell Anderson. Published by Doubleday, Doran & Co., Inc., Garden City, N. Y.

"Men in White," by Sidney Kingsley. Published by Covici, Friede, Inc., New York.

"Dodsworth," by Sinclair Lewis and Sidney Howard. Published by Harcourt, Brace & Co., New York.

"Ah, Wilderness," by Eugene O'Neill. Published by Random House, New York.

"They Shall Not Die," by John Wexley. Published by Alfred A. Knopf, New York.

"Her Master's Voice," by Clare Kummer. Published by Samuel French, New York.

"No More Ladies," by A. E. Thomas.

"Wednesday's Child," by Leopold Atlas. Published by Samuel French, New York.

"The Shining Hour," by Keith Winter. Published by Doubleday, Doran & Co., Inc., Garden City, New York.

"The Green Bay Tree," by Mordaunt Shairp. Published by Baker International Play Bureau, Boston, Mass.

1934-1935

"The Children's Hour," by Lillian Hellman. Published by Alfred Knopf, New York.

"Valley Forge," by Maxwell Anderson. Published by Anderson House, Washington, D. C. Distributed by Dodd, Mead & Co., New York.

"The Petrified Forest," by Robert Sherwood. Published by Charles Scribner's Sons, New York.

"The Old Maid," by Zoe Akins. Published by D. Appleton-Century Co., New York.

"Accent on Youth," by Samson Raphaelson. Published by Samuel French, New York.

"Merrily We Roll Along," by George S. Kaufman and Moss Hart. Published by Random House, New York.

"Awake and Sing," by Clifford Odets. Published by Random House, New York.

"The Farmer Takes a Wife," by Frank B. Elser and Marc Connelly.

"Lost Horizons," by John Hayden.

"The Distaff Side," by John Van Druten. Published by Alfred Knopf, New York.

1935-1936

"Winterset," by Maxwell Anderson. Published by Anderson House, Washington, D. C.

"Idiot's Delight," by Robert Emmet Sherwood. Published by Charles Scribner's Sons, New York.

"End of Summer," by S. N. Behrman. Published by Random House, New York.

"First Lady," by Katharine Dayton and George S. Kaufman. Published by Random House, New York.

"Victoria Regina," by Laurence Housman. Published by Samuel French, Inc., New York and London.

"Boy Meets Girl," by Bella and Samuel Spewack. Published by Random House, New York.

"Dead End," by Sidney Kingsley. Published by Random House, New York.

"Call It a Day," by Dodie Smith. Published by Samuel French, Inc., New York and London.

"Ethan Frome," by Owen Davis and Donald Davis. Published by Charles Scribner's Sons, New York.

"Pride and Prejudice," by Helen Jerome. Published by Doubleday, Doran & Co., Garden City, New York.

1936-1937

"High Tor," by Maxwell Anderson. Published by Anderson House, Washington, D. C.

"You Can't Take It with You," by Moss Hart and George S. Kaufman. Published by Farrar & Rinehart, Inc., New York.

"Johnny Johnson," by Paul Green. Published by Samuel French, Inc., New York.

"Daughters of Atreus," by Robert Turney. Published by Alfred A. Knopf, New York.

"Stage Door," by Edna Ferber and George S. Kaufman. Published by Doubleday, Doran & Co., Garden City, New York.

"The Women," by Clare Boothe. Published by Random House, Inc., New York.

"St. Helena," by R. C. Sherriff and Jeanne de Casalis. Published by Samuel French, Inc., New York and London.

"Yes, My Darling Daughter," by Mark Reed. Published by Samuel French, Inc., New York.

"Excursion," by Victor Wolfson. Published by Random House, New York.

"Tovarich," by Jacques Deval and Robert E. Sherwood. Published by Random House, New York.

1937-1938

"Of Mice and Men," by John Steinbeck. Published by Covici-Friede, New York.

"Our town," by Thornton Wilder. Published by Coward-McCann, Inc., New York.

"Shadow and Substance," by Paul Vincent Carroll. Published by Random House, Inc., New York.

"On Borrowed Time," by Paul Osborn. Published by Alfred A. Knopf, New York.

"The Star-Wagon," by Maxwell Anderson. Published by Anderson House, Washington, D. C. Distributed by Dodd, Mead & Co., New York.

"Susan and God," by Rachel Crothers. Published by Random House, Inc., New York.

"Prologue to Glory," by E. P. Conkle. Published by Random House, Inc., New York.

"Amphitryon 38," by S. N. Behrman. Published by Random House, Inc., New York.

"Golden Boy," by Clifford Odets. Published by Random House, Inc., New York.

"What a Life," by Clifford Goldsmith. Published by Dramatists Play Service, Inc., New York.

1938-1939

"Abe Lincoln in Illinois," by Robert E. Sherwood. Published by Charles Scribner's Sons, New York and Charles Scribner's Sons, Ltd. London.

"The Little Foxes," by Lillian Hellman. Published by Random House, Inc., New York.

"Rocket to the Moon," by Clifford Odets. Published by Random House, Inc., New York.

"The American Way," by George S. Kaufman and Moss Hart. Published by Random House, Inc., New York.

"No Time for Comedy," by S. N. Behrman. Published by Random House, Inc., New York.

"The Philadelphia Story," by Philip Barry. Published by Coward-McCann, Inc., New York.

"The White Steed," by Paul Vincent Carroll. Published by Random House, Inc., New York.

"Here Come the Clowns," by Philip Barry. Published by Coward-McCann, Inc., New York.

"Family Portrait," by Lenore Coffee and William Joyce Cowen. Published by Random House, Inc., New York.

"Kiss the Boys Good-bye," by Clare Boothe. Published by Random House, Inc., New York.

WHERE AND WHEN THEY WERE BORN

(Compiled from the most authentic records available.)

Abba, Marta	Milan, Italy	1907
Abbott, George	Hamburg, N. Y.	1895
Abel, Walter	St. Paul, Minn.	1898
Adams, Maude	Salt Lake City, Utah	1872
Adler, Luther	New York City	1903
Adler, Stella	New York City	1904
Aherne, Brian	King's Norton, England	1902
Akins, Zoe	Humansville, Mo.	1886
Alexander, Katherine	Arkansas	1901
Alexander, Ross	Brooklyn, N. Y.	1904
Allenby, Peggy	New York	1905
Allen, Adrianne	Manchester, England	1907
Allgood, Sara	Dublin, Ireland	1883
Anders, Glenn	Los Angeles, Cal.	1890
Anderson, Judith	Australia	1898
Anderson, Maxwell	Atlantic City, Pa.	1888
Andrews, A. G.	Buffalo, N. Y.	1861
Andrews, Ann	Los Angeles, Cal.	1895
Anglin, Margaret	Ottawa, Canada	1876
Anson, A. E.	London, England	1879
Arling, Joyce	Memphis, Tenn.	1911
Arliss, George	London, England	1868
Ashcroft, Peggy	Croydon, England	1907
Astaire, Fred	Omaha, Neb.	1899
Atwell, Roy	Syracuse, N. Y.	1880
Atwill, Lionel	London, England	1885
Bainter, Fay	Los Angeles, Cal.	1892
Baker, Lee	Michigan	1880
Bankhead, Tallulah	Huntsville, Ala.	1902
Banks, Leslie J.	West Derby, England	1890
Barbee, Richard	Lafayette, Ind.	1887
Barrett, Edith	Roxbury, Mass.	1904
Barry, Philip	Rochester, N. Y.	1896
Barrymore, Ethel	Philadelphia, Pa.	1879
Barrymore, John	Philadelphia, Pa.	1882
Barrymore, Lionel	London, England	1878

492

Barton, James .... Gloucester, N. J. 1890
Baxter, Lora .... New York 1907
Beatty, Roberta .... Rochester, N. Y. 1900
Beecher, Janet .... Chicago, Ill. 1884
Behrman, S. N. .... Worcester, Mass. 1893
Bell, James .... Suffolk, Va. 1891
Ben-Ami, Jacob .... Minsk, Russia 1890
Bennett, Richard .... Cass County, Ind. 1873
Bergner, Elisabeth .... Vienna 1901
Berlin, Irving .... Russia 1888
Best, Edna .... Sussex, England 1900
Binney, Constance .... Philadelphia, Pa. 1900
Blackmer, Sidney .... Salisbury, N. C. 1896
Boland, Mary .... Detroit, Mich. 1880
Bolger, Ray .... Dorchester, Mass. 1906
Bondi, Beulah .... Chicago, Ill. 1892
Bordoni, Irene .... Paris, France 1895
Bowman, Patricia .... Washington, D. C. 1912
Brady, Alice .... New York 1892
Brady, William A. .... San Francisco, Cal. 1863
Braham, Horace .... London, England 1896
Brent, Romney .... Saltillo, Mex. 1902
Brian, Donald .... St. Johns, N. F. 1877
Brice, Fannie .... Brooklyn, N. Y. 1891
Broderick, Helen .... New York 1891
Bromberg, J. Edward .... Hungary 1903
Bruce, Nigel .... San Diego, Cal. 1895
Bryant, Charles .... England 1879
Buchanan, Jack .... England 1892
Buckler, Hugh .... Southampton, England ... 1886
Burke, Billie .... Washington, D. C. 1885
Burton, Frederick .... Indiana 1871
Byington, Spring .... Colorado Springs, Colo. ... 1898
Byron, Arthur .... Brooklyn, N. Y. 1872

Cabot, Eliot .... Boston, Mass. 1899
Cagney, James .... New York 1904
Cahill, Lily .... Texas 1891
Calhern, Louis .... New York 1895
Cantor, Eddie .... New York 1894
Campbell, Mrs. Patrick ...... England 1865
Carlisle, Alexandra .... Yorkshire, England 1886
Carlisle, Kitty .... New Orleans, La. 1912

Carminati, Tullio .... Zara, Dalmatia 1894
Carnovsky, Morris .... St. Louis, Mo. 1898
Carpenter, Edward Childs ..... Philadelphia, Pa. 1871
Carr, Alexander .... Russia 1878
Carroll, Earl .... Pittsburgh, Pa. 1892
Carroll, Leo G. .... Weedon, England 1892
Carroll, Nancy .... New York City 1906
Catlett, Walter .... San Francisco, Cal. 1889
Cawthorne, Joseph .... New York 1868
Chandler, Helen .... Charleston, N. C. 1906
Chaplin, Charles Spencer ..... London 1889
Chase, Ilka .... New York 1900
Chatterton, Ruth .... New York 1893
Cherry, Charles .... England 1872
Christians, Mady .... Vienna, Austria 1907
Churchill, Burton .... Toronto, Can. 1876
Claire, Helen .... Union Springs, Ala. 1908
Claire, Ina .... Washington, D. C. 1892
Cliffe, H. Cooper .... England 1862
Clifford, Kathleen .... Charlottesville, Va. 1887
Clive, Colin .... St. Malo, France 1900
Coburn, Charles .... Macon, Ga. 1877
Cohan, George M. .... Providence, R. I. 1878
Cohan, Georgette .... Los Angeles, Cal. 1900
Colbert, Claudette .... Paris 1905
Collier, Constance .... Windsor, England 1882
Collier, William .... New York 1866
Collinge, Patricia .... Dublin, Ireland 1894
Collins, Charles .... Frederick, Okla. 1904
Collins, José .... London, England 1896
Collins, Russell .... New Orleans, La. 1901
Colt, Ethel Barrymore .... Mamaroneck, N. Y. 1911
Colt, John Drew .... New York 1914
Conklin, Peggy .... Dobbs Ferry, N. Y. 1912
Connolly, Walter .... Cincinnati, Ohio 1888
Conroy, Frank .... London, England 1885
Cook, Joe .... Evansville, Ind. 1890
Cooper, Gladys .... Lewisham, England 1888
Cooper, Violet Kemble ...... London, England 1890
Cornell, Katharine .... Berlin, Germany 1898
Corrigan, Emmett .... Amsterdam, Holland 1871
Corthell, Herbert .... Boston, Mass. 1875
Cossart, Ernest .... Cheltenham, England 1876

Coulouris, George .... Manchester, England 1906
Courtenay, William .... Worcester, Mass. 1875
Courtleigh, Stephen .... New York City 1912
Coward, Noel .... Teddington, England 1899
Cowl, Jane .... Boston, Mass. 1887
Craven, Frank .... Boston, Mass. 1880
Crews, Laura Hope .... San Francisco, Cal. 1880
Crosman, Henrietta .... Wheeling, W. Va. 1865
Crothers, Rachel .... Bloomington, Ill. 1878
Cumberland, John .... St. John, N. B. 1880
Cummings, Constance .... Seattle, Wash. 1911

Dale, Margaret .... Philadelphia, Pa. 1880
Dalton, Charles .... England 1864
Danforth, William .... Syracuse 1869
Davis, Donald .... New York 1907
Davis, Owen .... Portland, Me. 1874
Davis, Owen, Jr. .... New York 1910
Day, Edith .... Minneapolis, Minn. 1896
De Cordoba, Pedro .... New York 1881
Digges, Dudley .... Dublin, Ireland 1880
Dinehart, Allan .... Missoula, Mont. 1889
Dixon, Jean .... Waterbury, Conn. 1905
Dowling, Eddie .... Woonsocket, R. I. 1895
Dressler, Eric .... Brooklyn, N. Y. 1900
Dressler, Marie .... Cobourg, Canada 1869
Dudley, Doris .... New York City 1918
Duncan, Augustin .... San Francisco 1873
Dunn, Emma .... England 1875
Dunning, Philip .... Meriden, Conn. 1890
Dupree, Minnie .... San Francisco, Cal. 1875
Durante, Jimmy .... New York City 1893

Edney, Florence .... London, England 1879
Eldridge, Florence .... Brooklyn, N. Y. 1901
Ellerbe, Harry .... Georgia 1905
Ellis, Mary .... New York 1900
Ellinger, Desirée .... Manchester, Vt. 1895
Elliott, Gertrude .... Rockland, Me. 1874
Elliott, Maxine .... Rockland, Me. 1871
Emery, Gilbert .... Naples, New York 1875
Emery, Katherine .... Birmingham, Ala. 1908
Emerson, John .... Sandusky, Ohio 1874

Errol, Leon ....Sydney, Australia 1881
Ervine, St. John Greer ....Belfast, Ireland 1883
Evans, Edith ....London, England 1888
Evans, Maurice ....Dorchester, England 1901

Fairbanks, Douglas ....Denver, Colo. 1883
Farley, Morgan ....Mamaroneck, N. Y. 1901
Farmer, Frances ....Seattle, Wash. 1914
Farnum, William ....Boston, Mass. 1876
Farrar, Geraldine ....Melrose, Mass. 1883
Fassett, Jay ....Elmira, N. Y. 1889
Faversham, William ....Warwickshire, England ...1868
Fenwick, Irene ....Chicago, Ill. 1887
Ferber, Edna ....Kalamazoo, Mich. 1887
Ferguson, Elsie ....New York 1883
Field, Sylvia ....Allston, Mass. 1902
Fields, Lew ....New York 1867
Fields, W. C. ....Philadelphia, Pa. 1883
Fischer, Alice ....Indiana 1869
Fitzgerald, Barry ....Dublin, Ireland 1888
Fletcher, Bramwell ....Bradford, Yorkshire, Eng...1904
Fontanne, Lynn ....London, England 1887
Foster, Phœbe ....New Hampshire 1897
Foy, Eddie, Jr. ....New Rochelle, N. Y. 1906
Franklin, Irene ....St. Louis, Mo. 1878
Frederick, Pauline ....Boston, Mass. 1884
Friganza, Trixie ....Cincinnati, Ohio 1870
Frohman, Daniel ....Sandusky, Ohio 1850

Gahagan, Helen ....Boonton, N. J. 1902
Garden, Mary ....Scotland 1876
Gaxton, William ....San Francisco, Cal. 1893
Gaythorne, Pamela ....England 1882
Geddes, Norman Bel ....Adrian, Mich. 1893
George, Grace ....New York 1879
Gerald, Ara ....New South Wales 1902
Gershwin, George ....Brooklyn, N. Y. 1898
Gershwin, Ira ....New York 1896
Gielgud, John ....London, England 1904
Gillmore, Frank ....New York 1884
Gillmore, Margalo ....England 1901
Gish, Dorothy ....Massillon, Ohio 1898
Gish, Lillian ....Springfield, Ohio 1896

Glaser, Vaughan .... Cleveland, Ohio 1873
Gleason, James .... New York 1885
Golden, John .... New York 1874
Gordon, Ruth .... Wollaston, Mass. 1896
Gottschalk, Ferdinand .... London, England 1869
Granville, Charlotte .... London 1863
Granville, Sydney .... Bolton, England 1885
Greaza, Walter .... St. Paul, Minn. 1900
Green, Martyn .... London, England 1899
Green, Mitzi .... New York City 1920
Greenstreet, Sydney .... England 1880
Groody, Louise .... Waco, Texas 1897
Gwenn, Edmund .... Glamorgan, Wales 1875

Haines, Robert T. .... Muncie, Ind. 1870
Hall, Bettina .... North Easton, Mass. 1906
Hall, Laura Nelson .... Philadelphia, Pa. 1876
Hall, Natalie .... North Easton, Mass. 1904
Hall, Thurston .... Boston, Mass. 1882
Halliday, John .... Brooklyn, N. Y. 1880
Halliday, Robert .... Loch Lomond, Scotland ...1893
Hamilton, Hale .... Topeka, Kansas 1880
Hampden, Walter .... Brooklyn, N. Y. 1879
Hannen, Nicholas .... London, England 1881
Hanson, Gladys .... Atlanta, Ga. 1887
Harding, Lyn .... Newport, England 1867
Hardwicke, Sir Cedric .... Lye, Stourbridge, England..1893
Harrigan, William .... New York 1893
Harris, Sam H. .... New York 1872
Harrison, Richard B. .... London, Ontario 1864
Hart, Vivian .... Texas 1905
Haydon, Julie .... Oak Park, Ill. 1910
Hayes, Helen .... Washington, D. C. 1900
Hector, Louis .... England 1882
Heflin, Van .... Walters, Okla. 1909
Heineman, Eda .... Japan 1891
Heming, Violet .... Leeds, England 1893
Hepburn, Katharine .... Hartford, Conn. 1907
Herbert, Evelyn .... Brooklyn, N. Y. 1900
Hobart, Rose .... New York 1906
Hoey, Dennis .... London, England 1893
Hopkins, Arthur .... Cleveland, Ohio 1878

Hopkins, Miriam .... Bainbridge, Ga. 1904
Holmes, Taylor .... Newark, N. J. 1872
Howard, Leslie .... London, England 1890
Howard, Sydney .... Oakland, Cal. 1891
Hull, Henry .... Louisville, Ky. 1893
Hunter, Glenn .... Highland Mills, N. Y. 1896
Huston, Walter .... Toronto 1884
Hutchinson, Josephine .... Seattle, Wash. 1898

Inescort, Frieda .... Hitchin, Scotland 1905
Ingram, Rex .... Dublin, Ireland 1892
Irving, Isabel .... Bridgeport, Conn. 1871

Jagger, Dean .... Columbus Grove, Ohio ... 1904
Janis, Elsie .... Delaware, Ohio 1889
Joel, Clara .... Jersey City, N. J. 1890
Johann, Zita .... Hungary 1904
Jolson, Al .... Washington, D. C. 1883
Johnson, Chic .... Chicago, Ill. 1891
Johnston, Moffat .... Edinburgh, Scotland 1886
Joy, Nicholas .... Paris, France 1892

Kane, Whitford .... Larne, Ireland 1882
Kaufman, George S. .... Pittsburgh, Pa. 1889
Kaye, A. P. .... Ringwood, England...... 1885
Keane, Doris .... Michigan 1885
Keith, Ian .... Boston, Mass. 1899
Keith, Robert .... Scotland 1899
Kelly, Walter C. .... Mineville, N. Y. 1875
Kennedy, Madge .... Chicago, Ill. 1890
Kerrigan, J. M. .... Dublin, Ireland 1885
Kerr, Geoffrey .... London, England 1895
Kershaw, Willette .... Clifton Heights, Mo. 1890
Kilbride, Percy .... San Francisco, Cal. 1880
King, Dennis .... Coventry, England 1897
Kingsford, Walter .... England 1876
Kingsley, Sydney .... New York 1906
Kirkland, Alexander .... Mexico City 1904
Kirkland, Muriel .... Yonkers, N. Y. 1904
Kruger, Alma .... Pittsburgh, Pa. 1880
Kruger, Otto .... Toledo, Ohio 1895

Landi, Elissa .... Venice, Italy 1904
Landis, Jessie Royce .... Chicago, Ill. 1904

Larimore, Earl .... Portland, Oregon 1899
Larrimore, Francine .... Russia 1898
Lauder, Harry .... Portobello, Scotland 1870
Laughton, Charles .... Scarborough, England 1899
Lawrence, Gertrude .... London 1898
Lawson, Wilfred .... London, England 1894
Lawton, Frank .... London, England 1904
Lawton, Thais .... Louisville, Ky. 1881
Lederer, Francis .... Karlin, Prague 1906
Le Gallienne, Eva .... London, England 1900
Leiber, Fritz .... Chicago, Ill. 1884
Lenihan, Winifred .... New York 1898
Leontovich, Eugenie .... Moscow, Russia 1894
Levy, Benn .... London, England 1900
Lewis, Mabel Terry .... London, England 1872
Lillie, Beatrice .... Toronto, Canada 1898
Locke, Katherine .... New York 1914
Loeb, Philip .... Philadelphia, Pa. 1892
Loftus, Cecilia .... Glasgow, Scotland 1876
Logan, Stanley .... Earlsfield, England 1885
Loraine, Robert .... New Brighton, England... 1876
Lord, Pauline .... Hanford, Cal. 1890
Lorraine, Lillian .... San Francisco, Cal. 1892
Lou-Tellegen .... Holland 1881
Love, Montagu .... Portsmouth, Hants 1877
Lunt, Alfred .... Milwaukee, Wis. 1893

Macdonald, Donald .... Denison, Texas 1898
Mackay, Elsie .... London, England 1894
MacKellar, Helen .... Canada 1896
March, Fredric .... Racine, Wis. 1897
Margo .... Mexico 1918
Marshall, Everett .... Worcester, Mass. 1902
Marshall, Herbert .... London, England 1890
Massey, Raymond .... Toronto, Canada 1896
Matthews, A. E. .... Bridlington, England 1869
McClintic, Guthrie .... Seattle, Wash. 1893
McCormick, Myron .... Albany, Indiana 1906
McIntyre, Frank .... Ann Arbor, Mich. 1879
Meek, Donald .... Glasgow, Scotland 1880
Meighan, Thomas .... Pittsburgh, Pa. 1879
Menken, Helen .... New York 1901
Mercer, Beryl .... Seville, Spain 1882

Meredith, Burgess ....Cleveland, Ohio 1909
Merivale, Philip ....Rehutia, India 1886
Merman, Ethel ....Astoria, L. I. 1909
Mestayer, Harry ....San Francisco, Cal. 1881
Miller, Gilbert ....New York 1884
Miller, Marilyn ....Findlay, Ohio 1898
Mitchell, Grant ....Columbus, Ohio 1874
Mitchell, Thomas ....Elizabeth, N. J. 1892
Mitzi (Hajos) ....Budapest 1891
Moore, Grace ....Del Rio, Tenn. 1901
Moore, Victor ....Hammonton, N. J. 1876
Moran, Lois ....Pittsburgh, Pa. 1909
Morley, Robert ....Semley, Wiltshire, England.1908
Morgan, Claudia ....New York 1912
Morgan, Helen ....Danville, Ill. 1900
Morgan, Ralph ....New York City 1889
Morris, Mary ....Boston 1894
Morris, McKay ....San Antonio, Texas 1890
Muni, Paul ....Lemberg, Austria 1895

Nagel, Conrad ....Keokuk, Iowa 1897
Nash, Florence ....Troy, N. Y..............1888
Nash, Mary ....Troy, N. Y..............1885
Natwick, Mildred ....Baltimore, Md. 1908
Nazimova, Alla ....Crimea, Russia 1879
Nielsen, Alice ....Nashville, Tenn. 1876
Nolan, Lloyd ....San Francisco, Cal. 1903
Nugent, J. C. ....Miles, Ohio 1875
Nugent, Elliott ....Dover, Ohio 1900

O'Brien-Moore, Erin ....Los Angeles, Cal. 1908
O'Connell, Hugh ....New York 1891
Odets, Clifford ....Philadelphia 1906
Oldham, Derek ....Accrington, England 1892
Olivier, Laurence ....Dorking, Surrey, England..1907
Olsen, Ole ....Peru, Ind. 1892
O'Malley, Rex ....London, England 1906
O'Neill, Eugene Gladstone .....New York 1888
O'Neill, Nance ....Oakland, Cal. 1875
Ouspenskaya, Maria ....Tula, Russia 1876
Overman, Lynne ....Maryville, Mo. 1887

Pemberton, Brock ....Leavenworth, Kansas 1885
Pennington, Ann ....Philadelphia, Pa..........1898

Perkins, Osgood .... Boston, Mass. 1892
Perry, Margaret .... Denver, Colo. 1913
Philips, Mary .... New London, Conn. 1901
Pickford, Mary .... Toronto 1893
Pollock, Channing .... Washington, D. C. 1880
Post, Guy Bates .... Seattle, Wash. 1875
Powers, James T. .... New York 1862
Powers, Leona .... Salida, Colo. 1900
Powers, Tom .... Owensburg, Ky. 1890
Price, Vincent .... St. Louis, Mo. 1914
Pryor, Roger .... New York City 1901

Quartermaine, Leon .... Richmond, England 1876

Rains, Claude .... London, England 1889
Rambeau, Marjorie .... San Francisco, Cal. 1889
Rathbone, Basil .... Johannesburg 1892
Reed, Florence .... Philadelphia, Pa. 1883
Rennie, James .... Toronto, Canada 1890
Revelle, Hamilton .... Gibraltar 1872
Richman, Charles .... Chicago, Ill. 1870
Ridges, Stanley .... Southampton, England 1891
Ring, Blanche .... Boston, Mass. 1876
Robinson, Edward G. .... Bucharest, Roumania 1893
Robson, May .... Australia 1868
Rogers, Mary .... Rogers, Ark. 1916
Roos, Joanna .... Brooklyn, N. Y. 1901
Ross, Thomas W. .... Boston, Mass. 1875
Royle, Selena .... New York 1905
Ruben, José .... Belgium 1886
Rumann, Siegfried .... Hamburg, Germany 1879

Sanderson, Julia .... Springfield, Mass. 1887
Sands, Dorothy .... Cambridge, Mass. 1900
Santley, Joseph .... Salt Lake City 1889
Savo, Jimmy .... New York City 1895
Sawyer, Ivy .... London, England 1897
Scheff, Fritzi .... Vienna, Austria 1879
Schildkraut, Joseph .... Bucharest, Roumania 1896
Scott, Cyril .... Ireland 1866
Scott, Martha .... Jamesport, Mo. 1914
Segal, Vivienne .... Philadelphia, Pa. 1897

Wynyard, Diana .... London, England 1906
Wynn, Ed. .... Philadelphia, Pa.........1886

Yorke, Oswald .... London, England 1868
Young, Roland .... London, England 1887
Yurka, Blanche .... Bohemia 1893

Ziegfeld, Florenz, Jr. .... Chicago, Ill. 1868

NECROLOGY

June 18, 1939—June 15, 1940

Anderson, Mary (Navarro), actress, 80. Famous beauty and actress on American and British stage; debut at 14 as Juliet in "Romeo and Juliet" in Louisville, Ky. (1875); first appearance in New York as Pauline in "The Lady of Lyons"; retired in 1899; collaborated with Robert S. Hitchins in dramatizing "The Garden of Allah." Born Sacramento, California; died Worcestershire, England, May 29, 1940.

Basshe, Em Jo, playwright, 40. Holder of Guggenheim Fellowship (1931) for creative work in theatre; wrote "Adam Solitaire," "Earth," "The Centuries," etc. Born Russia, died New York, October 29, 1939.

Benson, Sir Frank, actor and manager, 81. Leading Shakespearian actor in Great Britain for more than fifty years; knighted by King George V (1916); played many seasons at Stratford-on-Avon Memorial Theatre, of which he was a Governor; toured Canada and United States in 1913; awarded Croix de Guerre for activity in World War I; pensioned by Britain for his support of English drama. Born Airesford, England; died London, England, December 31, 1939.

Bentley, Irene, actress and singer, 70. Noted musical comedy star at turn of century; first appeared in "Little Christopher" (1895); later in "It Happened in Nordland," etc.; first starred in "Wild Rose"; played "The Belle of New York" in London; retired in 1910; widow of Harry B. Smith, lyric writer. Born Baltimore, Maryland; died Allenhurst, New Jersey, June 3, 1940.

Brady, Alice, actress, 47. Daughter of William A. Brady, producer; first appearance (1909) with Robert Mantell in "As You Like It"; sang in light opera; stage successes included "Mourning Becomes Electra," "Forever After," "The Bride of the Lamb," etc.; received Academy award (1938) for performance of Mrs. O'Leary in film "Old Chicago"; featured in 32 films including "Bought and Paid For," "When Ladies Meet," etc. Born New York City; died New York, October 28, 1939.

Campbell, Mrs. Patrick, actress, 75. First success "The Second Mrs. Tanqueray"; played Juliet opposite Sir Johnstone Forbes-Robertson; co-starred with Sarah Bernhardt in "Pelléas et Mélisande"; toured with Ben Greet troupe; first American tour in 1901; debut in motion pictures at 65 in "The Dancers." Born Kensington, London, England; died Pau, France, April 9, 1940.

Clive, Edward E., actor, producer and director, 64. First appeared London in "The White Heather" (1898); eventually in 1,159 plays; fourteen years as head of his own stock company in Boston; first appearance in New York (1912) as Marley's Ghost in "Christmas Carol." Born Monmouthshire, England; died North Hollywood, California, June 6, 1940.

Connolly, Walter, actor, 52. Debut in Norfolk, Virginia, in "Classmates" (1908); in New York as Sylvius in "As You Like It"; four years with Sothern-Marlowe; supported Madge Kennedy, Pauline Lord and other stars; pictures include "Bitter Tea of General Yen," "Victor Herbert," etc.; stage rôles in "Your Uncle Dudley," "The Late Christopher Bean," "The Bishop Misbehaves," etc. Born Cincinnati, Ohio; died Beverly Hills, California, May 28, 1940.

Elliott, Maxine (Jessie McDermot), actress, 69. Famous beauty and actress, 1890 to 1920; first appearance with E. S. Willard touring in "The Middleman"; first starred in "Her Own Way" (1903); appeared in "The Chaperon" at the opening of Maxine Elliott's Theatre, New York (1908); London debut (1895) in "Two Gentlemen of Verona"; married Nat Goodwin, toured Australia and later played with him in "The Cowboy and the Lady," "An American Citizen," etc.; last Broadway appearance in "Trimmed in Scarlet" (1920); appeared in films in "The Eternal Magdalen" and others. Born Rockland, Maine; died Juan Les Pins, Cannes, France, March 5, 1940.

Evarts, William H. (William Hentz), actor, 73. Played more than 2,000 rôles in 59 years on stage, in stock and vaudeville; first appearance with Joseph Jefferson; lately in radio plays. Born Roxbury, Massachusetts, died South Portland, Maine, June 6, 1940.

Faversham, William, actor, 73. Career began with "The Swiss Cottage," London (1886), and ended with "Lord and Lady Algy" in Montclair, New Jersey (1932); first appearance in New York as Dick in "Pen and Ink," (1887); leading man for Minnie Maddern Fiske, Maude Adams, etc.; leading man at Empire Theatre (1893 to 1901); debut as a star in "A Royal Rival" (1901); remembered in "The Squaw Man," "Aristocracy," "Sowing the Wind," etc. Born London, England; died Bay Shore, Long Island, New York, April 7, 1940.

Finch, Flora, comedienne, 71. Pioneer in films after early career as a Shakespearian actress with Ben Greet; teamed with John Bunny from 1910 to 1915 in 260 moving picture shorts; began film career in Biograph studios in New Jersey in 1907; last few years played stock bits in Hollywood; first Hollywood film was "Quality Street" (1927); last "The Shop Around the Corner"; last appearance on stage in "Poppy" with W. C. Fields. Born England; died Hollywood, California, January 4, 1940.

Galli, Rosina, dancer, 45. For 18 years première danseuse of Metropolitan Opera House; child dancer at La Scala at 6; later première danseuse at La Scala; famous as Princess in "Le Coq d'Or" (1918) and Ballerina in "Petruschka" (1925); wife of Giulio Gatti-Casazza. Born Naples, Italy; died Milan, Italy, April 30, 1940.

Girardot, Etienne, actor, 83. Originator of title rôle in "Charley's Aunt" (1893); supported Ellen Terry, Mrs. Fiske and William Collier; film career started with Vitagraph in Brooklyn, New York; important recent rôle in "The Hunchback of Notre Dame." Born London, England; died Hollywood, California, November 10, 1939.

Graham, George, actor, 64. Forty-one years in theatre; first appearance in "The Black Tulip" with Cyril Maude, London (1899); with Maude for three years; with Forbes-Robertson in New York (1906); with James K. Hackett in "Mr. Hopkinson"; subsequently appeared with John Drew, George Arliss, Arthur Byron, etc.; was playing Polonius to Maurice Evans' Hamlet when he died. Born Dorchester, England; died Chicago, Illinois, November 16, 1939.

Harlan, Otis, actor, 75. First appearance (1887) in Charles Hoyt's "A Hole in the Ground"; later in "A Black Sheep," "A Stranger in New York," "A Night and Day," etc.; with Weber and Fields; Capt. Andy in "Show Boat" in films; Diamond Jim, etc. Born Zanesville, Ohio; died Martinsville, Indiana, January 20, 1940.

Hatton, Fanny Locke, playwright, 69. Assistant drama editor and critic on *Chicago Herald* (1914); co-authored with her husband, Frederick Hatton, and Leo Ditrichstein, "The Great Lover"; with her husband, "Years of Discretion,"

"Squab Farm," "Lombardi, Ltd.," etc. Born Chicago, Illinois; died New York, November 27, 1939.

Heyward, DuBose, playwright, novelist and poet, 55. Best known for his novel "Porgy," dramatized in collaboration with his wife, Dorothy K. Heyward (1927); later with a George Gershwin score produced as an opera, "Porgy and Bess" (1935); other plays: "Brass Ankle," "Mamba's Daughters," etc.; wrote motion picture version of "Emperor Jones." Born Charleston, South Carolina; died Tryon, North Carolina, June 16, 1940.

Johnsrud, Harold, actor, 35. Started career with "The Prisoner" at the Provincetown Theatre, New York (1927); played in "Channel Road," "Uncle Vanya," "Winterset," etc.; was playing D'Alcala in "Key Largo" at the time of his death. Born Spokane, Washington; died New York City, December 24, 1939.

Kidder, Kathryn, actress, 71. Thirty-five years a leading American Shakespearian actress; co-starred with Frederick Warde and Louis James; created Dearest in "Little Lord Fauntleroy"; starred in "Madame Sans Gene"; last appearance in "Remember the Day" (1935); wife of Dr. Louis Kaufman Anspacher, playwright. Born Newark, New Jersey; died New York, September 7, 1939.

Leslie, Amy, actress and drama critic, 85. Forty years drama critic of *Chicago Daily News;* popular on Broadway under name of Lillie West in Gilbert and Sullivan operas; retired as prima donna of "Castles in the Air" with De Wolf Hopper. Born West Burlington, Iowa; died Chicago, Illinois, July 3, 1939.

Lowe, Robert, actor, 64. Long career on stage dating back to "The Girl I Left Behind Me"; supported Blanche Walsh; played in "Lightnin'," "Seventh Heaven," etc. Born Washington, D. C.; died New Dorp, Staten Island, New York, September 21, 1939.

McMillan, Lida (Snow), actress, 71. Forty-nine years on American stage; debut (1889) Chicago, in "Lost in New York"; with Dearborn Stock Co., Chicago; supported George M. Cohan in "The Tavern," Stuart Robson in "The Comedy of Errors," Walter Huston in "Elmer the Great"; last seen in New York in "Prologue to Glory" (1938). Born Cincinnati, Ohio; died New York, March 29, 1940.

Moore, Raymond, producer, 42. Pioneer in Summer theatre movement; founder and owner of Cape Playhouse, Dennis,

Massachusetts, where Bette Davis and others started. Born Baltimore, Maryland; died New York City, March 8, 1940.

Phillips, Albert, actor, 65. Career in stock companies in New York, Chicago, Cleveland, Kansas City and Philadelphia; remembered in "The Littlest Rebel," "An American Tragedy," etc.; played General Grant in "Abraham Lincoln" (1919); last appearance as Stephen Douglas in "Abe Lincoln in Illinois" (1939). Born Edwardsville, Indiana; died New York, February 24, 1940.

Polaire, Mlle. (Emilie Marie Bouchard), French actress and singer, 59. Appeared in French cafés, light opera and drama; appeared in New York in "Le Visiteur" in 1910, when she was billed as "the ugliest woman in the world." Born Algeria; died Champigny-sur-Marne, France, October 14, 1939.

Roberts, Florence, actress, 79. Career covered sixty years beginning with "Hoop of Gold" in Brooklyn, New York, 1870, and ending with rôle of grandmother in "The Jones Family" film this year; starred in "Zaza," "Camille," etc.; fifteen years in Philadelphia stock. Born Isle of Man, England; died Hollywood, California, June 6, 1940.

Shea, Thomas E., actor and playwright, 79. Toured United States and Great Britain with his own stock company for half a century; proud of having acted before King George V and Queen Mary of England, King Albert of Belgium and King Alfonso of Spain in "The Trial of Mary Dugan" at a London theatre. Born East Cambridge, Massachusetts; died Cambridge, Massachusetts, April 23, 1940.

Templeton, Fay, musical comedy actress, 74. Star of musical comedy in late nineties; remembered as Buttercup in "Pinafore," Mary in "Forty-five Minutes from Broadway," etc.; many years with Weber and Fields music hall revues; first performance 1869; last important appearance in "Roberta" in 1934. Born Little Rock, Arkansas; died San Francisco, California, October 3, 1939.

Tetrazzini, Luisa, singer and actress, 68. Famous coloratura soprano; debut Florence, Italy (1895); American debut with Hammerstein in "La Traviata" (1908); appeared with Metropolitan, Chicago and Boston Opera Companies; repertory included forty operas; awarded gold medal of Royal Philharmonic Society of London (1912). Born Florence, Italy; died Milan, Italy, April 28, 1940.

Thomashefsky, Boris, actor, author, impresario and producer, 75. Founder and leading personality of New York Yiddish theatre; composed and orchestrated many operas; wrote several hundred plays and translated classics into Yiddish; appeared in Yiddish versions of many Shakespearian plays; on Broadway in English play "The Singing Rabbi" (1931). Born Kiev, Russia; died New York, July 9, 1939.

Unger, Gladys Buchanan, playwright, 55. First play "Edmund Keen," produced London, 1902; most recent (written in collaboration with Marcella Burke) "Tonight We Dance," produced Chicago, 1939, with Ruth Chatterton in leading rôle; others "Ladies of Creation," "Experience Unnecessary," "Nona," "Two Girls Wanted," etc.; adapted many French plays; wrote many motion pictures. Born San Francisco, California; died New York, May 25, 1940.

Weber, L. Lawrence, producing manager, 68. Operated Broadway theatres, including Longacre (for 20 years) and Little Theatre with John Golden and F. Ray Comstock; other partnerships with Weber and Fields and Harry H. Frazee with whom he produced "No, No, Nanette," "Little Jesse James," "Cobra," etc.; active in formation of Metro Pictures; one of the founders of Columbia Burlesque Wheel; treasurer Producing Managers Association; member Board of Governors League of New York Theatres. Born New York City; died New York, February 22, 1940.

Winter, Winona, actress, 52. More than thirty years in musical comedy and vaudeville; daughter of William Banks Winter, minstrel; appeared with Harry Lauder, Julian Eltinge, Will Rogers and Elsie Janis. Born Huntsville, Alabama; died Hollywood, California, April 27, 1940.

THE DECADES' TOLL

(Persons of Outstanding Prominence in the Theatre
Who Have Died in Recent Years)

	Born	Died
Aborn, Milton	1864	1933
Ames, Winthrop	1871	1937
Anderson, Mary (Navarro)	1860	1940
Baker, George Pierce	1866	1935
Belasco, David	1856	1931
Benson, Sir Frank	1859	1939
Bernhardt, Sarah	1845	1923
Campbell, Mrs. Patrick	1865	1940
Crabtree, Charlotte (Lotta)	1847	1924
De Koven, Reginald	1861	1920
De Reszke, Jean	1850	1925
Drew, John	1853	1927
Drinkwater, John	1883	1937
Du Maurier, Sir Gerald	1873	1934
Duse, Eleanora	1859	1924
Fiske, Minnie Maddern	1865	1932
Galsworthy, John	1867	1933
Gorky, Maxim	1868	1936
Greet, Sir Philip (Ben)	1858	1936
Herbert, Victor	1859	1924
Patti, Adelina	1843	1919
Pinero, Sir Arthur Wing	1855	1934
Pirandello, Luigi	1867	1936
Rejane, Gabrielle	1857	1920
Rogers, Will	1879	1935
Russell, Annie	1864	1936
Schumann-Heink, Ernestine	1861	1936
Sembrich, Marcella	1859	1935
Shaw, Mary	1860	1929
Sothern, Edwin Hugh	1859	1933
Terry, Ellen	1848	1928
Thomas, Augustus	1857	1934
Yeats, William Butler	1865	1939

INDEX OF AUTHORS

513

INDEX OF PLAYS AND CASTS

517

INDEX OF PRODUCERS, DIRECTORS AND DESIGNERS

522